THE OXFORD HANDBOOK OF

ANIMAL ORGANIZATION STUDIES

THE OXFORD HANDBOOK OF
ANIMAL ORGANIZATION STUDIES

Edited by
LINDA TALLBERG
and
LINDSAY HAMILTON

Great Clarendon Street, Oxford, OX2 6DP,
United Kingdom

Oxford University Press is a department of the University of Oxford.
It furthers the University's objective of excellence in research, scholarship,
and education by publishing worldwide. Oxford is a registered trade mark of
Oxford University Press in the UK and in certain other countries

© The Several Contributors 2023

The moral rights of the authors have been asserted

First Edition published in 2023

Impression: 1

All rights reserved. No part of this publication may be reproduced, stored in
a retrieval system, or transmitted, in any form or by any means, without the
prior permission in writing of Oxford University Press, or as expressly permitted
by law, by licence or under terms agreed with the appropriate reprographics
rights organization. Enquiries concerning reproduction outside the scope of the
above should be sent to the Rights Department, Oxford University Press, at the
address above

You must not circulate this work in any other form
and you must impose this same condition on any acquirer

Published in the United States of America by Oxford University Press
198 Madison Avenue, New York, NY 10016, United States of America

British Library Cataloguing in Publication Data

Data available

Library of Congress Control Number: 2022932391

ISBN 978-0-19-284818-5

DOI: 10.1093/oxfordhb/9780192848185.001.0001

Printed and bound by
CPI Group (UK) Ltd, Croydon, CR0 4YY

Links to third party websites are provided by Oxford in good faith and
for information only. Oxford disclaims any responsibility for the materials
contained in any third party website referenced in this work.

Foreword

It was a great pleasure and privilege to be invited to write this short prologue for the first handbook of the emergent field of Animal Organization Studies. As I read the introduction and the contributions, I realized that I too had been part of an academic group that failed to consider animals. In the late '90s I returned to academia after a decade of absence. At the time Human-Animal Studies (the term I use, although others prefer different terms) was emerging as a multidisciplinary field, drawing mainly on disciplines located in the humanities and social sciences, that recognized and then explored, the complex significance of animals in human lives and in their social and cultural worlds.

I had previously written on human-animal relations and was attracted to the field. I became a member of a School of Business and Social Sciences where I developed a course entitled 'Animals, Cultures, and Societies'. The failure, above, was that although I spoke with my sociology and anthropology colleagues about animals, I never thought of speaking with colleagues who taught courses on business, management, and organization about them because, surely, animals would not figure in their worlds? I now appreciate the frustration of the editors who commented to me that, after presentations of their animal-centred research, they were often asked, 'But why animals?'

Business Studies has a focus on commodities and human social relations and Management Studies and Organization Studies has human labour and social relations as a focus—please forgive my very crude reductionism. A key theme of this volume is a call to recognize animals as more than commodities, entities, or objects in the context of business enterprises and the myriad organizations that are founded on them. Just to keep with the notion of value for a moment: it is a theme that expands to consider and explore the nature of the lives of animals in these contexts, and perhaps ways to improve them and the relationships they have with humans and humans have with them. In part, this involves a decentring of humans, but it also involves a recentring of humans with animals. Different animals, in different ways, have value in these contexts and in questioning and rethinking notions of value in these contexts we are led to reconsidering animal lives and interspecies relationships.

The remit of the volume, however, is much wider than enterprises and organizations. Whenever, and wherever, humans and animals associate there are systems of management and organization to structure, sometimes to encourage and sometimes discourage, the encounters and the relationships. These range, for example, from the relationships in the most intimate spaces of homes to farms, laboratories, equestrian centres, parks and other leisure spaces, the shared human-animal habitats of cities, zoos, animal sports, tourist activities, and wildlife watching, to the organizing of relationships in vast national parks and conservation areas. Here the editors and authors offer insights and fresh awareness that, I hope, will prompt and encourage colleagues from other disciplines to think about the nature, structures, and practices of management and organization as key elements of human-animal relations.

The first part of the introduction is a fine manifesto for the possibilities of what Animal Organization Studies can aspire to and might become. The editors have decided on this term to open a field rather than fencing it in/off with terminological fixities and restricted perspectives. This is an invitation to participate and I very much enjoyed the varied participations here. The theoretical sections set out a new world of thinking for me and others showed how such thinking can offer new perspectives on practices and empirical settings. As an ethnographically-focused social anthropologist interested in human-animal relations, I am always interested in specificities, not the human and the animal, but the engagements of particular people with particular animals in particular contexts. I found all this in the rich interdisciplinarity of the chapters.

I return to that bemused question, 'But why animals?' This volume offers an important reply and multifaceted response. Now the question should not be 'Why?' but 'How?'

Garry Marvin
Professor of Human-Animal Studies
University of Roehampton

Contents

List of Figures — xi
List of Tables — xiii
Editor Biographies — xv
Chapter Author Biographies — xvii

Editors' Introduction — 1
LINDA TALLBERG AND LINDSAY HAMILTON

PART I ORGANIZING ANIMALS: PAST, PRESENT, FUTURE

1. From Interesting to Influential: Looking Forward with Multispecies Organization Studies — 17
   KENDRA COULTER

2. Breeding Profits: Animals as Labour and Capital in Euro-American History — 28
   AMANDA REES

3. Posthumanist Praxis and the Paradoxes of Agency, Responsibility, and Organization in the 'Anthropocene' — 42
   RICHIE NIMMO

4. COVID-19 and Zoonotic Disease: Manufacturing and Organizing Ignorance within the Animal-Industrial Complex — 57
   CAROLINE CLARKE, CHARLES BARTHOLD, AND MATTHEW COLE

5. Organizing a Real that Is Yet to Come: A Critical Inquiry of Education in Animal Organization Studies — 73
   HELENA PEDERSEN

PART II ORGANIZING ANIMAL ENCOUNTERS: KNOWING, MEANING, AND MATERIALITY

6. *More-than-Human* Leadership? Studying Leadership in Horse–Human Relationships   87
   ASTRID HUOPALAINEN

7. Reconfiguring the Senses: Sensor Technologies and the Production of a New Sensorium in Cattle Farming   101
   CAMILLE BELLET

8. Working the Dog: The Organization of Space, Time, and Labour in Multispecies Homes   115
   ERIKA CUDWORTH

9. Social Media Images of Urban Coyotes and the Constitution of More-than-Human Cities   129
   CHRISTIAN HUNOLD

10. Imagining Stories of and with Animals at Work: Care, Embodiment, and Voice-Giving in Human-Equine Work   145
    LUCY CONNOLLY

11. Wild Pedagogies for Doing Multispecies Organizational Ethnography: Using the Tracking Craft of the Southern African San   159
    HARRY WELS AND FRANS KAMSTEEG

12. Guided by a Lizard: Respectful Organizing and Symmetric Reciprocity with Totem Animals   179
    KARL-ERIK SVEIBY AND TEX SKUTHORPE

13. 'Secret Squirrel Reports for Duty': How the Use of Animal Metaphors Can Assist Our Learning of Workplace Interactions   194
    STEPHANIE RUSSELL

14. Big Hat, No Cattle: Using Animal Metaphors to Frame Strategic Human Resource Management   210
    TRICIA CLELAND SILVA

PART III SUSTAINABILITY, IDENTITY, AND ETHICS: ANIMALS IN PRODUCTION AND CONSUMPTION SYSTEMS

15. Animal Organization Studies and the Foundational Economy: Infrastructures of Everyday Multispecies Life   227
BRYONY GOODWIN-HAWKINS

16. How Can We Reduce Speciesism? A Psychological Approach to a Social Problem   241
DORIS SCHNEEBERGER

17. A Handshake between Anthropocentricism and Capitalism: Reflections on Animal Life within Industrial Food Systems   258
DINESH JOSEPH WADIWEL

18. Barbaric, Feral, or Moral? Stereotypical Dairy Farmer and Vegan Discourses on the Business of Animal Consumption   272
NIK TAYLOR, HEATHER FRASER, NAOMI STEKELENBURG, AND JULIE KING

19. Tinkering with Relations: Veterinary Work in Dutch Farm Animal Care   288
ELSE VOGEL

20. Stockfree's Short Shadow: Shifting Food Systems Towards Sustainability by Re-thinking Veganism as a Performative Practice of Production   300
STEFFEN HIRTH

21. Honeybee Bias and Bee-washing: Effects of Vertebrate-centric Care?   313
OLIVIA DAVIES AND THOMAS D.J. SAYERS

22. Empathy and Inclusion: A Philosophical Reading of the Ethics of Nonhuman Animals in Organizations   331
ELISA AALTOLA

PART IV CARE, CULTURES, AND AFFECT IN ANIMAL WORK RELATIONS

23. Olly the Cat: Excerpts from a Feline Ethnography in Business and Management Studies — 349
    DAMIAN O'DOHERTY

24. Catching Crab Truth in Seawater: On Rockpooling, Affect, and Charisma — 368
    LINDSAY HAMILTON

25. When Disaster Hits, Dissonance Fades: Callings and Crisis at an Animal Shelter — 383
    LINDA TALLBERG AND PETER J. JORDAN

26. Husky Kennels as Animal Welfare Activists: Multispecies Relationships as Drivers of Institutional Change — 397
    JOSÉ-CARLOS GARCÍA-ROSELL

27. Robotic Animals in Dementia Care: Conceptions of Animality and Humanity in Care Organizations — 409
    DAVID REDMALM, MARCUS PERSSON, AND CLARA IVERSEN

28. Te Ao Māori and One Welfare in Aotearoa New Zealand: The Case of Kurī, Dog Registration, the Law, and Local Councils — 425
    JANET SAYERS AND RACHEL FORREST

29. Dogs at Work: Gendered Organizational Cultures and Dog-Human Partnerships — 442
    NICKIE CHARLES, REBEKAH FOX, MARA MIELE, AND HARRIET SMITH

Index — 457

Figures

11.1 Visual expression of 'ontological mutability' (Guenther, 2020b): San rock art. Photo source: Copy of rock shelter images on photographic paper by Harald Pager, Ndedema Gorge in the Drakensberg, South Africa, courtesy Rock Art Research Institute, University of the Witwatersrand. — 163

11.2 Tracking the landscape with all your senses. Samuel Bak's 'Landscape with five senses', (oil on canvas, 80x104cm). Photo source: Dorotheum Vienna, auction catalogue 26.11.2019. — 165

11.3 Leopard spoor on the road (in circle). Photo source: Harry Wels. — 166

11.4 Lion spoor (no circle). Photo source: Harry Wels. — 166

12.1 The sand goanna, detail of painting 'Journey of Knowledge' by Tex Skuthorpe. Copyright: The authors. — 180

12.2 Painting of The Crane and the Crow—a Law story by Tex Skuthorpe. Copyright: The authors. — 187

16.1 Baseline measures of speciesism. — 248

16.2 Overview results. The last line shows which aspect each EP named as being most memorable for them in the research process. 'Videos' = videos of human and NHAs shown in the workshop; ' ATE' = 'alien thought experiment'; 'CCP' = 'crash course philosophy (video)'; 'TE' = 'thought experiments (in general)'. — 250

16.3 Results for Herb. — 252

18.1 Cows (Heather Fraser, 2021). — 273

21.1 Top row: examples of four bee species of the insect order Hymenoptera—European honeybee, neon cuckoo bee, hylaeine bee, and blue banded bee. Rows two-four offer a glimpse into the diversity of other insect groups, all of which contribute to their local ecology whether it be through predation, herbivory, pollination, or as food for other organisms. Displayed left to right (insect order in parentheses): paper wasp (Hymenoptera), flower-feeding march fly (Diptera), drone or flower fly (Diptera), bee fly (Diptera), skipper butterfly (Lepidoptera), thorn bug (Hemiptera), weevil (Coleoptera), fan beetle (Coleoptera), spotted ladybird (Coleoptera), green lacewing (Neuroptera), praying mantis (Mantodea), and dragonfly (Odonata). (Copyright: Thomas Sayers). — 315

22.1	Types of empathy.	337
24.1	At the edge of the sea, seaweed covers the craggy rocks and pools. Photo by Michael Richardson-Moore on http://www.unsplash.com.	372
24.2	The craggy coastline, a liminal zone imbuing fear of nature's tentacular power. Photo by Jamie Street on http://www.unsplash.com.	379
27.1	The Joy for All Pup. Press photo, used with permission from the manufacturer.	413
27.2	The Joy for All Cat. Press photo, used with permission from the manufacturer.	413
28.1	A Māori man lets Premier Richard Seddon know what he thinks about the dog tax. Used with permission from the Alexander Turnbull library. By Ashley Hunter, 1898, Reference Number: 23009191.	426
28.2	Kai Time with Kurī. Used with permission from the National Library of New Zealand. By Charles Hemus, 1849–1925. Kai time. [ca 1900] Reference Number: A-367-030.	428

Tables

12.1 A glossary of useful terminology (adapted from Ash et al. 2003; Giacon 2021; Skuthorpe 2019).   184

12.2 Examples of the human—totem animal inter-acts.   190

Editor Biographies

Linda Tallberg is an Assistant Professor in Management and Organization at Hanken School of Economics (Finland). Her research focuses on nonhuman animals in management and organization, emotions, multispecies methods, crystallization, critical and human-animal studies, animal voice, and ethics. She has published on these topics in *Work, Employment and Society, Journal of Organizational Ethnography, Management Learning,* and *Journal of Business Ethics*.

Lindsay Hamilton is a Senior Lecturer in Management at the University of York (UK). Her interests include human-animal interactions in organizations, and multispecies ethnography. On these themes, she has published in journals such as *New Technology, Work and Employment, Management Learning* and *Organization* and has written two books: *Animals at Work* (2013) and *Ethnography after Humanism* (2017), both with Nik Taylor.

Chapter Author Biographies

Elisa Aaltola is a Philosopher specializing in moral psychology, and animal and environmental ethics, working at the University of Turku (Finland). She has published extensively and her publications include *Varieties of Empathy: Moral Psychology and Animal Ethics* (2018), *Animal Suffering: Philosophy and Culture* (2012), and *Animal Ethics and Philosophy: Questioning the Orthodoxy* (co-edited, 2014) in addition to around 40 peer-reviewed articles.

Charles Barthold is a Senior Lecturer at the Open University. Charles employs a variety of critical approaches to organization studies in relation to power and resistance in the context of contemporary economic, environmental and social issues. This includes discourses of anthropocentrism. Charles has published *Resisting Financialization with Deleuze and Guattari* (2018).

Camille Bellet is a Wellcome Trust Research Fellow in Humanities and Social Science at the Centre for the History of Science, Technology, and Medicine (CHSTM), University of Manchester. She has a background in veterinary medicine and a PhD in Epidemiology and specializes in public health and human-animal studies.

Nickie Charles is Professor and Director of the Centre for the Study of Women and Gender, University of Warwick, UK. She is Principal Investigator on the Leverhulme-funded project, 'Shaping inter-species connectedness: training cultures and the emergence of new forms of human-animal relations' and has published widely in animal studies.

Caroline Clarke is a Senior Lecturer in Organization Studies at The Open University. She enjoys a variety of research interests, including a focus on first-opinion veterinary surgeons. More recently, she has developed an interest in critical animal studies and the Anthropocene. She has published in journals such as *Human Relations, Organization Studies,* and *The Veterinary Record*.

Matthew Cole is a Lecturer in Criminology at The Open University. His work focuses on the sociology of veganism/anti-veganism and extending a zemiological perspective on social harms of nonhuman animals. His first book, *Our Children and Other Animals*, co-written with Kate Stewart, explores the childhood socialization of human domination of other animals.

Lucy Connolly received her PhD in Business and Management from Maynooth University in 2020. Her thesis focused on human-animal relationships and the practice of care in equine-related organizations. She is interested in the ethical implications of the use of animals within our institutions, as well as eco-conscious and feminist approaches to business and management.

Kendra Coulter is the Chancellor's Chair for Research Excellence and Associate Professor in Labour Studies at Brock University (Canada) and a fellow of the Oxford Centre for Animal Ethics. She is the author of *Animals, Work, and the Promise of Interspecies Solidarity* (2016) and co-editor of *Animal Labour: A New Frontier of Interspecies Justice?* (2020).

Erika Cudworth works at Leicester's De Montfort University, UK. She is interested in intra-species relations and practices at various scales, from the relative privilege of homes in the global north, to practices of securitization and warfare, and the global Animal-Industrial Complex; and in the use of intersectional feminist and complexity approaches.

Olivia Davies is an Independent Academic and Filmmaker. She completed her PhD in Management and Organisation Studies at Monash University, Australia, focusing on the entanglement of humans and other animal species that work together. Her main research interests include more-than-human theory and methodologies, and audio-visual methods of data collection, analysis, and publication.

Rachel Forrest is Associate Professor (BSc Zoology, Postgraduate Diploma in Laboratory Technology, PhD Molecular Genetics), and was born and raised in Marton, New Zealand. Paternally, she is of Ngāti Maniapoto descent, while maternally she has strong European roots. Rachel's research focuses on improving the health and wellbeing of both animals and humans.

Rebekah Fox is a Cultural Geographer with a long-standing interest in human-animal relations. She is a Research Fellow at the University of Warwick, UK. Her research centres on the importance of animals in everyday life, including changing relationships with companion animals and the use of innovative methods in multispecies research.

Heather Fraser is a Critical Social Worker whose work focuses on violence and abuse, for humans and non-human animals. She coordinates the Master of Social Work Program at Queensland University of Technology. Visual and narrative methods, and animal assisted and art interventions are her other specialties.

José-Carlos García-Rosell is a Senior Lecturer of Responsible Tourism Business at the Multidimensional Tourism Institute, Faculty of Social Sciences, University of Lapland, and Adjunct Professor in Tourism at the Faculty of Tourism, University of Maribor. He works in the fields of corporate social responsibility, business ethics, and responsible management education.

Bryonny Goodwin-Hawkins is an Interdisciplinary Researcher in Rural and Regional Studies. Her work examines the legacies of economic change, and explores paths towards sustainable, inclusive futures. She is Senior Research Fellow at the Countryside and Community Research Institute and affiliated with the National Innovation Centre for Rural Enterprise (NICRE).

Steffen Hirth is Research Associate in the project EU 1.5° Lifestyles at the University of Münster. He obtained his PhD in Sociology at the Sustainable Consumption Institute (SCI), the University of Manchester and holds a degree in Social and Economic Geography from the Johannes Gutenberg University of Mainz.

Christian Hunold PhD, is a Professor in the Department of Politics, Drexel University, Philadelphia, USA. A scholar of environmental politics and political theory, Hunold's current work examines how the blurring of human and nonhuman worlds 'after nature' generates new forms of eco-political receptivity and reflexivity. He serves on the editorial board of *Environmental Politics*.

Astrid Huopalainen is a Senior Lecturer in Organization and Management at Åbo Akademi University, Finland. Her research focuses on posthuman theorizing, gender, embodiment, and the socio-materiality of organizing. She cares dearly for nonhuman animals and seeks to advance animal welfare and voice through her research and everyday praxis.

Clara Iversen is a Reader (Docent) in Sociology and a Senior Lecturer in Social Work. Her work concerns interactional resources for accomplishing shared understanding in various social work settings, including suicide helplines and dementia care.

Peter J. Jordan is Professor of Organizational Behavior and the Acting Director of the Work Organization and Wellbeing Research Centre at the Griffith Business School, Griffith University, Australia. Peter's current research interests include emotional intelligence, discrete emotions in organizations, and employee entitlement in organizations.

Frans Kamsteeg is an Associate Professor of Organization Studies at Vrije Universiteit Amsterdam. He teaches organizational ethnography and culture theory. His research comprises identity formation in South African Higher Education, the neoliberal impact on academia, including reflections on 'whiteness', and most recently, the role of non-human sentience in organizations.

Julie King is a Medical Anthropologist who explores and researches in the areas of gender and disability inequality and social inclusion. Her research methods are focused on giving voice to people who are often powerless in society and much of her work has been conducted in the global south. She currently coordinates the Social Work Honours Program at the Queensland University of Technology.

Mara Miele is Professor in Human Geography at Cardiff University, UK. Her research interests include animal geography, Science and Technology Studies (STS), and geographies of science, focusing on practices of animal welfare science and its advances in the field of animal emotions. She is currently working on a Leverhulme Trust funded project *Shaping Inter-species Connectedness* (2018–21).

Richie Nimmo is a Senior Lecturer in Sociology at the University of Manchester (UK), where he researches and teaches human-animal relations and environmental sociology. He has published numerous articles on human-animal-technology assemblages and society-nature interactions.

Damian O'Doherty is Professor of Management and Organization Theory at Liverpool University Management School where he is research director for the Work, Organization and Management Group. He is senior editor at *Organization* and has published widely in business and management studies.

Helena Pedersen is an Associate Professor in Education and Senior Lecturer at the Department of Pedagogical, Curricular and Professional Studies, University of Gothenburg. She is author of *Schizoanalysis and Animal Science Education* (2019), *Animals in Schools: Processes and Strategies in Human-Animal Education* (2010), and co-editor of the Critical Animal Studies book series (Brill).

Marcus Persson is an Associate Professor of Sociology at Linköping University, Sweden. His research focuses on the use of new technology and social transformation. He is currently involved in several research projects on the use of robots in working life and its impact on interpersonal relationships, work environment, and professional values.

David Redmalm is a Senior Lecturer at Mälardalen University, Sweden. He studies human-animal relations in various settings such as riding schools, urban space, multispecies homes, and organizations, and the different and often overlapping roles given to nonhuman animals in these contexts—as symbols, companions, adversaries, consumption objects, and co-workers.

Amanda Rees is a Historian of Science and Reader in Sociology at the University of York, UK. She has researched and published extensively in the field of human-animal studies, most recently *Animal Agents* (2017) and *Human* (2020), co-authored with Charlotte Sleigh.

Stephanie Russell is employed within the Corporate Programmes team in the Faculty of Business and Law at Anglia Ruskin University, Cambridge. Her research interests are in the field of remote working, organizational behaviour, and human-animal studies, with a focus on ethnographic and qualitative methodologies.

Doris Schneeberger works at the Institute of Change Management and Management Development at the Vienna University of Economics and Business (Austria). She obtained her PhD (Philosophy) at the University of Salzburg on possible future universal declarations of nonhuman animal rights. Her current research focus lies in the emerging field of animal organization studies.

Harriet Smith is a Research Associate in the School of Geography and Planning, Cardiff University. Her primary research focus is in developing novel methodologies, incorporating arts based and visual methods for more-than-human research. Her current role is on the Leverhulme Trust funded project 'Shaping interspecies connectedness: Training cultures and the emergence of new forms of human animal relations'.

Janet Sayers is Associate Professor (PhD Sociology, MBS (Dist)) and a second-generation British-originating Pākehā. Her work is focused on the interface between animals and organizations with a focus on ethical issues. She has published in journals such as *Organization*; *Gender, Work and Organization*; *Journal of Business Ethics*; and *Academy of Management Learning and Education*.

Thomas D.J. Sayers is an Ecologist, Nature Videographer, and Independent Academic. He completed his PhD in Ecology at the University of Melbourne, Australia, specializing in pollination ecology and overlooked pollinators. He is passionate about macro photography; a technique which he uses to showcase the beauty and importance of invertebrates.

Tricia Cleland Silva is a Postdoctoral Researcher at Hanken School of Economics in an Academy of Finland project and teaches at Metropolia University of Applied Sciences in the master's programme of Health Business Management. Her creative home base is at Metaphora International, a family business she co-founded with her husband in 2015.

Naomi Stekelenburg is a Researcher Advocate at Queensland University of Technology (Queensland, Australia). Her research interests centre around how emotions such as disgust are harnessed to reinforce restriction and boundaries on 'non-acceptable' human and other animal bodies.

Karl-Erik Sveiby is Professor Emeritus at Hanken School of Economics (Finland). Previous appointments include honorary professorships at Queensland University of Technology, Griffith University and Macquarie Graduate School of Management in Australia, and Hongkong Polytechnic University. His current research interests are responsible organizing, critical innovation studies, and knowledge management.

Nik Taylor is a Public Sociologist whose research focuses on mechanisms of power and marginalization expressed in/through human relations with other species. Her teaching, at the University of Canterbury, New Zealand, focuses on human-animal violence links and scholar-advocacy; she is also Co-Director of the New Zealand Centre for Human-Animal Studies.

Else Vogel is a Faculty Member of the Department of Anthropology at the University of Amsterdam. She currently holds a 'Veni' grant from the Dutch Research Council for the project 'Veterinary concerns: navigating clashing values in farm animal care', which examines human-animal relations in intensive livestock production.

Dinesh Joseph Wadiwel is a Senior Lecturer in Human Rights and Socio-Legal Studies at the University of Sydney. He is author of *The War against Animals* (2015), co-editor of *Foucault and Animals* (2017) and *Animals in the Anthropocene: Critical Perspectives on Non-Human Futures* (2015), member of the Multispecies Justice research group at the University of Sydney, and Chair of the Australasian Animal Studies Association.

Harry Wels is an Associate Professor of Organization Studies at Vrije Universiteit Amsterdam and in African Studies at the African Study Centre Leiden. His research is on multispecies ethnography in the context of wildlife conservation in southern Africa. His teaching is mainly on qualitative research methodologies in the context of a multisensory approach to multispecies worlds.

EDITORS' INTRODUCTION

LINDA TALLBERG AND LINDSAY HAMILTON

THE United Nations (UN) conference on Climate Change in Japan in 1997—and the resultant Kyoto Protocol—is often heralded as the historic moment at which climate change and environmental sustainability became the basis of economic, social, and political reorganization. Yet when the world's media refocused on Japan in July 2021 for the spectacle of the Olympic Games, it was unsettling to reflect that the intervening 24 years had not witnessed significant improvements in humanity's custodianship of planetary materials—animals, insects, vegetation, fossilized and mineral matter, and so on—and was living with and through a series of devastating events including a global pandemic and extreme weather events including tsunamis, flash floods, and forest fires. Had any of the environmental challenges identified at Kyoto been resolved? Had the international politics of whose task it was to lead on carbon reduction been ironed out? Rather than tackling the legacies of humanity's reliance upon fossil fuels, the global situation appeared much worse and, to many commentators, politically and economically insoluble. The limited crowd numbers at the Olympic Games served as a stark reminder of this concerning state of affairs, and the recent surge in fuel prices as a result of international conflict has underlined this concern in a time of extremes.

Such issues have been of increasing interest to those in the Business School (as a generic if contentious term) particularly in political economy, critical marketing, green accounting, corporate responsibility, and sustainability studies just as they inform and extend (increasingly vocal) public discourses on ethics, environmental citizenship, and planetary conservation. Important questions, therefore, continue to arise about the nature of contemporary organization and organizing practices; who are these for, exactly? Who benefits from the operation of increasingly globalized capital markets? What place is there for the nonhumans, such as animals, in all this organization; do they hold the lowly status of objects, resources, or bodies in which value is stored, only to be released through increasingly sophisticated extractive industrial processes? Or, can they be conceived of as workers, colleagues, and co-producers of organizational value, meaning, and wellbeing? What place is there for multispecies companionship, solidarity, and mutual value creation today and in the future, if any?

Given that it is increasingly acknowledged both in popular and academic literature that human and nonhuman animals do not dwell in separate spheres, neatly subdivided by borderlines between wilderness and civilization, subject and object, organization theory needs to respond more comprehensively to this more-than-human shift in outlook. In fact, as many theorists maintain, our fates are intertwined, often through commercial or organizational entanglements which serve to press our interactions together. The effects of these touching spheres of experience can be felt in the equally calamitous impacts of forest fires that obliterate nonhuman animals as well as human habitations, for example, but they are also felt in the rather more mundane context of consuming nonhuman animals or their by-products around the family dinner table, when one animal becomes food for another. The species are mixed together in a number of other commercially organized settings such as travel, leisure, care, and hospitality, as a number of the chapters in this book attest, and which collectively highlight that there is more to these contact points than the dyad of hunter-prey (a questionable practice distinction in itself). Hence, the importance of including nonhuman animals in our theoretical as well as empirical studies of commercial activity is of growing significance if we are to better account for the nonhumans who not only intersect and affect our lives but who are themselves deeply affected by our activities, thoughts, and feelings.

While the acceleration of habitat loss, climate change, and extinction has certainly broadened scholarly interest in this agenda, opening up the scope for study beyond specialist subfields and bringing it into the mainstay of business, management, and organization studies, we feel that it is timely to draw together those with an interest to help drive forward new agendas and ways of advancing thought on nonhuman animals and our relationships with them. Our aim in this handbook is to offer readers a starting point for thinking through the implications of this argument in their own studies and research. The chapters in this volume complement but also extend and draw together the growing portfolio of business scholarship which has resulted in conference streams and in special issues on nonhuman animals in business, management, and organization journals to date, such as *Gender, Work and Organization* (2019), *Culture and Organization* (2018), *Organization* (2016), and *Journal of Business Research* (2008). The increased interest demonstrates that business, management, and organization studies are beginning to take serious note of 'the animal question' but it is also important to give shape to that growing canon of work.

We start from the point that human-animal interactions are not reducible to binary positions of oppressor and oppressed, and while we retain a critical awareness of (and focus on) such a power-laden relationship, we also seek out cases of subtle, nuanced relationships that operate along collegiate, companionable lines. We foreground hard-to-describe mixed species relationships, and examine emotions, affect, and epistemology. In addition, we search for cultural, semiotic, and symbolic points of connection that inform us about the meaning of a broad range of experiences in a world populated by lifeforms other than humans. We seek to frame these enquiries through the overarching lens of commercial exchange and organization of human activities. Here we ask, and seek to provide some preliminary answers to, the questions: Where do animals fit in the contemporary organization and organizing? How should we characterize and theorize our relationships with the nonhuman world? And, perhaps most importantly, could we (human animals) behave more ethically in our relationships with nonhumans? Although this book attempts to respond to these questions by setting out the sorts of thinking and empirical research that we feel best constitutes the broad world of Animal Organization Studies—a new discipline in its own right—this book is intended to provide a starting point for further work at a time when more of us ask ourselves what it should mean to be human in this intense period of accelerated capitalism and climate crisis, a time which others have described as the posthuman condition in the Anthropocene.

As to how such a discipline of animal organization scholarship should be defined, it is hard to draw neat intellectual borderlines around it and we do not aim to limit its development or to exclude important writing from this emerging canon. It is perhaps fair to say, however, that this collection introduces and overviews the multidisciplinary work of over 40 key theorists and researchers who aim to draw focus towards nonhuman animals by taking a less anthropocentric line on matters of business, management, or organization. This may be because they hold an interest in the ethics, philosophy, and the role of nonhuman animals in workplaces or other organized spaces; nonhuman animals in systems of production, consumption, or capital exchange; or because they are pursuing research methods or ways of educating multispecies inclusion. Equally, they may have been selected because their empirical endeavours have emancipated nonhuman animals from the base condition of objects by producing accounts that resist humanist exclusion. These are the overarching thematic connections that have prompted us to make the selection of the chapters included in this formative volume and it is these objectives that we feel best sums up the Animal Organization Studies sphere of inquiry (but we also acknowledge that this could just as easily be called Nonhuman Organization Studies, Multispecies Organization Studies, Human-Animal Organization Studies, Posthuman Organization Studies, or indeed any number of different things). By trying to expose the workings of social and economic norms, such as those that unequivocally place certain nonhuman animal species in the category of food or objects of commercial value, there are a number of basic ways of configuring the discipline we have begun to define.

First, we perceive this to be unashamedly philosophical, and often, critical in its treatment of many aspects of the current status quo. In this endeavour, there is overlap with Critical Management Studies, Human-Animal Studies, and Critical Animal Studies, all of which take a broad view of the social and economic conditions by which power relations are underscored and gain traction. At the more strident end of this continuum, there are arguments against capitalist modes of organizing which are often presented as exploitative or unethical in their ramifications for nonhuman animal lives as well as marginalized human groups. These often encapsulate activist positions as well as advocacy scholarship. Other writers take a different line, however, by exposing the acting and affective capacities and behaviours of nonhuman animals, as well as the ways they often exist independently of humans, but use these to tell a less polemic story, nonetheless seeking to resist humanist bias in their broad emancipatory agenda.

Second, Animal Organization Studies is concerned with knowledge politics, the complexities arising from the very different heuristic and cognitive processes of nonhuman animals and humans as well as the persistent human dilemma and challenge of knowing nonhuman animals. In this there is also a recognition that humans are animals and, as such, Animal Organization Studies encompasses both human and nonhuman animal relationships in a broader multispecies focus than Organization Studies (which traditionally only considers human animals). Third, Animal Organization Studies is about mapping the points of connection and contact between different actors and forms of agency. In this aspect, there is a strong empirical drive to show and demonstrate (rather than just theorize) how nonhuman and human lives are entangled, enmeshed, and mutual in many ways.

Fourth and finally, Animal Organization Studies is interdisciplinary. By spanning a range of critical and questioning positions, we seek to broaden its scope beyond straightforward critique. Hence, this is not a discipline that is equivalent to animal rights, welfare, or liberation, although these aspects can be part of it when considering nonhuman animals in a critical manner. Animal Organization Studies seeks to resist recourse to human norms and assumptions to primacy but draws on many strands of thought about the philosophy, ethics, and theory of the human-animal boundary, interactions, and responsibilities, as well as those keen to explore the new and growing techniques and cases of multispecies research methods and theorization. It brings together Organizational Studies with writings from the broader humanities including Geography, Sociology, History, and Science studies, subjects which have, since the 1970s, sought to explore interspecies entanglements and intersections via specialized interdisciplinary academic journals such as *Animals*, *Anthrozoös*, and *Society & Animals*. Unique in its encompassing of a wide range of scholarship to focus on human-nonhuman animal interaction, we envision Animal Organization Studies to use a wide range of theoretical resources, such as Critical Management Studies, Critical Theory, ethics of care, feminism, ecofeminism, postcolonialism, Actor-Network Theory, affect theory, poststructuralism, and posthumanism (among others), to provide different, and at times overlapping, theoretical groundings to developing knowledge and understanding of the lived experiences of different species as they come into contact (or avoid one another) in human organized spaces such as tourist resorts, offices, farms, homes, and shelters. The book also includes aspects of technological innovations, such as robots and sensor systems, relevant to understanding and developing human-nonhuman animal relationships especially in the future.

Contributions to this Volume

To create this volume, we invited academics from different geographical regions, backgrounds, academic seniority, perspectives, and disciplines to write chapters on nonhuman animals in organization and organizing. To create a new field of Animal Organization Studies, many of the authors are from outside business studies, and the volume includes a range of Human-Animal Studies and Critical Animal Studies scholars from other disciplines, including sociology, philosophy, anthropology, politics, geography, and ecology. As organizing activities cut across most academic fields in one way or another, we asked these animal scholars to consider aspects of business and organizing in their work while our business scholars were more focused on engaging with the nonhuman animal question in aspects of Organizational Studies.

As readers might notice in the breadth of terminology used, we have deliberately not restricted chapter authors to stay consistent with certain words across the whole volume in efforts to showcase the diversity of conceptualizations, perspectives, and disciplinary conventions across nonhuman animal-focused research. To that end, some authors prefer 'multispecies' or 'more-than-human' and some refer to nonhuman animals as 'animals' while others prefer 'nonhuman animals'. This conceptual variety we see as enriching the project of opening up to life beyond a traditional humancentric focus in a multidisciplinary sense and we hope that those readers new to the interdisciplinary fields of Human-Animal Studies, Critical Animal Studies, and Animal Studies receive a taste of these specialized fields through this volume's inclusive conceptual positionings. This is also to allow interested readers to consider language in a deeper, more meaningful sense and we urge them to investigate further terms that pique their interest from the variety of references included in this work.

We have organized this book into four main themed parts. It was difficult to devise and maintain lines of demarcation between the chapters and parts, and many of them have relevance to several areas of inquiry and focus. Nonetheless, for simplicity and to aid the reader's understanding of the contents in this volume, Part I focuses on the historical, present, and future aspects of organizing nonhuman animals. This provides both historical and contemporary context for our later sections. Part II looks at aspects of knowing, meaning, and materiality in how we organize human-nonhuman animal encounters. It considers the way that nonhuman animals may be experienced by humans, in proximity or at a distance, and also considers some of the representations that humans make of nonhuman animals and their repertoires of activity. Part III consists of chapters related to nonhuman animals in production and consumption systems, specifically regarding themes of sustainability, identity, and ethics. Here, we consider the importance of nonhuman animals to economic activities of various types and also reflect on the 'rights' and 'wrongs' of global systems that incorporate nonhuman animal bodies and their by-products. Finally, Part IV brings the volume more specifically into the world of work with themes related to care, cultures, and affect in animal work relations. This part is also concerned with the ethics of the mixed species setting, but draws focus to specific work settings where such issues can be considered in context.

Part I Organizing Animals: Past, Present, Future

From the very outset of the volume in chapter 1, Kendra Coulter argues for a more attentive and ethically engaged field of organization studies to develop more compelling, proactive, and forward-looking scholarship. Coulter suggests that including a multispecies focus in organizational studies offers much-needed diagnostic and analytical insights that reflect the current realities of human-animal labour and relations. She argues that this is needed if we seriously aim to recognize the physical, psychological, emotional, and intergenerational harm many forms of human labour and production cause to other species—and to particular groups of people. Hence, the chapter considers the ways that organization scholars can build from a deeper understanding of the present, in order to offer valuable and nuanced ideas, proposals, and provocations focused on possible futures that includes multiple species of life.

In chapter 2, Amanda Rees provides a historical context for animal organizational studies by examining selected aspects of human-animal relationships as they evolved from the early-modern period to the present day. She explores how late eighteenth-century 'improvers' turned animals into factories for converting sunlight into profit, and how nineteenth-century social mobility created the modern-day 'pet' industry. Spanning a range of time periods, Rees considers the exponential growth of interest in wild animals in the twentieth century, the mechanics and profitability of their display in captivity, and the strategies for their study in the field, before turning to the growth of interest in animal agency and anthropomorphism in twenty-first-century analysis and scholarship and its implications for the livestock industry. Fundamentally, Rees charts the different contexts in which animals are regarded as raw materials, as tools or as people—and asks what this can tell us about wider human(e) relationships in the Anthropocene.

In chapter 3, Richie Nimmo zooms in on this particular theme, specifically, how the Anthropocene remains an essentially contested concept despite its increasing prevalence across multiple disciplines and fields. The chapter argues that anyone committed to thinking seriously about sustainability and what used to be called society-environment relations, must now engage with the Anthropocene and its paradoxes and challenges. The discussion undertakes a critical posthumanist reading of nonhuman animals in the Anthropocene with particular attention to the central paradoxes around agency and responsibility, and the implications for various influential approaches to environmental politics and green social transition. The chapter concludes with a call for a posthumanist praxis that embraces forms of environmental organization and politics which understands the Anthropocene as a crisis of human-animal relations and becoming human with others in a more-than-human world—a challenge inescapable to all of us.

In chapter 4, Caroline Clarke, Charles Barthold, and Matthew Cole provide a timely focus on how ignorance is both manufactured and organized in the animal-industrial complex (AIC), an aspect which has led to the emergence of many zoonotic diseases, including COVID-19. Clarke and colleagues discuss how—in our human need to satisfy demand and maximize profit—animals are bred and kept in poor conditions, without adequate space, light, or ventilation, as well as suffering long periods of transportation that lowers their immune system and heightens their stress levels. Despite these practices, Clarke, Barthold, and Cole argue that the root cause of pandemics has been persistently ignored. The chapter asks an important (and urgent) question: why, given the millions of lives, and trillions of dollars lost to COVID-19, there is still no urgent public debate about the root causes of pandemics?

In chapter 5, Helena Pedersen considers how humans might learn to respond to the challenges identified in previous chapters. Here, Pedersen uses the animal-industrial complex (AIC) as a framing concept and analytic tool for drawing our attention to the role and function of educational institutions as previously unexplored organizational contexts. The chapter delineates a rationale for critical inquiry but also explores AIC work education drawing on Deleuze and Guattari's thoughts in the continental philosophy tradition, works in sociology of education and Pedersen's own ethnographic fieldwork.

Part II Organizing Animal Encounters: Knowing, Meaning, and Materiality

In considering the contact points between humans and other animals, chapter 6 opens this section with an exploration of 'more-than-human' leadership in horse-human relationships within the Finnish equestrian culture. Drawing on ethnographic research on horse-human interactions, Astrid Huopalainen analyses how horses and humans *co-construct* relational leadership dynamics in time and space. By taking the fine-grained, affective, nonverbal, and largely overlooked characteristics of the horse-human relationship seriously in leadership research, the chapter extends the study of leadership into a posthuman or 'more-than-human' terrain and, by so doing, opens up novel possibilities for conceptualizing and researching leadership.

In chapter 7, Camille Bellet examines close and distant contact with animals through a case of new digital technologies in cattle farming organizations. She explains how new sensor technologies can be positive for certain aspects of animal farming and support farmers in their daily work, while there are also downsides and drawbacks. Drawing on a sample of documentary sources in France and the United Kingdom, the chapter examines the imaginary world built around new sensor technologies in cattle farming. Bellet argues this underlies broader norms and powers, conventions and etiquettes vis-à-vis sensory practices and human-animal relations in cattle farming, and at a broader social level, defines what rural modernity is and should be. The chapter suggests that by reconfiguring the senses and producing a new sensorium in cattle farming, advancing technologies are reconfiguring human relations with cows in dramatic ways.

In chapter 8, Erika Cudworth examines how time and space are organized in specific ways around paid human work, walking with dogs, and within the home, suggesting a multispecies organizing of everyday practices and spaces. Rather than focusing on organized animal relations as in the previous chapter, here Cudworth focuses on aspects of the mundane in everyday spaces, considering the home and the outside spaces of dog and human walking as important arenas in which organizing relations cohere. The chapter draws on an ethnographic study in two different UK field sites—the Lea Valley Park in East London, and a village in the East Midlands of England—finding that the activity of walking, homespace, and time are organized by both dogs and their human companions in ways that involve compromise, labour, and accommodation. In consideration of the constant negotiations in myriad small details, the chapter poses human working life as difficult for multispecies households, as work can compromise the wellbeing of some humans and many dogs.

In chapter 9, Christian Hunold draws attention from the domestic to the cityscape and explores the organization of space shared between people and urban coyotes. Due to the ubiquity of smart phones and the growing abundance of coyotes in US cities in the past 10 years, there has been a proliferation of urban coyote images in social media posts which form the empirical grounding of the chapter. The images typically reveal coyotes routinely inhabiting human-built infrastructure in mundane urban settings and the wild animal serves as the natural pole on a nature-culture continuum. Hunold explores the organization of urban spaces and how the ordinariness of images destabilize the prevailing wild-animal-out-of-place storyline and contribute to the normalization of coyotes as urban dwellers in multispecies landscapes characterized by fast-paced environmental change. To this end, the chapter analyses ways urban coyote images engage with the Anthropocene's evolutionary possibilities of hybridity, unsettled mixtures, and indeterminacy.

In chapter 10, Lucy Connolly highlights a distinctive multispecies methodology. She uses the Listening Guide method for interpreting interview transcripts and explores how narrative practices construct human-horse caring relationships at work. The Listening Guide method offers a 'way in' to access the construction of relationships between animal and human, and how humans engaged in human-animal work come to understand the nature of their roles in the context. This chapter is grounded within the ethic of care framework, specifically addressing embodied caring imagination. In the stories, the participants are heard 'giving voice' to the horses by literally speaking their side of the conversation and this represents one way of trying to include animal voice in research.

In chapter 11, Harry Wels and Frans Kamsteeg continue the theme of experiencing, sensing, and learning by presenting a way to conduct multispecies organizational ethnography through a reiterative combination and cycle of 'Observation', 'Becoming with', and 'Reflexivity'—which they call OBR—based on the tracking craft of the Southern African San. The chapter not only highlights the importance of Indigenous knowledges of the animals in question, it also argues for a 'wild pedagogy' in teaching and researching. The wild pedagogy is where humans are decentred and multisensorial realities are considered. To lend empirical depth to this argument, the chapter illustrates the San's animated worldview and cosmologies which always include nonhuman sentience in animals (and plants), in non-hierarchical ways.

In chapter 12, Karl-Erik Sveiby and (sadly, deceased Indigenous custodian) Tex Skuthorpe, illustrate another Indigenous perspective which foregrounds animals as socially significant actors with their own unique crafts and wisdom. Here, the relational ontology of the prehistoric community of the Australian Nhunggabarra First People and their stories give a unique insight in how precolonial humanity organized respectful relationships with animals. The chapter highlights the value of this viewpoint for the present day. The relational constructivism as an epistemology explicitly describes activities, interactions, and power relations in this community and the chapter calls for respectful reciprocation in human-animal interactions, even if they may sometimes appear difficult to understand from a present-day point of view.

In chapter 13, Stephanie Russell examines the meanings attributed to animals in a Western business setting. In describing a 'Gung Ho' work-culture, she depicts a range of telling animal metaphors and animal costumes in her case study of Fireco. Drawing on Actor Network Theory (ANT), the chapter highlights the important role of nonhumans in shaping our learning of complex workplace issues. Russell argues that the ANT lens provides insights to the power relations shared amongst human and nonhuman actors, and that these result in more intelligible, accessible, and inclusive workplace practices when all employees understand, embrace, or, where appropriate, challenge them. The chapter prompts us to reflect on the ways we consider animals as emblems and totems of organizational value.

In chapter 14, Tricia Cleland Silva continues methods of narrative interpretation, this time in terms of Strategic Human Resource Management (SHRM) stories that include animal metaphors. The chapter opens a discussion to the limitation of multispecies research within human management fields and calls for more open-minded, inductive, and inclusive approaches to research that involves, or at least acknowledges, all the species within the context of study. However, this requires researchers to be held accountable for the stories they tell and be critical of the limitations to human-centric storytelling. Using the Texan saying 'Big Hat, No Cattle', the chapter contrasts real and imagined stories about management and animals.

Part III Sustainability, Identity, and Ethics: Animals in Production and Consumption Systems

Providing important context to the developing discussion of ethics, capital exchange, and consumption, in chapter 15, Bryonny Goodwin-Hawkins shares insights of infrastructures of everyday multispecies life in the foundational economy. She describes shared human and animal lives, labour, and products, and discusses the absence of animals in foundational economy thinking. Helpfully, the chapter identifies potential ways to review our economic foundations through a multispecies lens. The chapter does so through examples from the agri-food sector and working across three key themes: shared everydays, revaluing human-animal foundations, and prioritizing wellbeing, all to create a shared and sustainable future through 'good lives' for both humans and animals.

Chapter 16 draws focus away from economic matters to the personal and psychological realm of experience. Doris Schneeberger uses a compassionate methodology with a qualitative interventionist research design in order to examine whether certain interventions reduce speciesism, the term that describes the relegation of certain species to lower status on the basis of their capacities or appearance. Schneeberger explains that speciesism distorts human thinking, perceptions, and research efforts while causing suffering and harm to countless sentient beings. Thus, the chapter tests management doctoral students' levels of speciesism through 'the speciesism scale' completed prior and after a designed intervention of reducing speciesism. The chapter takes a psychological approach to the bigger social problem of speciesism, arguing for a positive and optimistic approach to learning about other animals and their experiences.

In chapter 17, Dinesh Joseph Wadiwel continues the thematic focus on ethics and the (mis)treatment of nonhuman animals. The chapter argues that the two intertwined forces of anthropocentrism and industrial capitalism dominate relationships and entire economies. Wadiwel explores how our contemporary modality of hierarchical anthropocentrism materializes in practices and institutions which are designed to pin down nonhuman animals, establishing a continuing 'war like' relation of violence, domination, and death in our relationship to them. Questioning this dyad, the chapter describes how these systematic forms of violence interact with nonhuman animals within the capitalist food system and draws on Marx's value theory to examine how animals are positioned as raw materials and labour within production. The chapter prompts deeper thinking about the ways that humans have become oriented towards the extraction of surplus and how animals have been positioned as consumption commodities designed to enable the reproduction of human life. The chapter ends by calling for radical transformation in our societal systems that promote a wider conception of flourishing that moves beyond the human.

In chapter 18, Nik Taylor, Heather Fraser, Naomi Stekelenburg, and Julie King, turn to the everyday challenges of change. This chapter analyses a struggle over morality in the business of meat consumption and production through two projects: *The Dairy Farmers' Wellbeing Project* (2017–19) and the *Vegan Wellbeing Project* (2019–20). Animal farming is still etched in the dominant masculine representations of 'true' 'Kiwi' and 'Aussie' national identities in spite of the worldwide rise in veganism and the plant-based industry. The competing gendered discourses about the ethics and morality of using animals for food, clothing, entertainment, and testing are enlivened by emotive social media discussions and the chapter explores the competing discourses impacting markets, jobs, and future industry directions. This chapter serves as a reminder of the highly contentious nature of both food production work and food consumption practices.

In chapter 19, Else Vogel focuses on Dutch veterinary practices in intensive farming. In the Netherlands, veterinarians play a key role in the continuation, regulation, and innovation of industrial livestock production and Vogel details how veterinarians treat animals, coach farmers, perform animal welfare procedures, or otherwise try to achieve 'good' farm animal care. Describing the different roles veterinarians use in livestock production, the chapter highlights different practices of *doing good*—each with its own care and accountability relations, and particular promises, challenges, and limits. What emerges is that while ethicists and animal activists elevate the relation to the animal as the primary ethical relationship, in practice veterinarians are entangled, and operate in a web of relations.

In chapter 20, Steffen Hirth contributes to a powerful critique of the extant food system with a practice approach that draws on overlapping themes of sustainability and ethics. The chapter considers the academic, policy, and public debates that have increasingly led to calls for the adoption of more plant-based diets. Yet, in spite of acknowledging livestock's 'long shadow' (i.e. its high environmental footprint) and the need to transform food systems towards sustainable practices, vegan and vegetarian diets still cause fierce debates between people with different dietary identities. The chapter argues that identity-based understandings of who or what is considered as a 'vegan' obfuscate necessary changes in production and provisioning practices. Thus, the chapter develops a wider understanding of vegan food practices through stockfree organic agriculture's organization, biomateriality, and its 'short' shadow.

In chapter 21, Olivia Davies and Thomas D.J. Sayers take focus away from mammals, and draw our gaze to insects and, specifically, invertebrate animals. In addition to debating the ethics of having (or not having) a backbone, the chapter extends the theme of sustainability in terms of the ways in which organizations attend (or not) to our invertebrate companions, moves which hold significant ecological and social implications. The chapter draws attention to some of these dimensions in relation to the important ecological and economic activity of insect pollination through an empirical focus on the interrelated organizational phenomena of honeybee bias and 'beewashing'. The authors propose acts of more-than-vertebrate care which can only take place through intimate moments of relationality; are always entangled with and influenced by other unique, situated forces; and, emerge through the intersection of multiple 'lifetimes', the outcomes of which are never singular, pre-determined, or concluded once-and-for-all. The chapter also discusses what this might entail for various insect-pollinated systems of commercial importance.

In chapter 22, and concluding this part in a more explicitly philosophical way, Elisa Aaltola explores the potential uses and moral dimensions of empathy within organizations. The three fundamental questions raised in this chapter are: What are the social and moral benefits of empathy? How do these benefits manifest in de facto animal ethics? And should organizations seek to enhance empathy so as to better pay heed to the wellbeing of nonhuman animals? To start answering these, the chapter introduces six different varieties of empathy and analyses their potential role in making sense of the perspectives and moral consideration of nonhuman animals. Hence, Aaltola's empathy framework contributes to a new type of organizational philosophy that demonstrates how to pay attention to the experiences and moral worth of nonhuman animals.

Part IV Care, Cultures, and Affect in Animal Work Relations

This part turns to lived social, organizational, and work experiences with animals; or at least the idea of animals. To commence, in chapter 23, Damian O'Doherty draws on ethnographic research at Manchester Airport, not usually associated with nonhuman life. Yet here, 'Olly the cat' served as totem and guide during his fieldwork and the chapter calls for animal studies in management and organization research to go beyond a human-centred speciesism in which animals serve as symbols, representations, or projections of all-too-human preoccupations and anxieties. Hence, O'Doherty suggests a 'feline politics' that requires new sensitizing concepts and language in order to trace the way in which organization proliferates and unfolds, in feline moves, through other-than-human inflected patterns of disorganization and disorder.

In chapter 24, Lindsay Hamilton presents rockpools and the acts of rockpooling as an affective encounter between species. The chapter highlights the value of charisma as a theoretical framing of the intertidal zone which is explored as a space of both material and semiotic 'assemblage' made possible by the playful and child-like acts of curatorship through the particular valuation of target species, such as fish and crabs. The chapter uses vignettes, stories, and legends to consider how a range of positive and negative feelings, senses, and emotions can play out in both real and imagined encounters at the seashore. Hamilton explains that charisma and affect are of considerable value for explaining how and why some species draw the focus of human attention, care, and conservation efforts, while other species receive little or no interest or care.

In chapter 25, Linda Tallberg and Peter J. Jordan discuss callings and disaster in an animal shelter. Using affective multispecies ethnographical material, the chapter discusses how wellbeing in human-animal work is entangled across species when a natural disaster reframed wellbeing for the multispecies organizational actors. Using a posthumanist lens on animal dirty work, the authors illustrate how a crisis revealed insights into dissonance and wellbeing for humans and animals. The chapter suggests that care-based animal organizations, such as those in the animal welfare sector, need to better consider the interconnectedness of multispecies wellbeing in designing their organizational policies and processes as ideological values are core for many workers who ascribe to having a work-calling. Hence, the chapter calls for more attention to interspecies wellbeing at work and in organizations, as fundamentally, wellbeing is deeply entangled in affective relationships.

In chapter 26, José-Carlos García-Rosell discusses corporate activism of animal welfare within the context of dog sledding tourism in northern Finland. Using institutional theory and care ethics, the chapter illustrates how a group of tourism husky kennels engage in political action to improve the living and working conditions of sled dogs. García-Rosell suggests this theoretical framework contributes to approaching animal welfare activism in terms of an ethical position that is driven by justice and care experienced through multispecies relationships in this business-context. In addition, the chapter explores the motivation of the small business owners as well as the barriers to, and strategies for, their political struggle of improving animal working lives.

In chapter 27, David Redmalm, Marcus Persson, and Clara Iversen explore the topic of robotic animals in dementia care organizations. Based on the chapter's empirical data, the authors discuss ideas of animality that shape the robots and their application in care organizations and find that the robot animals connect with a fundamental mammalian aspect of our humanity. However, the authors point to concerns of patients' dehumanization when robots replace human-to-human interaction, and the robots are thus treated as a threat to human dignity. Hence, the chapter examines how notions of animality (if not living breathing animality) and a biopolitical understanding of the human as mammal play an integral role in robotized care organizations.

In chapter 28, Janet Sayers and Rachel Forrest discuss the Te Ao Māori ontology (Māori worldview), which sees the interconnectedness and interrelationship of all living and non-living things, to analyse human-kurī (dog) relations in Aotearoa New Zealand. Based on collaborative action research, as well as archival materials and Indigenous resources, the chapter discusses One Welfare—an influential approach to understanding the vital relationship between human and animal wellbeing in a variety of industries and organizations—and a need for both a transdisciplinary approach and partnership with Māori (the tangata whenua or Indigenous people of Aotearoa New Zealand), around human-nonhuman-environmental interfaces to do with human and animal health. Serving as a reminder of the importance of alternative ways of seeing and thinking about animals, Sayers and Forrest use their detailed case materials to show the legal, political, and economic nature of an act so apparently mundane as dog keeping.

In chapter 29, Nickie Charles, Rebekah Fox, Mara Miele, and Harriet Smith maintain a canine focus by examining the practicalities of dog training. In two case study settings, they show how relations between humans and dogs are constructed and explore how different organizational cultures shape interspecies working relationships. Using a gendered lens, and drawing on the theories of emotion and affect, they address the idea of partnership in two contrasting organizations. They find that partnerships are controlled by the organization, interspecies affective ties are instrumentalized to meet organizational goals, and dog-human relationships only persist insofar as they contribute to these goals. The chapter asks whether the differences in the way the organizations construct this relationship and the work they do in cases of partnership failure can be understood in terms of their gendered cultures and the gendered work the dogs are trained to do.

The content, rationale and methodological background of these collected chapters, far from producing a definitive or final version of Animal Organization Studies, offers a selective window into the possibilities open to new and established scholars. We hope that in this collected set of theoretical, empirical and methodological writings, readers will find inspiration to think differently, experiment with different perspectives, and reflect on their own practices and values with the nonhuman world.

PART I
ORGANIZING ANIMALS: PAST, PRESENT, FUTURE

CHAPTER 1

FROM INTERESTING TO INFLUENTIAL

Looking Forward with Multispecies Organization Studies

KENDRA COULTER

It is organizational activity, particularly that of for-profit organizations, which causes the most harm to the largest number of animals. This fact should be kept front-of-mind when thinking about animals and organizations. I would argue that this fact means organizational researchers ought to take human-animal relations and multispecies issues seriously. At the same time, some organizational sites contain more ethical, solidaristic, and caring interspecies patterns, or practices that are more complex and warrant additional consideration. As a result, organizational analyses can not only help to critique and disrupt normalized patterns of violence and exploitation, but also to identify more promising and sustainable alternatives.

The latter can be accomplished by unpacking existing organizational cultures and practices, and by developing new and better ways of thinking and working with—and for—other species. In other words, multispecies organization studies can be both responsive and proactive. In this chapter, I argue that it is precisely this combination of conceptual and social goals that will help build ethically engaged and intellectually nuanced multispecies organization studies. The result would be compelling and influential scholarship that enriches organization studies itself, complementary fields of study, and ideally, real worlds of work.

To develop this argument, I begin by synthesizing the most salient dimensions of the intellectual terrain of organization studies, particularly given the international scale of this volume. Then I will focus on a particularly significant set of organizations, those in industrial animal agriculture, what is widely called factory farming. I will briefly outline the multifaceted, multispecies impacts of this approach to agriculture. Then I suggest alternatives as part of engaging in proactive thinking and exemplifying how organization studies can move beyond the diagnostic to the generative. I illustrate how existing labour process theory and other scholarly concepts can be enlisted and reshaped for multispecies organization studies, as well as integrate new analytical concepts to help reflect and recognize the realities of animals' labour and interspecies workplace relations. Crucially, I emphasize that multispecies organization studies ought to consistently take the wellbeing of both humans and other animals seriously. In other words, a multispecies organization studies ought to not only consider the interesting, but also conceptualize and produce research that can be influential, beyond the academy.

Organization Studies in Context

The chapters in this collection explore the intersections of work, organizations, and animals from various theoretical and geographic perspectives. Authors are also situated in different academic disciplines and scholarly fields. Some are primarily scholars of work and employment, broadly conceived, normally based in workplace or labour studies programmes or in management/business schools. Others are predominantly animal studies scholars based in different cognate disciplines who have begun to integrate research on and analyses of labour and/or workplaces.

This breadth is noteworthy for a few reasons. It reflects a growing recognition of the importance of studying work and workers when thinking about animals—and vice versa. At the same time, it means while we have a common interest in the multispecies nature of organizations, we have different areas of expertise, varied levels of knowledge about the sociology of work, labour studies, and organizations, and we are likely operating with distinct disciplinary and ontological expectations. These variances are further shaped by the geographic contexts in which we undertake academic labour in ways that are worth highlighting.

Indeed, I posit that a significant difference among organizational scholars, broadly conceived, is how we have been initiated into this academic domain, and what the dominant contours of our respective educational trajectories have been and continue to be. More specifically, because of distinct national academic cultures and/or disciplinary conventions, we may have different views on what the underlying goals of scholarly work are and ought to be. I have seen this tension on display at organization studies conferences, for example, and deem it important to address this metaphorical elephant in the room, particularly given the focus of this volume, and my argument in this chapter. Are scholars to study the world as it is and shed light on pressing, complex, misunderstood, or not well-known dynamics, including types of work and workers for academic purposes? Is this project to be pursued with dispassion in the pursuit of objectivity? Or is there a place for ethics and for scholarship that promotes greater fairness, equity, and justice? Conversely, is the role of scholarship to imagine and articulate transformative goals? In other words, to boldly imagine something different and paint utopian pictures, thereby articulating and encouraging larger projects of change?

The preferred or perhaps enforced answers to these questions will depend, in part, on disciplinary training and location. As a decidedly interdisciplinary scholar who both travels across and among different cognate disciplines and contributes to transdisciplinary scholarship in the fields of work and labour studies and different constellations of animal studies, I have seen these tensions play out in many ways, sometimes leaving people operating in (or retreating to) separate academic silos (or silos within silos), and/or, quite honestly, seeming like they are speaking different languages. For some scholars, engaging in generative scholarship that moves beyond describing and unpacking things as they are in order to consider how they *might be* is simply not an option. These acts of disciplinary disciplining may manifest particularly in publishing, and other forms of research support can reject such attempts, as can the requirements of different national, academic systems (including lists of 'acceptable' journals). For others, the place of utopian imaginings can serve decidedly small 'p' political intellectual goals and be welcome. At the same time, it is important to note that gender, ethnoracial identities, class, and other social factors can figure in noteworthy ways when academics are determining who is permitted to engage in proactive scholarship, and who is not.

These dynamics undoubtedly affect the ability for researchers to take up my call for organizational scholarship that is both responsive and proactive, and I am cognizant of these and other structural constraints shaping the larger academic terrain and researchers' abilities to engage in the sorts of work they deem of greatest importance. Indeed, I am grateful for the conceptual freedom and ability to take risks and forge new paths afforded by my tenured position in a scholarly field that welcomes politically engaged research and writing, my labour union, and the principles of academic freedom.

Overall, I see value in both 'as things are' research and in ambitious 'as things could be' research. At the same time, I argue that there is a pressing need for scholarship that fits between these two poles, for diagnostic scholarship that includes generative and solution-oriented propositions that are more achievable or actionable in the here and now. My hope is that this chapter can help readers see ways to transcend this perceived or real binary. In my view, critique is crucial, but not enough, on its own. Data gathering is essential, but insufficient as a solitary end goal. Remaining exclusively in the realm of the ambitiously imaginary can be an escape from having to address the messiness of real challenges in the world of work, including the barriers to change, and there is a need not only for bold utopian thinking, but also practical, actionable articulations that can be taken up now.

Crucially, I am not suggesting that ethical principles and goals replace the process of rigorous research and analysis by any means. Data matters. Evidence can broaden and/or challenge our perspectives in modest and major ways. Nuance is critically important. An ethically engaged engine can drive a multispecies or animal organization studies that values data of different kinds and is rooted in evidence, in the service of improving work-lives—those of fellow humans and of other animals. What I have called the promise of interspecies solidarity (e.g. Coulter, 2016a; 2016b), an ethical and political commitment rooted in empathy that invites us to envision and pursue progressive changes at local and larger levels for and with other animals, can further motivate and propel rigorous, attentive scholarship that simultaneously confronts the realities of human-animal labour today, and uses these priorities and processes to develop and advance solutions and alternatives, in the short, medium, and longer terms. I hope organization researchers feel neither apprehensive about making recommendations when it comes to the wellbeing of other species, nor that grand speculation is the only acceptable kind of forward-facing scholarship. Instead, I assert that there is value in generative approaches to organization studies that exist somewhere on the practical-utopian continuum and see great need for proposals that can be enlisted and adopted in organizations to improve the work-lives and experiences of members of other species and of our own.

Critical Data in Multispecies Organization Studies

In surveying the broad terrain of animals, organizations, and work, the sheer volume, breadth, and diversity of multispecies dynamics becomes clear (Coulter, 2016a). Other species have always been interconnected with humans' livelihoods in different ways and some patterns have remained consistent, while others have changed, been intensified, been improved, or become more damaging. There are also recent and nascent patterns, particularly when it comes to how our species engages animals in the formal provisioning of physical, psychological, and/or emotional care for people.

Determining who and what we want to study are not only intellectual decisions but are also political and ethical choices. So too are the questions we ask (and methods we use, an important dimension, one that is beyond the scope of this discussion and well-considered elsewhere: see e.g. Birke and Thompson, 2018; Coulter, 2018; Hamilton and Taylor, 2012). There is important multispecies, interspecies, and animal-centric research being undertaken as multispecies labour and organization studies develops. Each of these emphases can garner different as well as complementary data and insights. Here I will focus on a particularly significant, challenging, and damaging arena, namely industrial animal agriculture, precisely because of the scale and depth of its harm for animals, first and foremost, but also for humans and our shared environment.

Homo Sapiens first made a living through foraging/hunting-gathering and this was the primary way we survived for most of human history. Some foraging groups, particularly when environmental and geographic conditions were favourable, became more sedentary and began to farm. Humans have engaged in subsistence farming for thousands of years, and small-scale horticulture continued through the feudal and capitalist eras. It is only in the last few decades that a markedly different approach to agriculture has been created and expanded, an industrialized intra- and international system of for-profit, corporatized food production. In most countries of the global north, large agribusinesses, Concentrated Animal Feed Operations (CAFOs), and highly mechanized slaughtering facilities have become the dominant approach to agriculture, a process dubbed factory farming to emphasize the parallels between for-profit organizations producing inanimate objects like cars, and this hegemonic approach to agriculture. The core differences are that the corporate animal agriculture chain is not an assembly line, but a disassembly line, and the individuals involved are not inanimate objects, but rather sentient beings. This system exemplifies a core piece of what Barbara Noske (1989; 1997) has called the 'animal-industrial complex' (see also Twine, 2012). She proposed this term to capture the network of actors and organizations in both the private and public sectors that promote and defend industrialized and corporatized violence against animals.

This shift has been damaging to people and particularly to other animals. This system of normalized harm forms the foundation of so much economic activity and is impossible to ignore when thinking about animals and organizations. Smaller, family-owned farms are increasingly rare in countries around the global north. International agribusinesses are also contributing to the dispossession of communal and smallholder land and restricting the ability for peasants and other local people to pursue even modest livelihoods across the global south. Corporate consolidation means that a small number of agricultural corporations now own much of the food production and processing system. In some cases, such as with Tyson Foods in the United States, the same company may own all or many stages of the process—from the genetic engineering of breeding hens to the hatcheries and eggs to the trucks that drive those eggs to the feed that is provided for the chickens during their short lives. These processes are intended to maximize the number of animals that can be kept and then killed, the speed at which this happens, and the profit that can be generated (Wadiwel, 2020).

This corporate chain also disproportionately harms racialized and poor people, whether they are workers within the facilities and/or live nearby. Workers are at risk for both physical and psychological harm and crime rates and pollution in the areas around slaughtering facilities also increase (Cartwright et al., 2012; Fitzgerald, 2010; Fitzgerald, Kalof, and Dietz, 2009; Leibler and Perry, 2017; Leibler, Janulewicz, and Perry, 2017; Jacques, 2014). Injury and illness rates in slaughterhouses are higher than manufacturing averages. In plants killing and processing larger animals like cows, horses, and pigs, the risk to workers is even greater (Stull and Broadway, 2013). Racialized workers, women, immigrants, migrant workers, and/or undocumented people heavily populate slaughterhouse workforces (Pachirat, 2011; Stull and Broadway, 2013).

A sizeable body of scientific research has established that industrial agriculture is a leading cause of climate change, biodiversity loss, and species extinctions (see e.g. Caro, Davis, Bastianoni, and Caldeira, 2014; Gerber et al., 2013; Heffernan, Salman, and York, 2013; Ripple et al., 2014; Román-Palacios and Wiens, 2020). The health risks are also significant. Keeping thousands or tens of thousands of animals together in the tight, cramped conditions that characterize intensive confinement increases the risk of disease transmission among animals, and the likelihood of zoonotic (animal-human) transfer. Whether the next pandemic is viral or bacterial, intensive confinement is increasing the danger (see e.g. Akhtar, 2012; Chin et al., 2020; Hoelzer et al., 2017).

The damage done to animals by factory farming is difficult to properly capture. Most animals intended to be consumed are kept indoors in windowless facilities. Gestation crates for female pigs that allow them to stand up and lie down, but not move or turn around are illegal in a number of European countries, but widely used in North America and countries around the world, including China. Most chickens are held in rows of stacked battery cages within which they cannot move around or spread their wings. Milk is produced only by cows who have given birth, so females are impregnated repeatedly over a three- to four-year period after which they, too, are slaughtered. Calves are commonly removed from their mothers the day they are born. Female calves are taken to become milk producers themselves, while the males are usually kept largely immobile and solitary for three to four months before being slaughtered for veal.

Undoubtedly, there is some heterogeneity across farms and national contexts (Wilkie, 2010), but these practices are commonly established as industry standards. The sheer number of animals involved (tens of billions globally) and the depth of the physical, psychological, emotional, and intergenerational suffering are shocking, and unequivocally warrant the attention of anyone interested in organizations and animals. Noske (1989) argues that these billions of animals are examples of alienated animal labour. I have suggested that we can see female animals required to produce babies, eggs, or milk as engaged in a kind of coerced body work. Correspondingly, I have noted that these animals are prevented from engaging in their own forms of care work with their own families (Coulter, 2016a; 2016b).

Given the facts, I would argue that these widespread, damaging practices warrant more than identification and analysis. Undoubtedly, critique is warranted, from multiple distinct and overlapping angles. But the case of factory farming is significant not only because of the scale and severity of the suffering, but also because it should be challenged, and alternatives offered. That such a normalized, industrial system both forms the foundation of the food system and causes so much interspecies and multispecies harm demands recognition from organization scholars.

For reasons of workers' health, safety, and wellbeing, animal ethics, environmental preservation, and racial and global justice, this is an issue which does not simply warrant minor reforms. Instead, this is a serious socio-political and organizational challenge that calls for organization scholars to contribute to the generation and pursuit of alternatives to such severe violence and widespread suffering. This is neither an extreme nor utopian position. Factory farming is increasingly about the fundamentals of human health and, given the facts, confronting industrial animal agriculture is a logical and necessary task.

The Work of Generative Thinking

Many alternatives to factory farming exist and are continuously being developed. Plant-based foods and cultured meat and dairy are both receiving a growing amount of private-sector investment and developing and expanding as a result. Whether such developments offer opportunities to diversify and decentralize the food system is still uncertain, as are the kinds of jobs that will be created. In a similar vein, the role or potential involvement of the public sector is yet to be determined.

These are important developments that can help eliminate and replace animal suffering and dangerous, low-quality work for people, and are noteworthy for their potential to create what I call humane jobs. I have proposed the concept of humane jobs as a pithy term to help propel a new approach to animals and labour, one predicated on respect for all species (Coulter, 2016c; 2017). Similar to the idea that good, green jobs can help us transcend real and perceived divisions between environmental preservation and quality work, the concept of humane jobs can be enlisted responsively or proactively to assess and propose work that benefits both people and animals.

The idea of 'creating more humane jobs' is two-fold (see, in particular, Coulter, 2016c). It involves improving certain areas of work that already benefit animals (such as jobs in protection, various kinds of care work, etc.) in order to improve the working conditions and quality of life for people. It is also about creating new jobs and employment sectors that are underscored by a commitment to helping other species, not harming them. This is often achieved by replacing harmful practices (such as factory farming) with more ethical and sustainable alternatives that recognize people's need for livelihoods. The humane jobs framework can be employed to consider animal labour (Cochrane, 2020; Coulter, 2020a; D'Souza, Hovorka, and Neil, 2020), but it is primarily intended to generate better and new paid work for people in order to provide greater protections for other species.

As part of transitioning and replacing industrial animal agriculture, the prospects for urban employment in areas like food research and development, retail, service and hospitality, and so on, are clear. I also suggest that the end of factory farming could contribute to the development of more just, prosperous, and sustainable rural communities. After assessing existing practices, comparable examples, and new possibilities, as part of a commitment to fostering generative organization studies, here I highlight areas of potential. Unlike the corporatized status quo, the end of factory farming could create space for a resurgence of family farming, as well as a chance to diversify rural income sources. There will be new demand for more plant-based crops and proteins, including organic items, as well as the ingredients needed for new lab-created products. It is likely that some consumers will still want meat from dead animals, so animal farming will likely be part of the landscape, albeit on a smaller scale. Dining tourism that brings people onto real family farms could also thrive. Indeed, the end of factory farming does not mean the end of farming. Its demise could create conditions where the number of farmers would increase. Crucially, as part of intraspecies solidarity, the working conditions and wellbeing of the migrant workers who make so much fruit and vegetable farming possible should be taken more seriously, too, around the world.

There are also opportunities for re-imagining and expanding what farms do. For example, green care refers to a range of organized beneficial interactions with nature. It includes animal-assisted therapy, therapeutic horticulture, and care farms. Some of these kinds of programmes and farms already exist in various countries. Farms can be reshaped into places for children's and adults' learning, the delivery of health services, job training, among other programmes and services. This kind of expansion and diversification has the benefit of both providing valuable services and generating new green and humane jobs for people with varying levels of education and training, and from diverse backgrounds.

With a few exceptions, existing green care normally involves out-of-pocket user fees. Equity should be kept in mind if expanding green care, so it could be regulated and integrated with/into existing education, health care and One Health programmes (as is done in Norway, for example; see Garcia-Llorente, Rubio-Olivar, and Gutierrez-Briceno, 2018; Haugan et al., 2007). Moreover, if animals were going to be integrated as co-workers into therapy programmes, for example, their wellbeing, working conditions, and what I have called work-lives (see e.g. Coulter, 2020a; 2020b) need to be taken into consideration so the animals are properly respected on the job, as well as before and after their formal careers.

Indeed, animals would be part of a post-factory farming landscape. There would be fewer but happier animals, and the nature of human-animal relationships would likely change. Many people already work and interact with horses for leisure, sport, companionship, and sheer joy, for example, and the same could be true for other kinds of animals. Moreover, sub-cultures can celebrate and showcase heritage breeds, for example, and the inherent worth of these animals, minus the subsequent death sentence. More non-profit sanctuaries where animals can flourish without any expectations would also be beneficial.

Finally, as British writer George Monbiot (see, for instance, Monbiot, 2014) and others have argued in both academic and mainstream circles, there are many environmental reasons to allow some rural areas to be repopulated with native plant and animal species. This process is known as rewilding. Certain carefully planned opportunities for expanded recreation and learning in the country (such as hiking, birding) and some modest, strategic eco-tourism, including Indigenous-led initiatives and partnerships, could co-exist with rewilding (see e.g. Dashper and Buchmann, 2020; Fennell and Sheppard, 2021; García-Rosell and Tallberg, 2021; Kline and Rickly, 2021). This would also allow more wild animals to engage in their own forms of subsistence and care work, in processes of social reproduction that reproduce individuals and whole generations of their own species (Coulter, 2016a; 2016b). Moreover, the cumulative effects of wild animals' forms of labour contribute to what I have dubbed eco-social reproduction, as they also directly affect the health of local environments and ecosystems (ibid). Returning some land to other species is one small way to begin to make amends for the immense damage we have done to animals' families, cultures, and habitats, and to allow them to engage in their own self-initiated and self-organized forms of work.

The goal of these kinds of proposals, as part of pursuing a humane jobs transition away from factory farming, is for rural regions to become more sustainable, vibrant spaces for people and animals to respectfully co-exist. Rather than harming rural economies, the end of factory farming is an opportunity to create new income sources and humane jobs for diverse people. This kind of thinking is both responsive to an urgent and widespread organizational challenge and illustrates how we can extend our vocabulary and analysis to generate fodder for improvements and change.

Ironically, some might see this vision as utopian. Others may see this kind of approach as too reformist. Nevertheless, what I have done is provide one extended illustration of how an ethically engaged multispecies organization studies can be diagnostic, as well as proactive. There are many more such opportunities, and how specifically such work is pursued will vary depending on the particular contexts, organizations, and actors. It could undoubtedly include even more specific proposals than these.

To conclude, we can pursue scholarship that is nuanced and rooted in data, and simultaneously animated by pressing multispecies issues of concern and interspecies solidarity. There are many possibilities that emerge when we challenge ourselves to not recoil into silos, or to simply study safe topics, but rather to face and confront the damage humans do through our organizations, and how we could do better, for the wellbeing of other species and our own.

References

Akhtar, A. (2012). *Animals and public health: Why treating animals better is critical to human welfare*. New York: Palgrave Macmillan.

Birke, L. & Thompson, K. (2018). *(Un) stable relations: horses, humans and social agency*. London: Routledge.

Caro, D., Davis, S.J., Bastianoni, S., & Caldeira, K. (2014). Global and regional trends in greenhouse gas emissions from livestock. *Climatic Change, 126(1–2)*, 203–16.

Cartwright, M.S. et al. (2012). The prevalence of carpal tunnel syndrome in Latino poultry processing workers and other Latino manual workers. *Journal of Occupational and Environmental Medicine, 54(2)*, 198–201.

Chin, A. et al. (2020). Pandemics and the future of human-landscape interactions. *Anthropocene, 31*, 100256.

Cochrane, A. (2020). 'Good Work for Animals'. In C. Blattner, K. Coulter, & W. Kymlicka (Eds.), *Animal labour: A new frontier of interspecies justice?* (pp. 48–63). Oxford: Oxford University Press.

Coulter, K. (2016a). *Animals, work, and the promise of interspecies solidarity*. New York: Palgrave Macmillan.

Coulter, K. (2016b). Beyond human to humane: A multispecies analysis of care work, its repression, and its potential. *Studies in Social Justice, 10(2)*, 199–219.

Coulter, K. (2016c). Humane jobs: A political economic vision for interspecies solidarity and multispecies wellbeing. *Politics and Animals, 2(1)*, 67–77.

Coulter, K. (2017). 'Towards humane jobs: Recognizing gendered and multispecies intersections and possibilities. In M. Griffin Cohen (Ed.), *Climate change and gender in rich countries: Work, public policy and action* (pp. 167–82). Milton Park: Routledge.

Coulter, K. (2018). Challenging subjects: Towards ethnographic analyses of animals. *Journal for the Anthropology of North America, 21*(2), 58–71.

Coulter, K. (2020a). Toward humane jobs and work-lives for animals'. In C. Blattner, K. Coulter, & W. Kymlicka (Eds.), *Animal labour: A new frontier of interspecies justice?* (pp. 29–47). Oxford: Oxford University Press.

Coulter, K. (2020b). Horses' labour and work-lives: New intellectual and ethical directions'. In J. Bornemark, P. Andersson, & U. Ekström von Essen (Eds.), *Equine cultures in transition: Ethical questions* (pp. 17–31). Milton Park: Routledge.

Dashper, K. & Buchmann, A. (2020). Multispecies event experiences: Introducing more-than-human perspectives to event studies. *Journal of Policy Research in Tourism, Leisure and Events, 12*(3), 293–309.

D'Souza, R., Hovorka, A., & Neil, L. (2020). Conservation canines: Exploring dog roles, circumstances, and welfare status'. In C. Blattner, K. Coulter, & W. Kymlicka (Eds.), *Animal labour: A new frontier of interspecies justice?* (pp. 65–87). Oxford: Oxford University Press.

Fennell, D.A. & Sheppard, V. (2021). Tourism, animals and the scales of justice. *Journal of Sustainable Tourism, 29*(2–3), 314–35.

Fitzgerald, A.J. (2010). A social history of the slaughterhouse: From inception to contemporary implications. *Human Ecology Review, 17*(1), 58–69.

Fitzgerald, A.J., Kalof, L, & Dietz, T. (2009). Slaughterhouses and increased crime rates: An empirical analysis of the spillover from "the jungle" into the surrounding community. *Organization & Environment, 22*(2), 158–84.

Garcia-Llorente, M., Radha Rubio-Olivar, R., & Gutierrez-Briceno, I. (2018). Farming for life quality and sustainability: A literature review of green care research trends in Europe. *International Journal of Environmental Research and Public Health, 15*(6), 1282.

García-Rosell, J-C. & Tallberg, L. (2021). Animals as tourism stakeholders: Huskies, reindeer, and horses working in Lapland. In C. Kline & J.M. Rickly (Eds.), *Exploring non-human work in tourism: From beasts of burden to animal ambassadors* (pp. 103–121). Berlin: Walter de Gruyter.

Gerber, P.J. et al. (2013). *Tackling climate change through livestock: A global assessment of emissions and mitigation opportunities*. Food and Agriculture Organization of the United Nations.

Haugan, L. et al. (2006). Green care in Norway: Farms as a resource for the educational, health and social sector. In J. Hassink and M. van Dijk (Eds.), *Farming for health* (pp. 109–26). Dordrecht: Springer.

Hamilton, L. & Taylor, N. (2012). Ethnography in evolution: Adapting to the animal 'other' in organizations. *Journal of Organizational Ethnography, 1*(1), 43–51.

Hamilton, L. & Taylor, N. (2017). *Ethnography after humanism: Power, politics and method in multi-species research*. London: Palgrave Macmillan.

Heffernan, C., Salman, M., & York, L. (2013). Livestock infectious disease and climate change: A review of selected literature. *CAB Reviews, 7*(11), 1–26.

Hoelzer, K. et al. (2017). Antimicrobial drug use in food-producing animals and associated human health risks: What, and how strong, is the evidence? *BMC Veterinary Research, 13*(1), 1–38.

Jacques, J.R. (2015). The slaughterhouse, social disorganization, and violent crime in rural communities. *Society & Animals, 23(6)*, 594–612.

Kline, C. & Rickly, J.M. (Eds.). (2021). *Exploring non-human work in tourism: From beasts of burden to animal ambassadors.* Berlin: Walter de Gruyter.

Leibler, J.H. & Perry, M.J. (2017). Self-reported occupational injuries among industrial beef slaughterhouse workers in the midwestern United States. *Journal of Occupational and Environmental Hygiene, 14(1)*, 23–30.

Leibler, J.H., Janulewicz, P.A., & Perry, M.J. (2017). Prevalence of serious psychological distress among slaughterhouse workers at a United States beef packing plant. *Work, 57(1)*, 105–9.

Monbiot, G. (2014). *Feral: Rewilding the land, the sea, and human life.* Chicago: University of Chicago Press.

Noske, B. (1989). *Humans and other animals: Beyond the boundaries of anthropology.* London: Pluto Press.

Noske, B. (1997). *Beyond boundaries: Humans and animals.* Montréal: Black Rose Books.

Pachirat, T. (2011). *Every twelve seconds: Industrialized slaughter and the politics of sight.* New Haven: Yale University Press.

Ripple, W.J. et al. (2014). Ruminants, climate change and climate policy. *Nature Climate Change, 4(1)*, 2–5.

Román-Palacios, C. & Wiens, J.J. (2020). Recent responses to climate change reveal the drivers of species extinction and survival. *Proceedings of the National Academy of Sciences, 117(8)*, 4211–17.

Stull, D.D. & Broadway M.J. (2013). *Slaughterhouse blues: the meat and poultry industry in North America.* Belmont, CA: Wadworth.

Twine, R. (2012). Revealing the 'animal-industrial complex:' A concept and method for critical animal studies. *Journal for Critical Animal Studies, 10(1)*, 12–39.

Wadiwel, D. (2020). The working day: Animals, capitalism, and surplus time. In C. Blattner, K. Coulter, & W. Kymlicka (Eds.), *Animal labour: A new frontier of interspecies justice?* (pp. 181–206). Oxford: Oxford University Press.

Wilkie, R.M. (2010). *Livestock/deadstock: Working with farm animals from birth to slaughter.* Philadelphia: Temple University Press.

CHAPTER 2

BREEDING PROFITS

Animals as Labour and Capital in Euro-American History

AMANDA REES

INTRODUCTION

THE present-day understandings and practices that characterize the organization and management of human-animal relations are firmly rooted in a long history of more-than-human cultural and economic global entanglements. Awareness of this wider context is essential for a nuanced analysis in this emergent field of animal organizational studies: this chapter is thus intended to provide a broad historical perspective on the evolution of human-animal relationships from the eighteenth century up to the present day. This period—from the beginnings of the industrial revolution to the emergence of the posthuman—is characterized by a number of critical transformations in these relationships, which can be generally organized around the question of whether, and in which contexts, nonhuman animals were, and are, regarded as raw materials, as tools, or as quasi-people (Haraway, 2007; Thomas, 1983).

The industrial revolution itself was based on a series of significant shifts in how Europeans perceived and interacted with the natural world, as well as initiating transformative changes in human culture and communities at the local, regional, national, and global level. Animals, frequently to be found on the boundaries between nature and culture, both reflected and focused these transitions (Kete, 2011; Malamud, 2009; Senior, 2007). Over the course of the last three decades or so, scholars in the humanities and social sciences have been deeply engaged in exploring the ethical, commercial, and social consequences of these shifts (Kalof, 2007; Manning and Serpell, 1994; Philo and Wilbert, 2000; Rees, 2017a Urbanik, 2012;). This chapter will give an overview of the results of their research, beginning with livestock and the agricultural improvers of the late 1700s, moving through the creation of the pet industry and the mechanics and profitability of the control of vermin and display of wild animals, to the growth of interest in animal agency and anthropomorphism in twenty-first-century scholarship.

Domestic Economy

Domestic cattle and sheep arrived in Britain from continental Europe during the Neolithic period (Cummings and Morris, 2018; Ryder, 1964), while chickens are known from the Iron Age (Maltby et al., 2018). The origins of domestic pigs are slightly more confused; while domestic pigs arrived in Europe from the Near East in the Neolithic period, there is some evidence that the DNA of modern European pigs also derives from the European wild boar (Frantz et al., 2019). But what is particularly interesting here is that the bodies and behaviour of modern domestic livestock do not just differ from their wild ancestors: they are also very different even from their domestic progenitors. These differences are the result of a conscious series of decisions by humans about how to manage animals most effectively—in essence, about how to make animal bodies into more efficient factories for converting sunlight into financial profit.

From the early eighteenth century onwards, attitudes towards domestic livestock in Britain had started to shift considerably. Rather than looking at animals for what they were, increasingly agricultural reformers and improvers were considering instead what an animal could, or rather *should* be like. Edward Topsell, for example, advised his readers in 1658 that a sheep 'ought to be of a large body, so that their wool may be the more' (Topsell, 1658: 466), whilst also recommending that an ox should bought in March, when they are lean, so that 'if they should be unruly and stubborn, they may be the more easily tamed, before their flesh increase their strength' (ibid, 58). Essentially, farmers were being encouraged to regard their animals as raw material, which both could and should be improved. These endeavours were helped considerably by wider changes in land management practice—in particular, the Enclosure movement, whereby land once held in common was redistributed as private property. For livestock, what this meant was that their daily lives were now conducted under far closer human management: no longer allowed to roam woodlands and meadows for pasture and pannage, animals were instead penned into fields and yards. Their behaviour and their levels of productivity could be monitored more closely, and—crucially—their breeding could be controlled far more carefully. Animals who were not big enough, who were unruly, or who produced substandard wool, meat, or milk, would either be slaughtered or neutered (Wykes, 2004). In the first steps towards the eventual industrialization of livestock production, only the most productive would be admitted as parents to the next generation (Hribal, 2003).

Sam White's study of the history of Chinese pig breeds in Europe and North America demonstrates this phenomenon very clearly (White, 2011). In China, as the human population and pressure on the land grew, pigs came to live far more closely and commensally with humans much earlier, creating an ecological niche for themselves out of the waste and leftovers of the household and farm. In Europe, however, they maintained their traditional foraging semi-wild status: they were nominally under the control of human populations but fed themselves through the practice known as 'pannage'—primarily eating the nuts and fruits of the forest floor that were unwanted by humans. In roaming wild in this way, they had to fend for themselves, ranging widely, fighting off predators (in doing both, using up calories that might have been converted into human food) and mating as they pleased. But as European population densities increased in the seventeenth and eighteenth centuries, so too did the pressure to cut down the forests for farming: urbanization created a new niche in which pigs could scavenge—and the import of Chinese breeding stock accelerated the physical and psychological transformation of the nascent capitalist pig. Now, English farmers could work with animals that 'are very prolific, are sooner made fat than the larger kind, upon less provisions, and cut up, when killed, to more useful and convenient portions' (Beilby, 1800 in White, 2011: 107).

By the nineteenth century, breeders were learning to produce a range of different types of livestock breed, suited both to different geographical areas and a range of tastes in fashion, whether with regard to external appearance or internal production. The first native UK breed to be recognized was the Hereford. It was primarily associated with the work of Benjamin Thompkins, and valued for its 'economy in feeding, natural aptitude to grow and gain from grass and grain, rustling ability, hardiness, early maturity and prolificacy' (Cattle Site, 2021). The Scottish Aberdeen Angus emerged from the combined efforts of three farmers—Hugh Watson, William McCombie, and Sir George Macpherson-Grant, working from 1808 to the early twentieth century. The same period saw an emergent division of labour in cattle. Hitherto, the same animals had been expected by farmers to produce both meat and milk—the mid-nineteenth century saw breeds specializing. Alongside the beef Herefords now could stand the dairy Jersey, Friesans, and Ayrshire cattle. Poultry, too, in the mid-twentieth century and as a result of a series of 'Chicken of Tomorrow' contests organized by the American A&P store, would soon specialize into meat (broiler) and egg production.

This production of particular kinds of animals to human specification was not confined to livestock, of course. The nineteenth century, particularly the Victorian period, also saw a tremendous growth of interest in pet breeding, as Harriet Ritvo's work has clearly shown (Ritvo, 1987; 2010). In 1983, Keith Thomas had defined a pet as an animal that was kept in the home, that was given a name, was never eaten—and which played no economic role. But what later scholarly work has shown is the sheer extent of the economic activity that was inspired by the emergence of the pet industry and specific, ever more distinct, breeds and strains of animals. Before the nineteenth century, dogs were organized and managed according to their function—they could be hunters, herders, guard dogs, turnspit dogs, or lapdogs. From mid-nineteenth century onwards, dogs were known instead by their appearance—their culturally negotiated breed (Worboys, Strange, and Pemberton, 2018). In some cases, this related to their place of origin (Pekingese, Pomeranian, Chihuahua) or their behavioural characteristics (poodles, for their habit of playing in water/puddles, for example). In others, breeds were named for the individual, such as Louis Dobermann, most associated with their creation. Dog shows, modelled on the aristocratic cattle and livestock shows that had been a feature of eighteenth-century rural life, now emerged as part of the urban landscape, as the new middle classes learnt to negotiate status and identity in these new spaces by emulating their social superiors. At these shows, the biological attributes of these new breeds were socially negotiated and managed, often prioritizing fashion and aesthetic taste over the physical wellbeing of the animal. And at the same time, the institutions and accessories that we think of today as part of the pet world—breed clubs and societies, leads, coats, brushes, toys, dishes, books, specialized food—were also being produced. For the first time, you had dogs that were worth money not because they could do something, but simply because of what they looked like. Humans were willing to spend money on individuals and items that primarily functioned to express their own identity as an animal lover/pet owner.

Clearly, the emergence of capitalist modernity and the processes of industrialization and urbanization fundamentally reformulated human relationships with animals in Europe and North America. Domestic animals in particular were increasingly treated as biological capital through which profit (both financial and emotional) could be maximized by control of breeding, while also being mobilized as important signifiers of identity—living brands that could indicate the owner's wealth, status, class, race, gender, or point of geographical origin. But even as the sheer numbers of livestock animals and the popularity of pets grew, so too did concern with a much less welcome category of animal. Vermin had always been a problem for farmers—but it was one that became an issue of national security in wartime.

Commercial Competitors?

Charles Elton, a zoologist at Oxford, had been trying to understand how and why wild animal population levels varied since the early 1920s. In 1926, he was employed by the Hudson Bay Company to map the annual distribution of fur-bearing animals in the Arctic: fluctuations in these numbers had a major impact on the fur trade, and hence the economy of the entire Canadian Arctic region (Chitty and Elton, 1937). In 1932, he founded the Bureau of Animal Population at Oxford to study the issues of wild animal ecology, particularly with respect to disease and the relationship between wild and domestic animals. His team focused on animals of economic importance—fur-bearing animals and game birds, certainly—but also on those animals that caused economic damage. Voles, for example, destroyed young trees, and hence were of great interest to both government (the Forestry Commission) and industry (the Bryant and May match company) who funded some of Elton's initial work in England (Crowcroft, 1991). But it was with the outbreak of the Second World War that the Bureau had to step up: scientists and technicians throughout the United Kingdom were exempt from military service if their research benefited the war effort, and Elton and his team had a key role to play in the war on waste. The Bureau turned its attention to pest extermination.

Their focus was on rodents—the brown rat (found in the countryside), the black rat (found on the docks), and the mouse (found in domestic homes throughout Britain). At this point, little was actually known about rodent control—despite the vast range of poisons on offer, their efficacy at exterminating, or even just reducing, populations was not well understood. Elton's first efforts were to study the use of poison under controlled conditions—and in studying this, in a ramshackle laboratory attached to a pig farm, for the first time scientists started to understand the principles of rat behaviour. Rats, it appeared, avoided new objects like the plague—and if a rat survived ingesting poisoned food, then it would thereafter refuse that food. These are now fundamental principles that govern the use of laboratory rats in behavioural and cognitive psychological research—but they were discovered as part of the extremely pragmatic drive to eradicate food competitors in wartime conditions. Karen Sayer's history of the emergence of modern rat management (Sayer, 2017) charts the way in which ideas of efficiency and agricultural productivity became central to the scientific study of animal behaviour in the post-war period—even felines, it seemed, could potentially participate in the disciplined army of farm workers. Cats, Elton suggested in the mid-1950s, could be persuaded to form important sources of alternative labour in times of skills shortage, although the reward for their efforts (milk) did need to be carefully managed so as to maintain their productivity levels (Elton, 1953).

While some rodents could only contribute to national economic security by dying, others were being actively created in order to participate in the emergent field of genetics and medical research. Abbie Lathrop, a businesswoman from the American mid-West, began breeding mice, rats, and guinea-pigs in the early 1900s, supplying both the US government and rodent fanciers with animals. Her careful breeding records meant that her animals would become some of the most widely used lab mice strains in the world, critical to the study of cancer and the practices of modern biomedicine (Steensma et al., 2010). The historian Karen Rader has documented the way in which, during the early twentieth century, the mouse body became a mass-produced, standardized variable in and for experimental biology—the use of which in research was in turn dependent on the development of considerable commercial infrastructure, such as cages, handling equipment, feed, bedding, transport, and so forth (Rader, 2004). Laboratory rodents did not, of course, just play a role in cancer research, but were fundamental to the establishment of product safety and reliability in marketing drugs, food additives, beauty/grooming products, and cleaning chemicals. While concern for the welfare of laboratory rodents tended to lag behind care for nonhuman primates, dogs and cats, their exploitation still aroused strong opposition amongst members of the general public (Jasper and Nelkin, 1991; Petit, 2017). In this, rodents demonstrate most clearly the extent to which animal ethics are, in practice, treated as situational and context-dependent: in different geographical spaces (the home, the farm, the sewer, the laboratory) the same animal is subject to radically divergent standards of management and control.

This also, of course, applies to cultural spaces. Large mammalian predators such as wolves, foxes, badgers, coyotes, otters, and bears have seen their status change drastically over the course of the last century, veering from 'subject-to-eradication-programmes' vermin to 'hailed-as-symbols-of-the-wilderness' charismatic megafauna. The experience of wolves in the United States has been particularly significant here, given their role in the emergence of wilderness management as a profession, and the importance of hunting as a major commercial leisure activity. One of the key players in this new business, Aldo Leopold, was explicit—his 'profession began with the job of producing something to shoot'(Leopold, 1940: 343)—that is to say, the job of wildlife managers was to ensure that hunters had targets at which to aim. These targets would usually be elk or deer of some kind—which, of course, were also preyed on by wolves. If you wanted to produce lots of deer, it therefore followed that you had to get rid of the wolves. Since wolves were also a threat to the livestock owned by the farmers spreading across North America, it's not surprising that wolf eradication became the declared aim of the US Bureau of Biological Survey. As a result, by the 1950s, wolves were all but extinct in the continental United States (Coleman, 2004). The results weren't quite as anticipated—while deer populations did increase rapidly as a result of the demise of the wolves, they also crashed shortly thereafter, as the animals ate themselves out of their habitat. Aldo Leopold went on to become a key figure in the emerging conservation movement, realizing after seeing the 'fierce green fire dying' in the eyes of one wolf, that a new ethical standard was needed in land management theory and practice (Leopold, 1949; Lorbiecki, 2016). The reintroduction of wolves to Yellowstone National Park and elsewhere from the mid-1990s onwards has demonstrated just how central wolves are to managing the wild—that in fact, they themselves can be considered as active agents in land management (Jones, 2017).

Foxes and badgers have faced similar problems in the United Kingdom, as their iconic cultural status conflicted with their economic impact, creating significant ethical and legal problems. For British people in the nineteenth and early twentieth centuries, the killing of a fox by anyone other than a pack of hunting dogs was condemned as vulpicide—and novelists as disparate as Anthony Trollope and Edith Nesbit vividly described the shame associated with the act. The only right way to kill a fox was to hunt it on horseback with a pack of dogs: an activity considered equally horrific by many late twentieth- and twenty-first-century Britons. From the 1960s onwards, the effort to put an end to this activity has provoked considerable controversy and occupied much parliamentary time (Woods, 2000). The issue for badgers had less to do with hunting as a leisure activity—in this case, the problem was the economic harm caused by their alleged role as a disease vector, specifically for bovine TB (bTB). As Angela Cassidy has shown (Cassidy, 2012; 2019), the significant fictional role played by badgers in English literature (from an Anglo-Saxon riddle poem to *Wind in the Willows* and the *Animals of Farthing Wood*) has had a material impact on the management of this problem. Bovine TB, once a serious source of infection for the human population of the United Kingdom, was largely brought under control from the 1960s onwards, through a combination of regular testing and slaughter of infected animals. However, from the mid-1980s and through the 1990s, cases of bTB in cattle started to rise. This had a major economic and emotional impact on farmers, some of whom faced the slaughter of herds that had taken generations to build—and many of these farmers blamed badgers, who had been identified as carriers of bTB in 1971. A succession of government-inspired reports and trials, produced by some of the most influential scientists in the United Kingdom followed. But the conflict between the calls from conservationists and other public figures for the badger to be protected, and the needs of farmers to have their livelihoods safeguarded has proved intractable. The badger/bTB problem in many ways encapsulates the ongoing ethical dilemma of how to manage wild animals alongside industrial livestock production.

Wild Displays

It is important to remember that the industrialization and intensification of domestic livestock production happened during much the same period as the global growth in studies of wild animal behaviour. From the 1960s onwards, at the same time as cows, pigs, chickens—even mice—were increasingly treated as standardized biological machines, some scientists were beginning to talk and write about wild living animal groups in a way that emphasized the individuality and uniqueness of the social relationships that existed within them. Social relationships between domestic animals had been the subject of scrutiny for considerable time—the term 'pecking order' comes, of course, from Thorleif Schjelderup-Ebbe's observations of social dominance in the 1920s (de Waal, 2001). But these observations were revealing something more—the existence, perhaps, even of nonhuman animal culture.

Some of these studies took place in the United Kingdom on foxes and badgers (Macdonald, 1987; Neal, 1958), others in the United States on wolves and bears (Craighead, 1982; Mech, 1970). Some of the most interesting studies took place in East Africa, in the national parks of Kenya and Tanzania, and focused on chimpanzees, baboons, elephants, and lions (Goodall, 1986; Moss, 1988; Packer, 1994; Strum, 1987). Again, there was a long history in North America and Europe of observing and writing about wild animals (Lutts, 1990)—what was different about these studies was that they were being carried out in a systematic and (eventually) long-term manner. This was not a case of animal behaviour being watched in passing, or over the course of a week or a month. These scholars went to the field to learn about the social and ecological behaviour of wild-living animals over an extended period of time, and some of these studies (Jane Goodall's chimpanzee study at Gombe, Craig Packer's lion research in the Serengeti) have now lasted for more than half a century. In order to study animals systematically, it was clear to researchers from the very start that they needed to be able to identify individuals—fieldworkers needed to be sure that they weren't surveying the same population twice, or that attention wasn't being concentrated on one animal at the expense of another. Researchers tried a number of different ways of identifying individuals—ear notches, radio collars, leg rings, even (in the case of Bernhard Grzimek, dyeing a zebra's coat)—as well as simply learning to recognize ear or whisker patterns, or the type and number of notches in a dolphin's fin (Rees, 2017b). But once an individual was identified in this way, researchers also needed to be able to refer to them quickly, and one of the first big questions faced by animal field scientists was whether to use numbers or names. Numbers might appear more scientific, especially since names might carry unfortunate connotations—but even a number can become a name once it's in use.

As a result, observers got to know—and crucially, to write about, individuals— Goodall's David Greybeard, Dian Fossey's Digit, Cynthia Moss' Tuskless, Shirley Strum's Peggy—later on, and more infamously, Cecil, the lion killed in Zimbabwe by an American tourist on a hunting safari. Names and individual identification mattered, because they enabled researchers to link present-day actions with past events, to make possible connections between cause and effect—in essence, to record the history of these animal societies as it unfolded before them. In fact, many of these researchers literally wrote the history of their populations in the form of books written for the popular market, many of which became bestsellers (Fossey, 1983; Goodall, 1971)—partly to share the fascination they felt at watching the complexity and depth of nonhuman animal lives, but also to raise awareness of conservation projects and of the need to protect the habitat and integrity of these populations.

This was part of a notable growth of public interest in wild animals in the mid-twentieth century—nature programmes were a key element of the BBC's television schedules from the early 1950s onwards. *Zoo Quest*, which ran from 1954 to 1963 and was a joint production by the BBC and London Zoo, charted the adventures of the young David Attenborough as he travelled to exotic locations in order to capture animals for the Zoo (Gouyon, 2019). Each episode began and ended with Attenborough in the television studio, displaying and discussing the animals that he had brought back to the United Kingdom, and which the audience would soon personally be able to visit in the Zoo. A few years later, however, attitudes to wild animals, and the social and physical practices of displaying them, began to shift in at least some institutions. Whereas once the highlight of a trip to the zoo might have been the chimpanzee tea party or a ride on an elephant, increasingly audiences were being encouraged to sponsor individual animals, or pay a premium to care for the animals in 'zookeeper for a day' programmes (Grazian, 2015; Hancocks, 2003). Rather than presenting animals in cages, architectural reforms displayed them in naturalistic settings, with plenty of water, greenery, mud, or sand, depending on preference. Rather than being organized according to their taxonomic positioning (all big cats caged in one part of the zoo, all horned ungulates in another), animals were grouped according to their ecosystem of origin, with plains animals separated from jungle dwellers. Most interestingly, systems of control changed, with hidden walls and moats rather than bars used to ensure that the animals stayed where they had been put. The impression this gave to the audience, though, was that the zoo inhabitants were in some way 'choosing' to stay where they were, to engage with their human visitors by their persistent presence.

A structurally similar elision of human control and activity can be seen in natural history programming, where shots are chosen, edited, and angled so as to exclude evidence of any local human inhabitants. As Chris Sandbrook put it, after watching some of the outputs of the BBC's Natural History Unit, 'anyone unfamiliar with East Africa could be forgiven for thinking that there is an unbroken chain of natural wildlife habitat stretching from the Rwenzori in the west to Mount Kilimanjaro in the East. There isn't' (Sandbrook, 2013). This is part of the 'Myth of Wild Africa' narrative (Adams and McShane, 1996), where Western audiences are both encouraged to believe in the existence of an Edenic wilderness, untainted by human actions, and to think of the African continent as the location of this Eden, thereby literally erasing the existence of the people who live and work around the national parks. This way of displaying wild animals, with zoos on the one hand being presented as Noah's Ark beacons of conservation hope, while on the other, natural history documentaries depict an unspoiled, unpopulated landscape, can be taken to absolve their audiences from any sense of responsibility for looming Anthropocene extinctions, at the same time as it reproduces postcolonial power relationships (Jones et al., 2019). Westerners are needed, in this narrative, to protect the animals of Africa from Africans, with important consequences for wildlife management as well as the distribution of conservation resources, while wild animals, it seems, recognize their saviours by choosing to stay with them.

Agents, Objects, and the Posthuman?

One of the most notable recent shifts in scholarly studies of human-animal relationships has been a marked growth of interest in exactly this theme of animal agency—the ability of animals to make decisions and choices, and to actively shape the worlds in which they exist (Bhattacharyya and Slocombe, 2017; Rees, 2017a; Steward, 2009). This is an interest that in many ways parallels the steady growth in the tendency to treat pets as family members and quasi-people—a tendency that has been accompanied by an equivalent increase in the scope of the pet industry's activities. Seasonal festivities, for example, now often include treats or cards meant for the family dog or cat, and health insurance for pets can now regularly be found as part of health care packages. Even after death, it is possible to buy a coffin or a cremation plot for the animal's remains. This level of care and attention contrasts sharply with the treatment and cultural perception of livestock animals: living lives largely hidden from the public gaze, it is hard for consumers to recognize the presence of the once-embodied animal in ready meals, chicken nuggets, and pre-sliced meats displayed for purchase. Considerable linguistic and commercial practice has gone in to distancing humans from the animals they eat: the reality of industrial livestock lives is only really faced when the system breaks down, as with the BSE crisis of the 1990s, the foot and mouth epidemic (2000), and the horsemeat scandal (2013) in the United Kingdom.

The concept of agency can still, however, be applied to livestock. Domestication and human-controlled artificial selection did not just produce particular configurations of biological bodies, it also affected animal temperament and behaviour. Cattle—despite, or perhaps because of their size—are excellent examples of this. Unlike, for example, deer or sheep, domestic cattle show very high levels of cooperation with humans (notwithstanding the reasonably regular reports of farmers suffering injury or death as a result of an interaction with a cow). Indeed, if it wasn't for the willing cooperation of cows—voluntarily queuing up and standing still to be milked, for example, as opposed to having to be driven in and tied up—dairy farming would be an even more difficult profession to pursue than it already is. Lewis Holloway and Chris Bear's study of the evolution of milking systems, from the 'catheter milking' of the mid-nineteenth century to the robotic systems increasingly in use today, demonstrate this very clearly (Holloway and Bear, 2017). Their investigation of the co-constitution of human and bovine agency and subjectivity shows the significance of both technology and organizational systems to this process. The introduction, for example, of robotic milking machines ostensibly provides far greater freedom for both human and nonhuman partners: neither is now tied to particular milking times, and both are free to access the systems on demand. But regardless of the time at which the cow chooses to be milked, her output can now be measured and monitored at a very detailed level: not just her overall milk yield, but its quality can be judged alongside the amount of food ingested and medical treatment required. The cow's performance as a labourer can now be subjected to granular scrutiny, while the farmer now has, not just the costs of the new system to manage, but the impact of the new information on husbandry and marketing practices. In this context, it becomes again appropriate to ask, are animals part of the working class? Are they the tools through which profit is created, or do they themselves labour to produce that profit? When they eat grass and feed, and convert that raw material into muscle fibre, milk, or calves, do they represent farming capital or labour (Porcher and Schmitt, 2012)?

Even more significant, however, are the consequences of taking animal agency seriously for our understanding of human agency—and even, potentially, for the concept of the posthuman. As with the bovine example explored above, considering animal agency forces us to move away from a notion of agency as located in an individual mind, possessing free will, rationality, and self-awareness, and towards an idea of agency as emergent, relational, bounded, and mediated. Posthumanist debates emerged out of the blurring of the human-machine boundary and the elevation of a free mind above bodily limitations: animal agency, in many ways, returns us to a world of embodied responsibility.

Concluding Thoughts

Characteristic of human-animal relationships in the English-speaking world over the last two centuries or so has been an apparent tension between treating animals as quasi-persons whose preferences and motivations can be identified and (sometimes) respected, or as biological raw material to be reconfigured according to human need and sometimes with regard only to human whim. Neither position is sustainable. Twenty-first-century scholars might refer to pets as companions, but their position, while often indispensable, remains subordinate. Livestock might be dismissed as 'walking larders', but they remain, in Rhoda Wilkie's term, 'sentient commodities', and the emotional and cognitive challenges involved in living with animals born to die have to be carefully managed (Wilkie, 2010). Challenging the presumption that human-animal relationships are reducible to binary or dyadic analysis is, and will be, one of the fundamental challenges facing animal organizational studies. As the example of agency above demonstrates, taking animals seriously requires the rethinking of some foundational concepts for the social sciences and humanities: for organizational and management studies these theoretical frameworks will have key empirical and commercial consequences.

As this chapter has shown, relationships between humans and other animals are ambiguous, often contradictory, and governed by a series of situational ethics, whereby the treatment of an animal is determined, not so much by species or philosophy, as by physical context and individual history. But it's also important to remember that the treatment of animals reflects our own sense of human(e)ity, not just with the elision of local people in natural history displays and narratives, but—more disturbingly—with the mobilization of animal categories and metaphors to manage relationships between human communities. Most of these apparent paradoxes, whether in the context of wild animals, pets, vermin, or the industrial livestock industry, are rooted in the very clear distinction that is drawn between 'nature' and 'culture' in the Anglo-American and European world. It will be interesting to see how these develop—and what consequences this has for our sense of what it means to be human—when the consequences of climate change really begin to disrupt life in affluent Western economies.

References

Adams, J. & McShane, T. (1996). *The myth of wild Africa: Conservation without illusion.* Berkeley: University of California Press.
Anderson, V. (2004).*Creatures of Empire: How domestic animals transformed early America.* Oxford: Oxford University Press.
Bhattacharyya, J. & Slocombe, S. (2017). Animal agency: Wildlife management from a kincentric perspective. *Ecosphere, 8*(10), 1–17.
Cattle Site. (2021). Hereford: History. https://www.thecattlesite.com/breeds/beef/14/hereford/
Cassidy, A. (2019). *Vermin, victims and disease: British debates over bovine tuberculosis and badgers.* London: Palgrave Macmillan.
Cassidy, A. (2012). 'Vermin, victims and disease: UK framings of badgers in and beyond the bovine TB controversy. *Sociologica Ruralis, 52*(2), 192–214.
Coleman, J. (2004). *Vicious: Wolves and men in America.* New Haven: Yale University Press.
Craighead, F. (1982). *Track of the grizzly.* New York: Sierra Club Books.

Cummings, V. & Morris, J. (2018). Neolithic explanations revisited: Modelling the arrival and spread of domesticated cattle into neolithic Britain. *Environmental Archaeology. 27(1)*, 20–30.

Chitty, D. & Elton, C. (1937). Canadian arctic wildlife enquiry, 1935-6. *Journal of Animal Ecology, 6(2)*, 368–85.

Crowcroft, P. (1991). *Elton's ecologists: A history of the bureau of animal population*. Chicago: University of Chicago Press.

Elton, C. (1953). The use of cats in farm rat control. *British Journal of Animal Behaviour, 1*, 151–5.

Fossey, D. (1983). *Gorillas in the mist*. Boston: Houghton Mifflin.

Frantz, L. et al. (2019). Ancient pigs reveal a near-complete genomic turnover following their introduction to Europe. *Proceedings of the National Academy of Sciences, 116(35)*, 17231–8.

Goodall, J. (1971). *In the shadow of man*. London: Collins.

Goodall, J. (1986). *The chimpanzees of Gombe: Patterns of behaviour*. Cambridge, MA: Harvard University Press.

Gouyon, J-B. (2019). *BBC wildlife documentaries in the age of Attenborough*. London: Palgrave Macmillan.

Grazian, D. (2015). *American zoo: A sociological safari*. Princeton: Princeton University Press.

Hancocks, D. (2001). *A different nature: The paradoxical world of zoos and their uncertain future*. Berkeley: University of California Press.

Haraway, D. (2007). *When species meet*. Minneapolis: University of Minnesota Press.

Holloway, L. & Bear, C. (2017). Bovine and human becomings in histories of dairy technologies: Robotic milking systems and remaking animal and human subjectivity. *BJHS Themes, 2*, 215–34.

Hribal, J. (2003). Animals are part of the working class: A challenge to labour history. *Labour History, 44*, 435–53.

Jasper, J. & Nelkin, D. (1991). *The animal rights crusade: The growth of a moral protest*. London: The Free Press.

Jones, J. et al. (2019). Nature documentaries and saving nature: Reflections on the new Netflix series *Our Planet*. *People and Nature, 1(4)*, 420–5.

Jones, K. (2017). Restor(y)ing the 'Fierce Green Fire': Animal agency, wolf conservation and environmental memory in Yellowstone National Park. *BJHS Themes, 2*, 151–68.

Kalof, L. (2007). *Looking at animals in human history*. London: Reaktion.

Kete, K. (Ed.) (2011). *A cultural history of animals in the age of Empire*. London: Bloomsbury.

Leopold, A. (1940). The state of the profession. *Journal of Wildlife Management, 4*, 343–6.

Leopold, A. (1949). *A Sand County Almanac*. Oxford: Oxford University Press.

Lorbiecki, M. (2016). *A fierce green fire: Aldo Leopold's life and legacy*. Oxford: Oxford University Press.

Lutts, R. (2001). *The nature fakers: Wildlife, science and sentiment*. Charlottesville: University of Virginia Press.

Macdonald, D. (1987). *Running with the fox*. London: Unwin Hymans.

Malamud, R. (Ed.) (2009). *A cultural history of animals in the Modern Age*. London: Bloomsbury.

Maltby M. et al. (2018). Counting Roman chickens: Multidisciplinary approaches to human-chicken interactions in Roman Britain. *Journal of Archaeological Science: Reports. 19*, 1003–15.

Manning, A. & Serpell, J. (Eds.) (1994). *Animals and human society*. London: Routledge.

Mech, D. (1970). *The wolf: Ecology and behaviour of an endangered species*. Minneapolis: University of Minnesota Press.

Moss, C. (1988). *Elephant memories: Thirteen years in the life of an elephant family*. Chicago: University of Chicago Press.

Neal, E. (1958). *The badger*. London: Collins.

Packer, C. (1994). *Into Africa*. Chicago: University of Chicago Press.

Petit, M. (2017). The great cat mutilation: Sex, social movements and the utilitarian calculus in 1970s New York City. *BJHS Themes, 2*, 57–78.

Philo, C. & Wilbert, C. (Eds.) (2000). *Animal spaces, beastly places: New geographies of human/animal relations*. London: Routledge.

Porcher, J. & Schmitt, T. (2012). Dairy cows: Workers in the shadows? *Society and Animals, 20*, 39–60.

Radar, K. (2004). *Making mice: Standardizing animals for American biomedical research, 1900–1955*. Princeton: Princeton University Press.

Rees, A. (2017a). Animal agents? Historiography, theory and the history of science in the Anthropocene. *BJHS Themes, 2*, 1–10.

Rees, A. (2017b). Wildlife agencies: Practice, intentionality and history in 20th century animal field studies. *BJHS Themes, 2*, 127–49.

Ritvo, H. (1987). *The animal estate: The English and other creatures in the Victorian age*. Cambridge, MA: Harvard University Press.

Ritvo, H. (2010). *Noble cows and hybrid zebras: Essays on animals and history*. Charlottesville: University of Virginia Press.

Ryder M. (1964). The history of sheep breeds in Britain. *The Agricultural History Review, 12(1)*, 1–12.

Sandbrook C. (2013). The BBC's Africa as Middle Earth. In *Thinking Like a Human: Conservation for the 21st Century* https://thinkinglikeahuman.com/2013/01/18/the-bbcs-africa-as-middle-earth/

Sayer, K. (2017). The 'modern' management of rats: British agricultural science in farm and field during the 20th century. *BJHS Themes, 2*, 235–63.

Senior, M. (Ed.) (2007). *A cultural history of animals in the Age of Enlightenment*. London: Bloomsbury.

Steensma, D. et al. (2010). Abbie Lathrop, the 'Mouse Woman of Granby': Rodent fancier and accidental genetics pioneer. *Mayo Clinic Proceedings, 85(11)*, 83.

Steward, H. (2009). Animal agency. *Inquiry: An Interdisciplinary Journal of Philosophy, 5(3)*, 217–31.

Strum, S. (1987). *Almost human: A journey into the world of baboons*. London: Random House.

Thomas, K. (1983). *Man and the natural world: Changing attitudes in England, 1500–1800*. London: Allen Lane.

Topsell, E. (1658). *The history of four footed beasts and serpents*. London: E. Cotes https://quod.lib.umich.edu/e/eebo/A42668.0001.001:4?rgn=div1;view=fulltext

Urbanik, J. (2012). *Placing animals: An introduction to the geography of human/animal relations*. Lanham. Rowman and Littlefield.

de Waal, F. (2001). *The ape and the sushi master: Cultural reflections of a primatologist*. New York: Basic Books.

White, S. (2011). From globalised pig breeds to capitalist pigs: A study in animal cultures and evolutionary history. *Environmental History, 16(1)*, 94–120.

Wilkie, R. (2010). *Livestock/deadstock: Working with farm animals from birth to slaughter*. Philadelphia: Temple University Press.

Woods, M. (2000) 'Fantastic Mr. Fox? Representing animals in the hunting debate'. In C. Philo and C. Wilbert (Eds.), *Animal spaces, beastly places: New geographies of human/animal relationships* (pp. 182–202). London: Routledge.

Worboys M. et al. (2018). *The invention of the modern dog: Breed and blood in Victorian Britain*. Baltimore: Johns Hopkins University Press.

Wykes, D. (2004). Robert Bakewell (1725–1795) of Dishley: Farmer and livestock improver. *The Agricultural History Review, 52*(1), 38–55.

CHAPTER 3

POSTHUMANIST PRAXIS AND THE PARADOXES OF AGENCY, RESPONSIBILITY, AND ORGANIZATION IN THE 'ANTHROPOCENE'

RICHIE NIMMO

Introduction

Upon reading his daily newspaper in the early 1990s, the anthropologist of science Bruno Latour noted that 'A single thread links the most esoteric sciences and the most sordid politics, the most distant sky and some factory in the Lyon suburbs, dangers on a global scale and the impending local elections or the next board meeting. The horizons, the stakes, the time frames, the actors—none of these is commensurable, yet there they are, caught up in the same story' (1993: 1). The linking thread is the hole in the ozone layer, which connects scientists and aerosols, politicians and refrigerators, industrialists and inert gases. Latour's point was that what modern thinkers had long been accustomed to call 'nature' and 'society', or 'science' and 'politics', and treat as essentially separate albeit interrelated domains, are, in fact, constitutively entangled in heterogeneous and hybrid assemblages, which have become increasingly visible and pervasive in contemporary technoscientific societies. What was persuasive but contentious in the early '90s is almost self-evident now, as a glance at any serious newspaper on any given day will affirm. Stories about such 'more than human' phenomena as climate breakdown, collapsing biodiversity, and the spiralling degradation and toxification of the environment, now make the headlines almost as regularly as the staple fare of day-to-day political intrigues and power struggles. Indeed, hybrids of 'society' and 'nature' increasingly supply the explicit or implicit substance, context, or horizon of developments in national and international politics, from controversial green industrial strategies to legal battles over pesticides regulations, from vehicle emissions scandals to food and farming policies, and from disputes over fishing rights to the social and economic impacts of zoonotic diseases. The human world is no longer thinkable as a world in itself, relatively separate from nonhumans.

The notion of the 'Anthropocene' is made thinkable by this erosion of modernity's discursive and epistemic separation of 'nature' from human 'society'. The term emerged in earth systems science as a way to challenge the exclusion of human activity from studies of long-term physical changes in the earth system (Crutzen and Stormer, 2000). It proposed to acknowledge the birth of a new epoch in which the earth is shaped more profoundly by the aggregate impact of collective human activity than by all natural or nonhuman forces and processes combined, constituting a new geological age, dominated by humanity (Crutzen, 2002). It has subsequently been taken up in the social sciences and humanities, where it is widely employed as a means to signify the ontological and existential dilemma of the present historical epoch, an epoch in which, as Ulrich Beck wrote in a different tradition of thought, humanity is now 'confronted with the historically unprecedented possibility of the destruction through decision-making of all life on this planet' (Beck, 1992: 101). The Anthropocene emerges from this historical moment, in which the idea of nature as an 'environment' external to and relatively separate from society, having been cracking and creaking for several decades, now like a melting glacier begins its final collapse. It is not without irony that this is precipitated by the real collapse of ecosystems and animal populations around the world, in what has been called a 'biological annihilation' or 'sixth mass extinction' (Ceballos, Ehrlich, and Dirzo, 2017), albeit the first to be driven by humans.

Yet the Anthropocene remains a contentious and problematic concept. There is still little consensus over its scientific rigour or its veracity as a geological hypothesis. In the humanities and social sciences, where it is has proliferated rapidly, there is disagreement as to which of several alternative socio-historical periodizations it affirms, and on its merits as a way of understanding modern societies in relation to the natural or nonhuman world (Castree, 2016; Chakrabarty, 2018). This has given rise to some fundamental critique of the concept, which has nevertheless become practically inescapable for anyone committed to thinking seriously about socio-environmental relations. Even the alternative concepts which have been proposed by its critics, notably 'Capitalocene' and 'Plantationocene' (Haraway, 2015; Moore, 2017), invariably acknowledge and underline the discursive centrality of the 'Anthropocene' in framing these very debates. This chapter takes the view that whilst the Anthropocene is riddled with problems, contradictions, and tensions, these are also productive paradoxes, which, if navigated critically and carefully, can be potent heuristics in the toolkit of multispecies-ecological thinking, ethics, and organization.

Navigating the paradoxes of the Anthropocene requires some conceptual or cognitive map, which is provided here by another way of thinking made possible by the erosion of the great divide between humans and nonhumans, namely posthumanism. Encompassing a series of interrelated ontological, epistemological, and theoretical developments across the humanities and social sciences, posthumanism is defined by its attempt to critique and supersede the Enlightenment conception of the human being as an autonomous, rational, and self-knowing sovereign actor, separate from and elevated above nonhumans and 'nature' (Braidotti, 2013; Wolfe, 2010). Posthumanist scholars have not only deconstructed this conception of humanity for its hubris and exceptionalism, they have linked it to the global ecological crisis, understood as a consequence of unrelenting anthropocentrism in a more-than-human world (Plumwood, 2002). Rather than deifying humanity as a transcendent master actor and world-builder, posthumanism responds to escalating anthropogenic destruction by advocating and practising ontological and ethical humility about humanity (Kopnina, 2018; Nimmo, 2019). Thus, posthumanism posits a relational ontology in which humans are but one actor among many in a heterogeneous living world, neither autonomous of nonhumans nor perfectly self-knowing, self-determining, or rational. Instead humans are constituted within perpetually unfolding, complex, and 'messy' relations with other agents and forces, which cross-cut and confound the imagined boundaries of the human domain (Barad, 2003; Haraway, 2003; Latour, 1993). This chapter pursues a critical posthumanist reading of the Anthropocene, paying particular attention to what I suggest are its central paradoxes around agency, responsibility, and multispecies relations. The effective navigation of these paradoxes confronts contemporary organization as an ethical and political imperative in the context of the burgeoning ecological and climate crises of our time. For organizational analysis, the significance is manifold, since our understandings of our place in time and history, space, nature—indeed our very conception of who 'we' are and what it is to be human—have practical consequences for our conduct, for how we organize commercial and other forms of activity, in short for our relations with others, both human and nonhuman.

Anthropocene and the Anthropos

If the Anthropocene is a descriptive and diagnostic concept, proposing that we recognize a new geological epoch dominated by human activity, it is also didactic, inscribing the present as a moment of existential crisis and calling for urgent socio-ecological transformation. In acknowledging that human activity is now the dominant material force acting upon earth, disrupting its 'natural' cycles, reshaping the interlocking systems of the biosphere, and altering planetary ecology, the Anthropocene warns that this is radically destabilizing the conditions for human as well as nonhuman life, and compromising the prospects for human flourishing in the future by making a less hospitable earth (Rockstrom et al., 2009; Steffen at al., 2004). Though couched in the fairly cautious scientific language of 'planetary boundaries' and the need to maintain a 'safe operating space for humanity', this is unmistakeably a call to action; having demonstrated remarkable disruptive and destructive power, humanity must urgently find a way to divert this into radical socio-environmental change if we are to avert the ecological catastrophe towards which we are hurtling on our present trajectory. Thus, the Anthropocene concept insists that we must take responsibility for the unintended planetary consequences of our species' activity and change our mode of living in order to ensure a liveable planet for future generations. This represents a powerful framing of the ecological crisis, but one that is deeply problematic in several respects.

The 'Anthropo-cene' interpolates humanity as the key actor, the sovereign collective agent both responsible for the disruption of the biosphere and uniquely capable of acting reflexively at a global level in order to consciously master and take control of the unintended consequences of its collective activity. This re-inscribes the archetypical Enlightenment humanist conception of 'man' as world-historical master actor and self-saviour, consciously reshaping himself and nature through rational action shaped by objective knowledge (Leiss, 1994; Merchant, 1980). Feminist and decolonial scholars have rightly subjected this to trenchant critique for its role in aligning an ostensibly universal 'humanity' with the socio-historically situated knowledges, rationalities, and interests of elite, global north, white men (Dhawan, 2014; Plumwood, 1993; Plumwood, 2002). But there are signs that this Eurocentric, colonial, and gendered conception of humanity is being tacitly reinscribed at the centre of environmental-political discourse under a new cloak of universality provided by the 'Anthropocene' (Crist, 2013; Mitchell, 2014; Schulz, 2017; Simpson, 2020).

A grossly homogenizing concept, 'humanity' can brush over critical distinctions of all kinds. One is the distinction between wealthy elites located predominantly in the global north, who have contributed disproportionately to the aetiology of the climate and ecological crises over generations through their financial control of extractive and polluting industries as well as their own ultra-high-consumption lifestyles, and those who have found themselves expropriated, dispossessed, and exploited by these elites (Baskin, 2019; Marquardt, 2018). Plainly, the global rich and the global poor are neither equally responsible for the environmental crisis nor equally impacted by its effects (Malm and Hornborg, 2014). The global poor are far more vulnerable to a wide range of environmental impacts, less able to evade or protect themselves against the effects of environmental disruption, and affected more immediately and severely by climate disasters and adverse environmental phenomena (Gonzalez, 2017). This axis of socio-environmental inequality overlaps and intersects with global and regional legacies and relations of empire, colonialism, and gender inequality, with people in the global south disproportionately bearing the brunt of environmental degradation in its immediate social and economic impacts (Dengler and Seebacher, 2019). In short, environmental degradation and ecological disruption act as powerful magnifiers of entrenched historically-transmitted structural inequalities. By centring and foregrounding the 'human', Anthropocene discourse tends to background pivotal questions of environmental justice and obscure the role of socio-economic, neo-colonial, and gender relations in shaping and producing the ecological crisis.

The centring of the 'anthropos' also tends to conflate human activity with the ecological impacts of capitalism, a historically specific form of economic and social organization, as though this were synonymous with humanity (Malm and Hornborg, 2014;

Moore, 2016). This is highly distortive given that environmental-historical analysis amply demonstrates the uniquely expansionary, extractive, and pollutive dynamics of capitalism in both its mercantile-colonial and industrial forms (Malm, 2016; Moore, 2017; Wark, 2016). The appropriation and depletion of nonhuman sources of value has been integral to the reproduction of capitalist accumulation throughout its history, bound up with capital's propensity to exhaust the health or vitality of human and nonhuman entities caught up in the circuits of commodity production. In this sense environmental degradation is not a contingent effect of capitalism but is internal to its logic. Moreover, the mass production and consumption regimes engendered by post-Second World War capitalism underpinned the 'great acceleration' (Steffen et al., 2015; Gorg et al., 2019), that period of just a few decades during which the great majority of global environmental impacts have accumulated, from carbon emissions to soil degradation, and from ocean pollution to species mass extinction. Today, just 100 companies are responsible for 71 per cent of global greenhouse gas emissions, amounting to almost 1 trillion tonnes (Griffin, 2017). Recognizing the centrality of capitalist relations of production, extraction, exploitation, and accumulation in driving the 'anthropogenic' changes in the biosphere is therefore indispensable.

A critical Anthropocene politics then must already be posthuman in the sense that it must disaggregate the 'anthropos' at the heart of the concept, undoing its masking of the entangled roles of capitalist accumulation regimes, colonial continuities, and gender inequalities, in asymmetrically shaping the causes and contours of the global socio-environmental crisis. Yet a post-capitalist, decolonial, and ecofeminist response to the Anthropocene only takes us so far, providing some answers to questions of responsibility and environmental justice, but without addressing the question of organization—that is, how to accomplish the necessary transition from our present state of escalating crisis to a transformed mode of socio-ecological existence. Where is the transformative agency which could accomplish the necessary transition from our current crisis trajectory? Whilst eco-socialist thinkers grasp the socio-environmental struggle as class struggle, and decolonial scholars point to subaltern struggles with neo-colonial regimes of extraction and exploitation, Anthropocene discourse offers no political theory of socio-ecological transformation. The lacuna tends to be filled by the least overtly political, most ostensibly neutral, and therefore most hegemonic conceptions of environmental change.

Managing the Biosphere?

In its original articulation in the natural sciences, the Anthropocene did not really collapse the nature-society divide but simply bridged it, positing two interlocking but asymmetrical systems. Nature was conceptualized as the global geo-bio-sphere, a great planetary organism upon which human society depends but which is being increasingly disrupted and degraded by the impacts of human activity (Crutzen, 2002;

Steffen et al., 2004). Society, on this model, is both within and against nature, a part of nature which has become dysfunctional. It follows that human society must manage its relationship with nature more rationally and sustainably in order to ensure human survival (Bierman et al., 2009). Notwithstanding the preference for organic rather than machine metaphors, this Anthropocene ontology has some fundamental commonalities with the old mechanistic ecology of modernism long associated with anthropocentric rationalizations of environmental degradation as well as with instrumental defences of nature, namely the view of nature as a complex machine, the value of which lies in its usefulness to human beings (Merchant, 1980; Plumwood, 1993). Both conceptualize humans and nonhumans as existing in essentially distinct albeit functionally interrelated domains, and both imagine 'nature' as an external, singular, and encompassing object-system upon which human society depends.

This way of thinking about nature is so entrenched in modern culture that it can be difficult to see its strangeness, anthropologically. To facilitate this, it can be contrasted with indigenous cosmologies which understand humans and nonhumans as interconnected entities or kin, not within a singular 'nature' but within holistic living worlds imbued with agency, spirit, and meaning, a perspective from which the Anthropocene's systems-thinking looks distinctly modern and dualist (Inoue and Moreira, 2016; Taylor, 2021). It also fails to capture the constitutive hybridity of a lifeworld in which we constantly eat, drink, inhale, and absorb the products of our techno-industrial infrastructure, with potentially profound but ill-understood effects on our own biology or 'nature' (Alaimo, 2010; 2017). It does not capture the implications or significance, for example, of a world in which every one of us has detectable levels of certain radioactive particles and residues of industrial chemicals and plastics in our bodies, illustrating that the Anthropocene is also within. In short, it does not break decisively with the modernist vision of humanity-as-knowing-subject acting upon object-nature. For posthumanist, ecofeminist, and Indigenous thinkers alike, this way of thinking is both constitutive and symptomatic of the socio-ecological crisis the Anthropocene purports to diagnose. In its separation of humans from nonhumans, its othering of 'nature' as an external entity, and its elevation of humanity into would-be global managers of the biosphere, it proposes to solve the problems of anthropocentrism using the tools of anthropocentrism.

The most starkly anthropocentric readings of the Anthropocene are found in neoliberal, transhumanist, and ecomodernist imaginaries, which see 'the end of nature' as a realization of transcendent human power and creative potential, a marker of our having finally domesticated not only numerous other species but now the planet itself (Abbinnett, 2019; Crist, 2013). Having brought the earth under our control, at least potentially, we have thereby brought within reach the dream of abolishing nature as a limit or constraint on our techno-economic development, freeing us to pursue our full human potential as 'god species' or masters of the earth (Ellis, 2009; Lynas, 2011). It follows that the main problem with human domination of the biosphere is that it hasn't yet gone far enough. This is the ontology most closely aligned with large-scale 'techno-fix' responses to climate change, most notably geo-engineering mega-projects, from solar radiation management, to cloud thinning, to carbon capture, which propose to fix the unintended consequences of modernity's domination-and-control ecology by elevating those same principles to a higher level, wherein humanity increasingly intervenes directly in problematic aspects of the earth system and its 'natural' cycles. In this rationale, given that we are already geo-engineering the planet, albeit haphazardly and inadvertently, it is not such a radical break to propose to do so deliberately and rationally in an effort to take control of the consequences of our collective activity (Asafu-Adjaye et al., 2015; Ellis, 2009). In this view, living in the Anthropocene means living in a world which has been fully humanized, rendering such Indigenous or romantic notions as kinship with agential natures redundant, and the only question is how best to organize and manage our human living space, the anthropo-sphere.

Where geo-engineering embraces the 'end of nature' as an opportunity to extend human potential, a contrasting proposal argues that a proportion of the earth's land and oceans—initially 30 per cent, before progressing to half—should be 'set aside for nature'. Humans would either be excluded entirely or strictly forbidden from farming, fishing, logging, mining, hunting, or any other economic activities in these areas (Kopnina, 2016; Wilson, 2016). This is a reinvention of modernist conservation, with nature reasserted as pristine wilderness separate from humans, who need to be kept at bay in the interests of nature-protection (Lorimer, 2015). If realized it would represent a dramatic shrinking of the current human footprint on the biosphere and a concomitant expansion of 'wilderness'. A laudable aim, but it becomes toxic in its implications as soon as it is worked-through at the level of lived politics. There is seldom any critical consideration by Half-Earth proponents of the politics of selecting, enforcing, and policing these human-free zones, nor of the potentially devastating impacts on the communities making their livelihoods, often very precariously, within or bordering these areas (Buscher et al., 2017; Schleicher et al., 2019). Thus, though Half-Earth may at first look like the antithesis of geo-engineering, appearing to resist the colonization of nature via a strategy of withdrawal, the idea of protecting and conserving a pristine nature via the enforced exclusion of humans engenders a politics of socio-environmental domination. It translates into the authority of predominantly global north organizations and agencies to speak for a singular 'nature' and to enforce their vision of socio-environmental relations in its name.

Displacing people from designated 'nature' zones and policing their exclusion is counterproductive as well as unethical, since the whole conservation agenda thereby becomes quite reasonably perceived by those communities as the livelihood-denying imposition of alien authorities (West et al., 2006). Such proposals overlook the gains that have been made within the field of conservation in recent decades by moving towards approaches grounded in a recognition that those who live within or near to areas of wilderness are not just a threat to the biodiversity of those areas but also key to their protection, which can only be achieved through their active involvement in forging local socio-ecologies that are economically and environmentally viable for them (Ellis et al., 2019; Oldekopp et al., 2016). It follows that proposals for environmental transition must not only eschew anthropocentric and a-social conceptions of humanity and of an overarching and unitary human agency, they must also eschew the neo-colonial violence of environmental enclosures that flows from this. This cannot be the work chiefly of external, global north agencies and organizations, whether acting as would-be managers of a global 'nature' or as enforcers of new territorial boundaries, but must be socially grounded and embedded in the live realities and socio-environmental struggles of the most ecologically vulnerable and precarious communities.

A vision of environmental transformation which better acknowledges and foregrounds the role of social divisions and inequalities in the politics of socio-ecological change can be found in 'Green New Deal' agendas. Though radical in the context of hegemonic neoliberalism with its preference for incremental, market-based consumer environmentalisms, Green New Deal politics essentially revamps the central contention of ecological modernization thinking, by proposing that the capitalist imperative of perpetual economic growth can be reconciled with socio-ecological sustainability via 'green growth' (Jacobs, 2013). This is to be achieved by means of large-scale public investment in renewable energy, green infrastructure, and business, alongside ambitious state-sponsored job creation schemes in green industries and the radical reduction of social inequality through fiscal and economic restructuring (Barbier, 2010; Klein, 2019; Sanders, 2019). In this vision, the key driver of ecological degradation—industrial capitalism—is reimagined as a potential engine of socio-ecological transformation, if only it can be suitably steered by the right political formations, using the right economic and industrial strategies, and mobilizing the right technologies (Klein, 2019; Sanders, 2020). There is much to admire in this as a challenge to neoliberalism's disproportionate responsibilization of individual consumers, emphasizing instead the capacity and responsibility of states to spearhead collective socio-environmental change, as well as the need for a transition consistent with principles of social and economic justice. Its adequacy as a response to the enormity of the ecological crisis is nonetheless questionable.

Having emerged from the thinking, research, and campaigning activities of multiple environmental organizations and social movements over many years, what the US, European Union (EU), and UK versions of the Green New Deal that have made it to the stage of concrete proposals or policy programmes have in common, is their focus on energy and transport infrastructures, industrial and manufacturing strategy, and the housing and construction sectors, as the key areas of policy intervention through which to secure socio-environmental objectives. The key objective across these areas is decarbonization, and the relationship of the nation-state to the global biosphere is conceived and measured predominantly in terms of the quantities of carbon emitted by national economies. A consequence of this framing is to de-emphasize aspects of the ecological crisis which are interconnected with, but irreducible to, climate change, notably the precipitous decline in vertebrate and invertebrate populations around the world (Ceballos, Ehrlich, and Dirzo, 2017), the rapid destruction of biodiverse habitats and the few remaining areas of 'ecological integrity' (Plumptre et al., 2021), and the loss of fertile land, soil, and clean water. In this broader ecological context, driving a transition away from fossil fuels is absolutely urgent and necessary, but far from sufficient.

'Green growth' thinking also tends to background ecological problems less amenable to being addressed via state or corporate-led techno-industrial solutions, especially those which require de-growth, disinvestment, and retraction, rather than strategic investment and new technologies, and those which pivot upon the collective relationship of global north consumption practices to production assemblages and relations in environmentally fragile regions. Instead it focuses principally upon neo-Keynesian sustainability measures such as expanding renewable energy production, mass-producing electric vehicles, and retro-fitting buildings to maximize their energy efficiency. There is for example relatively little attention given to industrial agriculture, animal farming, meat and dairy consumption, land use, and food policy, especially at a global scale. Where these are addressed, the proposals are insipid when compared with the far bolder agendas on energy and infrastructure. The result is a distinctly urban, techno-industrial, and global north vision of both the causes of the ecological crisis and its solutions. It is also an anthropocentric vision in which human-animal relations are backgrounded and animals themselves are a marginal presence, reduced to collateral damage.

Animals in the Anthropocene

Some striking statistics are helpful in grasping the Anthropocene as a mode of species relations. In 2020 the global biomass of all living organisms was for the first time outweighed by 'anthropogenic mass', defined as the total mass embedded in inanimate solid objects produced by humans (Elhacham et al., 2020). This has been doubling about every 20 years for the past century, whilst the total mass of plants—which make up 90 per cent of biomass—has steadily declined. Within the category of biomass, humans and domesticated livestock constitute 96 per cent of the global biomass of mammals (Bar-On et al., 2018), with humans making up 36 per cent, livestock 60 per cent, and wild animals just 4 per cent. Among birds, 70 per cent of the total global biomass of birds is made up of domesticated chicken and other 'poultry', whilst just 30 per cent is wild birds, accounting for over 10,000 species. Indeed, the most populous mammal on earth by a large margin is the broiler chicken, leading some to suggest that the most apt future marker of the Anthropocene will not be the dramatic rise in parts per million of carbon dioxide, nor the traces of radioactive particles from post-1945 nuclear tests and leaks, nor the proliferation of microplastics, but the ubiquity of fossilized chicken bones from the 50 billion slaughtered annually (Bennett et al., 2018). Another measure is that the proportion of the world's landmass which is unmodified by human farming, construction, industry, or mining, has shrunk during the last century from 85 per cent to 23 per cent (Watson et al., 2018), whilst the rate of species extinction is estimated to be 1000 times higher than the background or 'natural' rate, as a direct consequence of human activities (Pimm et al., 2014), with populations of wild animals falling by an average of 60 per cent since 1970 (Grooten and Almond, 2018).

A posthumanist ethics and politics must grasp the Anthropocene as a crisis of a whole way of being human in a more-than-human world, not just a crisis in our management of the global environment. It must challenge the widespread tendency to dislocate climate change from species extinction, biodiversity loss, and ecosystem breakdown, and to focus almost exclusively on climate goals, instead foregrounding the transformation of species relations as a key means to address the climate crisis and to mitigate those of its impacts that are already 'locked in'. On this view, our constitutive entanglement with nonhumans offers our best opportunity to realize other modes of becoming human. We will only address the Anthropocene crisis as a species which knows its fate to be inseparable from that of the other animals in this dynamic living world. Moreover, by thinking with animals it is possible to reconcile the Anthropocene's call to action with a posthumanist insistence upon ontological and epistemic self-effacement. The politics consistent with this are not only ecocentric, they involve acting relationally through and within multispecies assemblages, rather than acting upon nature conceived as an external system and an object of techno-managerial control.

Concrete proposals in this spirit include so-called 'rewilding', including the reintroduction of species and restoration of degraded eco-systems, reforestation to increase biodiversity on land formerly used for grazing, as well as restoring mangroves, seagrass meadows, swamps, and wetlands (Brown, McMorran and Price, 2012; Monbiot, 2013; Taylor, 2005). Crucially, rewilding in a posthumanist mode is not about attempting to recreate a romanticized historical 'wild' exclusive of humans, but rather to forge a wilder more-than-human world in the future, a 'rambunctious garden' rich with relations of interspecies flourishing and human-animal co-habitation (Jorgensen, 2015; Marris, 2013). With its emphasis on the future and on giving nonhumans greater scope to co-construct new wilds with humans, rather than striving to recreate pristine historic wilds purified of humans, this is perhaps better thought of as 'wilding' than 'rewilding'. It must also, crucially, mean an absolute reduction in animal agriculture, which is the only way to address 'livestock's long shadow' of massive greenhouse gas emissions, habitat loss, and accelerating anthropogenic extinction (Hirth, 2020; Steinfield et al., 2006). Moreover, there is a need for a clear-eyed understanding that these things will not and cannot be effective alongside economic business as usual and continued growth—capitalism cannot be 'offset'. What is needed is radical transformation, of energy, transport, and industrial systems—all those things consistent with Green New Deal thinking, but there must also be large-scale retrenchment—pulling back, ramping down, scaling back, which means a new economics entirely. Posthumanism challenges the human exceptionalism underpinning orthodox growth-based macro-economics, pointing to the ecological necessity of 'post-growth' or 'de-growth' models (Jackson, 2016; Reichel and Perey, 2018). The assumed centrality of perpetual growth and of GDP as a measure of the health of economies, even in Green New Deal agendas, must be displaced by a new emphasis on social and ecological goals, maintaining human welfare and reducing social inequalities in the context of dramatic reductions in resource-use, material throughput, and environmental impacts. There is no space for magic thinking on this—it means shrinking economic activity and planned techno-industrial retrenchment, especially in the global north (Mastini et al., 2021). A challenge to growth is inescapably, of course, a challenge to the very logic of capital, underlining again the need for post-capitalist thinking and politics in the Anthropocene.

One might object that the foregoing visions are still predicated upon some conception of human separation from 'nature', and of human organization and management of other species and habitats. But there are many forms of management, stretching from domination and control to something better described as stewardship. We are inextricably entangled with others, other animals, other species and ecosystems, hence our ethics and politics must not stop at a conception of humanity as separate from the nonhumans that not only make human life possible but give it much of its richness. From this perspective, to overlook or disavow connection and thus 'response-ability' is anathema. Yet such an ethics of entanglement can be partly differentiated from an ethics of forbearance, restraint, and conscientious withdrawal. The latter proceeds less from a celebration of relational becoming than from an affect or structure of feeling embedded in humility and hospitality towards alterity and a commitment to avoid colonizing the autonomy of the other (Nimmo, 2016). Where an ethics of entanglement seeks to become-with-nonhumans more ethically and symmetrically, an ethics of disconnection or exclusion seeks to limit the relentless expansion of the human domain in an effort to respect and protect what remains of nonhuman autonomy (Giraud, 2019). For this posthumanist sensibility the Anthropocene is a crisis of human domination, which cannot be addressed solely by enfolding nonhumans ever more closely within humanity's embrace, but must also involve letting go, allowing nonhumans to escape the colonizing dynamic, if it is to prevent multispecies stewardship from sliding into anthropocentric domination. The world is not mere raw material for a human project of enlightened self-mastery and self-realization, even one that may claim to incorporate nonhuman others within its relational self-becoming.

Conclusion

This discussion has drawn upon a posthumanist sensibility in critically reflecting upon some tensions and paradoxes in the concept of the Anthropocene, from which to draw out what I have argued are some necessary components of a posthumanist ethics and politics for the socio-ecological crisis. It began by highlighting how the concept of the Anthropocene was preceded and made possible by strands of thinking positing the end of the discursive separation of 'nature' or the 'environment' from 'society' or 'culture', which has been central to modernist ontology, epistemology, ethics, and politics. The Anthropocene is symptomatic of this erosion of the 'great divide', even if its post-dualist vision is a partial one, underpinned by the earth-systems thinking and geology from where the concept emerged. As such, the Anthropocene does not so much deconstruct the society-nature and human-nonhuman divides as bridge them, functionally and causally, by foregrounding the massive bio-material impacts of human activity upon the planet. It nevertheless undermines the notion of nature as a sphere relatively unaffected by humans, constituting a stable stage or background for human civilization and human history. In the Anthropocene we have a 'nature' that is finite, malleable, and in the process of being disrupted in its fundamental processes. In that sense nature, or the bio-material environment, is something that is increasingly produced by humans, even as humanity remains fundamentally dependent upon that bio-material environment.

Yet this conceptualization remains problematic and contested. The key problems include its tendency to de-emphasize critical questions of environmental justice, political economy, capitalist ecology, colonial continuities, and gender inequalities. All of these can be traced to the Anthropocene's interpolation of 'humanity' or the 'Anthropos' as the key socio-environmental agent both responsible for the ecological crisis and capable of its solution. This has the effect of backgrounding multiple axes of environmental injustice and inequality as well as the more-than-human assemblages within and through which 'human' agency emerges and is made possible. But the question of agency cannot be left at critique, with no sense of what is to be done or by whom. The Anthropocene is a didactic and activist concept, stressing the catastrophic implications of the ecological crisis as simultaneously a crisis for human civilization and for the biosphere, and demanding an urgent response. Hence, no form of environmental quietism or fatalism, whether emanating from romantic, melancholic, or misanthropic sentiments, is ultimately consistent with the spirit of the Anthropocene as a call to action. The Anthropocene demands posthumanist praxis as well as posthumanist theory. Yet it signally fails to furnish a theory of environmental transformation.

Various agendas in contemporary environmental politics can be read as responses to the Anthropocene with their own visions of socio-ecological transformation, including geo-engineering proposals to technologically intervening in large-scale planetary and climatological processes, Half-Earth proposals to set aside a proportion of the planet 'for nature', and Green New Deal plans to restructure capitalist economies and create sustainable 'green growth'. Exploring the rationale and implications of these in light of a posthumanist ethical and political sensibility, each turns out to be defective in some critical way, from the Promethean techno-managerialism of geo-engineering, to the neo-colonial logic of enclosures underpinning Half-Earth, to the urban and global north asymmetry of Green New Deals. The common root of their particular inadequacies is their common tendency to understand the Anthropocene as a crisis of human relations with 'nature' as an external environment. Posthumanist praxis must embrace forms of environmental organization and politics which understand the Anthropocene as a crisis of human-animal relations and of a whole way of becoming human with others in a more-than-human world.

References

Abbinnett, R. (2019). The Anthropocene as a figure of neoliberal hegemony. *Social Epistemology, 33*(4), 367–79.

Alaimo, S. (2010). *Bodily natures: Science, environment, and the material self*. Bloomington: Indiana University Press.

Alaimo, S. (2017). Your shell on acid: Material immersion, Anthropocene dissolves. In R. Grusin (Ed.), *Anthropocene feminism*. Minneapolis: University of Minnesota Press, 89–120.

Asafu-Adjaye, J. et al. (2015). *An ecomodernist manifesto*. The Breakthrough Institute: http://dx.doi.org/10.13140/RG.2.1.1974.0646

Barad, K. (2003). Posthumanist performativity: Toward an understanding of how matter comes to matter. *Signs, 28(3)*, 801–31.

Barbier, E.B. (2010). *A global Green New Deal: Rethinking the economic recovery*. Cambridge: Cambridge University Press.

Bar-On, Y.M., Phillips, R., & Milo, R. (2018). The biomass distribution on earth. *PNAS, 115(25)*, 6505–11.

Baskin, J. (2019). Global justice and the Anthropocene: Reproducing a development story. In F. Biermann & E. Lovbrand (Eds.), *Anthropocene encounters: New directions in green political thinking*. Cambridge, Cambridge University Press, 150–168.

Beck, U. (1992). From industrial society to risk society: Questions of survival, social structure and ecological enlightenment. *Theory, Culture and Society, 9(1)*, 97–123.

Bennett, C.E. et al. (2018). The broiler chicken as a signal of a human-reconfigured biosphere. *Royal Society Open Science, 5(12)*, 180–325.

Braidotti, R. (2013). *The Posthuman*. Cambridge: Polity.

Brown, C., McMorran, R., & Price, M.F. (2012). Rewilding—A new paradigm for nature conservation in Scotland? *Scottish Geographical Journal, 127(4)*, 288–314.

Büscher, B. et al. (2017). Half-earth or whole earth? Radical ideas for conservation, and their implications. *Oryx, 51(3)*, 407–10.

Castree, N. (2016). The Anthropocene and planetary boundaries. In *International Encyclopaedia of Geography: People, the Earth, Environment and Technology*, John Wiley and Sons Lt.: Hoboken, New Jersey, US https://onlinelibrary.wiley.com/doi/abs/10.1002/9781118786352.wbieg0027.pub2

Ceballos G., Ehrlich, P.R., & Dirzo, R. (2017). Biological annihilation via the ongoing sixth mass extinction signaled by vertebrate population losses and declines. *Proceedings of the National Academy of Sciences of the USA, 114(30)*, 6089–96.

Chakrabarty, D. (2018). Anthropocene time. *History and Theory, 57(1)*, 5–32.

Crutzen, P. (2002). Geology of mankind. *Nature, 415*, 23.

Crutzen P.J. & Stoermer, E.F. (2000). The Anthropocene. In W. Steffen (Ed.), *Global change: Newsletter 41 of the IGBP (International Geosphere-Biosphere Programme)*, Royal Swedish Academy of Sciences, Stockholm, 17–18.

Crist, E. (2013). On the poverty of our nomenclature. *Environmental Humanities, 3(1)*, 129–47.

Dengler, C. & Seebacher, L.M. (2019). What about the global south? Towards a decolonial feminist degrowth approach. *Ecological Economics, 157*, 246–52.

Dhawan, N. (2014). *Decolonizing enlightenment: Transnational justice, human rights and democracy in a postcolonial world*. Opladen: Verlag Barbara Budrich.

Elhacham, E. et al. (2020). Global human-made mass exceeds all living biomass. *Nature, 588*, 442–4.

Ellis, E. (2009). Stop trying to save the planet. *Wired*, Opinion, 05/06/2009: https://www.wired.com/2009/05/ftf-ellis-1/

Ellis, E., Pascual, U., & Mertz, O. (2019). Ecosystem services and nature's contribution to people: Negotiating diverse values and trade-offs in land systems. *Current Opinion in Environmental Sustainability, 38*, 86–94.

Giraud, E.H. (2019). *What comes after entanglement? Activism, anthropocentrism, and an ethics of exclusion*. Durham, NC: Duke University Press.

Gonzalez, C.G. (2017). Global justice in the Anthropocene. In L. Kotze (Ed.), *Environmental law and governance for the Anthropocene*. Oxford: Hart Publishing, 219–240.

Gorg, C. et al. (2019). Scrutinizing the great acceleration: The Anthropocene and its analytic challenges for socio-ecological transformations. *The Anthropocene Review, 7(1)*, 42–61.

Griffin, P. (2017). *CDP Carbon Majors Report 2017*. CDP Worldwide.

Groote, M. & Almond, R.E.A. (Eds). (2018). *World Wildlife Fund, Living Planet Report—2018: Aiming higher*. Gland, Switzerland.

Haraway, D. (2003). *The companion species manifesto*. Chicago: Prickly Paradigm Press.

Haraway, D. (2015). Anthropocene, Capitalocene, Plantationocene, Chthulucene: Making kin. *Environmental Humanities, 6*, 159–65.

Hirth, S. (2020). Food that matters: Boundary work and the case for vegan food practices. *Sociologia Ruralis, 61(1)*, 234–54.

Inoue, C.Y.A. & Moreira, P.F. (2016). Many worlds, many nature(s), one planet: Indigenous knowledge in the Anthropocene. *Revista Brasileira de Politica Internacional, 59(2)*, e009.

Jackson, T. (2016). *Prosperity without growth: Foundations for the economy of tomorrow*, 2nd Edition. London: Routledge.

Jacobs, M. (2013). Green growth. In R. Falkner (Ed.), *The handbook of global climate and environment policy*. Hoboken: John Wiley, 197–214.

Jorgensen, D. (2015). Rethinking rewilding. *Geoforum, 65*, 482–8.

Klein, N. (2019). *On fire: the burning case for a green new deal*. London: Allen lane.

Kopnina, H. (2016). Half the earth for people (or more)? addressing ethical questions in conservation. *Biological Conservation, 203*, 176–85.

Kopnina, H. (2018). Anthropocentrism and post-humanism. In H. Callan (Ed.), *The international encyclopaedia of anthropology*. Hoboken: John Wiley.

Latour, B. (1993). *We have never been modern*. Cambridge, MA: Harvard University Press.

Leiss, W. (1994). *The domination of nature*. Kingston: Queen's University Press.

Lorimer, J. (2015). *Wildlife in the Anthropocene: Conservation after nature*. Minneapolis: University of Minnesota Press.

Lynas, M. (2011). *The God species: How the planet can survive the age of humans*. London: Fourth Estate.

Marquardt, J. (2018). Worlds apart? The global south and the Anthropocene. In T. Hickmann et al. (Eds.), *The Anthropocene debate and political science*. London: Routledge, 200–218.

Malm, A. (2016). *Fossil capital: The rise of steam power and the roots of global warming*. London: Verso.

Malm, A. & Hornborg, A. (2014). The geology of mankind? A critique of the Anthropocene narrative. *The Anthropocene Review, 1(1)*, 62–9.

Marris, E. (2013). *Rambunctious garden: Saving nature in a post-wild world*. London: Bloomsbury.

Mastini, R., Kallis, G., & Hickel, J. (2021). A Green New Deal without growth? *Ecological Economics, 179*, 106–832.

Merchant, C. (1980). *The death of nature: Women, ecology and the scientific revolution*. New York: Harper.

Mitchell, A. (2014). Making a 'Cene'. *Wordly* (blog), 23 February 2014.

Monbiot. G. (2013). *Feral: Rewilding the land, sea, and human life*. London: Penguin.

Moore, J.W. (2016). *Anthropocene or Capitalocene? Nature, history, and the crisis of capitalism.* Oakland: PM Press.

Moore, J. (2017). The Capitalocene, Part I: On the nature and origins of our ecological crisis. *Journal of Peasant Studies, 44(3)*, 594–630.

Nimmo, R. (2016). From over the horizon: Animal alterity and liminal intimacy beyond the anthropomorphic embrace. *Otherness, 5(2)*, 13–45.

Nimmo, R. (2019). Posthumanism. In P. Atkinson et al. (Eds.), *Sage research methods foundations*. London: Sage.

Oldekop, J.A. et al. (2016). A global assessment of the social and conservation of protected areas. *Conservation Biology, 30*, 133–41.

Pimm, S.L. et al. (2014). The biodiversity of species and their rates of extinction, distribution and protection. *Science, 344(6187)*, 1246752.

Plumptre A.J. et al. (2021). Where might we find ecologically intact communities? *Frontiers: Forests and Global Change, 4(626635)*, 1–13.

Plumwood, V. (1993). *Feminism and the mastery of nature.* London: Routledge.

Plumwood, V. (2002). *Environmental culture: The ecological crisis of reason.* Abingdon: Routledge.

Reichel, A. & Perey, R. (2018). Moving beyond growth in the Anthropocene. *The Anthropocene Review, 5(3)*, 242–9.

Rockström, J. et al. (2009). Planetary boundaries: Exploring the safe operating space for humanity. *Ecology and Society, 14(2)*, 1–24.

Sanders, B. (2019). *The Green New Deal.* https://berniesanders.com/issues/green-new-deal/

Schleicher, J. et al. (2019). Protecting half of the planet could directly affect over one billion people. *Nature Sustainability, 2*, 1094–6.

Schulz, K.A. (2017). Decolonising the Anthropocene: The mytho-politics of human mastery. In M. Woons and S. Weier (Eds.), *Critical epistemologies of global politics*. Bristol: E-International Relations, 46–62.

Steffen, W. et al. (2004). *Global change and the earth system: A planet under pressure.* Berlin: Springer.

Steffen, W. et al. (2015). The trajectory of the Anthropocene: The great acceleration. *The Anthropocene Review, 2(1)*, 81–98.

Steinfield, H. et al. (2006). *Livestock's long shadow: Environmental issues and options.* Food and Agriculture Organisation of the UN.

Simpson, M. (2020). The Anthropocene as colonial discourse. *Environment and Planning D: Society and Space, 38(1)*, 53–71.

Taylor, P. (2005). *Beyond conservation: A wildland strategy.* London: Earthscan.

Taylor. M.B. (2021). Indigenous interruptions in the Anthropocene. *PMLA, 136(1)*, 9–16.

Wark. M. (2016). *Molecular red: Theory for the Anthropocene.* London: Verso.

Watson, J.E.M. et al. (2018). Protect the last of the wild. *Nature, 563*, comment, 31 October 2018, 27–30.

West, P., Igoe, J., & Brockington, D. (2006). Parks and peoples: The social impact of protected areas. *Annual Review of Anthropology, 35*, 251–77.

Wilson, E.O. (2016). *Half-Earth: Our planet's fight for life.* New York: Liveright.

Wolfe, Cary. (2010). *What is posthumanism?* Minneapolis: University of Minnesota Press.

CHAPTER 4

COVID-19 AND ZOONOTIC DISEASE

Manufacturing and Organizing Ignorance within the Animal-Industrial Complex

CAROLINE CLARKE, CHARLES BARTHOLD, AND MATTHEW COLE

> Pandemics such as the COVID-19 outbreak are a predictable and predicted outcome of how people source and grow food, trade and consume animals, and alter environments. (Key message 7, United Nations Environment Programme and International Live-stock Research Institute, 2020: 7)

RECENTLY, scholars in management and organization studies (MOS) have been prolific in their focus on the coronavirus pandemic. For example, there is great interest and speculation about the ways in which our day to day working lives will change, and what form this may take (Spicer, 2020), as well as important discussions concerning how systemic gender, race, and class inequalities have been further illuminated and exacerbated by the working practices adopted during this period (e.g. Milliken et al., 2020). Of particular concern has been frontline workers, whose activity has become enmeshed within debates about what constitutes necessary, or key work; those, deemed indispensable by the government to sustain and keep us alive. Paradoxically, the majority of this activity remains synonymous with low-skilled labour, the minimum wage, or any unpaid invisible work like caring, for it is simultaneously constituted as *valuable*, but not *valued*.

These topics are laudable, but despite the proliferation of words that have been devoted to the grave effects of the pandemic, the highly compelling question '*How on Earth Did We Get Here?*' seems conspicuous by its absence; a debate largely eschewed by management and organization studies scholars, the media, and politicians alike. In this chapter, we argue that COVID-19 is merely the canker of a far more serious and endemic disease—misplaced human conceit. One consequence of this is a naturalized and sedimented superiority complex that has encouraged a tendency in humans to treat everything, and everyone, purely as a profitable resource, permitting us to cycle through numerous and relentless means–end calculations and justifications that wreak havoc on our planetary host and its habitability. Our main contribution to this book focuses on COVID-19, the (deliberate) forms of ignorance that surround our relationship with animals, and the consequences that flow from practices that are rooted in *anthropocentricism*—a 'desire to determine human specificity over and against those beings who/that threaten to undermine that specificity' (Calarco, 2008: 53).

By drawing from different disciplines of critical animal studies, critical management studies, and ecosophy (Guattari, 1992) through a marriage, not so much of convenience but of serendipity, we suggest ways to challenge damaging organizational practices, especially those contained within the powerful animal-industrial complex (henceforth AIC). We also explore how different forms of *agnoses* (ignorance) are fundamental for the survival of the AIC, while simultaneously closing down posthuman, alternative, or necessary 'truths' about our place in a wider entangled network. The latter could be harnessed as antidotes, to both anthropocentricism and the (neglected) problem of speciesism, to promote an awakening, or reconstitution, of how to live a good and sustainable life alongside the Others with whom we share our planet. In short, this chapter provides support and momentum for transforming our scholarly work into growing a theoretical and practical field of animal or multispecies organization studies.

ASYMMETRICAL ANIMAL-HUMAN RELATIONSHIPS

> The animals of the world exist for their own reasons. They were not made for humans any more than black people were made for white, or women were created for men. (Walker, 1982: 14)

We have sketched out how the current pandemic has its roots located in an anthropocentric preoccupation with exclusively human concerns. Notwithstanding the efforts of the animal rights, vegan, and environmental movements, the dominant historical trajectory has been the accelerating instrumentalization of the planet and the life it sustains, as a resource pool to be drained solely for human benefit. Paula Arcari argues that the COVID-19 pandemic 'should be a moment that instigates serious reflection on our profligate use and careless treatment of other animals' (2021: 187). However, at the time of writing the experience of COVID-19 has not been marked by a thoroughgoing process of human self-reflection on the damage wrought by this historical intensification of anthropocentrism. Conversely, discourses foregrounding human health above any other consideration predominate (Taylor et al., 2021). In many cases, the agnoses that preceded the pandemic have intensified. This has included relative inattention to millions of laboratory animals sacrificed in pursuit of COVID-19 vaccines, abandoned companion animals used and then discarded as temporary sops for lockdown-induced loneliness, and the millions of victims that are one consequence of 'meat'[1] packing' being declared 'essential' work. Human supremacism was perhaps nowhere more starkly illustrated than in the mass murder of millions of nonhuman animals held captive in 'fur farms', shortening their already truncated and immiserated lives (Taylor et al., 2021).

The AIC is the anthropocentric 'organisation' par excellence, insofar as it represents the conceit that humans are the sole legitimate organizers—mostly for profit motives— of the lives and deaths of the other inhabitants of the planet. In other words, the AIC is the inverse of Alice Walker's famous quotation that opens this section; its anthropocentric commitment to subjugating nonhuman animals to human interests is the basis of the abyssal asymmetry of power that characterizes human-nonhuman animal relations. In the context of critical animal studies, the term AIC was coined by anthropologist Barbara Noske in 1989, indicating the extent to which nonhuman animal exploitation was industrialized as well as organized by interlocked state and non-state actors in a 'complex'. More recently, sociologist Richard Twine defined the AIC as a 'partly opaque and multiple set of networks and relationships between the corporate (agricultural) sector, governments, and public and private science. With economic, cultural, social and affective dimensions it encompasses an extensive range of practices, technologies, images, identities and markets' (2012: 23). Simply put, Big Agriculture has vested interests in securing their 'business as usual' practices, throughout the current pandemic and beyond. Complacency and exeptionalism legitimise the transformation of animal bodies into profitable commodities, via the production of agnoses, and adiaphorization (Clarke and Knights, 2022), regardless of suffering.

A key problem in challenging this state of affairs is how the consumption of animal products has taken on a sedimented sense of being 'natural', as ever greater quantities of consumption have become normalized. The more animal products are consumed, the more profits can be generated from them, such that normalizing their consumption right from childhood makes good business sense (Cole and Stewart, 2014). To this end Big Agriculture pours huge resources into marketing, shaping our tastes through the manipulation of the symbolic meanings of animal products, and by conferring an aura of high status, luxury, and the good life, despite mass production cheapening the products (and nonhuman animals' lives). Alongside the AIC, such endeavours are supported by the media and the state, through direct promotion (Molloy, 2011; Nibert, 2016) or tacitly via nutrition guidelines, education curricula, or school meals. The nexus of shared AIC interests creates and sustains 'invented needs' (Marcuse, 2002 [1964]) for animal products. One example is the hegemonic assumption that dogs must eat flesh-based 'pet food', which now accounts for nearly 25 per cent of meat consumption (Ward and Oven, 2019). The flipside of animal product are rarely promoted - the denial of the harms they

---

[1] In this chapter we place 'meat' (and like terms) in quotation marks, to denote its status as a euphemism for the flesh of nonhuman victims of the AIC. The ubiquity of such euphemisms are intrinsic to the perpetuation of agnoses that obscure the anthropocentric roots of zoonotic disease.

cause, to humans (chronic diseases of consumption, and as we'll see, zoonotic diseases); to the planet (climate change, deforestation, pollution, and the squandering of land, soil, and fresh water) and most of all, to other animals themselves—the animals caught in the AIC, and those exterminated as their natural habitats are destroyed to sustain increasing demand.

Organizing Animal Resources and Ignoring the Consequences: A Sting in the Tale/Tail

> I think we're challenged as mankind has never been challenged before to prove our maturity and our mastery, not of nature, but of ourselves. (Carson, 1962: 427)

If the conceit of human-animals (2) stretches towards an imaginary where the exploitation of nonhuman animals, and the biosphere more generally, has no repercussions then surely this erroneous view must now be unravelling? (Wright and Nyberg, 2015). In spite of mounting evidence concerning our anthropogenic practices and their effects (e.g. forest fires, rising tides, species extinction, plastic pollution, global heating, melting ice caps, and the current COVID-19 pandemic), it remains unclear as to if, rather than when, there will be any cessation in our hubris that *we* are masters of the universe (Plumwood, 2002).

Anthropogeny

Depicted elsewhere as 'the revenge of Gaia'—describing a time when the Earth fights back (Lovelock, 2007), Michael Moore, director of *Planet of the Humans*, suggests that COVID-19 should be viewed as a form of moratorium, as though 'Mother Nature has put us in the time-out room' to reflect on our actions (The Hill, 2020). Notwithstanding our reservations concerning how both Lovelock and Moore construct 'nature' as somehow separate, or external to humans, which is surely part of the problem, we concur; anthropocentric practices of organizing and exploiting so-called resources have serious and *known* consequences, even if this knowledge is not widely shared. One such consequence created the conditions of possibility for COVID-19 to emerge. Zoonotic disease[2] is reported to account for 60 per cent of known human infectious disorders, but new and emerging zoonoses are increasing in frequency and severity and responsible for 75 per

---

[2] Zoonotic disease is where infectious diseases in nonhuman animals cross over or 'jump' to humans and infect them. Many zoonotic diseases are potentially lethal.

cent of all novel diseases (Morse et al., 2012). Without radical change, requiring new and 'ambitious lines of enquiry' (UNEP, 2020: 4), additional pathogenic diseases—especially if they cannot be treated through antibiotics—are likely to engender even more lethal pandemics, with possible death rates exceeding 50 per cent for those infected (Greger, 2020; Smart and Smart, 2017;). As the next pandemic waits in the wings, the inseparable, entangled issues of climate change promise other horrific events, even extinction, unless 'humans are capable of stemming their drive to species suicide' (Chomsky, 2021).

Considering such prophecies of omnicide from zoonotic pathogens, and/or climate disaster, perhaps the most vital question for organizational scholars is '*how can we stop ourselves returning again to a similar situation in the future?*'. Institutions such as the World Health Organisation (WHO) and the United Nations Environment Programme (UNEP) have already identified and provided ample empirical evidence concerning the destructive consequences of specific contemporary ways of organizing, particularly in relation to the treatment of nonhuman animals. In their report 'Preventing the Next Pandemic: Zoonotic Diseases and How to Break the Chain of Transmission' (UNEA, 2020), they identify seven drivers of zoonotic disease. All are anthropogenic,[3] and linked with the AIC:

1. Increasing demand for animal protein
2. Unsustainable agricultural intensification
3. Increased use and exploitation of wildlife
4. Unsustainable utilization of natural resources accelerated by urbanization, land use change, and extractive industries
5. Travel and transportation (humans and other animals)
6. Changes in food supply chain
7. Climate change

Quammen (2012: 39) explains how these complex problems are primarily due to 'the convergence of two [ecological and medical] forms of crisis on our planet', such that when they 'intersect, their joint consequences appear as a pattern of weird and terrible new diseases'. Similarly, Smart and Smart describe zoonoses as emerging 'from complex constellations of very disparate influences' (2017: 33)that are already well documented, demonstrating how the emergence of COVID-19 was expected, rather than exceptional. As no single driver of zoonotic disease alone can explain the emergence of COVID, explanations must necessarily be nuanced by incorporating a broad number of contributors. Nevertheless, we have already witnessed the (preferred) option of identifying something/someone to blame, through increased racial abuse towards Chinese nationals 'responsibilized' for the COVID outbreak (e.g. Elias et al., 2021).

Since all seven drivers of zoonotic disease are anthropogenic and relate to our treatment of nonhuman animals, it appears that governing authorities have learned few

---

[3] Relating to, or as a result of, the activities of human beings in relation to 'nature'.

lessons over the last three decades. This is despite multiple zoonotic dress rehearsals, most notably: 'mad cow' disease (where herbivores were fed cows' brains to become cannibals) (Adams, 1997); AIDS; swine flu; avian flu; MARS; SARS; and Ebola. With future pandemics being predicted in terms of *when*, not *if* (Benatar, 2007; Greger, 2020; UNEP, 2020), why do so few of us know about the risks concerning animals and pandemics, and why is this vital issue not being debated within this COVID-19 context? Were we to ignore (how could we?) the suffering and anguish resulting from 3.1 million *confirmed* human deaths at the time or writing (29 April 2021), and move straight to the so-called rational bottom line, in economic terms the pandemic is devastating—estimated to be in the region of trillions of dollars. As prevention clearly seems preferable to any cure (Greger, 2020; UNEP, 2020), on this basis alone it is perplexing and unconscionable that transparent debate about risk factors and future pandemics have not taken place in the public domain. To explore the reason for this absence we revisit the intensive (and potentially dangerous) organizational practices underpinning the USD trillion of the animal-industrial complex ('meat' production alone is worth USD 1640 billion (OECD FAO, 2021)), to examine how knowledge is unevenly disseminated.

Knowledge/Power Relations

In their book *Agnotology—The Making and Unmaking of Ignorance*, Proctor and Scheibinger (2008) suggest that ignorance, in common with knowledge, comes in various forms that are neither natural or neutral, but distributed in specific ways. In its purest and most basic form, ignorance is simply *knowledge-not-yet-discovered*, or an *absence-of-knowledge*, for example the question of what happens to us when we die. By contrast, the question of what causes a pandemic cannot be an *absence-of-knowledge*, since clear documented evidence from multiple peer-reviewed sources regarding the link between pandemic risk and the ways we treat and eat nonhuman animals existed long before COVID-19 broke (Madhav et al., 2018; Morse et al., 2012; Smart and Smart, 2017). One of many examples can be found in the article 'The Chickens Come Home to Roost' (Benatar, 2007), warning us of the high probability that a zoonotic disease emerging from the wet markets in China could cause a pandemic. Of particular interest is the author's observation about how the root cause is persistently sidestepped:

> [C]hanging the way humans treat animals— … ceasing to eat them, or at the very least, radically limiting the quantity of them that are eaten—is largely off the radar as a significant preventive measure. (Benatar, 2007: 1545)

While there can be little doubt that such knowledge already existed, how many of us were aware of the risks associated with industrial farming? Since Benatar's work was published, a full-blown global pandemic, with the most likely cause just as predicted, has struck, so how has this changed our knowledge of human-animal relations? Greger writes:

In this new Age of Emerging Diseases, there are now billions of animals overcrowded and intensively confined in filthy factory farms for viruses to incubate and mutate within. Today's industrial farming practices have given viruses billions more spins at pandemic roulette. How can we stop the emergence of pandemic viruses in the first place? Whenever possible, *treat the cause*. (Greger, 2021: 1; emphasis added)

Benatar (2007) accurately prophesied that following an actual pandemic outbreak, public debate and discourse would focus almost exclusively on the creation and rollout of a vaccine scheme, largely because 'this relieves humans of any need to improve their treatment of animals at all' (p. 1546). Tendencies towards *apathy* not only prevent us from taking action, for example considering alternatives such as plant-based food, but they also prohibit us from examining the root cause of pandemic outbreaks, sustaining ignorance in relation to zoonotic risks and the mass consumption of 'meat'. The last 18 months of deep immersion in a global pandemic confirms that this debate remains firmly off the agenda (Taylor, 2021).

As we have argued, an *absence-of-knowledge* does not adequately account for this situation, so we must consider other explanations. Proctor suggests the term *absent knowledge*—the 'deliberate production of ignorance in the form of strategies to deceive' (2008: 8). These can be deliberately crafted and used as both an 'active construct' or 'strategic ploy' (at 8) to intentionally censor, fail to disclose, or conceal information, for example the very techniques used by the tobacco industry to stall empirical confirmation of the causal link between cigarettes and lung cancer. Similar tactics can be found on the topic of climate change and denialism funded by oil corporations, exploiting what Bowden et al. call 'the production of reflexive ignorance, which reinforces skepticism around scientific authority and defends particular economic interests' (2021: 397). All forms of absent knowledge can spread ignorance, through a variety of techniques including 'secrecy, stupidity, apathy, censorship, disinformation, faith, and forgetfulness' (Proctor, 2008: 2), but they must be actively and continually reinforced and remade, to prevent particular forms of knowledge becoming widely *knowable*.

Within the animal-industrial complex, the proven link between pandemics and our treatment of nonhuman animals could be construed as *concealed absent knowledge*, concerning the damaging, yet profitable organizational practices that both Organization Studies scholars and lay persons have broadly failed to identify. Proctor states that 'many companies cultivate ignorance as a kind of insurance policy: if what you don't know can't hurt you' (2008: 25), but this is dangerous as it frequently serves to obfuscate a form of structured truth that requires interrogation. Regarding the AIC, we argue that our enemy is complacency and ignorance, while their allies are in forms of *knowledge suppression*:

> One of the best things modern animal agriculture has going for it is that most people … haven't a clue how animals are raised and 'processed.' … the less the consumer knows … the better. (Cheeke, 2003)

In his book, *How Not To Die in a Pandemic*, later updated into an article, Greger describes avian (or bird) flu as a far more lethal form of zoonotic disease than COVID-19, with a far higher potential to kill, referring to COVID (in comparison) as a mere 'dress rehearsal'.

Given the weight of scientific evidence establishing the link between our treatment of animals and the emergence of zoonotic disease, it is clear that those organizing the corporate slaughterhouses or industrial chicken factories in which animals/birds suffer, do so not out of scientific ignorance but by taking *calculated risks*. It has long been documented that a lack of ventilation and space cause stress and lower immune systems in animals (Urrutia, 1997), yet we continue to adopt a strategy of profit maximization simply because the cost of improvements might be outweighed by the loss in production (Bell et al., 2004). The process of manufacturing ignorance also requires the naturalization, the seduction, and constitution of particular practices such as eating 'meat'-based junk food, as being so taken for granted that they lie beyond challenge. Consider this quote from the editor of *Poultry*:

> I'm not as worried about the U.S. human population dying from bird flu, as I am that there will be no chicken to eat. (Thaxton, 2005 as cited in Greger, 2020: 336)

Organizations engaged in the AIC hope to externalize the risk of potential zoonoses for the public to escape accountability. So far, as illustrated by COVID-19, this calculated risk has paid off, for when zoonotic disease morphs into global devastation and pandemic status, the economic costs are shifted from the industry onto public health departments. Reductionist explanations that focus only on how people are affected means that, 'many important features will be missed' (Smart and Smart, 2017: 27), not least the set of organizing practices that will usher in the next pandemic, as well as 'the ecological catastrophe into which we are hurtling on our present trajectory' (Nimmo, chapter 3 in this volume). In a most anthropocentric manner, we declare 'war' on the coronavirus, while ignoring our own actions in bringing it into being, lest we must confront any uncomfortable changes required in enacting our daily lives. Partly through the perpetuation of different forms of *agnoses*, animal consumption is not only naturalized, habitual, and experienced by many as a—culturally constructed—pleasant gastronomical experience, it is also big business. For instance, the AIC through 'meat' production makes around USD1640 billion a year (OECD FAO, 2021), which excludes the extremely profitable 'pet' food industry whose products are increasingly 'meat'-based, and account for a staggering '*one-quarter* of all the meat consumed in the United States, equivalent to the meat devoured by twenty-six million Americans' (Ward and Oven, 2019: ix, emphasis added).

We suggest this might partly account for Benatar's bewilderment as to why tackling the root cause is consistently off the radar. Further, we contend that profit and the protectionist practices by the agri-industry may also inform some of the perplexing contradictions found within the UNEP report, insofar as it clearly sets out seven anthropogenic and zoonotic drivers of the pandemic, alongside 10 specific policy recommendations, yet is carefully crafted so that words such as 'vegan', 'vegetarian', 'plant-based', or even 'reduced consumption of "meat"' never feature explicitly. In addition, on page 32 of the report, concerns are expressed due to the '*over*-exploitation', rather than the *exploitation of* animals, while simultaneously furnishing the reader with the Convention of Migratory Species statement—the biggest 'threat affecting most species' is their 'consumptive use' (UNEP, 2020). This amplification and suppression of parts of the story are what Proctor describes as the uneven geographical and political distribution of knowledge because 'like ignorance it occupies space and takes us down one path rather than another ... has a face, a house and a price—there are people attached, institutions setting limits, and costs in the form of monies or opportunities lost' (2008: 26).

While we would not go so far as to claim the UNEP report is a form of what Proctor (2008) calls 'alibi research'—that which purports to be studying the issue, but not really addressing it in practice—it is certainly a partial and anthropocentric view on how to maintain and regulate, rather than disband, particular harmful consumptive practices. For example, there is an inevitable emphasis on tightening regulations and inspection practices (which have already been proven not to be adhered to) by advocating a '*farm to fork*' approach along the '*entire consumptive chain*' for the purpose of ensuring that ingesting animals will not harm human-animals (UNEP, 2020: 47; emphases added). While the complex processes involved in transporting animals from their rearing location to the plate is problematized, it simultaneously normalizes how billions of nonhuman animals are bred for the explicit purpose of ending up on our forks while ignoring the stressing and immune-lowering effects on them (O'Keefe, 2005). What initially looks like an encouraging, evidenced-base reporting on the drivers of zoonotic disease, could also be interpreted as a set of anthropocentric recommendations and actions to sustain these exploitative practices. Perhaps the agenda becomes obvious when we notice that the report aims to understand 'the threats [zoonoses] pose to *human health*' (UNEP, 2020: 4; emphasis added).

Despite the UNEP's declared intentions of 'how to minimize the risk of further devastating outbreaks?' and to pursue 'an ambitious line of enquiry', does it satisfy these aims and questions? We argue it does not, as it eschews more radical ways to 'address the root causes' of zoonotic emergence' (UNEP, 2020: 50) and fails to protect us from future threats. Moreover, the suggestions merely help us consume animals-as-resources while also identifying how this is risky and problematic. One effect is that the UNEP report contributes to a form of 'reflexive ignorance' (Bowden et al., 2021) by not addressing the central issue of the mass consumption of 'meat'. Furthermore, the UNEP's claim about the reduction of risk is disingenuous in that 'according to the CDC, the leading candidate for the next pandemic is a bird flu virus known as H7 N9, which is a hundred times deadlier than COVID-19. With an apparent case fatality rate of nearly 40% ... as a flu virus, [it] has the potential to blanket the globe' (Greger,

2021: 3). Were the report to sincerely follow an ambitious line of enquiry, it should at least consider a more radical rethink of human-animal relations; how we can reduce, even abolish, our routine practices of consuming nonhuman animals' parts by replacing them with alternatives, for example plant-based products. Suggestions such as these would contribute to the alleviation of the zoonotic drivers referred to as 1, 2, 3, 5, 6, and 7, and perhaps also number 4 (UNEP, 2020: 15; Greger, 2021). At the very least, the UNEP report could have recognized that not radically transforming human animal relations—within the framework of the AIC—would involve reproducing the current level of zoonotic risk, and identify how default 'no action' strategies perpetuate and increase zoonotic threats.

Returning to Proctor's ideas (2008) around knowledge and ignorance, we must pay attention to the questions they pose: 'who is ignorant and why?' and 'what keeps ignorance in one place, and why?' We have shown how this is not an *absence-of-knowledge-not-yet-discovered* because 'the public health community has been shouting from the rooftops for years about the risks posed by factory farms' (Greger, 2021: n.p.). Rather it is a deliberate suppression of a lucid recognition of the risk of the AIC and its concomitant practices. In the final section of this chapter, in the context of ecosopy and MOS, we briefly consider how to address the coalescence of the widespread and often deliberate ignorance vested on consumers, the protectionist mechanisms surrounding the AIC, and the anthropocentric tendencies underpinning our organization of nonhuman animals and scholarly work.

Towards Multispeciest Organization?

> At the heart of our response to zoonoses and the other challenges humanity faces should be the simple idea that the health of humanity depends on the health of the planet and other species. If humanity gives nature a chance to breathe, it will be our greatest ally as we seek to build a fairer, greener and safer world. (UNEP, 2020: 4)

While agreeing with the spirit and intention of this quote (which aims to move beyond the agnoses strategies of the AIC which we discussed earlier), particularly the first part, we also recognize how it exemplifies precisely the anthropocentricism it might seek to avoid; the idea that as humans we can suddenly 'take' full and rational control of any remedial action required, while also deciding what a 'fair' world might look like, to whom, and for whom, is highly problematic (e.g. Coulter, chapter 1 in this volume; Barthold and Bloom, 2020). In other words, now that zoonotic disease (and climate issues) threaten the very survival of human-animals we must take urgent action and assert our autonomy, primarily *to save ourselves*. However, in acknowledging how we have already made a mess of 'controlling' environmental resources by extracting far more than we have contributed, this ontological divide between nature and humans is sustained

(Bonneuil and Fressoz, 2016), and we are once again urged to rely on the same (slightly altered) practices to remedy the very problem we created. Further, the use of the word 'nature' constitutes it as somehow *apart from* 'humanity', which feeds the fundamental misrecognition of ourselves as discrete autonomous individuals (Lacan, 2006), rather than acknowledging how we are always already entangled and 'as interrelated and indispensable to each other as the different organs in our body' (Watts, 2011; see also Latour, 2017). As Butler (2021: n.p.) observes 'Who now could deny that to be a body at all is to be bound up with other living creatures, with surfaces, and the elements, including the air that belongs to no one and everyone?', and yet the acknowledgement of being vulnerable to zoonotic disease easily punctures our fragile constructions of detachment. It also reminds us that we are animals, just like other animals, and there is no biological barrier between the pangolin and us, an inconvenient truth that our anthropocentrism seeks to dampen or obscure.

In response to agnoses about the AIC and zoonotic diseases, one alternative way of viewing the world would be to amplify 'ecosophical' (Bignall et al., 2016) perspectives that radically 'challenge the conceptual foundations upon which modern Western philosophy rests' (p. 456). In recognizing how each and every part of the planet forms the whole, these provide an antidote to the anthropocentric tendencies of viewing ourselves at the top of a hierarchy, entitled to treat everything and everyone as a means to an end; even when this involves damaging the earth system that sustains all forms of life. Posthumanism (Wolfe, 2010) is one such ecosophical perspective, for it respects diversity and difference (Diprose, 1994) and seeks to dismantle dominant hierarchies of identities that lead to Othering and violence, so as to facilitate ethical and embodied engagement with the Other, and all the others. Without such embodiment (e.g. Braidotti, 2011; Pullen and Rhodes, 2014), there is a danger that everything, and everyone, is capable of being transformed into a mere object, as evidenced by the neoliberal-capitalist ideologies of 'service benefit' accounting (Bignall et al., 2016), towards a solely 'logical control of the world' (Negri, 2004: 4). Were we to recognize that each and every species within our universe is *always already* mutually entangled (Barad, 2007: 141), we would be no more inclined to inflict harm on others (be it animal, vegetable, or mineral) than pit our own bodily organs against each other. For this reason, a posthumanist perspective has the potential to provide an alternative and beneficial body of knowledge to address particular agnoses' techniques that have brought us the anthropocene, particularly misinformation about ecological practices that need not inflict harm, violence, or disaster on others (Braidotti, 2019; Smart and Smart, 2017).

Indigenous philosophies provide another ecosophical approach (Guattari, 2000) that is arguably more radical than posthumanism insofar as it does not originate from the hegemonic Western post-enlightenment conception of human-animals. Notably, Bignall et al. (2016) write that Indigenous philosophies 'provide a long tested alternative to Western humanism' and offer relevant remedies for life in the anthropocene because of their 'more than human' perspective, taking as its starting point the belief that human-animals are 'inseparable from a constitutive connection to the natural world' (p.457) through a 'sacred ecology' (p. 471). Unlike Western humanism, Indigenous philosophies experience their relationship with mountains and rivers not merely as a contextual backdrop, but rather as a *living* form of interconnectivity, to the extent that its inhabitants claim to 'experience the wellness or ill-health of the environment as an aspect of their own cultural health as an Indigenous Nation' (p. 469; see also Descola, 2013).

Arguably, ecosophical approaches would have the potential to inform organizational studies of nonhuman animals, which have mostly failed to interrogate the AIC and are therefore complicit in the oppressive practices of speciesism that underpin the latter (Noske, 1989). A marginalized group which has contributed to the study of speciesism in organizations (e.g. Clarke and Knights, 2019; 2021; Cunha et al., 2019; Krawczyk and Barthold, 2018; Labatut et al., 2016) has not received the attention that MOS bestows on other 'isms', and complicitous silence sustains platitudes of corporate social responsibility and business ethics, obfuscating rather than radically challenging, normative and taken-for-granted modes of anthropocentrism. The consequences of this neglect are significant in rendering us both complacent and ignorant about the organization of animals and their effects in terms of 'corporate irresponsibility' (Mena et al., 2016).

On a final note, the knowledge produced in these encounters might help us to resist the construction and weaponization of ignorance in relation to nonhuman animal exploitation, through the dissemination of academic knowledge in the form of public debate, or for example, through universities' curricula.

Conclusion

> But although the logos is common, most people live as if they had their own private understanding. (Heraclitus as cited in Johnstone, 2014: 4)

In this chapter we argue that it is incumbent on MOS scholars to engage with important and interdisciplinary challenges that have effects at local, national, and global levels. Further, by exploring how zoonotic disease is transmitted, as just one consequence of our treatment and organization of nonhuman animals, it behoves us to 'unmake' the ignorance surrounding the origins of the COVID-19 pandemic, as an attempt to stall or eradicate the certainty of future pandemics. This is perfectly feasible, since these are problems that have both their origins and solutions in human behaviour, but it must include being cognizant and sharing our understanding of *all* the social, economic, and health costs that flow from the AIC. This is vital because not only have states and corporations failed to prepare and protect the world from a crisis they knew was coming, they also knowingly enabled it, by ignoring warnings and the adoption of profit-maximizing strategies in relation to mass scale rearing and slaughtering of nonhuman animals. It is clear we cannot rely on these organizations to keep us safe, but in turn they are shielded by our ignorance, partly through their denial of responsibility, but also by withholding knowledge to ensure it is *absent*, rather than knowable.

Something that could be explored in terms of academic knowledge is critical or *agonistic dialogue* (Parker and Parker, 2017) with alternative organizations, which develop processes that are more ethical towards other animals and would thereby mark a departure from the AIC's practices. As one example, this could include vegan organizations that develop economic logics that enable distance from the AIC. Further avenues might include non-governmental organizations (NGOs) and social movement organizations (e.g. animal rights activists) that aim to resist the hegemony of the AIC and its effects and current agnoses. Critical dialogue should include other animals within the framework of socio-material processes (Barthold and Bloom, 2020; Kalonaityte, 2018), as opposed to an anthropocentric conception of dialogue only involving 'rational' white men (e.g. the US Founding fathers). We are also in a privileged position to discuss speciesism and zoonosis with students, which could be disseminated through graduate and postgraduate curricula.

REFERENCES

Adams, C.J. (1997). 'Mad cow' disease and the animal industrial complex: An ecofeminist analysis. *Organization and Environment, 10(1)*, 26–51.

Arcari, P. (2021). The Covid pandemic, 'pivotal' moments, and persistent anthropocentrism: Interrogating the (il)legitimacy of critical animal perspectives. *Animal Studies Journal, 10(1)*, 186–239.

Barad, K. (2007). *Meeting the universe halfway: Quantum physics and the entanglement of matter and meaning.* Durham: Duke University Press.

Barthold, C. & Bloom, P. (2020). Denaturalizing the environment: Dissensus and the possibility of radically democratizing discourses of environmental sustainability. *Journal of Business Ethics, 164(4)*, 671–81.

Bell, D., Robertson, S., & Hunter, P.R. (2004). Animal origins of SARS Coronavirus: Possible links with the international trade in small carnivores. *Philosophy Trans R Soc. London B Biological Science, 359[1447]*, 1107–14 https://doi.org/10.1098/rstb.2004.1492.

Benatar, D. (2007). As the chickens come home to roost. *American Journal of Public Health, 97(9)*, 1545–6.

Bignall, S., Hemming, S., & Rigney, D. (2016). Three ecosophies for the Anthropocene: Environmental governance, continental posthumanism and Indigenous studies. *Deleuze, 10(4)*, 455–78.

Bonneuil, C. & Fressoz, J.B. (2016). *The shock of the Anthropocene: The earth, history and us.* London: Verso.

Bowden, V., Nyberg, D., & Wright, C. (2021). 'I don't think anybody really knows: Constructing reflexive ignorance in climate change adaptation. *The British Journal of Sociology, 72(2)*, 397–411.

Braidotti, R. (2011). *Nomadic theory: The portable Rosi Braidotti.* New York: Columbia University Press.

Braidotti, R. (2019). *Posthuman knowledge.* Cambridge: Polity Press.

Butler, J. (2021). Creating an inhabitable world for humans means dismantling rigid forms of individuality. *Time 2030*, available at: https://time.com/5953396/judith-butler-safe-world-individuality/

Calarco, M. (2008). *Zoographies: The question of the animal from Heidegger to Derrida*. New York: Columbia University Press.

Carson, R. (1962). *Silent spring*. Boston: Houghton.

Cheeke, P.R. (2003). *Contemporary issues in animal agriculture*, 3rd Edition. Upper Saddle River: Prentice Hal.

Chomsky, N. (2021). Chomsky warns of humanity's drive to 'species suicide' amidst climate and nuclear threats. An interview with Richard Baker, available at: https://redactionpolitics.com/2021/02/09/chomsky-species-suicide-climate-emergency-nuclear-threat

Clarke, C. & Knights, D. (2019). Who's a good boy then? Anthropocentric masculinities in veterinary practice. *Gender, Work and Organization, 26(3)*, 267–87.

Clarke, C. & Knights, D. (2022). Milking it for all it's worth: Unpalatable practices, dairy cows and veterinary work? *Journal of Business Ethics, 176*, 673–688.

Cole, M. & Stewart, K. (2014). *Our children and other animals: The cultural construction of human-animal relations in childhood*. Farnham: Ashgate Publishing, Ltd.

Cunha, M.P.E., Rego, A., & Munro, I. (2019). 'Dogs in organizations. *Human Relations, 72(4)*, 778–800.

Descola, P. (2013). *Beyond nature and culture*. Chicago: University of Chicago Press.

Diprose, R. (1994). *The bodies of women: Ethics, embodiment and sexual difference*. London: Routledge.

Elias, A., Ben, J. Mansouri, F., & Paradies, Y. (2021). Racism and nationalism during and beyond the COVID-19 pandemic. *Ethnic and Racial Studies, 44(5)*, 783–93.

Greger, M. (2020). *How to survive a pandemic*. London: Bluebird.

Greger, M. (2021). Primary pandemic prevention. *American Journal of Lifestyle Medicine*, 15598276211008134.

Guattari, F. (1992). Pour une refondation des pratiques sociales. *Le Monde Diplomatique*, October, 26–27.

Guattari, F. (2000). *The three ecologies*. London: Athlone Press.

Kalonaityte, V. (2018). When rivers go to court: The Anthropocene in Organization Studies through the lens of Jacques Rancière. *Organization, 25(4)*, 517–32.

Krawczyk, V.J. & Barthold, C. (2018). The affordance of compassion for animals: A filmic exploration of industrial linear rhythms. *Culture and Organization, 24(4)*, 268–84.

Johnstone, M.A. (2014). On 'Logos' in Heraclitus. *Oxford Studies in Ancient Philosophy, 47*, 1–29.

Labatut, J., Munro, I., & Desmond, J. (2016). Animals and organizations. *Organization, 23(3)*, 315–29.

Lacan, J. (2006). *Écrits*. New York: W.W. Norton and Company.

Latour, B. (2017). *Facing Gaia: Eight lectures on the new climatic regime*. Cambridge: John Wiley and Sons.

Lovelock, J. (2007). *The revenge of Gaia: Why the earth is fighting back and how we can still save humanity*. Vol. 36. London: Penguin UK.

Madhav, N. et al. (2018). *Pandemics: Risks, impacts, and mitigation*. Washington: The World Bank.

Marcuse, H. (2002) [1964]. *One-dimensional man: Studies in the ideology of advanced industrial society*. London: Routledge.

Milliken, F.J., Kneeland, M.K., & Flynn, E. (2020). Implications of the COVID-19 pandemic for gender equity issues at work. *Journal of Management Studies, 57(8),* 1767–72.

Mena, S. et al. (2016). On the forgetting of corporate irresponsibility. *Academy of Management Review, 41(4),* 720–38.

Molloy, C. (2011). *Popular media and animals.* Basingstoke: Palgrave Macmillan.

Morse, S.S. et al. (2012). Prediction and prevention of the next pandemic zoonosis. *The Lancet, 380(9857),* 1956–65.

Negri, A. (2004). *Subversive Spinoza: (UN) contemporary variations: Antonio Negri.* Manchester: Manchester University Press.

Nibert, D. (2016). Origins of oppression, speciesist ideology, and the mass media. In N. Almiron, M. Cole, & C.P. Freeman (Eds.), *Critical animal and media studies: Communication for nonhuman animal advocacy* (pp. 74–88). London: Routledge.

Noske, B. (1989). *Humans and other animals.* London: Pluto Press.

OECD-FAO. (2021). *OECD_FAO Agricultural Outlook 2021–2030.* OECD Publishing. Paris:, https://doi.org/10.1787/19428846-en.

O'Keefe, T. (2005). Starting on the farm. *Watt Poultry USA,* Juni, S. 12–16 June.

Parker, S. & Parker, M. (2017). Antagonism, accommodation and agonism in critical management studies: Alternative organizations as allies. *Human Relations, 70(11),* 1366–87.

Plumwood, V. (2002). *Feminism and the mastery of nature.* London: Routledge.

Proctor, R.N. (2008). Agnotology: A missing term to describe the cultural production of ignorance (and its study). In R.N. Proctor & L. Schiebinger (Eds.), *Agnotology: The making and unmaking of ignorance* (pp. 1–36). Stanford: Stanford University Press.

Proctor, R.N. & Schiebinger, L. (Eds.) (2008). *Agnotology: The making and unmaking of ignorance.* Stanford: Stanford University Press.

Pullen, A. & Rhodes, C. (2014). Corporeal ethics and the politics of resistance in organizations. *Organization, 21(6),* 782–96.

Quammen, D. (2012). *Spillover: The powerful, prescient book that predicted the Covid-19 coronavirus pandemic.* New York: Random House.

Smart, A. & Smart, J. (2017). *Posthumanism: Anthropological insights.* New York: University of Toronto Press.

Spicer, A. (2020). Organizational culture and COVID-19. *Journal of Management Studies, 57(8),* 1737–40.

Taylor, C., Struthers Montford, K., & Kasprzycka, E. (2021). Introduction: Critical animal studies perspectives on Covid-19. *Animal Studies Journal, 10(1),* 1–6, available at: https://ro.uow.edu.au/asj/vol10/iss1/2.

Thaxton, Y.V. (2005). Are you prepared for AI? *Poultry,* April–May, page 5.

Twine, R. (2012). Revealing the 'animal-industrial complex'—A concept and method for critical animal studies? *Journal for Critical Animal Studies, 10(1),* 12–39, available at: http://www.criticalanimalstudies.org/volume-10-issue-1-2012/.

The Hill. (2020). Michael Moore: Mother nature sending warning, people to 'time-out rooms' with pandemic, available at: https://thehill.com/hilltv/rising/495081-michael-mooremother-nature-sending-warning-people-to-time-out-rooms-with.

Urrutia, S. (1997). Broilers for next decade: What hurdles must commercial breeders overcome? *World Poultry, 13(7),* 28–30.

United Nations Environment Programme and International Live-stock Research Institute. (2020). *Preventing the Next pandemic: Zoonotic Diseases and How to Break the Chain of Transmission*. Nairobi: United Nations Environment Programme and International Livestock Research Institute.

Walker, A. (1982). *The color purple*. New York: Pocket Books.

Ward, E. & Oven, A. (2019). *The clean pet food revolution: How better pet food will change the world*. Lantern Books.

Watts, A. (2011). *The book: On the taboo against knowing who you are*. London: Vintage.

Wright, C. & Nyberg, D. (2015). *Climate change, capitalism, and corporations*. Cambridge: Cambridge University Press.

Wolfe, C. (2010). *What is posthumanism?* Minneapolis: University of Minnesota Press.

CHAPTER 5

ORGANIZING A REAL THAT IS YET TO COME

A Critical Inquiry of Education in Animal Organization Studies

HELENA PEDERSEN

Introduction: Animals and the Problem of Education

EDUCATION is often viewed as a preventative measure to all kinds of social problems and as a tool to create sustainable future societies. Education is also seen as a common good; the right to education as a fundamental human right, a tool for equality and public and individual welfare, as well as for national progress and development. Education is supposed to make us become better human beings and make our nation-states prosper. This arguably idealist view of education has been contested by critical education theorists (including Giroux,1981; McLaren, 1998; Morrow and Torres, 1995) who claim that education reproduces social inequalities rather than alleviating them. In these critical education discourses animals have, until recently (e.g. Kahn, 2003; Kopnina and Cherniak, 2015; MacCormack, 2013; Repka, 2019; Russell and Spannring, 2019; Wallin, 2014), been conspicuously absent. Animal bodies have been fundamental for the development and dissemination of knowledge and skills at different levels and in different spaces of our educational institutions, but rarely have these educational institutions been configured as an agent of power, a system of exploitation, and a *problem* for animals.

This chapter attempts to reverse the anthropocentric gaze on education and scrutinize education as a problem for animals. Analysing education as part of animal organization studies is an absolutely crucial undertaking in this respect. Few institutions in Western society accommodate the entire human population to the extent that education does, and it normally permeates many years, even decades, of a person's life. Education guides our perceptions of society as well as what positions are accessible to us in different societal sectors and arenas. In brief, education exerts an impact on our lives difficult to compare with any other institution or organization. It acts on everybody who is caught up in its system, sometimes with our ostensible compliance and at other times, more coercively (cf. Perriton and Reynolds, 2004). Education is engaged not only, or even primarily, in knowledge dissemination and training, but also in subjectivity production (cf. Starkey et al., 2019): it guides us in who we are (and who we may become) in relation to other people, as well as animals, and organizes our relations with them; at every level from education policymaking and partnerships with animal industries, to micro-level intersubjective 'encounters' with animals in schools (Pedersen, 2010a; 2019).

This chapter is concerned with the former aspect: The embeddedness of education in animal industries that, as we shall see, goes beyond the notion of 'partnership'. In my book, *Schizoanalysis and Animal Science Education* (Pedersen, 2019), I ask the overarching question: what is the function of education in the animal-industrial complex (A-IC)? Approaching this question as a key problem for animals utilized in the education system as well as for animal organization studies, I will first give a brief account of some significant intersections of the A-IC and animal organization studies in the most relevant literatures. Then, I will explore what work education does in the A-IC. Here, I will draw on Deleuze and Guattari's ([1980] 2004) thoughts, work within the field of sociology of education and experiences from my own ethnographic fieldwork. I will conclude with some reflections on the A-IC as an organizing concept[1] for critical animal organization studies and suggestions for further research.

The Animal-Industrial Complex in Animal Organization Studies

In their introduction to the special issue of 'Animals and Organization' in the journal *Organization*, Labatut, Munro, and Desmond (2016: 319) aptly remark that the 'discussion of ethics in relation to the animal is organizational from top to bottom'. Labatut et al. (2016) identify three key themes, or 'problematics', in animal organization studies: agriculture and the biosocial organization of nature/culture; ethics as the organization of the animal; and the politics of animal resistance. In the same journal, Doré and Michalon (2017) pose the question of what makes human-animal relations 'organizational', proposing the rather abstract notion of 'anthropozootechnical agencement'

---

[1] Twine (2012) has offered a detailed and helpful analysis of the A-IC as an organizing concept for critical animal studies generally. In the present chapter I do not intend to reiterate Twine's work but rather add to it by including education as an often overlooked key actor in the A-IC.

(derived from Actor-Network Theory and Deleuzian ontology) to analyse the organizational characteristics of these relations. Both Labatut et al. (2016) and Doré and Michalon (2017) address the industrialized animal production system as a key problem and case study, respectively, for animal organization studies. Likewise, Lennerfors and Sköld (2018) note in their editorial to the special issue on 'The Animal' in the journal *Culture and Organization*, that an emerging body of scholarship in management and organization studies is concerned with industrial food systems, the organization of animal suffering, and mass slaughter these systems are specializing in.

The overarching organizing concept of the Animal-Industrial Complex (Noske, 1997; Twine, 2012), connecting exploitative 'anthropozootechnical' and biosocial human-animal relations as they materialize and become enacted across a range of societal institutions and production sites, is not, however, explicitly engaged in these studies. Sayers (2016: 374) touches on this, arguing that 'factory-farming is part of the modern global capitalist industrial complex' and also points out that the factory farm has become a node for organizing activism as a form of 'influential collective resistance which radically challenges existing capitalist models of production'. Focusing on pigs in industrial production systems, Sayers (2016: 373) further notes that the objectifying language of industrial agriculture constitutes pigs as an 'instrumental resource or an inert material from which all value is extracted', and the pigs' powerlessness in this system is reinforced by zoological, biological, genetic, and other forms of knowledge about them.

Importantly, Sayers (2016) approaches knowledge production about animals as an inherent dimension within the organization of their exploitation in the animal-industrial complex (cf. Cole, 2011; Williams, 2004). Knowledge production in the A-IC relies on, as Noske (1997) has remarked, intimate partnerships between science, food production systems, capital, and government institutions. Research and development, and the dissemination of knowledge in fields such as animal science and its various specializations (e.g. livestock science, meat science, dairy science, animal genetics; see Twine, 2010) take place to a large extent at agricultural universities and other institutes of higher education. Thus, the education system is, arguably, a key actor in how we think about and organize our relationship with animals, although rarely addressed as such. This chapter seeks to contribute to these debates by offering a provisional analysis involving both the A-IC and education, and, in particular, the connections between them.

With the concept of 'the animal industrial complex', Barbara Noske (1997) referred to the embeddedness of animal-based industries in a capitalist fabric, pointing to an expanding interpenetration of agriculture, advanced technology, financial interests, and government institutions as multinational processing industries are working to take control over the various stages of animal production by, for instance, contract farming. Building on Noske's work, Twine (2010; 2012) has given a sociological account of the development and operations of biotechnologies through an increasing exploitation of animals, supported by animal science as a field of research in service of a knowledge-based bio-economy (see Pedersen, 2019). Perhaps the A-IC is best conceptualized as a transnational institutional aggregate where different animal industries not only are approaching and overlapping each other, but also tend to rely on and consolidate each other in diverse ways.

A site where the exploitative, brutal, and indifferent nature of the A-IC and its organization becomes painfully concrete is the slaughterhouse. Siegfried Giedion (1948) offers an architectural history analysis of the mechanization processes in the organization of animal slaughter. The industry that has given us diabolical innovations, such as Judas sheep and other 'decoy animals' (Pedersen, 2013; 2019; Williams, 2004) to control the animal flows passing through the various stages of slaughter, has also invented a repertoire of other machines such as (examples taken from pig slaughter) hog-hoisting devices, hog traps and suspension devices, conveyor belts, hog-scraping and hog-cleaning machines, and spine-cleaving machines; devices described by Giedion (1948: 232) as 'medieval instruments of torture'. From an organization studies perspective, the main point here may not be the cold rationality and effectiveness of the slaughter process itself, but rather the effectiveness by which the act is rendered completely neutral (Norwood, 2015).

While some contemporary organization scholars have taken an anthropocentric approach and analysed the effects on slaughterhouse workers of routinized killing of animals (Baran, Rogelberg, and Clausen, 2016), ever since the publication of Upton Sinclair's famous novel *The Jungle* (1906), a 'genre' of eyewitness accounts from inside slaughterhouses has appeared in fiction, journalism, and scientific literature. These accounts, many of which attempt to represent slaughter process experiences from the animals' perspective, have been documented by authors such as Noëlie Vialles ([1987] 1994), Sue Coe (1995), Gail Eisnitz (1997), Eric Schlosser (2002), Jonathan Safran Foer (2009), Lina Gustafsson (2020), and Timothy Pachirat (2011). Timothy Pachirat's (2011) ethnographic study is of particular interest to animal organization studies. As an academic seeking employment undercover at a US slaughterhouse, Pachirat offers insights into the absurd organization of the slaughterhouse as a workplace as well as the rationale of the spatial layout of the building. This layout separates the workers from having an overview of the slaughter process through a Fordist division of labour; it separates the workers from their supervising managers, *Panopticon*-style; it separates the animals from each other and, ultimately, from their own subjectivity; and it separates the entire slaughter business from public insight (Pachirat, 2011; Pedersen, 2013; 2019; Vialles, 1994). Pachirat remarks that distancing is a power mechanism, pointing to a number of non-governmental organizations (NGOs) whose political work for change involves attempts to decrease the distance between the public and the violent acts (such as WikiLeaks, PETA, Human Rights Watch, Amnesty International). Activist strategies against the animal production system are, however, frequently subject to co-optation by the meat industry, which, at any moment, may turn slaughter into an event of visual consumption, a spectacle, and a marketing strategy (Göransson, 2017; Parry, 2010; Shukin, 2009), taking advantage of animal subjectivity as a tool for enhancing production efficiency through 'humane slaughter' techniques (Williams, 2004) . In contrast to the critical eyewitness accounts of animal slaughter mentioned above, in these cases, the event of 'eyewitnessing' takes on a different modality and function of affirming and celebrating the efficient, hyper-rational, and hygienic administration of death performed in a clearly defined, designated space (Pedersen, 2010b). The cruel situation and destiny of the animals, however, remains the same.

Shifting focus from slaughterhouse organization to the animal production site, Noske (1997) draws on the Marxian notion of alienation in order to theorize what is at stake for the animals in large-scale systems of production: First, they are alienated from their own products; more specifically, from their own bodies and their offspring. 'The relationship between the production- and laboratory-animal and its [sic] own body', writes Noske (1997: 18), 'has almost become grotesque'. In the machinery of animal production, the animal's own body has become the very cause of her misery as 'an alien and hostile power confronting the animal' (Noske, 1997: 18).[2] Alienation from offspring not only means the forced separation of mother and her newborn that often takes place shortly after birth (Noske, 1997), but also the animal's alienation from her sexuality and biological reproduction process through forced insemination and other invasive technologies. Second, animals are alienated from productive activity as their bodies are forced to be useful for one single capacity, such as producing meat, eggs, or milk, and the whole animal is subordinated to this one 'activity'. Third, animals are alienated from their fellow-animals as they are either removed from their own societies and relationships with species-kin, or have these societies and relationships grossly distorted by being crowded together in large numbers. Fourth, animals are alienated from their environment by being incarcerated in factories or laboratories during their short lives. Fifth, animals are alienated from species life as they are totally incorporated in a production system where they become reduced to raw materials, production tools, and machine appendages. One sector of the animal-industrial complex where the alienation, incorporation, and commoditization of animal life has intensified is the 'poultry' industry, which, from an organization perspective, has blurred the boundaries between corporate interests, research and development in animal science, and food production management systems (Boyd, 2001; Labatut et al., 2016; Watts, 2000). In all these examples from the animal-industrial complex, a de-animalization process (Noske, 1997) depriving animals of everything that constitutes a life, is built into the organizing structure of animal agribusiness.

As noted above, the animal-industrial complex does not always operate through blatant power exertion and overt violence but can involve more refined techniques relying on acknowledgement on animal subjectivity and agency, rather than deprivation and de-animalization. An example of such techniques, more subtle in their manifestation of power, is robotic milking technologies used to extract milk from cows' bodies without the immediate physical presence of humans, and that allow

---

[2] Barbara Noske's Marxian analysis of the animal's alienation from her own body should not be understood as a downplaying or obscuring of human power, agency, and responsibility at the animal production site. Rather, I suggest it should be viewed as an effect of the organization and institutionalization of systematic animal exploitation. For a partly similar (albeit anthropocentric) phenomenological analysis of human pain, see Elaine Scarry (1985). See also Wadiwel (2015).

cows a certain degree of autonomy in the milking process (Holloway, 2007). Lewis Holloway's Foucauldian analysis argues that in such systems of dairy production, technology, the spatial organization of the premises, the cow's body, and subjectivity all come into play—and are co-produced—under a regime of disciplinary power presenting itself as animal-friendly and benign. Such regimes of disciplinary power in robotic systems of dairy production align with similar developments in animal-centred welfare science that appear as a benevolent alternative to conventional 'factory farming' models. Through what Matthew Cole (2011) terms 'quasi-therapeutic' claims to know individual farmed animals, their behaviour, and preferences, the animals themselves are co-opted into the knowledge-generating processes and positioned as active contributors to the improvement of their own welfare. Of course, there are distinct limits to the agency they are afforded since the preference to avoid slaughter and continue living is beyond reach for these animals and outside the welfare science discourse; at the same time, it makes their slaughter appear as more acceptable in the eyes of the public (Cole, 2011). Hence, these 'progressive' innovations in animal science and ethology are ultimately designed to be put to work against the animals' own interest since they consolidate animal slaughter more firmly beyond the realm of public scrutiny and critique.

THE WORK OF EDUCATION IN THE ANIMAL-INDUSTRIAL COMPLEX

As demonstrated above, animal production and killing is embedded in, and feed back into, expert knowledge in animal science and management (Pedersen, 2019; Twine, 2010). To begin to grasp the workings of scientific knowledge production in the animal-industrial complex, it is necessary to analyse the education system as a vital actor in the A-IC. Pierce (2013) argues that educational institutions form a terrain where life and its mechanisms are targeted by a range of production and control regimes, and that education has become part of a biocapitalist landscape where the dissolution of restrictive barriers to the commodification of life takes place. Anne Sauvagnargues (2016) describes the embeddedness of education in industrial production systems as follows:

> The industrial machine is built on a scientific machine with a cognitive output. This scientific machine capitalizes on the cognitive factor from elementary school to the university, according to complex networks (*arborescences*) of teaching, research, laboratories, institutes and companies, as well as circuits of finance, research funds, foundations, economic investment in education, research, production and commercialization. These elements not only make the fabrication of artifacts possible, but even more, they make them profitable by producing humans capable of using them and especially of purchasing them. (Sauvagnargues, 2016: 188)

Hence, teaching, from elementary school to university, together with economic investments in education at all levels, constitute a condition for industrial production processes. They contribute, as Sauvagnargues points out above, to forming human subjects capable of (and keen on) using, purchasing, and assisting in the production of animal commodities (Pedersen, 2019). The centrality of education in the animal-industrial complex is also briefly described by Noske (1997: 23), noticing that agribusiness companies 'sometimes run their own courses in university departments, which in turn actively conduct and give impetus to rationalization measures that are being implemented in agriculture and animal husbandry'. These concise accounts begin to map out the multiple couplings between the formal education system and the animal-industrial complex, comprising not only the food production system, but the pharmaceutical industry, the horseracing industry, even fur farming (as a source of animal carcasses for dissection training in veterinary education). The animal industries are not only active at university level; they also reach out to schools through films, books, farm visits, products in the school cafeteria, advertising, vending machines, sponsorships, and even through offering complete lesson plans designed to fit with the school curriculum and its learning objectives (Cole and Stewart, 2014; Göransson, 2017; Linné and Pedersen, 2016; Repka, 2019; Rowe, 2013; see also Trachsel, 2017). Meneka Repka (2019: 102) has conceptualized these outreach and partnership strategies as a 'process of reciprocal value sharing between institutions', enacted through various forms of curricula.

At the beginning of this chapter, I suggested that animal organization studies need to critically address not only the organization and management of animal bodies, subjectivities, movements, behaviour, suffering, and killing, but also the animal-industrial complex as an organizing *concept*. An in-depth conceptual analysis, I argue, requires an understanding of the work of education in the A-IC as this reveals something about the A-IC that may otherwise be overlooked. While here I can only address briefly how an understanding of education can contribute to a conceptual analysis of the A-IC significant to animal organization studies, I develop the analysis in more detail elsewhere (Pedersen, 2019). Importantly, what an understanding of education in the A-IC helps us see is that the A-IC is neither a cross-institutional infrastructure, an ideological superstructure, nor a deterministic omnipotent phenomenon (although it may accommodate aspects of all three) (Pedersen, 2019). Rather, when connecting with education, the A-IC constructs, to draw on Deleuze and Guattari ([1980] 2004: 157), 'a real that is yet to come, a new type of reality'. That is, education creates new realities in the virtual realm, by working with students' still undeveloped potentials (supposed to be developed in certain directions and not others). This means that education, for instance animal science education, not only has a regulatory function, but also a vitalizing one (Pedersen, 2012). Education communicates and connects. Education requires conformity, but also supports and encourages, and recommends appropriate behaviour, attitudes, and allies to students. Especially in animal science education programmes directly involved in the A-IC such as veterinary education and vocational animal caretaker education, students may develop feelings of professional pride, knowledgeability, and expertise (and take on the authority that comes with it), and privileged affiliation with specific professional communities (Pedersen, 2010a; cf. Smith and Kleinman, 1989). Education may even work by excitement, desire (Pedersen, 2019), and what Jane Bennett (2001) has called 'enchantment'—a mood of lively and intense engagement with the world. Animal science education also tends to relieve tension embedded in controversial animal-related issues (such as animal experimentation or meat eating). In doing so, it offers students liberation from feelings of guilt towards animals when engaging in, or complying with, harm inflicted onto them as part of their education (cf. Arluke and Hafferty, 1996). In this manner education guides students in navigating and balancing potential ethical conflicts arising from the contradictions produced within their education (Pedersen, 2010a). In all these ways, education points to new realities (Deleuze and Guattari [1980] 2004) for students; a promissory real as a future professional that is within reach and yet to come—and so does the animal-industrial complex, when the two work in symbiosis.

As a concrete example of how the embeddedness of education in the A-IC can organize such new realities for students in a particular school, I draw on my ethnographic field studies in upper secondary school where I have followed an animal caretaker education class. Animal caretaking is a specialization within the vocational Natural Resource Use Programme in Sweden, designed to prepare students for a variety of animal-handling professions in, for instance, zoos and aquariums, pet shops, veterinary clinics, and research laboratories. These schools often keep animals for training purposes. The school where I carried out fieldwork housed an authentic rodent lab on its premises; a little world of its own, a miniature replica of a 'real' animal laboratory. It was located in a separate designated area of the school building and presented as being used for studies of genetics, for 'providing food for predators' kept at this school, and for learning 'how to take care of a lab in a proper way' (Pedersen, 2008: 136). According to one teacher, no animal experiments were carried out in the lab. Still, learning 'how to take care of' included, for the students, becoming familiar with two large carbon dioxide containers placed on the floor, used for killing animals. Like a real animal research lab, this one was also closed to the public, and during the school's 'open house' event when the public was invited to visit the school and learn about its activities, visitors were prevented from entering the lab: a huge flower pot was placed in the middle of the staircase leading to the room, and a hand-written sign on the door explained that 'the animals need calm and quiet' (Pedersen, 2008: 137). This school lab directly connects animal science education to the pharmaceutical branch of the animal-industrial complex. It organizes life conditions for both animals and students in education by providing learning of specific kinds of knowledge and skills (and not others), coding animals for specific kinds of roles and relations (and not others). It also points forward to a real that is yet to come for the students by configuring the pharmaceutical industry as a significant future employer for them. These new realities for students however rely on—paradoxically—a reproduction of a perpetual *status quo* of exploitative conditions for animals in society.

Conclusion

As Anne Sauvagnargues (2016: 188) has pointed out, industrial systems of production rely on a crucial cognitive factor provided by all levels of the education system and its 'arborescences' of economic investments. Hence, as we begin to unfold the multiple ways in which education, knowledge production, teaching, and learning is embedded in the animal-industrial complex, education emerges as not only a central actor in, but a *condition for* the A-IC. Understanding the A-IC as an organizing concept for critical animal organization studies thus requires analyses of the multifaceted, dynamic, and productive functions of education in the A-IC. The productive dimensions of education are of key importance here. Rather than solely focusing on the coercive and sometimes oppressive tendencies of education that critical education scholars have alerted us to, entangled with these overt manifestations of power exist in daily activities of teaching and learning another repertoire of strategies employing desire, enchantment, and friendly guidance of students to develop their still unrealized potential in certain directions (and not others). This, I argue, takes on certain manifestations with the presence of animals in education. Education organizes promissory futures (cf. Starkey et al., 2019) by engaging students' hopes and dreams as aspiring professionals in the animal sectors—as veterinarians, animal scientists, zoo workers—or, as the particular empirical example from the animal caretaker school in this chapter has shown, animal technicians in research laboratories. These promissory future career prospects for students rely however on a *reproduction* of present arrangements of animal exploitation.

While this chapter has only begun to provisionally sketch the work of education in the A-IC, a question I explore in further detail elsewhere (Pedersen, 2019), critical animal organization scholars could develop this work by scrutinizing what is at stake for the animals as well as the students who are caught up in the intersections of different educational settings (formal and nonformal) and the A-IC. More importantly, future research can connect with social movement studies and resistance studies to further explore Sayers' (2016: 374) claim that the factory farm has become a node for organizing activism as a form of 'influential collective resistance which radically challenges existing capitalist models of production'. What could be potential roles of education in such collective resistance, and how could education point to another 'real that is yet to come' (Deleuze and Guattari [1980] 2004: 157) that liberates both students, animals, and education itself from the atrocities of the animal-industrial complex?

References

Arluke, A. & Hafferty, F. (1996). From apprehension to fascination with 'dog lab'. The use of absolutions by medical students. *Journal of Contemporary Ethnography*, 25(2), 201–25.

Baran, B.E., Rogelberg, S.G, & Clausen, T. (2016). Routinized killing of animals: Going beyond dirty work and prestige to understand the well-being of slaughterhouse workers. *Organization, 23(3),* 351–69.

Bennett, J. (2001). Commodity fetishism and commodity enchantment. *Theory and Event, 5(1):* doi:10.1353/tae.2001.0006.

Boyd, W. (2001). Making meat: Science, technology, and American poultry production. *Technology and Culture, 42,* 631–64.

Coe, S. (1995). *Dead meat.* New York: Four Walls Eight Windows.

Cole, M. (2011). From 'animal machines' to 'happy meat'? Foucault's ideas of disciplinary and pastoral power applied to 'animal-centered' welfare discourse. *Animals, 1(1),* 83–101.

Cole, M. & Stewart, K. (2014). *Our children and other animals: The cultural construction of human-animal relations in childhood.* Farnham: Ashgate.

Deleuze, G. & Guattari, F. ([1980] 2004). *A thousand plateaus: Capitalism and schizophrenia.* London: Continuum.

Doré, A. & Michalon, J. (2017). What makes human–animal relations 'organizational'? The description of anthrozootechnical agencements. *Organization, 24(6),* 761–80.

Eisnitz, G.A. (1997). *Slaughterhouse.* New York: Prometheus Books.

Foer, J.S. (2009). *Eating animals.* London: Hamish Hamilton.

Giedion, S. (1948). *Mechanization takes command: A contribution to anonymous history.* New York: Oxford University Press.

Giroux, H. (1981). *Ideology, culture and the process of schooling.* Philadelphia: Temple University Press.

Gustafsson, L. (2020). *Rapport från ett slakteri.* Falun: Natur and Kultur.

Göransson, M. (2017). *Ätbara andra.* Göteborg och Stockholm: Makadam Förlag.

Holloway, L. (2007). Subjecting cows to robots: Farming technologies and the making of animal subjects. *Environment and Planning D: Society and Space, 25,* 1041–60.

Kahn, R. (2003). Towards ecopedagogy: Weaving a broad-based pedagogy of liberation for animals, nature, and the oppressed people of the earth. *Journal for Critical Animal Studies, 1(1),* 36–53.

Kopnina, H. & Cherniak, B. (2015). Cultivating a value for non-human interests through the convergence of animal welfare, animal rights, and deep ecology in environmental education. *Education Sciences, 5,* 363–79.

Labatut, J., Munro, I., & Desmond, J. (2016). Introduction: Animals and organizations. *Organization, 23(3),* 315–29.

Lennerfors, T.T. & Sköld, D. (2018). The animal. *Culture and Organization, 24(4),* 263–7.

Linné, T. & Pedersen, H. (2016). With care for cows and a love for milk: Affect and performance in Swedish dairy industry communication strategies. In A. Potts (Ed.), *Meat Culture* (pp. 109–28). Leiden and Boston: Brill.

MacCormack, P. (2013). Gracious pedagogy. *Journal of Curriculum and Pedagogy, 10(1),* 13–17.

McLaren, P. (1998). *Life in schools. An introduction to critical pedagogy in the foundations of education.* New York: Longman.

Morrow, R.A. & Torres, C.A. (1995). *Social theory and education. A critique of theories of social and cultural reproduction.* Albany: State University of New York Press.

Norwood, B.E. (2015). Siegfried Giedion (2013) mechanization takes command: A contribution to anonymous history. *Culture Machine,* 1–12: 576–1383-1-PB.pdf (culturemachine.net)

Noske, B. (1997). *Beyond boundaries: Humans and animals.* Montréal: Black Rose Books.

Pachirat, T. (2011). *Every twelve seconds: Industrialized slaughter and the politics of sight*. New Haven and London: Yale University Press.

Parry, J. (2010). Gender and slaughter in popular gastronomy. *Feminism and Psychology, 20(3)*, 381–96.

Pedersen, H. (2008). Learning to measure the value of life? Animal experimentation, pedagogy, and (eco)feminist critique. In R. Sollund (Ed.), *Global harms: Ecological crime and speciesism* (pp. 131–49). New York: Nova Science Publishers.

Pedersen, H. (2010a). *Animals in schools: Processes and strategies in human-animal education*. West Lafayette: Purdue University Press.

Pedersen, H. (2010b). Terror from the stare: Visual landscapes of meat production. *Antennae: The Journal of Nature in Visual Culture, 14*, 34–38

Pedersen, H. (2012). Education, animals, and the commodity form. *Culture and Organization, 18*, 415–32.

Pedersen, H. (2013). Follow the Judas sheep: Materializing post-qualitative methodology in zooethnographic space. *International Journal of Qualitative Studies in Education, 26(6)*, 717–31.

Pedersen, H. (2019). *Schizoanalysis and animal science education*. London and New York: Bloomsbury Academic.

Perriton, L. & Reynolds, M. (2004). Critical management education: From pedagogy of possibility to pedagogy of refusal? *Management Learning, 35(1)*, 61–77.

Pierce, C. (2013). *Education in the age of biocapitalism: Optimizing educational life for a flat world*. New York: Palgrave Macmillan.

Repka, M. (2019). Intersecting oppressions: The animal industrial complex and the educational industrial complex. In A.J. Nocella II et al. (Eds.), *Education for total liberation: Critical animal pedagogy and teaching against speciesism* (pp. 99–118). New York: Peter Lang.

Rowe, B.D. (2013). It IS about chicken: Chick-fil-A, posthumanist intersectionality, and gastroaesthetic pedagogy. *Journal of Thought, 48(2)*, 89–111.

Russell, C. & Spannring, R. (2019). So what for other animals? Environmental education research after the animal turn. *Environmental Education Research, 25(8)*, 1137–42.

Sauvagnargues, A. (2016). *Artmachines: Deleuze, Guattari, Simondon*. Edinburgh: Edinburgh University Press.

Sayers, J.G. (2016). A report to an academy: On carnophallogocentrism, pigs and meat-writing. *Organization, 23(3)*, 370–86.

Scarry, E. (1985). *The body in pain: The making and unmaking of the world*. New York and Oxford: Oxford University Press.

Schlosser, E. (2002). *Fast food nation*. London: Penguin Books.

Shukin, N. (2009). *Animal capital: Rendering life in biopolitical times*. Minneapolis and London: University of Minnesota Press.

Sinclair, U. (1906). *The jungle*. New York: Grosset and Dunlap Publishers.

Smith, A.C. III & Kleinman, S. (1989). 'Managing emotions in medical school: Students' contacts with the living and the dead. *Social Psychology Quarterly, 52(1)*, 56–69.

Starkey, K., Tempest, S., & Cinque, S. (2019). Management education and the theatre of the absurd. *Management Learning, 50(5)*, 591–606.

Trachsel, M. (2017). The presence of 'pork' and the absence of pigs: Changing stories of pigs and people in Iowa. In D. Nibert (Ed.), *Animal Oppression and Capitalism*. Vol. 1 (pp. 76–94). Santa Barbara: Praeger.

Twine, R. (2010). *Animals as biotechnology: Ethics, sustainability and critical animal studies.* London and Washington, DC: Earthscan.

Twine, R. (2012). Revealing the 'animal-industrial complex'—A concept and method for critical animal studies? *Journal for Critical Animal Studies, 10(1),* 12–39.

Vialles, N. ([1987] 1994). *Animal to edible.* Cambridge: Cambridge University Press.

Wadiwel, D.J. (2015). *The war against animals.* Leiden and Boston: Brill Rodopi.

Wallin, J. (2014). Dark pedagogy. In P. MacCormack (Ed.), *The Animal Catalyst: Towards Ahuman Theory* (pp. 145–62). London: Bloomsbury.

Watts, M.J. (2000). Afterword: Enclosure. In C. Philo & C. Wilbert (Eds.), *Animal spaces, beastly places: New geographies of human-animal relations* (pp. 292–304). London and New York: Routledge.

Williams, A. (2004). Disciplining animals: Sentience, production, and critique. *International Journal of Sociology and Social Policy, 24(9),* 45–57.

PART II

ORGANIZING ANIMAL ENCOUNTERS: KNOWING, MEANING, AND MATERIALITY

CHAPTER 6

MORE-THAN-HUMAN LEADERSHIP?
Studying Leadership in Horse–Human Relationships

ASTRID HUOPALAINEN

INTRODUCTION

HUMAN–ANIMAL relationships and the co-creation of meaning across species boundaries have received ever-growing scholarly attention in the interdisciplinary field of Human–Animal Studies (HAS), in which horse–human relationships have also been extensively examined (e.g. Birke, 2007; 2009; Birke and Thompson, 2017; Brandt, 2004; Schuurman and Franklin, 2016; Game, 2001; Maurstad et al., 2013; Schuurman, 2021; 2019; 2021). In the field of organization studies, nonhuman animals are increasingly acknowledged as sensory agents, individuals, and organizers in their own right who participate (or not) in co-creating our organized world (e.g. Satama and Huopalainen, 2019; Huopalainen, 2020; Sayers, 2016; Tallberg et al., 2020; O'Doherty, 2016; Skoglund and Redmalm, 2017). Today, human animals increasingly co-habit and share lives with nonhuman animals so that *humanimal* life stories, histories, and lived experiences intertwine. Similarly, human–horse relationships are increasingly defined through (species) boundary-crossing and co-becoming (Schuurman and Franklin, 2016; 2019), although horses do not co-habit human homes like most other pets. In contemporary equestrian culture, horses are largely perceived as observant animal companions (Birke, 2007; Schuurman and Franklin, 2019) or coaches to be respectfully cared for. More broadly, we might notice a historical shift in the place of the horse in contemporary Western society, from serving the human as an industry worker or military worker (Swart, 2010) to increasingly serving the human as a tourist worker (Dashper, 2017b; 2020), leisure companion, friend, and therapist (Solala, 2020).

As domesticated (and subordinated) flight animals controlled by humans, horses have worked for and with humans throughout our shared history (Birke, 2007; Birke and Thompson, 2017; Schuurman, 2017; 2021). Historically, horses have served humans in bloody wars with imperial and colonial purposes (Swart, 2010), for communication purposes, as vehicles, as (forest) industry workers (Solala, 2020), and in agriculture (Schuurman, 2019), sports, entertainment, gambling, leisure, and tourism (Dashper, 2017a; 2020). In organization studies, the horse industry, with its multiple agents, participants, and relations, has relatively rarely been studied (for exceptions, see Dashper, 2020). This appears somewhat surprising, given that horses and humans share a long joint history, including in the areas of management, leadership, and organization. Horses connect with (human) leadership discourses, representations, and practices in multiple ways. For example, equine-assisted leadership training, with its *join-up* and *follow-up* exercises of (re)connecting nonverbally with horses in a training ring, has become an increasingly popular tool for leaders' self-development (Birke, 2007; Kelly, 2014) over the past 20 years.[1] Commonly, equine-assisted leadership training is said to develop (human) affective capabilities that go beyond cognition, such as body language, presence, and affective engagement with the surrounding world. With horses, which are animals sensitive to these matters, embodied presence and body language cannot be *faked*.

In this chapter, I will explore the co-creation of the relational leadership dynamics between horses and humans in particular situated contexts. I work from the posthuman viewpoint (Haraway, 2003; 2008; Sayers et al., 2021) that problematizes human exceptionalism, anthropocentrism, and dominance over all other animals. Specifically, my aim is to introduce the transformative, finely grained horse–human relationship and its affective possibilities and (un)stable relations (Birke and Thompson, 2017) to leadership research. Here, leadership is conceptualized in line with the relational leadership approach (Uhl-Bien, 2006; Uhl-Bien and Ospina, 2012) as socially constructed, processual, and emerging. In horse–human relationships, humans need to co-create leadership not through interactions with other humans (Kelly, 2014), but through leader–follower relationships with sentient animals with their own *raison d'être*. Flesh-and-blood horses sense and relate to human animals *differently* than other humans. I will discuss how the posthuman decentring of the human might extend the concept of leadership to ethically include nonhuman animals and invoke different subjectivities (Sinclair and Wilson, 2002). Throughout, I seek to do justice to the ethical complexity of the horse–human relationship by shifting ordinary knowing positions and taking relationality, horse agency, and individuality seriously.

Historically, the horse–human dyad holds strong symbolic power, especially from the viewpoint of masculine leadership. The management concept itself derives from the Latin expression *maneggiare* (O'Doherty, 2016; Staunæs and Raffnsøe, 2019) and refers historically to the hands-on, physical ability 'to handle and train horses' (Hammond,

---

[1] Different kinds of equine-assisted leadership programs have been developed, ranging from anthropocentric and traditionally masculinist programmes to more receptive forms of training that build on Indigenous-American horsemanship philosophies and develop the human ability to reflexively listen to, *whisper to*, and engage with horses (Staunæs and Raffnsøe 2019).

2016: 133). Today, the word *management* is still largely perceived as an activity of controlling—not horses—but humans, resources, and finances. Etymologically, management goes back to the 'art' or practice of directing or training a horse 'by holding its reins in the hand' (Staunæs and Raffnsøe, 2019: 63), which evidently points to a *human*-led activity of directing and disciplining the animal. Different violent actions and punishing materialities, such as reins, whips, saddles, bits, and spurs have been, and still are, part of these controlling activities. The anthropocentric view of horse–human interactions largely ignores the power, agency, wellbeing, and sensibility of the horse in shaping and co-creating mutual activities. Moreover, the violence enacted towards a distressed horse as witnessed during the Tokyo Olympics has, among other events, raised further debate about animal wellbeing in equestrian culture.

Theoretically, I combine insights from the literature on relational leadership (e.g. Uhl-Bien, 2006; 2021; Uhl–Bien and Ospina, 2012) and horse–human relationships (Birke, 2007; Dashper, 2017b; 2020; Maurstad et al., 2013; Staunæs and Raffnsøe, 2019) to develop situated and in-depth understandings of how *more-than-human* leadership relationality materializes in situated practices within the Finnish sociocultural equestrian context. In so doing, I conceptualize horses as active, conscious subjects with agency (Birke and Thompson, 2017; Schuurman, 2019) that participate—and sometimes rightfully refuse to participate—in co-creating leadership dynamics. Methodologically, I draw on ethnographic and autoethnographic research material on horse–human interactions at the stables and the manège, as well as interviews with riding instructors in Finland. This allows me to analyse how horses and humans co-construct leadership in situated relationships. This chapter is structured as follows. First, I present theoretical literature on the evolving horse–human relationship and relational leadership. Second, I briefly discuss the methodological considerations of my study before turning to the analysis, in which I focus on the leadership dynamics in horse–human relationships. Finally, I conclude and discuss the implications of my study, including how the insights presented could go beyond the equestrian context.

Conceptualizing Horse–Human Relationships

In contemporary society, it is broadly accepted that animals 'should be cared for as individuals and that their subjective experiences should be appreciated' (Schuurman, 2021: 10). While humans interpret and care for animals differently across different spatial and temporal contexts, humans have traditionally acted in a position of dominant power *over* all other animals in the world (e.g. Huopalainen, 2020; Sayers et al., 2021; Tallberg et al., 2020). Whereas some animals are compassionately cared for, humans continue to exploit, objectify, violate, abuse, and mistreat others. For a long time, research in HAS and Critical Animal Studies (CAS) has problematized the gendered, racialized, and power dynamics of human–animal relationships. Likewise, the growing posthumanist literature has further problematized the human/animal dualism, human exceptionalism, and dominance (e.g. Haraway, 2003; 2008). I adopt the posthumanist viewpoint of relationality in addressing horse–human relationships as mutually co-created becomings (e.g. Dashper, 2020; Schuurman, 2021). Rather than treating relationships as fixed or static, this perspective emphasizes boundary-crossing, care, co-being, and mutual encounters with animals (Haraway, 2008; Schuurman, 2021). From this perspective, the boundaries between human/animal, nature/culture, and body/mind become inherently blurred.

Who are horses, then, as individuals and sentient beings? What are their thoughts, feelings, and perceptions of the world? What is it like to live the kind of domesticated life they live, and how do we come to understand each other? The horse is a curious flock animal—observant, conscious, and sensitive. Like other animals, horses experience feelings, emotions, and intentions. Following scholars (e.g. Birke, 2007; Schuurman, 2021; Dashper, 2017a; 2017b; 2020) who have extensively studied horse–human relationships, I conceptualize horses as conscious subjects with their own prior experiences, personalities, and characters. Horses' actions have meanings for themselves (Schuurman, 2021). At times, horses also cooperate, work with, and share mutual experiences with humans. Humans craft connectedness and proximity with horses in many ways. 'That there is an art to how humans relate to horses has been acknowledged since the ancient Greeks, when Xenophon published his *Art of Horsemanship*', Birke (2007: 219) reminds us. Meanwhile, humans interpret horse animality, agency, and voice differently, depending on the context. Throughout history, humans have associated horses with respect, mystique, beauty, authority, power, wealth, consumer luxury, and dominance. In the context of equestrian culture, Birke and Hockenhull (2015) approach horses as nonhuman friends who affect and *change* how humans structure, build, and make sense of (mutual) relationships. Developed in care work, animal work, groundwork, and riding, the horse–human relationship spills over multiple spaces, situations, and contexts.

Riding constitutes an embodied, sensory, and relational activity. Whereas riding has traditionally been an upper-class privilege in the Western context, today's horse riding is a popular sport, although it is an expensive form of leisure. Riding is also a business of riding schools, paying clients, and management training. Both classical riding and more advanced equestrian art in the form of dressage emphasize shared experiences, subtle cooperation, and mutual understanding between horses and humans to reach beauty, precision of movements, cross-species communication, and mutual response. However, riding activities have traditionally been human centred, and historically, humans have rarely considered how their actions can enhance the wellbeing of the horse. Whereas horses are increasingly recognized for their beneficial effects on human wellbeing,[2] this

---

[2] Today, equine-assisted activities and interventions designed to improve human mental health and wellbeing are common, and therapeutic riding, to give an example, constitutes an established equine-assisted activity for people with physical disabilities.

viewpoint also risks reproducing an anthropocentric understanding of the horse as a useful tool or object for human pleasure, wellbeing, and exploitation. From the perspective of CAS, riding is a problematic practice of human dominance over the animal, especially as uneven power relations, violent acts, and punishing materialities are part of these practices. Following feminist researchers (e.g. Birke et al., 2004; Birke, 2007; Brandt, 2004; Game, 2001), I view riding less as a form of domination or physical exercise and more as part of a continuum of cross-species relation-building and co-being of genuinely seeking to listen to and relate to the horse (Brandt, 2004; Game, 2001). For humans, learning to interpret and getting to know horses individually can still be difficult. A horse might also prefer doing something else to being ridden in the first place. Birke (2007: 219) discusses riding as a co-created practice based on *horsemanship*—'an ability to understand what the horse is thinking and feeling and to act accordingly, with sensitivity'. This is also close to how I approach riding. Next, I turn to the literature on relational leadership to discuss what *bringing in* horses might do to the conceptualization of leadership.

From Relational Leadership to Posthuman or *More-than-Human* Leadership

> [A]applied to leadership, a relational perspective changes the focus from the individual to the collective dynamic. (Uhl-Bien, 2006: 662)

I approach leadership as a dynamic form of co-creation between leaders and followers (Uhl-Bien, 2006; 2021) in space and time. To investigate how horses and humans co-construct leadership together, one has to focus closely on the emerging processes and accomplishments of horse–human dyads rather than personal traits or characteristics. Mainstream leadership research has long focused on individual leaders and their personalities, behaviours, abilities, and leadership styles (Carroll et al., 2008; Alvesson and Sveningsson, 2003; Yukl, 2012). Despite the shift of attention from (human) individuals and behaviours to the relations, practices, and processes through which leadership materializes in organizations, leadership research remains dominantly *human*-centred, focusing on human actions, expressions, and practices. In this way, the agency, potential, and significance of various nonhuman actors in co-constructing this joint activity have been fairly overlooked.

Inspired by affective pedagogies of learning leadership (Staunæs and Raffnsøe, 2019) from multispecies encounters, I argue that organizational scholars could learn something valuable from connecting with horses and analysing the practical actions that horse–human dyads co-produce. Historically, horses have been associated with powerful leaders through statues, paintings, and visual and textual representations of

White imperials, war heroes, and kings and queens on their majestic horses. For example, one might think of prominent celebrity horses, such as Bucephalus of Alexander the Great, or Napoleon's white war horse Marengo participating in the Battle of Waterloo in 1815. More recently, Kim Jong-un was depicted on a picturesque snow-white horse in the North Korean mountains, much like a topless Vladimir Putin was captured mounting a horse out in southern Siberia's *wilderness*. These images represent only a few well-known examples of ruthless dictators portrayed on the horseback as hallmarks of macho-masculinity, much like the archetype of the self-made, entrepreneurial *Marlboro man* carelessly riding into the sunset. In these cases, horses are used to both enhance the symbolic power and image of the human leader and make human leaders more accessible, which is often the case with mounted police units moving along and encountering citizens in urban spaces (Schuurman, 2021). Relatedly, in their article about the first dogs in the White House, Skoglund and Redmalm (2017) show how the animals (and breeds) represent particular leadership values.

In more recent years, *horse girls* and leadership have been scholarly investigated, with riding and stable cultures portrayed as unique forms of leadership training (Forsberg, 2012; Zetterquist Blokhuis, 2019). Today, horse-assisted leadership learning (Kelly, 2014; Staunæs and Raffnsøe, 2019) and horse handling sessions (Birke, 2007) are increasingly offered for corporate management for how to lead *differently* by attuning to others, learning to respond in embodied ways to movement, subtle changes, and so on. Simultaneously, these examples provide lucrative business opportunities and management fashions. To be able to lead, handle, and *manage* a horse—a strong, large, muscular, and potentially dangerous prey animal with a sight radius of 360 degrees—requires mutual trust, experience, listening, and understanding. Relating to horses and their wellbeing then requires care and sensitivity, as well as practical leadership experience.

How can you lead others if you are unable to relate to others or 'unable to develop an acute sense of your environment and other creatures?', Staunæs and Raffnsøe (2019: 60) ask. Studying the affective possibilities and opening of the interacting senses regarding how to *learn to be affected* is important here. Uhl-Bien (2006: 655) defines relational leadership as 'a social influence process through which emergent coordination (i.e. evolving social order) and change (e.g. new values, attitudes, approaches, behaviors, and ideologies) are constructed and produced'. From this perspective, leadership is co-created though the everyday interactions between actors. Evidently, the literature assumes that these actors are human, but in this chapter, I demonstrate how nonhuman animals are part of co-constructing relational leadership. Leadership is not only socially constructed but also socially distributed (Uhl-Bien, 2006). It is constantly being shaped and reshaped in connection with actors and their surrounding environments (Crevani et al., 2010).

The established relational leadership literature emphasizes verbal language, dialogue, and conversation in the co-construction of leadership relationality (Hosking, 2011; Uhl-Bien, 2006; Ryömä and Satama, 2019) within the context in which leadership takes place. In horse–human relationships, the role of verbal language is less important than nonverbal negotiation, embodied presence, and affective attunement. While horses and humans co-construct meaning in mutual encounters, power is always present. Precisely as Denis, Langley, and Sergi (2012: 266) point out, 'not all organizational actors are equal when entering interactions'. This is especially true in human–animal relations, where nonhuman animals and humans might gain agency and power in different ways.

Methodological Considerations

My interest in horses and the close relationships I have developed with them have mattered to the writing of this chapter. I write as someone who cares for horses, seeks to craft connectedness with horses, and is familiar with horses in the role of an amateur/hobby rider for the last 25 years. Methodologically, I draw on in-depth ethnographic research material on horse–human interactions at the stables and the manège of one riding school in Helsinki, combined with autoethnographic material and four interviews with professional riding instructors conducted in 2020–21. Gaining access was an informal process, as I knew riders and staff at the riding school from before. The gathered empirical material allows me to closely analyse how horses and humans co-construct leadership relationally. In ethnographic observations, close attention is given to the subtle and largely nonverbal aspects of the leadership dynamics between horses and humans working together. Horse wellbeing and good care were a central priority in the riding school where I conducted my observations.

Difficult ethical questions concerning representation, voice, power relations, and relationality are always part of multispecies ethnographies (e.g. Hamilton and Taylor, 2013; 2017). Multispecies research invites critical reflection regarding how to ultimately include, interpret, voice, and do animals justice (ibid). Dashper (2017b; 2020) emphasizes horses' limited ability to express consent in daily training and practice. The same goes for expressing consent in being part of research. Generally speaking, horses do not voluntarily participate in training sessions initiated by humans, and I also need to reflect upon the asymmetric power relations between riders and horses. Although the horse cannot express itself verbally in human language, it communicates through body language, movements, and gestures. I also believe that horses can express joy and happiness about co-being with humans, about participating in riding or training sessions with humans, for example, by moving in a relaxed yet energetic manner and swinging their tail freely and evenly, ears pointing to the direction of the human.

Analysis: Three Episodes of *More-than-Human* Leadership

In organizations, relationships are constantly negotiated among members (Cunliffe and Eriksen, 2011). Similar negotiations occur between horses and humans in their daily interactions. In what follows, I present three examples of how more-than-human leadership emerges contextually. Specifically, the relational leadership perspective allows me to zoom in on the micro-level activities that co-constitute leadership in the particular space of species boundary-crossing and co-becoming.

Relational Co-being and Listening to the Horse in Multispecies Leadership

I sat and observed a riding lesson one early October evening at a manège in Helsinki in autumn 2020. It was relatively cold, and I sat in the audience of an otherwise empty manège. It was, after all, still COVID-19 times. Six horses with their riders trot along and keep sufficient distance from one another, which is a matter of safety in riding. 'Do not think like a human; think like a horse. Find your common language!', Sarah, the riding instructor, tells her students from the middle of the training space. I have heard this articulation before. Attuning to the horse matters for relational leadership to emerge. Sarah repeatedly instructs the riders to shift their perspective towards the horse and *sense* the horse in order to achieve rhythm, flow of movements, and balance. 'Be gentle, sit properly, and focus on her [the horse]', she continues, while carefully observing the horse–human dyads moving past her in trot. 'Yes, good, pet her for trusting you, for becoming more relaxed, and for "letting go". Very nice rhythm!' Being gentle is of utmost importance, like rewarding the horse for the smallest things done right. The horses move in a relaxed yet energetic manner, with their necks relaxed and ears pointed towards the riders. At this very moment, it looks like they might enjoy the lesson.

'The act of riding entails close and intimate interspecies body-to-body communication, based on trust and mutual understanding', Dashper (2020: 15) suggests. This complex process of relational negotiation and cross-species communication invites questions, such as the following: Where are you? Where are you going? Are you okay leading–following–leading–following? In this cooperation and ongoing process of negotiation, the distinct boundaries between the leader and the follower become blurred (Uhl-Bien, 2006; Uhl-Bien and Ospina, 2012). To Staunæs and Raffnsøe (2019), leadership is rarely (only) about verbally shaping relationships with others—it is, to a significant extent, about embodied listening and learning to be(come) affected to perform more caring, perceptive, and ethically sound ways of leadership. As a practice, riding requires continuous sensory attention and relational listening (Koivunen and Wennes, 2011). What the horse cannot tell the rider in a shared verbal language, the rider must learn to understand nonverbally and kinesthetically from the horse's point of view. Ideally, riding is about making the horse move just as beautifully as horses move by their own *horsy* nature.

The horse only agrees to follow the rider if they convince the horse to collaborate in subtle, *horse-like* ways. A clumsy or inexperienced rider forcing the horse could probably make the horse move forward but not in a rhythmic or beautiful manner.

'Sometimes, when the rider asks the horse to make certain movements, they unconsciously physically hinder it', instructor Lotta explains. 'Also, if you treat the horse as a tool, nothing will ever work. It is you, the rider, who can invite cross-species communication through availability and by setting the tone for your collaboration. If you force the horse, you break your bond. You never develop if you don't understand each other. The horse does nothing, nothing at all, to consciously irritate the human' (Interview with Lotta). Schuurman (2012) also emphasizes trust, a relaxed state of the mind, and the creation of positive emotions in the horse–human relationship. This was something that the riding instructors I spoke to also emphasized, both during the observed riding lessons and outside of them. Constantly encouraging, petting, and giving credit to the horse creates a relaxed horse that is receptive to the rider's smallest signals in collaboration. This care is part of good horsemanship and is a condition for relational leadership to emerge.

Taking the Side of the Horse

Way back in time, in spring 1992, Baronesa threw me off the saddle during one of our weekly riding lessons at the manège of the La Chevalerie stables in Rhode-Saint-Genèse, Belgium. This happened regularly to the extent that eight-year-old me, quick to get back in the saddle, saw the reoccurring event as a rite of passage into the equestrian world. Baronesa, a Spanish mountain pony with a prominent mane, was not always in the mood of practising the art of rising trot with an inexperienced kid bouncing up and down in the saddle. Who would? Rather, she took the lead in the situation by creating momentary disorganization—making sudden jumps or speedy sprints across the manège to shake me off—while I was learning to communicate meaningfully with her. While Baronesa did exactly what she wanted, my job from an inexperienced position in the saddle was to learn and develop, to become a rider who is good enough to gain her trust and respect. Back then, my Finnish riding instructor, Päivi, introduced the *glass horse* metaphor: 'Imagine riding a horse made of porous glass. The horse will break beneath you if you don't carefully adjust your own bodily movements and *move together with the horse!*' When I eventually developed as a rider and found a shared sense of softness, balance, rhythm, and tempo together with Baronesa, which is necessary for horse–human co-being, I could also better sense and enable Baronesa's movements without disturbing her trot. Our cooperation, co-being, and bond developed (Autoethnographic notes).

Shared everyday experiences develop the horse–human relationship, in which unexpected events may occur and challenge this relationship. What the above example demonstrates is that riding, leading, and following are about developing the ability to *get in the body* in order to achieve contact, relationality, and cross-species collaboration. As sensitive animals, horses sense subtle differences in other beings' bodily tensions and muscle tone (Staunæs and Raffnsøe, 2019). Therefore, carefully adjusting human bodily movements to horse movements matters for relationality as both horses and humans attune to each other.

Mismatchings?

Leadership between humans and horses is not (solely) a human-led activity in which humans perform leadership, and the horse acts as the follower. Rather, this processual activity is co-constructed with and by animals. As conscious agential subjects (Birke and Thompson, 2017; Schuurman, 2019), horses participate—and sometimes refuse to participate—in co-constructing relational leadership dynamics. Horses are sensitive to how human bodies (unintentionally) communicate stress, nervousness, and insecurity, as well as to presence, care, and confidence (Game, 2001; Staunæs and Raffnsøe, 2019). This was something that I regularly observed during fieldwork. Depending on the situation, the horse sometimes lacks the interest or willingness to follow or be led by the human. Sometimes, the horse leads the human (as portrayed empirically above) and not the other way around. Horses and humans do not always understand each other. Sometimes, the horse attempts to (momentarily) break free from existing work practices in order to gain agency that differs from the view of the human rider. My analysis suggests that horse–human leadership requires relational listening from both actors and that it embodies surrender, co-being, and presence by making oneself available to each other (compare Game, 2001; Staunæs and Raffnsøe, 2019). Embracing nonviolent training methods and caring for horses by making oneself affectively available to and carefully listening to the horses are conditional for relational leadership to emerge. In this way, multispecies relationality and trust can be viewed as an invitation to connect—over and over across time and space—to become leaders, followers, and companions.

DISCUSSION AND CONCLUSIONS

Leader–follower dynamics emerge in horse–human relationality in time, space, and place. In this chapter, I moved away from authoritative, masculine understandings of the horse–human relationship towards posthuman perspectives emphasizing care, co-being, and learning from horses. Empirically, I illustrated how horses and humans co-create leadership relationally by sensing, attuning towards, and listening closely to each other. Turning to the understudied equestrian context allowed me to i) investigate closely under-researched practices in order to further problematize anthropocentric understandings of leadership; ii) develop novel, more species-inclusive understandings of the same; and iii) shift ordinary knowing positions to further develop the ethical complexity of the horse–human encounter. In what follows, I discuss these aspects further, including how these insights go beyond the equestrian context.

Studying leadership in horse–human relationships develop the relational, collective, and plural leadership paradigm in which more-than-human leaderful relationships are conceptualized as the very situated, day-to-day content of leadership work (Crevani et al., 2010; Crevani, 2015). Empirically, I demonstrated how leadership is a co-created process between bodies of different species communicating in subtle ways. In the ever-changing multispecies relationship—sometimes in sync and sometimes clashing—leadership materializes through relational listening and cross-species communication negotiated in the moments-to-moments where species meet. In existing leadership research, the leader's actions, the leader's persona, the spoken and written word, conversations, and discourses have been largely emphasized. The relational leadership literature has also emphasized verbalizations of leadership relations (Uhl-Bien, 2006; Uhl-Bien and Ospina, 2012) in favour of embodied and nonverbal aspects. My empirical material suggests that the nonverbal, affective, and subtle embodied aspects matter significantly to the development of more-than-human leadership in the horse–human context. This, I believe, is a valuable insight for other empirical contexts where these aspects have not yet received the scholarly attention they deserve.

Studying relational leadership in horse–human relationships challenges the dominantly anthropocentric view of leadership. Working with a horse is different from working with humans, and it adds another level of complexity to understanding leadership *beyond* human relations at work. By interacting with humans in their own ways and on their own terms, horses co-produce leadership actions with humans. Despite misunderstandings, horses and humans can (learn to) communicate respectfully and be affected by each other. Based on my study, developing more-than-human leadership requires human care for, connectedness with, and sincere interest in the Other's worldview (Staunæs and Raffnsøe, 2019). Attuning towards nonhuman animals requires a willingness to learn from this mutual encounter: how can we humans learn and *change* from this meeting? Experiences with horses make felt and tangible the complexity of embodied, ethical encounters (Staunæs and Raffnsøe, 2019). Meeting the Other in uneven power relations can be an inherently uncomfortable experience. As researchers, we must continuously reflect upon matters of ethics and care, asking whether and how we can do justice to those we study. Considering horses as individuals with agency, voice, and their own rights—or even as ethical subjects—presents further possibilities for improving horse welfare, interspecies care, and the quality of horse–human relations in posthuman futures.

The horse–human relationship suggests possibilities of knowing otherwise and doing other-worlding (Haraway, 2008). Listening closely, considering the perspective of the Other, and attuning to body language, gestures, and affective moods are important not only to how we co-construct leadership relationships with nonhuman animals but also to how we might envisage more sustainable forms of leadership in human-centred workplaces. Could we not consider learning to lead humans in the caring way we lead and follow horses, emphasizing listening, relationality, and presence? The care, gentleness, and respectful agenda in horse–human relationships could translate into human-centred workplaces and the ways in which everyday interactions between humans at work could be done differently. There is more to be learned about sensitive and attuned leadership practices for humans, too, and whether this would make for more ethical leadership. Moreover, shifting the dominant knowing position helps us humans (re)imagine the world through less aggressively managerialist lenses and (re)consider existing dominant power relations. This shift might even help us develop more caring, ethical modes of connecting with, understanding, and interpreting Others in the world. Finally, an ontological and epistemological shift in established knowing and power positions may also 'help us prompt new questions' (Staunæs and Raffnsøe, 2019: 73) about relational leadership, as well as the ethical possibilities that emerge in leader–follower encounters. This shift appears vital in creating more humane leadership and workplaces.

References

Alvesson, M. & Sveningsson, S. (2003). Managers doing leadership: The extra-ordinarization of the mundane. *Human Relations, 56(12)*, 1435–59.

Birke, L. (2007). 'Learning to speak horse': The culture of 'natural horsemanship'. *Society and Animals, 15*, 217–40.

Birke, L. (2009). Interwoven lives: Understanding human/animal connections. In I.T. Holmberg (Ed.), *Investigating human/animal relations in science, culture and work* (pp. 18–33). Uppsala: Centrum för genusvetenskap, Uppsala University.

Birke, L., Bryld, M., & Lykke, N. (2004). Animal performances: An exploration of intersections between feminist science studies and studies of human/animal relationships. *Feminist Theory, 5(2)*, 167–83.

Birke, L. & Hockenhull, J. (2015). Journeys together: Horses and humans in partnership. *Society and Animals, 23(1)*, 81–100.

Birke, L. et al. (2011). Horses' responses to variation in human approach. *Applied Animal Behaviour Science, 134*, 56–63.

Birke, L. & Thompson, K. (2017). *(Un)stable relations. Horses, humans and social agency.* London: Routledge.

Brandt, K. (2004). A language of their own: An interactionist approach to human–horse communication. *Society and Animals, 12(4)*, 299–316.

Carroll, B., Levy, L., & Richmond, D. (2008). Leadership as practice: Challenging the competency paradigm. *Leadership, 4(4)*, 363–79.

Crevani, L. (2015). Relational leadership. In I.B. Carroll, J. Ford, & S. Taylor (Eds.), *Leadership: Contemporary critical perspectives* (pp. 188–211). London: Sage Publications.

Crevani, L., Lindgren, M., & Packendorff, J. (2010). Leadership, not leaders: On the study of leadership as practices and interactions. *Scandinavian Journal of Management, 26(1)*, 77–86.

Cunliffe, A.L. & Eriksen, M. (2011). Relational leadership. *Human Relations, 64(11)*, 1425–49.

Dashper, K. (2017a). *Human-horse relationships in equestrian sport and leisure.* Abingdon: Routledge.

Dashper, K. (2017b). Listening to the horses: Developing attentive interspecies relationships through sport and leisure. *Society and Animals, 25(3)*, 207–24.

Daspher, K. (2020). More-than-human emotions: Multispecies emotional labour in the tourism industry. *Gender, Work and Organization, 27(1)*, 24–40.

Denis, J.L., Langley, A., & Sergi, V. (2012). Leadership in the plural. *Academy of Management Annals, 6(1)*, 211–83.
Forsberg, L. (2012). *Manegen är krattad: Om flickors och kvinnors företagsamhet i hästrelaterade verksamheter*. Luleå: Luleå tekniska universitet.
Game, A. (2001). Riding: Embodying the centaur. *Body & Society, 7(4)*, 1–12.
Hamilton, L. & Taylor, N. (2012). Ethnography in evolution: Adapting to the animal 'other' in organizations. *Journal of Organizational Ethnography, 1(1)*, 43–51.
Hamilton, L. & Taylor, N. (2013). *Animals at work: Identity, politics and culture in work with animals*. Leiden: Brill Academic Press.
Hamilton, L. & Taylor, N. (2017). *Ethnography after humanism: Power, politics and method in multi-species research*. London and Storbritannien: Palgrave Macmillan.
Hammond, G. (2016). *The language of horse racing*. London: Routledge.
Haraway, D.J. (2003). *The companion species manifesto: Dogs, people, and significant otherness*. Chicago: Prickly Paradigm Press.
Haraway, D.J. (2008). *When species meet*. Minneapolis: University of Minnesota Press.
Hosking, D.M. (2011). Telling tales of relations: Appreciating relational constructionism. *Organization Studies, 32(1)*, 47–65.
Huopalainen, A. (2020). Writing with the bitches. *Organization*. Published online before print, DOI:10.1177/1350508420961533
Kelly, S. (2014). Horses for courses: Exploring the limits of leadership development through equine-assisted learning. *Journal of Management Education, 38(2)*, 216–33.
Koivunen, N. & Wennes, G. (2011). Show us the sound! Aesthetic leadership of symphony orchestra conductors. *Leadership, 7(1)*, 51–71.
Labatut, J., Munro, I., & Desmond, J. (2016). Animals and organizations. *Organization, 23(3)*, 315–29.
Maurstad, A., Davis, D., & Cowles, S. (2013). Co-being and intra-action in horse–human relationships: A multi-species ethnography of be(com)ing human and be(com)ing horse. *Social Anthropology, 21(3)*, 322–35.
O'Doherty, D.P. (2016). Feline politics in organization: The nine lives of Olly the cat. *Organization, 23(3)*, 407–33.
Ryömä, A. & Satama, S. (2019). Dancing with the D-man: Exploring reflexive practices of relational leadership in ballet and ice hockey. *Leadership, 15(6)*, 696–721.
Satama, S. & Huopalainen, A. (2019). 'Please tell me when you are in pain': A heartbreaking story of care, grief and female–canine companionship. *Gender, Work and Organization, 26(3)*, 358–76.
Sayers, J. (2016). A report to an academy: On carnophallogocentrism, pigs and meat-writing. *Organization, 23(3)*, 370–86.
Sayers, J., Martin, L., & Bell, E. (2021). Posthuman affirmative business ethics: Reimagining human–animal relations through speculative fiction. *Journal of Business Ethics*. DOI: https://doi.org/10.1007/s10551-021-04801-8
Schuurman, N. (2012). 'Hevoset hevosina': Eläimen ja sen hyvinvoinnin tulkinta (PhD thesis). Joensuu: University of Eastern Finland. Available at: https://epublications.uef.fi/pub/urn_isbn_978-952-61-0665-6/urn_isbn_978-952-61- 0665-6.pdf
Schuurman, N. & Franklin, A. (2016). In pursuit of meaningful human–horse relations: Responsible horse ownership in a leisure context. In J. Nyman & N. Schuurman (Eds.), *Affect, space and animals* (pp. 40–51). London: Routledge.

Schuurman, N. (2017). Horses as Co-Constructors of Knowledge in Contemporary Finnish Equestrian Culture. In T. Räsänen & T. Syrjämaa (Eds.), *Shared Lives of Humans and Animals. Animal Agency in the Global North* (pp. 37–48). London Routledge.

Schuurman, N. & Franklin, A. (2019). Interpreting animals in spaces of cohabitance: Narration and the role of animal agency at horse livery yards. In J. Bornemark, U. Ekström von Essen, & P. Andersson (Eds.), *Horse Cultures in Transformation: Ethical Questions* (pp. 225–39). London: Routledge.

Schuurman, N. (2021). Animal work, memory, and interspecies care: Police horses in multispecies urban imaginaries. *Cultural Geographies, 28(3),* 547–61.

Sinclair, A. & Wilson, V. (2002). *New faces of leadership.* Melbourne: Melbourne University Press.

Skoglund, A. & Redmalm, D. (2017). 'Doggy-biopolitics': Governing via the first dog. *Organization, 24(2),* 240–66.

Solala, H. (2020). Hevosvetoinen yhteiskunta. Hevosen taloudellinen merkitys Suomessa 1800- ja 1900-lukujen vaihteessa. In T. Räsänen & N. Schuurman (Eds.), *Kanssakulkijat. Monilajisten kohtaamisten jäljillä* (pp. 256–82). Helsinki: Suomalaisen Kirjallisuuden Seura.

Staunæs, D. & Raffnsøe, S. (2019). Affective pedagogies, equine-assisted experiments and post-human leadership. *Body & Society, 25(1),* 57–89.

Swart, S. (2010). *Riding high: Horses, humans and history in South Africa.* Johannesburg: Wits University Press.

Tallberg, L., Huopalainen, A., & Hamilton, L. (2020). Can methods do good? Ethnology and multi-species research as a response to Covid-19. *Ethnologia Fennica, 47(2),* 103–12.

Uhl-Bien, M. (2006). Relational leadership theory: Exploring the social process of leadership and organizing. *The Leadership Quarterly, 17(6),* 654–76.

Uhl-Bien, M. & Ospina, S. (2012). *Advancing relational leadership research: A conversation among perspectives.* Charlott: Information Age.

Uhl-Bien, M. (2021). Complexity and COVID-19: Leadership and Followership in a Complex World. *Journal of Management Studies, 58(5),* 1400–1404.

Yukl, G.A. (2012). Effective leadership behavior: What we know and what questions need more attention. *Academy of Management Perspectives, 26(4),* 66–85.

Zetterquist Blokhuis, M. (2019). *Interaction between rider, horse and equestrian trainer—A challenging puzzle* (PhD thesis, Södertörns högskola).

CHAPTER 7

RECONFIGURING THE SENSES

Sensor Technologies and the Production of a New Sensorium in Cattle Farming

CAMILLE BELLET

INTRODUCTION

FEET on the ground, hands on the phone, and eyes on the screen. This may be the twenty-first-century figure of the modern farmer as imagined by most technocrats (policymakers, scientists, and investors in agricultural technology (AgTech)) in France and the United Kingdom (UK). In both countries, tech advocates expect wearable technologies connected to phones and tablets, such as sensors, animal collars, and implanted fleas, to help cattle farmers 'work smarter' (Rugg, 2020)—that is, to monitor their barns and animals[1] remotely, while allowing robots to clean buildings, milk animals and treat them autonomously.

While agricultural technology can be positive for certain aspects of animal farming and support farmers in their daily practice, there are also downsides. In this chapter, I challenge the recurring assumptions made by French and British advocates of cattle sensor technologies. More specifically, I question the sensorial norms established through the use of sensor technologies which, I argue, underlie broader powers, conventions and etiquettes *vis-à-vis* sensory practices and human-animal relations in cattle farming. My argument is that sensor technologies reconfigure the senses and produce a new sensorium in cattle farming, i.e. an 'experiential envelope' of what humans (farmers, and vets, for example) could feel or experience as animal sensation in the first place (adapted from Paterson, 2018: 71). This, I argue, may ultimately reconfigure human relations with cows and cattle farming organizations.

---

[1] In this chapter, I mostly use the terms 'humans' and 'animals' as shorthand for the more accurate but longer terms 'human and nonhuman animals.'

France and the UK both soar in a recent ranking of the world's most innovative countries in agricultural technology (AgFunder, 2020). With nearly 250 AgTech start-ups and cooperative associations, France has in recent years accelerated the technological modernization of its agricultural landscape. According to the French government (Bournigal et al., 2015), 79 per cent of French farmers use the Internet, 70 per cent install professional applications on their phones for daily agricultural work, and the use of business applications in agriculture has increased by 110 per cent between 2013 and 2015. In the UK, too, agricultural technology aims to 'transform' (Rugg, 2020), revitalize, and 'deliver a new golden era' (Morrison, 2019) for farming communities. As early as 2015, the UK invested in several AgTech catalyst and centres worth £160 million to boost the integration of British farmers into an increasingly digitized global agrifood system (AgFunder, 2018).

Among investments, animal sensor technologies are particularly flourishing (Thrive, 2019). This is part of an emerging culture of 'smarter' animal farming—or precision livestock farming (PLF)—in which scientific forms of rationalizations such as agricultural robotics, artificial intelligence (AI), and autonomous systems are expected to help farmers boost efficiency and animal productivity while reducing production costs and the negative effects of intensive animal farming.

As in many other countries, PLF represents for many French and British technocrats a solution—or 'technological fix' (Jasanoff and Kim, 2015: 106)—to the future sustainability of animal farming in a context of increasing demand for animal products and food insecurity (Bournigal et al., 2015; Deloitte, 2019; EU, 2017; UK Parliament, 2015). PLF is also expected to bring substantial benefits for the daily life and work of farming communities. Several articles in the French and British media claim (Bothorel, 2018; Maddyness, 2018) that with sensor technologies, farming work will be less repetitive, less difficult, less stressful, less tiring, and at the same time, safer, more enjoyable, and more fulfilling.

Particularly in the cattle sector, the steady decline in the number of farmers since the 1950s (Pflimlin et al., 2009) has resulted in enormous market pressures and an increase in herd size. Therefore, cattle sensor technologies are expected to take pressure off farmers and encourage young people into cattle farming (Andonovic et al., 2018; Berckmans, 2017). As the following excerpt from a European Commission report on PLF notes (EU, 2017: 7):

> Farmers struggle to cope with the increased size of their herds ... and have less time to keep an eye on the health and welfare of individual animals ... PLF offers a solution to overworked farmers by employing sensors, cameras and microphones using sophisticated algorithms to continuously monitor every single animal ... PLF will reduce stress in farmers by enabling them to act more effectively and achieve a better work/life balance, while gaining greater recognition for their efforts.

As if obvious, the report then concludes: 'benefits include healthier, happier animals and an improved economic performance for farms.'

The purpose of this chapter is twofold. First, by complementing a renewed interest in the role of senses and sensory practices in work and organizations, it explores the biopolitics of the senses in cattle farming as articulated within the 'sociotechnical imaginaries' (Jasanoff and Kim, 2015) of cattle sensor technologies in France and the UK. Drawing on a purposive sample of documentary sources (scientific, media, and official), the chapter examines how 'collectively imagined forms of social life and social order' (Jasanoff and Kim, 2015: 4) are reflected in cattle farming through cattle sensor technologies and are carried by an 'ocular metaphor' (Kavanagh, 2004) of Western capitalist and extractivist imaginations. Second, the chapter suggests how such sociotechnical imaginaries, rooted in an elitist Western tradition of human exceptionalism where humans and eyes are unique and distinctive from animals and the other senses, closes down, in turn, the creative opportunities for interspecies sensory exchanges and learning possibilities offered by cattle sensor technologies. In making that case, the chapter begins with a review of the literature on the role of senses and sensory practices in cattle farming organizations. It then provides a detailed description of the sociotechnical imaginaries built around cattle sensor technologies in France and the UK and concludes with some reflections on the meaning and implications of such imaginaries.

Senses and Sensory Practices in Cattle Farming Organizations

For Cooper (2007: 1548), 'the existential basis of human organization lies in the work of the human organs and senses rather than in the conscious intentions and purposes of its individual members.' The senses, Cooper continues, are 'tentacles and feelers' that project themselves and, therefore, individuals into their environment. Senses like sight, touch, taste, smell, and the entire body, help humans to understand an otherwise 'invisible and meaningless' environment. They are both the triggers and the instruments for human social practices and actions, shapers of human work and organizations (see also Lefebvre, 1991).

The study of the 'practico-sensory realm of social space' (Lefebvre, 1991: 15) is not new in organization studies and many have been interested in how the senses craft social spaces, give meaning to individuals and their environments while governing their organization of, for example, homes (Burley et al., 2007), clinics (Gardner and Williams, 2015), schools (Ramsey, 2008), events (Mauksch, 2017), and slaughterhouses (Hamilton and McCabe, 2016; McLoughlin, 2019). These studies have shown that social organizations are not static loci. Rather, they are ongoing processes, products of unsettled and malleable social interactions and sensory practices, of which humans and their senses are only a part.

In the particular context of farming, Quinn and Halfacre (2014) expose how the organization and configuration of the agricultural place is a product of daily explorations and sensory immersion with animals, plants, buildings, machines, and landscapes. The sensory engagement of farmers with their surroundings produces what Holloway and Morris (2014) call 'a particular kind of aesthetic response', an 'enchantment' (Herman, 2015), at the origin of farmers' daily awareness, knowledges, and practices. As Herman (2015: 103) claims, farming is 'not purely a business or mechanism for policy implementation but can also be an immersive lifestyle grounded in embodied, experiential relations.' The senses and sensory practices of farmers within their environment not only construct their workplace, rather, they also build farmers' sense of place, a 'homeplace' (Mack, 2007: 375).

Tacit professional knowledges and practices often emerge from multisensory immersions. In her study, Mack (2007: 382) shows, for instance, how Norwegian seafarers share knowledge 'on the decks and bridges, down in the engine rooms into the galleys and cabins' which 'hold a deep reservoir of memories that accumulate throughout voyages; wherein much of the art and craft related to seafaring has traditionally passed from one generation to the next.' Sensory experiences and encounters—in this case, with the sea, the machines, the wind, and the birds—give seafarers a means to reflect, engage, and understand their daily life and work on the boat. Likewise, sensory, embodied, and experiential practices give farmers a unique knowledge and understanding of their daily life and activities (Herman, 2015; Jones, 2013). Bates (2019: 6) describes this as an agricultural 'sensescape'—that is, a landscape of 'interwoven processes of visualisation, memory, emotion, and thought' that give farmers a continuous understanding of the needs of their lands, plants, and animals and how to protect them for future generations (Herman, 2015: 104).

From the choice of clothing, tool, mode of travel, to the type, duration, and form of practices (harvesting or bringing cattle to the barn, moving on foot or motor vehicle), to the sensations and feelings provoked by these practices, the senses permeate the body and mind of farmers. They produce sensory atmospheres, affecting farmers' mood and resilience daily (Adams-Hutcheson, 2019; Bates et al., 2019; Burley et al., 2007; Mack, 2007). The senses can indeed 'lift [their] spirits' (Adams-Hutcheson, 2019), 'promote [their] sense of well-being' (Bates et al., 2019) (e.g. when they help a cow to give birth) or, on the contrary, plunge them 'in a murky, bone-chilling pall, limbs heavy and lethargic' state (Adams-Hutcheson, 2019: 1007). But such bodily sensations are not only the result of what constitutes their close environment (its matter and its living). They are also the product of a sensorium produced in this environment, configured by standards and conventions surrounding sensory practices and sensations. As Mack (2007) argues, some environments control and lock in the senses, make them dull and silent rather than vibrant and cognizant. In the next section, I briefly explore the biopolitics of the senses and sensations in cattle farming organizations.

DIFFERENT SENSES AT WORK?

In their book, Hamilton and Taylor (2017) note that scientists often struggle to consider a more-than-human perspective when trying to understand their environment. They explain, in particular, how scientists have 'a tendency to consider what other species mean to humans rather than considering or seeking to understand how humans and animals *co-constitute* the world' (Hamilton and Taylor, 2017: 2; original emphasis). Although in principle more-than-human, sensory studies in farming have often, too, 'fall[en] into the trap of prioritising human knowledge' (Hamilton and Taylor, 2017: 7), as well as their senses and sensations.

While animals are often acknowledged as present during the interviews and ethnographies (see e.g. Adams-Hutcheson, 2019; Herman, 2015), and while they imbue the study atmosphere with an 'affective background' through their presence, body, and smell (Adams-Hutcheson, 2019: 1011), animal senses and sensory experiences are often missed and lost in scientific productions. Part of the reason, is that scientists working on the farm mostly centre their research on their own senses and sensations: they converse with their fellow humans while projecting their own sensory and emotional experiences into the space (of the farm) and onto an 'other' (the animal), who is otherwise absent from these conversations. Using Lefebvre's (1991: 16) words, I argue, however, that animal senses and sensory practices are not only a 'precondition' of what Adam-Hutcheson (2019: 1012) calls the 'multisensory daily tasks of farming', but their 'formulation'. Farming spaces (e.g. the barns, milking-sheds, farmhouses) and farming practices are all shaped by animal senses and sensory practices: their sight, smell, touch, sound; their body and sensations (e.g. curiosity, pleasure, resistance, boredom), which must also be included in the production of knowledge of the material and lived realities of cattle farming (Jones, 2013).

To be clear, human sensations are always mediated by *human* senses and sensory practices. They are also essential 'instruments of process' (Cooper, 2007: 1555) for creating and fostering 'new ideas and knowledges about human-animal relationships' (Hamilton and Taylor, 2017: 4). However, some senses and sensory practices are more inclusive and open to animal sensory and 'knowledge-practices' (Holloway and Morris, 2014) than others. In this chapter, in particular, I question the frequent assertion made by scientists of the sole 'importance of looking, and looking, and looking, at animals' (Holloway and Morris, 2014: 10)—an assertion frequently reiterated by advocates of cattle sensor technologies. Such questioning should not only benefit the field of human-animal studies or any studies exploring the relations and entanglements between humans and other sensory beings in organizations, but also help create a science *beyond* the visual—that is, a science shifting away from the 'vision centred interpretation of knowledge, truth, and reality that has characterized the western philosophical tradition' (Kavanagh, 2004: 445, see also Bates et al., 2019; Islam et al., 2016; Strati, 1999).

Sight and sound have traditionally been more valued in Western discourses than other senses, like touch and smell—a valuation which continues to current times. Sight has often been referred to as the 'noblest sense' (Bynum and Porter, 1993: 2) because of its link to the 'eye of the mind' and the divine light—that is, the religious truth of heaven (Kavanagh, 2004). 'Not far away from the noblest sense' (Bynum and Porter, 1993: 2), sound too, centres attention on human language and the exercise of speech (Kavanagh, 2004), which together with writing—a 'visual exercise' (Kavanagh, 2004: 449)—constitute what I would call the two 'perfect' and 'tidiest' sensory practices of traditional Western knowledge-practices—that is, two forms of knowledge-making sensory practices perceived, especially by scientists, as more absolute, chaste (see e.g. Gilman, 1993), more apprehensible (compared to touch, e.g., that is difficult to isolate from a specific sense organ; see e.g. Paterson 2018), clean and safe (see e.g. Palmer, 1993). As Hannah Arendt (1978: 122) explains so well, 'emphasis and interest have shifted entirely from contemplating to speech, from nous [mind] to logos [word]' and, in the context of new digital technologies, from word to data too.

As Tuan (1977: 183-4) notes, however, 'while the visual quality of a place is easily tallied, the feel of a place takes longer and is … a unique blend of sights, sounds, smells and a unique harmony of natural and artificial rhythms.' Sight, for Tuan, is only one of the instruments by which humans understand and internalize their environment. Indeed, not everything is translatable by visual appreciation and it is the combination and 'flexible' (Cooper, 2007: 1567) composition of different senses and sensory practices that allow humans to understand their place and organizations. To this, I would add that the diversification of sensory practices as 'instruments' (Cooper, 2007) of knowledge also represent a source of social inclusion (see e.g. the work of Lupton and Lipps (2021) on inclusive museums) that should be expanded to the more-than-human. In the light of what I have explored so far, I now return to the sociotechnical imaginaries of cattle sensor technologies in France and the UK and reflect on its meaning and implications for farming and its inhabitants.

Producing a Modern Sensorium in Cattle Farming

For many French and British tech advocates, cattle sensor technologies are the future of cattle farming—from the restricted use of agrochemicals and antimicrobials to the conservation of resources such as soil and water, to the improvement of agricultural working conditions (Barth, 2016), to the welfare of the farmed animals (Case, 2021; Halachmi et al., 2015). This imaginary intersects with what Cooper (2009: 249) calls a Western 'modern thinking of technology' that views cattle sensor technologies as instruments 'to extend human knowledge and control' in farming (e.g. overuse of chemicals, resources, agricultural working conditions, and animal wellbeing).

By allowing continuous and remote monitoring of individual cows, sensor technologies are, for example, expected to help farmers better recognize and respond quickly to cows' individual needs (e.g. for water, food, and health care). They are also expected to replace a 'good number of arduous farming tasks' (Maddyness, 2018) considered as rather repetitive and unrewarding, such as cow heat detection, body condition scoring, and lameness scoring (Halachmi et al., 2019). By collecting vast volumes of individual cow data directly processed by software and what are called 'smart algorithms', cattle sensor technologies are also expected to increase the 'ability' of humans (including farmers) to understand complex cattle systems (Neethirajan, 2020a: 2; see also Ezanno et al., 2021). Setting aside the know-how and sensory knowledge-practices of the farmer-cow dyad, imagined sensor technologies provide, in sum, both knowledge and prediction of 'anomalies' (Neethirajan, 2020a: 2), 'precision' (Neethirajan, 2020b), better understanding (e.g. of cow diseases and stress), and quick fixes to problems (e.g. challenges of insemination, greenhouse gas emissions, and antibiotic use). With them, farmers make 'better decisions quicker' as articles in the media put it (Gregory, 2020).

Advocates also value cattle sensor technologies for their 'speed', their connectivity to the global value chains and markets, their unlimited memory (by their storage capacity), and their capacity to 'extract' and 'accumulate' both internal (in the body) and external (in the environment) signals and information (Carolan, 2018; Ezanno et al., 2021; Neethirajan, 2020a) to make the 'hidden', 'discernible' (Paterson, 2018), and the enigmatic, intelligible. At no point in this quest for progress and knowledge of the animal, is there any question of interspecies exchanges and communications; multisensoriality; or technological flexibility, randomness, and changeability—so many concepts that inherently compose the day-to-day life, work, and profession of cattle farmers and that modern sensor technologies seem expected to oust. As an online press article sums up so well (Bothorel, 2018): the new '[farmers] get the results on [their] cell phone, [they] don't even need the manual anymore, to touch the soil.'

By reconfiguring the senses, imagined sensor technologies produce, however, a new sensorium in cattle farming dominated by what Kavanagh (2004: 445) calls, the 'primordial position of the ocular metaphor.' Indeed, the modern individual cow comes to be centred on, if not abbreviated to, the human eye (Kavanagh, 2004: 448). Every idea of individual cow data (e.g. temperature, movement, sound) implies a visual image—the creation of graphics and photography accessible to the human eye for the human understanding of the cow's condition, the cow's health and wellbeing. However, the rational and 'fixed point of view' (Kavanagh, 2004: 451) that comes with visual quantification and 'metricization' (Paterson, 2018: 73) (i.e. the ability to measure) normalize the way humans sense and understand cows. This maintains what Levin calls a sensory 'civil order' (cited in Kavanagh, 2004: 452) from which the deviant (the 'abnormal') should be known. This dialectic of human-animal distancing, Nimmo (2021: 11) explains as the 'exploitation and appropriation at the heart of capitalism' and large-scale industrial animal production.

Nor do cattle farmers emerge unscathed from these pristine, orderly, and 'noble' (see e.g. Bynum and Porter, 1993) imaginaries of sensory modernity. The 'imagined figure of the good farmer', as Kuch et al. (2000: 535) note, appears 'increasingly data-savvy' and requires, some experts believe, 'acculturation' (Ezanno et al., 2021: 10)—as a kind of scientific and technological proselytism in farming areas. Indeed, many attempts have been made in France and the UK to persuade cattle farmers that sensor technologies are 'the future' (Barth, 2016), the way to be progressive, and connected to modernity and the global world. According to one leading communications services company in the UK, sensor technologies have 'the potential to *boost* rural communities' (Gregory, 2020; emphasis added) as if rural communities were too slow or too 'dusty'. In France, too, the terms 'modernity', 'future', 'progress', and 'connectedness' flood the lexicon of pro-tech national surveys (Lachia, 2018). Some say that sensor technologies will help to connect remote areas and transform 'one of the *oldest* sectors into one of the most high-tech' (Lowemberg-Deboer, 2015: 2; emphasis added). Others say that these technologies will replace old traditional tools like 'paper and pencil', making farmers real 'ageekulturists' (Bothorel, 2018)—a play on words of the modern 'geek' (techie) culture and 'agriculturist' (farmer). But as the website of one of the world's leading AgTech companies, Alltech, indicates, 'the promise of digital technologies' in agriculture leans more towards a model of futuristic, monochrome, and sanitized city than a sensory and socially diverse farming ecology. The visual representation[2] used by the company Alltech to illustrate its own vision and fantasy of what modern cattle farming and cattle sensor technologies are and should be shows indeed a cow's face, affixed to an image of a suspension bridge, illuminated at night, similar to the one that spans the Golden Gate and whose lines connect constellation points frequently used in big data and global AI imaginaries. All these symbolize human progress, modernity, and enlightenment in a cowless city.

Through scientific rationalization of the senses and farmer sensorium, such vision of modernity risks, I argue, not extending (as Cooper puts it), but reducing the opportunities for multispecies know-how and sensory knowledge-practices in cattle farming. The Western idea of progress and modernity dependent and imbued with fast, standardized, cognitive, and capital-productive technologies is not new but represents only one, 'a certain kind' (Taylor, 2004: 9), of the many possible imaginaries of modernity through technology. It is these imaginaries that I discuss next in the final section of this chapter.

Final Discussion: Imaginaries of the Absurd?

As many have pointed out before (e.g. Miles, 2019; Nimmo, 2021), sociotechnical imaginaries of precision farming are often 'consistent with a productivist science' and 'has less to do with mitigating agricultural pollution [and the ill-being of both

---

[2] See the first image in archived version of the page at: https://web.archive.org/web/20220322110218/https://www.alltech.com/blog/bridging-data-gap-dairy-farming-promise-digital-technologies.

farmers and animals] than it does with advancing industrial modes of production' (Wolf and Wood 1997: 186). As explored in this chapter, the promotion of cattle sensor technologies is mostly driven by increasing herd size, increasing production volumes, as well as broader systems of normative incentives in cattle farming in France and the UK.

Expectations that sensor technologies will mitigate the negative effects of cattle farming on climate change and pollution, thereby protecting the environment and our ecology, are, however, somehow grandiloquent. Nothing guarantees that the production and degradation of cattle sensor technologies (e.g. their semiconductors and batteries) will not be more resource-intensive (e.g. in electricity, water, copper, and aluminium) and harmful to the environment. In addition, the recent global shortage of computer chips (Sweeney, 2021) have also shown to what extent computer technologies, such as sensor technologies, are not giveaways and that their implantation in most cattle farms, as desired by tech advocates, is not given yet.

The idea that, by constantly capturing individual cow data and measurements, sensor technologies allow farmers to take time off from the farm, get away from and better know their animals, is also just as naïve. It not only shows a certain ignorance and arrogance about what it means to know and connect with an animal for both the human and the cow, but it also shows a serious disregard of the role of cows as agents and teachers of good quality farming and farming professions (e.g. farmers and vets). From what has been described in this chapter, it will indeed be difficult to refute the fact that one of the key pillars of cattle farming practices and organizations are cows. Jones (2013: 429), for example, explains how cows motivate and give farmers pleasure at work by their presence, their 'intimate everyday encounters and the ways these are articulated through bodies', smell, touch, sensations, responses, and movements. Indeed, cows teach farmers what they are and how their life should be, with or without sensor technologies. Cattle farmers know their cows because they live, experience, and work with and through them constantly (Porcher, 2014). Cows allow farmers to develop what King-Eveillard et al. (2020: 15) call a 'farmer's eye and gut feelings.' Through this human-cow connection and sensory *proximities*, cattle farmers see what 'some people can't see' (Holloway and Morris, 2014).

For farmers, visual graphics, data, and measurements are just a plus, which, without contextual and multisensory knowledge-practices of everyday life and work with and through animals, can be unnecessary. Even worse, digital connectivity, visual graphics, data, and measurements can create doubts and bewilderment (e.g. as to data value), insecurity (e.g. as to data ownership and privacy), mental health problems and anxiety (e.g. as to human-animal connection loss) (Giersberg and Meijboom, 2021; Kling-Eveillard et al., 2020; Lachia, 2018; Scott et al., 2017). In one online press article, for example, a French farmer explains how technology can be tiring, making farmers feel overwhelmed with data coming from countless sources and unable 'to disconnect from their phones and tablets, to stop constantly checking software, sensors, stock markets and social media' (Bothorel, 2018). Such fatigue and concerns could be one reason for the slow adoption of sensor technologies by cattle farmers in France and the UK

(Lachia, 2018; UK Parliament, 2015), as well as future rejections and ill-being caused by cattle sensor technologies.

Currently obfuscating the peculiarities of rurality (in this case of the cow, the farmer, and the role of their mutual sensory practices and sensations), the sociotechnical imaginaries of cattle sensor technologies are problematic for at least four reasons. First, by losing the cow, these imaginaries reinforce the 'historical pattern of [human] concentration of [animal] assets' (Wolf and Wood, 1997: 181) and animal exploitation which is at the very origin of the many social and ecological crises that cattle sensor technologies are expected to mitigate (see also Bos et al., 2018; Nimmo, 2021). Second, it elevates an 'imagined future' (Jasanoff and Kim, 2015: 4) of human-animal relations in cattle farming compatible with large-scale industrial animal production (Stevenson, 2017), which is subject to the public's criticism (see e.g. Giersberg and Meijboom, 2021). Third, not only does this imaginary demean the animal, the cow's social value and agency in farming, but ultimately also the farmer for whom the cow matters and constantly participates in their personal and professional development and their wellbeing. Finally, by stabilizing such an understanding of human-animal sensory exchanges and knowledge-practices in cattle farming, such sociotechnical imaginaries standardize and normalize what I call agricultural technological modernism into something less rural, less animal, and less sensory.

There are things 'townies [urban people] can't understand'. This is what Alex, a cattle farmer told Adams-Hutcheson (2019: 1016) when describing the effects of drought on their cows and the turmoil they felt listening to their incessant bellowing. Agricultural technologies, and in particular cattle sensor technologies, can 'open up new and even unpredictable possibilities' (Cooper, 2007: 1554), new directionalities of human-animal sensory exchanges, and understanding in and around farming. But to offer such possibilities, to 'liberate and allow for [new sensory and organizational] experimentation' (Carolan, 2018: 75) in cattle farming, a new 'programmability' (Paterson, 2018: 82) of cattle sensor technologies must be found. This includes a new language of technological modernism in agriculture which includes the rural, the animal, and the senses beyond the visual. A language which not automatically calibrates farmer and cattle senses to produce capital, industrial efficiency, and productivity. Rather, a language that produces uncertainties and questions what Brain (2015: 133) would call 'every dimension of the [cow] medium': from the sensory and material aspects of cow health and wellbeing; to the conditions of their perception by humans; to their social and political conditions in farming.

Acknowledgments

Camille Bellet currently receives funding from the Wellcome Trust as part of her Wellcome Trust Research Fellowship in Humanities and Social Science, 'Investigating 'smart' animal health: Digital sensing and the reorganisation of healthcare in cattle farming' [219799/Z/19/Z], and is hugely grateful for Wellcome's ongoing support.

References

Adams-Hutcheson, G. (2019). Farming in the Troposphere: Drawing together affective atmospheres and elemental geographies. *Social & Cultural Geography, 20(7)*, 1004–23.

AgFunder. (2018, 10 October). 'How the UK is becoming a global leader in agritech.' Retrieved from https://agfundernews.com/how-the-uk-is-becoming-a-global-leader-in-agritech.html.

AgFunder. (2020). '2020 European agri-foodtech investment report.' Retrieved from https://agfunder.com/research/2020-european-agri-foodtech-investment-report/.

Andonovic, I. et al. (2018). Precision livestock farming technologies. https://pure.strath.ac.uk/ws/portalfiles/portal/85734728/Andonovic_etal_GIoTS_2018_Precision_livestock_farming.pdf.

Arendt, H. (1978). *The life of the mind/thinking*. New York: Harcourt Brace Jovanovich.

Barth, B. (2016, 28 January). 'Technology is becoming more and more pervasive in the age-old craft of animal husbandry.' Retrieved from https://modernfarmer.com/2016/01/wearable-devices-livestock/.

Bates, V. et al. (2019). Beyond landscape's visible realm: Recorded sound, nature, and wellbeing. *Health & Place, 61*, 102271. https://doi.org/10.1016/j.healthplace.2019.102271

Berckmans, D. (2017). General introduction to precision livestock farming. *Animal Frontiers, 7(1)*, 6–11.

Bos, J.M. et al. (2018). The quantified animal: Precision livestock farming and the ethical implications of objectification. *Food Ethics, 2*, 77–92.

Bothorel, M. (2018, 4 May). 'Ageekulteurs: le smartphone est dans le pré.' Retrieved from https://centtransitions.wordpress.com/2018/05/04/ageekulteurs-vers-lagriculture-de-demain/.

Bournigal, J-M. et al. (2015). 30 projets pour une agriculture compétitive & respectueuse de l'environnement. Ministère de l'agriculture, de l'agroalimentaire et de la forêt. https://agriculture.gouv.fr/sites/minagri/files/rapport-agriculture-innovation2025.pdf.

Brain, R.M. (2015). *The pulse of modernism: Physiological aesthetics in fin-de-siècle Europe*. Seattle: University of Washington Press.

Burley, D. et al. (2007). Place attachment and environmental change in coastal Louisiana. *Organization & Environment, 20(3)*, 347–66.

Bynum, W.F. & Porter, R. (1993). Introduction. In W.F. Bynum & R. Porter (Eds.), *Medicine and the five senses* (pp. 1-6). Cambridge: Cambridge University Press.

Carolan, M. (2018). 'Smart' farming techniques as political ontology: Access, sovereignty and the performance of neoliberal and not-so-neoliberal worlds. *Sociologia Ruralis, 58(4)*, 745–64.

Case, P. (2021, 8 March). 'Immigration rules risk further exploitation of farmworkers, research finds.' Retrieved from https://www.fwi.co.uk/business/business-management/staff/immigration-rules-risk-further-exploitation-of-farmworkers-research-finds.

Cooper, R. (2007). Organs of process: Rethinking human organization. *Organization Studies, 28(10)*, 1547–73.

Cooper, R. (2009). The generalized social body: Distance and technology. *Organization, 17(2)*, 242–56.

Deloitte. (2019). 'Smart livestock farming potential of digitalization for global meat supply.' Retrieved from https://www2.deloitte.com/content/dam/Deloitte/de/Documents/operations/Smart-livestock-farming_Deloitte.pdf.

EU. (2017). 'Precision farming: Sowing the seeds of a new agricultural revolution.' Retrieved from https://cordis.europa.eu/article/id/400295-precision-farming-sowing-the-seeds-of-a-new-agricultural-revolution.

Ezanno, P. et al. (2021). Research perspectives on animal health in the era of artificial intelligence. *Veterinary Research, 52,* 40–55.

Gardner, J. & Williams, C. (2015). Corporal diagnostic work and diagnostic spaces: Clinicians' use of space and bodies during diagnosis. *Sociology of Health & Illness, 37(5),* 765–81.

Giersberg, M.F. & Meijboom, F.L.B. (2021). Smart technologies lead to smart answers? On the claim of smart sensing technologies to tackle animal related societal concerns in europe over current pig husbandry systems. *Frontiers in Veterinary Science, 7,* 588214.

Gilman, S. (1993). Touch, sexuality and disease. In W.F. Bynum & R. Porter (Eds.), *Medicine and the five senses* (pp. 198–224). Cambridge: Cambridge University Press.

Gregory, R. (2020, 4 September). 'Smart technology could help transform rural communities.' Retrieved from https://www.wales247.co.uk/smart-technology-could-help-transform-rural-communities.

Halachmi, I. et al. (2015). Discussion: How PLF delivers added value to farmers. In I. Halachmi (Ed.), *Precision livestock farming applications. Making sense of sensors to support farm management* (pp. 113–118). The Netherlands: Wageningen Academic Publishers.

Halachmi, I. et al. (2019). Smart animal agriculture: Application of real-time sensors to improve animal well-being and production. *Annual Review of Animal Biosciences, 7,* 403–25.

Hamilton, L. & McCabe, D. (2016). 'It's just a job: Understanding emotion work, de-animalization and the compartmentalization of organized animal slaughter. *Organization, 23(3),* 330–50.

Hamilton, L. & Taylor, N. (2017). *Ethnography after humanism. Power, politics and method in multi-species research.* London: Palgrave MacMillan.

Herman, A. (2015). Enchanting resilience: Relations of care and people-place connections in agriculture. *Journal of Rural Studies, 42,* 102–11.

Holloway, L. & Morris, C. (2014). Viewing animal bodies: Truths, practical aesthetics and ethical considerability in UK livestock breeding. *Social & Cultural Geography, 15(1),* 1–22.

Islam, G., Endrissat, N., & Noppeney, C. (2016). Beyond 'the eye' of the beholder: Scent innovation through analogical reconfiguration. *Organization Studies, 37(6),* 769–95.

Jasanoff, S. & Kim, S-H. (2015). *Dreamscapes of modernity: Sociotechnical imaginaries and the fabrication of power.* Chicago: University of Chicago Press.

Jones, O. (2013). 'Who milks the cows at Maesgwyn?' The animality of UK rural landscapes in affective registers. *Landscape Research, 38(4),* 421–42.

Kavanagh, D. (2004). Ocularcentrism and its others: A framework for metatheoretical analysis. *Organization Studies, 25(3),* 445–64.

Kling-Eveillard, F. et al. (2020). Farmers' representations of the effects of precision livestock farming on human-animal relationships. *Livestock Science, 238,* 104057.

Kuch, D., Kearnes, M., & Gulson, K. (2020). The promise of precision: Datafication in medicine, agriculture and education. *Policy Studies, 41(5),* 527–46.

Lachia, N. (2018, 20 November). 'Usages du numérique en élevage Bovin Laitier.' Retrieved from https://agrotic.org/observatoire/2018/11/20/dossier-n3-usages-du-numerique-en-elevage-bovin-laitier/.

Lefebvre, H. (1991). *The production of space.* United-Kingdom: Wiley-Blackwell.

Lowenberg-DeBoer, J. (2015). The precision agriculture revolution: Making the modern farmer. *Foreign Affairs, 94(3),* 1-3.

Lupton, E. & Lipps, A. (2021). *The senses: Design beyond vision*. New York: Princeton Architectural Press.

Mack, K.S. (2007). Senses of seascapes: Aesthetics and the passion for knowledge. *Organization, 14(3)*, 373–90.

Maddyness. (2018, 11 May). 'L'innovation, un terreau fertile pour les agriculteurs?' Retrieved from https://www.maddyness.com/2018/05/11/linnovation-un-terreau-fertile-pour-les-agriculteurs/.

Mauksch, S. (2017). Managing the dance of enchantment: An ethnography of social entrepreneurship events. *Organization, 24(2)*, 133–53.

McLoughlin, E. (2019). Knowing cows: Transformative mobilizations of human and non-human bodies in an emotionography of the slaughterhouse. *Gender, Work & Organization, 26*, 322–42.

Miles, C. (2019). The combine will tell the truth: On precision agriculture and algorithmic rationality. *Big Data & Society, 6(1)*, 1–12.

Morrison, O. (2019, 27 June). 'UK farmers look to technology to solve productivity crisis.' Retrieved from https://www.foodnavigator.com/Article/2019/06/27/UK-farmers-look-to-technology-to-solve-productivity-crisis#.

Neethirajan, S. (2020a). The role of sensors, big data and machine learning in modern animal farming. *Sensing and Bio-Sensing Research, 29*, 100367.

Neethirajan, S. (2020b). Transforming the adaptation physiology of farm animals through sensors. *Animals, 10*, 1512.

Nimmo, R. (2021). Replacing cheap nature? Sustainability, capitalist future-making and political ecologies of robotic pollination. *Environment and Planning E: Nature and Space, 5(1)*, 426–446.

Norton, T. et al. (2019). Review: Precision livestock farming: Building 'digital representations' to bring the animals closer to the farmer. *Animal, 13(12)*, 3009–17.

Palmer, R. (1993). In bad odour: Smell and its significance in medicine from antiquity to the seventeenth century. In W.F. Bynum & R. Porter (Eds.), *Medicine and the Five Senses* (pp. 61–68). Cambridge: Cambridge University Press.

Paterson, M. (2018). The biopolitics of sensation, techniques of quantification, and the production of a 'new' sensorium. *Resilience: A Journal of the Environmental Humanities, 5(3)*, 67–95. https://www.jstor.org/stable/10.5250/resilience.5.3.0067.

Pflimlin, A., Faverdin, P., & Béranger, C. (2009). Un demi-siècle d'évolution de l'élevage bovin. Bilan et perspectives. *Fourrages, 200*, 429–64

Porcher, J. (2014). *Vivre avec les animaux*. Paris: La Découverte.

Quinn, C.E. & Halfacre, A.C.H. (2014). Place matters: An investigation of farmers' attachment to their land. *Human Ecology Review, 20(2)*, 117–32.

Ramsey, C. (2008). Managing to learn: The social poetics of a polyphonic 'classroom'. *Organization Studies, 29(4)*, 543–58.

Rugg, A. (2020, 5 September). 'Smart technology could help transform rural communities.' Retrieved from https://www.leaderlive.co.uk/news/18699717.smart-technology-help-transform-rural-communities/.

Scott, D.A., Valley, B., & Simecka, B.A. (2017). Mental Health Concerns in the Digital Age. *International Journal of Mental Health and Addiction*, 15, 604–613.

Stevensons, P. (2017). Precision livestock farming: Could it drive the livestock sector in the wrong direction?' CIWF. https://www.ciwf.org.uk/media/7431928/plf-could-it-drive-the-livestock-sector-in-the-wrong-direction.pdf.

Strati, A. (1999). *Organization and aesthetics*. London: Sage Publication Ltd.
Sweeney, M. (2021, 21 March). 'Global shortage in computer chips 'reaches crisis point.' Retrieved from https://www.theguardian.com/business/2021/mar/21/global-shortage-in-computer-chips-reaches-crisis-point.
Taylor, C. (2004). *Modern social imaginaries*. Durham/London: Duke University Press.
Thrive. (2019, 23 September). 'Animal agtech market map: 95 startups innovating for the livestock farming industry.' Retrieved from https://thriveagrifood.com/7167-2/.
Tuan, Y.F. (1977). *Space and Place: The Perspective of Experience*. Minneapolis, MN: University of Minnesota Press.
UK Parliament. (2015, 21 September). 'Precision farming.' Retrieved from https://post.parliament.uk/research-briefings/post-pn-0505/.
Wolf, S.A. & Wood, S.D. (1997). Precision farming: Environmental legitimation, commodification of information, and industrial coordination. *Rural Sociology, 62(2)*, 180–206.

CHAPTER 8

WORKING THE DOG

The Organization of Space, Time, and Labour in Multispecies Homes

ERIKA CUDWORTH

Richard Scarry's *What Do People Do All Day?* first published in 1968, is one of the most popular illustrated books for children, and being a child of 1966, it was my favourite. The title appears to be a misnomer, given that there are no people, only animals, undertaking a wide range of human jobs and roles in 'Busytown'. In his meticulous analysis of Scarry's text, sociologist John Levi Martin identifies 20 kinds of animal and 132 occupational categories, mapping the status of jobs to the socio-logics of species (2000: 206). For example, feminized labour is overwhelmingly performed by feminized animals such as cats and rabbits, 'dirty' and unskilled jobs by pigs (as exemplifiers of the working-class body) and authoritative jobs are undertaken by predators such as lions, bears, and foxes (Levi Martin, 2000: 215–23). What do dogs do all day? Busytown dogs are placed in trusted positions in a range of public services, particularly law enforcement. Levi Martin's well-made point is that there is a hidden language or code inscribed in children's books, which teaches children 'what kinds of people do what kinds of things' (2000: 225). However, the hierarchical categorization of animals indicates ways in which real creatures are socially situated in naturalized categories. Scarry depicts pigs as greedy, dirty, and unskilled, a comfortable popular stereotype perhaps, given the particularly tortuous treatment of these animals in farming systems. The role of dogs in law enforcement is one we recognize beyond children's fiction, one in which these relatively privileged animals, commonly in closer relationships with humans, are seen to work collaboratively (Smith et al., 2021).

This chapter is concerned with the 'doings' of two privileged species—humans and dogs—living together in relatively privileged homes; and with what they 'do all day'. The kinds of doings which are the focus of this chapter are some of those familiar to feminist organization studies such as balancing the demands of home, work, and caring labour. The way in which space and time is organized, both in and outside of the home is considered, reflecting Doré and Michalon's (2017) observation that our relations with nonhuman animals are organizational, and that everyday life and practices involving animals are scripted. The chapter examines how time and space are organized in specific ways around paid human work, walking with dogs, and within the home. In so doing, the chapter contributes to moves critiquing anthropocentric assumptions which form the basis of much of the study of organization(s) (Sayers, 2016); by suggesting that the organization of everyday practices and spaces are multispecies. The role of animals has been under-researched in organization studies until recently (Hannah and Robertson, 2016; Labatut et al., 2016; Sage et al., 2016), despite their omnipresence in organizations. When animals are discussed, this tends to be in the context of workplaces such as veterinary surgeries (Clark and Knights, 2019) or slaughterhouses (Hamilton and McCabe, 2016). When animals kept as companions or 'pets' are discussed, this is often related to public presentation (Skoglund and Redmalm, 2017). This chapter, however, focuses on aspects of the mundane in everyday spaces, considering that the home and the outside spaces of dog and human walking as important arenas in which organizational relations cohere.

In previous work, I have suggested that humans are entangled in complex systemic relations of domination with nonhuman animals that I have called anthroparchy (Cudworth, 2011). The household is a site in which anthroparchal relations intersect with other systemic relations, of patriarchy, capitalism, and so on. Within the home and in public spaces of walking, dog companions are commodities, legally defined as objects that are 'owned'. Dogs are nearly always part of anthroparchal structures of reproduction—the product of the puppy breeding industry, often subject to its nexus of violence. As commodities, dogs may be passed from one household to another, or abandoned to shelters or the street, and the 'rescue' dog is a product of this systemic violence. The Western household is a key site of consumption, where the bodies of domesticated animals not considered 'pets' may be stored, prepared and consumed as food by both human occupants and companion cats, dogs, and others (Cudworth, 2016). For many nonhuman creatures, a human home is a site of neglect, violence, and abuse. As feminist animal studies scholarship has found, cats, dogs, and other animal companions may be implicated in forms of gendered domestic violence (Flyn, 2000). Alternatively, 'pets' may be neglected, or treated with cruelty in this privatized space, relatively obscured from public view. Pet owners, along with their animal companions, may also face discriminatory and exclusionary practices in relation to making a home, as competitive private rental markets make it difficult for multispecies households to rent (Power, 2017). This acknowledgement of the macro and micro relations of power is more than a caveat to what follows. However, while the organization of time and space is fundamentally shaped by human power, the agency of dogs in relations with specific humans and contexts needs to be acknowledged.

In thinking through the relational organization of time and space in dog-human lives in this chapter, I draw on material from an ethnographic study in two field sites—the Lea Valley Park in East London, and a village in the East Midlands in England. There was an initial period of intensive immersion in the London site—daily observations were undertaken while walking with dogs over the course of a calendar year and kept in the form of an ethnographic diary. The diary recorded events, interactions, and routines of dogs and humans in the space of 'dog walking', noting interactions between individual dogs and humans and interactions within and across walking 'packs' (of human(s) and dog(s)). Fifty-two semi-structured interviews were undertaken, 37 with people walking dogs on the marshes that form part of the Lea Valley Park, followed by a second phase of 15 interviews with people walking dogs around a village in rural Leicestershire. More women than men were both observed walking (suggesting perhaps that dog walking is gendered care work) and found willing to participate (perhaps indicating women are less reserved about speaking about their home lives and the qualities of their relationships, as suggested by Charles and Aull Davies, 2008).

Most of the interviews were 'walk and talk' or mobile interviewing, accompanying informants as they went about their daily routines and asking questions along the way (Hall, Lashua, and Coffey, 2006). I worked in a 'research pack', accompanied by the dogs who share my home. My interviewees were people who walk dogs regularly and have close bonds with them. All participants shared homespace, and Varner (2002) would describe these households as those where humans understand dogs mainly as 'domestic partners' and occasionally as 'companion animals' but not as 'mere pets'. It should be noted that this data was collected prior to the COVID-19 pandemic, which has impacted everyday life in all of the areas considered in this chapter (and suggests a further project!). In the sections which follow, I consider human-animal organization in three areas: dog walking, in relation to paid employment, and in the management of homespace. It is with this last area that we will begin.

The Multispecies Household and the Organization of Private Space

It is estimated that 59 per cent of UK households have 'pets', and the most popular of these is the dog, with an estimated 33 per cent of households containing a total of 12.5 million dogs in 2019–20 (PMFA, 2021). Across Europe there are an estimated 85 million dogs and within European Union (EU) countries 24 per cent of households contain at least one (FEDIAF, 2018: 4–5, 8). Everyday lives, then, are often likely to be multispecies lives. Key reasons given by UK dog owners for living with dogs include that 'they make me happy' (51 per cent), 'for love and affection' (47 per cent), and companionship (35 per cent) (Statista, 2021). Survey data indicates that animal companions are considered family members (Harris, 2015); while qualitative studies suggest this is due to the qualities of the relationships involved (Charles, 2014). Charles (2016: 11) also finds that while animals can be human-like in their intimacies with family members, they are sometimes seen as being 'better at being family' than human members of a household because they provide affection without strings.

In living together, humans and dogs invoke a number of practices and meanings of home such as intimacy, love and care, and privacy. Home is a space for the expression of self, while also a space humans control; albeit that dog owners also adapt to living with dogs (Cudworth, 2021). Varner (2002) suggests there are three models of organization of human-dog households, each with a different quality of relationship depending on the degree to which dogs are incorporated into indoor space. Households having a high level of incorporation are those where human participants understand dogs as 'domestic partners'. In households where there are restrictions on the use of space by dogs, dogs are 'companion animals' rather than partners; and those dogs who are 'mere pets' are in households where they are excluded from homespace, for example, chained or caged in yards. In the UK, exclusion of dogs from the space of home is rare. Nonhuman animals specifically impact on the space of home. Gabb (2008) has suggested that being seen as a family member is reflected in the fact that private spaces within the Western home (such as bedrooms and bathrooms) are open to animal companions. In my research, dogs were companions or partners, and for most interviewees, dogs were allowed free rein of homespace, thus statements such as these were common:

> He's allowed all over the home.
>
> ... they've got the whole house to themselves.

Few attempts were made to restrict where dogs might go, and for some, this was a point of principle enabling the free expression of dogs:

> I wouldn't want a dog that was so regimented that it can only sit in a certain place.
>
> I don't want to have a dog and then say, 'oh you can't go here' and, 'you can't go there'.

Charles' (2016: 7) research indicates an absence of physical boundaries and the sharing of space, including beds; and more than half of my interviewees shared beds and bedrooms with dogs. Some co-sleepers told of a dog's ability to reorganize spaces of sleeping, to acquire and maintain space, and to move sleeping human bodies:

> I've got a king size bed and he takes up most of it so I usually find that I'm across the top or wedged into a really small bit of the bed and he's stretched out over the whole thing...

For a third of interviewees however, dogs were excluded from certain areas (particularly bedrooms) or trained not to sit on the furniture. Here, the spatial organization of home was subject to the drawing and redrawing of boundaries for both humans and dogs. Sometimes this was for practical reasons, such as the size of dog: 'he's not allowed up on the sofa because then there'd be no room for anybody else'; while others considered marking space for humans only as an issue of training and minimizing unwanted dog behaviour. For a few, marking space for humans-only was a constant 'battle of wills' while others had effectively given up on reorganizing the household to limit dog use of space:

> ... We found that he couldn't cope with round door knobs but the lever sort of door handle he could open easily. So, I put some cabin hooks on the doors with those handles, 'that will sort it' kind of thing; but no, he'd bang the door or jump up and [then] they would be open.

In all homes, dogs had space for their exclusive use. This ranged in form and scale from human beds and rooms of a home, to pieces of furniture, dog crates, dog beds, blankets, and baskets. Many interviewees discussed the need for dogs to have 'their own space' where they could escape from humans and be relatively undisturbed; and this was seen as important for dog wellbeing.

Philo and Wilbert (2000: 13) suggest that there is a distinction between human constructions of 'animal space' and animals' constructions of space, which they refer to as 'beastly places'. These reflect animal understandings of the organization of space and may be transgressive. In my research I encountered numerous stories of household damage caused by dogs: chairs and kitchen cupboards which were 'gnawed', sofas 'completely wrecked', rugs and cushions 'eaten', and wallpaper 'stripped' from walls. There were a variety of responses to such damage including disguise ('we've put a blanket over it'), confining dogs to various parts of the home or concern that destructive behaviour results from separation anxiety or boredom and action taken to mitigate this.

A further issue of friction was the challenge posed by canine ingenuity and sense of smell to the human organization of kitchen space and storing of food. Matter out of sight is not necessarily out of sniff:

> We put food away and in bags and cupboards and stuff and he can smell bloody anything. A door doesn't stop him smelling and he's so clever, he can open doors. He's more clever than my husband, he can close them too! [laughing]

My interviewees had numerous tales of food stolen from cupboards, kitchen work surfaces, shopping bags, and pockets. There was surprise at the ability of dogs to encroach on spaces from which they were forbidden: some dogs were able to open refrigerators and undo zips in bags. Those who attempted to organize space through restricting dog access often found this was breached by dogs working their way around barriers and prohibitions—moving to the bedrooms when banned from sofas, scaling a wall and into a neighbouring garden when prevented from using part of 'their' garden, for example. Controlling dogs' movement around the home was challenging, but controlling their smell, another matter entirely:

> Well, he farts a lot.... I mean he just creates an *atmosphere* [laughing] a thick fug, a thick fug of horror [pause for extended laughter]. And always nearest to me as well. And sometimes, well bloody hell, phew! God.

You take your eye off of him [while out walking] for one fucking minute and there he is—covered in Chanel No.5 [fox poo]. He loves it. He just *loves* it. I wash him of course ... but it just lingers. I think he pretty much always smells slightly of shit. My house must stink [laughing].

What is strongly apparent in the organization of multispecies homes is embodied practices. Both dog and human bodies assert themselves in the private space of home. The multispecies home involves compromise—while humans have the upper hand, the organization of space is an arena of challenge and change. Dog-human spatial negotiation is also an arena of embodied affectivity—in all the discussions of spatial organization, people laughed, at both their dogs and themselves.

Venturing Outside: Time, Space and the Organization of Walking

The Kennel Club of Great Britain (2022) suggests a minimum of 30 minutes a day for all breeds of dog, and often between one and two hours (depending on age), yet one in five dog owners in the UK do not walk their dogs daily (Derbyshire, 2010). For those who do, qualitative research indicates that dogs motivate people to walk from a sense of responsibility (Knight and Edwards, 2008). My research focused on those for whom walking with dogs is key to organizing time on a daily basis: 'First walk at half past six ... then I'll take them on a proper walk, about half nine, quarter to 10, and then I go again just after lunch'. A routine of walking such as this, was a key structuring device in the day of all interviewees. For many, this was something 'you have to negotiate' with dogs. Times and places of walking are not always a decision made exclusively by human walkers:

It has to be the right time, doesn't it [to partner]? Set walks.... We took him down to the seaside ... Walked for hours. But he still wants to go, when he comes back, to where he always goes ... he's quite controlling.

On individual walks most dogs are, to differing degrees (depending on the attitude of their humans) at least able to have some influence over the route taken and the time spent. Dogs may change route to greet other 'packs' (of human and dog walkers, Cudworth, 2017), or engage in extended play which modifies the direction of the walk or the time spent engaging with other dog walkers, something captured in the fieldnotes:

'The woman with her Bassett and Beagle are'? I want to convey it's the three of them, rather then the woman being most significant?

The time involved in walking dogs was something to be enjoyed. Some said that walking the dog(s) was 'frequently the high point of my day'. Dog walking was seen as a necessity whatever the weather: 'It doesn't matter if it's raining, or snowing or cold, I'll go out. And I wouldn't do that if I didn't have a dog'. Where there were negative aspects these came in the form of concern that 'old dogs can restrict your walking quite a bit'. Some would take older dogs out even when they were unable to walk (in backpacks, trolleys, or prams) in order to continue the processes of both human and canine socializing. While others have found that walking dogs is an important catalyst to social interaction (McNicholls and Collins, 2000), my interviewees stressed the importance of socializing for dogs.

Routine exchanges with regular walkers, often over years, means that human walkers accumulate much knowledge about other people and their dogs, and what people know about other packs is a significant feature of the diary data. In some cases, friendships were made as a result of the friendships established between dogs, and the repeated interactions of their humans over time. For those dog walkers with children the friendships of dogs are often compared to the relationships made through younger children:

> [The dog has] got her friends that she knew when she was a puppy, so they become your friends, like having children, with their parents ... there's lots of people that I know with dogs the same age that we met when they were puppies and all end up walking and meeting and chatting.

The demands of dog walking led to additional demands on the time of people living with dogs. While previous research found that dogs encourage a sense of community and lead to increased household connectivity (McConnell et al., 2011; Westgarth et al., 2007), I also found that relationships of caring obligation were often fostered as a consequence of the routine practice of walking. For those walking dogs this might mean sharing dog walking or dog-sitting responsibilities while people are working, walking dogs when people are ill, or providing other care work for those within dog-walking communities, including shopping, child care, assisting with veterinary visits, and so on. These kinds of reciprocal care for other dog walking packs have led me to refer to the relational networks formed through dog walking as 'posthuman communities' (Cudworth, 2017), which are not only more-than-human, but in being so, are qualitatively altered in nature.

The walking of dogs was a significant structuring device for the day. For the majority of those interviewed, who were working, most days began with a walk and returning home after work was often the trigger for a second walk. As one put it, 'during the week, it's like a walk-work-walk sandwich'. Some organized their walks to fit around work or what they felt their dogs would like to do, while others organized meeting and walking with other packs of dog and human walkers. This was usually for socializing, but there was also an element of mitigating risk for women who considered that 'it's nice to have someone to go [a]round with in the winter when you're up early and it's so dark'. In addition to walking being temporalized and spatialized, it is also time-hungry activity. Most interviewees used the phrase 'a proper walk', clearly defined as relatively long—45 minutes would be a minimum, but this would more likely be an hour or longer, and would involve spaces dogs were understood to enjoy (parks, forest, beach, fields) with time spent off-leash. For most interviewees, a 'proper' walk was a daily activity with some dogs being walked in this way twice a day, and others having a second (or in some cases third or fourth) walk that might be shorter and perhaps on the street. Walking therefore, took up a significant amount of time for my interviewees, and it was sometimes set up as a demand on people's time that was in tension with those of paid employment. All interviewees were asked what they thought could improve their lives with dogs, and the kind of response below, was common:

> Not having to work! Yes, absolutely, not working [laughing]. Then you wouldn't have to worry about your dogs not getting enough exercise.

> When I started working full time again a really big thing was walking—I have to make sure that Millie walks.

We now turn to the ways in which lives are organized in relation to paid employment and the tensions attending this for those living with dogs.

Negotiating Public and Private: Organizing Home and Work

For my interviewees, it was not hair, mud, mess, or walking in the rain which was considered the 'worst thing' about living with a dog, but the impact of work. Other studies have found that one of the main reasons people give as to why they do not have a dog companion is that they are working and do not have enough time, rather than not 'liking' dogs (Westgarth et al., 2007: 2). Most were conscious of, and sometimes expressed guilt about, the length of time dogs may be left home alone and could become 'bored' or 'lonely'.

Apart from assistance animals, dogs are generally excluded from (and understood to be out of place in) workspaces (Charles and Wolkowitz, 2018). It is not surprising therefore, that only five dogs in the sample were regularly taken to workplaces: a book binder, a charity fundraising office, a solicitor's office, and an acupuncture clinic. For some dogs, walking to an office and being expected to sleep under a desk was what was required. While this means that dogs are not left home alone, a dog is not expected to actively participate and some were unable to adapt to this passive role. A number of interviewees had experimented with taking dogs to work but had found the 'dog under the desk' role too dull for dogs and this led to tensions for them at work. For a tiny minority, dogs were permitted more of a free rein within the workspace, and in only one case, taking dogs to work develops into a specific ongoing role so that 'work' outside the home becomes part of shared life. Most dogs, therefore, were left at home when people were 'at work'.

A small number of interviewees were not in any kind of employment. About a third worked part time, and in many cases, this seemed related to the anxiety many felt about leaving dogs alone:

> I haven't worked much since I've had the dogs. I worked at the old peoples' home when I had Poppy, but it was just short shifts and then in the village I worked in the jewellery shop and that was half days, so it worked.
>
> When I was working full time I just couldn't have a dog.

Some people had moved from full- to part-time working even when this was not desirable or had proved a financial burden, or had moved towards home working because they had worried that their dogs had been left too long. Others felt they could not contemplate a return to full-time employment even if this were desirable, or alternatively, that they needed to be working fewer hours. Some were conscious of their dependency on family members and friends providing day care:

> So the whole work thing, yeah, I've been lucky there [as the dog is able to stay with her sister or her father when she is working] but I don't know what I'd do [without that support].

Those who worked full time often expressed guilt about the impact of their working hours on their dog while also juggling schedules in order that dogs are not left excessively:

> She's never left longer than five hours and we both can work from home so often during the week she'll be with one of us for stretches and [name of partner] can take her into her office.

Some of those working full time used 'doggy day-care'; either a set up where large numbers of dogs go to a day-care centre (in the rural study site, dogs would be collected and returned home by one popular local centre in a purpose-designed mini-bus) or where dogs are dropped off or picked up by dog walkers either just for a walk during the day or for all-day care. This was usually seen as a very positive experience for dogs:

> She loves it there so much that she always wants to get in the van if she sees it going round the village. We even send her there one day a week even if we are at home all day so she doesn't miss out.
>
> She just adores [name of dog walker] and spending the day there. Lots to do, lots of walks and there's always crumpets for tea [laughing].

The concerns people have about dogs being negatively affected by the impact of human work reflect the kinds of tension between demands of work and home found in literature on work and childcare (Drobnič, 2011). Employers were unsympathetic in terms of making allowances for illness or death of dogs and were generally hostile to dogs being brought to workplaces. For those who had moved to part-time working to accommodate a dog, the decision was often necessitated by a lack of flexibility and understanding on the part of their employer. In juggling working commitments, schedules of partners, and care for children, other human relatives, and other animal companions, as well as organizing dogs to be dropped off or collected by friends, relatives and dog-care services, my human interviewees went to considerable lengths to accommodate living with dogs in their daily routines. Only those with a high degree of autonomy in their working environment (who worked at home or for themselves) were able to manage the demands of work without experiencing conflict and anxiety.

For those with younger children, care work for dogs and care work for children became part of the same issue around which formal work had to be organized:

> … it has a massive impact how I work my work so that I can pick up [name of son] primarily, to save on child-minding fees but also so that Sam [name of dog] is not left all on his own all day because you can't do that. So that's a massive [pause] that is a big thing. I would work, I would have a different job or y'unno I would work differently if we didn't have Sam.

Similarities were also drawn between the social elements of dog walking and walking children to school and spending time at the school gates. Labours of exercising, feeding, playing with and entertaining dogs, of spending quality time with them and providing love and affection can be seen as similar to the labour involved in care for children, as reproductive labour. There were stories of periods of incredibly intense care work, with anxious dogs, rescue dogs who had experienced trauma, puppies, and in particular, older and ill dogs resulting in human carers having disrupted sleep and routines, being unable to work, go on holiday, or leave an animal alone.

There is, however, a darker side to the keeping of dogs as companions. In the UK alone, approximately 1.5 million dogs are suffering from separation anxiety at any one time (Bradshaw, 2012: 173). UK charities have voiced significant concern about levels of separation anxiety in dogs, with estimates of up to 85 per cent of dogs suffering when left alone, 50 per cent of whom are managing their emotions so effectively that their human owners are generally unaware there is a problem (RSPCA, 2019). Whatever the working hours, the dog waiting at home for their humans to return from work is ready to greet and welcome, to provide affection, and to provide companionship or a walk at the end of a human working day. They have negligible agency in changing this relation. Elsewhere I have suggested that being a human companion is not always an easy role for a dog and that it requires self-management, both physically and emotionally. Dogs also engage in various forms of care work for humans: they greet, provide company and affection, they may endure but also often seek tactile encounters and this can constitute active intervention in response to human emotions (Cudworth, 2022).

The public world of human paid work affects both humans and dogs, and often to the detriment of both. Human companions of dogs significantly modify their days and their working lives to accommodate caring for dogs. The juggling of time, responsibility, and labour invites similarities with other caring responsibilities, as do the costs involved (of part-time working or day-care).

Concluding Discussion: Working Time, Space, and Species

This chapter has focused on how the lives of relatively privileged humans and dogs are organized. The people interviewed for this project were engaged in a wide variety of working practices, but it was for a very small minority that human working life did not pose difficulties for the multispecies household. The space of home is modified in certain ways to accommodate or restrain dogs, and the use of homespace by dogs has implications for the idea of home and for reproductive labour. The most time-consuming form of reproductive labour human companions undertake for dogs is walking, and juggling the time spent walking and 'being with' dogs in relation to the demands of paid work is a challenge. There are parallels that might be drawn between caring for dogs and caring for children and other human 'dependents'—cleaning and tidying up, entertaining, socializing, feeding, and otherwise making sure that needs are met, for example in terms of exercise or the provision of external services such as day-care.

The evidence of separation anxiety among the millions of dogs left at home while humans work is sobering; as are the statistics for those dogs who do not get proper exercise and time to socialize with other dogs. The inspiration for the chapter comes from an interviewee's discussion of 'working work' (quoted above) to fit around her responsibilities for her child and her dog. While 'pet'-friendly employment is rising in some occupations and countries, this is limited in the UK. Those interviewees who were not retired or without significant control over their working patterns, experienced conflicted feelings about responsibilities for work and 'home'. They exhibited anxiety and concern about the quality of their dogs' lives, and the compromises working life necessitated, while the pressure on their time outside work was intensified by dog-related labour. Human-centrism drives our relations with other animals and even those who try to live as best they can with the dogs-of-their-heart are challenged by anthroparchal relational structures. This is not one-way-traffic that situates dogs as victims of human power. Dogs are agential beings who challenge human ideas of homespace, while their close relations with individual humans enable them to make effective decisions while walking. However, dogs and often also their humans, have relatively little power in negotiating with employers.

Focusing on the space/time/agency nexus, my arguments resonate with those who consider that humans organize with animals and that animal agency constitutes human capacities to organize. Sage et al. (2016) suggest an organizational conceptual triad of 'invitation', 'exclusion', and 'disturbance' that speaks usefully to the data presented here.

Their notion of 'disturbance' describes the ongoing renegotiation of boundaries or relational boundary work where humans are compelled to reflect on the likes and dislikes of animals and to consider what their bodies might do. Dog domestic companions muddy homespace and realize their beastly designs. In attempting to exclude dogs from certain spaces, their humans are often unsuccessful and faced with what dog bodies are able to do. In their demands for care, attention, and space, I consider that dogs disorganize human time and space on a daily basis. Sage et al. (2016) use the idea of 'invitation' to describe a strengthening of relations between human and animal actors in ways that collectively transform roles and action. The organization of walking involves elements of disturbance but is a practice that emerges through collective agency and with transformational potential. As such, it can be seen as involving 'invitation', as can elements of practice within homespace where collective fate is constituted and developed.

When it comes to the impact of work on human and dog lives however, we are in different territory. Sage et al. (2016) use the term 'exclusion' to capture the most usual boundary work organizing human-animal relations, where animals are excluded spatially and temporally. I have understood this sociologically as inscribing anthroparchy in social structures wherein animals are marginalized, exploited, and/or oppressed. The dogs in my study were usually excluded from human workspaces, and such working environments were usually those in which caring responsibilities for dogs were not considered significant. Work time/space is understood to be human exclusive. In turn, the impact of work time on the lives of dog domestic companions was a source of anxiety for my interviewees, and led to extra pressure in juggling caring and work commitments. While living with a dog companion and being able to offer a responsible and caring home is a privilege, my data also suggests that this impacts on the kinds of work and work hours some of my interviewees were able to undertake.

Could dog responsibilities not be 'worked' a little differently? This chapter is written as the UK emerges from the second national 'lockdown' due to the COVID-19 pandemic. There is concern about sky-rocketing levels of separation anxiety in the burgeoning population of 'lockdown dogs' and dogs more widely, with the return to work after a year or more of so many people working from home. Yet other possibilities surely suggest themselves. Homeworking combined with time in formal workspaces has been shown to be efficient and effective, while walking and time spent with animal companions has been seen as positively contributing to people's mental health. Reorganizing the times and spaces of formal work for those living with dogs as domestic companions might not transform what people and dogs 'do all day' in all the ways this is necessary and desirable, but it would intervene to lower anxiety and promote flourishing for dog and human companions.

References

Bradshaw, J. (2012). *In defence of dogs*. London: Penguin.
Charles, N. & Aull Davis, C. (2008). My family and other animals: Pets as kin. *Sociological Research Online*, 15(5) http://socresonline.org.uk/13/3/4.html

Charles, N. (2014). 'Animals just love you as you are': Experiencing kinship across the species barrier. *Sociology, 48*, 715–30.

Charles, N. (2016). Post-human families? Dog-human relations in the domestic sphere. *Sociological Research Online*, 83–94, available at: http://www.socresonline.org.uk/21/3/8.html.

Clarke, C. & Knights, D. (2019). Who's a good boy then? Anthropocentric masculinities in veterinary practice. *Gender, Work and Organization*. 26(3) 267–287.

Charles, N. & Wolkowitz, C. (2018). Bringing dogs onto campus: Inclusions and exclusions of animal bodies in organizations. *Gender, Work and Organization* https://doi.org/10.1111/gwao.12254

Cudworth, E. (2011). *Social lives with other animals: Tales of sex, death and love, 26*(3), 303–321. Basingstoke: Palgrave.

Cudworth, E. (2016). On ambivalence and resistance: Carnism and diet in multispecies households. In A. Potts (Ed.), *Critical perspectives on meat culture* (pp. 222–42). Brill: Leiden, Boston.

Cudworth, E. (2017). Posthuman community in the Edgelands. *Society and Animals, 25*(4), 384–403.

Cudworth, E. (2021). Muddied living: Everyday practices in multispecies households. *International Journal of Sociology and Social Policy, 41*(3/4), 424–39.

Cudworth, E.(2022). Labors of love: Work, labor and care in dog-human relations. *Gender, Work and Organization, 29*(3), 830–844.

Derbyshire, D. (2010). Walkies? Fat chance: One in five dog owners too lazy to take their pets out every day. *Daily Mail Online*, 6 August. Retrieved on 20 March 2013, from http://www.dailymail.co.uk/news/article-1300658/Walkies-Fat-chance-One-dog-owners-lazy-pets-day.html?ito=feeds-newsxml

Doré, A. & Michalon, M. (2017). What makes human–animal relations 'organizational'? The de-scription of anthrozootechnical agencements. *Organization, 24*(6), 761–80.

Drobnič, S. (2011). Introduction: Job quality and work-life balance. In S. Drobnič & A. M. Guillén (Eds.), *Work-life balance in Europe: The role of job quality* (pp. 1–14). Basingstoke: Palgrave.

FEDIAF (The European Pet Food Industrial Federation). (2018). *Facts and Figures 2018*, Brussels: FEDIAF, available at http://www.fediaf.org.

Flynn, C.P. (2000). Battered women and their animal companions: Symbolic interaction between human and nonhuman animals. *Society and Animals, 8*, 99–127.

Gabb, J. (2008). *Researching intimacy in families*. Basingstoke: Palgrave Macmillan.

Hall, T., Lashua, B., & Coffey, A. (2006). Stories as sorties. *Qualitative Research, 3*, 2–4.

Harris. (2015). More than ever, petsmembers of the family. Harris poll, available at: https://theharrispoll.com/whether-furry-feathered-or-flippers-a-flapping-americans-continue-to-display-close-relationships-with-their-pets-2015-is-expected-to-continue-the-pet-industrys-more-than-two-decades-strong/.

Hamilton, L. & McCabe, D. (2016). 'It's just a job': Understanding emotion work, de-animalization and the compartmentalization of organized animal slaughter. *Organization, 23*(3), 330–50.

Hannah, D. R. & Robertson, K. (2016) 'Human-animal work: A massive, understudied domain of human activity'. *Journal of Management Inquiry, 26*(1), 116–118.

Kennel Club UK. (2022). 'Dog Breeds A-Z' Retrieved on 17 March 2022 from https://www.thekennelclub.org.uk/search/breeds-a-to-z/#J

Knight, S. & Edwards, V. (2008) 'In the company of wolves: the physical, social and psychological benefits of dog ownership'. *Journal of Aging and Health, 20*(4), 437–455.

Levi Martin, J. (2000). What do animals do all day?: The division of labour, class bodies and totemic thinking in the popular imagination. *Poetics, 27*(2–3), 195–231.

McConnell A.R. et al. (2011). Friends with benefits: On the positive consequences of pet ownership. *Journal of Personal Social Psychology, 101*(6), 1239–52.

McNicholls, J. & Collins, G.M. (2000). Dogs as catalysts for social interactions: Robustness and effect. *British Journal of Psychology, 91*, 61–70.

PFMA (Pet Food Manufacturers Association. (2021). Pet population 2021. Retrieved from https://www.pfma.org.uk/pet-population-2021.

Philo, C. & Wilbert, C. (Eds.) (2000). *Animal spaces, beastly places: New geographies of human–animal relations*. London, New York: Routledge.

Power, E.R. (2017). Renting with pets: A pathway to housing insecurity? *Housing Studies, 32*(3), 336–60.

RSPCA. (2019). Our bid to help 7m dogs suffering from separation anxiety. Retrieved from https://www.rspca.org.uk/whatwedo/latest/details/-articleName/2019_03_06_7m_dogs_could_be_suffering_from_separation_anxiety.

Labatut, J., Munro, I., & Desmond, J. (2016). Introduction: Animals and organizations. *Organization, 23*(3), 315–29.

Sayers, J. (2016). A report to an academy: On carnophallogocentrism, pigs and meat-writing. *Organization, 23*(3), 370–86.

Sage, D. et al. (2016). Organizing space and time through relational human–animal boundary work: Exclusion, invitation and disturbance. *Organization, 23*(3), 434–50.

Skoglund, A. & Redmalm, D. (2017). 'Doggy-biopolitics': Governing via the first dog. *Organization, 24*(2), 240–66.

Smith, H. et al. (2021). Becoming with a police dog: Training technologies for bonding. *Transactions of the Institute of British Geographers*, 46(2) 478–494.

Statista. (2021). *Reasons for dog ownership in the UK*. [Accessed 26 03 2021]. https://www.statista.com/statistics/797008/reasons-for-dog-ownership-united-kingdom-uk/

Varner, G. (2002). Pets, companion animals and domesticated partners. In D. Benatar (Ed.), *Ethics for everyday* (pp. 450–75). New York: McGraw Hill.

Westgarth, C. et al. (2007). Factors associated with dog ownership and contact with dogs in a UK community. *BMC Veterinary Research, 3*(5), available at http://biomedcentral.com/1746-6148/3/5.

CHAPTER 9

SOCIAL MEDIA IMAGES OF URBAN COYOTES AND THE CONSTITUTION OF MORE-THAN-HUMAN CITIES

CHRISTIAN HUNOLD

Introduction

SEVERAL years ago, two images of coyotes photographed in urban settings circulated widely in the US media. One image, taken in 2009, shows a coyote napping in a light rail car in Portland, Oregon. In the other, taken in 2015, a coyote stands on the flat roof of a bar in Queens, New York. At the time these images made the news, they were widely understood to show a wild animal utterly lost in the city. As such, the images reinforced the widely held belief that humans and wild predators inhabit categorically different worlds, both spatially and ecologically. Framed as being out of place in the city, the coyote in these images served as the natural pole on a nature-culture continuum and a seat on a commuter train and a rooftop served as the cultural pole. I do not mean to suggest that coyotes belong on trains or rooftops, but rather that the images' newsworthiness traded on the self-evident absurdity of mundane urban spaces as places for encounters with coyotes.

More recently, however, the ubiquity of smart phones and the growing abundance of coyotes in North American cities have led to a proliferation of images showing coyotes in urban settings, particularly on social media. Coyotes are regularly caught on camera in locales as seemingly inaccessible to a mid-sized wild carnivore as Manhattan's Central Park, for example. I argue that the circulation on social media of countless images that reveal coyotes as residing in urban settings, as opposed to being ostensibly lost in them, foregrounds processes of multispecies place-making whereby particular 'multispecies landscapes assemble and emerge' (Aisher and Damodoran, 2016: 294) in distinctive ways, shaped by place-specific meanings, local knowledge, and social-ecological dynamics. Unlike natural resources and ecosystems, places such as the neighbourhood parks studied in this chapter resist universalizing claims-making; they are not given but formed, materially and discursively, through interspecies encounters. '[P]laces contain human and also nonhuman stories, meanings and significance. A place is not simply materially carved out of space.... places are also remembered, experienced, felt, discussed and imagined' (Aisher and Damodoran, 2016: 294, 299). Much of this multispecies place-making involves struggles for control and negotiations of acceptable levels of risk, but at times what emerges from this 'throwntogetherness' (Crevani, 2019) are novel expressions of kinship and ways of being well together in multispecies neighourhoods (Acampora, 2004; Houston et al., 2018; Steele, Wiesel, and Maller, 2019).

This chapter approaches practices of multispecies place-making through visual methods (Bencherki, 2020; Jarzebowska, 2021) to highlight that pictures help tell stories about the practices of accommodation that structure conflict/co-existence among humans and coyotes in urban spaces. I say 'conflict/co-existence' rather than 'co-existence' because, following Srinivasan (2019), any empirically plausible conception of cohabitation with free-roaming canids must acknowledge the full spectrum of these interspecies relations, including conflict. Relying on visual methods, I weave together insights from human-animal studies (Barua, 2016; Blue, 2016), new materialist thinking (Bennett, 2009), and recent work within organization studies on space and animals (O'Doherty, 2017) to better understand how multispecies conflict/co-existence remakes urban locations though practices of accommodation. Being neither exclusively human nor entirely nonhuman, such practices of accommodation reveal and respond to the challenges of facilitating human cohabitation with coyotes in urban spaces usually managed to satisfy primarily human needs. I am not primarily interested in analysing the representational content or in assessing the symbolic value of the visual materials being considered here. I ask not what images of urban coyotes show, but what they do; how such images do not just represent space and place, but how the joint activities of coyotes and humans revealed by social media imagery are remaking neighbourhood parks in San Francisco and Philadelphia as places that accommodate the recreational needs of humans (and their companion dogs) and the needs of wild canids smaller than a gray wolf but larger than a red fox.

I intend to show how our stories of co-inhabiting these spaces with coyotes come to be made real through visual accounts of place-making (Bencherki, 2021). 'New political stories that focus on living together and sharing spaces with other animals might help humans to accept a certain amount of risk and see [coyotes] in a different light' (Meijer, 2019: 179). Meijer's hopeful sentiment, prompted by experiments with nonlethal methods of managing graylag geese in the vicinity of Schiphol Airport, informs my analysis of how storying interspecies relations on social media structures urban green spaces as multispecies dwellings (Cnossen, de Vaujany, and Heafliger, 2020; Crevani, 2019). Following a brief overview of more-than-representational visual methodologies relevant to my inquiry, I explore how social media images of coyotes from San Francisco and Philadelphia are remaking neighbourhood parks in these cities as places that include coyotes as fellow urban dwellers.

Virtual Contact Zones and More-than-Representational Visual Methodologies

According to Gwendolyn Blue, 'digital technologies are not simply a neutral means of visualizing a preexisting world. Rather, they intervene in the world by rendering certain elements visible, sensible, and public' (Blue, 2016: 46). Consider professional wildlife photography as a medium of visual communication. Commercial wildlife photographers rely on a rich arsenal of portrait photography techniques to showcase wild animals in radiant light and vibrant colour. Telephoto lenses, shot wide open, set off animals' emotionally engaging facial features against pleasingly out-of-focus backgrounds. Insofar as animals are shown situated in identifiable landscapes, these settings are often at once both visually dramatic and generically exotic, such as a snow-capped mountain range or a vast savannah bathed in the warm glow of the setting sun. Without fail, human-made artifacts remain outside the frame so as to maintain the illusion that charismatic wild animals inhabit an idealized wilderness, as opposed to the side of the road or the grounds of an ecotourism lodge where they are more reliably encountered and photographed. In his analysis of how such virtual images of 'spectacular' encounters with charismatic wild animals contribute to the production of lively commodities for nature conservation organizations and for the wildlife tourism industry, Barua (2016) highlights how such sanitized virtual contact zones purge ecological context and nonhuman agency from human-animal relationalities:

> Encounters are engineered such that they have a fetishistic currency of their own, circulating with immense velocity, but at the cost of effacing the ecologies of animals with no room for the subject to respond. (Barua, 2016: 734)

Commodified images of charismatic wildlife harness appealing nonhuman physical attributes to elicit specific human emotional responses, so as to trigger charitable donations to conservation organizations or to increase safari vacation bookings. Such imagery does not invite critical reflection regarding power asymmetries, exclusions, and inequalities that structure relations between human and nonhuman animals (Giraud, 2020). On the contrary, commodified interspecies virtual contact zones help perpetuate a blindness to the mutual entanglements and shared ecologies of all living beings. However, if, as Chakrabarty (2009) observes, human beings are now reshaping the planet with the power of a geophysical force, like tectonic plates or volcanoes, ecological ignorance of this sort is all the more troubling. In his response to the chokehold on our eco-political imagination of this 'learned invisibility', Schlosberg (2016) hopes that a reflexive 'politics of sight' might render *everyday* multispecies entanglements more visible and pull us out of our immersive ignorance.

In what follows, I explore how everyday multispecies worlds reveal themselves in virtual interspecies contact zones that are, in Barua's terms (2016), decidedly *un*spectacular. The photos and videos considered here are not the work of visual media professionals. They are posted on social media by people who encounter a coyote during a walk in the neighbourhood park or while running an errand. Motion blur, dull lighting, and haphazard framing make for images that have more in common with snapshots in a family photo album than with carefully staged encounters with charismatic wildlife. However, the normative potential of such images to enhance our ecological receptivity and to figure out better ways of relating to one another across species boundaries, I argue, lies precisely in their (often unwitting) inclusion of urban coyotes' ecological context. Because of smart phone cameras' wide field of view, most users' unfamiliarity with conventions of professional wildlife photography, and the unplanned nature of the encounters themselves, these images render visible the daily activities of urban coyotes and their relationships with humans and (in many cases) their dogs: trotting along a residential street, napping in someone's yard, watching people in a park, or being curious about a dog.

Materialist entanglement theories from Bennett's (2009) new materialism to Barad's (2007) intra-action and Haraway's (2008) becoming-with imply, for my purposes, that social media images of urban coyotes have the capacity, in principle, to 'open public life and space to the creative intervention of human and more-than-human entities and forces' (Blue, 2016: 46). 'More-than-representational' visual methodologies consider 'what images reveal about the ebbs and flows of relations emergent between bodies' (Margulies, 2019: 4). The work such images perform is varied, and includes fostering more attentive ways of seeing in familiar contexts (Thomsen, 2015), accessing the affective liveliness of human-animal relations including those with 'scary' predators (Hanisch, Johnston, and Longnecker, 2019), distributing political agency across species (Blue, 2016), and questioning and reformulating concepts such as belonging and otherness (Blue and Alexander, 2015: 154). Insofar as social media images of urban coyotes do not rob the animals of their voices or their ecological contexts, I contend, they help constitute cities (and our understanding of them) as more-than-human spaces.

Social Media Images and *Living Well* with Urban Coyotes?

Though urban coyotes' status may be undergoing a cultural transformation (Flores, 2017), their membership in urban society remains contested, with 'dominionistic' and 'negativistic' attitudes still outnumbering more positive attitudes towards the animals (Fidino, Herr, and Magle, 2018). As opportunistic, generalist predators with a taste for goose eggs and rodents (and lacking natural predators of their own when they live in cities) coyotes function as apex predators in urban ecologies (Gehrt, 2007). Though coyotes who inhabit cities are more or less tolerated by their human neighbours, they are neither admired wild animal nor beloved pet (Hunold and Lloro, 2022). In fact, coyotes arouse mixed feelings because they occasionally prey on cats and small dogs and get involved in territorial disputes with dogs (Elliot, Vallance, and Molles, 2016: 1345).

Encounters with coyotes pose some, albeit minor physical risks to adult humans. Though only two humans have been killed by coyotes in recent decades, there were 367 attacks on humans in the United States and Canada from 1977 to 2015 (Baker and Timm, 2017), with a recent upward trend likely reflecting increased interactions with coyotes in urban and suburban areas. Attacks on young children, particularly toddlers, can cause serious injury, and such incidents invariably fuel anxieties about living alongside coyotes, often with deadly consequences for the animals. In March 2021, for example, an exceptionally aggressive young male coyote who, during an eight-month period, had bitten five people, including a two-year-old, in the San Francisco Bay Area town of Moraga was trapped and killed by United States Department of Agriculture Wildlife Services personnel. Several uninvolved coyotes were killed before the culprit could be trapped and identified by a DNA match (Bahr, 2021). For urban coyotes, visibility remains a double-edged sword.

Social media images of coyotes, dogs, and humans co-inhabiting everyday urban spaces engage the eco-political challenges of learning how to *live well* with wild nonhuman animals in urban settings (Luther, 2018: 192). I analyse human-coyote interactions in neighbourhood parks in San Francisco and Philadelphia. At times, these interactions generate new political stories of multispecies hospitality and neighbourliness, but not always. Perceptions of coyotes as menacing wild predators also persist in these spaces. Precisely what it means to *live well* with urban coyotes remains contentious. As we shall see, some vernacular practices of living alongside urban coyotes clash with municipal wildlife management policies that tend to view all interactions with coyotes through a conflict lens, leaving little room for the co-inhabitants to explore relationships that do not centre an expectation of conflict. An implicit goal of the more-than-human practices of accommodation involved in urban place-making, I argue, is to work out a set of shared expectations capable of guiding co-inhabitation of shared spaces by attending to the organization of spatial and temporal arrangements. This involves the distribution of entanglement and disentanglement so as to preserve everyone's autonomy by limiting unwanted intimacy between species (Britton and Hunold, 2021: 3; Rutherford, 2018). This resonates with O'Doherty's (2017) exploration of the ways that the human environment of the business-class airport lounge is carefully zoned to include certain actors (in this case, travellers, consumers, or 'loungers') while deploying spatial tactics that exclude less desirable 'others' through a carefully arrayed series of physical and symbolic screens. In a multispecies setting like the contemporary cities I explore, however, there is a need to discover and practise a relational interspecies etiquette (von Essen, Allen, and Tickle, 2020; see also Michelfelder, 2018), albeit one that operates along similar lines of exclusion, boundary-maintenance, and screening.

Buena Vista Park Coyotes, San Francisco

In October 2018 a male coyote known to reside in the Haight-Ashbury and Buena Vista neighbourhoods of San Francisco was observed with lacerations to his face and body, injuries likely sustained in an altercation with another canid. The injured coyote was the breeding male of a family living in Buena Vista Park and Corona Heights Park, two adjacent hilly neighbourhood parks that feature wooded walking trails, tennis courts, and dog runs. Coyotes are territorial animals who live in family groups comprised of a breeding pair and their pups; occasionally, offspring from a previous litter remain in their birth territory until they reach sexual maturity and disperse in search of their own territory. Thus, families may vary in size from two up to perhaps six or seven individuals at a time (Simons, 2020). The injured coyote was well known to local residents, who in August 2016 had named him 'Carl'. Images of Carl lying 'all curled up and barely moving' in the morning sun were posted to Buena Vista Park Coyotes (BVPC), a public Facebook group.

Created in 2016 by a resident who enjoyed observing and photographing the coyotes, BVPC features myriad images and videos showing coyotes, dogs, and humans encountering one another in and around these neighbourhood green spaces. A revealing facet of BVPC is that most images of mere sightings garner only a few innocuous responses such as 'Lovely!', 'So beautiful!', and the like. Residents are used to seeing coyotes in the park. Preservation and restoration of San Francisco's remaining undeveloped areas along with a move to nonlethal management of native predators around the turn of the century have led to a resurgence of coyotes in the city, from which they had been absent for many decades (Todd, 2018). San Francisco social media are teeming with images of coyotes exploring the neighbourhoods abutting the city's green spaces. According to official estimates, between 50 and 100 coyotes live in the city, though numbers fluctuate throughout the year because, as with other wild animals, juvenile mortality is high. Coyotes are native to California, including the Bay Area, and their presence in San Francisco today is remarkable primarily because until the end of the twentieth century coyotes found within city limits were routinely killed (Todd, 2018).

The coyotes shown on BVPC appear to make no effort at concealment and images of coyotes engaged in everyday activities such as walking, hunting, playing, and sleeping in close proximity to human visitors abound on the Facebook group. Though some misgivings about predation on free-roaming cats and the potential for territorial disputes with dogs remain in San Francisco (Todd, 2018), residents are generally not startled by their presence and do not appear to view them as being out of place in these spaces. Regular park visitors identify individual coyotes, notably burly dark-coated Carl and his slender light-coloured mate, as easily as they recognize their own dogs. Some coyotes, to the consternation of animal control officers and some coyote advocates, have learned which humans may be persuaded to hand out dog kibble. Park rangers enforce wildlife regulations by posting educational signage regarding the presence of coyotes and by occasionally ticketing scofflaws who do not keep their dogs leashed or who are caught feeding coyotes. Though coyotes' right to reside in San Francisco appears to be a settled question, negotiating the terms of interspecies etiquette to guide co-inhabitation remains a work in progress on BVPC. Attempts to work out what it means to *live well* with the neighbourhood's coyotes in this virtual encounter zone vacillate between appeals to professional wildlife management practices that seek to limit conflict by forbidding most interactions between coyotes and humans (and their dogs) and testimonials to lived experiences that point to the emergence in these parks of new forms of kinship among humans, dogs, and coyotes. The conflict-prevention perspective is enshrined in policy and law; the more relational approach remains a vernacular, dissident perspective practised by some coyote rebels who play with dogs and by some human rebels who let their dogs engage with friendly coyotes.

Images posted on BVPC prompted by disturbances of routines in the lives of the coyotes make these fault lines visible. Injuries are one such disturbance. In December 2017, for example, Carl was observed favouring an injured hind leg, which healed in a matter of weeks. His recovery was chronicled in several images taken during this period. The wounds he sustained in 2018 were about a week old when they were noticed. Carl was getting around and appeared to be in fairly good condition in spite of his injuries. Several posters recalled his recovery from the previous injury and hoped he would pull through again. Concern for his wellbeing drove speculation about what interventions might assist in his recovery. In the 2018 incident some posters worried that a deep laceration across his mouth might prevent him from drinking and feeding adequately. However, San Francisco wildlife officials do not attempt to administer veterinary care to wild animals who are not immobilized by their injuries. As it happened, Carl's injuries healed on their own. A comment on an image of Carl and his mate walking in Corona Heights Park taken a year and a half later reads: 'Carl's mouth scar is healed but I wonder if it bothers him as he eats. And that leg is still stiff' (BVPC, 9 May 2020).

The 2018 incident prompted speculation whether dogs rather than coyotes might have attacked Carl. There are fenced off-leash dog runs in both parks. Some dog walkers, however, let their dogs off the leash outside these approved spaces, and complaints of dogs chasing coyotes are a staple on BVPC. Coyotes, for their part, defend their territory from canine intruders, particularly while caring for pups in late winter and spring. A coyote standing his ground may be experienced as unsettling by anxious dog walkers:

> Carl wouldn't leave the path this morning (even when I shouted and clapped) so Crosby and I had to turn around!!! Getting bold. (BVPC, 2 February 2017)

More persistent challenges such as coyotes 'escorting' unwanted dogs from their territory by following them (and their human) can be emotionally intense, even for longtime residents:

> Hi folks, just a note that two coyotes just chased me and my leashed dog (50 pound Border Collie mix). I had to *sprint* down from the top of the hill all the way down the fire road and into the street at Upper Terrace and Buena Vista Ave West before they held off. They were nipping at both of us with their teeth bared the entire time. Pretty terrifying. (BVPC, 29 June 2020)

Given that running from coyotes might encourage them to give chase, the original poster elaborated on her decision to run rather than stand her ground:

> I screamed at them (have been encountering them for years) and walked away, and they tore after me with teeth bared so that's why I ran. (BVPC, 29 June 2020)

Physical violence between domestic dogs and coyotes is only a small part in a broad spectrum of canine-to-canine interactions (Boydston et al., 2018). Dog-coyote interactions reported on BVPC range from mutual indifference and avoidance to curiosity to mutual play, and only rarely escalate to moments of tense conflict—even if violent encounters attract much attention given that peaceful interactions are rarely remarked upon and that coyote-dog interactions perceived as being *too* friendly invite censure on BVPC. Occasional scuffles and injuries aside, however, no dog or coyote is known to have been killed in Buena Vista Park or Corona Heights Park as a result of inter-canine violence.

Even so, pet owners' understandable concern for the safety of their dogs inflects social media discussions of urban coyotes across North America. However, posters on BVPC rarely blame coyotes for defending themselves from aggressive dogs. Rather, they blame careless dog owners for not leashing dogs and for not respecting coyotes' personal space even when dogs are leashed. In this perspective, respect for the needs of Carl and his family is best expressed by leashing one's dog and by resisting coyotes' entreaties for handouts in order to 'keep them wild'. Crossing ontological boundaries is bound to lead to misunderstandings and therefore best avoided. People who are known to feed coyotes are roundly condemned on BVPC. Responses to a video posted on BVPC that shows Carl standing on a bluff overlooking a footpath barking and yipping excitedly for about 20 seconds illustrate the arguments in this debate. Interspersed with Carl's continuous vocalizations are half a dozen barks made by the dog belonging to the person filming the video.

To one viewer Carl's apparent agitation suggested that the person filming the video had allowed his leashed dog to get too close to what sounded, to her ears, like a distressed coyote. One longtime park visitor resisted this interpretation of distress, however, and countered that several dog walkers had been reporting that Carl appeared to want to play with their dogs. In fact, the video's author implied precisely that in the discussion thread: 'This particular coyote followed us out of the park, after dropping a tennis ball in front of my pup. I'll leave interpretations of that to others' (BVPC, 18 August 2018). Proper leash-walking etiquette is often discussed by group members, with some advocating for strict adherence to canine social distancing rules and others seeing no harm in their leashed dog exchanging greetings with a coyote, provided both canines consent to this activity. Those in the social distancing camp make a categorical distinction between wildness and domestication which implies that all interactions between coyotes and dogs inevitably spell disaster for members of both species. This non-relational account of existing alongside but not *with* urban wild animals, informed by the tenets of professional wildlife management aimed at conflict prevention, leaves little room for interspecies games that might result in positive experiences for the participants (von Essen, Allen, and Trickle, 2020: 152). Whenever a heretical dog owner suggests that a coyote seems to enjoy playing with their dog—as indicated, for example, by play-bowing—they are castigated by those who abhor even such seemingly innocuous boundary crossings as taking the first step on the road to ruin. In this view, a tennis ball dropped by a coyote at a dog's feet as an invitation to play signals the emergence of a doomed multispecies mélange rather than an expression of canine joy or interspecies kinship.

If, however, some coyotes are known by regular park visitors to associate safely with their dogs (and their humans), how might these coyotes be incorporated into the more demanding norms of cooperation and reciprocity usually reserved for human relationships with companion animals (Donaldson and Kymlicka, 2011)? Successful cooperation with coyotes based on mutual respect, it turns out, is well-documented. For example, coyotes who live on sheep ranches where they are not persecuted form stable family groups who learn that livestock guard dogs mean business. The resident coyotes generally stay away from sheep, repel intruding coyotes, and pass this knowledge on to their pups. Adhering to rudimentary rules of interspecies etiquette is not beyond the capacity of these wild canids (Walkaboutlou, 2018). Scientific confirmation in the late 1990s of the 'predator paradox' that the more predators are removed, the more livestock is killed has persuaded even state agricultural extension services to recommend that livestock managers leave resident coyotes' family structure intact (Shivik, 2014). Similar accounts exist for Australia's dingoes in areas where ranchers have stopped killing them (Emmott, 2020). The relational, interactional, and practical organization (Bencherki, 2021) of livestock farms differs greatly from that of urban parks, but the point remains that, where they are encouraged to do so, coyotes actively participate with human and nonhuman others in the constitution of the spaces they inhabit (Van Patter, 2021).

Even to gesture at exploring such more relational possibilities of being well together, however, is to invite censure on BVPC. Posters who approve of the coyotes' presence in these spaces tend to see coyotes (and dogs) as passive victims-in-waiting and/or as objects to be controlled rather than as sentient beings with lived experiences who are capable of learning and who may be trusted to make safe choices. Here it would be remiss of me to ignore that some contributors to BVPC vehemently object to accommodating coyotes in the city. One of these sceptics is resigned to the coyotes' presence while insisting (despite evidence to the contrary) that they 'do not control things' and, further, warning that 'the coyote issue is heading for disaster' insofar as an ever-expanding coyote population will condemn the neighbourhood's companion animals to become prey for starving coyotes. Such doom-mongering does not appear to resonate widely on BVPC, even though dog walkers have had to contend with the fact that coyotes have profoundly altered the experience of walking one's dog in Buena Vista Park and Corona Heights Park. Residents continue to debate how canine agency—coyote as well as dog—might be acknowledged and appropriately accommodated in their neighbourhood. Thus far, however, only a few dissenters have admitted to relaxing control and letting members of both species work out for themselves how to balance canine-to-canine intimacy and autonomy in these shared spaces.

Wissahickon Valley Coyotes, Philadelphia

As in San Francisco, coyotes have become more abundant in East Coast cities. Coyote sightings in New York City, Philadelphia, and Washington, DC regularly make the local news and are reported on social media. In these cities, however, face-to-face encounters with coyotes are less common and, when they do occur, more fleeting than in San Francisco. Though coyotes have been photographed in New York City's Central Park, Philadelphia's Fairmount Park, and Washington's Rock Creek Park, there are no spaces in these cities where coyotes are as relaxed around humans as in San Francisco's parks. The dense vegetation of East Coast woodlands, moreover, offers manifold opportunities for concealment by wild animals who do not wish to be observed by humans. As a result, human-coyote relationalities in these cities emerge primarily in virtual contact zones rather than in embodied interactions. That is to say, few people who spend time in Philadelphia's parks are even aware of the presence of coyotes, and of those who are even fewer have encountered a coyote in person.

There is an additional wrinkle regarding co-inhabiting East Coast cities with coyotes. The animals found in New England, New York, and Pennsylvania are a hybrid of both coyote and wolf parentage that originated in southern Ontario around the turn of the twentieth century (Way and Lynn, 2016). Eastern coyotes, or 'coywolves', are notably larger than their Western forebears, so much so that they do not even register as coyotes for some first-time observers who just assume they have come face to face with a scruffy large dog. Reports of someone learning that these canids are in fact coyotes are common on Philadelphia social media. So are accounts of someone reporting a coyote sighting to friends or relatives only to have their sanity questioned, presumably because coyotes are so strongly associated with the American West that claims of their presence in Philadelphia engender disbelief. Coyotes may have been inserting themselves into the city for a few decades, but they are only just beginning to insert themselves into the public imagination. The largely virtual nature of people's interactions with urban coyotes, along with accounts of deer-hunting coywolves, may go some way towards explaining the prominence of 'scary wild predator' narratives in social media discussions about Philadelphia's coyotes.

In July 2018 a member of Friends of the Wissahickon (FOTW), the official Facebook page of the eponymous volunteer friends-of-the-park organization, posted an image of a tan-coloured Eastern coyote cantering across a lawn on the SugarLoaf Campus of Chestnut Hill College, located in Northwest Philadelphia. Coyotes are most abundant in the city's northwest neighbourhoods of Chestnut Hill, Mount Airy, Andorra, and Roxborough. These leafy neighbourhoods cluster around the steep wooded hillsides of Wissahickon Valley Park, a 2,042-acre green corridor that connects the city with its suburbs to the north. The Valley's forest and adjacent meadows are rich in the small mammals such as rabbits, groundhogs, squirrels, chipmunks, and voles that comprise the bulk of the coyote diet. Eastern coyotes weigh 35–55 lbs, however, and are capable of killing the white-tailed deer that abound in this part of the city.

The image of the loping coyote posted on the FOTW Facebook page was accompanied by a well-intentioned but clumsily worded public service announcement that asked people to mind their cats and dogs while, at the same time, seeking to assuage concerns that Eastern coyotes, like wolves, hunt in packs that go after unwary family dogs and, by extension, human children. Eastern coyotes' short summer coat, as on the individual pictured in the Facebook image, reveals the animals' deep chest and muscular body, features that emphasize their wolf parentage. Though Eastern coyotes do hunt cooperatively in pursuit of deer, there have been no reports in Philadelphia of coyotes attacking dogs (or children). Thus primed, however, the exchange that followed on Facebook unleashed much scepticism about the wisdom of tolerating these wild predators in an urban setting. In addition to many posts asserting that coyotes routinely kill pets for food, the persistent myth that cunning coyotes will lure dogs into an ambush to be torn to pieces by 'the pack' also made an appearance:

> They most definitely will go after your pets. And they may look alone but that one coyote will annoy your big dog until it chases it and that's when the pack comes from every side. (FOTW, 28 July 2018)

One post went a step further and took issue with coyotes' carnivorousness as such. This person viewed 'out-of-control' coyotes as pests, as wanton killers not only of pets but also of wildlife:

> There are dead deer all over back in Schuylkill Valley Nature Center from these yotes, they should be put down. (FOTW, 28 July 2018)

In this thread prompted by the image of the SugarLoaf coyote, however, reports of pets attacked or killed by coyotes all stemmed from posters who live or used to live in the American Southwest. Posters with personal knowledge of Pennsylvania's coyotes, such as a farmer from the Philadelphia suburbs, testified to their unproblematic co-existence with livestock and pets. Most encounters with coyotes in Philadelphia are brief, however, and thus afford limited opportunities to get to know coyotes as they are, as opposed to how they are imagined (or feared) to be. There is no 'Carl', beloved survivor of hardships and occasional playmate to dogs. The novelty of encountering coyotes in the neighbourhood is captured by several comments in the thread:

> I saw it and thought 'that's a weird looking fox'! (FOTW, 28 July 2018)

> I did hear a neighbor mention that she saw 3 coyotes together eating her trash in the early morning. She didn't realize they were coyotes, she called them 'wild dogs'. (FOTW, 28 July 2018)

> My house backs up to the park at the bottom of Cathedral Rd and was watering grass two weeks ago and looked to my right and there was one standing 30 feet away looking at me. It was really nice/healthy looking and was more grey in color, not ratty like that. (FOTW, 28 July 2018)

Expressions of more positive feelings about coyotes also figure among the responses to the SugarLoaf coyote: 'So cool!', 'I like coyotes'. These posters tend to argue for keeping cats inside and not letting dogs roam in areas where coyotes are present. In this coyote-friendlier perspective, sensible pet-keeping practices go a long way towards enabling co-existence. Keeping cats indoors does all wild animals a favour, after all, and dogs are required to be leashed in Wissahickon Valley Park anyway. Even these generally supportive posts, however, stop short of reimagining human/animal and nature/culture binaries (emphasis added):

> These are wild animals. Plain and simple. *Out of their element for sure*, but they should not be put down. They and their wildness should be respected. You should be responsible with your pets—coyotes or not—and this should most definitely raise your level of awareness for the care and attention you take. (FOTW, 28 July 2018)

Given the virtual nature of most encounters between humans and coyotes in Philadelphia—virtual as far as humans are concerned, at any rate; urban coyotes are closely attuned to human habits and time their own movements to minimize unwanted encounters (Gehrt, Brown, and Anchor, 2011)—social media discussions of interspecies etiquette remain necessarily somewhat abstract, focused on prescriptions such as not letting companion animals roam unattended. Even coyote-friendly participants in such exchanges, however, do not think that coyotes *belong* in Philadelphia, exactly. Rather, coyotes rate as one more source of potential trouble people need to take into account while visiting neighbourhood parks. However, since coyotes are evidently doing well in the Wissahickon and not actually causing humans any trouble, accommodating their wildness, in this view, seems to require little more than being aware of their presence and not interfering with their lives.

Conclusion

This willingness to leave urban coyotes alone has limits. As Teresa Lloro and I have noted elsewhere (Hunold and Lloro, 2022), some intra-urban ontological boundaries appear to remain fixed insofar as residents are willing to live among coyotes, but still believe their presence is unnatural. This perception of unnaturalness has a spatial dimension, coming into play where coyotes stray from the urban green spaces that people imagine as the most appropriate habitat for urban wild animals. Residents articulate a categorical distinctiveness, *within* cities, of green spaces to which coyotes, if they must live in cities, ought to be confined and of residential areas where their presence tends to arouse suspicion. When it comes to coyotes, some urban spaces are evidently more legitimately multispecies than others. Politically speaking, city streets in residential neighourhoods cannot easily accommodate coyotes, even if a coyote's behaviour seems to suggest otherwise.

For example, in late April 2018, a healthy young coyote found in a South Philadelphia neighourhood was cornered and captured by police and subsequently euthanized by the Pennsylvania Game Commission on the grounds that the animal was 'too friendly and docile' and therefore might pose a danger to the public were he to return to an urban setting. The comments section of a *Philadelphia Inquirer* story (Gantz, 2018) covering the incident were rife with disapproval of the decision to kill the coyote. The story was accompanied by images of the coyote cowering behind a dumpster and, once captured, awaiting execution in a transport cage. Wildlife officials' catch-22 approach to risk management, whereby a coyote's showing too much aggression and showing too little both trigger a death sentence, struck many people as absurd. The young coyote had done nothing wrong and was apparently healthy, so why had he not been set free in a suitable location outside the city? Not a single comment, however, asked why the coyote had been interfered with in the first place, or why he had not been released nearby. After all, the very same stretch of South Philadelphia where he was captured features areas of green space along the Delaware River, with abundant prey and plenty of cover.

In Philadelphia, increased visibility of urban coyotes has been met with greater ambivalence than in San Francisco where encounters with coyotes have been commonplace for some time. San Francisco's virtual contact zone of Buena Vista Park Coyotes, for all of its clashing storylines, prefigures how uneasy toleration might develop into something more like genuine hospitality and mutual respect. How humans respond to the discovery of wild predators living in their midst may be determined, to some extent, by the two species' mutual attunement. It is likely no coincidence that North American cities tend to embrace a hands-off approach to managing urban coyotes once tempers stoked by discovery of their presence subside (Hunold and Mazuchowski, 2020). New political stories about living alongside coyotes may, with time, emerge in cities like Philadelphia too. After all, as Rutherford contends, Eastern coyotes/coywolves embody the Anthropocene's most interesting conceptual elements and 'call into question ... the "purifying logic" we apply to the nonhuman world, pointing instead to the evolutionary possibilities of hybridity, of unsettled mixtures, of indeterminacy' (Rutherford, 2018: 215). However, for the time being new political stories about 'what the coywolf might teach us about living well in the Anthropocene' (Rutherford, 2018: 207; see also Weckel and Wincorn, 2016) are still struggling to assert themselves against old truths about what is natural and unnatural in how urban wild animals use the spaces they share with us, and who gets to decide such questions.

References

Acampora, R. (2004). Oikos and domus: On constructive co-habitation with other creatures. *Philosophy & Geography, 7(2)*, 219–235.

Aisher, A. & Damodaran, V. (2016). Introduction: Human-nature interactions through a multispecies lens. *Conservation and Society, 14(4)*, 293–304.

Bahr, S. (2021). Coyote that attacked five in the Bay Area is finally caught. *The New York Times*, 12 March, https://www.nytimes.com/2021/03/12/us/coyote-killed-california-bay-area.html.

Baker, R.O. & Timm, R.M. (2017). Coyote attacks on humans, 1970–2015: Implications for reducing the risks. *Human-Wildlife Interactions, 11(2)*, 120–32.

Barard, K. (2007). *Meeting the universe halfway: Quantum physics and the entanglement of matter and meaning*. Durham, NC: Duke University Press.

Barua, M. (2016). Lively commodities and encounter value. *Environment and Planning D: Society and Space, 34(4)*, 725–44.

Bencherki N. (2021). Using video methods to uncover the relational, interactional and practical constitution of space. In S. Grosjean & F. Matte (Eds.), *Organizational video-ethnography revisited* (pp. 99–116). London: Palgrave Pivot. https://doi.org/10.1007/978-3-030-65551-8_6

Bennett, J. (2009). *Vibrant matter: A political ecology of things*. Durham, NC: Duke University Press.

Blue, G. (2016). Public attunement with more-than-human others: Witnessing the life and death of Bear 71. *GeoHumanities, 2(1)*, 42–57.

Blue, G. & Alexander, S. (2015). Coyotes in the city: Gastro-ethical encounters in a more-than-human world. In K. Gillespie & R-C. Collard (Eds.), *Critical animal geographies: Politics, intersections and hierarchies in a multispecies world* (pp. 149–63). London, New York: Routledge.

Boydston, E.E. et al. (2018). Canid vs. canid: Insights into coyote–dog encounters from social media. *Human-Wildlife Interactions, 12(2)*, 233–42.

Britton, J.L. & Hunold, C. (2021). Bordering processes and pony wildness on Assateague Island. *Society & Animals* (published online 30 March). https://doi.org/10.1163/15685306-BJA10042

Chakrabarty, D. (2009). The climate of history. *Critical Inquiry, 35(2)*, 197–222.

Cnossen, B., de Vaujany, F.-X., & Haefliger, S. (2020). The street and organization studies. *Organization Studies* (published online 7 May). DOI: 10.1177/0170840620918380.

Crevani, L. (2019). Organizational presence and place: Sociomaterial place work in the Swedish outdoor industry. *Management Learning, 50(4)*, 389–408.

Donaldson, S. & Kymlicka, W. (2011). *Zoopolis: A political theory of animal rights*. Oxford: Oxford University Press.

Elliot, E.E., Vallance, S., & Molles, L.E. (2016). Coexisting with coyotes (*Canis latrans*) in an urban environment. *Urban Ecosystems, 19(3)*, 1335–50.

Emmott, A. (2020). The dingo as a management tool on a beef cattle enterprise in western Queensland. *Australian Zoologist* (published online 9 October). https://doi.org/10/7782/AZ.2020.033

Fidino, M., Herr, S.W., & Magle, S.B. (2018). Assessing online opinions of wildlife through social media. *Human Dimensions of Wildlife, 23(5)*, 482–90.

Flores, D. (2017). *Coyote America: A natural and supernatural history*. New York: Basic Books.

Gantz, S. (2018). Coyote captured in city center euthanized. *Philadelphia Inquirer*, 27 April, https://www.inquirer.com/philly/health/environment/coyote-captured-in-center-city-euthanized-20180427.html

Gehrt, S.D. (2007). Ecology of coyotes in urban landscapes. In D.L. Nolte, W.M. Arjo, & D.H. Stalman (Eds.), *Proceedings of the 12th wildlife damage management conference*, https://urbancoyoteresearch.com/sites/default/files/resources/ecologycoyotes.pdf.

Gehrt, S.D., Brown, J.L., & Anchor, C. (2011). Is the urban coyote a misanthropic synanthrope? The case from Chicago. *Cities and the Environment, 4(1)*, Article 3.

Giraud, E.H. (2020). Disentangling ourselves from animals. *The Philosopher, 108(1)*, 51–6.

Hanisch, E., Johnston, R., & Longnecker, N. (2019). Cameras for conservation: Wildlife photography and emotional engagement with biodiversity and nature. *Human Dimensions of Wildlife, 24(3)*, 267–84.

Haraway, D. (2008). *When species meet*. Minneapolis: University of Minnesota Press.

Hunold, C. & Mazuchowski, M. (2020). Human-wildlife coexistence in urban wildlife management: Insights from nonlethal predator management and rodenticide bans. *Animals, 10(11)*, 1983.

Hunold, C. & Lloro, T. (2022). There goes the neighorhood: Urban coyotes and the politics of wildlife. *Journal of Urban Affairs, 44(2)*, 153–173.

Houston, D. et al. (2018). Make kin, not cities! Multispecies entanglements and 'becoming-world' in planning theory. *Planning Theory, 17(2)*, 190–212.

Jarzebowska, G. (2021). 'Four-legged terror' or 'ultimate New Yorker'?: Urban rat videos and their media reception. *Society & Animals* (published online 8 January).

Luther, E. (2018). Urban wildlife organizations and the institutional entanglements of conservation's urban turn. *Society & Animals, 26(2)*, 186–96.

Margulies, J.D. (2019). On coming into animal presence with photovoice. *Environment and Planning E: Nature and Space, 2(4)*, 831–49.

Meijer, E. (2019). *When animals speak: Toward an interspecies democracy*. New York: New York University Press.

Michelfelder, D.P. (2018). Urban wildlife ethics: Beyond 'parallel planes'. *Environmental Ethics, 40(2)*, 101–17. DOI: 10.5840/enviroethics201840212

O'Doherty D.P. (2017). Animals and organization: Feline politics and the nine lives of 'Olly the Cat'. In *Reconstructing Organization* (pp. 215–43). London: Palgrave Macmillan.

Schlosberg, D. (2016). Environmental management in the Anthropocene. In T. Gabrielson et al. (Eds.), *The Oxford handbook of environmental political theory* (pp. 193–210). Oxford: Oxford University Press.

Shivik, J.A. (2014). *The predator paradox: Ending the war with wolves, bears, cougars, and coyotes*. Boston: Beacon Press.

Simons, E. (2020). A new alpha coyote takes over in San Francisco's Presidio. *Bay Nature Magazine*, 24 January, https://baynature.org/2020/01/24/a-new-alpha-coyote-takes-over-in-san-franciscos-presidio/.

Srinivasan, K. (2019). Remaking more-than-human society: Thought experiments on street dogs as 'nature'. *Transactions of the Institute of British Geographers, 44(2)*, 376–91.

Steele, W., Wiesel, I., & Maller, C. (2019). More-than-human cities: Where the wild things are. *Geoforum, 106*, 411–15.

Thomsen, D.C. (2015). Seeing is questioning: Prompting sustainability discourses through an evocative visual agenda. *Ecology and Society, 20(4)*, Article 9.

Todd, K. (2018). Coyote tracker: San Francisco's uneasy embrace of a predator's return. *Bay Nature Magazine*, 2 January, https://baynature.org/article/coyote-tracker-san-francisos-uneasy-embrace-of-a-predators-return/.

Rutherford, S. (2018). The Anthropocene's animal? Coywolves as feral cotravelers. *Environment and Planning E: Nature and Space, 1(1–2),* 206–23.

Van Patter, L.E. (2021). Individual animal geographies for the more-than-human city: Storying synanthropy and cynanthropy with urban coyotes. *Environment and Planning E: Nature and Space,* December.

von Essen, E., Allen, M., & Tickle, L. (2020). Game of drones: On the moral significance of deception in modern sport hunting. *The Philosophical Journal of Conflict and Violence, 4(2),* 137–57.

Walkaboutlou. (2018). Observations of coyote behavior on ranches, by 'Walkaboutlou'. Coyote Yipps, https://coyoteyipps.com/2018/10/09/observations-of-coyote-behavior-on-ranches-by-walkaboutlou/.

Way, J.G. & Lynn, W.S. (2016). Northeastern coyote/coywolf taxonomy and admixture: A meta-analysis. *Canid Biology & Conservation, 19(1),* 1–7.

Weckel, M. & Wincorn, A. (2016). Urban conservation: The northeastern coyote as a flagship species. *Landscape and Urban Planning, 150,* 10–15.

CHAPTER 10

IMAGINING STORIES OF AND WITH ANIMALS AT WORK

Care, Embodiment, and Voice-Giving in Human-Equine Work

LUCY CONNOLLY

INTRODUCTION

In noting that 'humans behave differently with animals than they do with other people' Hannah and Robertson (2017: 117) indicate the potentially fertile territory that human-animal work (HAW) provides for organizational theory. Defining HAW as 'human work that is substantially focused on live *non-hum*an animals' (Hannah and Robertson, 2017: 116), such work as it pertains to horses offers the opportunity for particularly significant insights. Engaging with horses is more dangerous than caring for cats or dogs (Brandt, 2009), given their size, speed, and their having 'the mental and physical characteristics of a prey animal rather than a predator' (Keaveney, 2008: 444). The fact that horses are ridden adds an extra element to an embodied relationship (Brandt, 2009; Maurstad, Davis, and Cowles, 2013).

Noting the specialized nature of the relationship of care between human and horse, Finkel and Danby (2019: 389) use the term 'equiscapes' which are 'viewed as leisure "working" environments, where investments in time, resources and emotions are framed in work discourses in order to legitimize efforts and expenditure'. Having horses as companions, then, is 'work', even if not for financial return. The extra dimension added by remunerated, instrumental equine work that makes it 'human-animal work' (Hannah and Robertson, 2017) provides possibilities for a similar richness to that which appears in the context of recreational equine experiences. Such work may involve breeding horses, training them to be ridden, teaching others how to ride, or even coaching people how to train their own horses to be ridden. Equine work may also involve the running of a livery yard—the care of other people's horses for a fee—and would include such duties as mucking out stables, feeding, exercising, worming, and grooming the horses under their care. For their part, horses have been constructed as similarly engaging in 'work', whether it be the emotional labour of keeping people safe (Dashper, 2020) or the combined partnership of shared embodied activities to achieve a common goal (Birke and Hockenhull, 2015; Brandt, 2009).

This chapter explores how the narrative practices of 20 participants engaging in human-equine work construct caring relationships between themselves and the horses with whom they work. It demonstrates, through use of the Listening Guide method (Gilligan and Eddy, 2017; Sorsoli and Tolman, 2008; Woodcock, 2016) for interpreting interview transcripts, how they make use of their caring imaginations to construct voice on behalf of these horses. While acknowledging that such constructions do not claim to reflect the reality of the lived experiences of horses, this novel use of the Listening Guide method acknowledges the power implicit in both the interview process and such narrative constructions, while also enabling a window into the creation of the two-sided relationship necessary for the completion of care, where only one party in the relationship has 'voice'.

'Voicing' Animals

While animals do not possess verbal language akin to what humans have, the term 'voice' is used to describe utterances made by animals, or indeed the effect of these utterances, for example on the hunting field (Marvin, 2009). Here, a 'mute' (p. 37) hound is of no value and silence is, more broadly speaking, considered to be the burden of the 'dumb beast' without ability to have or express thoughts. While Suen (2015: 12) offers the possibility of seeing the silence of animals as 'an active form of resistance that conjures its own power', history has seen humans deliberately silence animals so as not to hear their voices, for example during painful experimentation procedures (Luke, [1992] 2007). Furthermore, verbal language has been used for 'the manufacturing of consent within the human population for the oppression and exploitation of the animal population' (Stibbe, 2001: 147). It achieves this through terms of objectification and ownership, turning pigs into pork, 'an instrumental resource or an inert material from which all value is extracted' (Sayers, 2016: 373). Silencing animals enables humans to 'speak over' the animals' own forms of communication, leaving them vulnerable to domination (Hamilton and Taylor, 2013). However, to achieve some sort of representation in our social spaces, nonhumans may need someone to 'give voice' to their side of the story. 'Speaking for', therefore, can become an action 'necessary for both animal liberation *and* animal exploitation, despite their conflicting goals' (Suen, 2015: 14).

'Giving voice' to animals is an activity achieved in relation, rather than in opposition. Such relationships are developed through time spent in interaction, observation, and the 'empathetic partaking of the perspective of the other' (Sanders and Arluke, 1993: 384). In the case of horse-human relationships, Birke, Hockenhull, and Creighton

(2010) show how knowledge surrounding how best to care for horses is situated within social networks, where humans and horses alike are seen to have a degree of agency. The voices of the human-animal workers in this chapter's research speak to understand what is going on in both their own bodies and those of the horses. They 'give voice' to their belief in what these bodily responses mean, both by constructing narratives for themselves and for me as the interviewer, and by literally 'voicing' the equine' side of the 'conversations' between them as caregiver and cared-for. This interaction of body and voice enables the construction of caring practices which are informed by direct experiences, empathetic relationship (Slote, 2007) and critical, imaginative reflection (Hamington, 2004). If the act of 'giving voice' by human-animal workers is to be heard in our organizational enquiry, then a technique which is flexible enough to capture the innovative ways this voice can be presented, yet sensitive enough to the ethics that pertain to such dynamics, is required. This chapter offers the Listening Guide method as one possible technique through which we can explore the construction of the animal voice.

Using the Listening Guide to Hear the Equine 'Voice'

This research takes place within a social constructionist framework, with relationships acting as sites where 'the world comes to be what it is for us' (Gergen, 2009: 3). Consistent with this philosophy of knowledge production, I utilized a form of 'active' interviewing (Holstein and Gubrium, 1995) where both interviewer and participant co-construct meaning. As a co-producer of knowledge, my form and tone of questioning, as well as my own silences and interruptions, influenced the narrative that was produced (Mishler, 1986). While the interviews carried out were informal in nature, a set of questions was prepared and adjusted during the early stages of fieldwork, focusing particularly on stories of care, interaction, and relationships in their work with horses.

The research used a technique of purposive sampling from the population of interest which resulted in there being 20 participants, including horse breeders, trainers, coaches, yard managers, and livery managers. There was no distinction as to gender during the sampling process, to acknowledge that all genders 'can position themselves alike in the ways they describe caregiving' (Holstein and Gubrium, 1995: 26). Overall, the group is coherent in that their work with horses, either full- or part-time, can be considered a job, one which is undertaken for, amongst other reasons, a level of financial return. The interviews were recorded with the participants' consent and anonymized.

Derived from care theory (see Brown and Gilligan, 1992; Gilligan, 2015), the 'Listening Guide' method involves attending to voices of relationship through a number of 'listenings' which can be adapted to suit a particular research question. An emerging technique, it has already been utilized to uncover different voices contrapuntally expressed as the mental processes of one person or narrator (Gilligan et al., 2006;

Gilligan, 2015; Sorsoli and Tolman, 2008). It generally requires at least four different 'listenings' of the text or transcript. The first is to assess the 'plot' of the narrative and the researcher's response to what is heard, as well as to the participant themselves. This listening also provides the opportunity to note any words or themes that stand out, as well as potentially sensitive information to be omitted from further interpretation. This acts to maintain trust and protect the relationship with the participant as foremost in the research process (Clandinin and Connelly, 2000).

The second listening is to attend to the voice 'I' in the text. This allows the researcher to note how the participant speaks of themselves before the researcher does (Brown and Gilligan, 1992; Gilligan et al., 2006). This stage 'represents an attempt to hear the person, agent or actor, voice her or his sense of agency, while also recognizing the social location of this person who is speaking' (Mauthner and Doucet, 1998: 130). The third and subsequent listenings are for voices of relationship. These listenings are informed by the research question, which is used 'as a touchstone and to listen for and identify voices that inform the inquiry' (Gilligan and Eddy, 2017: 79). During this phase, the researcher is enabled to go back through the transcript to identify any patterns, reflecting this method's iterative nature and the need to 'fine-tune' (Gilligan et al., 2006: 266). The final listening involves the writing of a memo outlining what was learned from the interview and how it answers the research question. Further iterative moves can occur when analysing across several interviews as new voices and themes arise, requiring a fresh look at voices already heard in previously analysed transcripts (Gilligan et al., 2006).

In a turn particular to the nature of my research question, voice poems were also created for the horses themselves. This was done by highlighting on the text each time the participant 'gave voice' to the horse by literally speaking for them, thereby attributing subjectivity, preferences, and beliefs (Regan, 2004) to them. In passages where the participant gave voice to their own 'I', as well as to the horse, these 'poems' reveal how the two voices interact, where they are in conflict and where in harmony (Gilligan et al., 2006; Gilligan, 2015), accepting that the 'voice' of the horse is but another voice of the participant themselves. In this way, the Listening Guide provides a template that is structured, while encouraging flexibility and innovation (Woodcock, 2016). It is this very innovation that reveals the creation of the animal voice as a way of accessing the expression of empathy that is required if we are to 'speak for' (Suen, 2015) and advocate, rather than 'speak over' (Hamilton and Taylor, 2013) or silence their representation in our social spaces.

The Listening Guide in Action—'Diane'

To illustrate the Listening Guide in action, I provide an exemplar, 'Diane', and outline the steps taken during each of the various listenings. Diane is a coach and trainer, with whom I spoke for over an hour. As well as fulfilling the definition of a human-animal worker that underpins this research, the innovative nature of Diane's work and her openness to discussing it with me, even though we had never met before, contributed significantly to my findings.

First Listening

Listening to the audio recording again refreshed the interview in my mind as some time had passed since we had talked. It allowed me to tune in once more to Diane's voice and our conversation.

> **Excerpt from memo of first listening:**
>
> Diane speaks thoughtfully, often pausing as she considers her responses to my questions deeply. I can hear her constructing her ideas while I listen back over the audio, with her stopping sentences and sometimes trailing off, 'I don't know', as she tries to put shape on her thoughts which are, in many ways, unknowable, but not less important for that. I appreciate her efforts as it is clear to me while listening that she is really engaging with the subject matter openly and honestly with her, sometimes incomplete, sentences emphasizing how unknowable some of these interactions are … Also, the relationship between us as interviewer and participant sounds relaxed and comfortable, with a good rapport developed. I obviously felt comfortable enough, where elsewhere I might be silent, to share that I have a pony, have done horsemanship courses, etc., which would be seen as a risk, but I think enhanced our rapport and facilitated an open and thoughtful discussion.

The next phase of the first listening involved going through the transcript again to highlight any pertinent ideas, feelings, and themes. I also reviewed the entry in my reflective diary written upon arriving home after the interview, as well as any notes taken during, immediately after, and at the transcription phase. During this read through, I also highlighted passages for omission from further analysis. These included those contributions that I was asked to omit, references to others, potentially sensitive passages, and those not addressing Diane's experience of her work. For transparency, the page numbers and details of these passages, as well as the reasons for omission, were logged. Details of Diane's background with horses, where and how she learned her caring practices (Hamington, 2004) with horses, were also noted. I familiarized myself further with the emerging themes and concepts and noted these insights, together with the relevant page numbers, to assist in the later stages in the Listening Guide process.

Second Listening

I listened to the recording of Diane's interview again. This time, I underlined on the transcript every time 'I' appears, taking note of those passages pertaining to horse-human interaction. I did not include those passages that were omitted after the first listening. I then reproduced these 'I' poems on a separate sheet. This process revealed the words and expressions that arise most often with the 'I', across a range of physical, emotional, and mental processes, for example, 'I hurt', 'I fear', 'I feel', 'I love', as well as 'I know', 'I think', 'I wonder'. The negations of such expressions were also revealed, such as 'I don't think', 'I don't know'. I also noted the 'he/she' and 'we' that arise when she speaks of and with the horse:

Excerpt from transcript of interview with Diane:

D: One of them has— like the time I hurt my back really badly a few years ago and one of them was off for the whole summer. Like he was— there was just something he wasn't putting his head up as high and he was slightly lame but not full— not anything that I could— like the vet could pick up or anything. It was just a slight little offness. And I remember one day I went to this guy for my back and I came back feeling really, really good and I went down to the field and I was— it sounds stupid, but I was really trying to tell him I was okay. And he was like, like he was 15 or 16, he turned into a five-year-old. And he started running up and down and his head was higher than it had been all summer. He kept whinnying and calling me up the field like when I was walking away from him, he kept whinnying and kept calling and like so I totally think he was carrying some of that for me.

I hurt	
	he was-
	he wasn't putting his head up as high
	he was slightly lame
not anything that I could-	
I remember	
I went to this guy	
I came back feeling really, really good	
I went down to the field	
I was-	
I was really trying to tell him I was okay.	
	he was like, like he was 15 or 16,
	he turned into a five-year-old.
	he started running up and down
	his head was higher
	He kept whinnying and calling me up the field
I was walking away from him	
	he kept whinnying and kept calling
I totally think	
	he was carrying some of that for me.

Separating out when Diane uses 'I' and 'he', enabled me to see the interaction of these two bodies, how Diane expresses the human pain worn by the horse, followed by the relief of pain for both. I interpreted this as an instance of Diane's caring imagination, where an exchange of empathy and the joint knowledge of experiencing the world through flesh (Hamington, 2004) is constructed.

Next, I took note of any passages where Diane 'speaks for' the horses and wrote this down, parallel to the 'I' poems and in the relevant order. This produced a total of seven human-horse 'voice poems' and drew my attention to the utterances of the horses, many of which were missed on the first reading. These seven voice poems revealed to me 'conversations' between Diane and her horses, stripped back to where both parties to the conversations are positioned in relation to the other. While Diane's own side is voiced during the interview narrative itself, the horses' sides are 'voiced' by her using direct speech, as if they are present and 'talking' themselves. Each passage of 'speech' from the horse is either a response to, or initiating a response from, Diane. They provide insight into how Diane imagines what the horses are feeling and thinking in each corresponding moment. Voicing their side appears to facilitate Diane in her own imaginative construction of their points of view:

Third Listening

Example of voice poem:

D: And so, like three or four of them right in front of me, one came and drank from a puddle, another came and drank from the trough or went to the trough, wet his mouth and came out again. And it's like they're just kind of saying <u>'Here come on, check this'</u>. Even though <u>I had seen</u> it, <u>but I was still checking</u> them all to see if they were okay, they're just like giving me the heads up.

'Here come on, check this'.

I had seen
but I was still checking

This listening was informed by the research question of how the roles of caregiver and cared-for are narratively constructed in human-animal work. I therefore sought to investigate voices of caring relationships and interaction. This listening was also inspired by the previous listenings for the 'I' and the expressed 'voice' of the horses. I asked myself 'where is the horse?' in each of these passages and 'what are they doing?' when responding to, or with, Diane.

In this listening, moments of harmony are expressed through the construction of desire on the part of the horse, as well as occasions when horse and human are constructed as being in connection with each other. Moments of conflict are expressed through the appearance of resistance on the part of the horse. I noted all the passages where the interactions appeared to reveal instances of these states and examined how Diane responds in each of the passages. These responses were then read as moments of caregiving, acted bodily but recounted narratively, using her sense of speech to report on the giving of care through sight, hearing, and sense of touch. In return, the horses' physical actions, such as jumping or running away, stopping, failing to move, etc., were all 'voiced' as imaginatively constructing a mental process on the part of the horse that was acting upon, or reacting to, Diane as caregiver.

All the passages involving interaction between Diane and a horse were documented in a similar way to highlight any recurring themes.

> *Excerpt from memo of third listening:*
>
> D: We always teach them that, how to come off pressure away from the horsebox and then we were just at a standstill and I don't know (.) I don't know how it came to me but I was try—really trying to tell her it was okay, but I just got the feeling that she didn't feel she'd enough space, that she was going to run on top- that she felt she was going to damage me if she came in, so like we—we just tried taking out the partition then … so I was just rubbing her shoulder and, eh, I was really trying to tell her you know 'it will be okay, it will be okay' and then she just took a step in and then took another step and we just walked in through and out— like gave her a break when we came out. So, it's like getting her in, then taking the pressure off and letting her out, so it's like job done. It's not like getting her in and closing up and going.

Annotations:
- Use of 'we' to denote herself and the horse together.
- Diane's use of 'gut' feeling, from physical proximity? Her gut informing caring imagination, how the horse feels, sharing physicality.
- Fear as care on the part of the horse, doesn't want to injure. Horse here expressing resistance actually as a way of practicing care?? Diane's caring imagination, that is how she reads it.
- Diane's response to improve situation. Who is 'we'? Assume another human?
- Horse responding to care. Given choice and breaking down resistance.
- 'We' here is Diane and the horse acting together. Importance of taking it slowly, giving horse a break. Horse and human in connection.
- Use of physical contact to express care. Care as embodied. Shoulder rub means 'it will be okay' in that moment, articulated as such in the context of the interview with me. Importance of touch & feel.

Fourth Listening

This final listening was carried out to gain an overall view of how the interview with Diane contributed to the research question. Over the course of the entire analysis stage, more clarity regarding the substance of the themes and concepts began to arise.

'Oh my God! She speaks horse!'

The second listenings proved particularly useful in revealing the constructed voice of the horses, when the participants 'speak' for their horses. Lining these horse 'voice poems' up in parallel to the 'I' poems allowed me to see how the participant locates both parties to these 'conversations'. In this way, the horses are made present in the narratives and their 'speech' is constructed as either a response to, or initiating a response from, the human participant. This listening revealed the link between how the horses' bodies are spoken of and how their 'speech' reflects these bodily movements. Careful examination highlights the points at which the horses 'speak' and then the imagined explanations of this speech.

Following others making use of this method (see e.g. Davis, 2015; Gilligan et al., 2006; Gilligan and Eddy, 2017; Sorsoli and Tolman, 2008), I make use of different fonts to offer a window into my interpretation process. **Bold** is used to highlight the 'voice' of the horse and *italics* are used to highlight the imagined thought processes that give rise to the horse 'talking', while <u>double underline</u> is used to highlight the bodily movements of the horses that are 'translated' into thoughts and, eventually, speech.

If we return to the voice poem in the excerpt from Diane's transcript above, the horses' 'voice' is constructed from their apparent behaviour. They 'ask' for care, specifically that Diane checks their water:

> DIANE: And so, like three or four of them right in front of me, <u>one came and drank from a puddle, another came and drank from the trough or went to the trough, wet his mouth and came out again</u>. And it's like they're just kind of saying **'Here come on, check this'**. Even though I had seen it, but I was still checking them all to see if they were okay, *they're just like giving me the heads up.*

Even though she was already aware of it, Diane does not miss their giving her 'the heads up' as she sees it. She voices their direct request to her that she sort out their water. The horses are constructed as knowing who their caregiver is and how to communicate with her to make their preferences known, by moving their bodies in the direction of the solution.

Similar voice poems were heard across all the interview narratives. Another coach and trainer, Tina, describes a moment, expressed through the horse's body but vocalized by Tina, when her horse is constructed as realizing that the human understands her:

> TINA: ... And I would start walking towards her middle where you'd put the saddle, start walking. And every time I'd see <u>the breathing start to change</u>, I'd stop and step back away from her and go away from her. Every time. And after about six or seven times it was the most hysterical thing. I— I went to— to walk towards her and <u>she didn't breathe harder</u> and I walked up and I put a hand on her. And <u>then she started to tense just a little bit</u> and I took the hand off and I walked away again. <u>And she went (gestures turning her head right around and making a quizzical face)</u>. *She realized that I was paying attention to her opinion and what she thought about things and was reacting to what she thought about things.* And she was— I mean, <u>she nearly fell over</u>. *She couldn't— She couldn't believe it.* She— **'Oh my God! You know what I—? You understood that? Oh my God! She speaks horse!'**

The mare's bodily movements appear to be constructed as reflecting a thought process, that is that Tina cares about her opinion. This thought process is then given voice. An almost dancelike movement can be visualized between Tina and the horse. As Tina steps forward, the horse reacts, causing Tina to step back. This movement is interpreted by the horse as Tina respecting her preferences, thereby building trust and connection. 'Speaking horse' is a way for Tina to demonstrate how she believes the horse felt understood in that moment. In this way, being understood is articulated through 'speaking' the language of another.

Geraldine, another coach and trainer, tells a similar story of a working partnership between her and one of the horses in her riding school. In this passage, coach and horse are constructed as creating knowledge together to care for the rider and teach them to hold their body in the most correct and effective way:

> Geraldine: … there's one there called (names horse) <u>who will do literally what the rider says but in a way where she's going</u> 'Get a clue! I'm doing this sideways coz you're sittin' sideways.' … 'Come on, figure it out!' And you know, when you're teaching with her and then <u>she'd be looking at you</u> kind of going 'Go on tell her what to do properly' … And then when she does it right, *she's really happy again*. She's like 'Yeah!' *She gets really kind of content that the person's figured it out.*

Here, Geraldine becomes someone who can read her horses' expressions and know what they are thinking. The horse is presented as imploring the person on her back to read her movements as a sign that they are asking the wrong questions. Rather than acting out of self-preservation, Geraldine imagines the horse as wanting the rider to get it right and attributes joy to her when the rider finally figures it out. In this way, the horse is constructed as participating as a teacher rather than just as a prop in the context of the lesson.

Discussion: 'What If They Could Talk?'

During the data collection phase, this question proved to be a nice talking point as it provided an opportunity for the participants, and indeed myself, to let loose our imaginations and create alternative worlds where horses could speak and understand speech in our terms. Naturally, such a dynamic would fundamentally change the nature of human-animal work. It is therefore not surprising that they do not all express a desire for such a possibility to come true. Where they answer that they would like if the horses could speak, this was based on improving welfare outcomes and the opportunity for dialogue with the different characters they had constructed in their narratives. Where they elect to stick to the status quo, a world where horses cannot talk, they imagine hearing negative things or are rejecting what they believe to be the dishonestly verbal world of humans. Overall, the ability to speak on the part of the horse does not appear to be a requirement for the participants. A competent caregiver is constructed by the participants as one who is skilled at embodied interaction, at reading the horses, and 'listening' with their eyes, ears, and sense of feel. As a result, the response 'but they do speak!' is not uncommon across their narratives.

Noddings (2013: 19) describes various ways in which the cared-for can be responsive to the caregiver, beyond verbal acknowledgement: 'The one cared-for sees the concern, delight, or interest in the eyes of the one-caring and feels her warmth in both verbal and body language'. While recognizing that 'we inevitably consider response in relation to human response' (Noddings, 2013: 151–2), she speaks of the responsiveness of animals, again expressed through bodily actions such as the 'purring, rubbing, nibbling' (p. 156) of her cat. She refers to her own bodily processes, such as hearing and seeing, when describing how she becomes moved to care. The bodily aspect of care, therefore, appears as a natural element in its practice. According to Hamington (2004: 69), the caring imagination is one aspect of this embodied care, along with caring knowledge and caring habits: 'When we come to care about that which we have experienced only indirectly or not at all, the caring imagination draws from its wealth of tacit body knowledge to make the connecting leap'.

This caring imagination interacts with embodied caring knowledge 'to create points of departure for developing responsive interconnections that inform action' (Phillips, 2016: 477). This is a process that is intellectual as well as felt in the body, as meaning is created upon further critical reflection (Hamington, 2004). Thus, care is enabled through narrative practice (Lawrence and Maitlis, 2012) as the roles of both caregiver and nonverbal cared-for can be imaginatively constructed. The participants in this research suggest that the silence of the nonverbal animal provides an opportunity to get away from the verbal, to enter the world of their own bodies, which in turn facilitates the development of their own empathetic engagement with embodied others (Hamington, 2008). They appear to trust their imaginations to provide them with accurate knowledge and do not necessarily require verbal instruction.

Anthropomorphism, the attribution of human thoughts and beliefs to nonhumans, is something that is generally feared by those who work with animals (Karlsson, 2012) and the participants in this study no less so. A number express their desire to avoid it or clarify that they do not approach their horses in this way, presumably aware of the potential for error when projecting human perspectives onto a nonhuman other. Despite this, each one of their narratives includes horse 'voice-poems' or occasions where they give verbal speech to the horses' sides of the conversations that they construct. This seems to confirm Karlsson's (2012) contention that avoiding anthropomorphism entirely is not possible when seeking to learn about animals. While not perfect, 'the aim must never be to forbid a certain kind of symbol when communicating thoughts on animals, but to describe animals well' (Karlsson, 2012: 719). Hamington (2008: 184) appears to agree, stating how the practice of anthropomorphizing 'often represents an imaginative or playful attempt to understand animals'. Others have spoken of the potentially positive aspects to the use of anthropomorphism with horses, including its role in maintaining welfare and the human-horse relationship (Thompson and Clarkson, 2019). The projection of various human emotions onto horses by their caretakers would appear to have some support in the scientific literature (Hötzel, Vieira, and Leme, 2019). The participants in this chapter's research seem to make use of anthropomorphic 'voicing' as an attempt to understand their horses and to empathetically imagine what they are 'saying'. By revealing the link between embodied interaction and voice-giving, the human-animal workers in this research appear to be attempting to make the connection between the behaviour of the horses and what they are 'thinking'. Translating these thoughts into words gives them a way to imagine the needs of the horses and to respond as best they can.

In conclusion, this chapter demonstrates the ability of the Listening Guide method to reveal constructions of voice on behalf of another and, as such, has applicability to other scenarios of human-animal interaction. While seeking to represent the point of view of this other, the participants herein are similarly offering an additional construction of themselves. The practice of voice-giving appears to facilitate understanding in themselves by connecting them with their own felt experiences and bodily habits. I therefore suggest that the Listening Guide technique may have applications in more ethnographic methods, perhaps even an auto-ethnography in an animal-related context. Its flexibility and sensitivity to context may facilitate the researcher themselves to 'feel' the various sensations in their own bodies and examine how they construct voice by analysing their own narratives of care, thereby directly experiencing their personal constructions of the animal voice, as well as the construction of an alternative voiced self.

The application of the Listening Guide to other contractual animal-based contexts, particularly dairy, beef, sheep, and pig farms, or any such industry where the body of the animal becomes the product, might offer interesting insights. Such a care-based methodological approach could be taken to understand the experience of farmers who move from a caregiving role to having to send their animals to slaughter. This could be a response to Anthony (2012), who suggests that an ethic of care approach might offer a counter to the invisibility of animals in a mechanized, industrial, 'hands-off', farming system.

In this research, there arose some occasions where the horses are constructed as acting as caregivers towards their humans. Utilizing the Listening guide method to investigate this idea might have merit. While work has been done on the role of assistance animals (see Charles and Wolkowitz, 2019; Hunter, Verreynne, Pachana et al., 2019), exploring voice-giving from the other side, that is, animals 'giving voice' to humans, in such contexts as special needs supports (Suen, 2015), might reveal additional thought-provoking results.

By placing the duties of relationship at its core, the Listening Guide method emphasizes the importance of ethical behaviour as part of the research process. I believe this technique has much to offer the study of human-animal interaction and I hope that it becomes more widely, and innovatively, used within this sphere of scholarship.

References

Anthony, R. (2012). Building a sustainable future for animal agriculture: An environmental virtue ethic of care approach within the philosophy of technology. *Journal of Agricultural and Environmental Ethics, 25,* 123–44.

Birke, L. & Hockenhull, J. (2015). Journeys together: Horses and humans in partnership. *Society and Animals, 23,* 81–100.

Birke, L., Hockenhull, J., & Creighton, E. (2010). The horse's tale: Narratives of caring for/about horses. *Society and Animals, 18,* 331–47.

Brandt, K. (2009). Human-horse communication. In A. Arluke & C. Sanders (Eds.), *Between the species: Readings in human-animal relations* (pp. 315–20). Boston: Pearson Education Inc.

Brown, L.M. & Gilligan, C. (1992). *Meeting at the crossroads: Women's psychology and girls' development.* Cambridge, London: Harvard University Press.

Charles, N. & Wolkowitz, C. (2019). Bringing dogs onto campus: Inclusions and exclusions of animal bodies in organizations. *Gender, Work and Organization, 26(3),* 303–21.

Clandinin, D.J. & Connelly, F.M. (2000). *Narrative inquiry: Experience and story in quality research.* San Francisco: Jossey Bass.

Dashper, K. (2020). More-than-human emotions: Multispecies emotional labour in the tourism industry. *Gender, Work and Organization, 27,* 24–40.

Davis, B.R. (2015). Harmony, dissonance, and the gay community: A dialogical approach to same-sex desiring men's sexual identity development. *Qualitative Psychology, 2(1),* 78–95.

Finkel, R. & Danby, P. (2019). Legitimizing leisure experiences as emotional work: A posthumanist approach to gendered equine encounters. *Gender, Work and Organization, 26(3),* 377–91.

Gergen, K.J. (2009). *An invitation to social constructionism.* London: SAGE.

Gilligan, C. (2015). The listening guide method of psychological inquiry. *Qualitative Psychology, 2(1),* 69–77.

Gilligan, C. et al. (2006). On the listening guide: A voice-centered relational method. In S.N. Hesse-Biber & P. Leavy (Eds.), *Emergent methods in social research* (pp. 253–71). California, London: Sage Publications.

Gilligan, C. & Eddy, J. (2017). Listening as a path to psychological discovery: An introduction to the listening guide. *Perspectives in Medical Ethics, 6,* 76–81.

Hamington, M. (2004). *Embodied care: Jane Addams, Maurice Merleau-Ponty and feminist ethics.* Urbana and Chicago: University of Illinois Press.

Hamington, M. (2008). Learning ethics from our relationships with animals: Moral imagination. *International Journal of Applied Philosophy, 22(2),* 177–88.

Hamilton, L. & Taylor, N. (2013). *Animals at work: Identity, politics and culture in work with animals.* Leiden: Brill.

Hannah, D.R. & Robertson, K. (2017). Human-animal work: A massive, understudied domain of human activity. *Journal of Management Inquiry, 26(1),* 116–18.

Holstein, J. A., & Gubrium, J. F. (1995). *The active interview.* SAGE Publications, Inc. https://dx.doi.org/10.4135/9781412986120

Hötzel, M.J., Vieira, M.C., & Leme, D. (2019). Exploring horse owners' and caretakers' perceptions of emotions and associated behaviors in horses. *Journal of Veterinary Behavior, 29,* 18–24.

Hunter, C. et al. (2019). The impact of disability-assistance animals on the psychological health of workplaces: A systematic review. *Human Resource Management Review, 29(3),* 400–17.

Karlsson, F. (2012). Critical anthropomorphism and animal ethics. *Journal of Agricultural Ethics, 25,* 707–20.

Keaveney, S.M. (2008). Equines and their human companions. *Journal of Business Research, 61,* 444–54.

Lawrence, T.B. & Maitlis, S. (2012). Care and possibility: Enacting an ethic of care through narrative practice. *Academy of Management Review, 37(4),* 641–63.

Luke, B. ([1992] 2007). Justice, caring, and animal liberation. In J. Donovan & C.J. Adams (Eds.), *The feminist care tradition in animal ethics* (pp. 125–52). New York: Columbia University Press.

Marvin, G. (2009). Creating and representing foxhounds. In A. Arluke & C. Sanders (Eds.), *Between the species: Readings in human-animal relations* (pp. 34–9). Boston: Pearson Education Inc.

Maurstad, A., Davis, D., & Cowles, S. (2013). Co-being and intra-action in horse-human relationships: A multi-species ethnography of be(com)ing human and be(com)ing horse. *Social Anthropology, 21(3),* 322–35.

Mauthner, N. & Doucet, A. (1998). Reflections on a voice-centred relational method: Analysing maternal and domestic voices. In J. Ribbens & R. Edwards (Eds.), *Feminist dilemmas in qualitative research* (pp. 119–46). London: SAGE.

Mishler, E.G. (1986). *Research interviewing: Context and narrative.* Cambridge, MA: Harvard University Press.

Noddings, N. (2013). *Caring: A relational approach to ethics and moral education,* 2nd Edition. Berkeley, Los Angeles: University of California Press.

Phillips, M. (2016). Embodied care and planet earth: Ecofeminism, maternalism and postmaternalism. *Australian Feminist Studies, 31(90),* 468–85.

Regan, T. (2004). *The case for animal rights,* 2nd Edition. Berkeley: University of California Press.

Sanders, C.R. & Arluke, A. (1993). If lions could speak: Investigating the animal-human relationship and the perspectives of nonhuman others. *The Sociological Quarterly, 34(3),* 377–90.

Sayers, J.G. (2016). A report to an academy: On carnophallogocentrism, pigs and meat-writing. *Organization, 23(3),* 370–86.

Slote, M. (2007). *The ethics of care and empathy.* London, New York: Routledge.

Sorsoli, L. & Tolman, D.L. (2008). Hearing voices: Listening for multiplicity and movement in interview data. In S.N. Hesse-Biber & P. Leavy (Eds.), *Handbook of emergent methods* (pp. 495–515). New York, London: The Guilford Press.

Stibbe, A. (2001). Language, power and the social construction of animals. *Society and Animals, 9(2),* 145–61.

Suen, A. (2015). *The speaking animal: Ethics, language and the human-animal divide.* London, New York: Rowman & Littlefield.

Thompson, K. & Clarkson, L. (2019). How owners determine if the social and behavioural needs of their horses are being met: Findings from an Australian online survey. *Journal of Veterinary Behavior, 29,* 128–33.

Woodcock, C. (2016). The listening guide: A how-to approach on ways to promote educational democracy. *International Journal of Qualitative Methods, 15(1),* 1–10.

CHAPTER 11

WILD PEDAGOGIES FOR DOING MULTISPECIES ORGANIZATIONAL ETHNOGRAPHY

Using the Tracking Craft of the Southern African San

HARRY WELS AND FRANS KAMSTEEG

INTRODUCTION: WHY WILDNESS WORKS

ORGANIZATIONAL ethnography has gone through multiple 'turns' in its relatively short history. It started as a cultural turn in Western organization and management studies in the late 1970s, but has since then moved in many directions, often related to the constantly changing world of organizations and organizing itself (Rouleau, De Rond, and Musca, 2014). While for some it is predominantly a method, it has increasingly been promoted as a discipline (Neyland, 2008; Van Maanen, 2011; Ybema et al., 2009). There is a strong tendency towards discourse, narrative, and storytelling but given ethnography's focus on everyday sensemaking, its tales cover a huge variety of topics and fields (Van Maanen, 2010). However, the fields covered in organizational ethnography are primarily in the Western world and within those fields it is also mostly Western problems that are studied (Nkomo, 2011; Özkazanç-pan, 2008). In our contribution, we expand on one of the recent innovations in organizational ethnography, the 'species turn' (Kirksey and Helmreich, 2010), as it has been further developed by Wels in two articles in the *Journal of Organizational Ethnography* (2015; 2020). This turn fundamentally implies a decentring of the human and a shift towards including nonhuman sentient beings (animals and plants). Consequently, multispecies organizational ethnography has entered the debate on the Anthropocene and other –cenes (Harraway, 2016) that has gained considerable weight with the recent ecological crisis. This is by no means a simple move as it requires a fundamental rethinking of the paradoxical relation of (wo)man to the world, and the ways to study it.

In *The Wild Places* Robert Macfarlane (2007) explores how, on the one hand, humans have made tremendous efforts in ordering the wildness of this world by means of 'disenchantment', breaking its resistance, and reducing its lurking dangers. On the other hand, we have been appreciating and even extolling the richness and diversity of the same nature as *wilderness*. The ambiguous relationship that humans maintain with their wild environment consists of the desperate effort to reconcile the belief in human excellence—and the corresponding subjugation of everything nonhuman—with the equally powerful and boundless longing for an ever more vanishing wild nature. Although today's pristine wild places only seem to survive at the fringes of human domestication efforts, Macfarlane's (2007: 321) search for wild places in the United Kingdom ultimately leads him to discover that wildness is unexpectedly resilient but surprisingly showing itself mainly in the cracks of our tamed, cultured, and damaged environment.

Ethnography has always strongly been associated with fieldwork, the endeavour to make sense of what multispecies creatures do in a particular field. The term 'field' has long been understood as a demarcated area or space that humans somehow try to bring under control, physically and/or linguistically. It is hardly a coincidence that the same word, 'field' is used for working the land and bringing coherence to our thinking: both 'culture' and 'agriculture' refer to this human effort to control, 'tame', or 'domesticate' what is wild in the sense of untouched (pristine), unrestricted, and uncontrollable. Similarly, fieldwork as an ethnographic research skill has always aimed at mapping the field of study. Though fields could be wild and messy, ethnographers have reached for order. Until recently, we believed that whenever this 'wild' environment hit back, gaining full control again was just a matter of time. Anthropogenic thinking urges us to come to our senses and see 'wildness as "weaved with the human world"' (Macfarlane, 2007: 227) in what Kirksey (2015: 219) calls 'emergent ecologies' where new assemblages of interspecies collaboration start to flourish and explore 'wild possibilities' in the wrecked and blasted landscapes resulting from human destructiveness and wastefulness worldwide.

Tsing (2015) also writes about these ruined landscapes in her multispecies ethnography on matsutake mushrooms in which she tries to be open to and interpret multispecies relationships to try and understand 'entanglements' and 'indeterminate encounters' between humans and other animals. This is an endeavour concerned with 'trac[ing] the contingencies of unexpected connections' (Kirksey, 2015: 6) between humans, animals and other nonhuman life forms, and 'things' (Latour, 2020), also referred to as 'assemblages' (Haraway, 2008) or emergent ecologies (Kirksey, 2015) in the field of (networks of) organizations. This development in ethnographic thinking emerges from an acceptance of 'entanglements' between diversities of life forms as well as the overwhelming scientific evidence that the Cartesian binary between humans and animals can no longer be sustained (Bekoff, 2007; Bradshaw, 2009; De Waal, 2016;

Fudge, 2002; Meier, 2019; Noske, 1997; Reesink, 2021; Safina, 2015). As Calarco (2007: 149; emphasis in original) puts it, '(i)n brief, *we could simply let the human-animal distinction go*.

Based on shared sentience (Cambridge Declaration, 2012), sensemaking and agency (cf. Despret, 2016; McFarland and Hediger, 2009), life forms and 'things', become entangled in 'emergent ecologies' (Kirksey, 2015) and collaborative diversities made possible by multiple and mutual 'contaminations' (Tsing, 2015: 27–9), similar to what Haraway (2016: 58) conceptualizes as 'sympoiesis'. Humans certainly 'do not have the monopoly on meaning' (Fudge, 2002: 136); sensemaking is a process humans share with other sentient life forms.

Yet no matter the theoretical challenges involved in the 'species turn', in going beyond human exceptionalism, '(i)t [still] seems much easier to theorize about decentring the human than to walk the talk' (Pacini-Kechabaw et al., 2016: 149). Nevertheless, multispecies organizational ethnography aims to analyse and contribute to the re- and bewilderment of the wondrous but wounded world we live in. 'In modernity, mastery usurped mystery', as Macfarlane writes in his *Landmarks* (2016: 25). Following his subsequent plea for a re-wonderment about (wild) nature, now largely turned into what Tsing (2015) calls 'capitalist ruins' created by Western-style domination and exploitation, we need to undo the learning styles and school pedagogies that have come to cover the full field of teaching from kindergarten to academia. We need to move beyond the idea of human exceptionalism, built upon the idea that human bodies are merely the physical cloak of a superior mind that has not only tamed these bodies, but also domesticated and dominated all other living beings, and the wildness of their natural environment (Challenger, 2021).

The implications of this unlearning and 'relearning' for doing and teaching ethnography are not straightforward, for '(t)he challenge of decentring the human within the decidedly humanist practice of social science research cannot be underestimated' (Pacini-Kechabaw et al., 2016: 149). In other words, how do we methodologically go about empirically researching these posthuman emergings in the field (cf. Hamilton and Taylor, 2017)? How do we change the common ethnographic limitation to follow only human traces while observing, interviewing, and participating in 'the everyday' (cf. Atkinson, 2014; Hamersley and Atkinson, 2007)? What has the 'multispecies turn' done to develop a more inclusive set of ethnographic fieldwork methods that we can teach the next generation of fieldworkers? To achieve such an understanding a pedagogy is needed that is wild enough to picture the wildness within and around us and make a contribution to ecological resilience that 'unsettles' the social sciences and humanities (cf. Bird Rose et al., 2012).

To develop such a wild ethnographic pedagogy (cf. Jickling, 2018; see also Irwin, 2019) we propose to turn to the San people of Southern Africa, a hunter-gatherer community which itself has been largely domesticated but, nevertheless, displays a set of paradigmatic skills that can revitalize multispecies ethnography into a multisensorial fieldwork strategy capable of knowing the world by mapping its ecological landscapes.

By doing that it breathes new life into what has been linguistically and operationally instrumentalized for so long (Ijäs, 2017; Tomaselli, 2001; Verbuyst, 2021; Koot, 2018). Liebenberg et al. (2021: 7), including a number of San people, use the metaphor of 'tracking science' as an alternative and more inclusive term to 'citizen science', explicitly blurring standard differences between academic knowledge search and what has often been called Indigenous knowledge production. In their view 'tracking' is similar to gathering and 'monitoring' data, evidences, spores, tracks, and even facts: labels that suddenly lose their traditionally accepted meaning. They equate standard scientific operating procedures with the San tracking practice. Without claiming that these tracking skills will bring a final solution to the challenge of multispecies organizational ethnography, we think that the 'new found respect for non-academic knowledge ...' (Sagarin and Pauchard, 2012: 77), as presented by Liebenberg's San tracking science, literally provides new paths to explore (cf. Bradshaw, 2021: 197–8; Challenger, 2021: 99–106; Kimmerer, 2013; Du Plessis, 2018).

San Tracking Practices

As Tomaselli (2017: 9) argues, '(w)hile the bodies of knowledge and associated bodies of practice relating to multispecies ethnographies are relatively new in the Western academic enterprise, they have, of course, a long history amongst indigenous people who relied on their knowledge of the environment and fauna and flora, the seasons, climate, and astronomy, for their survival and livelihoods' (see also Cohn and Hasharon, 2012). As the San developed and taught each other their tracking skills from generation to generation over the many thousands of years that they roamed the wide arid landscapes of southern Africa (cf. Henn et al., 2011), we can only humbly take inspiration from their fieldwork forms of learning to revitalize, or 'wild', our own pedagogy for teaching and doing multispecies organizational ethnography with current generations of students.

Although their tracking skills are central in San cultural practice, focusing specifically on them could be regarded negatively, as contributing to what Prins (2009: 193) labelled as 'Kalahari San stereotypes' or 'postcard Kalahari San constructions': 'being short in stature, wearing animal skins, hunting with bow and arrow, herding animals, speaking click languages, being close to nature, or residing in a desert climate'. (Verbuyst, 2021: 283). These descriptions have led some anthropologists to label them as an example of 'repressive authenticity' (Wolfe, 1999, cited in Verbuyst, 2021, chapter 7) in which '(a)ny attempt by San people to live out a vision of San-ness that is radically different from the popularly recognized, ... San norm is treated with suspicion [and] regarded as inauthentic' (Ellis, 2015: 130). Hence, while we do focus on San tracking skills in this chapter, we view them as part of the broader ontological ideas about thinking inclusively and beyond binary oppositions, which resonates with current posthumanist thinking (Braidotti, 2019; Latour, 2020).

FIGURE 11.1 Visual expression of 'ontological mutability' (Guenther, 2020b): San rock art. Photo source: Copy of rock shelter images on photographic paper by Harald Pager, Ndedema Gorge in the Drakensberg, South Africa, courtesy Rock Art Research Institute, University of the Witwatersrand.

The San tracking skills are embedded in their cosmology and animated worldview, in which they have always considered nonhuman animals as sensemaking beings, next to humans (Guenther, 2020a; 2020b). Guenther (2020b: 27) claims that the San exhibit an 'ontological blending' that 'becomes ontological entanglement once the perspectivist component is added, that is, the perspective of the animal-other vis à vis the human, in which the former, viewing itself [sic] in the same exceptionalist terms as humans view themselves, views the latter, humans, as other-than-humanimal persons, creating a knot of ontological entanglements conducive to much overlapping or breakdown of species boundaries and identities'. This also means that the hunting and killing of animals by the

San is for reasons of unavoidable food supply, never out of greed, for sport, or without explicit expressed respect for the life they take. What Guenther (2020b: 1) refers to as the San's 'ontological mutability' (see Figure 11.1) also strongly informs their tracking skills (Liebenberg, 2012).

We now provide a description of the bodily and sensory nature of tracking in general and of San tracking skills in particular. In this description we try to convey that 'a study of their [San] view of human-animal relations ... may provide Westerners, specifically recent researchers, cognitive ethologists and other Western "anthrozoologists" who have jettisoned the Cartesian dualist perspective, with helpful clues and insights in their new and novel, intellectually recalibrated take on the age-old question of what is human' (Guenther, 2020b: 3).

For most academics, it is difficult to imagine what tracking means in the endless, vast, and arid landscapes of Southern Africa, with nothing other than your own sensory apparatus and interpretation at your disposal. This may not only be because of unfamiliarity with the Southern African landscapes but also because no matter that '(o)ur senses are our most elemental tools in building an observational understanding of ecological relationships, ... they are often underutilized and sometimes viewed with scepticism in a scientific context' (Sagarin and Pauchard 2012: 47). This difficulty can easily lead academics to brush aside the lifeworld of trackers for what it is, and (re)turn to theory and text, because this is what we are familiar with. But let us try to paint a picture based primarily on Liebenberg (2012) and Ijäs (2017), and some modest tracking experiences by one of us (mainly leading to failures: Wels, 2020: 360, n. 12).

Tracking is a bodily and sensory art (Liebenberg, 2012; Song, 2013); it has to be learned and trained by practicing it and not by reading about it. Tracking, as Tsing (2015) writes, is built on 'commitment to observation and fieldwork', (pp.159–60), the 'arts of noticing (p. 255)', 'searching with all the senses (p. 243)', and constantly needing to 'slow down', since you 'miss most ... if you move too fast'. In Tsing's study it is about tracking *matsutake* mushrooms, but sensuously slowing down is also valid for observing and tracking other kinds of life/beings. At the core of the endeavour is searching for spoor. The originally Dutch word 'spoor' simply means 'footprint' (Liebenberg, 2012: 111), 'the track or trail of an animal' (Walker, 1981: 15), or a mushroom of course.

These 'tracks and trails' are about much more than just 'footprints' though and include various 'signs of animal presence found on the ground or indicated by disturbed vegetation' including 'scent, urine and faeces, saliva, pellets, feeding signs, vocal and other auditory signs, circumstantial signs, blood spoor, skeletal signs, paths, homes and shelters. Spoor are not confined to living creatures. Leaves and twigs rolling in the wind, long grass sweeping the ground or dislodged stones rolling down a steep slope leave their distinctive spoor' (Liebenberg, 2012: 111). Tracking in vast landscapes is clearly the kind of multisensory and experiential skill that the San possess and multisensuous ethnographers dearly require (Stoller 1997; see Figure 11.2).

Paul John Myburgh, who has lived for extensive periods of time with San people and gone with them on many hunting trips, neatly describes their tracking:

FIGURE 11.2 Tracking the landscape with all your senses. Samuel Bak's 'Landscape with five senses', (oil on canvas, 80x104cm). Photo source: Dorotheum Vienna, auction catalogue 26.11.2019.

> The blood spoor on the sand ... with real hunger as a motive it follows that a wounded animal seldom, if ever, escapes a Bushman[1] hunter. Their ability to search for, to find and follow the faintest of signs in such vast and difficult terrain, is unparalleled. It is more than the following of footprints in sand, more than broken glass and blood spots, more than just physical signs ... it is to listen with your fingertips and look with your feet ... it is a feeling in the body that calls to the animal's life-body, and you follow these feelings in yourself as much as you follow the animal ... and in this way, predator and prey, *you come together in sacrifice and redemption*'. (Myburgh, 2013: 92; emphasis added)

---

[1] 'Bushman' is how the Khoisan are popularly known, but the term 'Bushman' is sometimes avoided as potentially offensive to the people to whom it refers, with San often being used instead. The 'Khoi' are considered closely related to the San as they share so-called click languages and therefore together are usually referred to as Khoisan. However, not everybody believes Bushman to be offensive and they sometimes use it themselves. It continues in widespread use (Bushman | Definition of Bushman by Merriam-Webster (merriam-webster.com), accessed 12 February 2021).

FIGURE 11.3 Leopard spoor on the road (in circle). Photo source: Harry Wels.

FIGURE 11.4 Lion spoor (no circle). Photo source: Harry Wels.

Guenther (2020a: 235) refers to blurring of boundaries as the 'sympathy bond' between hunter and prey based on 'reflexivity and relationality'. This is not a one-way superior feeling of predator over prey, because in relation to lions, it is the San that are the prey and as a result they know what it means to be hunted (p. 78; see also Charles Foster's description of being hunted below). This sympathy bond between hunter and hunted has led to a 'seemingly limitless abundance of ... animal-related rules and regulations' when to hunt and whom to hunt (Guenther, 2020b: 132) and a great respect for animals, even if hunted (Guenther, 2020a: 262). This 'relational connectedness may curb the potential for overexploitation inherent in hunting that is prosaic, functional and efficient ... ' (Guenther, 2020a: 261; see also Ham, 2020: 207–67).

Stander et al. (1997, in Ijäs, 2017: 188) state that 'a team of [San] trackers was able to identify the spoor of individual animals, with a 93.8% success rate of the 569 cases', meaning that they ultimately found almost every animal they were after, based on interpreting their tracking data correctly. This is a sure sign that the senses and the bodies of the San are attuned, and trained into reliable guides to tracking, which for them is a constant confirmation of their approach. The photos above (Figures 11.3 and 11.4), in a maybe somewhat simplified fashion, show some of the complexities of recognizing spoor, especially when you consider how you are supposed to find them in the vast landscapes of southern Africa.

From Tracking to the Learning Cycle of OBR

Liebenberg (2012) argues that the San hunting and tracking practices—finding and interpreting spoor, combined with hypothesizing about animal routes, reflects the basic structure of scientific reasoning. Similarly, Sagarin and Pauchard (2012: 77) contend that 'the beginnings of science were marked by the systematization of traditional observations'. Framed differently, it involves a reiterative combinative cycle of 'Observation', 'Becoming with', and 'Reflexivity', or OBR (Wels, 2020). We believe that exactly this cyclical framework is appropriate to the organization of multispecies ethnography in that it can be applied to researching both human and nonhuman animals and allows a non-hierarchical attitude towards nonhuman animals' sensemaking processes, agency, and even resistance (Colling, 2021; Hribal, 2011). Blattner et al.'s (2020) study of animal agency makes another compelling argument for such an approach.

While it is perhaps a generalization, ethnographers, including ourselves, often write about *observation*, the O in OBR, as key to the ethnographer's 'participant *observation*' tool (Bernard, 2006; Spradley, 1980), many, if not most, of our own ethnographic observations would never hold up as independent data. That is, in terms of systematics and consistency, our observations are always dependent and usually only make sense in combination with text from conversations, interviews, and written documents. Including nonhuman life forms in ethnographic research means that we have to become more systematic, consistent, and generally more serious about observation as a method on its own, and not necessarily in combination with other methods like participation or interviewing (cf. Nippert-Eng, 2015). A stronger focus on observation also means a drastic reduction of our 'addiction' to language and texts, which 'anaesthetizes all five senses' (Serres, 2016: 89).

Observation means to 'open [ourselves] up to the world' (Serres, 2016: 93); Haraway's (2016) 'worlding' and Latour's (2018) 'down to earth' point in the same direction. To strengthen and train our observational skills on their own, it is useful to add drawing to our repertoire of taking field notes (cf. Causey, 2017) which is a convenient way to avoid viewing text as the single form of data, although writing extensive field notes remains mandatory. Nippert-Eng (2015) and Causey (2017) provide very helpful observation exercises but learning observation by 'doing' with non-academic practitioners is equally, if not more, effective. One of the authors received such training while living in and visiting the Southern African bush alongside a group of rangers. They taught him four important lessons. First, they showed him that observation is always multisensorial. Second, they taught him that observation requires lots of patience. Little was to be gained, they said, by making 'instant' observations. Third, they stressed that observation involves 'reading the bush' by looking '*through* the bush' (instead of *at* or *in* the bush). Fourth, they showed him the limitations of isolated observations and instead to always look at the bigger picture of related and connected phenomena (Wels, 2020). We know from sports and music that even the talented need to study hard to master the required skills. Similarly, yielding ethnographic results is the fruit of intense and protracted training (cf. Sagarin and Pauchard, 2012: 45).

What helps tremendously in getting better at observation is when one actively tries 'becoming with' animal (and other nonhuman) sentience (the B in OBR). It implies that one empathizes with and tries to imagine why animals do what they do. Part of the San's success in tracking is that they 'become' the antelope, an eland they are after, for instance, as the tracker 'merges being human and animal' (Guenther, 2020a: 224; see also DuPlessis, 2018). It leads to a 'morphing of identities' and 'bring[s] about an experience ... of cross-species blurring of identity and alterity' (Guenther, 2020a: 7), a 'feeling and thinking antelope' (p. 239), 'eliciting an ontological shift in the hunter through intense sympathetic attunement to the prey animal' (p. 25). Haraway (2008: 25; emphasis added) writes about blurring boundaries between species in terms of 'the *dance* of relating', as hunters themselves describe it (Foster and Foster, 2000). Similarly, Tsing (2015) uses dance and dancing as metaphors for tracking and foraging matsutake mushrooms in the forest: 'The dance is a form of forest knowledge, though not codified in reports' (p. 241), but leading to the 'arts' and 'pleasure' of noticing (pp. 17–25, 279).

Similar to Haraway's (2008) 'becoming with', Aaltola's (2018 see also Ch.22 in this volume) conceptualization of 'embodied empathy' is helpful in imagining and training these therianthropic man-animal transformations of the San. Embodied empathy frees 'our somatic capacity to express and read mindedness ... a state of perception: one immediately perceives the mental states of others on account of the expressiveness of the body' (Aaltola, 2018: 208). As Fudge concludes '(w)hat is at stake ultimately is our own ability to think beyond ourselves' (Fudge, 2002: 22).

Trying to explain these demanding 'techniques' to a generally academic and 'Western' audience, Guenther (2020b: 9) refers to Charles Foster (2016) who tried 'becoming with' various animals iconic for the British landscape, like badgers, urban foxes, otters, swifts, but also red deer. Guenther (2020b: 9) writes: 'Charles Foster came closest to his goal—of being a red deer—when he had himself chased by a human hunter and his hound ... The experience, lasting several hours, peaked at the moment, near the chase's end, when 'mostly unconscious I was behaving very much like a hunted deer'. Tsing (2015) adds to elucidating what 'becoming with' means by showing how in the context of hunting mushrooms in the forest 'the [tracking] skill comes [with] the memory' and that '(w)ithout the dance of matsutake forests, memory loses focus' (Tsing, 2015: 244). A similar story of how just 'becoming with' the landscape can tap into the memory and knowledge of its constituent parts is told by William Ellis in a webinar about a herbalist in the South African province of Northern Cape, who maintained that interviewing him about his phenomenal knowledge of plants was useless. Only by physically, that is sensorially, being in the landscape, could he 'become with' it and share his knowledge with William.[2]

The O of 'observation' and the B of 'becoming with' culminate in the R of 'reflexivity,' as it is this 'translation' (cf. Tsing, 2015: 217–25) that connects the 'dots' of the O and the B through interpretation and sensemaking. According to Liebenberg (2012) tracking is not only about being able to follow spoor based on multisensory observations (cf. Pink, 2009) but also includes 'be(ing) able to *interpret* the animal's activities so that [one] can anticipate and predict its movements' (Liebenberg, 2012: 138; emphasis added). While this kind of interpretation is complicated enough in itself, its complexity is often aggravated by the partiality of data. '(T)racks may be partly obliterated or difficult to see, they may only show fractional evidence, so the reconstruction of the animals' activities will have to be based on creative hypotheses. To *interpret* the spoor, trackers must use their imagination to visualise what the animal was doing to create such markings' (Liebenberg, 2012: 150; emphasis added). Interpreting spoor can be trained, like the O and the B, by building knowledge repertoires that can inform interpretations (cf. Alvesson and Sköldberg, 2000: 250), such as those for animal behaviour, spoor variations, intra-species differences, weather conditions, climatic changes, vegetation cover, the diversities in the terrain and landscape, etc. Reflexivity, as Alvesson and Sköldberg (2000) frame it, has to do with raising the level of researcher awareness of the multiplicity and ambiguity of empirical data, helping towards better 'perceiving the mental state of others' (Aaltola, 2018: 208). This can be 'trained' and kept up to date through an ongoing development of one's 'interpretive repertoire' (ibid). This

---

[2] CRG Webinar: Walking with herders: Animal and plant ontologies in Namaqualand | African Studies Centre Leiden (ascleiden.nl), accessed 23 February 2021.

interpretive 'interplay' with O and R is not likely to be developed linearly but more probably in 'patches' and by 'indeterminate encounters' (Tsing, 2015: 218, 37) in order to live up to the ongoing improvisations that tracking requires.

Training the sensorium for OBR is not easily done but training the senses individually may result in them collectively 'seeing' more. Fortunately, the plasticity of the brain (Rosenblum, 2010) allows training the kind of 'empathetic mind' required for 'becoming with' (Krznaric, 2014) and developing reflexivity by building new interpretive repertoires (Tayar and Paisley, 2015). In the next section, the idea of OBR training will be explored in more detail as a form of 'wild pedagogy' (Jickling et al., 2018a; Winks 2019) to learn multispecies ethnographic methods beyond words (Wels, 2012).

Going Wild about Training OBR

The typical university is a place where teaching is done inside the concrete walls of lecture halls and laboratories in some sort of academic plant. The products of this academic industry are 'sold' as diplomas, journal articles, patents, and, last but not least, as qualified workers for the higher echelons of the labour market (Donskis, Sabelis, Kamsteeg and Wels, 2019), whom Serres (2016: 94) referred to as dwelling in 'the ivory tower of language'. Given its 'wild' inspiration from San tracking, taking teaching and training of OBR seriously as a methodological approach to multispecies organizational ethnography, thrives best in a '*wild* pedagogy'.

As described earlier, wildness questions control and domestication. What core elements, then, can be distinguished in a pedagogy that is deliberately 'self-willed' (Jickling, 2018b: 161)? Wild pedagogy thinking and practice is constituted by six key touchstones. It starts with recognizing (1) the agency and the role of nature as co-teacher. Subsequently, it stresses (2) wildness and challenging ideas of control of nature. From this, it follows that knowing the world is not a matter of following prescribed and simple paths but instead requires opening up for (3) complexity, the unknown, and spontaneity. Classrooms are not ideal pedagogical places but (4) locating the wild outdoor (near-by and far-off) helps this opening-up. This is not a quick-and-dirty trick to be learned but requires (5) time and practice. In sum, it means a pedagogical turn-over, (6) a cultural change that brings the world to students and urges them to think radically and politically (Jickling et al., 2018b; see also Green and Dyment, 2018).

OBR's wild pedagogy makes it a radical method that challenges the neoliberal character of present-day academia (cf. Bauman and Donskis, 2013: 131–67), which suffocates and undermines Humboldtian exploration and a multispecies (ethnographic) orientation. Von Humboldt's (1769–1859) combined observation and feeling, drawing and text, love for the outdoors, made him see 'the devastating environmental effects of colonial *plantations*' (Wulf, 2015: 5; emphasis added). Tsing (2015) uses the same *plantation* as a metaphor for, and the logic behind, the neoliberal world striving for control that comes at the price of devastating effects for the planet and people. In line with other posthumanist writers such as Latour and Haraway, Tsing uses tracking matsutake mushrooms in the woodlands as a powerful metaphor for 'intellectual life ... a source of many useful products emerging in unintentional design ... The image calls up its opposites: In assessment exercises, intellectual life is a *plantation* [that reduces the work of scholars to a number] ... Consider instead the pleasures of the woodland. There are many useful products there, from berries and mushrooms to firewood, wild vegetables, medicinal herbs, and even timber. A forager can choose what to gather and can make use of the woodland's patches of unexpected bounty. But the woodland requires continuing work, not to make it a garden but rather to keep it open and available for an array of species ... For intellectual work, this seems just right [and may lead to] the unexpected bounty of a nest of mushrooms ...' (2015: 286; emphasis added).

OBR precisely aims to explore the intellectual 'wildwood' (Deakin, 2007) Tsing describes. For OBR to be trained and multispecies organizational ethnography to flourish, academia's pedagogy should go wild,[3] that is, move away from the confines of the lecture halls, classrooms, 'labs and computers' (Sagarin and Pauchard, 2012: 10) and the 'addict[ion] to what is said' (Serres, 2016: 94). The 'ontological mutability' as described by Guenther (2020a, see above) together with the San-inspired tracking metaphor constitute the OBR wild pedagogical approach that we attempted with our Masters' students in Culture, Organization and Management from 2020 onwards.

We taught the programme's opening course 'Sensemaking in Organizations' at a goat farm in a forest on the outskirts of Amsterdam. Although '"sensemaking" is an increasingly influential perspective in ... organization studies' (Brown et al., 2015: 266), as a teaching subject it is largely focused on gathering textual data through interviewing and text analysis. Contrary to most organization studies, we present sensemaking in the double meaning of concrete perceptions with our five senses[4] combined with interpretive action of the mind, akin to a social constructivist perspective. Within a multispecies assemblage of smells, sounds, sights, touches, and tastes, students practised each and every individual sense, keeping rigorous field notes and writing reflexive vignettes in view of piecing together a (multi)sense-scape. For students and staff this outdoor course was a revelation. The forest-located goat farm, in the proximity of a major motorway and the national Dutch airport provided a multisensorial 'heaven'. Part of the ethics in this course is to sensitize the students as much as possible to an inclusive and less/non-hierarchical approach to nonhuman life forms—an aspect hardly emphasized or expected by students in organization sciences.

---

[3] We consciously stay away from the currently popular concept of 'rewilding' because we consider the term problematic for what we want to convey in this chapter. It is not about a 'going back' to something that started off wild (suggested by the prefix 're'). The wild we refer to is building an attitude to challenge, question, and straddle all sorts of assumed or taken-for-granted boundaries ranging from human-animal, mind-body, academic disciplines, academic-popular, important-unimportant, recognized-unrecognized, dream-reality, dead-alive, spiritual-secular, doing-thinking, etc.

[4] We refrain in this chapter from the debates around the number of senses and how historically thinking about the senses has led us to where we are now. See Jütte (2005), for a history of the senses.

As a process and an attitude, however, teaching sensemaking 'in the wild' is not simply implemented. Like San tracking, or mushroom foraging for that matter, it requires constant improvisation and sensitivity to changing contexts. We had no ready-made sensory toolkit but rather developed sensemaking experiments in multispecies settings on the spot. Our 'wild' OBR training in multispecies organizational ethnography required constant contextualization as we realized that no multispecies living landscape, whether in Southern Africa, the Netherlands, or elsewhere, is ever the same. Outside of the classroom, sounds, smells, touches, tastes, sights, the ingredients of 'doing sensemaking', constantly change and confuse the sensing actor.

The organization of education alone required high sensitivity from both teachers and students. Path-finding in the forest, changing weather conditions, constant interruptions by animals, visiting children and their parents, and the farm personnel meant that there was never a dull moment, or a moment to sit back. Both the teaching and the sensemaking field exercises automatically had a real-life feeling for the students. Indeterminate encounters of the full range of senses led to a heightened sense of awareness for experiencing a multispecies world: the strong animal smells and sounds, the rush in the trees because of a gust of wind, the touch of first raindrops on our skin and our laptops, the wasps going after our snacks, the constant change of colourations before our eyes during the day as a result of being outdoors, and the impressions of the built environment around us, ranging from planes arriving and leaving to the children's playground behind the goat shed, to the smell of chips from the restaurant.

How to make sense of this multi-sited, multispecies, and multi-organized reality in ethnographic terms was the task we set ourselves in this course. It was, in terms Liebenberg (2012) used for the art of San tracking, a true and original scientific journey. We regularly sent our students into the forest to do some tracking. One assignment was to develop a soundscape using only hearing while walking through the woods. Another assignment challenged the students to observe an unanimated farm object or an (animated) animal and try to interpret the goat farm's organization from their perspective. Students were also invited to smell and touch trees, plants, animals, soil, and report how they made sense of what they did, if at all. Both the field teaching and the assignment created a mixture of amazement, wonder, irritation, dullness, commitment, as well as frustration because the OBR-style sensemaking we made them try was not just exciting, but also difficult, time-consuming, and exasperating at times. Much of the difficulty and frustration students expressed had to do with how to report on what they 'sensed' in the field. Translating sensory experiences into text is certainly one of most complex challenges.

Despite its attempt to try and avoid language and text, OBR in multispecies organizational ethnography can only be made academically 'acceptable' when it is solidified in concrete field notes or a field journal (Farnsworth et al. 2014; Sagarin and Pauchard, 2012: 53–6). Fieldwork-based scientists, who practised OBR *avant la lettre*, all relied on field notes for their academic publications, some of which led to scientific revolutions and paradigm shifts in the direction that we also argue for in this chapter. Great examples in the natural sciences are found in any one of the founding people of ethology: Niko

Tinbergen (Kruuk, 2003), Jane Goodall,[5] and George Schaller (Canfield, 2011a; see also Drickamer and Dewsbury 2010). In anthropological fieldwork examples of the extensive use of and reliance on field notes are, for instance, Bronislaw Malinowski (Roldán, 2002), and among current day organizational ethnographers people like Pachirat (2011) and Ho (2009; see for more examples Ybema et al., 2009).

The students whom we pushed to observe, 'become with', and reflect, desperately struggled to find ways to express the results of their efforts. 'Since human memory is transitory and things that are not written down may slip away quickly' (Canfield 2011b: 14), even OBR can probably not survive academically without field notes, reports, and publications. It may take some time to find the ideal means to make sense of multispecies organizational ethnographic data. After all, lichens are not created out of algae and fungi in a day either (Sheldrake, 2020: 79–104; Tsing, 2015: 137–44). We may well need to train a few more classes at the goat farm.

THE WILD WAY FORWARD

For thinking of multispecies worlds in terms of multispecies organizational ethnographies, we need to start conceptualizing beyond most of our commonly accepted binaries distinguishing humans from all else on this planet. This is challenging and requires rethinking our theories, research methodologies, and teaching practices. Inspired by the tracking practice of a Southern Africa community of San hunter-gatherers we have tried to scratch the surface of all three levels. We have suggested how OBR can provide a way forward in how to operationalize the conceptual advances in actual multispecies organizational ethnographic field work practices. With our wild pedagogic teaching experiments we have lured our students towards a multispecies organizational ethnography outside of the traditional university classroom. Our hopes are that the pedagogy we propose may contribute to recognizing a more-than-human perspective on organization studies which in turn would lead to thinking more sustainably about the world we organize.

For a multispecies orientation humans need to know 'how to be animal' (or tree, or plant for that matter) in order to remove our alienation from the rest of planet earth and to descend from our human 'dream of greatness' and 'exceptionalism' (Challenger, 2021: 11–72, 204) into the living 'wild' world again. Contributing to this alienation is our addiction to language which tends to have our 'senses destroyed' (Serres, 2016: 106). With the example of the San's tracking skills, and the OBR approach derived from them, we propose a rethinking of the senses as a gateway to knowledge. There is enough 'wildness' left to be taught and studied, 'if we only stop in our tracks and look

---

[5] Jane Goodall's field notes digitized—Futurity (accessed 26 February 2021).

around us' and realize that we are explorers of the 'undiscovered country of the nearby' (Macfarlane, 2007: 225).

We agree, with Serres, that it is ironic that we argue for this using academic text and language to advocate our multisensory, multispecies organizational ethnography, just as we acknowledged the paradoxical use of textual field notes in order to 'capture' and 'translate' our OBR findings. Perhaps we can take some comfort from Challenger (2021: 89; emphasis added) who writes: 'When we recognise that we are social primates whose beliefs about the world and others change to fit the relationship we want, our *hypocrisies become more predictable*'. This is what we can offer animal organization studies.

References

Aaltola, E. (2018). *Varieties of empathy. Moral psychology and animal ethics.* London, New York: Rowman and Littlefield.

Alvesson, M. & Sköldberg, K. (2000). *Reflexive methodology. New vistas for qualitative research.* London, New Delhi: Sage Publications.

Atkinson, P. (2014). *For ethnography.* Los Angeles: Sage Publications.

Bauman, Z. & Donskis, L. (2013). *Moral blindness. The loss of sensitivity in liquid modernity.* Cambridge, Malden: Polity Press.

Bekoff, M. (2007). *The emotional lives of animals. A leading scientist explores animal joy, sorrow, and empathy—and why they matter.* Novato: New World Library.

Bernard, H.R. (2006). *Research methods in anthropology.* Lanham: Altamira Press.

Bird Rose, D. et al. (2012). Thinking through the environment, unsettling the humanities. *Environmental Humanities*, 1, 1–6.

Blattner, C., Donaldson, S., & Wilcox, R. (2020). Animal agency in community: A political multispecies ethnography of VINE Sanctuary. *Politics and Animals*, 6, 1–22.

Bradshaw, G. (2009). *Elephants on the edge. What animals can teach us about humanity.* New Haven, London: Yale University Press.

Bradshaw, K. (2021). Humans as animals. *Utah Law Review*, 1, 185–209.

Braidotti, R. (2019). *Posthuman knowledge.* London: Polity Press.

Brown, A.D., Colville, J., & Pye, A. (2015). Making sense of sensemaking in Organization Studies. *Organization Studies*, 36(2), 265–77.

Calarco, M. (2007). *Zoographies. The question of the animal from Heidegger to Derrida.* New York: Columbia University Press.

Cambridge Declaration (2012). Available at: http://fcmconference.org/img/CambridgeDeclarationOnConsciousness.pdf.

Canfield, M.R. (Ed.) (2011a). *Field notes on science & nature.* Cambridge, MA, London: Harvard University Press.

Canfield, M.R. (2011b). Introduction. In M.R. Canfield (Ed.) *Field notes on science & nature.* Cambridge MA, London: Harvard University Press, 1-18.

Causey, A. (2017). *Drawn to see. Drawing as an ethnographic method.* Toronto: Toronto University Press.

Challenger, M. (2021). *How to be animal. A new history of what it means to be human.* Edinburgh: Canongate Books.

Cohn, I. & Asharon, R. (2012). Indigenous ways—fruits of our ancestors. *Journal of Adventure Education and Outdoor Learning*, 11(1), 15–34.

Colling, S. (2021). *Animal resistance in the global capitalist era*. Michigan: Michigan State University Press.

Deakin, R. (2007). *Wildwood. A journey through trees*. London: Hamish Hamilton.

Despret, V. (2016). *What would animals say if we asked the right questions?* Minneapolis, London: University of Minnesota Press.

Drikckamer, L. & Dewsbury, D. (Eds.) (2010). *Leaders in animal behaviour. The second generation*. Cambridge: Cambridge University Press.

Donskis, L., Sabelis, I., Kamsteeg, F. & Wels, H. (2019). *Academia in crisis. The rise and risk of neoliberal education in Europe*. Leiden: Brillp-Rodopi.

De Waal, F. (2016). *Are we smart enough to know how smart animals are?* New York: Norton.

Du Plessis, P. (2018). Tingling armpits and the man who hugs lions. In N. Bubandt (Ed.), *A non-secularAnthropocene: Spirits, specters and other nonhumans in a time of environmental change*. More Than Human. AURA Working Papers, 3, 97–106.

Ellis, W. (2015). *Ons is Boesmans*: Commentary on the naming of Bushmen in the southern Kalahari. *Anthropology Southern Africa*, 38(1–2), 120–33.

Erwin, D. (2019). Wild Pedagogies: Touchstones for re-negotiating education and the environment in the Anthropocene. *Journal of Adventure Education and Outdoor Learning*, 19(4), 374–5.

Farnsworth, J.S., Baldwin, L., & Bezanson, M. (2014). An invitation for engagement: Assigning and assessing field notes to promote deeper levels of observation. *The Journal of Natural History Education and Experience*, 8, 12–20.

Foster, C. (2016). *Being a beast. An intimate and radical look at nature*. London: Profile Books.

Foster, C. & Foster, D. (2000). The great dance: A hunter's story. Documentary film.

Fudge, E. (2002). *Animal*. London: Reaktion Books.

Green, M. & Dyment, J. (2018). Wilding pedagogy in an unexpected landscape: Reflections and possibilities in initial teacher education. *Journal of Outdoor and Environmental Education*, 21, 277–92.

Guenther, M. (2020a). *Human-animal relationships in San and hunter-gatherer cosmology. Therianthropes and transformation*, Vol. I. London: Palgrave Macmillan.

Guenther, M. (2020b). *Human-animal relationships in San and hunter-gatherer cosmology. Imagining and experiencing ontological mutability*, Vol. II. London: Palgrave Macmillan.

Ham, A. (2020). *The last lions of Africa. Stories from the frontline in the battle to save a species*. Sydney, London: Allen & Unwin.

Hamersley, M. & Atkinson, P. (2019)[2007]. *Ethnography: Principles in practice*, 4th Edition. Abingdon: Routledge.

Hamilton, L. & Taylor, N. (2017). *Ethnography after humanism*. London: Palgrave Macmillan.

Haraway, D. (2016). *Staying with the trouble. Making kin in the Chthulucene*. Durham, London: Duke University Press.

Haraway, D. (2008). *When species meet*. Minneapolis, London: University of Minnesota Press.

Henn, B.M. et al. (2011). Hunter-gatherer genomic diversity suggests a southern African origin for modern humans. *PNAS*, 108(13), 5154–62.

Ho, K. (2009). *Liquidated. An ethnography of Wall Street*. Durham: Duke University Press.

Hribal, J. (2011). *Fear of the animal planet. The hidden history of animal resistance*. Chico: CAAK Press.

Ijäs, M. (2017). *Fragments of the hunt. Persistence hunting, tracking and prehistoric art* (Unpublished PhD thesis, Aalto University, School of Arts, Design and Architecture, Department of Art).

Jickling, B. et al. (Eds.) (2018a). *Wild pedagogies. Touchstones for re-negotiating education and the environment in the Anthropocene.* London: Palgrave Macmillan.

Jickling, B. et al. (2018b). Wild pedagogies: Six initial touchstones for early childhood environmental educators. *Australian Journal of Environmental Education, 34*(2), 159–71.

Jütte, R. (2005). *A history of the senses. From antiquity to cyberspace.* Cambridge: Polity Press.

Kirksey, E. (2015). *Emergent ecologies.* Durham, London: Duke University Press.

Kirksey, E. & Helmreich, S. (2010). The emergence of multispecies ethnography. *Cultural Anthropology, 25*(4), 545–76.

Koot, S. (2018). The Bushman brand in southern African tourism: An indigenous modernity in a neoliberal political economy. In R. Fleming Puckett & I. Kazunobu (Eds.), Research and activism among the Kalahari San today: Ideals, challenges, and debates. *Senri Ethnological Studies, 99,* Osaka: National Museum of Ethnology (pp. 231–50).

Kruuk, H. (2003). *Niko's nature. A life of Niko Tinbergen and his science of animal behaviour.* Oxford: Oxford University Press.

Krznaric, R. (2014). *Empathy. Why it matters, and how to get it.* New York: Penguin.

Kimmerer, R.W. (2013). *Braiding sweetgrass. Indigenous wisdom, scientific knowledge, and the teaching of plants.* Minneapolis: Milkweed Editions.

Latour, B. (2020). *Het parlement van de dingen. Over Gaia en de representatie van niet-mensen* [The parliament of things. About Gaia and the representation of non-humans]. Amsterdam: Boom Uitgevers.

Latour, B. (2018). *Down to earth. Politics in the New Climatic Regime.* London: Polity Press.

Liebenberg, L. (2012) [1990]. *The art of tracking. The origins of science.* Cape Town, Johannesburg: David Philip.

Liebenberg, L. et al. (2021). Tracking Science: An Alternative for Those Excluded by Citizen Science. *Citizen Science: Theory and Practice, 6*(1), 1–16.

McFarland, S.E. & Hediger, R. (Eds.) (2009). *Animals and agency. An interdisciplinary exploration.* Leiden: Brill Academic Publishing.

Macfarlane, R. (2007). *The Wild Places.* London: Granta.

Macfarlane, R. (2016). *Landmarks.* London: Penguin.

Meijer, E. (2019). *When animals speak. Towards an interspecies democracy.* New York: New York University Press.

Myburgh, P.J. (2013). *The Bushman winter has come. The true story of the last band of /Gwikwe Bushmen on the Great Sand Face.* Cape Town: Penguin.

Neyland, D. (2008) *Organizational ethnography.* London: Sage Publications.

Nippert-Eng, C. (2015). *Watching closely. A guide to ethnographic observation.* Oxford: Oxford University Press.

Nkomo, S.M. (2011). A postcolonial *and* anti-colonial reading of 'African' leadership and management in organization studies: Tensions, contradictions and possibilities. *Organization, 18*(3), 365–86.

Noske, B. (1997). *Beyond boundaries: Humans and animals.* Montreal: Black Rose Books.

Özkazanç-Pan, B. (2008). International management research meets 'The rest of the world'. *Academy of Management Review, 33*(4), 964–74.

Pachirat, T. (2011). *Every twelve seconds. Industrialized slaughter and the politics of sight.* New Haven, London: Yale University Press.

Pacine-Ketchabaw, V., Taylor, A., & Blaise, M. (2016). Decentring the human in multispecies ethnography. In C.A. Taylor & C. Hughes (Eds.), *Posthuman research practices in education*. (pp. 149–167). London: Palgrave Macmillan.

Pink, S. (2009). *Doing sensory ethnography*. Los Angeles, London: Sage Publications.

Prins, F.E. (2009). Secret San of the Drakensberg and their rock art legacy. *Visual Arts*, 23(2), 190–208.

Reesink, M. (2021). *Dier en mens. De band tussen ons en andere dieren* [Animal and human. The bond between us and other animals]. Amsterdam: Boom Uitgevers.

Rouleau, l., De Rond, M., & Musca, G. (2014). From the ethnographic turn to new forms of organizational ethnography. *Journal of Organizational Ethnography*, 3(1), 2–9.

Roldán, A.A. (2002). Writing ethnography: Malinowski's field notes on Baloma. *Social Anthropology*, 10(3), 377–93.

Rosenblum, L.D. (2010). *See what I'm saying. The extraordinary powers of our five senses*. New York, London: W.W. Norton & Company.

Safina, C. (2015). *Beyond words. What animals think and feel*. New York: Henry Holt and Company.

Sagarin, R. & Pauchard, A. (2012). *Observation and ecology. Broadening the scope of science to understand a complex world*. Washington, London: Island Press.

Serres, M. (2016) [1985]. *The five senses. A philosophy of mingled bodies*. London: Bloomsbury.

Sheldrake, M. (2020). *Entangled life. How fungi make our worlds, change our minds, and shape our futures*. London: The Bodley Head.

Song. T. (2013). *Entering the mind of the tracker. Native practices for developing intuitive consciousness and discovering hidden nature*. Rochester (VT), Toronto: Bear & Company.

Spradley, J.P. (1980). *Participant observation*. New York: Holt, Rinehart & Winston.

Stander, P. E., Ghau, I. I., Tsisaba, D., Oma, I. I., & Ui, I. I. (1997) Tracking and the interpretation of spoor: A scientifically sound method in ecology. *Journal of Zoology*, 242(2), 329–341.

Stoller, P. (1997). *Sensuous Scholarship*. Pennsylvania: Pennsylvania University Press.

Tayar M. & Paisley V. (2015). Reflexivity, critical reflection, and mindfulness in experiential learning: Developing successful international business graduates. In V. Taras & M.A. Gonzalez-Perez (Eds.), *The Palgrave handbook of experiential learning in international business*. (pp. 464–483). London: Palgrave Macmillan.

Tomaselli, K. (2017). Ethical procedures? A critical intervention: The sacred, the profane, and the planet. *The Ethnographic Edge*, 1(1), 3–16.

Tomaselli, K.G. (2001). Rock art, the art of tracking, and cyber tracking: Demystifying the 'Bushmen' in the information age. *Visual Anthropology*, 14(1), 77–82.

Tsing, A. (2015). *The mushroom at the end of the world. On the possibility of life in capitalist ruins*. Princeton, Oxford: Princeton University Press.

Van Maanen, John (2010) A song for my supper: More tales of the field. *Organizational Research Methods*, 13(2), 240–55.

Van Maanen, J. (2011) Ethnography as work: Some rules of engagement. *Journal of Management Studies*, 48(1), 218–34.

Verbuyst, R. (2021). *Khoisan consciousness. Articulating indigeneity in post-apartheid Cape Town* (Unpublished PhD thesis, Ghent University).

Walker, C. (1981). *Signs of the wild*. Cape Town: Struik.

Wels, H. (2020). Multi-species ethnography: Methodological training in the field in South Africa. *Journal of Organizational Ethnography*, 9(3), 343–63.

Wels, H. (2015). 'Animals like us': Revisiting organizational ethnography and research. *Journal of Organizational Ethnography*, 4(3), 242–59.

Wels, H. (2012). Research methodologies without words. Paper presented at the Minding Animals Conference, 3-6 July, Utrecht, The Netherlands..

Winks, L. (2019) Wild Pedagogies. *Environmental Education Research*, 26(2), 303–4.

Wolfe, P. (1999). *Settler colonialism and the transformation of anthropology*. London: Cassell.

Wulf, A. (2015). *The invention of nature. The adventures of Alexander von Humboldt. The lost hero of science*. London: John Murray.

Ybema, S. et al. (Eds.) (2009). *Organizational ethnography. Studying the complexities of everyday life*. Los Angeles, London: Sage Publications.

CHAPTER 12

GUIDED BY A LIZARD

Respectful Organizing and Symmetric Reciprocity with Totem Animals

KARL-ERIK SVEIBY AND TEX SKUTHORPE IN MEMORIAM

I am sitting in a four-wheeler rattling along a dirt track on my first 'walkabout' in the Australian bush and am completely lost. It is stinking hot inside and I'm thirsty and longing for some fresh air. Beside me, a relaxed Tex at the wheel is telling me that we are now entering Nhunggal country, his mother's land. Suddenly, a fearsome-looking creature jumps onto the track from the right, the biggest lizard I have ever had the misfortune to encounter, more than a metre long [Figure 12.1 below]. It freezes upright in what looks like a threatening position. Tex stops the car, and shuts down the engine:

'Stay in the car and don't move' he says and gets out. From my safe position in the vehicle, I watch. Slowly, slowly, Tex walks toward the lizard and stops a couple of metres away. The lizard is still frozen in the same position. He looks at the lizard but does not say anything that I can hear. The lizard moves its head and seems to relax.

Then it continues its run and disappears in the bush. The encounter took less than a minute. Tex re-enters the vehicle as if nothing special had happened and we continue. He points to the right. 'She is a sand goanna mother. Her nest is over there, not far away. We must not go there; our tracks may attract predators to her nest. She is out foraging. There's water over there.' He points further down the track to the left.

In the above vignette, Tex explains that the sand goanna, a common lizard species all over Australia, was his totem animal. He was showing respect to his 'sister' through his 'true form' as her 'brother'. This time his respectful inter action yielded an exchange of knowledge whereby he got information about the location of her nest with newly-hatched children—her most valuable secret—and that he will help her to protect this secret. In exchange he learned the way to her waterhole, which might one day save his life.

FIGURE 12.1 The sand goanna, detail of painting 'Journey of Knowledge' by Tex Skuthorpe. Copyright: The authors.

Through vignettes like these, this chapter invites the reader to visit prehistorical Australia, made alive in the contemporary world by the Nhunggabarra Law stories. The chapter draws on stories and conversations with their custodian, Tex Skuthorpe,[1] a man who devoted his life to safeguarding the oral history and cultural heritage of the Nhunggabarra. As will become clearer, such First Peoples' organizations and ontologies are closer to nature and offer the promise of distinctive organizational solutions which are arguably more compatible with animals than many exploitative Western organizations. The solutions can be summarized by one word: *Respect*. This is an important concept among the First Peoples of Australia; to be respectful does not convey the conventional meaning of today—that is, a feeling of veneration or subservience—but has a much deeper meaning which will be explained in what follows.

The purpose of highlighting the present-day value of ancient Indigenous voices and stories is to contribute a unique case of how humanity once organized distinctive and respectful relationships with animals. This is relevant to the development of our current Animals and Organizations discourse because it blends an (often marginalized) Indigenous epistemological lens, drawn from communities and individuals through history, with the theoretical framings of relational ontology and relational constructivism

---

[1] Tex Skuthorpe was a Nhunggal man, the last custodian of his people's Law stories, painter, and teacher of his people's culture. He devoted his life to teaching his culture to young Aboriginal offenders in prisons and we collaborated for more than 20 years. The paintings by Tex and the Law stories are his people's gift to humanity (published in full in Sveiby and Skuthorpe, 2006).

(Hosking, 2011) to provide a different reading of the meanings attributed to animals as totemic social actors.

The Nhunggabarra of Australia

Very little is known about how the First People lived in the fertile Australian southeast Riverine landscapes. These are semi-arid flatlands in north-west New South Wales stretching from the south Queensland mountain-ridges and are criss-crossed by rivers that either flood the flatlands or dry up depending on rainfall in the mountains in patterns governed by the climate. People, like the Nhunggabarra, were living a semi-sedentary life in small villages along the riverbeds as witnessed by the early explorer Thomas Mitchell (1846). The focus of this chapter is on the organization of the Nhunggal community, which is one of 26 closely networked communities, here referred to as the Community of Communities (CoC). A tentative estimate of the population is around 1000 people and between 15,000 and 20,000 people in the CoC before the British occupation in 1788 (Sveiby and Skuthorpe, 2006). Today, only a handful of the Nhunggabarra (*-barra* = people) remain, their language is not spoken, and their lands are farmed and owned by others.

Fortunately, a treasure trove of Nhunggabarra Law stories remain. They are the main source of data for this chapter because they contain the rules of conduct: how to interact and how to organize society for achieving respectful relationships with the animals on their lands. These stories have been traditionally transmitted by Tex's ancestors throughout the disturbances of the nineteenth and twentieth centuries virtually untouched; a 200-year-old time capsule. The stories are a unique link to precolonial times and can thus be a more reliable source about how their society was meant to function than many European eyewitness reports of that time.

The First Peoples of Australia arrived possibly as long as 65,000 years ago (Clarkson et al., 2017) from the north-west, and then dispersed across the continent (Flannery, 1994). A skeleton find dated at 45,000–50,000 years ago at Lake Mungo (Bowler et al., 2003), some 700 km south-west from Nhunggal land, gives a tentative date for arrival of the ancestors of the First Peoples in Australia's south-east. They lived on their island continent until 1788, untouched by the guns, germs, and steel that devasted many First Peoples' lives elsewhere on the planet (Diamond, 1999).

Although classified as 'hunter-gatherers' by anthropologists (Barnard, 1999), they invented an entirely different way of farming than the peoples of the Fertile Crescent, which became the dominant way to organize relationships with animals in the rest of the world. Neither the first white explorer, Sir Thomas Mitchell, nor the settlers could fathom that this was an elaborate horticultural organization of 'farms without fences' (Gammage, 2011), cultivated by highly educated and competent people, who had respectful relationships with animals. It had taken an enormous human effort over thousands of years to achieve this type of organization. However, these organizing efforts started crumbling due to the viruses unwittingly introduced by the British colonialists, and up to 90 per cent of the First Peoples in the most densely populated areas of the southeast succumbed to disease (Butlin, 1993), with the Nhunggabarra among the hardest hit. Atrocities and massacres committed by the early white settlers completed the tragedy (Sveiby and Skuthorpe, 2006: 220). The remaining chapter is organized in three sections, beginning with how Tex guided me to discover his people's knowledge. First, I will share some of my own bewilderment when I, as a Westerner and newcomer, tried to figure out how to conduct the research and make sense of what I learned from Tex.

Discovering the Knowledge: A Mystery and Its Resolution

When we first met, I asked Tex:

KE: *What was your people's most valuable resource?*
Tex: *It was Knowledge.*
KE: *What is your people's word for knowledge?*
Tex: *I don't think we have one.*
KE: *???*

His answer was so unexpected that I realized that my questions were widely off the mark. To understand the Nhunggabarra's ontology and meanings of the Law stories, I needed to leave behind my Western ontology (Hosking, 2011) and enter a process of relating.

Many years later I asked Tex: *What would have been the right questions?*

Tex: *You and I walked together, and we talked about what we saw, the plants, the trees, the animals, and we shared each other's views. Walking the land gave us the feel, the smells. We will have different experiences. Both ways are right.*

Tex and I visited the places featured in the stories and camped in his country on several occasions. I took field notes and photos, trying to make sense of what I experienced; a kind of embedded ethnography (Lewis and Russel, 2011) that included inquiry, many conversations, and shared experiences. Gradually, over several years of working together, Tex also paid a visit to my mother's land in the north of Sweden and we established a close relationship.

However, our walks were nothing in comparison to those done in precolonial times. The pubescent Nhunggal boy was sent out alone into the bush to find his way to a neighbouring community in the CoC. He lived there, learning their ways to inter-act respectfully, and then continued to the next community. When he had lived in all the communities and returned home, he would be around 30–32 years old! He would go through an examination before being declared an adult and thus fit to marry a woman from one of the other communities.

The community placed less emphasis upon the education of young Nhunggal girls because they were considered to be more mature. In puberty, a girl learned how to inter-act respectfully as a mother, and she was introduced to the role as the custodian of the land by the women at home. When she moved to her husband's community, she began learning the practices of her husband's home community and its land care.

The most valuable knowledge was based on practical activities which they learned by doing and by inter-acting with competent experts, *knowing-how to inter-act respectfully*. Their stories are the 'Law Book', which I refer to as '*scripts*' because they were intended to be performed orally, or as theatre and dances, emulating the animals' inter-actions. The distinctions between action, *knowing-how* to do something, and *script knowledge*[2] (knowing that something exists), are all essential epistemological ingredients of the methodology.

Leaving the Western ontology took a long time. Over and over again, when I believed that I had understood, and I tested my interpretation of the stories, Tex explained that it was the opposite. The final piece of the puzzle is found in the dictionary of the Nhunggabarra's *Yuwaalayaay* language (Ash et al., 2003) and in my personal conversations with one of its editors, John Giacon (2021). These revealed that there are no specific words for 'knowledge' or 'respect' in the dictionary, but the verb *winanga* covers both concepts. *Winanga* can be both transitive and intransitive and, depending on the suffix (*-y* or *-li*), mean several activities: to understand, to know, to remember, to think, to love (Ash et al., 2003; Giacon, 2021). Hence, *winanga* has a much deeper and holistic meaning in Aboriginal languages than what is usually meant by the English word 'respect'. I will return to this issue in the reflection section.

The theoretical positioning is of a relational ontology based on relational constructivism, because it expands social constructivism to other life forms than humans (Hosking, 2011). The respectful relations with the totem animals are, therefore, understood as 'inter-acting: (a) a performance (b) that involves a coming together (c) of "whoever and whatever" thereby (re)constructing person-world relations as (d) relational realities' (Hosking, 2011: 53).

Based on the stories and the vignette above, through drawing on this theoretical framing, I understand *winanga* as a normative ethical behavioural guide for action: *knowing how to always inter-act respectfully with all life forms*. These life forms include people, the land and its animals (including insects), trees, rivers, the air, and the diseased ancestors (their spirits were believed to be alive in the *Warrambul*).

This definition of respect is local to the Nhunggabarra, the Nhunggal land's geography, and the *Yuwaalayaay* language. Elsewhere in Australia, explanations in English and words used, vary depending on the local language, environmental conditions, and situations. Referring to both totem animals and people, Tex stated: *When showing respect, you allow them to see you in your true form; authentic, as you are*. Based on these

---

[2] Hosking (2011) uses the term 'aboutness knowledge' referring to the conceptual knowledge of scientists.

Table 12.1 A glossary of useful terminology (adapted from Ash et al., 2003; Giacon, 2021; Skuthorpe, 2019).

Terms of reference	Meaning
Aboriginal	The original people of Australia (politicised term). Synonym: First People.
Biiwii	Sand goanna, a common lizard species in Australia. Tex's totem animal.
Burruguu / The Dreaming	The time of creation which is still going on "everywhen" (Stanner, 1953). "The Dreaming" is early anthropologists' attempt to generalise the variety of belief systems that were incompatible with any known Western Judeo-Christian belief systems.
Corroboree	Educational event with entertainment, eg. Law story performances
Longnecked turtle	The Nhunggal Land's totem animal, not to confuse with the individual totem animals.
Nhungga	The Kurrajong tree widely cultivated by the Nunggabarra. The leaves were used as fodder during droughts. Edible seeds were used for baking. Roots of old trees were tapped for water during droughts.
Nhunggabarra	The Kurrajong people. *-barra* = "people from"
Nhunggal	Used as adjective when speaking English. eg. Nhunggal woman/man
Rainbow Serpent / Garriya	A mythical creature that created the riverbeds for the water to flow. It could take many forms. On Nhunggal land it also appeared as a vicious giant crocodile *Garriya*.
Warrambul	1. The Milky Way. 2. Water channels that hold water only during flood times.
Winanga -y or -li	Verb: To understand, to know, to remember, to think, to love, "Respect"
Yurrti	Totem. Animals which obeyed the Law in the *Burruguu* and were turned into people.
Yuwaalayaay	A language in the *Gamilaraay* family, spoken by the Nhunggabarra,

linguistic aspects and the relational framing of the case presented next, I develop a concept for describing the Nhunggabarra with their totem animals as a *symmetrically reciprocal relationship*. Table 12.1 includes a glossary of terminology that can help assist understanding what follows.

Burruguu (the Creation) and the Rainbow Serpent Story

The earth gave birth to a snake, and it wriggled all over the earth making all the riverbeds as it went. The snake then asked for the frogs to be born. The frogs were born in sacks of water, so the snake tickled them and made them laugh. They laughed so hard that the sacks burst, releasing the water and filling all the riverbeds.

With the coming of water to the land, all the plants, trees, birds, and animals were made. In the Burruguu one of the laws that the animals learned was about certain places they could not go. Some of the animals broke the law by going to these places and they were turned into hills, mountains and valleys. These animals that broke the law became Law totems. In Nhunggal country, the animal that broke the law was the Longnecked turtle, and so this creature became the Law totem for the Nhunggal people.

Tex: *The animals that did not break the law were turned into Aboriginal people; it describes how Aboriginal people got all their different yurrti (totems)—from the animals who were rewarded by becoming human.* (Sveiby and Skuthorpe, 2006: 4).

The Creation story differs from the other Law stories as it was not intended to emulate animal behaviours. Instead, it explains the origin of the relationship between animals, humans, and the Nhunggal land. Based on my many conversations with Tex, I have constructed the following interpretation of the ontology: Both *biiwii*-lizards and *biiwii*-humans are the earthly multiple manifestations of one single *biiwii*-spirit in the Warrambul. Some of the *biiwii*-lizard manifestations were behaving disrespectfully whereas the *biiwii*-turned-human manifestations were rewards to those *biiwii*-lizards that had acted respectfully. When the *biiwii*-lizard manifestation dies, it disintegrates back into the Earth. When the *biiwii*-human dies, their earthly manifestation (the body) returns into the Earth while the spirit travels to the Warrambul and continues to live there forever, as a spirit together with their ancestors at the campfires, the stars. This is their reward for having behaved respectfully to both totem animals and humans. The Longnecked turtle totem was the Nhunggal Land's totem animal (not to be confused with the humans' totem animals).

This relational ontology was still guiding activities when Tex was a teenager: '*I remember this old bloke in the 1960s, who continued to perform the dance of the giant emu* [a species that had gone extinct since colonization]. *Every year he dressed up and painted himself and performed the dance. He had the role to perform the dance and he was convinced that in doing so, he kept the giant emu alive in the Warrambul*' (Sveiby and Skuthorpe, 2006: 8).

The Nhunggabarra had learned, through acts of trial and error during thousands of years, how to inter-act with the animals and different practices to care for the habitats that the animals were feeding from. If they failed, they knew that the animals would perish and the people with them. Tex expressed the tasks to achieve this, simply, as: '*Keep All Alive*'. However, of most importance was the Land's totem animal. If the Longnecked turtle became extinct, the Nhunggal land would die, and as a consequence, all Nhunggal people too. This shows how the totem system was linked to the local ecosystem and the land; if the land dried out, the water-dependent turtle would certainly die.

Tex's relationship with his totem animal began in childhood when he was sent out into the bush by the elders with gradually more difficult tasks. He started by observing and slowly learning about their family life, parenthood, birth and death, and how they acquired their food. When he returned, he was asked to relate what he had learned and to reflect about its meaning. The elders never criticized him, just said: 'hmm, there's more to it'. He knew that he had passed a test when he was given another, more difficult task. In this way, he began knowing-how to inter-act respectfully, and he became a member of the informal collective of all the sand goanna totem people in Australia. These are all kinfolk and Tex had relatives in every corner of Australia. All he needed to do on his journeys was to ask for the sand goannas, and he would be welcomed as a son by the oldest sand goanna couple, and as a brother by the other sand goanna people.

INTER-ACT RESPECTFULLY! A LAW STORY

Totem animals feature prominently in the Law stories. Generally, the storyline is that they inter-act disrespectfully and, thus, get punished. A Law story was meant to be learned by everyone in the community, and was designed with a dramatic plot to be performed at educational events (called '*corroborees*', see Table 12.1).

THE CRANE AND THE CROW

Garraagaa, the crane, was a great fisherman. He could catch many fish by hunting them out with his feet, from underneath the logs in the creek. One day, **when he had a great many on the bank of the creek,** *Waan, the crow, who was white at that time, came up and asked the crane to give him some fish. The crane* **told the crow to wait until the fish were cooked** *but the crow was hungry and impatient. He kept bothering the crane, who told him to wait. Eventually, the crane turned his back. The crow sneaked up, and was just about to steal a fish, when the crane saw him,* **seized a fish and hit the crow right across the eyes with it.** *The crow felt blinded for a few minutes. He fell on the burnt black grass around the fire and rolled over and over in his pain. When he got up,* **his eyes were white** *and the rest of him black, as crows have been ever since. The crow was determined to have his revenge. He waited for his chance and one day saw the crane fast asleep on his back with his mouth wide open. He crept quietly up to him and* **stuck a fish bone right across the root of the crane's tongue.** *The crane woke up, and when he opened his mouth to yawn, he felt like choking. He tried to get the thing out of his throat, and in the effort, he made a strange scraping noise—'gah-rah-gah, gah-rah-gah'. But the fish bone could not be moved, and still* **the only noise a crane can make is 'gah-rah-gah'**—*the name by which he is known.* (See figure 12.2 below).

To analyse this story, I apply relational constructivist theory. The bolded texts refer to the *inter-acts* (**b**) and *power-to* and *power-over* (**g**) according to Hosking (2011: 52).

GUIDED BY A LIZARD 187

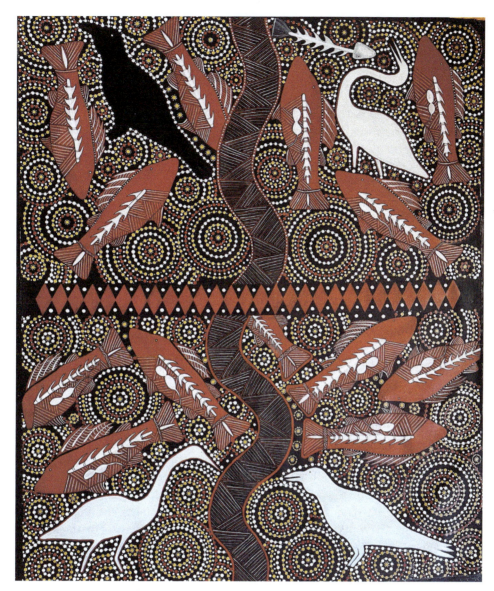

FIGURE 12.2 Painting of the Crane and the Crow—a Law story by Tex Skuthorpe. Copyright: The authors.

Crane and Crow are totem animals and, hence, also humans. Crane is performing (**b**) his *power-to* fish (**g**) from a position of *power-over* (**g**) a hungry Crow, who performs an act of begging (**b**). Crane responds with a *power-over* precondition (**g**) to cook the fish (**g**). This is the first chain of micro-level inter-acts.

Next, Crow attempts to steal (**b**) a fish and Crane hits him (**b**) with a fish (**b**) and Crow gets burned, a further physical micro-level inter-act. The inter-action continues when

Crane sleeps, which gives Crow temporary *power-to* (g) revenge by putting a fishbone in Crane's throat, the final micro-level inter-act.

Cranes and Crows were of course familiar to all, both children and adults. What was visible only to the initiated adults were three concealed disrespectful inter-acts. First, Crane should share his fishing *power-to* (g) fish with Crow instead of trying to preserve his *power-over* (b) Crow, making him dependent. Second, the Crane uses his *power-over* (b) a weaker totem animal, (a fish on dry land), as a weapon, which kills the fish. Finally, Crane is fishing too much, thereby endangering the breeding stock in the river, which will cause problems for the communities downstream, (the dot-painted big circles in Figure 12.2 above). This will lead to a breakdown in the relationship between the local Nhunggal ontology and the local ontologies of the downstream communities, a serious threat to the regional ontology of the whole CoC.

Organizing Respectfully with Collectives

The individual activities were coordinated by collectives with *power-over* specific Law story ontologies, and I will cover the three most important ones for this chapter. First, every adult was a member of a local protection collective for their particular totem animal. They maintained their own regional ontologies and relational processes (Hosking, 2011), covering the whole CoC. If the *biiwiis* disappeared from an area on the local Nhunggal land the *biiwii*-people would blame themselves; they would perform ceremonies, inter-acting with the *biiwii*-spirit in the *Warrambul* to figure out where and how they had shown disrespect against its earthly manifestations. They would alert the *biiwii* collective in the other communities, who would join the inter-action to understand what the root cause of the problem could be. In the case of disagreements, the full *biiwii* totem CoC collective gathered to arrive at a decision through dialogue and consensus.

The Marriage Law ontology was maintained by the women's collective and gave them the power to plan marriages, a regional ontology covering the whole CoC. This, in addition to the education ontology, had consequences for each local community's unmarried men and all married women from another community, creating an extraordinary blending of individual and regional ontologies. Kinship, then, defined the relational boundaries of organizing the CoC and its ontology.

The women inherited the land from their mothers and, as a collective, they were hence custodians of all the lands in the CoC, a regional ontology that gave them power over the most valuable natural resource, and a major responsibility to care for the local community relationships with the Land. Tex expressed it as: '*Care for the Land and the Land will care for you*'.

The Intergenerational Scope of *Knowing-how* and Scripts

In 1788, the community of 26 communities consisted of collectives responsible for specific areas of *knowing-how* that only assembled when called upon. Some 20 Law collectives have been identified, among them the 'pillars' mentioned previously.
Via the Marriage Law collective, the women had the *power-over* three intergenerational *knowing-how* areas: all the lands in the CoC, marriage planning, and thereby, what kind of *knowing-how* the married couples' children would be trained to perform. For example, Tex was given the role of Law story custodian, because both his parents were of Law totems. Except for the totem collectives, the male collectives' power was restricted to their home community.

The power of *knowing-how* was visible also in gender relations. Childcare, marriage planning, and Land care were women's tasks. The stories' script emphasizes collective decision-making and warn women from breaking-up into factions. Their power should be vested in collectives for counterbalancing men's individual physical strength and violent tendencies. Hence, the Nhunggabarrra would probably not fully understand today's gender discourse. For them, there were tasks they had to do, and in some of these, gender mattered. This gave women more power over the long-term, intergenerational survival of the people than the men. Men and women were different, yet equal.

Farms Without Fences

The Nhunggabarra used several methods to care for the animals. The primary tool was to ignite slow-intensity fires in small areas according to the seasons. They planted Kurrajong trees, which in addition to the variety of resources they produced (see Table 12.1), offered shade from the burning sun to both animals and humans. These, and many other practices, created an array of vegetation fertilized by the ash to attract the totem animals. In this way, the Nhunggabarra did not need fences to keep domesticated animals from running away—the animals came to them.

The main source of meat in Nhunggal country was several species of fish and crustaceans produced by the rivers. Their fish farms were the antitheses of today's industrial salmon farmers, who buy the fingerlings 'from the market', feed them with 'prepared commercial fish feed available in the market', and then keep the fish in cages or tanks until slaughter time (Roy's farm, 2021). In contrast to these present-day practices, the Nhunggabarra and the other communities along the rivers had developed other strategies for maximizing the yield. They kept the water clean from debris and constructed safe havens and hatching nurseries from tree branches where water was still, thus shielding the fingerlings from predators. They used different sized nets for fishing, but never hooks, as they would harm the fish. As a result, Mitchell (1846: 222) saw 'water being beautifully transparent, the bottom was visible at great depths, showing large fishes in shoals, floating like birds in mid-air'.

These systems of fish traps suggest that the First Peoples of south-east Australia knew, what has since been confirmed by science: bigger fish are the most valuable for sustaining a population and, therefore, should not be killed. Not only do big female fish produce larger quantities of eggs, but larvae from bigger fish also grow faster, and have a much higher survival rate than those spawned by smaller fish (Leahy, 2005).

TOPICS FOR REFLECTION

I will begin with the obvious issue of killing and eating totem animals and then reflect on the relational methodology applied. The kangaroo totem collective's members were not allowed to kill kangaroos, but they could eat the meat. This same rule applied to all totem animals. Before addressing this issue, I suggest the reader returns to the Creation story, the glossary (Table 12.1), and the text about the ontology of the Nhunggabarra.

Table 12.2 summarizes the four examples mentioned in this chapter, and shows how the totem relationship, over time, benefitted both the collective of wild animals and the collective of humans. The temporal aspect is important according to most Western ontologies, but this was not an issue for the Nhunggabarra. They knew that provided that the hunters followed the prescribed inter-acts in their ceremonies, the *biiwii* spirit in the *Warrambul* gave its consent to kill one of its manifestations on Earth. Therefore, the human-animal relationship can be said to be *symmetrically reciprocal*.

Table 12.2 Examples of the human–totem animal inter-acts.

Inter-acts	Type of resource	Beneficiary
Tex and the *biiwii* direct communication	Exchange of knowledge	Both animals and humans
Horticultural practices	Good fodder and shade	Both animals and humans
Caring for the land	Information about animal health	The animals
	Activities to solve problems	Both humans and animals
Kangaroo	Good fodder, shade, and healthy life	The animals
Respectful culling	Animal's life	The humans
Fish	Clear healthy water, good fodder, and protection against predators	The animals
Respectful culling	Animal's life	The humans

According to the Nhunggabarra totem ontology humans and other beings do not exist in time; their ontology had 'a complex spatial-temporal quality and its "metaphysical heart" (Porr, 2018: 396) encapsulating a oneness of "body, spirit, ghost, shadow, name, spirit-site, and totem",' (Stanner 1953; 25). I also refer the reader to the animals in figures 12.1. and 12.2. They are 'x-ray' paintings; the patterns inside the animals are neither decorations nor entrails, but Nhunggal sacred symbols, which illustrate that the knowledge of the totem animals makes them more valuable alive than dead.

I have chosen Hosking's (2011) version of relational constructivism as the theory for this chapter for several reasons: the theory resonates with what I experienced as a researcher and the Law stories explicitly describe activities, inter-actions, and power relations. In the section on 'Discovering the Knowledge', I have tried to convey how my relationship with Tex started from completely different selves and ontologies, then gradually developed into softer differentiations when I understood that, here, was a mystery in need of inquiry, and we had shared a number of experiences together. Tex, as a teacher of his people's culture and his self being scarred by the dominant white Western culture of today's Australia, had rarely experienced honest inquiry from a white person. But his response to my questions was a gift, as he communicated knowledge as art since the performative power of the scripts had been lost (Sveiby and Skuthorpe, 2006).

Our common language was English, but we were both speaking a foreign language. I had learned it voluntarily, but his English had been forced on him by the colonial powers—an abusive act of power which in one stroke also destroyed a vital source of *knowing-how*. The importance of the knowledge embedded in the Indigenous languages is now acknowledged in Australia, but far too late. As in my example of the word 'respect' shows, our 'relational process ... opened up possibilities' (Hosking, 2011: 52), but not satisfactorily. As the *Yuwaalayaay* language include words that contain multiple references to the local cultural context and its eco-system, Tex decided to do a painting of each Law story to complement its script (included in Sveiby and Skuthorpe, 2006).

The loss of the language also impacted the Law stories. What once were rich oral and visual performative scripts for people of all ages to learn the *knowing-how* to inter-act respectfully with each other and their totem animals, was reduced to written texts in English. Fortunately, Tex had learned how to interpret them from the Nhunggabarra elders in their own language, and our walks and dialogues, along with his paintings, helped make them sufficiently clear for my research purposes.

Relational processes 'have a historical quality in the sense that acts always supplement earlier performances and have implications for how a process will go on' (Hosking, 2011: 55). This feature has been applied for understanding prehistorical people's relationships with animals in archaeology and anthropology (see Brown and Walker, 2008). I also hypothesize that the performances of the Law stories' scripts were intentionally amended this way for the Nhunggabarra and the CoC historically up until 1788. For example, the Law stories portray an ambivalent political history shifting between male-driven autocratic organizing and collective organizing. The women's collectives' power over the intergenerational development of the CoC visible in the last version of the stories had probably developed as solutions for preventing future conflicts, while the Law story scripts were amended to classify such inter-actions as disrespectful.

Concluding Thoughts

This chapter presents a unique case from an Australian First People to show humanity once organized respectful relationships with animals, understood by using relational constructivism. The derived concept from the Law stories, *symmetrically reciprocal relationships*, summarizes what *respect* and *being respectful* meant in terms of the people's activities for/with the animals, and how they organized their society. The case also underscores the importance of ontologies that support individual activities and practices along with epistemologies that enable the deep involvement of the researcher.

The distance in time to their fully functioning society is a mere 200 years, but the distance between their respectful ontology towards all life-forms and our Western ontologies is infinite. We are, instead, counting down to a time in the near future when the whole planet Earth has had enough of our disrespectful ontology towards all life-forms, and the animals we call humans will perish. Will we succeed in turning the trend around?

I hope that the chapter will inspire future research to explore these ontologies further and to develop practices that will support respectful relationships for animals in today's organizations. Tex summarizes the key message from his people to us alive today: 'Respect All, Keep All Alive and Look after the Land', then: 'Land will look after You and We will All Survive.'

References

Ash, A. Giacon, J., & Lissarrague, A. (2003). *Gamilararaay, Yuwaalaraay and Yuwaalayaay dictionary*. Alice Springs: IAD Press.

Barnard, A. (1999). Modern hunter-gatherers and early symbolic culture. In R.I. Dunbar, M. Knight, & C. Power (Eds.), *The evolution of culture: An interdisciplinary view*, p.51–68. 2nd Edition. Edinburgh: Rutgers University Press.

Bowler, J. et al. (2003). New ages for human occupation and climatic change at Lake Mungo Australia. *Nature, 421*, 837–40.

Brown, L.A. & Walker, W.H. (2008). Prologue: Archaeology, animism and non-human agents. *Journal of Archaeological Method and Theory, 15(4)*, 297–9.

Butlin, N.G. (1993). *Economics and the dreamtime: A hypothetical history*. Cambridge: Cambridge University Press.

Clarkson, C. et al. (2017). Human occupation of northern Australia by 65,000 years ago. *Nature, 547*, 306–310.

Diamond, J.M. (1999). *Guns, germs, and steel, the fates of human societies*. 2nd Edition. New York: Norton.

Flannery, T. (2002). *The future eaters: an ecological history of the Australasian lands and people.* (1st ed, 1994). New York: Grove Press

Gammage, B. (2011). *The biggest estate on earth: how Aborigines made Australia.* Sydney: Allen and Unwin.

Giacon, J. (2021). Email conversation.

Hosking, D.M. (2011). Telling tales of relations: Appreciating relational constructionism. *Organization Studies, 32(1),* 47–65.

Leahy M. (2005). Let the big fish go to save the species, viewed 16 March 2021, New Scientist Newsletter.

Lewis, S.J. & Russell, A.J. (2011). Being embedded: A way forward for ethnographic research. *Ethnography, 12(3),* 398–416.

Mitchell, T.L. (1846). *Three expeditions into the interior of Australia.* Vol. 1, Limited facsimile edition. London: Boone.

Porr, M. (2018). Country and relational ontology in the Kimberley, Northwest Australia: Implications for understanding and representing archaeological evidence. *Cambridge Archaeological Journal, 28(3),* 395–409.

Roy's Farm, https://www.roysfarm.com/fish-farming/#Feeding.

Stanner, W.E.H. (1953). *White man got no Dreaming. Essays 1938-1973.* Canberra: The Australian National University Press and Scholarly Information Services/Library.

Sveiby, K. & Skuthorpe, T. (2006). *Treading lightly: the hidden wisdom of the world's oldest people.* Sydney: Allen and Unwin.

CHAPTER 13

'SECRET SQUIRREL REPORTS FOR DUTY'

How the Use of Animal Metaphors Can Assist Our Learning of Workplace Interactions

STEPHANIE RUSSELL

INTRODUCTION

ANIMAL metaphors are common in most cultures, so much so that we hardly even notice they are there. Animals can be used to describe people; both as a source of derision (Bame et al., 2013) and to socially exclude (Andrighetto et al., 2016). Organizations have long been known to use animals as their commercial logo, for example: Twitter, World Wildlife Fund (WWF), Lacoste, Jaguar, and Swarovski all have animal logos. While people's identification with animals enables them to relate to the organization behind the logo, however, there are exceptions. On the one hand, the alligator used on the Lacoste brand could be seen, at first glance, as fear-inducing if it were applied to an organization specializing in security. But Lacoste has designed it as a symbol of comfort. Swarovski, on the other hand, chose the logo of a swan to reflect grace, beauty, and elegance—a fitting metaphor and symbol for a jewellery brand. Metaphors themselves are known in the social science and literary fields as a means by which to make and partake in organizational stories (Bame et al., 2013); as a development of language (Pinker, 1993) and 'constitute a primary and enduring means of understanding human experience' (Bell and Clarke, 2014: 252). This chapter opens with a brief ethnographic vignette that illustrates the pervasive nature of animal metaphors in business life and highlights the role of nonhuman animals in contributing to the creation of an inclusive, moral, and productive workplace.

I like animal metaphors. Do you remember when we discussed how many we could get into one conversation—'you're as busy as a queen bee and Dan is always beavering away'. That was a start! (Laughing). Animal metaphors work for me, but when Richie started talking about dressing up as one of them ... it all went downhill (laughing). (Informal conversation, field notes).

The vignette above took place between two colleagues in the case study organization, Fireco. The individuals were discussing how they enjoyed using animal metaphors as a means of helping them to understand certain behaviours demonstrated by their colleagues, (or themselves), and it provided a clear link to the organizational culture—*Gung Ho*. *Gung Ho* is a fable of a wise Indian grandfather who advocates that organizational cultures should be structured around three key principles, which originated from watching animals. What became disconcerting for employees of Fireco, was when one of the team leaders suggested that these metaphors could be translated into costumes, and, even worse, when one of them was encouraged to dress up as an animal. The latter appeared unpalatable, because its unconventionality dramatized the organizational culture, leaving some employees feeling awkward when having to translate the culture, whilst wearing a costume. In exploring this case, this chapter offers a different take on what Labatut et al. (2016) discussed as the, animal at work. Here the animals are not 'real' but inferred through metaphors, brought to life through the assemblage of costumes and artifacts, which steers us towards recognizing the role that nonhumans play during the process of translation (Latour, 1987).

In extending an analysis of this organization's distinctive form of animal work, the chapter draws on the theoretical framing of Latour's (1987; 1991) Actor Network Theory (ANT), to provide an approach to the use of networks within organizations, which consist of both human and nonhuman actors. Using ANT encourages us to step away from easy assumptions of 'omniscient' humanity as the only gauge of how we may think about, and measure, agency within an organization. It broadens our thinking about the role that animals in a metaphorical/symbolic sense have on individuals' ways of behaving in workplaces, and the mechanisms of translating organizational culture into meaningful practice. Animals have the capacity to change the space in which organizational actors manage and interact with each other. This chapter shows how that takes place practically, as people experiment with the use of costumes, as one means by which organizational culture can be co-created by humans and nonhuman actors.

The chapter has two main goals. First, to contribute through the lens of ANT, the role played by an assemblage of agents, (costumes and artifacts), in translating organizational culture and raising awareness of human interaction in organizations. This provides the starting point for a discussion about what animal metaphors offer us as organizational scholars, in enhancing our understanding of the agency of both animals and humans where animal metaphors (or costumes) are used. The second contribution, through the use of ethnographic data, is to add practical insight into how culture is translated through agents within a network. Animals, in the symbolic sense, can provide insights into admirable attributes which are then created and shared amongst workplace employees to build a more inclusive and team-orientated culture. The empirical findings focus on the use of metaphors and costumes to convey the *Gung Ho* culture to employees, adding insights into the unique characteristics of the individuals (and animals) working at Fireco. These demonstrate that the heterogeneous network is always precarious, especially as animals have a 'lively subjectivity' and, as 'corporeal beings' (Nimmo, 2019: 120), add to the messy nature of organizational networks, and the cultures which frame them. In the next section, I set out the theoretical framework of the chapter before discussing how the interrelationships between animal metaphors and organizational culture create meaning amongst employees and enhance their understanding of 'appropriate' workplace interactions.

ANT: An Analytical Approach to Human-Animal Interactions

ANT emerged in the 1980s out of constructivist approaches to social sciences and from ethnographic studies of laboratories (Callon, 1984; Latour and Woolgar, 1979;). It has enabled a more accessible inquiry into a range of fields of academic practice, including the economy (Callon, 1998) and consumer goods (Cochoy, 2007). ANT was advanced in the 1990s and 2000s, as a way of providing an alternative approach to the study of social sciences, offering us a way of viewing the world, in that it entails a basic ontological claim that all entities are 'constituted and reconstituted in shifting and hybrid webs of discursive and material relations' (Latour, 1988 cited in Farias et al., 2020: xx). ANT has been at the forefront of providing a lens through which the social and organizational world is considered in a way which reflected a profoundly different orientation, both ontologically and methodologically (Nimmo, 2019).

Mol (2010: 265) argues, that ANT consists of 'a rich array of explorative and experimental ways of attuning to the world'. Actors can come in many forms (technology, object, machines, text, animals) and all can interact through relations with others (Law, 1992; Nimmo, 2019). These actors engage in 'translation' (Callon, 1984; Law, 1992) which can be seen as an 'enactment of materially and discursively heterogeneous relations' (Law, 2008: 141). Latour's (2018) more recent work is on climate change and ecological crises, but other work has explored architecture (Färber, 2020) and health care (Beisel, 2020), through the lens of ANT.

ANT theorists argue that 'knowledge' is not generated through the privileged human being, but it is a product, or effect, of a heterogeneous network (Callon, 1984; Law, 1992; 2008). The network consists of a process 'in which bits and pieces from the social, the technical, the conceptual and the textual are fitted together' (Law, 1992: 2). ANT provides a strong argument which acknowledges that the interrelated parts all participate in the creation of their surroundings. They shape it, through their interactions, and their own internal desires—in equal measure (Nimmo, 2019). It is not led by humans, nor is it dominated by power relations originating from one powerful actor. Any object can influence and change the social environment, be that an organization, a culture, a technology, the written word, or in this case, an animal. ANT also has the capability of providing us with a moral lens through which we view actors sensitively and are aware of their underlying assumptions (Mol, 2010), and the terms which frame their actions. Viewed in this way, a network is not bound by power relations, but illustrates 'the basis for a shared, relational system that co-produces value' (Hamilton and Mitchell, 2018: 9).

Studies are progressively moving towards more recognition of these interrelationships, between the agents of a network, both human and animal. The study of Manchester Airport Group (O'Doherty, 2016; also Ch. 23 in this volume), directs us to think about how multispecies interactions can have positive benefits for the ethnographer and the organization. 'Olly the Cat' was recognized as not just a 'symbol', but contributed to a wider ontological insight into the potential role that nonhumans play in creating and challenging cultural spaces, including questioning the role of management behaviour. More recently, Knight and Sang (2020) explored the recruitment and careers of police dogs and found that the dogs were deemed to be 'good' nonhuman animals in the organizational setting of the police, rather than just 'tools' of their owners. These studies are valuable starting points to indicate the fundamental role that ANT has, as a moral theory, but also as an analytical approach. Its value is captured by Williams-Jones and Graham (2003: 290) who state that it enables an 'unpacking… which has been simplified or buried'.

Wadham (2021: 110) brought to our attention the role that ANT plays as an 'epistemological position' and Cerolo (2009: 534) acknowledges that it 'offers a novel view both of social interaction and of those who can legitimately participate in it'. The heterogeneous interaction between diverse actors, enables ANT to dispense with a key pillar of anthropic thinking—in that rather than only using humans as the yardstick to measure agency (Nimmo, 2019), instead ANT encourages us to think of the agency of nonhuman animals, bacteria, bees, worms, and global viruses.

The use of animal metaphors and their associated costumes, are not reflective of a superior 'human world' (Taylor, 2011: 212), but rather animals, people, and inanimate objects, are co-creators of the workplace environment and culture in which they exist. They are tied together reflecting an 'interspecies solidarity' (Coulter, 2015), enabling us to construct meaning and engage equally in collective 'sense-making' (Weick, 1979). As Dowling et al. (2017: 824) stated 'beings, things and objects previously ignored as active agents' are now being brought to the fore. When applied to organizational studies, it is these co-constitutive relationships that enable us to understand the interaction between animals and humans in a more enlightened way. ANT encourages us to not have pre-conceived judgements about the role of actors, and their capacity to impact on, or within a network, but instead to go beyond seeing humans as the most powerful actor, when instead, they are just one part of a wider precarious network of relational actors.

Animal Metaphors and Organizational Culture

A key feature of ANT is the notion of interrelationships, social interaction, and relational meaning constructed through outcomes between agents (Latour, 1992; 2005). Starting with metaphors but visually seen through costumes and artifacts, is one way of achieving this representation of meaning, providing an easy-to-understand illustration of organizational culture, potentially enabling actors to communicate in ways that adjectives alone may hinder. This enables 'fresh ways of seeing, understanding and shaping the [organizations that we work in]' (Morgan, 2006: 5).

The use of animals to describe others (Andrighetto et al., 2016; Bame et al., 2013; Haslam et al., 2011;) has been one of the most widespread uses of metaphors. Metaphors have long been used as a way of defining everyday life; a way of highlighting certain aspects of a phenomenon (thought, feelings, behaviour, communication) and bringing it into being, whilst obscuring others (Bell and Clarke, 2014; Morgan, 2006;). The use of metaphors enables us to identify and resolve problems and Pinker (2007: 249) argued, 'People can not only ignore metaphors, but can question and discount them, and analyze which aspects are applicable and which should be ignored'.

Metaphors can help to 'translate' thought or behaviour, and create meaning alongside other actors. Bame et al. (2013), draws our attention to how animal metaphors can be used to maintain positive cultural changes, by encouraging people to reflect on animal behaviours (e.g. the horse bully, the snake bully, the howling monkey), prior to recruitment and selection, and in doing so, avoid recruiting potential 'bullies'. In a similar vein, but taking a more critical stance, Andrighetto et al. (2016) warned us against using animal metaphors for exclusionary purposes. When the metaphors of giraffe, worm, and bear were used to describe people, they had detrimental cultural consequences, leading to bullying and social exclusion, arguably challenging ANT's moral lens.

The connection between animals and organizational culture is not new. Shelley (2007–21) founded the Organizational Zoo which entertainingly profiles common behaviour types found in organizations. Animals in the hierarchy are reflective of that seen in an organizational culture, and through caricatures the strength and weaknesses of each animal/human behaviour is portrayed. On the Organizational Zoo website, the value of metaphors are explained, with the intention of making working life more manageable:

> The Organizational Zoo is a safe, engaging and creative way to explore relationships. It's exciting to see how much constructive conversation about behaviour is stimulated when people interact around the Zoo concept.

The humorous reference to animals adds to the growing body of practitioner literature around organizational culture, which speaks of the dysfunctionality of outdated management ideologies of the 1980s and 1990s. In the early 1980s, literature on corporate culture began to challenge the traditional separation of work and play (Deal and Kennedy, 1982). Peters (2003), a particularly strong critic, argued that the focus should not be on conformity, rationality, and unitary values, but instead on what Owler and Morrison (2020) have promoted as 'fun at work'.

More recently, the use of animal metaphors and observing animals in the literal sense has added rich insights into how we can use them to reimagine workplace roles, and improve current practice, such as the underrepresentation of female leaders (Smith et al., 2020). This has far-reaching consequences and is commendable, in that animals, (in their symbolic or literal sense), can 'shape not just our language but also our ways of thinking and acting' (Andrighetto et al., 2016: 630).

Gung Ho! Culture: Squirrels, Beavers, and Geese

Ken Blanchard and Sheldon Bowles (1998) are the authors of *Gung Ho*. In the foreword to the book, Blanchard states that it provides 'secrets to help people make work better' and *Gung Ho* provides an 'inspirational story on how to energise and empower your people'. Although the lack of reference to shareholder demands, inequality, profit, or resistance is evident within *Gung Ho*, it must be acknowledged that Fireco is still focused on productivity.

The first principle of *Gung Ho* was revealed by watching squirrels running to a feeder, stuffing their cheeks with sunflower seeds, and taking them back to the forest ready for winter. It was explained that squirrels do this to survive, and it reflects their ability to engage in 'worthwhile work' (Blanchard and Bowles, 1998: 35). Applying the Spirit of the Squirrel, it is suggested that employees should be encouraged to understand 'how we make the world a better place' (Ibid: 56). The second principle of *Gung Ho* is the 'Way of the Beaver', which was demonstrated by watching beavers repairing their dam, following a flood. It is argued that beavers are 'in control of achieving [their] goal' (Ibid: 93). This is cultivated in organizations when managers 'define the playing field and the rules of the game. Then you have to get off the field and let the players move the ball' (Ibid: 79). Employees work best when they feel valued and "[t]heir thoughts, feelings, needs and dreams are respected, listened to, and acted upon' (Ibid: 85). The third and final principle of *Gung Ho,* was observed in a flock of geese flying south for the winter. As the geese flew by in their V formation, they were honking at each other. It is asserted that this sound was a reflection of their happy, enthusiastic cheering of their fellow geese. The Gift of the Goose is a reflection of people being complimented and celebrated by their colleagues. In *Gung Ho* it was said that the goose is a reflection of 'teamwork' (Ibid: 133) whereby individuals engage in morning 'huddles' which end with a 'victory yell' (p. 93).

The three principles of *Gung Ho*, are offered as a means by which the translation of, often complex, management and cultural practices, can be transferred to employees in a fun, engaging, and easy to understand manner, very much like the Organizational Zoo. The use of animals, and the adoption of the culture in the case study organization, adds practical insight into ANT's network of agents and their co-constructed interactions. It offers us organizational insights into how human interaction can be learnt through observing animals and using animal metaphors. Before extending this line of enquiry empirically, it is perhaps important to offer some context for the case study which follows.

Fireco, the case study organization used in this chapter, is located in the north of England and is involved in international sales within the construction industry in 120 countries worldwide. The company designs and manufactures leading-edge technology, as well as providing independent customer support. The company prides itself on being able to support customers with first-hand software, products, and tools from training to consultancy. The data collected for this chapter was part of a two and a half year project that involved 10, 2-hour interviews, 30 hours of meeting observations, informal gatherings and documentary evidence. The data for this chapter also included spontaneous invitations to coffee/lunch and site inspections with employees.

The data collected was qualitative in nature, and the research employed an interpretive technique, to encourage one 'to describe, decode, translate and otherwise come to terms with the meaning, not the frequency' (Van Maanen, 1979: 520) of the events as they emerged. To investigate the value and role that animal metaphors, (and costumes), play in organizational life, involved drawing attention to how animals (symbolic or literal), have the capacity to conjoin with humans in the creation and resolution of cultural workplace interactions.

'Going the extra mile': Animal metaphors and cultural 'buy in'

> "You have to be contributing to teamwork, you have to recruit the right people who are going to do worthwhile work....you also have to teach people self-responsibility ... we can't roll up like a hedgehog, we have to get out there and be acting like squirrels and beavers, and teach our employees to work together like geese. It's really fun! Oh sorry, do you have a clue what I'm talking about? (laughing). These are the animals Ken talks about, have you heard of them?"

The above quote was expressed by Mick, (a marketing manager), who explained how the principles of *Gung Ho* were able to spread the values of the organizational culture, via the animal metaphors. Mick's humorous response, as he explained his alignment to Fireco's culture, demonstrates the value that metaphors can have in translating cultural values into meaningful actions. Employees within Fireco showed affinity to the culture as many viewed their jobs as 'worthwhile' in terms of 'making a difference' (Kim, sales coordinator). The use of animal metaphors in creating a high level of enthusiasm became evident when Melanie, (an export manager) indicated that she was truly following 'the way of the beaver'.

> "I've been at Fireco for fourteen years and to still have such enthusiasm now shows something. I align myself to the Way of the Beaver – it's really easy to remind yourself of the need to complete worthwhile work"

The animal metaphors were used during the recruitment process which aimed to ensure that the 'right' people were employed. For example, Sarah, (a corporate social responsibility officer) commented:

> "In my interview I was asked to describe situations which showed the core values, so where I showed courage, teamwork, commitment. I was asked to draw on specific examples... like, when did you show support for others in your team, what qualities make you a committed team player".

Gary, (an HR advisor), spoke of the need to ensure that people working within Fireco 'go outside their normal circle of habits', and explained how the animal metaphors enabled the organization to reflect on their current 'individualistic' culture, and move towards one which was collaborative and teamwork focused:

> "... teamwork was the one that we really needed to sort out. We had to introduce it as a value. Individuals were earning lots and lots of money, but then there were others who weren't. We used the metaphor of the goose. We changed the team payment; so yes, teams could earn a lot of money but that relied on the high earners helping the others – it brought people together. We say to people 'you are geese, remember, not lions.'"

Gary indicated how the metaphor of the goose, and the value of teamwork, managed to fundamentally shift the culture to one that showcased the reliance all actors had on one another. Rather than a powerful, dominating individual taking charge, all employees were responsible for a successful outcome. Viewed through the lens of ANT, this reinforces the agency of multiple actors in the network (Latour, 2005). In Gary's example, the symbolic goose has as much agency as he, or his colleagues have. The goose plays a fundamental role in helping Fireco to translate the desired behaviour, (collaborative, productive and supportive team player), and clarify what was deemed 'right' and 'wrong'. In contrast, the lion metaphor was not deemed desirable. Shelley (2007-2021) referred to lions as 'aggressive leaders who ruled the pride through fear' and this was not the appropriate behaviour that Fireco promoted amongst its employees. Using animals in this symbolic, metaphorical way, highlights a fundamental role of nonhuman animals, what Latour (1992) refers to as the 'missing masses'. ANT encourages us to see workplace networks through a moral and analytical lens—it provides an exploration of the inter-relational ties between actors (Latour, 1991; 2005), not a lens through which to view power. In this way, the goose shaped the ideal of the successful Fireco employee.

The cultural value of 'self-responsibility' through the Spirit of the Squirrel resulted in employees generating ' … dialogues [and] conversations that allow the 'voice' of these unspoken stakeholders … to be heard' (Waddock, 2011: 205 cited in Connolly and Cullen, 2018: 419). This is explained below by Greg (a team leader):

> "It doesn't matter where people work – in the warehouse, at home, out on the road, in the boardroom, they can all come up with ideas. We don't shackle people in here, we say to them, use the squirrel metaphor to remind yourself that you are self-responsible. Show us what you can do; be brave. It's a case of 'how would you solve this problem, find your own solution'".

Greg's statement: 'we don't shackle people', implies that employees are not deprived of freedom, quite the opposite, they are encouraged through the squirrel metaphor to demonstrate self-responsibility. This challenges previous human-centric interactions, prompting us to place ' … value on the responsibilities arising out of the bonds of these relationships' (Connolly and Cullen, 2018: 408). ANT encourages us to think of the moral worth of including all agents in cultivating positive organizational change and re-thinking our perspectives on nonhuman actors, thereby providing ' … a more rounded understanding of what work is and how it creates value' (Hamilton and Michell, 2018: 14).

In further conversations, it was revealed that Fireco trusted people to work from home, without having to engage in 'micro-management' (Alvesson and Sveningsson, 2003). The squirrel and the beaver metaphor provided the frame of reference to help shape and create a culture of trust and honesty. Kim, (a sales co-ordinator), explained:

> " … these cultural values are how you live your life. If you do these things right, then everything else will follow; the animals are great to remind you of the need to be trustworthy and show integrity. I totally believe in them and everything they stand for".

When employees were absent from the office, they still knew what was expected of them by managers—a valuable offering for organizations, who may have more homeworkers, than ever, in the future.

'Animals help to resolve [our] problems'.

During the empirical fieldwork observations and through informal conversations with employees, it became clear that the use of animal metaphors was gradually being replaced with a more practical initiative—dressing up in animal costumes. This rather quirky practice was one means of trying to make the culture appear 'fun' and to encourage people to bring out 'their inner clown' (Bolton and Houlihan, 2009: 557). Employees were urged to be innovative and excited by their work, even if this resulted in a 'laissez-faire approach to norms ... a 'joyous anarchy' in which 'zanies' and mavericks are hired and celebrated' (Fleming and Sturdy, 2008: 573).

If the training message was focused on taking 'self-responsibility' then a beaver costume was used. Bob, (a team leader), explains:

> " ... he's [a beaver] made of real stuff ... you know, he's got a stuffed beaver on his head ... some people don't like it because it's furry. But removing that away from it, I mean it's just a beaver. It's at least manmade, although I think he might have some ears on his head" (laughing)

The costumes led to the merging of home and work-life, explained by Kelly, (a sales co-ordinator), who made her own beaver outfit to use with her young son:

> "You take parts of *Gung Ho* into your home life. The dressing up [at work] is hilarious ... especially when Bob comes in with the beaver outfit on! (laughing). But it has definitely helped with my young son. He's five now, and a bit of a handful, but we've actually got a similar costume to the one used here for us, and we've replicated the training session with him. So, we use the costume to tell him that 'Mr Beaver expects you to behave and be responsible at school, he's watching you' (laughing). I've spoken to the other guys here and they've done the same with their children ... the animals help to resolve problems"

Kelly's reference to *'animals help to resolve problems'* reveals that animals can assist in improving and resolving our work challenges (recruiting the 'right' people, breaking down hierarchies, creating honesty and trust), but it also exposes the mutuality between humans and animals. Employees had to work with the costume to show their alignment to the culture, and the costumes only became agentic by being worn by the humans. This interdependence (Coulter, 2015) reinforces that networks are co-defined by the complexity of agents operating within them (Latour, 1992; 2005). The admirable traits of beavers, transferred through the beaver costume, conveyed to the next generation that these animals have qualities which humans could learn from, by adopting similar traits. ANT (Latour, 1992; 2005) offers us this rich, analytical, and moral perspective by not reducing the animal and human to binary agents, but recognising the value of both. For example, it can be questioned, whether the powerful message of 'worthwhile work', would have been quite so impactful had Kelly simply told her son to 'behave in a worthwhile way'.

Further, Kim explained how the animal metaphors helped to create trusting relationships, and provide reassurance at a team event, which consisted of her having to stand on a six-foot wooden pole and fall backwards into the arms of her colleagues below. The animals reminded the team of the qualities needed to work together, even when faced with uncertainty.

" ... six foot may not sound high, but when you're up on the sixth step that means your head is eleven foot off the ground ... me, being a big girl, I didn't want to do it. But my team told me to think about the animals....they shouted up to me 'geese don't say to each other 'I don't trust you to fly in formation behind me'' ... I was told to trust the team, and let my eyes follow the ceiling, and I would just fall back, and so I did, and they caught me!"

'Trust', demonstrated here, illustrates that it is a necessary and essential condition for co-operative engagement. The notion of 'companion trust' (Newell and Swan, 2000: 1295), describes trust based on judgements of goodwill and a moral obligation that both parties will be open and honest. Kim was reminded that the geese never question their fellow companions, instilling in her the belief and confidence she needed to undertake the activity. Despite the differences between humans and animals, the latter were still relied on in the above example by employees to achieve the task at hand. The goose metaphor helped Kim to succeed, reflecting the need for us to consider the 'unique qualities of animals... as significant in their own ways' (Hamilton and Mitchell, 2018: 15).

'Too animally?'

In this section, I explore how animal metaphors and the costumes resulted in resistance and organizational mockery; an important reminder that the 'lively' nature of animals (Nimmo, 2019), renders the network precarious (Law, 1992). Ross, (a sales coordinator), was not an avid supporter of the costumes:

"The costumes don't do it for me, the people look ridiculous in them and I'm not sure what message they're meant to be getting over. We just take the mick out of Bob when we're down the pub with him, can't help but tease him after he's done a training session (laughing). How can we take him seriously when he's standing in front of us with a furry beaver head on? (laughing)."

Ross's explanation of the costumes appeared to mock the organizational culture and whilst having 'fun at work' (Wadham, 2021) should be encouraged, it reminds us of the 'messy comingling' (Dashper, 2020: 34) of the network assemblage, which is only ever transient (Law, 1992). Resistance through humour was also evident when Phil, (a sales co-ordinator), stated:

Under *Gung Ho*, we're told that we should be living the values....the values are told to us through the dressing up events. So, maybe they just want us to all come in dressed up as an animal....ah, that's it, isn't it? (laughing and clicking his fingers). Now, I know where I've been going wrong all of these years, I just need to get a beaver outfit on, sit at my desk in it, and charm the customers. Then I'll stop getting told off, excellent!

Phil expressed to me that he was often told by his colleagues that he was not 'embracing the culture' but despite this, he continued to resist and used his humour to challenge the metaphorical display and translation of the animal behavioural traits.

Moreover, Matthew (a former team leader), explained how the costumes resulted in him withdrawing from his former role:

> "There was such reluctance for people to volunteer to do this training... where you have to dress up I mean... we had Craig, the recruiter, who told us that we would be expected to wear costumes... well the outfits were good....but it was the concept behind it. You felt stupid, I hated drama at school and that is what it is. You have to be in role, play act to the whole organization, who then thinks you're an idiot... I could only do it for so long...".

Matthew was required to act, as he described it, in a dramatical way, showing his 'inner clown' (Bolton and Houlihan, 2009: 557). For those individuals to whom this felt uncomfortable, the animals did not offer them comfort, nor did they 'solve a problem'. Quite to the contrary, they created a problem, so much so that Matthew withdrew from being a trainer.

Discussion and conclusion

Animal metaphors provoke our thinking of the interrelationships between humans and nonhumans, and like the employees of Fireco, encourage us to think about work relationships differently. The collective 'sense-making' (Weick, 1979) of Fireco's organizational culture was challenged—what it meant in practice, why the values were important, and how behaviour could be influenced through using animal metaphors as a reference point. This is important for organizations, be that for recruitment and selection, or to create organizational loyalty.

The animal metaphors, and the associated costumes, provided an alternative means for Fireco employees to learn and embrace the culture; the animals brought to life the organizational setting and helped to transfer ambiguous ideas into easy-to-understand behaviour and practices. ANT (Latour, 1992; 2005) equips us with this lens, enabling the subjectivity of all agents, (e.g. animals, technology, written work, objects), to be recognised (Nimmo, 2019). Having animal metaphors at the core of organizational life, enables us to work with them in a symbolic sense, but also, I would argue, in a literal one. By being more mindful of how squirrels, beavers and geese operate in their own habitat, by watching them and then adopting the same traits, which are deemed 'right' for the workplace, meant that Fireco employees learnt more about each other, themselves and animals in general through the stories. To have to demonstrate 'worthwhile work', encouraged a consideration of the hard work that beavers do when building their dam each winter, and the commitment that geese make to remain part of the wider 'formation'. Focusing on this co-production of lived experience, we can more fully understand how animal metaphors can participate and shape networks (Callon; 1984; Law, 1992).

If organizational studies is made practically intelligible through embodied enactment, the use of animal metaphors provides us with a visual means by which to facilitate workplace interaction (Morgan, 2006). A more authentic expression of ideas, feelings, concerns, and resistance may be possible, that words alone would limit. In this chapter, the distinctive contribution provided by ANT is that it has destabilised previous perceptions of workplace power relations, by acknowledging the ability of all agents to create an outcome (intended or not) (Nimmo, 2019). Animal metaphors and costumes are universally recognised, regardless of the context or location (e.g., if we think of the 'furry movement' to spread happiness). It is unlikely that in the literal sense, a lion, beaver, fox, or bee, will behave or be interpreted differently whether they are being spoken about in the UK, Australia, or Japan. Animal metaphors are, therefore, able to be used as an accessible means of thinking about complex workplace issues. Metaphors originate from the literal animal itself, so for organizational purposes, it is hugely valuable in being able to compare employee behaviour worldwide. We can consider for a moment the documentary 'Lucy the Human Chimp' (The Guardian, 29th April, 2021), which was a moving, first person account, reflecting on an intense, inter-species bond,- portraying friendship between human and animal; a testament to the blurriness of the inter-related assemblages of networks (Callon, 1984; Nimmo, 2019) binding us together.

Animals, and the costumes, cannot 'speak' in the same literary sense as humans, but they still 'spoke' to the employees of Fireco. They aided the translation (Callon, 1984) of cultural and social interaction, and redefined one's perception of what work is—not a labour process of exchange, under a capitalist structure (Braverman, 1976), but an environment where there is no divide, where learning, achievement and respect is encouraged. Rethinking our emphasis away from using abstract narrative (honesty, trust, worthwhile work), which is complex in its epistemological subjectivity, enables us to place more emphasis on the tangible animal qualities and the learnings we can acquire by adopting them. We have no need to deny nonhuman agents the rights and duties accorded to humans (Law, 1992) as they remind us of our morality (Latour, 1992) and the ethical duty we have to each other.

Operating as one agent in the network means that we should speak less and listen more. ANT enables us to acknowledge that we do not have to be the same as another agent in order to create strong working relationships and foster solidarity with them. This chapter has hopefully started to shine a light on an alternative reading of human-animal interaction in heterogeneous assemblages, and the role these play in shaping our workplaces. As Carol Emschwiller (cited in Kelemen et al., 2020: 694) stated:

"Maybe it's animalness that will make the world right again: the wisdom of elephants the enthusiasm of canines, the grace of snakes, the mildness of anteaters".

References

Alvesson, M. & Sveningsson, S. (2003). Good visions, bad micro-management and ugly ambiguity: contradictions of (Non-) leadership in a knowledge-intensive organization. *Organization Studies, 24(6)*, 961–88.

Andrighetto, L. et al. (2016). Excluded from all humanity: Animal metaphors exacerbate the consequences of social exclusion. *Journal of Language and Social Psychology, 35(6)*, 628–44.

Blanchard, K. & Bowles, S. (1998). *Gung ho! How to motivate people in any organization.* London: Harper Collins.

Bame, R. et al. (2013). Using animal metaphors to create and maintain positive changes in the workforce. *Journal of Diversity Management, 8(2)*, 51–62.

Bell, E. & Clarke, D.W. (2014). 'Beasts, burrowers and birds': The enactment of researcher identities in UK business schools. *Management Learning, 45(3)*, 249–66.

Beisel, U. (2020). What might we learn from ANT for studying healthcare issues in the majority world, and what might ANT learn in turn?' In A. Blok, I. Farías, & C. Roberts (Eds.), *The Routledge companion to actor-network theory* (pp. 246-55). London: Routledge.

Bolton, S.C. & Houlihan, M. (2009), Are we having fun yet? A consideration of workplace fun and engagement. *Employee Relations, 31(6)*, 556–68.

Braverman, H. (1976). *Labor and monopoly capital.* New York: Monthly Review Press.

Callon, M. (1984). Elements of a sociology of translation: Domestication of the scallops and the fisherman of St Brieuc Bay. In J. Law (Ed.), *Power, action and belief: A new sociology of knowledge. Sociological Review Monograph Series, 32 (1)* 196-233.

Callon, M. (1998). *The Laws of the Market.* Oxford, Malden: Blackwell Publishers/Sociological Review.

Cerulo, K. (2009). Nonhumans in Society. *Annual Review of Sociology, 35*, 531–52.

Connolly, L. & Cullen, J.G. (2018). Animals and organisations: An ethic of care framework. *Organization & Environment, 31(4)*, 406–24.

Coulter, K. (2015). *Animals, work, and the promises of inter-species solidarity.* London: Palgrave Macmillan.

Cochoy, F. (2007). A brief theory of the 'Captation' of publics: Understanding the market with little red riding hood. *Theory, Culture & Society, 24(7–8)*, 203–23.

Dashper, K. (2020). More-than-human emotions: Multispecies emotional labour in the tourism industry. *Gender, Work & Organization, 27(1)*, 24–40.

Deal, T. & Kennedy, A. (1982). *Corporate Cultures: The rites and rituals of corporate life.* Reading: Addison-Wesley.

Dowling, R. Lloyd, K., & Suchet-Pearson, S. (2017). Qualitative methods II: 'More-than-human' methodologies and/in praxis. *Progress in Human Geography, 41(6)*, 823–31.

Färber, A. (2020) How does ANT help us to rethink the city and its promises? In A. Blok, I. Farías, & C. Roberts (Eds.), *The Routledge companion to actor-network theory* (pp. 264-72). London: Routledge.

Farias, I., Blok, A., & Roberts, C. (2020). Actor-network theory as a companion. An inquiry into intellectual practices. In A. Blok, I. Farías, & C. Roberts (Eds.), *The Routledge companion to actor-network theory* (pp. xx-xxxv). London: Routledge.

Fleming, P. & Sturdy, A. (2008). 'Just be yourself'. Towards neo-normative control in organisations? *Employee Relations, 31(6)*, 569–83.

Hamilton, L. & Mitchell, L. (2018). Knocking on the door of human-animal studies: Valuing work across disciplinary and species borderlines. *Society and Animals, 26*, 1–20.

Haslam, N., Loughnan, S., & Sun, P. (2011). Beastly: What makes animal metaphors offensive? *Journal of Language and Social Psychology, 30(3)*, 311–25.

Kelemen, T.K. et al. (2020). The secret life of pets: The intersection of animals and organizational life. *Journal of Organizational Behavior, 41(7)*, 694–7.

Knight, C. & Sang, K. (2020). 'At home, he's a pet, at work he's a colleague and my right arm': Police dogs and the emerging posthumanist agenda. *Culture and Organization, 26(5-6)*, 355–71.

Labatut, J., Munro, I., & Desmond, J. (2016). Animals and organizations. *Organization, 23(3)*, 315–29.

Latour, B. (1987). *Science in action*. Cambridge, MA: Harvard University Press.

Latour, B. (1991). Technology is society made durable. In J. Law (Ed.), *A Sociology of monsters: Essays on power, technology and domination* (pp. 103–31). London: Routledge.

Latour, B (1992). Where are the missing masses? Sociology of a few mundane artefacts. In W. Bijker & H. Law (Eds.), *Shaping technology-building society. Studies in socio-technical change* (pp. 225–59). Cambridge: MA: MIT Press.

Latour, B. (2005). *Reassembling the Social—An Introduction to Actor-Network-Theory*. Oxford: Oxford University Press

Latour, B. (2018). *Down to Earth. Politics in the New Climatic Regime*. Cambridge: Polity Press.

Latour, B. & Woolgar, S. (1979). *Laboratory life: The social construction of scientific facts*. Beverly Hills: Sage.

Law, J. (1992). Notes on the Theory of the Actor Network: Ordering, Strategy and Heterogeneity (pp. 1–11). Published by the Centre for Science Studies, Lancaster University, Lancaster LA1 4YN. Retrieved at http://www.comp.lancs.ac.uk/sociology/papers/Law-Notes-on-ANT.pdf

Law, J. (2008). Actor-Network Theory and Material Semiotics. In B.S. Turner (Eds.), *The New Blackwell Companion to Social Theory* (pp. 141–58). Oxford: Blackwell.

Mol, A. (2010). Actor-network theory: Sensitive terms and enduring tensions. *Kölner Zeitschrift für Soziologie und Sozialpsychologie. Sonderheft, 50(1)*, 253–69.

Morgan, G. (2006). *Images of organization*. London: Sage Publications.

Newell, S. & Swan, J. (2000). Trust and inter-organizational networking. *Human Relations, 53(10)*, 1287–1328.

Nimmo, R. (2019). Biopolitics and becoming in animal-technology assemblages. *Journal of History of Science and Technology, 13(2)*, 118–36.

O'Doherty, D.P. (2016). Feline politics in organization: The nine lives of Olly the cat. *Organization, 23(3)*, 407–33.

Owler, K. & Morrison, R.L. (2020). 'I always have fun at work': How 'remarkable workers' employ agency and control in order to enjoy themselves. *Journal of Management and Organization, 26(2)*, 135–51.

Peters, T. (2003). *Re-imagine! Business excellence in a disruptive age*. London: Dorling Kindersley.

Pinker, S. (1993). *The language instinct*. New York: William Morrow.

Pinker, S. (2007). *The stuff of thought*. Viking, New York: Viking.

Shelley. (2007–21). The organizational zoo. A guide to workplace survival. Retrieved from https://www.organizationalzoo.com/

Smith, J.E. et al. (2020). Obstacles and opportunities for female leadership in mammalian societies: A comparative perspective. *The Leadership Quarterly, 31(2),* 1–15.

Taylor, N. (2011). Can sociology contribute to the emancipation of animals? In N. Taylor & T. Signal (Eds.), *Theorizing animals: Re-thinking humanimal relations* (pp. 201–20). Leiden, Netherlands: Brill.

The Guardian (2021, 29 April). 'They all got on as one family': The story of a woman who lived with chimps'. Retrieved from https://www.theguardian.com/film/2021/apr/29/lucy-the-human-chimp-hbo-max-documentary

Van Maanen J. (1979). Reclaiming qualitative methods for organizational research: A preface. *Administrative Science Quarterly,* 24(4), 520–26.

Waddock, S. (2011). We are all stakeholders of Gaia: A normative perspective on stakeholder thinking. *Organization & Environment,* 24, 192–212

Wadham, H. (2021). Relations of power and nonhuman agency: Critical theory, clever hans, and other stories of horses and humans. *Sociological Perspectives, 64(1),* 109–26.

Weick, K.E. (1979). *The social psychology of organizing,* 2nd Edition. Reading, MA: Addison-Wesley.

William-Jones, B. & Graham, J.E. (2003). Actor-network theory: A tool to support ethical analysis of commercial genetic testing. *New Genetics and Society, 22(3),* 271–96.

CHAPTER 14

BIG HAT, NO CATTLE

Using Animal Metaphors to Frame Strategic Human Resource Management

TRICIA CLELAND SILVA

THE metaphor 'big hat, no cattle' historically originates from southern United States (Texas) and implies someone or something appearing to be of a value, and yet, under close inspection, reveals no substance: 'He is full of talk and acts like he knows more than anyone else, but he's "big hat, no cattle"'. This metaphor can be used for scientific inquiry to evaluate strategic human resource management's (SHRM) contribution to understanding the management of people. SHRM, as a field of knowledge, developed from the early 1980s to explore the human resources (HR) function's impact on enhancing employees' performance to achieve competitive advantage. Through a multispecies metaphor conceptual frame of 'big hat, no cattle' in its original use (Skinner, 1981) and subsequent application (Guthrie et al., 2011) to the field of SHRM, this chapter critically explores the researchers' conceptualization of managing 'resources' to obtain competitive advantage through control and performance measurements based on profit. By contextualizing the metaphor's use to situate the authors' interpretation of SHRM as a concept, the chapter facilitates a discussion of the accountability of the researchers' moral reasoning of the strategic value of human and nonhuman animals.

Specifically, close reading techniques are used to deconstruct metaphors that may appear insignificant on the surface, and yet, are situated in knowledge productions which are political (Clarke, 2005:18) and have material consequences for the implicated actors who are either physically or discursively present in the situation of inquiry (Clarke et al., 2018: 76). As such, the empirical questions of this chapter are the following: how do the authors interpret the chosen metaphor 'big hat, no cattle' to explain their scientific inquiry into the field of SHRM at a time-specific, historical-cultural-political context? And, who is included in and excluded from this inquiry? The chapter concludes with a call to expand the scope of conceptualizing the 'management' (process) of 'strategic resources' (product) through metaphors and storytelling with a multispecies perspective. This call provides an opportunity to critically examine scientific inquiry as 'human action defining a moral and practical world' (Rabinow and Sullivan, 1987: 20–1). Throughout, the central analytic point is that examining metaphors and stories to frame the interpretation of the researcher in a multispecies context, provides an opportunity to hold future researchers more accountable as to what and who they include and exclude from their studies.

Strategic Human Resource Management: A Field of Scientific Inquiry

The starting point of Human Resource Management (HRM) as a field of study[1] was Taylorism or Scientific Management, but it was solidified by the research of Elton Mayo (Mayo, 1933) whose Hawthorne studies documented and revealed that workers are more productive through social engagement, rather than financial compensation and physical working conditions (Kaufman, 2014). Before the field was labelled HRM, it was conceptualized as personnel management or personnel administration. In the 1980s, the field began to incorporate strategy with the aim of competitive advantage in an increasingly globally integrated market. Central to this strategic focus was top management aligning the organizational goals with employee performance through the HR function. This function could take on different forms, but there were four foundational schools: human relations, labour relations, personnel administration, and industrial engineering (Skinner, 1981: 109).

After a decade of these schools applied to practice, the field shifted to the 'Resource-Based View' which states that organizations' 'valuable, rare, and costly to imitate resources' can contribute to sustained competitive advantage (Barney et al., 2001: 648). This analytical shift from personnel management to humans as strategic resources (Shaw, 2021) has produced a substantial body of research that examines potential bundles or systems of HR policies and practices to influence firms' performance. These systems are called 'high-performance work systems' (HPWS) and are widely believed to improve organizational performance through their impact on employee competencies and motivation (Guthrie et al., 2011: 1672).

Performance management and quantified measurement or, in most cases, financial indicators, have received much attention by SHRM scholars who have made careers and legacies from this scientific contribution to the field (see Kaufmann's (2012) critical review). Indeed, SHRM scholars have contributed to the debate on intrinsic motivation of

---

[1] As in the historical review of HRM by Kaufman (2014), the chapter situates the development of contemporary HRM and SHRM from the American perspective.

employees and subsequent performance, and yet, the success of the resources remains as quantified financial indicators of the organization's annual profit. Interestingly, although the field has frequently referenced and justified the field's contribution to the Hawthorne study, it has moved far from the original insights of observing the workers at General Electric and has drawn more from Taylorism by trying to control resources in quantifiable ways.

As in other fields of management that predominantly apply positivist approaches to research, there has been critical attention paid to HRM as a field of study and practice. For instance, the relationship between HRM rhetoric and reality (Watson, 1995); HRM practices as mostly disciplinary to create order and power effects (Townley, 1993: 523); the debate on HRM performance which has been intense but inclusive to financial rewards (Gerhart, 2007), and researchers exploring HRM 'beyond managerialism' (Delbridge and Keenoy, 2010: 804). More recently, Cooke argues that studies of HRM concepts, mindsets, and practices require contextualization to interpret what is happening and tailor solutions to the realities of the workplace (Cooke, 2018; Cooke et al., 2021). She advocates that HRM researchers require introspective analysis of their own intellectual and social upbringing, as well as theoretical orientation, when approaching and navigating the field. To address positivist trends of decontextualization in HRM research, she calls for 'a more open-minded, inductive, and inclusive approach to indigenous research that may present very different contexts, ways of contextualizing, and knowledge paradigms from the dominant discourses prevailing in HRM research' (Cooke, 2018: 3). In the next section, this chapter takes up Cooke's call through the application of the method, Metaphor Conceptual Frame (MCF), to the SHRM field.

As scientific inquiries are 'situated knowledges' which are 'woven of social relations' (Haraway, 2004c: 187), science is not objective. It is performed by humans who have a class, gender, culture, species, and biological context, as well as a methodological context. In this regard, the method applied in this scientific inquiry draws on a multispecies lens (Hamilton and Taylor, 2012) to address 'institutional ethnocentrism' (Johnson et al., 2006: 532), 'cultural ethnocentrism' (see Siebers et al., 2015), and anthropocentrism (such as Lestel and Taylor, 2013). As Haraway's work advocates (2004a, b, c), we cannot remove 'story telling' from science or our 'self' in relation to the subject or 'other'. We need to own the stories we tell, and scrutinize the stories we have been told, which on the surface, may have appeared as essential truths: 'Big hat, no cattle'!

INTERPRETING SCIENTIFIC INQUIRY: A MULTISPECIES METAPHOR CONCEPTUAL FRAME

> The practices of interpretation involve storytelling, different ways of organizing and representing the world, and different ways of making the world appear real. (Denzin, 2007: 459)

Interpreting the world through metaphors is an exploration into creative possibilities to reframe our perceptions or 'see the world anew' (Barrett and Cooperrider, 1990: 222). Metaphors are social constructs, which allow people to 'conceptualize one mental domain in terms of another' (Lakoff, 1993: 203) and play a central role in the development of human thought and intersubjective meaning-making. Metaphors facilitate the interpretation of multiple meanings by opening lived experiences to multiple actors and symbolic dimensions, which, through rational thought and physical senses, may have been underacknowledged. As described by Vince and Broussine (1996), metaphors are windows to the 'soul' of the social system (p. 59) and a way of 'reaching into the subjective terrain of unconscious experience' (p. 60).

Storytelling through metaphors provides an imaginary space to explore a story that collectively unites the actors (Cleland Silva and Fonseca Silva, 2019). It also allows the story to become alive or 'living' (Boje, 2011), and the actors to engage in critical awareness of their values and social interactions which mirror the stories they tell, and are told (White, 1995). In organizations, metaphors can be used to interpret one's environment and to support the management of work and practices (Greve, 2017: 402). Specifically, metaphors can be used as an opportunity to facilitate change or address underlying problems within an organization. As Gibb (2006) points out, metaphors are vehicles, which influence responses, even if the receivers are not consciously aware of them.

Conceptual metaphor theory (CMT) started with the book *Metaphors We Live By* (Lakoff and Johnson, 1980) and is defined as 'understanding one domain of experience (that is typically abstract) in terms of another (that is typically concrete)' (Kövecses, 2017: 13). This definition captures conceptual metaphors as a process and a product: the process is cognitive understanding of a domain and the product is the resulting conceptual pattern. CMT is often experimentally tested by studying the effects of metaphorical frames on individual reasoning through at least two levels of analysis: words versus concepts (Brugman et al., 2019: 3). The choice of analysis 'frames' the target domain in different ways, highlighting some aspects and backgrounding others (Lakoff and Johnson, 1980). A frame is understood here as a set of expectations that participants bring to the activity or occasion (Tracy, 1997).

Scholars who frame concepts through metaphors (see e.g. Holman, 2016; Moses and Gonzales, 2015; Ohl et al., 2013), as done is this chapter, identify references at the larger discourse level associated with the metaphor (Bateson, 1972; Goffman, 1974). For instance, to explore deeper the concept of HRM in reality beyond rhetoric, Watson (1995) entitled his article 'In search of HRM: Beyond the rhetoric and reality distinction or the case of the dog that didn't bark'. He introduces the metaphor to frame his arguments that, in the workplace, there is a divide between practices labelled as HRM and the theoretical development of the HRM field:

> The concepts and language of HRM are perhaps most usefully seen as discursive resources which both managers and academic writers make use of—or refuse

to make use of—in their occupational practices. [This article] [i]llustrates this argument with ethnographic material gathered in an organization in which many of those activities frequently labelled 'HRM' occur but where the notion of HRM is not used. The dog does not bark. (Watson, 1995: 6)

Further into Watson's text, the metaphor reappears from a story about Sherlock Holmes, a literary detective from the Victorian era created by author Arthur Conan Doyle. The story is about a dog present in an event where violent activities took place which Holmes and his assistant were investigating (Watson, 1995: 9). As he recounts the story, he reveals that the dog did not bark during the event, and therefore, the detectives conclude that no crime had taken place. Using the direct words of Sherlock: 'it is one of those cases where the art of the reasoner should be used rather for the sifting of details than for the acquiring of fresh evidence' (quoted in Watson, 1995: 9).

Inspired by the story, Watson (the scholar not Sherlock's sidekick) takes the meaning of the 'dog does not bark' metaphor to frame his ethnographic data of dialogues between the management researcher (himself) and two managers to not focus on more evidence but rather the actual 'reasoners' involved in HRM theories and practices:

[T]he most valuable way to study HRM is to look at it as a concept, label or rhetorical construct which both managers and academics utilize in making sense of trends in work activity and in pursuing their own projects in life—be they projects of doing managerial work and managing a managerial career or projects of doing academic work and managing an academic career. (Watson, 1995: 6)

To expand on this, I now turn to CMT in order to include a multispecies lens, as animals in management inquiry have historically been silenced as implicated subjects (Sayers, 2016) and 'unwitting bearers of human culture' (Hamilton and Taylor, 2012, quoted by Knights and Clarke, 2021: 2). A multispecies lens recognizes 'humans and animals as mutually constituted through entangled relations and everyday practical enactments of living' (Knights and Clarke, 2021: 2). And as Schön reveals (1993, quoted by Cameron, 2017: 430), 'the way an issue is framed can powerfully affect not only how the issue is understood but also what sort of solutions can be considered'. Returning to the central metaphor of the chapter; 'big hat, no cattle', this was first applied to the field of SHRM in *Harvard Business Review* (Skinner, 1981) and was later used to analyse managers' perceptions of the strategic function of HRM and high-performance work systems (Guthrie, 2011).

In the following sections, I proceed as follows: First, I contextualize the authors' metaphor use to frame the concept of HRM by abstracting the text, which makes cultural, historical, and political references. Then, I examine the authors' interpretation of the metaphor through its use in the text; and then connect the metaphor's interpretation and use to the authors' contribution to the SHRM field of study. The data analysis is written with the authors' text in *italics* and the referents to the context and HRM concept are underlined through the frame of the metaphor 'big hat, no cattle'.

'Big Hat, No Cattle': Managing Human Resources (Skinner, 1981)

The Context

Skinner (1981) describes the context of his research as *60 years* after the Hawthorne *experiment* (p. 106) and in the *US industry* (p. 106). The HRM concept is described as used *now* after calling the field *'human relations', 'personnel management', 'labor relations'* since *World War II* (p. 106). Skinner writes that HRM *'seems to be mostly good intentions and whistling in the dark or averting unionization. And the results of the 1970s suggest that we may not even be holding our own. The poor management of the workforce in this country is damaging the nation and our [American] standard of living. It is making us uncompetitive with the Japanese and some other Asians, the West Germans, and many others'* (p. 107).

He continues this point with a paragraph of *anti-establishment seeds* of the *1970s* (p. 109):

> *People instinctively resent forces that manage and control them-big business, directors, the industrial establishment, the boss, the boss's boss. The anti-establishment seeds sown in the late 1960s and early 1970s are bearing fruit, and more employees than ever are unwilling to subject themselves wholly to an organization or the discipline of a trade, profession or team.*

Skinner (1981) indicates that *'he does not wish to exaggerate the gloomy aspects of this picture. As surely modest progress has occurred nearly everywhere. For the most part, sweatshops are a thing of the past. Workplaces are better lit and ventilated and are generally safer than in the past. The atmosphere at work is less coldly formal, and decision making more participative. Managers are more aware of feelings and relationships and make fewer overt demands of employees. Few "bulls of the woods" charge about offices and factories'* (p. 107).

Within the context of society, Skinner (1981) writes: *'Some will argue that we've been doing many things and that it is societal factors such as the "declining work ethic", "the new breed", and the "new sociology" that are eroding management's efforts. Regardless, in most companies the results of enlightened people management are simply more comfort, more relaxation, more freedom from pressure, more security, more benefits, and higher pay, not more productivity and loyalty'* (p. 107).

Drawing directly from Skinner's metaphor frame, I proceed to write my own interpretation of the context he describes in relation to the management of people at work:

In 1981, managing people is important to most workplaces _everywhere_ [read: Western industrial democracies], and poor management continues to damage American standards of living. Management of employees made modest progress from the gloomy sweatshops, where 'bulls of the woods' once charged offices and factories. Workplaces are better lit and ventilated and the atmosphere less coldly formal with participative decision-making. Managers are also more aware of feelings and relationships. Yet, with the anti-establishment seeds sown in the late 1960s and bearing fruit [read: early 1980s], employees were not willing to be controlled through poor management as before unionization and World War II. Although some justified the civil unrest to societal factors such as the 'declining work ethic', 'the new breed', and the 'new sociology', enlightened people management continue to focus solely on extrinsic rewards for employee's work with material comforts such as higher pay rather than understanding deeply how to keep people loyal and productive.

The Interpretation

Most often, metaphors are used in storytelling to frame an abstract experience in terms of a concrete example. At the beginning of his article, Skinner tells a story to draw our attention to the metaphor 'big hat, no cattle'.
He writes (1981: 106):

> In the Dallas airport the other day I saw many tall, well-dressed, and impressive-looking men wearing large, immaculate Stetson cowboy hats. As I walked by one such hat-wearer, I noticed two middle-aged, sunburned men in faded jeans standing nearby. They eyed the same fellow, looked him up and down, and then said quietly to the other, 'Big hat, no cattle'.

This story gives the metaphor 'big hat' a gender [read: men], a constructed identity [read: cowboy], a context [read: Stetson whose creator John B. Stetson created the original hat of the pioneering American West and has been referred to as 'Boss of the Plains'], and a reference to a group with physical commonalities [read: tall, well dressed, impressive-looking].

The 'no cattle' implies the implication of cattle associated with a Stetson cowboy hat or a person who looks like a cowboy but has no specific purpose beyond hat-wearer. The observers are middle-aged sunburned men in faded jeans standing nearby. Through the metaphor's reference to the hat-wearer, one of the observers disassociates himself and the other observer from the many tall, well-dressed, and impressive-looking men wearing large, immaculate Stetson cowboy hats although they all are in the same airport and of the same gender.

The observers can be a reference to employee alienation, which Skinner describes throughout his article, but directly addresses on page 112: '*If managers continually fail* to listen, communicate, explain and anticipate, and in every way nurture commitment, and mutual understanding, employees will inevitably become _alienated_.' The alienation comes with the _macho belief_ [read: domineering arrogance] that the 'big hat' such as HR programmes or management can solve and fix poor morale or low productivity without getting at the basic underlying cause (p. 112).

The 'no cattle' refers to agency of the cattle to leave if not treated with care and respect by the cowboy, no matter how big the hat. As in SHRM, the value of people as 'resources' remains quantifiable; the intrinsic value of the employees is ignored, running the risk of people, like cattle, not returning to work unless under coercive control (see Skinner, 1981: 112). Skinner indicates going beyond the impressive big hat and focusing attention on the cowboy's habits, skills, values, and beliefs of how to treat cattle with long-term thinking. In reference to HRM, he writes that the supervisors need to return to the _basics_ and do them _better_ (p. 113). He writes: '[W]orst of all is supervision—the oldest and most written about management skills. The business schools neglect it, and economics, schedules, costs, and time pressures allow careless and inhumane practices to characterize it' (p. 113).

Skinner's main contribution to the HRM field is that organizations need to understand the extrinsic and intrinsic value of people at work. To go beyond the old adage '_people are people_' by focusing on doing the basics better by '_simply treating people with care and respect_' through long-term investment in tailored and considerate solutions (Skinner, 1981: 113). Lastly, Skinner advocates that '_employees are _stakeholders_ in the enterprise as their interest in the conditions of employment and work are as real as those of stockholders and managers. The problem is not whether to keep them involved in the management of the enterprise, _but how_' (1981: 112–13).

BIG HAT, NO CATTLE? THE RELATIONSHIP BETWEEN USE OF HIGH-PERFORMANCE WORK SYSTEMS AND MANAGERIAL PERCEPTIONS OF HR DEPARTMENTS (GUTHRIE ET AL., 2011)

The Context

This article is written by authors situated in three different countries: _USA_, _Ireland_, and _Republic of China_ (Guthrie et al., 2011: 1672) as these countries are listed with institutional affiliations of the primary author (USA) to the third author (Republic of China). Data is drawn from two _surveys_ (one survey focusing on _general management practices_ and the other on _human resource practices_ (p. 1675) sent to _managing directors_ (such as

CEOs) and _senior HR managers_ of _241 companies in the Republic of Ireland_ of which _132 completed the survey_ between _May 2006 and October 2006_ (p. 1676).

The authors assert that the research design does not include several contextual moderators, limiting the study's results (p. 1681). This limits also the metaphor frame due to the authors' omissions.

Drawing from past _empirical evidence_ (p. 1675) in the field of SHRM that _High-Performance Work Systems (HPWS)_ help _foster higher levels of human and social capital_ (p. 1675), the authors _propose_ (p. 1675) that HPWS _positively influence manager's perceptions_ of the _strategic value_ of _HR departments_. They also agree with _the link between HR practices and human and social capital_ by using a 2004 study by Youngt and Snell. The authors' starting point to their research contribution to HRM are the following hypotheses (p. 1675):

> H1: _Greater use of HPWS_ will be _associated with managers' perceptions that HR departments_ have _greater levels of strategic value_ for their firms.
>
> H2: The _human and social capital_ of a firm's workforce will _mediate_ the relationship between the use of HPWS and managers' perceptions of HR department strategic value.

Drawing from the authors' references to Skinner's metaphor frame, I proceed to write my own interpretation of how the authors describe the context of their study of SHRM:

In 2011, authors from the United States, Ireland, and China wanted to contribute to the SHRM field by proposing a study about the relationship between _managers' perceptions_ and strategic value of the HR function. They hypothesize that through the concepts of _high-performance work systems (HPWS)_ and _human and social capital_, they could prove a positive relationship between the greater use of HPWS and managers' perceptions that HR departments have strategic value for their firms. Companies' _HR managers_ and _Managing Directors_ are the study's participants, and are located in the _Republic of Ireland_.

The Interpretation

Unlike Skinner, whose analysis of the metaphor included societal factors, educational and work systems, managers, and the employees, the authors of this study focus solely on the _HPWS_ and the _managers' perceptions_. The employees' perceptions and other contextual factors are not included (see Guthrie et al., (2011: 1681) for the research design's limitations).

The metaphor 'big hat, no cattle' frames the positive relationship of the _HPWS_ and _the managers' perceptions_ of its _strategic value_. In other words, using the multispecies metaphor conceptual frame of Skinner: the _hat-wearers_ (Skinner, 1981: 106) are asked about the functionality of the hat from their perspectives devoid of their surroundings.

Although the authors mediate for the factor *human capital* (*acquisition HR and developmental HR* (Guthrie et al., 2011: 1675)) into the studied relationship, the *human capital* in reference to Skinner's story becomes the <u>sunburned men in faded jeans nearby</u> (Skinner, 1981: 106) rather than active participants in the relationship. These observers are a part of the same 'social arena' as they identify with the hat-wearers but are excluded.

The authors' title questions Skinner's metaphor choice ('*Big hat, no cattle?*') and assert their scepticism in the first paragraph (p. 1672) and in the discussion of their findings. For instance, in the first paragraph of the discussion (p. 1681), they reassert their original claim to question the metaphor:

> Skinner (1981) used the metaphor of '<u>big hat, no cattle</u>' to describe the gap between the rhetoric and the reality of the strategic value of HR departments. In ensuing years, despite cumulating evidence that HR practices can affect firm performance, HR departments are often viewed, collectively, as function that is more bureaucratic than strategic (e.g. Stewart 1996; Barney and Wright 1998; Hammonds 2005). (Guthrie et al., 2011: 1681)

> Through extensive research of empirical studies and theories within SHRM, the authors justify their study by asserting that the 'big hat' does matter, it is just a means of asking the cowboys to wear it well.

The authors set out to test the premise that would refute Skinner's metaphor and arguments. The authors' contribution to SHRM is based on Barney and Wright's 1998 study, which suggests that a fundamental contributor to the problems of 'big hat, no cattle' is the failure of the HR departments to engage in activities that build workforce capability. They assert that their original hypotheses of HPWS use would be associated with managers holding more favourable views of HR departments' strategic value. They further propose that this relationship would be mediated by a firm's relative levels of human and social capital. And yet, as indicated in their research limitations of their analysis and findings (p. 1681), <u>social capital</u> (*collaboration HR* (p. 1675)) and context is lost, and the managers become the central actors in the relationship. In other words, there still is '<u>no cattle</u>' but rather '<u>big hats</u>' and '<u>hat-wearers</u>', indicating that their contribution to the SHRM field is through the first half of Skinner's metaphor by excluding the other stakeholders and the cultural, historical, and political context of the metaphor.

IN SEARCH OF THE CATTLE? THE CONTEXT OF THE METAPHOR

> The point is to make a difference in the world, to cast our lot with some ways of life and not others. To do that, one must be in action, be finite and dirty, not transcendent or clean. Knowledge-making technologies, including crafting subject positions and ways of inhabiting such positions, *must be made relentlessly visible and open to critical intervention*. (Haraway, 1997: 36; emphasis in the original)

While submitting the first draft of this chapter, I wrote in the email to the editors that 'in search of the cattle, I almost got lost myself' (14 April 2021). Reflecting on this comment, I realize now that my own interpretation of 'big hat, no cattle' was positioned in relation to the human subjects being controlled and managed in quantifiable ways. I was not searching for the cattle, but rather my own scientific inquiry remained fixated on the 'big hat' and the material implications of women workers (my own subject position). In this way, I also lost the original purpose of this piece which was to include the cattle. My initial discussion and interpretation of 'big hat, no cattle' brought forth 'the Hawthorne study', in which the participants were mainly female workers who, through the method used by the researchers at the time, were able to tell their story in relation to work. In many ways, the women became visible in scientific inquiry, not only through the stories told, but how the researchers later retold the stories and included the women in the situation.

Researchers are storytellers through their chosen entry points of scientific inquiry. Which theories they apply and how they do it matters. It matters because the stories told have material consequences for those involved but, most importantly, also for those who are implicated and silenced. My main motivation in this chapter was to critically examine the interpretations of the metaphor 'big hat, no cattle' to challenge discourses of a field and hold accountable researchers' reasoning behind the application of the concepts. However, what I did not expect from my own method experimentation was that the gaze turned back at me, highlighting how researching is not removed, clean, or disconnected from human socially constructed reality. Scientific inquiry is relationally messy, emotional, performed, and powerfully positioned in a human-centric ecosystem.

Metaphors and storytelling 'bring consent and reconciliation with things as they really are' (Ardent, 1968: 102). In this chapter, I needed to reconcile with my own responsibility in a system of narratives that excludes species other than humans. In this way, the scientific entry point to interpreting the metaphor 'big hat, no cattle' is to ask the question: why are there no cattle? By analysing the metaphor for human-meaning making, the cattle were excluded even further. Now looking back at the metaphor 'big hat, no cattle', I would start by centralizing the cattle as a priority to investigating the situation for a few reasons. First, it impacts the way I interpret and approach the management of 'resources'. Second, it makes clear that knowledge-making is not innocent or clean, but based on our own sense of morality of who and what matters in our worlds.

To conclude with a paradox; this is not the end, but rather a beginning to a new story. Holding ourselves accountable to how our moral reasonings impact our understanding of a situation can make us realize that the evidence may have been there all along. By searching for 'fresh evidence', rather than questioning our own interpretation, limits seeing the situation as it really is. The cattle are there, right in front of us, and by solely focusing on the 'big hat', we continue to exclude the cattle from our storytelling and our responsibility to the material consequences of other species in our ecosystems.

References

Ardent, H. (1968). *Men in Dark Times*. New York: Harcourt.

Barney, J., Wright, M., & Ketchen Jr, D.J. (2001). The resource-based view of the firm: Ten years after 1991. *Journal of Management, 27(6)*, 625–41.

Barrett, F.J. & Cooperrider, D.L. (1990). Generative metaphor intervention: A new approach for working with systems divided by conflict and caught in defensive perception. *The Journal of Applied Behavioral Science, 26(2)*, 219–39.

Bateson, G. (1972). *Steps to an Ecology of mind*. New York: Ballantine.

Boje, D.M. (2011). *Storytelling and the future of organizations: An antenarrative handbook*. New York: Routledge.

Broussine, M. & Vince, R. (1996). Working with metaphor towards organizational change. In *Organisation development: Metaphorical explorations* (pp. 57–72).

Cameron, L. (2017). Using metaphor for peace-building, empathy and reconciliation. In E. Semino & Z. Demjén (Eds.), *The Routledge handbook of metaphor and language*. New York: Routledge: 426–442.

Clarke, A. (2005). *Situational analysis: grounded theory after the postmodern turn*. Thousand Oaks: SAGE.

Clarke, A., Friese, C.F., & Washburn, R.S. (2018). *Situational analysis: Grounded theory after the interpretative turn*, 2nd Edition. Thousand Oaks: SAGE.

Clarke, C. & Knights, D. (2021). Milking it for all it's worth: Unpalatable practices, dairy cows and veterinary work? *Journal of Business Ethics, 176*:673–688. DOI: https://doi.org/10.1007/s10551-020-04666-3.

Cleland Silva, T. & Fonseca Silva, P. (2019). Validating change through collaborative story craft. In *SAGE Research Methods Cases Part 2 (SAGE Research Methods Cases)*. Thousand Oaks: SAGE https://doi.org/10.4135/9781526478245

Cooke, F. (2018). Concepts, contexts, and mindsets: Putting human resource management research in perspectives. *Human Resource Management Journal, 28(1)*, 1–13.

Cooke, F.L., Xiao, M., & Chen, Y. (2021). Still in search of strategic human resource management? A review and suggestions for future research with China as an example. *Human Resource Management, 60(1)*, 89–119. Doi: https://doi.org/10.1002/hrm.22029

Delbridge, R. & Keenoy, T. (2010). Beyond managerialism? *The International Journal of Human Resource Management, 21(6)*, 799–817.

Denzin, N. (2007). Grounded theory and the politics of interpretation. In A. Bryant & K. Charmaz (Eds.), *Handbook of grounded theory* (pp. 454–72). Thousand Oaks: SAGE.

Gerhart, B. (2007). Modelling HRM and performance linkages. In P. Boxall, J. Purcell, & P.M. Wright (Eds.), *The Oxford handbook of human resource management* (pp. 552–80). Oxford: Oxford University Press.

Gibbs, R.W.J, Jr. (2006). Metaphor interpretation as embodied simulation. *Mind and Language, 21*, 434–58.

Goffman, E. (1974). *Frame analysis*. New York: Harper and Row.

Greve, L. (2016). Using metaphor as a management tool. In *The Routledge handbook of metaphor and language* (pp. 418–430). New York: Routledge.

Guthrie, J.P. et al. (2011). Big hat, no cattle? The relationship between use of high-performance work systems and managerial perceptions of HR departments. *The International Journal of Human Resource Management, 22(8)*, 1672–85.

Hamilton, L. A. & Taylor, N. (2012). Ethnography in evolution: Adapting to the animal 'other' in organizations. *Journal of Organizational Ethnography*, 1(1), 43–51.

Haraway, D.J. (1997). *Feminism and technoscience*. New York: Routledge.

Haraway, D.J. (2004a). A manifesto for cyborgs: Science, technology, and socialist feminism in the 1980s. In *The Haraway Reader* (pp.149–181). New York Routledge.

Haraway, D.J. (2004b). Morphing in the order: Flexible strategies, feminist science studies, and primate visions. In *The Haraway Reader* (pp.199–223). New York: Routledge.

Haraway, D.J. (2004c). Teddy bear patriarchy: Taxidermy in the Garden of Eden, New York City, 1908–36. In *The Haraway Reader* (pp.150–198). New York: Routledge.

Holman, M.R. (2016). Gender, political rhetoric, and moral metaphors in state of the city addresses. *Urban Affairs Review*, 52(4), 501–30.

Jasanoff, S. & Kim, S.H. (Eds.) (2015). *Dreamscapes of modernity: Sociotechnical imaginaries and the fabrication of power* (pp. 321–42). Chicago: University of Chicago Press,

Johnson, J.P., Lenartowicz, T., & Apud, S. (2006). Cross-cultural competence in international business: Toward a definition and mode. *Journal of International Business Studies*, 37(4), 525–43.

Kaufman, B. (2014). The historical development of American HRM broadly viewed. *Human Resource Management Review*, 24(3), 196–218.

Kövecses, Z. (2017). Conceptual metaphor theory. In E. Semino & Z. Demjén (Eds.), *The Routledge handbook of metaphor and language* (pp.13–28). New York: Taylor and Francis.

Lakoff, G. & Johnson, M. (1980). *Metaphors we live by*. Chicago: University of Chicago Press.

Lakoff, G. (1993). The contemporary theory of metaphor. In A. Ortony (Ed.), *Metaphor and thought*, 2nd Edition (pp.202--251). Cambridge: Cambridge University Press.

Lestel, D. & Taylor, H. (2013). Shared life: An introduction. *Social Science Information*, 52(2), 183–6.

Mayo, E. (1933). *The human problems of an industrial civilization*. New York: The Macmillan Company.

Moses, J.F. & Gonzales, M.H. (2015). Strong candidate, nurturant candidate: Moral language in presidential television advertisements. *Political Psychology*, 36(4), 379–97.

Ohl, J.J. et al. (2013). Lakoff's Theory of Moral Reasoning in Presidential campaign advertisements, 1952-2012. *Communication Studies*, 64(5), 488–507.

Rabinow, P. & Suillivan, W.M. (1987). The interpretive turn: a second look. In P. Rabinow & W.M. Sullivan (Eds.), *Interpretive social science: a second look*, 2nd Edition (pp. 1–30). University of California Press.

Sayers, J.G. (2016). A report to an academy: On carnophallogocentrism, pigs and meatwriting. *Organization*, 23(3), 370–86.

Shaw, J. (2021). The resource-based view and its use in strategic human resource management research: The elegant and inglorious. *Journal of Management*, doi:10.1177/0149206321993543

Siebers, L., Kamoche, K., & Li, F. (2015). Transferring management practices to China: A Bourdieusian critique of ethnocentricity. *International Journal of Human Resource Management*, 26(5), 251–573.

Skinner, W. (1981). Big hat, no cattle: managing human resources. *Harvard Business Review*, 59(5), 106–14.

Townley, B. (1993). Foucault, power/knowledge, and its relevance for human resource management. *Academy of Management Review*, 18(3), 518–45.

Tracy, K. (1997). Interactional trouble in emergency service requests: A problem of frames. *Research on Language and Social interaction*, 30(4), 315–43.

Watson, T.J. (1995). In search of HRM: Beyond the rhetoric and reality distinction or the case of the dog that didn't bark. *Personnel Review, 24(4),* 6–16.

White, M. (1995). *Re-Authoring Lives: Interviews and Essays.* Adelaide: Dulwich Centre Publications.

PART III

SUSTAINABILITY, IDENTITY, AND ETHICS: ANIMALS IN PRODUCTION AND CONSUMPTION SYSTEMS

CHAPTER 15

ANIMAL ORGANIZATION STUDIES AND THE FOUNDATIONAL ECONOMY

Infrastructures of Everyday Multispecies Life

BRYONNY GOODWIN-HAWKINS

INTRODUCTION

I write this chapter as the world enters a second year of a viral pandemic. Economies have stuttered, and the once familiar rhythms of daily life have given way to a locked down 'new normal'. COVID-19 will be remembered as a punctuating crisis for economics as much as for health. And, as crises are wont to do, the pandemic has raised critical questions about the lives we want to live, the world we want to bequeath to future generations, and the economic structures that enable—or disable—those visions.

Of course, there is nothing new about questioning modern, capitalist, globalized economies. Critical questions have flown for generations, from politicians' benches to philosophers' armchairs (and probably to therapists' couches). Debates have long simmered over what has value (Mazzucato, 2018), how governments should intervene (Mann, 2017), and who really benefits (Piketty, 2014). Into the new millennium, economic questions have increasingly engaged with our planetary capacities (Raworth, 2017) and the ecological and climate consequences (Moore, 2015). Already several years before the pandemic, the OECD's (2012) *Environmental Outlook* concluded that business as usual could no longer be an option.

If we are to truly re-imagine economies for just, inclusive, and sustainable futures, we need to remember that those futures are made upon a shared planet—shared among humans, of course, but also shared between humans and animals. With this posthumanist perspective in mind, in this chapter I bring animal organization studies into conversation with emerging thinking on the 'foundational economy'—the goods, services, and infrastructures that support our everyday lives. A growing number of foundational economy thinkers are interested in how these everyday necessities can be provided equitably, produced sustainably, and valued appropriately as the fundamentals for wellbeing. My contribution in this chapter is to apply these tenets to everydays that are shared with animals, and to foundational economic activities that incorporate animal lives, labour, and products.

I approach this task as an interdisciplinary researcher in rural and regional development. My guiding belief is that all places and their (multispecies) inhabitants matter, deserving positive futures, good work, and good lives. Too often, policies give preference only to certain places—usually large cities—as the 'engines' of economic growth; too often, presumptions about idyllic rurality mistake impoverished places for nature and nostalgia. My interest in the foundational economy is hence as an alternative to the economic structures and values that perpetuate uneven development. My interest in animal organization studies arises from my awareness that rural places are working places—and that work, labour, and organizations are not the domains of humans alone.

The chapter proceeds as follows. I begin below by outlining the growth of foundational economy thinking, and sketching some of the key ideas. Following this, I discuss the absence of animals in foundational economy thinking to date, identifying potential ways to review our economic foundations through a multispecies lens. I then think through these animal-foundational interconnections using examples from the agrifood sector and working across three key themes: shared everydays, revaluing human-animal foundations, and prioritizing wellbeing. My ultimate aim is to draw connections between the foundational economy and animal organization studies, encouraging you—the reader—to delve deeper and ask critical questions of your own.

The Foundational Economy

The foundational economy emerged as a concept only recently, offering a radical approach to economic policy (Bentham et al., 2013). Observing that 'the relationship between growth, jobs, prosperity and wellbeing has broken down' (Heslop et al., 2019: 5) in our current economic paradigm, foundational economy thinkers join those who, like advocates for 'doughnut' economics (Raworth, 2017) or the circular economy (Ellen MacArthur Foundation, 2013), seek sustainable and inclusive alternatives to profit and growth at all costs.

Importantly, the concept of a foundational economy draws from understandings that contemporary econom*ies* are diverse and plural, rather than singular and all-encompassing (Gibson-Graham, 2008). While aggregate statistics like GDP portray 'the economy', in reality economic development happens through multiple 'zones of activities with different characteristics' (Froud et al., 2020: 317). The foundational economy forms one of these 'zones', and comprises 'the group of heterogeneous activities delivering goods and services which *meet essential citizen needs and provide the infrastructure of everyday life*' (Froud et al., 2020: 319; emphasis added). These essential, everyday economic activities can be divided into a *material* domain, including the food we eat, the utilities that power our homes, or the pipes that run water to our taps, and a *providential* domain, including social 'goods' like education and health care (Foundational Economy Collective, 2018). Together, these provide 'the basic requirements of civilised life for all ... irrespective of their income and location' (Heslop et al., 2019: 6). In other words, the foundational economy undergirds everyday life for everyone, everywhere.

Being essential does not mean the foundational economy is fixed and unchanging. We will always need food, water, and shelter, but the foundational economy should not be confused with a simple hierarchy of needs. Everyday essentials evolve (Froud et al., 2020: 319). Broadband internet, for example, is widely recognized today as an essential infrastructure, but barely existed just a few decades ago. The foundational economy can change, adapt, and innovate. All too often, however, parts of the foundational economy are overlooked and taken for granted. Few in developed countries give much thought to running water—until we need a plumber. The COVID-19 pandemic has in some ways made the foundational economy more visible, with governments around the world flexing otherwise stringent lockdown restrictions to keep 'key workers'—from hospital staff to bus drivers and fruit pickers—on the job. The broader picture of an 'overlooked' economy also includes some things that are not essential per se, but nevertheless matter for our wellbeing (Froud et al., 2020). Again, the pandemic has highlighted some of these broader 'goods'. For instance, hair salons have often been prioritized for reopening.

A mistake that may lurk here is equating the foundational economy with low wage and low productivity sectors. Many 'key workers' are poorly paid. But far from being an innate characteristic of the foundational economy, low wages reflect deep-seated problems with what and who our current economic paradigm values. As the economist Mariana Mazzucato (2018: 271) observes, our current paradigm is locked in the tautological false belief that price *is* value: 'as long as a good is bought or sold in the market, it must have value ... rather than a theory of value determining price, it is the theory of price that determines value'. Similarly, many everyday services are characterized by low productivity. But to view this as a problem is to value outputs over outcomes—from health care to hairdressing, raising the output per worker is rarely a reasonable goal. What defines the foundational economy is *not* the economic performance of its parts, but 'the social value of services produced by the foundational economy and their contribution to well-being' (Froud et al., 2020: 318).

For foundational economy thinkers, the need to prioritize social value over economic measurement is critical. All too often, policies are designed to please statistics, rather than support wellbeing. GDP, for example, has become vaunted for measuring macroeconomic success, comparing development and diagnosing progress. Yet measuring GDP largely works to map 'winners' and 'losers' according to a narrow view of what counts, which offers little scope for alternative visions (Jones et al., 2020), including the foundational economy's 'unglamourous' yet essential contributions to human flourishing (Calafati et al., 2019; Heslop et al., 2019). As Martha Nussbaum (2011: 5) observes, 'real human importance is located not in GDP but elsewhere'. Recognizing the foundational economy as an intimate part of that 'elsewhere' requires also recognizing that a flourishing foundational economy cannot be measured by consumption nor wholly provided through market-based competition (Heslop et al., 2019), but must instead be pursued through objectives for wellbeing (Calafati et al., 2019).

There are already encouraging examples from policies and practices that support the foundational economy. Heslop et al. (2019) identify three trends that link the foundational economy to other emerging efforts to foster wellbeing through economic alternatives. First, local 'anchor institutions', such as schools and hospitals, are being increasingly encouraged to use their roles as employers, asset owners, and purchasers to strengthen local foundations and share the benefits with their communities. The 'Preston model' for community wealth-building, pioneered by local government in the post-industrial town of Preston, Northern England, is a widely cited example. Second, policy shifts are enabling some public services to be transferred (fully or partly) back to local ownership and/or decision making. Community energy is a notable example here. Third, the rise of sharing economies and mutual aid has helped to grow sharing and caring networks for everyday essentials, from hyper-local food co-operatives to community-led housing schemes. To date, the most explicit national policies have appeared in Wales, where the Welsh government's Foundational Economy Challenge Fund has joined an agenda set by the *Well-being of Future Generations Act* (Jones et al., 2020) to shape initiatives that 'directly target liveability and sustainability' (Froud et al., 2020: 317).

In this section, I have positioned foundational economy thinking as a necessary response to what Kate Raworth (2017) characterizes as 'twentieth century economics'—a limited and limiting view of what progress can and should be that has prioritized competition and consumption over wellbeing and sustainability. Revaluing the foundational economy does not ask us to abandon growth for good or give up on technological innovation (as the example of internet access shifting from a novelty to an essential demonstrates), but it does require attending to the everyday ingredients of good lives for all people, wherever they may live, and within the capacities of a healthy and habitable planet. Of course, this is a shared planet, and it is to our planet's animal inhabitants that I now turn.

The Foundational Economy and Animals

To date, foundational economy thinkers have had little to say about animals. Their concern, following a path to wellbeing framed by Nussbaum (2011) and Amartya Sen (1993) amongst others, has primarily been with people and places. In terms of countering the inadequacies of the current economic paradigm, this is a laudable concern and by no means a failing. However, as 'posthumanities' theorist Rosi Braidotti (2019: 40) observes, our growing realization that continued economic exploitation is unjust and unsustainable—and disastrously so in ecological terms—is also a call to move 'beyond humanist exceptionalism'. We are not, Braidotti reminds us, an exclusively human 'we', but relationally dependent upon multiple nonhuman others. If the goal of foundational economy thinking is to call attention to the foundations for wellbeing, then those foundations necessarily include human-animal relationships and that wellbeing cannot be reserved to humans alone.

In this sense, animal organization studies offers a useful bridge. Thousands upon thousands of organizations are nested within the foundational economy. Indeed, delivering the material goods and providential services necessary *every day* requires densely layered, intricate organization. As an economic domain, the foundational economy is also an inherently organizational domain. More so, viewing the foundational economy from an organizational perspective helps to refine focus from the generalized ideals of policy critique towards the practical realities of how goods are created and services are provided. What a multispecies perspective adds here—and why animal organization studies bridges concepts—is analytic purchase on the intrinsic role of animals and human-animal relations in many forms of work and organization.

Animal organization studies reflects an 'animal turn' in the social sciences (Buller, 2013), amidst wider critical recognition that disciplines fostered to focus on humanity and society originate in a 'Myth of Man' (Braidotti, 2019) that has proved both partial and harmful (Haraway, 2016). The 'posthuman predicament', as Braidotti (2019: 8) terms this scholarly *zeitgeist*, 'is not just a critique of Humanism ... [but] also takes on the even more complex challenge of anthropocentrism'. Influential interventions have ranged from theorizing 'cyborg' hybridity (Haraway, 2016) to re-enchanting vital materialism (Bennett, 2001). I acknowledge these literatures here as a backdrop to animal organization studies, yet set them aside as beyond my primary concern. I do, however, want to note two points. First, although posthumanism (and adjacent ideas) and heterodox economics emerge from different disciplinary lineages, they share a common conviction that existing paradigms have damaging consequences, and that redressing this 'predicament' requires approaching an entangled world through newly reappraised values and ways of noticing. Second, the posthumanist call to widen 'our' conceptual frames to include nonhuman others is directly applicable to rethinking economies.

Applying an animal organization studies lens on work and organizations to the foundational economy offers, I consider, perspectives that can beneficially expand both concepts, while magnifying the space for their common ground. Just as foundational economy thinking shifts attention to those sectors that are fundamental to our wellbeing, animal organization studies reveals the multispecies relationships within everyday economic activity and, more so, suggests that supporting 'our' wellbeing should include the wellbeing of nonhuman others, too.

These are broad brush principles, but we can readily begin to fill in some of the practical detail. Members of the Foundational Economy Collective (2018) suggest thinking about breakfast as a simple heuristic exercise. For most of us, the products, services, and infrastructures we interact with on a typical morning between waking up and eating breakfast are part of the foundational economy. Making a list is a startling exercise in noticing how many economic activities underlie our morning routines: water running from our taps, gas firing our central heating, the aroma of coffee, food to prepare. Where are the animals? Perhaps breakfast features milk, cheese, bacon, or honey; even cereals were partly produced by busy pollinators, and those keeping kosher diets will be all too aware that many fruits and vegetables harbour insect stowaways. Of course, before enjoying our own breakfasts, those of us with four-legged family members will be reminded whose hunger to prioritize; pets also interact with foundational infrastructures, from a filled water bowl to a warm radiator. Delving deeper, animal legacies might appear, too. In the United Kingdom, one well-known oats and muesli brand uses a horse and plough logo—a reminder that animal labour once played a central role in agriculture (as it continues to do elsewhere in the world). Today, oat production is mechanized, and the packets make their way to British supermarket shelves through supply chains travelling trunk roads that are, in another reminder of foundational animal labour, still called 'carriageways'.

As I hope this discussion has begun to tease out, multiple species are present within the foundational economy in multiple ways. Animal products and animal labour are certainly foundational. But domestic animals are also a reminder that there is not a clear-cut division between animal production and human consumption. Different species may produce and consume within the foundational economy in different ways at different times. The point is that the foundational economy is a multispecies domain, shared every day in interconnected relationships.

In the previous section, I noted three key themes in foundational economy thinking: attending to the everyday, revaluing what matters most, and, linking these ideas, prioritizing wellbeing over macroeconomic performance. In the next two sections, I shift these themes from their initial humanist frames to encompass animal interconnections. I draw my examples from the agrifood sector for convenience and consider mammals for simplicity, but of course the land-based food system is not the only foundational sector wherein animals produce and consume, nor do human-animal relationships within the foundational economy exclusively involve mammals (Buller, 2015). I suggest some routes towards broadening future research beyond these initial beginnings in my conclusion to follow.

Of Milking Parlours and Breakfast Tables

Just above, I suggested breakfast routines as a way to start thinking through how the foundational economy is present in our own lives—and then to follow the animals.

I want to sit with that theme a little longer, beginning with the example of milk. In many European countries (and those influenced by their colonial and/or culinary legacies), dairy products are a breakfast staple. This has a long agricultural history, and a shorter economic narrative. Eurasian peoples began consuming milk from cows, sheep, and goats at much the same time as these animals were being domesticated during the Neolithic period (Valenze, 2011)—the 'dawn' of agriculture. Making butter and cheeses emerged as a preservation method; in England, dairy became 'white meat' for the medieval poor, while the Low Countries were known for their milk production from around the fifteenth century (Valenze, 2011).

Milk, of course, requires milking—bringing humans and animals into intimate proximity. Historically, milking was typically a household activity, and humans and cows, for example, shared close connections. While we should avoid romantically imagining a friendly cow in every backyard, rural vernacular architectures offer a glimpse into everyday proximities. In the South Pennine uplands in Northern England, where I have carried out fieldwork, the 'laithe houses' of the seventeenth and eighteenth centuries combined living quarters for humans and animals in the same doughty stone building. Shared shelter made for shared sounds and smells, amid the shared rhythms of milking time.

Today, milking is still defined by close human-animal labour, but commercial dairy farmers no longer milk by hand. Milking machines of various kinds were pioneered in the mid-nineteenth century. By 1961, 85 per cent of the dairy herds in the United Kingdom were machine milked (Brassley, 2000). But this transition was viewed with anxiety by observers at the time: as well as raising new concerns about animal welfare, machine milking created dismay about monotonous human labour (Holloway and Bear, 2017). Monotonous or not, milking parlours are now highly organized workplaces. Over half a century of further development has seen technologies become increasingly sophisticated, with equipment able to record milk composition, detect potential animal health problems, and operate with lessening need for human intervention. These technologies both arise from and affect what humans and animals do in the milking parlour, reflecting agencies and subjectivities, and equally mediating these (Holloway and Bear, 2017). For example, machine milking responds to a farmyard rhythm, but also requires that cows live in herds. Because machines are more efficient, herds have been able to grow larger, and milk volumes have increased—and here I shift from production to consumption.

Historically, dairy produced at a domestic scale was often for household consumption, although surpluses were certainly sold or exchanged. Dutch farmers, for example, realized early that better nutrition for cows would increase milk yield and make a good profit (Valenze, 2011). However, growing urbanization was the crucial factor in commodifying milk. In his 1826 treatise *Der Isolierte Staat* (The Isolated State), German economist Johann Heinrich von Thünen pictured a central city surrounded by a providing countryside. In von Thünen's ideal model, concentric circles radiating from the city contained different types of agricultural land use (Woods, 2020). Dairy was prominently placed in the first circle: a vision of milk production ringing the city, so that perishable products could be quickly brought to market. Domestic dairy had become foundational.

Into the twentieth century, dairy grew as a significant industry. Production increased exponentially, and supply chains became longer and more complex. Partly, this was a story of modernization, enabled by research and technology and encouraged by national policies. Standardizing milk's fat, protein, and sugar content, for example, became both possible and desirable, making milk less of the farmyard and more of the factory (Atkins, 2010). Economic recovery after the Second World War brought a renewed 'productivist' drive in agriculture (Ilbery and Bowler, 1998). Fertilizers, insecticides, and hormones were developed to raise yields, production was intensified, and government subsidies supported price. Of course, large volumes had to be sold, and modernization and productivism were matched with the marketing of milk as pure and wholesome (DuPuis, 2002). Indeed, milk became a daily breakfast table staple not because it really reflected a traditional rural human-animal rhythm but because products need consumers.

Recently, growing recognition of the animal conditions and environmental costs of the dairy industry has led to a backlash against milk (Clay et al., 2020). Plant-based alternatives—'mylks'—have become increasingly ubiquitous, promising consumers thinner ecological footprints and consciences cleansed of animal welfare concerns. Clay et al. (2020) call this a 'palatable disruption', in which consuming one product over another is marketed as a solution to far more systemic problems. As they write, 'Mylks...encourage people to rebel just enough to switch from dairy milk to mylk while entreating them to remain devoted consumers of commodity mylk' (Clay et al., 2020: 945). I would also suggest that this palatable disruption deals with the posthuman predicament by creating a curious kind of 'postanimal' absence, in which animals are removed from consumption while animal products remain the norm. Like Britain's carriageways, mylks in the supermarket dairy aisle reflect the stories of how human-animal relationships have structured and re-structured foundational economic activities.

I have only skimmed milk's stories in this section, but I want to suggest that, if foundational economy thinking makes us more attentive to our breakfasts, animal organization studies might make us aware that other morning routines matter, too. Milk is a reminder of shared everydays and entanglements, representing ordinary embodied actions and social, economic, and technological histories alike. If food is a foundational good (Morgan, 2015), then we need to reflect on valuing what good is. I turn to this in the next section.

Of Rare Breeds and Knowing Provenance

In her book *The Value of Everything*, Mazzucato (2018) recounts the shift from eighteenth-century economic theories that located value in agriculture, to current celebratory perspectives on finance. I earlier cited Mazzucato's concerns that contemporary economics has come to put a theory of price over a theory of value, and in this section I want to return to the question of value in agriculture in order to illustrate how we might re-value the foundational economy through a human-animal frame.

Just above, I noted that machine milking has enabled bigger dairy herds. But, while this is true of the *number* of cows, it is not true of their genetic diversity. The legacy of agricultural productivism runs through bovine bloodlines, with generations of animals descending from systematic selection for favourable, productive traits. The typical dairy cow now produces around twice as much milk as a cow of 40 years ago (Oltenacu and Broom, 2010). In the United States, where the Holstein breed accounts for some 94 per cent of the national dairy herd and almost all of these cattle trace descent from one of two bulls, 9 million cows are estimated to be the genetic equivalent of fewer than a hundred animals (Gressier, 2021). There is evidence that selecting for milk yield has left these animals with deteriorating health and reduced lifespans (Oltenacu and Broom, 2010). This is clearly a problem of what gets valued and why.

Rare breed farming begins to suggest different conceptions of value. So-called 'rare' or 'traditional' livestock breeds are typically those that fell from favour after agricultural modernization meant more 'economic' breeds like Holstein cattle came to 'embod[y] innovation in farming practice, progressive thinking, and efficient husbandry' (Yarwood and Evans, 2006: 1311). Some rare breeds are today valued for their associations with particular places (Yarwood and Evans, 2006); others affectively mingle human and animal stories in shared lineages (Gressier, 2021). Reflecting on her ethnographic work with rare breed cattle farmers in Australia, Catie Gressier (2021) describes how these farmers understand the animals they breed and care for as a totality of traits: from their temperament and mothering ability, to their milk and meat. Here, a farmer's proud eye for a good animal means more than the market value of animal products.

Rare breed farming should not be mistaken for a rural idyll. The reason many conventional farmers select for productive characteristics is precisely because making a living farming is a hard economic reality. Gressier's (2021) farmers struggle to stay viable, and necessarily rely on off-farm income from a spouse or second job. Often, the holistic value they afford good animal lives is not matched by the prices markets place on animal products. This reflects the tremendous difficulties posed by an economic paradigm that tries to treat food as a tradeable commodity like any other (Morgan, 2015).

One way to revalue food is to revalue where food comes from. Geographical Indication (GI) schemes do so by certifying provenance—situating certain foods in stories of place and process and conveying that value to consumers. In the European Union (EU), GIs have been most famously used to protect niche products like champagne from cut-price competition, but there can be meaningful benefits at a local level that matter for humans and animals alike. For example, lamb from the Cambrian Mountains in Wales was awarded European GI protection in 2013. The designation followed several years of collaborative local action to support sustainable futures in a struggling upland region beset by demographic change and beholden to economic fluctuations (Goodwin-Hawkins, 2018). With farming a heartland for the Welsh language, the slow loss of local communities was also a loss of culture. Founded with support from the Prince of Wales, the Cambrian Mountains brand aimed to build better prices for local products and improve livelihoods. Crucially, to use the brand farmers must commit to sustainable land management practices and high animal welfare standards (Goodwin-Hawkins, 2018). The GI designation requires that: lamb is bred from ewes that are at least 80 per cent Welsh hill breeds; at least 75 per cent of the flock's annual dry diet also comes from the Cambrian Mountains; local slaughterhouses are used; and the lamb is traceable from 'fork to farm'. The designation also celebrates the region's traditional *hafod a hendre* seasonal grazing practices, and a culture of *cefnewid*, or cooperation, between farms for human-animal activities like shearing and gathering (Goodwin-Hawkins, 2018). For consumers, buying Cambrian Mountains lamb is buying a different set of values to commodity pricing. Value here is about the co-existing work and lives of humans and animals, through the seasons and across generations. Price can help sustain value in this holistic sense, but as I have been arguing, price poses problems when it becomes the driver for what *can* be valued.

I do want to sound a note of caution here, as conflating revaluing foundational sectors with re-pricing foundational goods returns us to the problematic tautology Mazzucato (2018) rightly critiques. From plant-based mylks to bucolic myths of artisanal production, consumerist solutions rarely redress systemic problems (Clay et al., 2020, Phillipov and Loyer, 2019). Indeed, too many people already face food poverty, and predicating animal wellbeing on human ability to pay risks entrenching inequalities further. The key point I want to make here is that foundational economy thinking asks us to reconceptualize the limited and limiting notion that goods and services that sell for little are worth little. Foundational economy thinkers hence mobilize a broader concept of social value—the contribution an economic activity makes to societal wellbeing—over economic performance. Animal organization studies suggests that *social* value alone might be all too exclusively human. There are no easy answers here, but beginning to notice the complex entanglements between humans and animals, economy and wellbeing, might help us ask better questions. With this in mind, I use the conclusion of this chapter to look towards future research.

Summary and Future Research Directions

In this chapter, I have worked to draw initial connections between animal organization studies and growing interest in the foundational economy. I began by describing the foundational economy as the material and providential goods, services, and infrastructures that support our everyday lives. This, I suggested, should make us reflect on the ways animals also share our everydays, whether through companionship, labour, or the ecological capacities of a single, shared planet. In brief examples from the agrifood sector, I drew attention to the ways everyday lives and economic foundations entail human-animal entanglements, and to the consequences and complexities of a modern economic paradigm that has put productivity over wellbeing.

A thriving and appropriately valued foundational economy undergirds our shared wellbeing, exactly because the foundational economy provides the essentials for everyday lives. Good lives should not be a solely human prerogative. There are many inequalities that are of human making and require human action, but advancing human wellbeing at the expense of other species is fundamentally flawed and does little to ensure sustainable futures for a shared planet. To revalue the foundational economy is necessarily to redefine good lives as shared lives, and requires shifting how we measure progress from prices and macroeconomic indicators towards more holistic benchmarks. There is a lot of work to do—and organization alongside.

I have only been able to stitch broad, initial ideas here in this chapter, but I want to conclude as I began by inviting others to pick up the threads. Let me thus offer five suggestions for future directions that research uniting animal organization studies and foundational economy perspectives might fruitfully take.

First, foundational sectors include domains where animal lives, labour, and products are particularly present. The food system is one example, but studies might tease out the animal implications of less obvious infrastructures and the human-animal interdependencies of other foundational goods. Scale matters, with room for ethnographic reflections on ordinary intimacies through to tracing dense supply chains. Second, understanding these interdependencies and the complexities they engender has important implications for how we approach revaluing the foundational economy. This should certainly include exploring how animal lives are valued in work, organizations, and economies, but there is equally a need to expand foundational economy perspectives to encompass everyday *animal* needs for material infrastructures (like water and warmth) and providential services (like veterinary care). Third, there are hints of animal histories lodged within foundational goods, services, and infrastructures from 'carriageways' to breakfast tables. Historical research on animals and animal products already exists, and there are opportunities to draw upon these findings to better historicize both the foundational economy and the origins of contemporary human-animal everydays. Fourth, alongside identifying animal presences, there is interesting potential to explore animal *absences* in the foundational economy. Research here might examine instances of foundational activities unintentionally displacing animals, or untangle the human-animal organizational consequences of efforts to intentionally replace animal labour and animal products, such as plant-based diets or lab-grown meat. Last, these suggestions so far perhaps echo a 'mammalian hegemony' (Buller, 2015). Foundational economy thinking's concern with *human* everyday lives has also located work to date in terrestrial space. Which animal lives might become imbricated if foundational activities were explored from the air (Adey, 2013) or the sea (Steinberg and Peters, 2015), for example?

Doubtless, many more connections can and will be made. These will lead us to greater empirical understanding, while also increasing the philosophical and political, ethical, and economic complications. For example, in this chapter I have repeatedly recalled that human and animal lives intertwine in everyday economic and organizational practices, but I have not substantively engaged with the philosophy of multispecies lives, including critical questions about the ethics of eating animals and animal products. These and other questions lurk, and here at least I will let them. Instead, I want to end with a rather more human-centric reflection. If we are to take multispecies 'good lives' as a normative—perhaps even utopian (Levitas, 2013)—goal for shared and sustainable futures, then it is nevertheless human work to puzzle the paths forward and confront the ways we do and do not speak justly for animals. Although what we have lately witnessed of the capacity of microscopic viral bodies to throw economies into disarray reminds us that policy decisions are never quite made by humans alone (much the posthumanist point), we cannot leave responsibility for the infrastructures of shared everyday lives to the whims of an imagined 'invisible hand'. We need to make the very real hands, and paws and claws, hooves, and fins, that inhabit the foundational economy visible so that we can make shared futures viable.

References

Adey, P. (2013). Air/atmospheres of the megacity. *Theory, Culture and Society, 30(7/8)*, 291–308.
Atkins, P. (2010). *Liquid materialities: A history of milk, science and the law*. London: Routledge.
Bennett, J. (2001). *The enchantment of modern life: Attachments, crossings, and ethics.* Princeton: Princeton University Press.
Bentham, J. et al. (2013). *Manifesto for the foundational economy*. CRESC Working Paper No. 131. Manchester: Centre for Research on Socio-Cultural Change.
Braidotti, R. (2019). *Posthuman knowledge*. Cambridge: Polity Press.
Brassley, P. (2000). Output and technical change in twentieth-century British agriculture. *Agricultural History Review, 48,* 60–84.
Buller, H. (2013). Animal geographies I. *Progress in Human Geography, 38(2),* 308–318.
Buller, H. (2015). Animal geographies II: Methods. *Progress in Human Geography, 39(3),* 374–84.
Calafati, L. et al. (2019). *How an ordinary place works: Understanding Morriston*. Foundational Economy Research Report, available at: https://foundationaleconomycom.files.wordpress.com/2019/05/morriston-report-v6-13-may-2019.pdf
Clay, N. et al. (2020). Palatable disruption: The politics of plant milk. *Agriculture and Human Values, 37,* 945–62.
DuPuis, E.M. (2002). *Nature's perfect food: How milk became America's drink*. New York: NYU Press.
Ellen MacArthur Foundation (2013). *Towards the circular economy 1*, available at: https://www.ellenmacarthurfoundation.org/assets/downloads/publications/Ellen-MacArthur-Foundation-Towards-the-Circular-Economy-vol.1.pdf Isle of Wight: Ellen MacArthur Foundation.

Foundational Economy Collective, (2018). *Foundational economy: The infrastructure of everyday life*. Manchester: Manchester University Press.

Froud, J. et al. (2020). (How) does productivity matter in the foundational economy? *Local Economy, 35(4)*, 316–36.

Gibson-Graham, J.K. (2008). Diverse economies: Performative practices for 'other worlds'. *Progress in Human Geography, 32(5)*, 613–32.

Goodwin-Hawkins, B. (2018). Mynyddoedd Cambrian Mountains Initiative. Rapid Appraisal, Horizon 2020 ROBUST Project.

Gressier, C. (2021). Bovine bloodlines. *Anthropology News*, available at: https://www.anthropology-news.org/index.php/2021/03/01/bovine-bloodlines/

Haraway, D. (2016). *Staying with the trouble: Making kin in the Chthulucene*. Durham, NC: Duke University Press.

Heslop, J., Morgan, K., & Tomaney, J. (2019). Debating the foundational economy. *Renewal: A Journal of Labour Politics, 27(2)*, 5–12.

Holloway, L. & Bear, C. (2017). Bovine and human becomings in histories of dairy technologies: Robotic milking systems and remaking animal and human subjectivity. *BJHS Themes, 2*, 215–34.

Ilbery, B. & Bowler, I. (1998) From agricultural productivism to post-productivism. In B. Ilbery (Ed.), *The Geography of Rural Change* (pp. 57–84). London: Longman.

Jones, R., Goodwin-Hawkins, B., & Woods. M. (2020) From territorial cohesion to regional spatial justice: The Wellbeing of Future Generations Act in Wales. *International Journal of Urban and Regional Research, 44(5)*, 894–912.

Levitas, R. (2013). *Utopia as method: The imaginary reconstitution of society*. Basingstoke: Palgrave Macmillan.

Mann, G. (2017). *In the Long run we are all dead: Keynesianism, political economy and revolution*. London: Verso.

Mazzucato, M. (2018). *The entrepreneurial state: Debunking public vs. private sector myths*. London: Penguin.

Moore, J.W. (2015). *Capitalism in the web of life: Ecology and the accumulation of capital*. London: Verso.

Morgan, K. (2015). The moral economy of food. *Geoforum, 65*, 294–6.

Nussbaum, M. (2011). *Creating Capabilities*. Cambridge, MA: Harvard University Press.

OECD. (2012). *OECD environmental outlook to 2050: The consequences of inaction*. Paris: OECD.

Oltenacu, P.A. & Broom, D.M. (2010). The impact of genetic selection for increased milk yield on the welfare of dairy cows. *Animal Welfare, 19(1)*, 39–49.

Phillipov, M. & Loyer, J. (2019). In the wake of the supermarket 'milk wars': Media, farmers and the power of pastoral sentimentality. *Discourse, Context and Media*, 32(December 2019), 1–8.

Piketty, T. (2014) *Capital in the twenty-first century*. A. Goldhammer (trans.). Cambridge, MA: The Belknap Press.

Raworth, K. (2017). *Doughnut economics: Seven ways to think like a 21st century economist*. New York: Penguin.

Sen, A. (1993). Capability and well-being. In A. Sen & M. Nussbaum (Eds.), *The quality of life* (pp. 30–53). Oxford: Clarendon Press.

Steinberg, P. & Peters, K. (2015). Wet ontologies, fluid spaces: Giving depth to volume through oceanic thinking. *Environment and Planning D: Society and Space, 33(2)*, 247–64.

Valenze, D. (2011). *Milk: A local and global history*. New Haven: Yale University Press.

Woods, M. (2020). Rural-urban linkages. In J. Duncan, M. Carolan, & J.S.C. Wiskerke (Eds.), *Routledge handbook of sustainable and regenerative food systems* (pp. 363–76). London: Routledge.

Yarwood, R. & Evans, N. (2006). A Lleyn sweep for local sheep? Breed societies and the geographies of Welsh livestock. *Environment and Planning A: Economy and Space, 38(7)*, 1307–26.

CHAPTER 16

HOW CAN WE REDUCE SPECIESISM? A PSYCHOLOGICAL APPROACH TO A SOCIAL PROBLEM

DORIS SCHNEEBERGER

EXPANDING our moral circle to include nonhuman animals is one of the great challenges faced by humanity in the twenty-first century (Anthis and Paez, 2021). Nonhuman animals (NHAs) are heavily involved in institutions and organizations created and dominated by humans—often involuntarily, and to their detriment. *Speciesism* (or, 'the unjustified disadvantageous consideration or treatment of those who are not classified as belonging to a certain species' (Horta, 2010: 1)) distorts human thinking, perceptions, and research efforts. It causes suffering and harm to countless sentient beings, both in the present and for the foreseeable future: consider here, for example, environmental degradation, world hunger, (the risks of) antibiotic resistance, pandemics, and climate change, and how these are linked to the current exploitation of NHAs by humanity.

In line with calls to management scholars to 'dare to care' (Adler and Hansen, 2012) and calls that have highlighted the need to incorporate compassion in our research and theorizing (Frost, 1999), the research question guiding my project is 'how can we reduce humanity's speciesism?' During this project, I was inspired by what management sciences term the 'compassionate methodology', which is 'deliberately and unapologetically engaged and activist' (Hansen and Trank, 2016: 360). I used a qualitative interventionist research design in order to examine whether certain interventions reduce the speciesism of my epistemic partners. I use the term 'epistemic partners' (EPs) (cf. Holmes and Marcus, 2008) to refer to my research participants or, a term more commonly used in psychology; 'test subjects'. I chose this term since making sense of the data and oral contributions was a collaborative process in which everyone involved in the research process contributed to co-produce insights into speciesism. Seven EPs (four male, three female, all doctoral students at the Vienna University of Economics and Business at the outset of the research process), underwent a series of interventions, designed to reduce their speciesism.

This study presents a psychological approach to the social and organizational problem of speciesism. It is a qualitative interventionist study with quantitative measurements measuring the speciesism of the EPs at three points during the process. These measurements are helpful in situating the EPs' processes in an objective/measurable dimension. The research design employed in this study is admittedly somewhat unconventional in management and organization studies. However, when aiming at a better understanding of 'critical organisational phenomena', 'some of the most significant contributions to management theory emerged from what might be…labelled "unconventional" organizational research' (Bamberger and Pratt, 2010: 665); therefore, an unusual research design may, in this case, prove illuminating.

The measurements showed that the interventions reduced the individual speciesism level of every EP. The extent of the reduction varied from a reduction of 1.17 (maximum) to 0.16 (minimum). In the discussion of these findings, I reflect on the diversity of these outcomes, using the psychoanalytic theory of defence mechanisms (Freud, 1984) and Lewin's theory of change (Lewin, 1947). The analysis of the empirical data using these two theories shows that the Freudian theory of defence mechanisms could be helpful in explaining why some individuals do not reach all three stages of Lewin's change process and why change processes might therefore turn out to be unsuccessful/incomplete.

The need to recognize the moral importance of NHAs and to defend this importance has already been discussed to a certain extent in organization studies (cf. Cunha, Rego, and Munro, 2019; García-Rosell and Tallberg, 2021; Labatut, Munro, and Desmond, 2016; Sayers, Hamilton, and Sang, 2019; Tallberg, García-Rosell, and Haanpää, 2021). This study could contribute to this discussion by fostering our understanding of how we can reduce individual speciesism levels and thus also reduce speciesism in our organizations and institutions. A series of interventions similar to the one employed in this study could be used in anti-speciesist trainings, workshops, and programmes within organizations. Reducing our speciesism is part and parcel of creating a world that is less plagued by violence, injustice, and suffering. It is a starting point of this chapter, then, that anti-speciesism helps us to expand our moral circle, and thus enables us to make ethically better decisions.[1] In the following sections, I describe the methods and research process in detail before moving on to a set of findings. These are discussed and final observations given in the context of some key psychological and organizational theories which provide the theoretical background for this study.

---

[1] At this point, I should like to provide some personal background information. I am a philosopher (NHA ethicist) as well as a psychoanalytical psychotherapist in training. Readers might find that this background has considerably influenced this research process, from designing the study to analysing and interpreting the empirical data.

Defending Others and Ourselves

Eating NHAs is a worldwide institution (Joy, 2020). A growing awareness of the atrocities that constitute how humans currently treat NHAs in factory farms and slaughterhouses has led many of us to distance ourselves from this institution and change our dietary habits, in order to reduce our contribution to NHA suffering and violence against NHAs. To many of us, making no attempt to do something to combat this atrocity, once we have caught a glimpse of the horrors that NHAs experience in the NHA industry, is simply not an option. There are sound reasons for taking further action, and not speaking up seems to represent a failure to render assistance and a failure of moral courage. We may have the goal of reducing NHA suffering and may try to influence other humans so that they too will reduce the NHA suffering they cause. Once we have arrived at this point, however, we may start to realize that attempting to influence humans so that they change the way in which they treat NHAs and reduce their speciesism is often akin to 'talking to a brick wall'. It is very hard indeed to inspire change. The reasons for the difficulty in changing human behaviour and attitudes lie in our psychological functioning, or as Dhont and colleagues (Dhont et al., 2020: 42) state: 'the psychological flexibility of our moral reasoning and behaviour is mind-boggling'.

An important psychological insight for those who aspire to change human attitudes and behaviours towards NHAs, is that when it comes to human psyches, attitude tends to follow behaviour, and not—as we might intuitively figure—the other way round (Dhont et al., 2020; Olson and Stone, 2005). This is one explanation of why it is so hard to have an anti-speciesist impact in a world where eating NHAs and their bodily products is heavily institutionalized. What is interesting to note is that a low speciesism score does not mean that a person does not exhibit speciesist behaviour:

> '[S]peciesism and ethical vegetarianism were—despite being strongly correlated—psychologically distinct factors. At first blush, this result might be surprising, as one might expect that endorsement of antispeciesism would consistently result in endorsement of ethical vegetarianism. However, this finding is consistent with previous research on the meat paradox (Bastian & Loughnan, 2017; Bratanova et al., 2011). People might endorse antispeciesism in the abstract or in domains where it does not conflict with their personal preferences, but they use specific beliefs and practices in the context of food (i.e., carnism; Monteiro et al., 2017; Piazza et al., 2015)' (Caviola, Everett, and Faber, 2019: 1017).

Another reason why inspiring change is so hard lies in how the human psyche tends to deal with cognitive dissonance. Psychologists speak of cognitive dissonance '[i]f a person knows various things that are not psychologically consistent with one another' (Festinger, 1962: 93). Loving (or even liking or simply empathizing with) NHAs and (killing and) eating them too is bound to cause cognitive dissonance. Our wish not to harm others clashes with the wish to eat NHA products. Often, our treatment of NHAs will be in conflict with our beliefs about them, and our affective states towards them (Loughnan, Bratanova, and Puvia, 2012). When 'knowing various things that are not psychologically consistent with one another', we 'will, in a variety of ways, try to make them more consistent' (Festinger, 1962: 93). When it comes to eating NHA products, we try to achieve this by adding certain rationalizations/justifications to our belief system, such as the '4Ns', according to which eating meat is normal, necessary, natural, and nice (Piazza et al., 2015).

In this study, alongside Lewin's theory of 'change in three steps' (Lewin, 1947), I reflect on my data through the lens of the psychoanalytical theory of defence mechanisms (Freud, 1984). It builds on the idea of the structural form of the human psyche, in which three intrapsychic forces are at work: ego, id, and super-ego (Freud, 1961). A positive image of ourselves and our own actions, as well as a belief system that is as free as possible of contradiction, is central to our psychological health and mental wellbeing. In order to maintain the latter, the ego employs a diverse range of defence mechanisms (Freud, 1984; Vaillant, 1992). Defence mechanisms are 'innate involuntary regulatory processes that allow individuals to reduce cognitive dissonance and to minimize sudden changes in internal and external environments' (Vaillant, 1994: 44).

Our superlatively efficient defence system protects our mental health and enables us to function, but unfortunately also hinders us when it comes to making moral progress. It contributes to conserving our behaviours, attitudes, and beliefs, even if these might need updating, since they have, after all, helped us to survive up to the present. The ego uses defence mechanisms automatically and vigorously, unbeknownst to us in our conscious experiences (Freud, 1984). This psychological defence system guards us against (currently) overwhelming demands from the super-ego as well as from outside of our own psyche (such as when non-/not-yet-vegans engage in ethical debates about veganism, for example). It therefore stands between us and moral progress, and only allows us to pass once the ethical demands do not seem overwhelming anymore.

The defence mechanisms in psychoanalytical theory are subdivided into more and less mature defence mechanisms (Cramer, 1987). Mature defence mechanisms are, for example; rationalization, intellectualization, and repression (ibid). Projection and denial are examples of immature defence mechanisms (ibid). The kinds of defence mechanisms that an individual employs will depend primarily on the psychological structure of the individual (Vaillant, Bond, and Vaillant, 1986). Depending on the maturity and health of our mental apparatus, our mental status quo, and the severity of the threat at a given moment, we employ more or less 'costly' defence mechanisms (Cramer, 1987: 598). If a threat is severe, and/or our mental constitution due to developmental or situational causes weakened, we might pay the price that is engendered by employing immature defence mechanisms: a more or less distorted perception of reality (ibid). We deny reality and lie to ourselves (even about ourselves), without realizing it. We might repress thoughts about the NHA industry, deny that we buy products from factory farms, lie (to ourselves) about how often we actually consume NHA products, project the devaluation and the guilt that we (do not want to/are not able to) feel when our actions are being criticized onto others and perceive them as their shortcomings, rather than our own (Freud, 1984).

How Change Happens

It may come as no surprise, that not only does Anna Freud's theory of defence mechanisms provide explanations when making sense of change when it comes to our actions and attitudes, so too does Kurt Lewin's theory of 'change in three steps', which are unfreezing, changing, and refreezing (cf. for a discussion of Lewin's model see Cummings, Bridgman, and Brown, 2016: 34). The interventions used in this study should ideally induce an 'unfreezing', cause anti-speciesist change, and a 'refreeze' at a less speciesist point. The simplicity of Lewin's model is striking; so is its legacy and applicability: some '[a]cademics claim that all theories of change are "reducible to this one idea of Kurt Lewin's"' (Cummings, Bridgman, and Brown, 2016: 34).

Freud's theory points out that our psyche is resistant to 'unfreezing'. It tries to avoid destabilization of the, so far successful, mental system. However, there are times and situations in our lives when we 'unfreeze' quickly, and are thus able to change quickly. These loopholes open up when our defence system is weakened due to crisis, or situations of mental destabilization. Crises are thus potentially highly transformative, as many will know from personal experience of tragedies or catastrophes, which have prompted a change of ways and lifestyle; in the end, often for the better. We can experience mental destabilization when we are in a state of shock and trauma. And this is where we return to advocacy for NHAs and reducing speciesism: witnessing the violence and suffering inherent in the current NHA industry is, for many, shocking and traumatic. Humans react differently to audio-visual images of the NHA suffering in the industry. These pictures, however, can elicit strong negative emotions and empathetic reactions (and spur anti-speciesist change). Fernández (2020), for example, conducted a study on the effectiveness of (violent) audio-visuals in promoting anti-speciesist attitudes and found that 'exposure to moral shock was decisive in the adoption of veganism and involvement in activism in most cases' (Fernández, 2020: 138).

Moral shock might be especially potent because it weakens our defence system and thereby accelerates change. Several studies have, however, concluded that other kinds of interventions can also be effective when it comes to reducing the consumption of meat. In their systemic literature review, including 22 studies with an experimental or quasi-experimental design, Harguess and colleagues showed that information about diverse aspects of the consumption of meat concerning NHA ethics, human health, and effects on the environment and climate, have, for example, brought about measurable changes: '[i]n general, increasing knowledge alone or when combined with other methods was shown to successfully reduce meat consumption behaviour or intentions/willingness to eat meat. Evoking emotions with animal images and making changes to the environment proved effective.' (Harguess, Crespo, and Hong, 2020: 1).

Methods and Research Process

Methods—The Speciesism Scale

The quantitative tool, which was used in this qualitative interventionist study, is the speciesism scale by Caviola and colleagues (Caviola, Everett, and Faber, 2019). It is empirically validated and consists of the following six items: '1) Morally, animals always count for less than humans. 2) Humans have the right to use animals however they want to. 3) It is morally acceptable to keep animals in circuses for human entertainment. 4) It is morally acceptable to trade animals like possessions. 5) Chimpanzees should have basic legal rights such as a right to life or a prohibition of torture. 6) It is morally acceptable to perform medical experiments on animals that we would not perform on any human' (Caviola, Everett, and Faber, 2019: 1017). The EPs chose their answers to each item on a 7-point scale from 'strongly disagree' to 'strongly agree'. For items 1, 2, 3, 4, and 6, 'strongly disagree' is the least speciesist answer, which receives 1 point, while for item 5, 'strongly agree' is the least speciesist answer possible (reversed scoring). An 'agree' for items 1, 2, 3, 4, and 6 means 2 points, a 'somewhat agree' 3 points, etc. (reversed again for item 5). The average of the answers to all items is the speciesism score. A higher score means higher speciesism, with a maximum score of 7 and a minimum score of 1.

This scale is the most precise tool for measuring speciesism to date. Previously, Dhont et al. (2014), Dhont, Hodson, and Leite (2016) and Piazza et al. (2015) proposed 'ad hoc measurement instruments' to enhance our understanding of how humans think about NHAs (Caviola, Everett, and Faber, 2019: 1017). Despite their significant merits, those instruments 'suffer from theoretical limitations and were produced without statistical validation and established scale development procedures' (p. 1017). The speciesism scale proposed by Caviola and colleagues fulfils important quality criteria: 'all items explicitly capture speciesism and the scale encompasses crucial aspects of the theoretical concept; experts in relevant fields validated all items; the scale consists of both abstract and empirical items; and does not contain items eliciting empirical and normative confounding factors' (p.1017).

The Research Process

The research process for this study began with individual, semi-structured interviews. In the first part of the interview, the EPs were confronted with diverse philosophical thought experiments. The first thought experiment that the EPs were asked to listen to, and reflect on aloud, was the 'alien thought experiment' by Richard David Precht (Precht, 2011: 144–6).[2] In this thought experiment, aliens land on our planet and enslave

---

[2] A video version of the thought experiment can be found online: '*HUMAN FLESH*—the *philosophical thought experiment* | #filosofix (2017) YouTube video, added by SFR Kultur [Online]. Available at https://youtu.be/tSUz6Rj5oo4 (accessed 23 May 2021).

humans in order to eat them and their bodily products. Since thought experiments often prompt a change in perspectives, they are especially powerful in fostering empathy and ethical reflection. In the second part, the EPs were asked questions about themselves, their studies, and their dietary habits. Their speciesism levels were measured after the first part of the interviews.

The second step of the research process, which happened several weeks later, was a workshop in which all EPs participated. At the beginning of the workshop, the EPs' levels of speciesism were measured. I then gave a short introduction to NHA ethics, and the participants watched a video[3] discussing speciesism and summarizing the most important arguments in NHA ethics. After this, the EPs watched nine short clips showing humans and NHAs. Some clips consisted of video footage from factory farms and slaughterhouses. This aspect was supposed to enable 'aesthetic inquiry', allowing 'felt meanings' (Hansen and Trank, 2016: 365). The aim of this part was to evoke affective empathy in the EPs. The EPs were asked to jot down the thoughts and feelings they had experienced whilst watching each clip; these notes were then sent to me after the workshop. Subsequent to the videos, a group discussion of approximately 30 minutes took place. At the end of the workshop, the speciesism levels of the EPs were measured again.

The third step of the research process was a final individual semi-structured interview. In this final interview, the EPs were asked what aspect of the whole research process was most memorable for them, or which aspect they found most helpful for themselves, in terms of broadening their understanding of the topic. They were asked if they thought that their speciesism levels had changed during the process and, if so, how they thought they had changed. They were then informed about the results of their measurements. These results were reflected on together. The EPs were then also asked about any changes in their dietary habits. In the process of data analysis, the three dominant analytical moves were 'asking questions', 'focusing on puzzles', and 'developing and/or dropping working hypothesis' (cf. Grodal, Anteby, and Holm, 2021). Since the research question was how to best reduce speciesism, the main goal of the analysis was to understand the reasons for changes in individual speciesism levels.

I recruited my seven EPs from amongst my peers (fellow doctoral students employed at the Vienna University of Economics and Business; three female, four male). I aimed for a diverse sample with a wide range of individual speciesism levels at the beginning of the research process (see Figure 16.1). The age range of my EPs was between 25 and 42. Their dietary habits ranged from 'vegan at home' to a diet including 'a lot of meat'. I chose a pseudonym for each of them inspired by the information that they provided during the research process.

---

[3] *Non-Human Animals: Crash Course Philosophy #42* (2017) YouTube video, added by CrashCourse [Online]. Available at https://youtu.be/y3-BX-jN_Ac (accessed 18 March 2021).

EP	Uva	Standard deviation	Leroy	Standard deviation	Tyrone	Standard deviation	Lacrima	Standard deviation	Hunter	Standard deviation	Herb	Standard deviation	Sentia	Standard deviation
Gender	f		m		m		f		m		m		f	
Age	25		39		42		29		31		37		30	
Diet	"unfortunately omnivorous"		"really likes eating meat"		omnivorous, tries to be vegetarian		eats meat a few times a year, vegan at home, vegetarian in restaurants		eats "a lot of meat", would like to reduce		"eats meat"		pescetarian, no dairy products, eats eggs, "very bad conscience" when eating NHA products	
Speciesism score 1st measurement	2.17	0.75	2.83	2.04	2.17	0.98	1.33	0.82	5	1.67	3.33	1.86	1.33	0.51

FIGURE 16.1 Baseline measures of speciesism.

FINDINGS AND DISCUSSION

A first (and distinctly uncontroversial) finding/hypothesis that can be deduced from the data (see Figure 16.1), is that lower speciesism scores seem to correlate with diets that include a lower amount of NHA products, especially meat. This is in line with previous research pointing to the existence of such a correlation (Caviola, Everett, and Faber, 2019: 1025).

When comparing the results of the first and third measurements of the individual speciesism levels (see Figure 16.2), we see that speciesism scores were reduced during the research process by 1.17 (Uva, Hunter), 1.16 (Leroy), 0.33 (Lacrima, Sentia), 0.17 (Tyrone), and 0.16 (Herb), respectively. A question that arises immediately is why there was a considerable reduction in some of the speciesism levels of some EPs (Uva, Hunter, Leroy), whilst there was only a small reduction in the speciesism levels of other EPs (Tyrone, Herb).

Lacrima's and Sentia's speciesism scores were also reduced by 0.33. It should be noted, however, that they had begun with a comparably low score (1.33), which was then reduced to the lowest score possible (1). Incidentally, Uva's speciesism score had also fallen to the minimum by the third measurement. However, in the final interview, Uva stated that even though she '*couldn't look at meat*'[4] (Uva, final interview) for several days after the workshop, she thereafter did resume eating meat. She thus 'recovered', and more or less went back to her previous dietary habits. Still, her actions changed, for at least a short period of time, after the interventions. This shows that a certain 'unfreezing', when it comes to her behaviour and (even if not lasting) change, occurred due to the interventions. However, after unfreezing and change, the third (and important) step of Lewin's change theory did not take place: the refreezing in a new position. Instead, there was a regression and a process of 'refreezing' again in a spot that was presumably close to the initial starting point. This might also have been prompted by the 'social pressures' to participate in the institution to eat NHA products that Uva reported (see the quote below). Uva's case exemplifies well that a low speciesism score can go together with speciesist behaviour (cf. Caviola, Everett, and Faber, 2019: 1017).

In order to explore which aspects might have caused the various reductions, I asked the EPs in the final interviews which aspects of the research process were especially memorable, or helpful for them, in terms of broadening their understanding of the topic (last line, Figure 16.2). As might have been suspected, different aspects were of significant for different EPs. Three EPs (Uva, Leroy, Tyrone) pointed to the videos from the NHA industry; three EPs (Lacrima, Hunter, Sentia) pointed to aspects that were employed to trigger changes in perspective (ATE = alien thought experiment; TE = thought experiments (in general)); three EPs (Lacrima, Herb, Sentia) pointed to input that provided rational NHA ethical argumentation (CCP = crash course philosophy (video)). These answers trigger the stipulation that a combination of interventions that employ diverse empathetic and rational abilities might be advisable when designing anti-speciesist interventions or workshops.

---

[4] The whole research process was conducted in German. The direct quotations included here are translations of the original German data.

EP	Uva		Standard deviation	Leroy		Standard deviation	Tyrone		Standard deviation	Lacrima		Standard deviation	Hunter		Standard deviation	Herb		Standard deviation	Sentia		Standard deviation
Gender	f			m			m			f			m			m			f		
Age	25			39			42			29			31			37			30		
Diet	"unfortunately omnivorous"			"really likes eating meat"			omnivorous, tries to be vegetarian			eats meat a few times a year, vegan at home, vegetarian in restaurants			eats "a lot of meat", would like to reduce			"eats meat"			pescetarian, no dairy products, eats eggs, "very bad conscience" when eating NHA products		
Speciesism score 1st measurement	2.17	0.75		2.83	2.04		2.17	0.98		1.33	0.82		5	1.67		3.33	1.86		1.33	0.51	
Speciesism score 2nd measurement	1.33	0.51		3	1.67		2	0		1	0		3.67	1.5		3.33	1.03		1.17	0.41	
Speciesism score 3rd measurement	1	0		1.67	0.52		2	0		1			3.83	1.47		3.17	0.75		1	0	
Reduction	1.17			1.16			0.17			0.33			1.17			0.16			0.33		
Memorable	Videos			Videos			Videos			ATE, CCP			TE			CCP			CCP, TE		

FIGURE 16.2 Overview results. The last line shows which aspect each EP named as being most memorable for them in the research process. 'Videos' = videos of human and NHAs shown in the workshop; 'ATE' = 'alien thought experiment'; 'CCP' = 'crash course philosophy (video)'; 'TE' = 'thought experiments (in general)'.

Naming a rational aspect as the most memorable/important aspect did not, of course, mean that the EPs were not (considerably) affected by other aspects. Herb, for example, exhibited an extensive use of rationalization as a defence mechanism throughout the research process: '*This unbearable video in this pig slaughterhouse, where the pigs were abused, . . . I didn't think, "Oh God, I am not allowed to eat pigs anymore", but how can you prevent these production methods from being possible at all. . . . . maybe I'm too cerebral when I look at these things*' (Herb, discussion during workshop). Nevertheless, he also stated in the discussion in the workshop that he was deeply affected by the videoclips emotionally (might suggest affective empathy): '*When I saw the cows, it devastated me just as much as it did with the pigs, as it did with the koalas*' (Herb, discussion during workshop).

When it comes to Herb, who '*eats meat*' (Herb, initial interview) and whose speciesism level was reduced by 1 point, it may be worth examining his journey a little more closely. He owes his pseudonym to the fact that in both the initial and the final interviews he mentioned the thought that plants could 'have feelings', too: '*The only thing that I always come up with is a bit of this whataboutism . . . : Where do I draw the line here? Plants are also beings, trees bleed . . . . I mean, if you get into a similar argumentation as with animals, what is excruciating, what is not, what does "suffering" mean, but in the end it doesn't resolve this argument. You can of course expand it in that respect, but, so, that's why this is actually not a real counter-argument, on the contrary, it shows the complexity of the whole thing, yes*' (Herb, final interview). He appeared quite conflicted, because, as he states, the ethical argumentation for veganism is strong, and he lacks robust arguments for eating NHAs (Herb, final interview). '*Actually, I can't really . . . I can't really justify why I eat meat. Why, I don't know, ... So, I would say, you also notice how I meander around that topic. But actually, my behaviour has not yet changed. But well, I would say I'm more interested in the subject now*' (Herb, final interview).

Even though Herb's behaviour might not have changed, and his speciesism seems at first glance only marginally affected by the interventions, upon taking a closer look at his answers in the three speciesism measurements (see Figure 16.3), it becomes apparent that a process of 'unfreezing' and (rather undirected) fluctuation is visible in the data. He changed his opinion on the moral value of NHAs (item 1, 6-4-4, reduction in speciesism). A similar shift towards less speciesism is also visible in item 6 on NHA experimentation (5-4-3). He fluctuated concerning NHAs in circuses (item 3, 2-4-3), NHAs as possessions (item 4, 3-4-3), and the legal rights of chimpanzees (item 5, 3-2-4). Herb might be in the earlier phase of forming a nuanced opinion on issues around NHA ethics. When I reflected with him about these results in the final interview, he explained that he had found it hard to provide his opinions in an intuitive way, and found himself instead entangled in rational reflections about what the items exactly mean and entail (Herb, final interview). His strong mature defence mechanisms thus, seemingly only allowed him to reach the first phase of Lewin's theory of change.

Another case set that demands further exploration in order to explain the comparably infinitesimal change is Tyrone's. His speciesism level was similarly reduced by only 0.17. Interestingly, in Tyrone's case, no comparable unfreezing can be detected in the quantitative data. Tyrone's answers mostly stayed the same in all three quantitative

Speciesism Scale Measurements Herb	1st measurement	SD	2nd measurement	SD	3rd measurement	SD
Morally, animals always count for less than humans.	agree	6	neither agree nor disagree	4	neither agree nor disagree	4
Humans have the right to use animals however they want to.	strongly disagree	1	disagree	2	disagree	2
It is morally acceptable to keep animals in circuses for human entertainment.	disagree	2	neither agree nor disagree	4	somewhat disagree	3
It is morally acceptable to trade animals like possessions.	somewhat disagree	3	neither agree nor disagree	4	somewhat disagree	3
Chimpanzees should have basic legal rights such as a right to life or a prohibition of torture.	somewhat agree	3	agree	2	neither agree nor disagree	4
It is morally acceptable to perform medical experiments on animals that we would not perform on any human.	somewhat agree	5	neither agree nor disagree	4	somewhat disagree	3
	3.33	1.86	3.33	1.03	3.17	0.75

FIGURE 16.3 Results for Herb.

measurements. They only changed concerning two items (number 1 and 3): There is a slight move towards a more speciesist stance in item 3 (1-2-2) and some anti-speciesist change when it comes to item number 1 (4-2-2). However, the anti-speciesist change in item number 1 ('Morally, animals always count for less than humans', 'somewhat agree' to 'somewhat disagree') might be important.

Although 'unfreezing' was not as detectable in Tyrone's speciesism scores, he reported changes in behaviour (compare that to Herb, as it was the other way round). When I asked Tyrone if his dietary choices were influenced by the research process, he answered: '*Yes, in general, when it comes to groceries... I try to be vegetarian if possible and I've also tried vegan days. I noticed that when I order Indian cuisine, it's relatively easy to eat vegan. If I eat Austrian cuisine or when I'm invited to someone's home, I realize that ... it's more the side dish that is vegan. But I notice that in the supermarket, for example, I have often put a piece of meat back again. Sometimes I did take it in the end, but often I also put it back*' (Tyrone, final interview).

While both Herb and Tyrone showed only an infinitesimal quantitative reduction in speciesism, in Herb's case, unfreezing was quite visible in the quantitative data. In Tyrone's case, unfreezing and change was not so much visible in his answers in the speciesism measurements, but in his behaviour (trying to buy vegetarian products, taking the piece of meat in the supermarket, and then putting it back). Herb might thus have been prompted to a stage of unfreezing but not yet change, while Tyrone actually reported behaviour and attitude change after the intervention. The strength of the defence mechanisms an individual employs could thus influence which stages of Lewin's change theory are reached in the change process.

When I asked him about his thoughts on the very small movement on the speciesism scale, Tyrone answered that social desirability (bias)—(i.e. 'the tendency of research subjects to give socially desirable responses instead of choosing responses that are reflective of their true feelings' (Grimm, 2010))—might have played a role in the first measurement (which took place in an oral form during the interview), causing his first speciesism score to be skewed towards a lower number. Tyrone stated that in the second and third measurement he was more honest, because he simply filled out the questionnaire online.

Summing up, Tyrone mentioned that he had learned a lot in the research process, and now has a more nuanced picture of the situation, and certainly no longer trusts the meat industry in the way that he did previously. Again, looking more closely revealed that the interventions achieved a certain kind of change, even if it was barely visible in the results of the speciesism measurements.

The thought that social desirability bias might have influenced Tyrone's answers goes well together with the fact that Tyrone also talked about the difficulties of not eating meat or other NHA products in social settings: '*I definitely notice in the family circle that meat is still such a fixed item ... that triggers certain discussions*' (Tyrone, final interview). In the initial interview with Uva, she mentioned those social pressures, too: '*[A]nd then grandma cooks something and you don't want to offend her, etc. I think there is a certain social pressure there, and then you like the taste of it, too, and I'm still looking for this incentive for myself a bit, or this point where I say, 'now I'll stop', or maybe find a solution to, at least, reduce it. Because I don't think I'll be able to make a really blatant cut overnight*' (Uva, initial interview).

Not only the social pressures of the institution of eating NHA products appeared repeatedly in the data, but also the wish to reduce one's intake of NHA products, or to become wholly vegetarian or vegan. Even Hunter, who earned this pseudonym because of his pastime, which includes killing nonhumans, stated that he'd like to become a 'reducetarian' (i.e. that he would like to reduce the amount of NHA products he consumes). However, for him, the prime reasons for this wish were not founded in NHA ethics, but were instead environmental reasons: '[K]eeping livestock is very expensive and unnecessarily pollutes our environment on many ... many levels.... I would very much like to continue to eat meat, but perhaps more consciously and less amounts of specific kinds of meat' (Hunter, initial interview).

Lacrima and Sentia were the ones who began the research process with very low speciesism scores initially (8). When asked about the most memorable or important part of the research process for them, they listed the thought experiments and the ethical arguments. This is interesting to note, since both of them reported intense levels of affective empathy while watching the videos in the workshop. Lacrima reported that she cried while watching four out of the nine videos. Her notes on what she felt and experienced while watching the videos in the workshop are telling: '*Cried, not able to watch the whole video, despair, hatred towards people who are able to do that; pain because of the state of the world that something like this is normal*' (Lacrima, workshop notes) and '*Insanity, anger, anger, anger, cruelty to animals, the look of the cows hurts so much, anger at the bureaucrats; anger that something like this is normal*' (ibid). In the discussion after watching the videos, Lacrima stated: '*My entire body still hurts*' (Lacrima, discussion in workshop). When trying to understand Lacrima's results and statements, it should be kept in mind that during the time in which the workshop took place, Lacrima was psychologically burdened by events in her private life (source of this information: personal correspondence several weeks after the interventions), which likely also played a role in how she reacted to the interventions in the workshop.

Thus, Lacrima reported a strong mental and physical reaction due to the interventions in the workshop (Lacrima, workshop notes). In the discussion after watching the videos, Hunter shared that he had asked himself whether we as consumers are responsible for the suffering that NHAs endure in the NHA industry. I responded that, of course, humans who breed and kill NHAs do so because we pay them to do it. This triggered one of the rare instances of what could be understood as an immature defence mechanism in this process, namely projection of guilt, responsibility, anger, and outrage. Lacrima commented: '*My thoughts at the end of this discussion were: I don't feel responsible for this suffering, structurally. I also think it's bad to give the responsibility to the consumer, to a certain extent, because it's all a system, it has a long tradition, it takes time to even question it. So, I see more of the responsibility in politics, to deal with and ban such things.... I find it dangerous to pass that on to the individual*' (Lacrima, discussion in workshop). Listening to Lacrima at this point in the discussion, I felt anger and outrage directed towards me. The amount of guilt that we as humans must shoulder in the light of what we do to nonhuman beings is perhaps too heavy to bear, and must therefore be projected. In a situation where one's defences are weakened by other stressors, we might regress and employ less mature defence mechanisms despite an actually mature psychological structure (Vaillant, 1994).

Concerning defence mechanisms in general, however, my EPs mainly employed mature defence mechanisms, such as rationalization and intellectualization, in order to calm their super-ego and conserve their morally questionable—as an NHA ethicist might put it, at least when it comes to their treatment of NHAs—behaviour and attitudes. This finding was certainly to be expected, considering the sample, which consists of doctoral students who have structurally mature psyches which, (among other factors), have enabled them to progress this far in their academic and professional lives.

Conclusion

It is important at this point to take a reflective pause; I felt guilty throughout the research process, for burdening my EPs, for confronting them with this kind of violence, for being critical, and for making them feel bad about themselves by challenging their behaviours and attitudes in various ways. Yet, I remain committed to an activist orientation and will continue to use scholarship to advocate for NHAs because 'being a bystander to suffering is not an option' (Singer, 2016: 40). Often, we might feel that, as individuals, we cannot have a significant impact when it comes to the atrocity of how human animals currently treat NHAs. How then can we reduce humanity's speciesism? The findings of this study exemplify that certain interventions can reduce speciesism markedly. We can make use of these interventions in order to reduce the speciesism present in our organizations and institutions. Once increasing numbers of humans develop anti-speciesist awareness, we might, in the near future, see leaders and managers offer training to their staff not just to reduce sexism, racism, ableism, and ageism in their organizations, but also speciesism.

Applying the psychoanalytical theory of defence mechanisms and Lewin's theory of 'change in three steps' to my empirical data has been thought-provoking. Future research could further investigate how defence mechanisms keep individuals from passing through all three of Lewin's stages of change (Uva experienced unfreezing and change, but not refreezing, and Herb only experienced unfreezing, but not change and refreezing, for example). Studying the psychological intricacies of speciesism and trying to understand how we can reduce it is important, because speciesism is a main cause of the incomprehensible amount of suffering we inflict on NHAs. Managers have an ethical responsibility to take the interests of those affected by their business activities into account. NHAs are severely affected by human economic and organisational activities. Business schools which take business ethics seriously should therefore also include anti-speciesist aspects in their curricula.

What might possibly be considerably more impactful than trying to change human attitudes in order to change human behaviour, is to change human behaviour and watch as the attitudes align themselves, (remember how humans first tend to change their attitudes only after they have changed their behaviour (Olson and Stone, 2005) and secondly tend to use rationalizations to make their attitudes less inconsistent with their behaviour (Loughnan, Bratanova, and Puvia, 2012)). Behaviour change can be achieved by transforming the NHA industry into an industry producing cultivated NHA products (which are produced by propagating cells and without killing NHAs, cf. Humbird, 2020). Transforming the supply side of the industry, thus basically ending NHA farming, will enable humans to make leaps in terms of anti-speciesist progress without having to change their dietary habits much. And at one point, when humans can have their steak, and NHAs keep their lives, too, '[t]he day may come when the rest of the animal creation may acquire those rights which never could have been withholden from them but by the hand of tyranny' (Bentham, 1789: 143).

References

Adler, N.J. & Hansen, H. (2012). Daring to care: Scholarship that supports the courage of our convictions. *Journal of Management Inquiry*, 21(2), 128–39.
Anthis, J.R. & Paez, E. (2021). Moral circle expansion: A promising strategy to impact the far future. *Futures*, 130, 102756.
Bamberger, P.A. & Pratt, M.G. (2010). Moving forward by looking back: Reclaiming unconventional research contexts and samples in organizational scholarship. *Academy of Management Journal*, 53, 665–71.
Bastian, B. & Loughnan, S. (2017). Resolving the meat-paradox: A motivational account of morally troublesome behavior and its maintenance. *Personality and Social Psychology Review*, 21, 278–99.
Bentham, J. (1789). *An Introduction to the Principles of Morals and Legislation*, available at: https://www.earlymoderntexts.com/assets/pdfs/bentham1780.pdf.
Bratanova, B., Loughnan, S., & Bastian, B. (2011). The effect of categorization as food on the perceived moral standing of animals. *Appetite*, 57, 193–6.
Caviola, L., Everett, J., & Faber, N.S. (2019). The moral standing of animals: Towards a psychology of speciesism. *Journal of Personality and Social Psychology*, 116(6), 1011–29.
Cramer, P. (1987). The development of defense mechanisms. *Journal of Personality*, 55(4), 597–614.
Cummings, S., Bridgman, T., & Brown, K.G. (2016). Unfreezing change as three steps: Rethinking Kurt Lewin's legacy for change management. *Human Relations*, 69(1), 33–60.
Cunha, M. P. e, Rego, A., & Munro, I. (2019). Dogs in organizations. *Human Relations*, 72(4), 778–800.
Dhont, K. et al. (2014). Social dominance orientation connects prejudicial human–human and human–animal relations. *Personality and Individual Differences*, 61, 105–8.
Dhont, K., Hodson, G., & Leite, A.C. (2016). Common ideological roots of speciesism and generalized ethnic prejudice: The Social Dominance Human–Animal Relations Model (SD-HARM). *European Journal of Personality*, 30, 507–22.
Dhont, K. et al. (2020). The psychology of speciesism. In K. Dhont & G. Hodson (Eds.), *Why we love and exploit animals—Bridging insights from academia and advocacy* (pp. 29–49). London, New York: Routledge.
Fernández, L. (2020). Images that liberate: Moral shock and strategic visual communication in animal liberation activism. *Journal of Communication Inquiry*, 45(2), 138–58.
Festinger, L. (1962). Cognitive dissonance. *Scientific American*, 207(4), 93–106.
Freud, A. (1984). *Das Ich und die Abwehrmechanismen*. Frankfurt am Main: Fischer.
Freud, S. (1961). *The ego and the id*. New York City: W.W. Norton & Co.
Frost, P.J. (1999). Why Compassion Counts! *Journal of Management Inquiry*, 8(2), 127–33.

García-Rosell, J. & Tallberg, L. (2021). Animals as tourism stakeholders: Huskies, reindeer and horses working in Lapland. In C. Kline, & J. Rickly (Eds.), *From beasts of burden to K9 security: The working animals of the tourism industry* (pp. 103–22). Berlin: De Gruyter.

Grimm, P. (2010). Social desirability bias. In J. Sheth & N. Malhotra (Eds.), *Wiley international encyclopedia of marketing*. Part 2. Marketing Research. (pp. 258–9). Hoboken, N.J.: John Wiley & Sons.

Grodal, S., Anteby, M., & Holm, A.L. (2021). Achieving rigor in qualitative analysis: The role of active categorization in theory building. *Academy of Management Review, 46(3)*.

Hansen, H. & Trank, C.Q. (2016). This is going to hurt: Compassionate research methods. *Organizational Research Methods, 19(3)*, 352–75.

Harguess, J., Crespo, N., & Hong, M. (2020). Strategies to reduce meat consumption: A systematic literature review of experimental studies. *Appetite, 144*, 104478.

Holmes, D. & Marcus, G. (2008). Collaboration today and the re-imagination of the classic scene of fieldwork encounter. *Collaborative Anthropologies, 1(1)*, 81–101.

Horta, O. (2010). What is speciesism? *The Journal of Agricultural and Environmental Ethics, 23*, 243–66.

Humbird, D. (2020). Scale-up economics for cultured meat: Techno-economic analysis and due diligence, available at https://doi.org/10.31224/osf.io/795su.

Joy, M. (2020). *Why we love dogs, eat pigs, and wear cows: An introduction to carnism*. Newburyport, MA: Red Wheel/Weiser.

Labatut, J., Munro, I., & Desmond, J. (2016). Animals and organizations. *Organization, 23(3)*, 315–29.

Lewin, K. (1947). Frontiers in group dynamics: Concept, method and reality in social science; social equilibria and social change. *Human Relations, 1(1)*, 5–41.

Loughnan, S., Bratanova, B., & Puvia, E. (2012). The meat paradox: How are we able to love animals and love eating animals? *Mind, 1*, 15–18.

Monteiro, C.A. et al. (2017). The Carnism Inventory: Measuring the ideology of eating animals. *Appetite, 113*, 51–62.

Olson, J.M. & Stone, J. (2005). The influence of behavior on attitudes. In D. Albarracín, B.T. Johnson, & M.P. Zanna (Eds.), *The handbook of attitudes* (pp. 223–71). Mahwah: Lawrence Erlbaum Associates.

Piazza, J. et al. (2015). Rationalizing meat consumption. The 4Ns. *Appetite, 91*, 114–28.

Precht, R.D. (2011). *Warum gibt es alles und nicht nichts?* München: Goldmann.

Sayers, J., Hamilton, L., & Sang, K. (2019). Organizing animals: Species, gender and power at work. *Gender, Work and Organization, 26*, 239–45.

Tallberg, L., García-Rosell, J.-C., & Haanpää, M. (2021). Human–animal relations in business and society: Advancing the feminist interpretation of stakeholder theory. *Journal of Business Ethics*, https://doi.org/10.1007/s10551-021-04840-1.

Singer, P. (2016). *The most good you can do: How effective altruism is changing ideas about living ethically*. New Haven: Yale University Press.

Vaillant, G.E., Bond, M., & Vaillant, C.O. (1986). An empirically validated hierarchy of defence mechanisms. *Archives of General Psychiatry, 73*, 786–94.

Vaillant, G.E. (1992). *Ego mechanisms of defense: a guide for clinicians and researchers*. Washington: American Psychiatric Press.

Vaillant, G.E. (1994). Ego mechanisms of defense and personality psychopathology. *Journal of Abnormal Psychology, 103(1)*, 44–50.

CHAPTER 17

A HANDSHAKE BETWEEN ANTHROPOCENTRICISM AND CAPITALISM

Reflections on Animal Life within Industrial Food Systems

DINESH JOSEPH WADIWEL

OVER the last century there has been an extraordinary expansion in the utilization of animals for food, and with this, the intensification of animal agriculture, with now hundreds of billions of land and sea animals confined within industrial production systems. This expansion expresses both the triumph of a hierarchical anthropocentrism that was inherent within the European enlightenment project, and the over-production of commodities as a means to generate capital. We find these two forces intertwined today in the factory farm; a symbolic handshake between anthropocentrism and industrial capitalism.

This chapter explores this relationship and its implications for the organization of animal life. Reflecting on my own process of developing a structural analysis of human violence towards animals, I explore how our contemporary modality of hierarchical anthropocentrism materializes in practices and institutions which are designed to pin down animals, establishing a continuing 'war like' relation of violence, domination, and death. The chapter then describes how these systematic forms of violence interact with animals within the capitalist food system. In the second part of the chapter, and drawing from the value theory of Karl Marx, I shall examine how animals are positioned as raw materials and labour within production, oriented towards the extraction of surplus and simultaneously as consumption commodities designed to enable the reproduction of human life. As I discuss, this analysis allows us to account for how anthropocentrism and capitalism produce remarkable and horrific forms of violence towards animals;

indeed, it perhaps indicates that animals under capitalism occupy a unique structural position.

THE WAR AGAINST ANIMALS

Within animal studies, posthumanism, and new materialisms, a variety of scholars have explored the way that anthropocentrism structures many human relationships with animals and nature (see e.g. Bennet, 2010; Braidotti, 2013; Tyler, 2012). While there are historically different forms of anthropocentrism, a particular focus of scholarship are the modalities of human superiority—or hierarchical anthropocentrism—which are attendant with European enlightenment rationalities. Tom Tyler describes this anthropocentrism as 'evaluative' insofar as it implies 'the bald belief or supposition that the human species is, in some sense, of greater importance and value than all else', and with this an imagined 'hierarchy, or chain of being, from the summit of which humanity gazes down on lesser creatures' (Tyler, 2012: 20–1). The development of this particular worldview was interconnected with European colonialism and underpins contemporary rationalities of racialization. As Claire Jean Kim notes, this same anthropocentrism shapes the way race was articulated within the colonial project, which placed humans and animals within the imaginary of the 'chain of being' (Kim, 2015; see also Kim, 2017). Through the colonial and settler colonial project, this anthropocentrism sought to displace and eliminate alternative ways of understanding and being in relation with animals, nature, and nonhumans (see TallBear, 2019).

This prevailing hierarchical anthropocentrism has had a historically unprecedented material effect on relations between humans and animals, something perhaps most starkly visible within contemporary global food systems. In 2019, some 81 billion land animals were slaughtered for human consumption (UN FAOSTAT, 2021). Figures on the numbers of fish killed annually for food are not officially defined by international governance organizations such as the UN Food and Agriculture Organization (UN FAO), however, it has been estimated that this could comprise up to 3 trillion animals per year across industrialized wild fish capture and aquaculture (see Fishcount, 2019; Mood and Brooke, 2012). It is no secret that such large-scale animal death requires the expansion of sophisticated intensified systems to manage the reproduction, life, and death of billions of animals (see Robinson et al., 2011: 43–59) and an ever-expanding intensification of adjacent industries such as feed production to enable this mass production to occur (see OECD, 2020: 32–6). The scale of this intensification is perhaps most apparent for fish used for human food globally. Industrial, mechanized forms of wild fish capture have traditionally accounted for most fish that humans ate during the twentieth century. However, following an explosion in the use of aquaculture since the 1990s—at a growth rate of around 9.5 per cent per year (UN FAO, 2014: 6)—farmed fishes now account for more than half of the fish consumed by humans (UN FAO, 2016: 2); an astonishing example of human capacity to completely transform its relations with sea animals within the space of a generation.

Whether these animal production systems are extensive or intensive, by necessity they most frequently involve imperious controls over reproduction (through human management of breeding); modalities of large-scale containment (such as fences, enclosures, concentrated feeding facilities); technologies of control and identification (e.g. cattle prods, branding, tail docking); moderate to total management of socialization, sexuality, food intake; and, of course, control over death, in particular in the systematic application of technologies of slaughter. Here, we can see that outright relationships of force shape the organization of most human-animal relations within food systems. Indeed, given that most directed human interactions with nonhuman animals occur within human food systems, it is not unreasonable to observe that our mainstay relations with most animals we have direct contact with involve relations of violence and domination.

How do we analyse this system-wide violence? Animal studies has a strong historical association with analytic moral philosophy. However, it was clear to me that contemporary moral philosophy has its limits in being able to explain large-scale structural violence. As a PhD student, I examined the practice of torture in the twentieth century, and sought to understand relations of violence, sovereignty, and power within contemporary nation-states. Torture in the modern era is best understood as a structural rather than individual phenomenon. There are certainly examples of where the practice of torture can be attributed to 'rogue' individuals, and momentary failures of individual ethics. Here, it is conceivable that moral philosophy has a place in setting standards for ideal or virtuous individual conduct. However, in most cases, when we look at the history of torture in human societies, we understand that the aim of torture regimes is to utilize violence, terror, and control of knowledge to enable a systematic domination of population. That is, the aim of the torture regime is to create a system-wide effect in relations of power and knowledge. As such, analytically, torture must be understood as structural: that is, exceeding individual moral failings and instead an element of society-wide power relations. Reflecting on this reality, I started to wonder whether a similar sort of analysis might be applied to thinking about violence towards animals. To what extent are acts of violence aimed at creating system-wide effects; that is, enabling a relation of power between humans and animals? To what extent is this violence and domination configured as a structural necessity for humans to enjoy freedom, pleasure, and flourishing only because this violence is imagined as unavoidable (in much the same way that torture regimes defend their violence in the name of peace and human security)? How does this violence interact with knowledge systems, constantly working to obfuscate, hide from view, and re-narrate itself as benign, acceptable, and part of the 'natural order of things'? My work as an animal studies scholar began when I started to apply what I had learnt about the structure of violence within human societies to examine the practices and rationalities that shaped human domination towards animals.

When I started doing this work, I could not avoid drawing a number of stark conclusions about the depth and intensity of human violence towards animals, and the implications that this had for human relations with animals. In my view, most direct human interactions with animals in food systems, in research, in sport, entertainment, and companionship, involve intense modalities of violence and control which aim at total domination, in a fashion that perhaps is best described with the term 'war'. Here, I was partly influenced by the German military theorist, Carl von Clausewitz, who described war as 'an act of violence to compel our opponent to fulfil our will' (Clausewitz, 2004: 15). The elegance of von Clausewitz's description of war cuts straight to the heart of the intention and rationality behind corporate acts of violence. While we might be distracted by the *forms* war takes (armies opposing each other, guns, tanks, air strikes, etc.), Clausewitz instead gives us an understanding of the logic of war. this logic—that war aims at using violence to create a state of dominion—is potentially applicable to a range of circumstances, including forms of violence directed by humans towards nonhuman animals. After all, the point of applying violence to animals systematically within our societies, is to direct these beings to fulfil human purposes, frequently against the wishes of animals themselves: this is why we deploy nets and hooks against fish in oceans and water ways; why cattle prods, whips, and dogs are used to herd sheep into pens and transports; why rabbits are restrained in experimental labs to enable the eye tests to be carried out; and why collars and leashes are utilized to guide companion animals through urban spaces. In all of these spaces, a mass organized violence aims to produce animal docility in the face of human prerogative, with the aim of bending animal agency towards 'fulfilling our will'.

In describing human violence towards animals as comprising a 'war', I was also influenced by Michel Foucault, and his own discussion of von Clausewitz and war, in his 1975-76 lectures at the College de France (Foucault, 2004). Here, Foucault takes up von Clausewitz's suggestion that 'war is policy pursued by other means' and inverts it, rendering the aphorism as 'politics is war pursued by other means'. From this, Foucault observes that the institutions of civil society carry within them a history of war-like conflict (Foucault, 2004: 50–1). Most societies, (and certainly postcolonial and settler colonial societies), are founded upon originary forms of violence, where a dominant force prevailed over other parties and established a legal order upon this site of conflict; this history establishes a form of society where war is internalized within the institutions of the civil political space:

> War is the motor behind institutions and order. In the smallest of its cogs, peace is waging a secret war. To put it another way, we have to interpret the war that is going on beneath peace; peace itself is a coded war. We are therefore at war with one another; a battlefront runs through the whole of society, continuously and permanently, and it is this battlefront that puts us all on one side or the other. There is no such thing as a neutral subject. We are all inevitably someone's adversary. (Foucault, 2004: 50–1)

For Foucault, the point of this articulation is to highlight the way in which forms of ongoing domination are inherent within the civil political sphere, typified in sovereignty as a political relation. Where sovereignty is often articulated through the implied consent of the liberal social contract, Foucault reminds us that it is instead founded upon war, dispossession, inequality, and continuing violence. For Foucault this is the foundation of contemporary forms of biopolitics, in particular State racism, which seeks to use the violence of the State to protect and nurture a biological population at the expense of all others: 'the more, "I—as species not individual—can live, the stronger I will be, the more vigorous I will be. I can proliferate" … The death of the other, the death of the bad race, of the inferior race (or the degenerate or the abnormal) is something that will make life in general healthier: healthier and purer' (Foucault, 2004: 255).

Of course, in describing this biopolitical violence which structures the logic of the contemporary nation-state, Foucault was not thinking about how this same logic might be applied to relations between humans and animals. However, in my view, this understanding is highly useful for making sense of the mainstay relations of violence and domination which characterize human relations with animals.

We can understand this in three, interconnected ways. First, the foundational division between humans and animals that are reproduced in prevailing forms of hierarchical anthropocentrism are imprinted by a fundamental form of conflict. Within the knowledge systems associated with this hierarchical anthropocentrism, we humans define ourselves through the violent disavowal of who we believe we are not: namely animals. This same antagonism shapes fundamental understandings of the political sphere; it is not accidental in this regard that Aristotle in describing 'man' as 'zoon politikon' is setting humans apart from other beings, those who, citing Homer, Aristotle describes as 'Tribeless, lawless, hearthless' (Aristotle, 1952: 446 [1253a]). And it is perhaps for this reason that Giorgio Agamben argues that 'the decisive political conflict, which governs every other conflict, is that between the animality and the humanity of man. That is to say, in its origin Western politics is also biopolitics' (Agamben, 2004: 80). To an extent this division is articulated in different formulations within the domain of European hierarchical anthropocentrism, including in the division between civilization and nature, a division that we could associate with what Val Plumwood described as 'the master story of Western culture' (Plumwood, 1993: 196); and in in racialized hierarchies which locate race within a continuum with animality (Kim, 2015; see also Kim, 2017).

Secondly, this violent separation between human and animal does not merely occur within the space of ontology or knowledge, but materializes in systematic forms of violence which are organized across the terrain of human-animal encounters. These relations are structured to enable a mass-scale violence that is almost beyond comprehension in terms of its expanse and intensity. The application of violence to literally trillions of animals requires massive mobilizations of resources, planning, logistics, and labour. On land, as we know, substantial territory must now be devoted to either grazing land for animals or for food that will be a feed crop for livestock systems (Mottet et al., 2017; UN FAO, 2009). Increasing forms of intensification push billions of animals into productive systems where their biological lives will be aligned with the production cycle of capital. In the seas, mechanized vessels hunt down trillions of fish annually to feed the voracious seafood business. In experimental labs, and often in concert with multinational pharmaceutical companies and cosmetics industries, millions of animals are contained and subject to experimentation as part and parcel of product testing and development. In sport and recreation, almost everywhere animals are contained, trained, made docile, made to perform, and extinguished when no longer useful. Finally, even in apparently benign forms of relationality, such as in companion animal relations, we find animals such as dogs subject to deep forms of control and dominion: bodily modifications and forced treatments such as sterilization; controls over movement, sexuality, and sociality; sequestration into tightly controlled private and public spaces, with strong legal controls over movement; use of persistent behavioural correction, discipline, and physical restraint devices such as leashes; and finally a general tolerance for disposability which grants human owners life and death powers, something I have described as 'privatised' form of dominion (Wadiwel, 2015: 177–201). All of this violence, carefully and continually orchestrated across multiple domains of human-animal relation, carries a veneer of civil peaceability. Our war against animals appears as benign, everyday, and lacking resistance. Civil institutions are arranged to carry out hostilities under the guise of peace.

Finally, the point of all of this is to establish a continuing state of dominion in order to solidify a set of relations that guarantee continuing pleasure and satisfaction to the victors of war. Our war against animals is so complete, so apparently without challenge, that it represents a kind of intoxication of power guaranteeing a seemingly unending process of victory. In a sense, from the perspective of organization, we find an elaborate arrangement of institutions, mechanisms, and labour forces globally which are driven to continue this unrelenting violence at all costs. The recent COVID-19 pandemic has only highlighted this reality. Despite the numerous outbreaks of the virus within human labour forces working 'shoulder to shoulder' in animal production and processing (see Lussenhop, 2020; News Wires, 2020; Reuben, 2020;) the institutional compulsion to continue production even at risk of human lives (see Evelyn, 2020; Mano, 2020;) highlighted the system imperative for this global violence against animals to continue unabated. Indeed, the poor conditions for human labour within animal agriculture—which extends in many parts of the world to low wage or forced labour in dangerous conditions—highlights the way that some human populations themselves are positioned as indirect recipients of harm in our war against animals.

The above analysis reveals something about the way in which a prevailing form of hierarchical anthropocentrism materializes and functions. The ontological separation between humans and nonhumans does not simply operate in the space of knowledge, but instead is materialized through excessive and continuous violence. This violence is spatially organized in such a way that is continued, unrelenting, and forms the core business-as-usual of a variety of institutions. However, it is 'hidden from view' so that materially and epistemologically it fails to generate human moral concern. Almost everywhere the traces of this violence are present, but they are rendered invisible, benign, everyday, and 'natural', through knowledge systems which continually suggest that animals and their lives can only exist for human benefit. Under this massive artifice is a driving demand to establish a state of dominion over nonhuman animals, to ensure that our opponents 'fulfil our will', and continue to deliver to us (humans) the spoils of war.

Animals and the Capitalist Food System

While the hierarchical anthropocentricism I have described above is an important structuring rationality for how we engage with animals, this is not the only axis that determines the forms by which power regulates human-animal relations. For example, as feminist animal studies theorists have described, patriarchal gender relations impact animal lives, for example in the shape of the reproductive controls applied to animals within animal agriculture (see April, 2019; Gillespie, 2018;) and in the gendered narratives and norms which fetishize meat as desirable and aligned to prevailing masculinities (Adams, 1990; Gruen, 1993). As these scholars have demonstrated, prevailing gender relations interact with anthropocentricism to shape the practices and technologies that dominate animal lives.

For example, as Kathryn Gillespie observes, central to the extensive controls over the reproductive labour of animals in meat and dairy production is a gendered approach to seeing bodies that is 'generally a reflection of the way the female animal body is viewed—that because biologically she can reproduce, "staying pregnant" must be the inherent function and purpose of her life' (Gillespie, 2014: 1329).

A different—and interconnected—axis which dominates the lives of animals within contemporary institutions is our prevailing economic system: namely capitalism. Here, I define capitalism as a social and economic relation that seeks to extract value from productive activity and reinvest this extracted value in the form of capital. It is important to note here that capitalism does not merely accumulate wealth and profits as an object. Instead, it seeks to create a productive value that continually, incessantly, seeks its own reinvestment in order to generate more value; what David Harvey has described as a 'bad infinity' (Harvey and Denvir, 2018). Today, we live in the midst of this bad infinity, with anthropogenic climate change a direct outcome of an economic system that mass produces commodities for the sake of capital accumulation in ways that fundamentally damage the ability of biological life on the planet to survive, flourish, and reproduce itself. This environmental crisis, and its interconnection with mass species extinction, is at least one dimension of the relationship between hierarchical anthropocentricism, capitalism, and animal lives. But another dimension is how capitalism has shaped relations with domesticated animals, particularly those within human food supplies. Animal husbandry is of course part of a long history of human-animal relations that stretches back millennia; however, capitalism radically transformed the shape of human domestication of animals. John Bellamy Foster and Brett Clark argue that intensification of animal agriculture is part and parcel of the 'metabolic rift' that signalled the arrival of capitalism and the disruption of previous relations of relative equilibrium with nature; a break in relations of production which 'encompasses the expropriation of corporeal beings, where nonhuman animals are reduced to machines in a system predicated on constant expansion, which ignores and increases their suffering' (Foster and Clark, 2018; Foster,

2000: 163–6). On a different, albeit related tangent, Jason Moore and Raj Patel argue that intensification of animal agriculture served a function for capitalism in reducing the costs of the reproduction of human labour, and that the process of making animal-based food 'cheap' required these forms of intensification, including for example, shortening the lives of broiler chickens in order to reduce the turnover time for this production (see Patel and Moore, 2018).

These perspectives allow us to look at the intensification of animal agriculture through a different light which takes in the interaction of anthropocentrism with capitalism. From the standpoint of traditional animal advocacy, the factory farm represents the most refined and brutal example of hierarchical anthropocentrism; the hotspot that perhaps most effectively puts on display the rationalities of our war against animals that I have described above. Arguably the emergence of radical animal rights movements were a response to the horrific realities of intensive animal agriculture, which express through their cold, rational, and purely instrumentalized utilization of animals the peculiar hostility of a prevailing anthropocentrism. Peter Singer's influential text, *Animal Liberation*, arguably responds to this horror, and identifies 'speciesism' as one way to describe the arbitrary and unjustifiable differentiation in our treatment of animals vis-à-vis humans (Singer, 1975: 21). However, we might observe that the factory farm isn't simply a monument to a prevailing hierarchical anthropocentrism, but also an example of the way in which capitalism has transformed food supplies, massively reorienting the place of animals within these systems. The factory farm represents the full immersion of animals within the rhythms of the production cycles of capitalism, interconnected with a global project of massification of animal products as a means of sustenance for human populations. It is for this reason that texts such as Singer's *Animal Liberation* are not so much treatises against anthropocentrism or 'speciesism' in isolation, but polemics against the *hybrid* relation between anthropocentrism and capitalism: that is, the factory farm as representing a meeting point between a violent anthropocentrism *and* the rationalized modalities of industrial capitalist food systems. A handshake between hierarchical anthropocentrism and capitalism.

We can make sense of this 'handshake' from at least three different vantage points which illustrate the unique relationship between animals and capitalism today. First, and most obviously, animals have been produced as commodities which become the means of subsistence for human populations. Here the investment of capitalist food systems is in efficient systems of production which allow for the transformation of living animals into dead meat; the latter representing a saleable commodity item for consumption. The tendency of these processes is towards intensification, and as I have described above, this requires an intense form of biopolitical management. There is a total and imperious management of reproduction, which coordinates life and death in relation to the product cycles of capitalism: for example, of the 75 million pigs in the United States, some 6.4 million sows are continuously 'farrowed' in order to produce litters of piglets, who will enable the creation of life to ensure the ongoing supply of death (USDA, 2019). This control over reproduction is central to dairy production, which relies on repeated insemination, pregnancy, and birth to enable continuous milk production (see Gillespie,

2014: 1326–7). There are further precise and relentless biopolitical controls over the life course of the animal in production, with management of factors such as sexuality, movement, sociality, lighting, and dietary intake, as well as carefully planned life cycles to ensure a product that can be sold at profit (see Wadiwel, 2015: 80–94).

This transformation in human diets has fundamentally realigned the biopolitical relation between human and animal populations: animals have been proliferated as raw materials to serve as a means of subsistence for the survival of human populations. This has implications for how we understand 'social reproduction' as a concept. Tithi Bhattacharya describes social reproduction as 'the complex network of social processes and human relations that produces the conditions of existence for that entity' (Bhattacharya, 2017: 2). Here, social reproduction is usually understood as comprising the forms of labour and energies required outside of formal production which facilitate that production; for example, the forms of care labour which while not formally 'priced' through wages, necessarily prop up the possibility of capitalism producing surplus. To an extent, the mass production of animal-based foods under capitalism has situated animals more prominently as resources for the reproduction of capitalism as a whole. As described above, we have seen an explosion in the use of animals for food. However, this growth in animal-sourced foods has not followed population growth in a linear way; instead, the growth rate of animals as food has exceeded the human population growth rate. In 1961, global per capita meat consumption, excluding fish and seafood, was at 23kg per person; by 2014 this had nearly doubled to 43kg per person (Ritchie and Roser, 2017). World per capita fish consumption has more than doubled (UN FAO, 2018). As discussed above, for Patel and Moore, this is part of capitalism's strategy for 'cheap food': by reducing the costs of animal-based food, this effectively reduced the wage cost of capitalism as a system. However, we can also note that this restructuring of human food supplies re-aligned human and nonhuman populations in relation to each other, so that human survival in a broad sense has become premised upon the production and reproduction of animal lives through animal agriculture. Indeed, if we were to summarize the above, we might note that under capitalism, animals have more and more become central for the reproduction of human life. This means that it isn't just that animals participate in the 'social reproduction' of capital; rather, as animal-based food increasingly enables all forms of human production, including social reproduction, we might observe that food animals under capitalism are increasingly a means for *the reproduction of reproduction itself.*

Secondly, we might also situate animals as *labour* within capitalism, and thus as a source of surplus. In the traditional Marxist view of labour, exploitation occurs through extraction of the difference between the value produced by labour power and the price of the wages paid to the worker (see Marx, 1986: 270–80). For Marx, the focus on the wage labourer as a primary site of exploitation was also accompanied by an understanding of the work of this labourer as focused upon an object external to the self, such that the archetypal labour relation involving a human worker expending labour power directly upon nature in order to fashion commodities as products (see Marx, 1986: 314–15). Feminist approaches to labour have challenged both of these assumptions, drawing attention to forms of unwaged labour which are (as discussed above) essential to social reproduction, and also highlighted the way in which the body of the worker themselves and its metabolic processes are drawn into production (see also Beldo, 2017 see; e.g. Cooper, 2008;); something we see in particular labour practices, for example, in commercial surrogacy work (see Pande, 2014). More recent work in animal studies and posthumanism has further challenged the anthropocentricism of Marxist conceptualizations of labour, by arguing that animals might well be considered labourers within production (see e.g. Barua, 2017; Blattner, 2020; Cochrane, 2016; Collard and Dempsey, 2013; Coulter, 2016; Hribal, 2003; Noske, 1997; Painter, 2016; Perlo, 2002; Stuart, Schewe, and Gunderson, 2013). My own view is that like human labour, one of the driving rationalities for animal use under capitalism is the extraction of surplus from the labour of animals; however, this surplus is extracted not as a difference between a wage and the value produced by labour, but instead the relationship between the value generated by the labouring being and the reproduction costs associated with this labour (see Wadiwel, 2018; 2020). From this perspective, processes of intensification seek to progressively extract this value by expanding 'yield' and reducing production turnover times. Arguably we can see this very clearly in attempts by animal agriculture to optimize 'feed conversion rates' (see e.g. Pierozan et al., 2016), enabling animal agriculture businesses to both expand yield and potentially reduce the time required for food animals to arrive at a saleable weight. Here, capitalism captures the metabolic activity of animals as 'labour', enabling the extraction of value by exploiting the difference between the value produced by animals themselves in their own growth and 'feed conversion' activities, and the system costs associated with the reproduction of life.

Thirdly, the above allows us to see something remarkable about the *structural position* of food animals under capitalism today. In the traditional Marxist scheme, the human proletarian occupied a unique structural position, representing a 'persona' who had only their labour power available to sell and nothing more in order to survive (see Marx, 1986: 270–80). In this reading, labour is treated as a 'variable' capital input into production, since the expenditure of labour power under capitalism is directly controllable through the manipulation of labour time and thus has the capacity to produce a surplus above reproduction time (Marx, 1986: 317); other 'constant' capital inputs to production do not have this same elasticity. This structural position of (human) labour is key to understanding capitalism as a social relation; capitalism is not merely an economic relation but also a force that organizes the social relations, since 'the social division of labour ... forms the foundation of all commodity production' (Marx, 1986: 471). However, in creating this understanding of capitalism as a social formation, Marx did not necessarily envisage capitalism as a force which interacted and organized animal lives as part of wider conceptions of 'social relations'. Yet, we might observe that capitalism not only organizes social relations with animals, it also produces a unique structural position for animals, particularly those in animal agriculture. Arguably the above processes—where animals are both transformed globally into a seemingly irreplaceable foundation of the reproduction of human populations, and that animals are simultaneously the targets for the extraction of surplus—highlight the way in which animal-based foods are not incidental to the evolution of capitalism, but are front and centre in relation to both the transformation of the means of human subsistence and as a labour force which is the object of exploitation. Nonhuman animals in the food system are not only raw materials that enter production as an 'input'; nor are they only raw materials that are brutally transformed into consumption commodities; nor are they only labour that is exploited by production processes. In truth, animals are a hybrid of these three positions; a unique conglomerate of 'constant' and 'variable' capital. Arguably this hybrid role of food animals suggests a differentiated structural position from the human worker, or at least most forms of human work under capitalism; and this in turn shapes human-animal exchange as a social relation. Today, the form of hierarchical anthropocentrism we see reflected in animals is a product of this unique structural position; food animals are continually produced and appear as a unique living combination of commodity and labour, and of course this position fundamentally informs the systems of violence which animals are exposed to on a systematic basis.

Conclusion

This chapter has described the way in which a prevailing hierarchical anthropocentrism interacts with market logics to organize the unique forms of violence that shape human-animal interaction in the contemporary era. I have first described the way in which this materializes into systematic practices of violence which apply to most animals that humans are in direct contact with, and are shaped by a rationality that aims at complete warlike domination. The aim of this violence is to establish an ongoing relationship of dominion; that is, to cement a model of human sovereignty over animals through widespread and systematically orchestrated violence. Secondly, I argue that this hierarchical anthropocentricism is interconnected today with the consolidation of capitalism as a prevailing and dominant economic system, in such a way as we could describe contemporary intensive animal agriculture as a 'handshake' between anthropocentricism and capital. Arguably this collaboration has produced the food animal as representing a unique structural position within contemporary societies, a hybrid of constant and variable capital that appears as both a commodity and as labour simultaneously. These logics in turn provide shape to the systems of violence experienced by many, if not most, animals in direct contact with humans; in other words, most human-animal relations today reflect the structural position of animals under capitalism, which is itself an outcome of an interaction with a prevailing hierarchical anthropocentricism.

The above analysis is in many respects grim by describing frankly the violence and domination that underpins human-animal relations. However, the object of this analysis is to provide an analytic frame to support change. Highlighting the interconnection between our contemporary prevailing hierarchical anthropocentrism and capitalism is sobering because of the enormity of the task presented for those invested in making transformative change on behalf of animals. However, it also highlights possible sites for alliance-building. At least one site for alliance is with anti-capitalist social movements, particularly those engaged in food systems, where common goals may be possible to realize which aim to end exploitation of both human and animal labour forces. Radical transformation is required; but perhaps there is scope in this radical imagination for a shared vision for societies that reduce and eliminate violence, and promote a wider conception of flourishing that moves beyond the human.

References

Adams, C.J. (1990). *The sexual politics of meat: A feminist-vegetarian critical theory*. New York: Continuum.

Agamben, G. (2004). *The open: Man and animal*. Stanford: Stanford University Press.

Aristotle. (1952). *Politics*. In R.M. Hutchins (Ed.), *The works of Aristotle*. Vol. 2 (pp. 445–548). Chicago: Encyclopaedia Britannica.

April, M. L. (2019). Readying the rape rack: Feminism and the exploitation of non-human reproductive systems. Dissenting Voices. 8.1, Article 8. https://digitalcommons.brockport.edu/dissentingvoices/vol8/iss1/8

Barua, M. (2017). Nonhuman labour, encounter value, spectacular accumulation: The geographies of a lively commodity. *Transactions of the Institute of British Geographers, 42(2)*, 274–88.

Bhattacharya, T. (2017). Introduction: Mapping social reproduction theory. In T. Bhattacharya (Ed.), *Social reproduction theory: Remapping class, recentering oppression* (pp. 1–20). London: Pluto Press..

Beldo, L. (2017). Metabolic labor: Broiler chickens and the exploitation of vitality. *Environmental Humanities, 9(1)*, 108–28.

Bennett, J. (2010). *Vibrant matter: A political ecology of things*. Durham and London: Duke University Press.

Blattner, C. (2020). Should animals have a right to work? Promises and pitfalls. *Animal Studies Journal, 9(1)*, 32–92. https://ro.uow.edu.au/asj/vol9/iss1/3

Braidotti, R. (2013). *The posthuman*. Cambridge: Polity.

Cochrane, A. (2016). Labour rights for animals. In R. Garner & S. O'Sullivan (Eds.), *The political turn in animal ethics* (pp. 15–32). London: Rowman & Littlefield International.

Collard, R-C. & Dempsey, J. (2013). Life for sale? The politics of lively commodities. *Environment and Planning A, 45(11)*, 2682–99.

Cooper, M. (2008). *Life as surplus: Biotechnology and capitalism in the neoliberal era*. Seattle: University of Washington Press.

Coulter, K. (2016). *Animals, work, and the promise of interspecies solidarity*. New York: Palgrave Macmillan.

Evelyn, K. (2020). Trump orders meat-processing plants to continue operating amid pandemic. *The Guardian*. 30 April 2020. https://www.theguardian.com/us-news/2020/apr/28/trump-executive-order-meat-processing-plants-coronavirus

fishcount.org.uk. (2019). Numbers of fish caught from the wild each year. fishcount.org.uk. At: http://fishcount.org.uk/fish-count-estimates-2/numbers-of-fish-caught-from-the-wild-each-year

Foster, J.B. (2000). *Ecology against capitalism*. New York: Monthly Review Press.

Foster, J.B. & Clark, B. (2018). Marx and alienated speciesism. *Monthly Review: An Independent Socialist Magazine.* 70(7) December 2018 https://monthlyreview.org/2018/12/01/marx-and-alienated-speciesism/.

Foucault, M. (2004). *Society Must Be Defended: Lectures at the College de France, 1975-76.* London: Penguin Books.

Gillespie, K. (2014). Sexualized violence and the gendered commodification of the animal body in Pacific Northwest US dairy production. *Gender, Place & Culture, 21(10)*, 1321–37.

Gillespie, K. (2018). *The cow with ear tag #1389.* Chicago: University of Chicago Press.

Gruen, L. (1993). Dismantling oppression. In G. Gaard (Ed.), *Ecofeminism: Women, animals nature* (pp. 60–90). Philadelphia: Temple University Press.

Harvey, D. & Denvir, D. (2018). Why Marx's capital still matters. *Jacobin.* 7 December 2018. https://www.jacobinmag.com/2018/07/karl-marx-capital-david-harvey

Hribal, J. (2003). 'Animals are part of the working class': A challenge to labor history. *Labor History, 44(4)*, 435–53.

Lussenhop, J. (2020). Coronavirus at Smithfield pork plant: The untold story of America's biggest outbreak. *BBC News.* 17 April 2020. https://www.bbc.com/news/world-us-canada-52311877

Kim, C.J. (2015). *Dangerous crossing: Race, species and nature in a multicultural age.* New York: Cambridge University Press.

Kim, C.J. (2017). Murder and mattering in Harambe's house. *Politics and Animals, 3*, 1–15.

Mano, A. (2020). Special report: How COVID-19 swept the Brazilian slaughterhouses of JBS, world's top meatpacker. *Reuters.* 8 September 2020. https://www.reuters.com/article/uk-health-coronavirus-jbs-specialreport-idUKKBN25Z1I4

Marx, K. (1986). *Capital.* Vol. 1. London: Penguin.

Mood, A. & Brooke, P. (2012). Estimating the number of farmed fish killed in global aquaculture each year. *Fishcount.org.uk.* http://fishcount.org.uk/fish-count-estimates-2/numbers-of-farmed-fish-slaughtered-each-year/study-to-estimate-the-global-annual-numbers-of-farmed-fish.

Mottet, A. et al. (2017). Livestock: On our plates or eating at our table? A new analysis of the feed/food debate. *Global Food Security, 14*, 1–8.

News Wires. (2020). Ghana's president says one person infected 533 with Covid-19 at fish factory. *France 24.* 11 May 2020. https://www.france24.com/en/20200511-ghana-s-president-says-one-person-infected-533-with-covid-19-at-fish-factory

Noske, B. (1997). *Beyond boundaries: Humans and animals.* Montreal: Black Rose Books.

OECD/FAO. (2020). *OECD-FAO Agricultural Outlook 2020-2029.* FAO, Rome/OECD Publishing, Paris. https://doi.org/10.1787/1112c23b-en.

Painter, C. (2016). Nonhuman animals within contemporary capitalism: A Marxist account of nonhuman animal liberation. *Capital & Class, 40(2)*, 1–19.

Pande, A. (2014). *Wombs in labor: Transnational commercial surrogacy in India.* New York: Columbia University Press.

Patel, R. & Moore, J.W. (2018). *A History of the world in seven cheap things: A guide to capitalism, nature and the future of the planet.* Carlton: Black Inc.

Perlo, K. (2002). Marxism and the underdog. *Society & Animals, 10*, 303–18.

Pierozan, C.R. et al. (2016). Factors affecting the daily feed intake and feed conversion ratio of pigs in grow-finishing units: the case of a company. *Porcine Health Management, 2(7)*, 1-8.

Plumwood, V. (1993). *Feminism and the mastery of nature.* London, New York: Routledge.

Reuben, A. (2020). Coronavirus: Why have there been so many outbreaks in meat processing plants? *BBC News*. 23 June 2020. https://www.bbc.com/news/53137613

Ritchie, H. & Roser, M. (2017). Meat and seafood production and consumption. Our World in Data. August 2017. https://ourworldindata.org/meat-and-seafood-production-consumption#per-capita-milk-consumption

Robinson, T.P. et al. (2011). *Global livestock production systems*. Rome: Food and Agriculture Organization of the United Nations (FAO) and International Livestock Research Institute (ILRI).

Singer, P. (1975). *Animal liberation*. London: Jonathan Cape.

Stuart, D., Schewe, R.L. & Gunderson, R. (2013). Extending social theory to farm animals: Addressing alienation in the dairy sector. *Sociologia Ruralis, 53(2)*, 201–22.

TallBear, K. (2019). Caretaking relations, not American dreaming. *Kalfou, 6(1)*, 24–41.

Tyler, T. (2012). *CIFERAE: A bestiary in five fingers*. Minneapolis, London: University of Minnesota Press.

UN FAO. (2009). *The state of food and agriculture: Livestock in the balance*. Rome: United Nations Food and Agriculture Organisation.

UN FAO. (2014). *The state of world fisheries and aquaculture: Opportunities and challenges*. Rome: United Nations Food and Agriculture Organisation.

UN FAO. (2016). *The state of world fisheries and aquaculture 2016. Contributing to food security and nutrition for all*. Rome: United Nations Food and Agriculture Organisation.

UN FAO. (2018). Is the planet approaching 'peak fish'? Not so fast, study says. Rome: United Nations Food and Agriculture Organisation. 9 July 2018. http://www.fao.org/news/story/en/item/1144274/icode/

UN FAOSTAT. Rome: UN Food and Agriculture Organisation. http://www.fao.org/faostat/en/

USDA. (2019). Quarterly hogs and pigs. United States Department of Agriculture. 27 June 2019. https://downloads.usda.library.cornell.edu/usda-esmis/files/rj430453j/3b591k937/5m60r2937/hgpg0619.pdf

Wadiwel: von Clausewitz, C (2004). *On War* (trans. J. J. Graham). New York: Barnes and Noble.

Wadiwel, D. (2015). *The war against animals*. Leiden: Brill.

Wadiwel, D. (2018). Chicken harvesting machine: Animal labor, resistance, and the time of production. *S A Q: The South Atlantic Quarterly, 117(3)*, 527–49.

Wadiwel, D. (2020). The working day: Animals, capitalism and surplus time. In C.E. Blattner, K. Coulter, & W. Kymlicka (Eds.), *Animal labour: A new frontier of interspecies justice?* (pp. 181–206). Oxford: Oxford University Press.

CHAPTER 18

BARBARIC, FERAL, OR MORAL? STEREOTYPICAL DAIRY FARMER AND VEGAN DISCOURSES ON THE BUSINESS OF ANIMAL CONSUMPTION

NIK TAYLOR, HEATHER FRASER,
NAOMI STEKELENBURG, AND JULIE KING

Introduction

The business of meat production and other forms of animal consumption has been globally institutionalized with most governments, such as those in New Zealand and Australia, providing large subsidies to ensure their continued viability. This transfer of public funds persists in spite of the now extensive evidence showing the significant negative impact animal agriculture has on the physical environs due to environmental acidification, heavy reliance on water, production of large quantities of waste that pollute the land and rivers, and associated production of greenhouse gas emissions (Howden et al., 2008; Rojas Downing et al., 2017). Much of the justification rests on the protection of rural and regional jobs—especially for traditional, non-Indigenous men—reflective of how animal farming is still etched in the dominant masculine representations of 'true' 'Kiwi' and 'Aussie' (read: settler colonialist) identities. Carnism, or the assumed naturalness of meat eating, and associated practices of animal consumption are, however, being challenged. Worldwide there has been a notable rise in veganism, especially by women, who have long been part of animal welfare and rights movements (Martinelli

FIGURE 18.1 Cows (Heather Fraser, 2021).

and Berkmaniene, 2018). Competing discourses about the ethics and morality of using animals for food, clothing, entertainment, and testing, have been enlivened by social media, where discussions can become intensely emotive, if not hostile (Phua et al., 2020).

In this chapter, we explore two polarized and competing discourses about the morality of animal farming and consumption advanced by dairy farmers and vegans respectively. As we show below, understanding how animals come to be positioned in organizations is important theoretically and conceptually to business, management, and organization studies. Our analysis is based on data drawn from two projects that we have recently conducted, *The Dairy Farmers' Wellbeing Project* (2017–19) and *The Vegan Wellbeing Project* (2019–20).* We show that the most polarized, popularized, and stereotypical view of vegans is that they are radical *ferals*, that is, a wild, undomesticated, and untamed group prone to taking drastic action. In countries like Australia where feral animals are routinely culled, to be called feral is far from an affectionate gesture. In contrast, animal liberation perspectives are often presented as viewing animal farmers (including dairy farmers) as barbaric, that is, a cruel, primitive, and uncivilized group who fail or refuse to see their involvement in systemic animal cruelty. This polarization is the result of a 'framing contest' (Schwartz, 2020: 8) that reduces complex controversy to two simplified and competing positions.

* Pseudonyms have been used for all interview material in this chapter.

At the centre of this dispute sit the lives and deaths of cows (and bulls, bobby (male) calves, and poddy (female) calves). No matter what attempts are made to create jobs or manage the environmental destruction of the dairy industry (such as deforestation and air and water pollution), or deal with the dietary problems dairy foods often cause (cholesterol, lactose intolerance), the issue of the treatment of cows remains: specifically, whether humans collectively have the right to maintain animal agribusiness; where in dairy farming, cows are forcibly impregnated, often dehorned and tail-docked, and ultimately sold for slaughter. Nevertheless, it is common for both dairy farmers and vegans to claim to care about cows in their struggle over morality. Effectively, cows often become *symbols* for both sides to represent their identities with their very bodies becoming sites of ideological and discursive dispute and control. For farmers, they are symbolic of their livelihoods, and a romanticized connection to the land. For vegans, they represent both voiceless beings in need of someone to speak for them, and the possibility of a different set of human-animal relationships based on care and respect.

The purpose of including Figure 18.1 (at the outset of the chapter) was to centre cows and their bodies within our analysis. At first glance it is an idealized view of dairy farming, with golden rays of sunshine and no hint of calves being separated from their mothers or being sent to slaughter. In this image, the cows have plenty of rich grass to consume, a stark contrast to the vast stretches of open, drought, and flood ridden plains on which most Australian cows live. However, on closer inspection, there are signs that life is not ideal: the cows have been dehorned and thanks to technology, have distended udders in which to produce more milk. There are also no bulls or bobby calves in sight. This leads us to contemplate how it is that cows' rights are invisibilized when farmers' views are represented as mainstream and commonplace. At the same time, vegan views are posited as radical and therefore open to dismissal in the argument that vegans focus only on the worst cases (Buddle et al., 2018). This line of thought allows for the maintenance of 'affected ignorance', which Schwartz (2020: 75) describes as:

> a kind of ignorance generated by what one knows but does not want to hear. It occurs when people refuse to acknowledge the connection between their actions and the resulting suffering of their victims, ask not to be informed of the practices causing the suffering, do not ask questions, or uncritically accept the dictates of custom and ideological constructions.

Two main choices are publicly represented: side with the 'barbaric' farmers or join the 'radical feral' vegans. The conventional romanticization of animal farmers, and the popular depiction of vegans as radical easily descends into a form of strategic vitriol setting the scene for a polarization that allows investors, producers, sellers, and consumers to sidestep animal cruelty issues. Accordingly, public debates are constrained and delimited to the point that discourses usually fail to consider even, for instance, whether or not products need to be sourced from animals, and how farmers might be supported to transition away from animal agribusiness.

Farmed animals are flesh and blood not just symbols. As O'Doherty (2016: 410) points out:

> The reduction of the animal to the role of symbol is rooted in a much deeper series of categories and dualisms upon which the late social scientific discipline—organisation studies—has been constructed and on the basis of which its knowledge practices proceed: nature/culture, representation/real, subject/object, theory/empirics, explanation/description, structure/agency, and so on.

Understanding the roles that animals play in organizations, in businesses, and in public discourses created about both, offers organization studies—and, indeed many other social sciences—an opportunity to re-assess their own intellectual foundations. It also begins to provide foundations from which different, more ethical, practices can be formulated.

Animals and Organization Studies

Until quite recently nonhuman animals have been largely overlooked in organization studies. As is the case in many fields/disciplines, when animals have been considered in organization studies, it has often been done for human benefit (e.g. Cunha et al., 2018; for notable exceptions see e.g. Hamilton and Taylor, 2012; Huopalainen, 2020; Sage et al., 2016; Sayers, 2016). While exceptions are still prone to marginalization and subject to niche status, this is slowly starting to change (Sayers, 2016), partly due to the critical organizational studies scholars who are interested in questions about power and domination and have shown how a myriad of organizational roles, practices, laws, and procedures relate to animals (Sayers, Hamilton, and Sang, 2019).

Despite such progress, there remain several barriers to the inclusion of animals in organization studies, not least of which is our lack of inclusive theories, concepts, and language that stems from an embedded anthropocentric epistemology. For example, Labatut et al. (2016: 316) point to three 'theoretical problematics' that arise from the inclusion of other animals in organization studies: (1) 'agriculture and the biosocial organisation of nature/culture', (2) 'ethics as the organisation of the animal', and (3) 'the politics of animal resistance'. The first problematic refers to the false dichotomy created between humans and animals; a longstanding divide used to naturalize and reify human supremacy, often done through transforming living animals into technological systems (Labatut et al., 2016: 317). The second refers to the historical (and repeatedly discredited) human assertion that animals cannot feel emotions and therefore cannot suffer. The third problematic—the politics of animal resistance—is more self-explanatory and reflects an interest in animal liberation. Despite these challenges, some scholars are attuned to including other animals in research on businesses and organizational cultures and recognize the need to study the roles of animals in animal agriculture in ways where the animals themselves do not remain abstract commodities (Connolly and Cullen, 2018; Hamilton and Taylor, 2017).

Animals, Organization, and Identity

Animals play important roles in organizational cultures often through the identities they provide for humans. For example, 'dirty work' with animals in the abattoir may provide 'spoiled identities' for humans (Hamilton and Taylor, 2013; McCabe and Hamilton, 2015), whereas voluntary work with species given elevated moral status such as dogs (Taylor, 2007) or horses (Hamilton and Taylor, 2012) may give workers self-esteem to such a degree this forms part of the glue keeping organizations together and functioning. As such, animals are part and parcel of human organizational culture in a temporal and symbolic sense.

However, what might be simply symbolic to us often has oppressive material effects for other animals. Precisely because animals are 'the unwitting "bearers" of human culture' they are often recast as human belongings, for instance when farmers brand 'their' livestock to mark proprietorship (Hamilton and Taylor, 2012: 45). Such branding is one of many identity-forming and maintaining processes that occur in animal agriculture—for the farmers who are declared the rightful owners and the animals now designated as livestock. Much of this identity-forming and maintenance work through human-animal relations also occurs more subtly at the level of discourse and symbolism. For instance, (male) farmers are conventionally taught to see themselves as the natural masters of 'their beasts', who are driven to be compliant. Agribusiness rests upon and encourages this tendency, for example, by the various discursive and symbolic manoeuvres designed to instigate a distance between humans and the animals they farm (Arcari, 2017; Hamilton and Taylor, 2012).

Hamilton and Taylor (2012: 70) showed there are tacit rules operating in the abattoir to routinize and normalize animal death. One of these rules is to consider animals as products as opposed to whole, sentient beings with personalities or any sense of individuality. These rules allow slaughterhouse workers to find some distance between their lived self and their 'killing self' (Hamilton and Taylor, 2012: 76), and to position other animals as beings whose oppression and death is legitimate and entirely normal. Similarly, farmed animals tend to be reduced to their biological products, and in so doing have their pain and suffering downplayed or ignored.

In dairy farming animals become milk, butter, and yogurt. In the meat industry animals become cuts of meat, such as legs, thighs, steaks, backstraps, and ribs (Sayers, 2016: 373). With reference to the pork industry, Stibbe (2003: 385) showed how technical and scientific language is used to 'covertly convey' the ideas that pigs are objects whose pain should be ignored. These discursive practices are not coincidental, serving to objectify and commodify animals into body parts and processes, and invisibilize their internment and slaughter. Language is key here, as Sayers points out (2016: 371), 'the problem starts with language ... and the answers also lie in language. Often, these discursive practices remain invisible but can have devastating effects.' But discourses and symbolism are not set in stone, they are constructed by human labour and, as such, they can be disrupted. Making the routinized violence inflicted upon animals visible can be a point of disruption (Burrell, 1997; Hamilton and Taylor, 2012). Understanding the discourses used by those in animal agriculture, and by those opposing it, is therefore key. In the remainder of this chapter we consider the various discourses used by farmers to normalize animal agriculture, and that used by vegans in attempts to disrupt it. The data we draw on to achieve this is taken from two different studies.

Study 1: The Dairy Farmers' Wellbeing Project (2017-19)

This study was funded by Animals Australia, which is an Australian-based animal protection and advocacy organization focusing on farmed animals. The project was designed to consider the issues affecting dairy farmers, their families, and their animals (livestock). The primary objective was to investigate whether farmers themselves identified (potential) links between their own wellbeing and the wellbeing of their livestock/animals. A total of 29 qualitative, individual interviews were conducted with eight dairy industry consultants and 21 dairy farmers (past or present), in South Australia, Queensland, New South Wales, and Victoria. Of the 21 dairy farmers, 10 are women and 11 are men. Of the eight consultants, there were three men and five women participants. Conversational, narrative interviewing was used purposively to unfold lived experiences of the dairy industry. Two methods of analysis were performed on the interview data: 1) thematic analysis (Braun and Clarke, 2006) using NVivo 12 Pro; and 2) critical narrative analysis (Fraser, 2004). Ethical approval was provided by Flinders University, South Australia, where the researchers worked at the time.

Overall, we found only a loose connection between dairy farmers' reports of their health and wellbeing, and that of their animals. Mostly, the farmers emphasized the economic precariousness of dairy farming and the negative implications this had for their health. Even with government subsidies, economic viability was a serious challenge. Most dairy farmers told us that they are no longer able to make a living through dairy farming alone. The notable exceptions were those in extended dairy farming families who processed their own milk and/or made dairy products such as cheese, custard, and yogurt. These options were not possible for most farmers given the costly infrastructure required to set up a milk processing plant, the specialized skills sets required to produce dairy products, and most crucially, access to a consumer market willing to purchase products at prices that are economically viable for farmers. Some farmers told us they were on the brink of collapse and did not know what would happen to them or their herds.

With regard to on-farm animal welfare practices, participants differed in regards to how quickly they separated calves from their mothers; whether they dehorned animals or docked their tails; and whether they succumbed to the pressure to 'get bigger (increase herd numbers) or get out (of the industry)'. Notwithstanding these important differences, the vast majority of cows, bulls, and calves used in the Australian dairy industry live prematurely short lives, and most of the farmers we interviewed recognized this. An important subset of stories that clearly (and quickly) emerged from our analysis was that of farmers' views of animal rights activists. While not all dairy farmers and consultants interviewed in this study expressed negative views about vegans and vegan activists, many brought up the issue of animal activism unprompted, and many held very strong views.

Vegan Activists as Out-of-Touch with the Realities of Rural Life

Many participants in our dairy study cast animal rights activists as urban dwellers who were disconnected from rural communities; people who did not understand the realities of the dairy farm, hurting farmers by giving the dairy industry bad press, especially on social media. By implication, this frames farmers as connected to rural communities and the land, as well as in most cases signalling a complex, ambiguous, and contradictory relationship with the animals who are 'sentient commodities' (Wilkie, 2005):

> **Sylvia:** They [Vegan activists] need to actually get onto a dairy farm and spend time with them and see what happens. [Current dairy farmer]
>
> **Julie:** It's very, very hard to stop misinformation on social media [By vegan activists] which can be a bit annoying. [Dairy industry consultant]
>
> **Allison:** Definitely an urban/rural divide now that's increasing, and because of that ... people are less and less connected to agriculture in Australia. And when you're less and less connected, then you have a lot less knowledge or accurate and honest knowledge ... *there is just facts of life on farms that aren't pretty, but that is just life,* just like humans die, animals die too. [Dairy industry consultant; emphasis added]
>
> **Valerie:** ... because it's so easy for someone to take a video and people that don't know what it is completely take it out of context ... There's plenty of things on, like animal liberation pages and stuff on Facebook where they've taken videos of horrible things that go on, but they don't actually understand the situation. So, *I'm not saying that there's not horrible things that go on,* but some things that are said to be horrendous are actually done because of all these other reasons, not because they think it's cruel or whatever, but they don't actually understand why you're doing it and they don't take the education and know why it's happening. [current dairy farmer; emphasis added]

This is a common refrain among those who find animal activist messages challenging to their status quo. As Buddle et al. (2018: 253) note, meat-eaters often dismiss activist messages about the lives of farmed animals as either extreme or as stemming from an ignorance about 'real' farming conditions. From the perspectives of these dairy participants, animal rights activists are wrong to challenge dairy farmers at all. Moreover, activists are certainly wrong to circulate social media pieces critical of the dairy industry, especially those that garner support in the wider public and do damage to industry brands and to farmers' identities as knowledgeable about, and connected to, the land. In two of the excerpts above, there is a significant and similar move taken by Allison (industry consultant) and Valerie (dairy farmer). It is their acknowledgement that agrifarming is brutal. However, such brutality is dismissed as normal and necessary as Allison admits 'there is just facts of life on farms that aren't pretty, but that is just life … '. Such justifications are echoed by meat consumers as Piazza et al. (2015: 126) demonstrate in their research into how omnivores use the '4 N's'—natural, normal, necessary, and nice—as the main justifications for the acceptability of eating meat not least because 'rationalizing enables omnivores to continue in a dietary practice that has increasingly come under public scrutiny'.

Animal Activists Unwilling to See Life from Farmers' Perspective

Some dairy farming interviewees expressed frustration, if not anger, at animal activism, particularly for activists' refusal to see the situation from the farmers' perspectives, a perspective that is presented as rational and normal through casting opposition as 'disconnection':

> Penny: And I think that's where the dialogue is missing. I feel like there is such a disconnection between the regional and urban communities, I'm going to assume that most of those people that are those people pointing fingers, saying 'You're doing a bad thing, you're doing a wrong thing', they have absolutely no connection to … the people and those regions that are doing that work … I think there's a lack of interaction, and in conversation and dialogue. [dairy industry consultant]
> Allison: … [there is a] lack of knowledge in today's society about the actual goings on, on a farm. I think there's a lot of misconceptions. The media only ever report the negative stories and doesn't report the good stories and I think animal activists are really hurting the industry. They [activists] have money and they provide a lot of misinformation that's not based on science or fact … it's very easy to portray the agricultural industry in a bad light. And I don't think farmers are very, as a breed, are very good at promoting all the good stuff they do. [dairy industry consultant]

These narratives argue against the legitimacy of animal activism occurring at all in the dairy industry. This in-group (i.e. farmers) and out-group (i.e. activists) identity management strategy (Ainsworth and Hardy, 2004) creates the farmer-as-expert identity who positions animal activists as those who 'have a lot of misconceptions' so they 'shouldn't point the finger' or compound the problem that 'the media only ever report negative stories' about dairy farming. It also positions the farmer as victim—of radical animal advocates who are seen as part of a wealthy public relations machine by farmers, who are struggling financially.

For these interviewees, there is an assumed shared identity of 'farmer' that carries with it certain understandings of their common world that animal activists cannot understand. Despite this, interviewees still distanced themselves from 'bad' farmers by arguing that activists have unfairly lumped all animal farmers in together, failing to recognize their differences, including how much some dairy farmers can care for their cows. Often, for our interviewees, this turned on the size of the farm with some smaller dairy farmers differentiating themselves from the large, industrial-scale farms that they admitted had a poor track record for animal welfare:

> **Kendra:** I mean smaller scale allows you to notice details … I think that when things are going wrong in a big system you see the outcome at the end when things are really—where all the animals are sick … I think that on a smaller scale you notice things—sick animals you know them by name or number or whatever. [dairy industry consultant]

While farmers portray activists as lacking in knowledge fear-mongers who use unfair moral shock footage, it is worth noting that journalists often deliberately seek stories that involve polarized viewpoints precisely in order to present them in terms of conflict (Schwartz, 2020). This was an argument put forward by the one dairy farmer who identified as vegan, who did not consume animal products herself and who described how she was rearing calves with their mothers rather than separating them shortly after birth. She was upset that vegans and their representative organizations ignored what she believed to be an alternative practice:

> **Clare:** And that's been my fight with the vegans. Why do you isolate anyone who's trying to say, I reckon we can do this better? … You've got the—you've got Animals Australia running those vegan photos of the cow and the calf together, and this'll be the last they ever spend time together. They're running all these photos and you see them everywhere—Vegan Society, Animals Protection Agency—but no one ever says, why don't we do this better? [current dairy farmer]

The Hurt and Disruptions Caused by Animal Protests

It should be noted, however, that while farmers may present themselves as victims of activism in some circumstances, the consequences of animal activism are very real for them. Some participants told stories about the hurt and disruption vegan activists caused. In the next excerpt Sylvia recalls a recent time when animal activists disrupted their public event, leaving participants initially stunned into silence:

> **Sylvia:** … a couple of months ago we were at a show and we do this fun thing called the Big Jersey Milk Off … just as we were about to start … we've got the music pumping. We've got all of our participants ready and their cups. And the vegans storm onto the centre of the oval placarding with their megaphones, and saying

really offensive things, like calling, naming and shaming dairy farmers as rapists and murderers and all of these—which they aren't! These dairy farmers love their cows, like they provide their income, they will do anything... And the dairy farmers were just silent for about 10 minutes; no one knew kind of what to do. And then a few of them started mouthing off... I know that one dairy farmer or two in particular couldn't sleep that night. It had actually got under their skin, and they were getting up to check their cattle to make sure that the vegans hadn't come in to let their cattle out or, you know, all sorts of things. [dairy farmer]

Sylvia said that the protestor 'had actually got under their [the farmers'] skin', not via the messages of animal emancipation but rather through fear of the loss of possessions in making them wonder about what other actions the activists might take, such as 'let[ting] their cattle out'. It is an intriguing fear, given letting cattle out is not known to be a vegan protest tactic, and may indicate farmers are unaware of animal activists' philosophies and tactics. Their distrust of animal activists ran deep and was shared by some of the dairy industry consultants we interviewed who also criticized animal activists' protest tactics:

> **Adam:** They [dairy farmers] feel personally attacked or something by some of the animal welfare [groups], like PETA, some of the more extreme groups, and take significant offense. [dairy industry consultant]
> **Amanda:** Well, I mean honestly, like I see ads and they're calling us rapists and murderers, I find that personally very offensive, because it's just not true. So, I just think that sort of ridiculous and over-emotive language should be taken out of the conversation and facts backed by evidence be used and not photo-shopped pictures should be at the forefront. [dairy industry consultant]
> **Kendra:** Please stop bashing the entire industry over one experience and maybe do a bit more research. So, it's that kind of thing, it's being brave enough to be vocal and actually say no you're wrong. And stand up to all of these smear campaigns. [dairy industry consultant]
> **Allison:** ... they're [activists] using shock tactics. [dairy industry consultant]

From these descriptions, animal rights activists are portrayed as ill-informed, privileged, and hostile people disconnected from rural life who lack compassion for farmers. They are troublemakers who take single but extreme examples of abuse of animals on farms and mistakenly publicize it as standard practice; people who use extreme, unethical 'moral shock' (Jasper, 1997) tactics that disrupt events and cause farmers direct harm. From this perspective, animal rights activists might fit the label of being *feral* (wild, undomesticated, and untamed).

Study 2: The Vegan Wellbeing Project (2019–20)

The Vegan Wellbeing Project aimed broadly to understand the social dimensions of vegan health and wellbeing. In recruitment of participants, we did not call for animal rights or vegan activists. Nor did we specifically ask vegans their views on dairy farmers. Rather, we asked more general questions about vegans' social health and wellbeing in a culture where meat-eating and other uses of animals' bodies in entertainment and testing are the norm. Participants could contribute photographs (with accompanying text if they chose) to the study website https://veganwellbeingproject.com/project/. We analysed the visual and written data to understand: (1) how vegans see themselves; (2) how public hostility towards veganism might negatively impact them; and (3) how they navigate public derision and its potential impacts on their health and wellbeing. Here, we discuss how vegans construct their own identities through the symbolic use of animals who are abused and oppressed by agribusiness.

Against Animal Cruelty

All participants in the Vegan Wellbeing Project signalled the importance of animal cruelty in the construction of their identities. Usually, this took the form of 'war stories' where they became aware of institutionalized animal abuse that were a 'catalytic experience' for them, enabling them to 'reconstruct their identity around moral and ethical issues' (Cherry, 2015: 61).

> Billy: The reason I am vegan is number one for the animals. I cannot support the cruelty involved with treating animals as commodities. Be it factory farming for animal-based food, fur farming, leather production, animal testing, I cannot have my money go to practices that cause pain and suffering to others.
> Em: I think the most difficult challenge for me being vegan is comprehending how rife and normalised sexual abuse is in animal exploitation ... Bestiality is frowned upon, however constructed in the context of non-human animal exploitation industries (agriculture, science, companion animal breeding etc), it is totally permissible and lawful.
> Rose: It took several more years of allowing myself to learn the truth about fish, dairy, and eggs until at last, I became vegan.

Self-directed discovery is a key part of becoming vegan for many such as Rose, Em, and Billy (above). In this narrative about vegan-inspired identity change, is the implied construction of farming as barbaric (primitive, cruel, and uncivilized). In their study of the archetypes, moral foundation, and narrative plots told by vegans, Napoli and Ouschan (2020) note there's often an inciting incident that promotes change to a vegan lifestyle, which often involves being exposed to detailed and disturbing information on normal(ized) farming practices. Chantal also speaks to this:

> Chantal: I was a vegetarian for about 25 years before I became vegan. I've been vegan for over 5 years now. I never realised the issues behind eating eggs and dairy products. It wasn't until a friend sent me some information on the way bobby calves are treated in New Zealand that I finally understood the cruelty behind dairy products.

This formation of a moral identity for vegans such as Chantal, rests upon the idea that animal farming is barbaric and cruel, and is a central part of the ethical challenge to carnism, or the assumed naturalness of consuming meat and dairy (Joy, 2010).

Challenging Carnism

For many vegans their diets operationalize their concerns about climate change, specifically the environmental destruction associated with the meat and dairy industries. However, the overarching reason for being vegan, rather than plant based, is to prevent animal cruelty. Some participants talked about hating 'meat' because it normalizes the killing of animals for food. A few honed the problem of supermarket shopping, namely the difficulty they have ignoring the everyday cruelty displayed on shelves:

> Tessa: … the feeling of alienation, I get almost every time I go grocery shopping.
> Linda: There are things you see in your daily life that most people just push to the back of their mind or make excuses for.
> Phoebe: … the way in which meat—death—is 'dressed up' both literally and figuratively (discursively) in contemporary Australian mainstream society.

For many vegans, standing at the deli bar or getting items located in or near the meat section of the supermarket can make for a distressing experience, in part because of the assumed normalcy of meat and dairy products:

> Phoebe: As I waited for my patties, I watched the people in front of me selecting their mountains of shaved meats; their indulgences and extravagances alongside the more everyday meat items … the way in which meat eating—and as a corollary, the slaughter of animals—is not only normalised but serves a range of social functions, which are enfolded into everyday practices which make 'speaking out against it' appear 'insane'.

Phoebe recognized it is easier for consumers to detach from the animals when their flesh is laid out as cuts of meat. Challenging this system was usually met with fierce resistance:

> Phoebe: It's easier to discredit the crazy vegan than to step back, look at the half shaven carcass in the glass cabinet and go, 'wait a minute, that is weird …'. I'm sure that if we were to swap out 'animal carcasses' for 'human carcasses', the overarching discourse of meat eating would abruptly lose the power of its normalcy.
> Tessa: I said it before, I'll say it again: meat eating is a fiercely guarded norm.

Frustration was also expressed at why people continue to consume these products when excellent alternatives are increasingly available:

> Frederick: Coles [supermarket chain] recently released a vegan version of the 'burger special sauce' which appears to [be an] imitation of the Big Mac sauce from McDonalds. Using all vegan ingredients, this burger represents an old-time

favourite without the death. My non-vegan sister ate one with me and commented on how great it tastes. It's times like this that makes me angry that we continue to normalise death for taste, especially when such great alternatives are available that are just as delicious.

Frederick called this story 'Hold the death', emphasizing that the pleasures of taste should not normalize death. It is one of the many stories we heard about food activism related to animal cruelty, or the process of examining where food comes from and the costs involved.

Collectively, participants from the Vegan Wellbeing project portrayed the production and consumption of animal products as barbaric; brutal practices done by unthinking people who failed to stop and consider the unethical nature of their behaviour. Animal farmers were not singled out but included in the dominant population who they saw as deliberately ignoring animal cruelty. From these perspectives, there is nothing natural or immutable about animal agribusiness.

Across the two cohorts of research participants, we have shown that vegans and farmers have internalized and participated in polarized narratives about farming practices, and that these narratives were inextricably tied to their own identity formation and management. Underlying this identity work are questions of morality, human nature, and animal purpose. However, these questions often fade into the background compared to the interests and narratives told by corporate interests of meat and dairy, which have produced complex technologies, procedures, and organizational imperatives that normalize the consumption of animal bodies as food and romanticize animal farmers. Carefully curated images of happy cows in green pastures are often the only images of 'livestock' consumers come close to.

Future Possibilities

What future possibilities exist for the movement away from animal agribusiness and into products and jobs not tied to the exploitation of animals? The short answer is that there are many promising possibilities, reflected in the rise of global vegan markets of all kinds (food, textiles, and cosmetics). Practical measures might start with: a) the promotion of vegan markets; b) the transfer of state subsidies from animal agricultural to vegan markets; and c) more dedicated efforts to help dairy (and meat) farmers to transition into other industries. But the challenge remains the sheer scale and might of agribusiness and how embedded it is in political organizing and the national psyche.

Dairy Australia (2022), a major animal agriculture lobby group, emphasise 'dairy careers' and the jobs the industry creates, particularly in rural areas. Dairy farming advocates such as Geoff Bell and Farmonline (2012, n.p.) promote the (uncritical) idea that the country was 'built upon the sheep's back' but express disappointment that 'The research tells us that nearly a third of all Australians do not appreciate the significance of agriculture to our national identity'.

There is no disputing the scale of the challenge given meat and dairy industries have so much corporate lobbying power. According to the Australian Bureau of Statistics (2020), animal agricultural commodities are worth billions of dollars in Australia alone. For example, in 2018–19 cattle and calves were worth $13 billion (up 7 per cent); sheep and lambs, $4 billion (up 5 per cent), pigs, $1 billion (up 7 per cent), and further livestock products such as wool, milk, and eggs were worth $10 billion. Meat and Livestock Australia (2019) reported that for the 2017–18 period in Australia there were 41,800 agricultural businesses involved in the cattle industry, with an estimated 172,000 people employed in the red meat industry alone, managing 26.4 million head of cattle, of which there were 2 million head of beef cows and heifers aged one year and over. Dairy Australia (2020) estimated the farmgate value (i.e. the value of a 'product' when it leaves the farm, minus any shipping or marketing costs) of the Australian dairy industry to be AUD$4.8billion, with 29 per cent of all milk production exported to countries such as China, from an industry employing some 43,500 people. Rural Skills Australia (2014) also estimates that indirect jobs in related service industries is in excess of 100,000. As we have shown through excerpts from the Dairy Farmers' Wellbeing Project and the Vegan Wellbeing Project, the business of meat production is deeply contested in Australia. However, until farming practices are publicly illuminated and detached from both big business and a sense of national identity, progressing into different markets will be extremely challenging.

Concluding Comments

Organization studies scholars can identify and chart particular networks and mechanisms of the animal-industrial complex to build a clearer picture of the entities and actors involved. In so doing, they must pay attention to the lived reality of the animals involved ensuring that they are 'rematerialized from varied capitalist processes of fragmentation and absenting' (Twine, 2012: 26). While detractors will argue that this is far from germane to organization studies, human-animal relations are central to organizations. As demonstrated in this chapter, studying human-animal relations in organizations can tell us much about symbolism, discourse, identity-formation, and the operation(s) and performance of power. As such, the inclusion of other animals in our fields of study has ramifications that speak to the very heart of multiple disciplines.

As Sayers et al. (2019: 244) point out, 'Questions of power, dominance and the role of the non-human belong firmly within the mainstream of critical organisation studies and deserve close attention from those already mindful of the difficulties that taxonomies, binaries and boundaries entail'. Additionally, as O'Doherty (2016) points out when discussing the impact Olly the cat had on a large organization in the United Kingdom, we should not reduce animals to passive vehicles for the 'symbolic projections of humans' (p. 415), because when we do, we close down possibilities—to notice different ways of organizing, to notice animal agency and resistance, and to challenge our long held and often erroneous beliefs about what our relationships with others might be.

Acknowledgements

We'd like to thank Animals Australia for funding the Farmers' Wellbeing Project and to the participants of both studies who gave so generously of their time. We would also like to thank Masters of Social Work student, Sandra Cookland and Research Assistant, Kate Walton for their work on the Farmers' Wellbeing Project. Finally, thanks to Craig O'Hara for creating the website for the Vegan Wellbeing Project.

References

Ainsworth, S. & Hardy, C. (2004). Critical discourse analysis and identity: Why bother? *Critical Discourse Studies, 1(2),* 225–59.

Arcari, P. (2017). Normalised, human-centric discourses of meat and animals in climate change, sustainability and food security literature. *Agriculture and Human Values, 34,* 69–86.

Australian Bureau of Statistics. (2020, May). *Value of agricultural commodities produced, Australia, 2018–19 financial year.* Australian Bureau of Statistics (abs.gov.au).

Buddle, E., Bray, H., & Ankeny, R. (2018). Why would we believe them? Meat consumers' reactions to online farm animal welfare activism in Australia. *Communication Research and Practice, 4,* 246–60.

Burrell, G. (1997). *Pandemonium: Towards a retro-organisation theory.* Sage: Beverley Hills, CA.

Cunha, M., Rego, A., & Munro, I. (2019). Dogs in organisations. *Human Relations, 72(4),* 778–800.

Dairy Australia. (2020). *Australian dairy industry in focus.* Dairy Australia. https://bit.ly/3gcralQ

Gillespie, K. (2018). *The cow with ear tag #1389.* Chicago: University of Chicago Press.

Hamilton, L. & Taylor, N. (2012). Ethnography in evolution: Adapting to the animal 'other' in organizations. *Journal of Organisational Ethnography, 1(1),* 43–51.

Hamilton, L. & Taylor, N. (2013). *Animals at work: Identity, politics and culture in work with animals.* Brill Academic Press: Boston and Leiden.

Hamilton, L. & Taylor, N. (2017). *Ethnography after humanism: Power, politics and method in multi-species research.* Palgrave: London.

Huopalainen, A. (2020). *Writing with the bitches.* Online First. DOI: 10.1177/1350508420961533

Howden, S., Crimp, S., & Stokes, C. (2008). Climate change and Australian livestock systems: impacts, research and policy issues. *Australian Journal of Experimental Agriculture, 48,* 788.

Jasper, J.M. (1997). *The art of moral protest: Culture, biography, and creativity in social movements.* Chicago: University of Chicago Press.

Joy, M. (2010). *Why we love dogs, eat pigs and wear cows: An introduction to carnism.* Conari Press: San Francisco.

Labatut, J., Munro, I., & Desmond, J. (2016). Animals and organisations. *Organisation, 23(3)*, 315–29.

Martinelli, D. & Berkmaniene, A. (2018). The politics and the demographics of veganism: Notes for a critical analysis. *International Journal for the Semiotics of Law, 31*, 501–30.

McCabe, D. & Hamilton, L. (2015). The kill programme: An ethnographic study of 'dirty work' in a slaughterhouse. *New Technology, Work and Employment, 30(2)*, 95–108.

Meat and Livestock Australia (2019). *Fast facts*. Retrieved 18/3/21, mla-beef-fast-facts-2019.pdf

Napoli, J. & Ouschan, R. (2020). Vegan stories: Revealing archetypes and their moral foundations. *Qualitative Market Research, 23(1)*, 145–69.

O'Doherty, D. (2016). Feline politics in organisation: The nine lives of Olly the cat. *Organisation, 23(3)*, 407–33.

PETA (n.d). *Animals are not ours*. Retrieved 20/3/21 Cow's Milk: A Cruel and Unhealthy Product | PETA

Phua, J., Venus Jin, S., & Kim, J. (2020). The roles of celebrity endorsers' and consumers' vegan identity in marketing communication about veganism. *Journal of Marketing Communications, 26(8)*, 813–35.

Piazza, J. et al. (2015). Rationalizing meat consumption: The 4Ns. *Appetite, 91*, 114–28.

Queensland Government State Development. (2021). Swickers bacon factory and Sunpork commercial piggeries. Retrieved 18/3/21 Swickers Bacon Factory and SunPork Commercial Piggeries | State Development, Infrastructure, Local Government and Planning.

Queensland Government (2020). Media release 13/2/20: *More beef means more jobs for the Darling Downs*. Retrieved 18/3/21, More beef means more jobs for the Darling Downs—Ministerial Media Statements.

Rojas-Downing, M. et al. (2017). Climate change and livestock: Impacts, adaptation, and mitigation. *Climate Risk Management, 16*, 145–63.

Sage, D. et al. (2016). Organizing space and time through relational human–animal boundary work: Exclusion, invitation and disturbance. *Organisation, 23(3)*, 434–50.

Sayers, J. (2016). A report to an academy: On carnophallogocentrism, pigs and meat-writing. *Organisation, 23(3)*, 370–86.

Sayers, J., Hamilton, L., & Sang, K. (2019). Organizing animals: Species, gender and power at work. *Gender, Work and Organisation, 26(3)*, 239–45.

Schwartz, B. (2020). The animal welfare battle: the production of affected ignorance in the Swedish meat industry debate. *Culture and Organisation, 26(1)*, 75–95.

Stibbe, A. (2003). As charming as a pig: The discursive construction of the relationship between pigs and humans. *Society and Animals, 11(4)*, 375–92.

Taylor, N. (2007). Never an it: intersubjectivity and the creation of personhood in an animal shelter. *Qualitative Sociology Review, 3(1)*. http://www.qualitativesociologyreview.org / ENG/archive_eng.php

Taylor, N. & Fraser, H. (2019). The Cow Project: Analytical and representational dilemmas of dairy farmers' conceptions of cruelty and kindness. *Animal Studies Journal, 8(2)*, 133–53, available at: https://ro.uow.edu.au/asj/vol8/iss2/10

Wilkie, R. (2005). Sentient commodities and productive paradoxes: The ambiguous nature of human-livestock relations in Northeast Scotland. *Journal of Rural Studies 21(2)*, 213–30.

CHAPTER 19

TINKERING WITH RELATIONS

Veterinary Work in Dutch Farm Animal Care

ELSE VOGEL

INTRODUCTION

'RESIST, veterinarian. This is not animal welfare!' [*Kom in verzet, dierenarts. Dit is geen dierenwelzijn!*] (NRC, 2017). This is the headline of a 2017 op-ed in a major Dutch newspaper. It is written by an organization of veterinarians called the Caring Vets. The op-ed was mostly signed by retired, companion-animal or ex-livestock veterinarians. It specified, however, that several vets working at the Netherlands Food and Consumer Safety Authority (NVWA) and in the intensive livestock production industry subscribed to the content of the piece but 'pulled out for fear of the possible consequences of openly supporting [the initiative]' (ibid). The 'bioindustry' of animals in food production has been a source of controversy in the Netherlands for decades, with activists speaking out about animal welfare issues such as battery chickens, veal crates, barn fires, and the disposal of young male animals as 'waste'. Concerns over the environmental effects and sustainability of keeping over 100 million farm animals in a densely populated country, where over half of the land is used for agriculture and horticulture, further increase the pressure on the livestock sector to change.

This op-ed was the first time that veterinarians joined the debate so publicly with such a critical, activist position in the media. The Caring Vets had thrown the 'cat among the pigeons', this much was obvious. Bringing their ethical concerns into the public eye had threatened an alliance between vets working in the livestock industry, and the farmers who they work with and who pay them. This became clear when the Royal Dutch Veterinary Association (KNMvD), responded with an open letter addressed to livestock farmers (Nieuwe Oogst, 2017). The letter seemed set on damage control. Its writers anticipated and expressed understanding for a possible emotional response of the farmers to the op-ed—'Angry? Sad? Or maybe just tired?'—and then emphasized the collective efforts of farmers and vets: 'Together we work very hard, often at ungodly hours, to produce food for citizens and consumers.' It then strategically restated the message of the op-ed: 'Who reads carefully, calmed after the initial emotion, will however see that the real message in the paper is: Veterinarian, keep being critical of the system in which you work and let's *together* make sure that the system continues to develop toward becoming even more sustainable' (ibid; emphasis added). Thus, the response of the Society did not take a stance for or against the content of the message, but rephrased it in a way that frames vets and farmers as a community with a common value orientation.

The response interpellated farmers as professionals who—like vets—are willing to change and look critically at their own work, while inviting an audience of concerned citizens to trust those involved to commit to improvement. Where the op-ed paints a picture of vets supporting 'business as usual', as uncritical cogs in the machine, the letter of the professional organization made it hard for its readers to accuse vets of complacency. Against the call to 'resist' of the Caring Vets, emerges the equally but quite differently normative invitation to 'continue to improve together'. In the response, we see a double move of translation of the initial critical message of the Caring Vets: on the one hand, it aimed to repair the public legitimacy of and trust placed in farming; on the other, it secured the veterinary profession's place within it. It is a crafty instance of managing relations; a skill which, or so I will suggest in this chapter, is crucial for veterinarians' involvement in the livestock industry.

In the Netherlands, vets play a key role in the continuation, regulation, and innovation of industrial livestock production. Extending studies of care in health care and farming (Mol, 2008; Mol et al., 2010; Singleton, 2012), this chapter details how vets treat animals, coach farmers, perform animal welfare procedures, or otherwise try to achieve 'good' farm animal care. In doing so, I draw on ethnographic fieldwork with veterinarians. As animal health care providers, they often have long-standing relations with farmers, their clients. They regularly visit farms, performing practical tasks, and advising the farmer about management and prevention issues around animal health.

Most of the veterinary practitioners I talked to worked in the dairy and pork industry, although many also occasionally treated animals other than cows or pigs, such as horses, goats, or pets. In total, I interviewed 20 veterinarians, recruited through the KNMvD and through a call in a professional journal for vets, and observed some of them in their work. I asked them about their daily work routines, and their vision of the profession and the livestock industry. I particularly inquired about the dilemmas they encounter in their work, while interacting with farmers and animals. In exploring the specificities of veterinary care, my question is not: *Do* vets working in the industry make a difference? Instead, I want to understand what is at stake in the practices through which vets aim to make a difference: *How* can vets make a difference, what action radius do they have, and what does their agency consist of? Rather than the problem being a matter of vets failing to 'do the right thing', I suggest the complexity lies in the many modes of 'doing good' that vets in farm animal care are engaged in.

Vets in Livestock Production

The job of veterinarians is to ensure good farm animal care; but what does this entail? The 'code for the veterinarian' [*code voor de dierenarts*] (2010) of the KNMvD states that vets 'should respect, promote, repair and/or guard the welfare and health of the animals in their care', recognizing the 'intrinsic worth' of the animal. In their op-ed, the Caring Vets remind their colleagues of these responsibilities. In so doing, they stress the relation of vets to animals as the primary ethical relationship. It is, however, only quite recently that the protection of animal suffering for the sake of the animal appears as a valid and even principal responsibility of veterinarians.

In his history of the Dutch veterinary profession, Offringa (1983) mentions the historically different 'value orientation' of medical doctors and veterinarians. Whereas doctors have been admired for their ability to save human lives, the veterinary profession gained its legitimacy primarily from its economic contributions. Predecessors of the current veterinarian performed practical work on farms, or fixed up horses during wars. Following the medical revolutions of Pasteur and Koch at the end of the nineteenth century, vets have played a crucial role in preventing the spread of zoonotic diseases and securing food safety which has further strengthened their academic and societal standing. It was mainly with the advent of pet culture, after the Second World War, that protecting animals from suffering became a central part of the veterinarian's vocation.

Mark, one of the vets I interviewed, active in the professional organization, explained it thus:

> We have many responsibilities: to the farmer of course, because he hires us. To the animal—we are animal doctors,[1] after all. To society we have a responsibility; think about the effects of using antibiotics.... I mostly work in the pig industry, and they also want me to contribute to their quality assurance schemes..... But the interests of the animal and those of the farmer, are sometimes completely contradictory. And the same goes for the animal and society, right; the animal wants antibiotics, but society says; be careful with that. And I am in the middle of all of it and have to weigh all those contradictory interests... I have to find a balance there.

While Mark explains all of this, he draws the various actors involved—farmer, animal, society, industry—on a piece of paper. In the middle, he writes 'vet', drawing arrows from the middle to all these interested parties. When he finishes, he pauses and underscores the arrow towards the farmer: 'And then my problem is that only one of those pays my bill.' What emerges from Mark's illuminating drawing, is that good care for farm animals involves fostering multiple 'objects of care' (Law, 2010). When veterinarians care for

---

[1] In Dutch, the common word for veterinarian is *dierenarts*, which translates literally as animal doctor.

farm animals, they also care for the farmer's livelihood, the consumer who will eat their meat, the animal's ecology, including the animals around it, and the credibility of laws, regulations, and their profession.

In relation to these objects of care, 'good' and 'bad' forms of caring for animals emerge. These 'goods' and 'bads', however, often do not align. There are tensions: what is good for a sick animal might not be good for a society in which antimicrobial resistance is on the rise. They cannot be added together in a single, overall calculus, that ends in an obvious verdict. In theory, and on Mark's piece of paper, it is possible to lay out all these different stakes and normativities, what is good and bad in relation to what. Such a form of ordering performs the relation between the different values relevant to veterinary care as *dilemmas*, as alternatives that present themselves, about which a vet or the farmer has to make a *decision*. This staged relation between various interests and ideals mirrors the representation of ethical questions in philosophy. Classical ethics, firmly rooted in the liberal tradition, focuses the ethical moment in the situation, a bifurcation point, where an individual, a *moral agent*, asks themselves: 'What should I do?'

Veterinary ethics, like medical ethics more generally, has thus concerned itself with formulating the moral conundrums central to the work of the vet, often with the practical aim of formulating rules or guidelines such as the code for the veterinarian. Bernard Rollin (2006: 27), for instance, posits as the fundamental ethical question in veterinary medicine: 'Does the veterinarian have primary allegiance to client or animal?'. He contrasts the model of the mechanic (staging clients as owners of property) with the pediatrician (framing clients as parents of the animals in their care). I work in a different scholarly tradition, however; one set in anthropology and another set in science and technology studies (STS), which explores care in practice (Mol et al., 2010) as a form of 'empirical ethics' (Pols, 2015; Willems and Pols, 2010). Such studies have shown that although dramatic ethical dilemmas do occur in health care, they are relatively rare. Most of what happens in care practices is more mundane, smaller, and immediate. And it does not necessarily hinge on *decisions* staged in delineated moments: what do I do now? Instead, it has to do with getting things practically realized.

Health care practitioners generally do not *choose* between different, often contrasting *goods* and *bads*, but aim to somehow work with them through *tinkering* (Mol, 2008). This might mean establishing routines through which dilemmas do not present themselves in the first place, or developing skills that help to reconcile incongruous demands.[2] Along the way, health care workers as well as patients improvise as they encounter what is and isn't possible from where they stand—physically, emotionally, financially, or in some other practical way. Like human health care, veterinary care is a complex practice, set amidst contentious sets of relations and diverging commitments. This begs the question how veterinarians deal with such complexities in practice. In the

---

[2] See farmers' 'skilled craftwork' in practising biosecurity (Higgins et al., 2018). See also Driessen's (2017) notion of 'will-work', which entails care workers' inventive strategies of aligning 'wanting' of professions and dementia patients; and Brüggemann et al. (2019) on how health professionals prevent and find ways out of potentially abusive situations.

following, I outline two different practices of 'doing good' that vets are involved in; daily veterinary care and the monitoring schemes of the state and industry. As we will see, tinkering is crucial to the work of veterinarians, too. In particular, I suggest managing relations, a mostly tacit skill that consists of non-technical, 'social' tinkering, is at the heart of veterinary work.

Improvement through Advice

On a grey day in November 2020, I join veterinarian Lukas on one of his regular visits to a farm. He visits this farm every month and knows his way around. He does not wait for the farmer to come out, but changes into an overall and boots, and hands me some as well. Since my pair are way too big for me, I shamble behind him into the calf pen, where Lukas gives the youngest calves an anesthetic through a syringe on their head, so they can be dehorned later. When that is finished, we move inside the house, where we meet Jack, the farmer, in the kitchen. Before the visit, back at the veterinary clinic, Lukas showed me a printout of the milk data of Jack's cows, supplied by the dairy company. Lukas carefully studied the data on protein, ureum content, and milk yield, explaining what the numbers mean. He paid particular attention to the 'Somatic Cell Count' of the farm as a whole and of the individual cows; a high cell count is a sign that a cow is fighting off an infection (often in the udders) and thus an indication of poor milk quality and animal health. Lukas showed me that at the particular farm we are visiting that morning, the overall cell count is rather high; 'there is probably an issue with sub-clinical mastitis'. And now, at the kitchen table, after a short conversation on Jack's recent doctor's visits for his painful hip, Lukas brings up the topic of the cell count.

Jack sighs and mentions that he vaccinated his cows for mastitis for some time, but stopped doing that. Lukas counters: 'I think it would be a good idea to continue.' He puts up his hands as if in surrender: 'I understand it is a lot of money though. It's your choice, you are the boss.' Jack seems to resist the topic, he shrugs and smiles, seemingly thinking: 'that's right'. Lukas tries again: 'If you ask me, what is the best way to tackle this, then there are four things ... '—and he counts them down on his hands: '1. Continue to vaccinate; 2. Use disinfectant foam on the teats prior to milking [to prevent cross-infection]; 3. Place an antibacterial foot bath so the cows go through that before they re-enter the barn; and 4. Split up your herd and keep your cows with a higher cell count separate, so they don't infect the others. Did you ever do something like this?' Responding to the second recommendation, Jack replies: 'well, using the foam takes me 15 minutes per milk round, so an extra half an hour a day, I just don't have the time for this. And separating the herd ... I tried this once, but it just wasn't feasible logistically, with the buildings I have.' 'It's a lot of work, I understand', says Lukas, rounding off the topic for now. On his next visit, Lukas will bring up the topic again, inquiring whether Jack has thought about implementing any of the measures he suggested.

This described visit highlights how the modern veterinary practitioner is no longer just a practical problem solver, but a consultant of herd health, offering their expertise to improve farm management. A lot of the daily work of vets nowadays, then, consists of giving advice, on topics of concern that either they or the farmer bring to the table. For the vets I talked to, a lot of pride and joy comes from being able to improving the lives of animals and that of their farmers through changes in biosecurity measures, equipment, food regimens, or vaccination schemes. When I ask what she enjoys most in her work, Karin, a pig vet, replies:

> With the nicest pig farmers, I just have ... I learn so much from them. Really, they learn from me and I from them. These are the most fun visits, because then you can talk about the issues where I think we can still really make a difference and they will take it [the advice] up.

Karin aims to 'make a difference', but to what exactly? As is clear from the way Lukas thinks along with the financial decisions the farmer has to make, vets are not just concerned with increasing the health and welfare of farm animals; they are also enrolled in the economic project of running the farm. In this practice of improvement, normative notions of what is good care for animals and the farm co-exist, and entwine with, considerations about what is financially and practically possible.

In Karin's depiction of her work as veterinary consultant, the veterinarian is positioned alongside the farmer. Both are enacted as care givers of animals on the farm. But they are not equals. Although most of the time, veterinarians feel like they can make a difference, advising is also a less immediate, less concrete 'intervention' than treating a sick cow, or facilitating a difficult birth. Improvement through advice is a process; it does not just 'happen' on one visit. And sometimes, it does not happen at all. As Lukas' interaction with Jack indicates, there are definite limits to what changes vets can make in the role of consultant. They can advise on a particular course of action, but in the end, the farmer is 'the boss' and decides what to do. In other words, vets can try to motivate, challenge, facilitate, and encourage farmers to do something, but they cannot force them. For many vets, this lack of agency can be frustrating. As Suzan, another pig vet, explained:

> One of the farmers I work with uses a lot of antibiotics for his pigs. And this is just a matter on which we are not finding each other ... He just ... is not bothered by it. Even if he is too high legally on his daily dosage. At some point I tried it with a joke: 'Well if you get into the hospital, no antibiotic will work for you, you will be resistant.' And he just laughed. So this is someone, however you approach him, you don't get to him.... I have tried convincing him in various ways that he needs to, for instance, heat his barn before the piglets enter; he won't. Sometimes there are mice droppings in the pens, because he hasn't cleaned them. So he is too lax, and I have told him so. But everything stays as it is.

What are Suzan's options here? She can refuse to be this farmer's veterinary consultant—but then he will find another, perhaps less critical vet to do the work. She might have lived up to her principles, but she will also have lost a client. If she is too outspokenly critical, she will risk being fired, and what has she done for these animals then? Most vets who encounter similar situations—and many do—will continue to try, and try again, to push or gently nudge the farmer to make changes on the farm, however small. One of the ways in which a farmer can be made to recognize the veterinarian as an ally and working partner, is by improving the relationship between them. This is part of the work of veterinarians, as Klara a dairy vet, illustrates:

> My way of working is very personal, I get close. I experience the family life. I usually know the kids, their names, where they go to school, what they do. I visit newborns, I attend weddings … Birthdays I try to avoid. You should be able to get to a professional relationship, I try to create something of a distance, so you can keep saying the things you need to say, or to prevent them asking too much of you. Sometimes it's necessary to take a step back, and let your colleague go a few times.

Often, farmer and vet work together for many years. The relationship of a farm's principal veterinarian to their farmer is professional, but most vets do not forget that there is also a pastoral quality to their bond (Law, 2010). There is a danger in this attachment, of which vets are well aware: too much understanding for the farmer can make one blind to the problems on the farm with regards to animal welfare and food safety. But if there is no trust, one will not accomplish much either. Klara describes her own reflective practice of shaping the relation with 'her' farmers, in which both attachment and distance is crucial. A productive '(de/a)ttachment' ensures Klara can be a support to the farmer, while also upholding her responsibilities to the farm animals under her care. At the same time, and importantly, a good relation also makes farmers accountable to veterinarians; it makes it harder to set their advice aside.

Improvement through Inspection

An important way in which concerns other than economic profit are being served in farming is through rules and regulations. Farmers in the Netherlands operate in a dense regulatory landscape; their work is governed by regulations pertaining to, among other things, housing and farm design, feed quality, medication use, and animal transport, variously meant to protect animal welfare, consumer safety, public health, and the environment. To ensure the enforcement of these rules, farmers are legally obligated to register information about their animals' health, as well as births, deaths, and medical treatments. At the dairy factory and the slaughterhouse, the milk and carcasses they deliver are carefully checked for pathologies and anomalies. These registration practices give the Dutch state, as well as representatives of the pork and dairy industry, a detailed look into the farm, at both the herd level and the level of the individual animal. If one of the values checked is out of range, farmers risk fines, losing permits, and loss of income.

Veterinarians' conduct is likewise governed through such regulations, which depict, for instance, which antibiotics can be prescribed for what health problem and when. Veterinarians, however, also *participate* in the governing of farmers. For instance, vets have a legal duty to report abuses to the NVWA. And while in some other European countries, inspection is done by official veterinarians employed by the state, in the Netherlands, the task of checking European legal requirements pertaining to food safety and animal welfare is delegated to independent veterinarians. So-called 'assured veterinarians' [*geborgde dierenartsen*] have the legal authority to conduct inspections and uphold European legislation for food safety and animal welfare on the farms where they work. Moreover, dairy and pig companies often mobilize vets as part of their quality assurance schemes. As experts in animal health, and as professionals who already visit farms regularly, veterinarians are thus asked to be the eyes and ears of the various governing bodies that farmers are accountable to.

One of these monitoring systems, approved and monitored by government, is called the 'Cow Compass' (CC), which performs an integral risk analysis of animal health and welfare on a farm. With the CC, farmers can meet legal requirements as well as demands of Dutch dairy cooperations to have a certified veterinarian perform yearly assessments of the herd. As part of the CC, the veterinarian reviews the general farm data available, for instance the Somatic Cell Count, medication use, and the number of sick and deceased cows. They then visit the farm and check the animals, paying particular attention to their health, behaviour, as well as the characteristics of the barn. The vet records all this information by answering a long list of questions, following detailed instructions on how to score particular values. For instance, when rating the quality of 'walking space' on a scale of 1 to 5, they cannot give a score higher than 3 if a barn floor is made of concrete rather than rubber.

The CC compiles all these questions into seven categories that are relevant to the health and wellbeing for cows: milking process, feeding and water, housing and husbandry, animal welfare, work routines, animal health and youngstock. The programme then assigns each of these aspects a score, again on a scale of 1 to 5, where 1 is risky and 5 is risk-free, and visually depicts these in a seven-pointed 'spider web'. A score below 3 means there are risks that require attention. Based on the inspection, the veterinarian writes a report that is sent to both the farmer and dairy company. The CC website promises that 'repeating the *Cow Compass* yearly will create an improvement cycle'[3] for the farmer, as risks and points to work on are flagged. When I visit veterinarian Tanja in the clinic where she works, she shows me what the CC looks like on the computer:

> Here for instance you see [scrolls down] food management … and that on this farm that water quality is inadequate, walking space too … Anyway that's how you score

---

[3] https://www.koemonitor.nl/koekompas/, last accessed 30 March 2022.

it. [points on the screen] Here's antibiotic use ... that is for young stock 8,36. So an average calf on this farm will be on antibiotics for 8,36 days a year. That is rather high, compared to other farms. So these are all things ... I will flag this with the farmer. You try to see where there are problems in the building or in the animals' health, and where we can add something.

The CC spans all aspects of animal husbandry that are relevant to veterinary care in dairy farming. For this reason, Tanja thinks the CC is 'a good tool', which helps her bring aspects of management to the farmer's attention that are important to animal health and wellbeing. At the same time, she feels its obligatory nature makes it difficult for farmers to take home the lessons it offers:

> It is now forced down the throats of the people who didn't want to do it. And that is not always easy. But well, they want to supply milk, so they will have to. But it is more fun with someone who is motivated than with someone who considers this an obligation.

Many vets explained to me that monitoring systems such as the CC are an important source of friction and irritation at the farm. For instance, Peter explained he recently had to conduct the assessment for a farm he visits every two weeks. Not only does he already have an intimate knowledge of the animals and the characteristics of the farm, he continuously works together with the farmer on optimizing the cows' health and wellbeing. For him, on that farm, the imposed 'improvement cycle' of the CC felt unnecessary, a disruption, and a waste of time—time for which the farmer pays the financial consequences. Rather than supporting his work, such obligatory assessments, then, entail activities that 'often seem "other" to the daily on-going care of the cattle', creating 'discrete moments of accountability that may displace or at least colonize embodied practices of "care"' (Singleton, 2010: 237).

Moreover, tensions ensue from the fact that the CC is not only meant to help the farmer and vet *improve* farm animal care; it is also an instrument to *prove* something to other parties. Schemes such as the CC provide the dairy industry with information of animal welfare at the farms their products originate from. This allows them to show the public and the government that their production systems abide by food safety and welfare standards. Although there are officially no direct consequences for the farmer if the CC results in bad evaluations, what will be done with the recorded information remains uncertain in the elaborate, complex, and shifting regulatory landscape around livestock production. Farmers suspect that the procedure that claims to help them, is meant to control them. Indeed, a vet told me that if the NVWA decides to check on a farm, the CC will be one of the first reports they will request as part of their inspection.

Through governance instruments such as the CC, then, the livestock industry, farmers, *and* vets are held accountable in specific ways to consumers, government, and ultimately the animal. But while performing their tasks of writing reports and scoring aspects on the farm, vets also become accountable to farmers for the nuisance and insecurity that these legislation and quality assurance schemes cause. Often, it falls upon vets to explain these schemes and their changes to farmers. Thereby, vets risk becoming the 'face' of the rules on the farm. One of the ways in which veterinarians mitigate this risk is by highlighting the performative nature of governance assemblages and the role both farmer and vet play within it. Rather than telling the farmer: 'It is not okay how you are treating these animals', several vets told me they would say something like 'what you are doing here is against the law' followed by 'hey, if the state inspectorate pays a visit, we will both get a huge fine'. Some would explicitly say: 'I'll put my inspector's hat on', and then proceed to assess the farm. With such remarks, the vet emerges as equally constrained to the farmer; both have to play their parts assigned to them by forces outside of their control. The critique, moreover, is delegated to 'the rules' and 'the law'. By separating themselves from their performative tasks, it is not the vet him/herself that asks the farmer to change; it is the state inspectorate, an absent-presence that threatens to hold both the farmer and vet accountable.

It is through such creative tinkering with words and positions that governance can be made sensitive to the specific embodied care work happening on farms. Although challenging for the vet, they are an important part of what makes governance 'work', how rules and regulations actually enact improvement on a farm. When I asked my informants whether it would be better if a veterinarian employed by the state or the industry performed the inspections, some predicted that bringing an 'outsider' to the farm, 'who would act as a policeman', would cause even more frustration and tensions. It is because of the trusted relation between vet and farmer that state supervision becomes more effective. A farmer's principal veterinarian is in a key position to translate legal and industry standards and regulations to the specificity of the farm and the farmer's situation.

Conclusion

In this chapter I have explored veterinary care in practice. I have shown how veterinarians often take on the role as advisor; but also increasingly figure as the farmer's inspector. Describing these different roles that vets take on in livestock production highlights that vets are not only juggling different *forms* of the good, but also are part of different practices of *doing good*. In farm animal care, the farmer and vet usually appear as a team. They work together on the health and wellbeing of animals, but also ensure that the farm as a business keeps running. While ethicists and animal activists elevate the relation to the animal as the primary ethical relationship, in practice veterinarians are entangled in, and operate in a web of relations. It is in tinkering with these complex relations, I suggest, that a different form of veterinary ethics is 'done'. This form of practised ethics, of care, is not so much focused on achieving a 'good', but on continuously changing a practice for the 'better'. It is not premised on judgement, but on improvement. It is a matter of trying over and over again.

Of course, this care practice has limits, risks, and challenges. In particular, vets struggle with the fact that they contribute their expertise mainly through giving advice to the client-farmer, who ultimately makes the final decisions. Therefore, the extent to which they can make a difference depends on the quality of the attachment to the farmer. It is this relationship, therefore, that is carefully managed.

In contrast to the uncertainty and slow tinkering that characterizes such care, legal rules and industry regulations hold the promise of control, transparency, and accountability. Increasingly, the veterinarian emerges as part of a governance apparatus, and is positioned as the farmer's auditor. At stake is keeping up standards on food safety and animal welfare. Potentially, the activities around inspection provide veterinarians with different ways of addressing concerns with the farmer, and ways of making a difference. In practice, however, they are also a source of friction, interfering with the work alliance between farmer and vet.

Vets' skill in tinkering with relations, once again, fills the 'gaps between [the] heterogenous assemblages' (Suzuki, 2021) in which they are involved. In his analysis of the work of a veterinarian in the culling of cattle during the 2001 Foot and Mouth Disease outbreak in the United Kingdom, John Law describes the nature of veterinary care as 'an improvised and experimental choreography for holding together and holding apart different and relatively non-coherent versions of care, their objects and their subjectivities' (Law, 2010: 69). This remains a relevant insight although the challenges veterinarians face in performing this choreography smoothly, I suggest, shed light on why vets rarely 'resist' in the way the Caring Vets, with whom I started this chapter, envision. Identifying, and speaking out against animal abuses would mean stepping out of the relations that make up daily veterinary care including, crucially, the relation to the animal. It is a mode of doing good that does not fit the care that veterinarians are involved in on a daily basis. In fact, it threatens the very relations that practice depends on. I suggest that exploring empirically what 'care' becomes in veterinary work on farms, and detailing how veterinarians navigate between contrasting values 'on the ground', can help strengthen veterinary care. Not by holding it up to abstract codes and standards, but by improving it on its own terms. By exploring these terms, this chapter hopes to have made a start in doing so.

References

Brüggemann, J., Persson, A., & Wijma, B. (2019). Understanding and preventing situations of abuse in health care—Navigation work in a Swedish palliative care setting. *Social Science & Medicine, 222*, 52–8. doi: 10.1016/j.socscimed.2018.12.035.

Driessen, A. (2017). Sociomaterial will-work: Aligning daily wanting in Dutch dementia care.' In J. Boldt & F. Krause (Eds.), *Care in healthcare: Reflections on theory and practice* (pp. 111 –133). London: Palgrave Macmillan.

Higgins, V. et al. (2018). Devolved responsibility and on-farm biosecurity: Practices of biosecure farming care in livestock production. *Sociologia Ruralis, 58(1)*, 20–39.

KNMvD. (2010). Code voor de Dierenarts. Viewed 11 August 2021, <https://www.knmvd.nl/code-voor-dierenarts/>.

Law, J. (2010). Care and killing: Tensions in veterinary practice.' In A. Mol, I. Moser, & J. Pols (Eds.), *Care in Practice: On tinkering in clinics, homes and farms* (pp. 57–72). Bielefeld: Transcript Verlag.

Mol, A. (2008). *The logic of care: Health and the problem of patient choice*. London: Routledge.

Mol, A., Moser, I., & Pols, J. (Eds.) (2010). *Care in practice: On tinkering in clinics, homes and farms*. Bielefeld: Transcript Verlag.

Nieuwe Oogst (2017, 29 June). 'Dierenartsenorganisatie wijst The Caring Vets terecht.' Retrieved from https://www.nieuweoogst.nl/nieuws/2017/06/29/dierenartsenorganisatie-wijst-the-caring-vets-terecht.

NRC (2017, 26 June). 'Resist, veterinarian. This is not animal welfare!' Retrieved from https://www.nrc.nl/nieuws/2017/06/26/kom-in-verzet-dierenarts-dit-is-geen-dierenwelzijn-11289973-a1564575?t=1627893573.

Offringa, C. (1983). Ars veterinaria: ambacht, professie, beroep. Sociologische theorie en historische praktijk. *Tijdschrijft Voor Geschiedenis, 93*(3), 407–32.

Pols, J. (2015). Towards an empirical ethics in care: Relations with technologies in health care. *Medicine, Health Care and Philosophy, 18*(1), 81–90.

Rollin, B.E. (2006). *An introduction to veterinary medical ethics: Theory and cases*, 2nd Edition. Ames: Blackwell Publishing.

Singleton, V. (2010). Good farming: Control or care? In A. Mol, J. Moser, & J. Pols (Eds.), *Care in Practice: On tinkering in clinics, homes and farms* (pp. 235–256). Bielefeld: Transcript Verlag.

Singleton, V. (2012). When contexts meet: Feminism and accountability in UK cattle farming. *Science Technology and Human Values, 37*(4), 404–33.

Suzuki, W. (2021). Improvising care: Managing experimental animals at a Japanese laboratory. *Social Studies of Science, 51*(5), 729–749.

Willems, D. & J. Pols. (2010). Goodness! The empirical turn in health care ethics. *Medische Antropologie, 22*(1), 161–70.

CHAPTER 20

STOCKFREE'S SHORT SHADOW

Shifting Food Systems Towards Sustainability by Re-thinking Veganism as a Performative Practice of Production

STEFFEN HIRTH

FOOD production and consumption are without a doubt in crisis. What makes 'good' food is an often fiercely led debate. Self-identifying as 'a vegan' naturally evokes a whole range of presumptions in other people. That many presumptions are negative (e.g. Cole and Morgan, 2011) may normatively obfuscate the biomaterial potential of vegan foods to help solve the climate, extinction, and biosafety crises we face (Hirth, 2019a). In this contribution, I suggest that part of the problem is a general focus on the identity of 'vegans' while the biomateriality and organization of vegan food provisioning practices is neglected. To gain understanding of veganism beyond an identity or lifestyle associated with consumption, I shed light on the vegan horticultural practice of stockfree organic agriculture (SOA) which omits animal by-products in crop cultivation. By examining it as a biomaterial and organizing practice, I focus on veganism, not as an *-ism*, (an ideology, identity, or lifestyle individuals adopt), but as a wider food practice and its potential to help overcome an unsustainable food system.

In the current food system, 'bad' food is a practical routine as much as 'good' or 'better' food a distinctive lifestyle choice. Conventional, non-seasonal, and highly processed ingredients from remote places and meals high in meat and dairy produced by poorly paid workers are the norm. It seems lucky that deciding against that is increasingly an option through alternative products. But should 'organic' and 'plant-based' consumption be an identity some people adopt while others are not willing to? And if the latter are just not able to change their lives, is it sufficient to enable them to make that choice? Should maintaining Earth as a relatively 'safe operating space' (Rockström et al., 2009) really be an 'option' among other options on the menu? Drawing on practice and organizing approaches, this contribution questions tendencies in food sustainability debates by which the shift towards 'good' food rather seems to depend on consumers' lifestyle choices than the types of foods made available in the first place and how their production is collectively organized. This contribution: (1) explores shortcomings in conceiving the practice of veganism and its transformative leverage as a consumer identity and lifestyle only, and (2) reconceptualizes it by reference to vegan agricultural practices as a wider, performative practice embedded in provisioning.

The notion of vegan food practices, I argue, may help to emphasize that, rather than just changes in consumption, reorganizing practices towards a sustainable food system will require changes in production, particularly degrowing the meat and dairy sector and conventional agricultural practices and replacing them with new ways of organizing food. Emerging from the vegan movement, one such alternative is SOA, also referred to as vegan organic, veganic, or biocyclic-vegan agriculture. Unlike animal-based organic and conventional agriculture, this horticultural method and certification forbids the use of animal by-products, such as manure or bone meal, as fertilizers in crop cultivation (Hagemann and Potthast, 2015; Hirth, 2021; Schmutz and Foresi, 2017; Seymour and Utter, 2021). By outlining the biomaterial specifics of foods cultivated in this way, I will show how SOA goes beyond the conventional framing of the term 'vegan' as an identity of consumers or any plant product, and shifts it towards a performative practice. I showcase the particular processes, relations, and materiality of organizing food veganly, and how this crosses the boundary of how 'vegan' is conventionally defined. The theoretical argument derived from that focus on processes, relations, and materiality is directed against food sustainability debates implying that sustainable transformations instead depend on behaviour change of individuals, adopting the 'right' identities, and living up to their values. In short, sustainability requires different food practices, not just changed dietary identities and lifestyles.

In line with practice and material turns, scholars of organizational food studies have recently emphasized that it matters not only how humans organize food, but also how food organizes our lives and practices considering that it 'has biomaterial qualities that invite, allow, demand, or resist certain forms of organizing' (Moser et al., 2021: 176). Here, I specifically focus on the differences in biomaterial qualities and fitted organizing practices along the lines of, first, animal-sourced or plant foods and, secondly, conventional or organic cultivation. Whether and how these biomaterialities are considered and affiliated with ostensibly immaterial identities and values of individual eaters matters for the pace and extent of food system transformations. Compared to plant foods, the biomateriality of feeding farm animals involves a disproportionately high land and resource use also referred to as 'Livestock's Long Shadow' (FAO, 2006). Reorganizing agri- and culinary culture as to favour plant rich foods is thus an effective lever to reduce the food system's social and ecological footprint. For example, the EAT-Lancet commission on a healthy diet within planetary boundaries emphasizes the need of 'substantially reducing *consumption* of animal source foods' (Willett et al., 2019: 3; emphasis added). However, in emphasizing reductions of consumption rather than production a pattern becomes visible by which the scope of action is limited to changes in demand. Transformative debates tend to focus on plant rich *diets* or vegan*ism*, rather than on reducing animal agriculture, wider food practices, and vegan provision. This implicitly renders change as a mere function of dietary choice and consumer lifestyles and veganism as an eating practice. But as I have argued before, veganism exhausts itself neither in eating nor in individuals' identities and lifestyles (Hirth, 2021). Against this background, I discuss how veganism conceived as a performative practice, not an identity or ideology, may help to better connect debates on dietary changes with the materiality of production and the common planetary interest in sustainable food systems.

Indeed, ever more salient symptoms of planetary crisis, such as the changing climate, deforestation, soil degradation, polluted over-fished oceans, and biodiversity decline at the rate of mass extinction, remind us of the urgency to change food systems (Ceballos et al., 2015; IPCC, 2019; Worm et al., 2006). With pandemic breakouts being facilitated by natural habitat destruction and quick viral transmission through air travel, the socio-ecology behind the COVID-19 crisis is linked to human domination over ecosystems and the globalized economy and society (IPES-Food, 2020; Settele et al., 2020). This suggests that we are already losing Earth as a relatively 'safe operating space' for us and our food systems (Rockström et al., 2009; Willett et al., 2019). It is also known that animal agriculture's large environmental footprint, and fossil fuel-based agricultural intensification play a major role in these crises and has lead global science and policy consortia to suggest societal shifts towards agroecology and plant-rich diets (e.g. IAASTD, 2009; IPCC, 2019; Willett et al., 2019). However, the prominent FAO (2006) report *Livestock's Long Shadow* did not result in immediate and direct problematization of animal agriculture (Bristow and Fitzgerald, 2011) and little has changed in practice.

In many so-called 'developed' countries, so-called 'plant-based' foods have gained undeniable salience in media, food industry, and retail, but they remain attributed to the moralized identity of a societal minority. Well aware of the stigma that comes with the term 'vegan' (Cole and Morgan, 2011), businesses often choose the innocuous 'plant-based' when they mean vegan food. Likewise, self-identification as 'vegan' is not for everyone—even if they are open to the idea of abstaining from animal-sourced foods. I have argued that tendencies to avoid a clear identity in public discourse are, perhaps paradoxically, symptomatic of a food (sustainability) debate that revolves around identity and little else (Hirth, 2019a). That the lines of dispute on 'good' or 'bad' food are centred on individuals' dietary identities—ranging from 'meat eaters' (carnists) to vegans—is paralleled by policy consortia's reductive focus on the demand lever which makes change dependent on shifts in dietary identities. However, recent research drawing on practice theory approaches suggests that identity and its divisive character could be a barrier to the widespread adoption of sustainable food practices (Dutkiewicz and Dickstein, 2021; Hirth, 2019b; 2021; Kurz et al., 2020). Therefore, I regard it as part of the problem that key debates seem to centre on dietary shifts, and thus variables that influence consumer decisions, rather than the actual output of animal agriculture in absolute terms, let alone the power-related political economic implications of a reduction (Fuchs et al., 2016).

By re-thinking veganism as a performative practice, this contribution explores how vegan food practices' *short shadow*—their biomaterial quality of requiring less land and resources (as none is used for the metabolic upkeep of farm animals)—can help address the sustainability problems deeply rooted in the wider organization of food provision, not just dietary identities. The following section summarizes the literature that explicitly conceives veganism as a practice and sketches the implications and pitfalls of conflating it with identity.

Approaching Veganism as Practice Not Identity

Practices are a theoretical construct directed against the assumption human subjects act rationally, autonomously, and unaffected by their social setting. Describing a social pattern of doing, a practice confines subjects or practitioners without ever subjecting them in absolute terms. Practices have been used to explain social stability and change in the context of discourse (Foucault 1980), everyday routines (Schatzki et al., 2001; Warde, 2005), and performativity (Barad, 2007; Butler, 1993; Gibson-Graham, 2006). As veganism has been examined with practice approaches and has relevance for 'materially constituting a sustainable food transition' (Twine, 2018: 166), I now rehearse the advantages for such a transition of conceiving veganism as performed practice, rather than moralized identity.

That veganism is often understood as an identity, rather than a practice, complicates its definition by directing the gaze from intersubjective action to subjective perception and self-representation. Self-identifying as 'a vegan' naturally evokes a whole range of presumptions in other people. Dutkiewicz and Dickstein (2021) emphasize that automatically conflating veganism with an animal rights ethic is inappropriate as there are different ethical bases for veganism. Therefore, their practice-based approach advises academics and activists to deploy a 'clear, neutral definition of veganism as a pattern of action'; their attempt at 'stripping "veganism" of any inherent ideological or political significance' (p. 14) aims at avoiding linguistic confusion caused by politically motivated debates denying that people exhibiting racist, sexist, or speciesist behaviour can also be vegans. That fascists, for example, can be vegans (Forchtner and Tomic, 2017; Wrenn, 2017)—undesirable as it may be for other vegans—is a social phenomenon of empirical importance which suggests a definition of the term vegan as a mere 'conduct-descriptive' practice of not eating or using any animal products (Dutkiewicz and Dickstein, 2021).

Another problematic consequence of veganism conceived as identity, is that a strong association with a minority identity may create tensions and anxieties when confronted with people of dissimilar attitude (or even with 'vegaphobia' see Cole and Morgan, 2011). This may also prevent people from performing vegan food practices in the first place. Addressing the efficacy of policies and behavioural campaigns aiming at societal shifts towards sustainability, Kurz et al. (2020) suggest that strong identification with veganism, or other 'moralized minority practice identities' (p. 87), may hamper those shifts as, for nonpractitioners, certain 'identity-defining behaviors might seem more self-defining than people are willing for them to be' (p. 95). They conclude that effective campaigns must offer easy ways to try out a practice without forcing a moralized identity upon them.

Here, I use practices to understand eating beyond individual food choices as a form of routinized, socially embedded behaviour (Warde, 2016) which also connotes that 'provisioning and consumption are inextricably entwined' (Barnett et al., 2011: 72). As veganism exhausts itself neither in eating nor in individuals' identities, I define it as a *food* practice, rather than just an *eating* practice (Hirth, 2019b; 2021). This broadens the scope to explore producer dimensions of vegan food practices as will be exemplified by the set of cultivation methods interchangeably referred to as SOA.

Conventionally, the term 'vegan', either describes an eating or lifestyle practice that involves the identity of being 'a vegan' or it is used as an essential property of plant foods—a carrot is seen as vegan per se. SOA challenges this conception in that its material-discursive practices omit animal by-products as fertilizers in crop cultivation. From this perspective, a carrot is not vegan per se; that status rather depends on the question whether it was nourished free from animal manure, bone meal, or other animal derivatives typically used for soil replenishment (Hirth, 2021). Re-thinking veganism in these terms channels our view away from a consumer identity or an essentialized property towards the *processes of materially cultivating* veganism—both in the agronomic and cultural practice sense.

A focus on processes of materialization resonates with Karen Barad's (2007) posthumanist, performative approach to 'material-discursive practices' in which humans are not the sole carriers of practices and nonhuman agencies are part of the boundary-making practices that are formative of matter and meaning (see also Cooren, (2020) for the context of organizational studies). The next section will outline the difference SOA makes by being the product of—in Barad's terms—'intra-acting' and 'entangled' human and nonhuman agencies, for example, human growers working with specific plants and their biomaterial capacity to recover nutrients in the soil. It is due to these soil-maintaining intra-actions, and the 'biomateriality of food' and its 'distinctive role in shaping and affecting organizing and organizations' (Moser et al., 2021: 175), that SOA can dispense with fossil and animal fertilizers and, thereby, omit some forms of violence intrinsic to animal-based agricultural practices. Later, I apply that notion of violence to discuss the detrimental effects of animal agriculture on biosafety and conservation. These examples will provide the context for some brief reflections on vegan food practices, and how they may be conceptualized to help overcome the political challenge of shifting food systems towards healthy, just, sustainable, and convivial practices.

Stockfree Sustainability: Omitting Violent Food Practices

Introducing stockfree organic agriculture (SOA) as a biomaterial practice involves distinguishing it from the various forms of violence entailed by conventional modes of organizing animals and crop cultivation. This includes violence against domesticated, 'wild', and human animals, as well as the life of the soil. Also referred to as veganic or vegan organic, SOA must be seen as a *value-driven* form of crop cultivation because it applies agroecological methods while deliberately refraining from using animal by-products (Schmutz and Foresi, 2017). Thus, the term stock*free* denotes a normative difference to stock*less* agriculture which depicts farmers who just happen to have no farm animals and may still use manure from other farms to fertilize crops.

As such, stockfree organic is intrinsically different, first, from conventional agriculture—based on minimal legal requirements—and, second, from 'conventional organic', that is, animal-based organic agriculture which is conventional from an SOA-perspective (Hirth, 2019b). While animal-based organic agriculture is dedicated to maintaining the life of the soil by forbidding synthetic fertilizers and pesticides applied in conventional farming, both involve the killing and exploitation of animals and, through that focus, have a high land footprint. To reflect on the intrinsic violence in current animal-based farming practices without simply drawing on the obvious aspect of slaughter, I will outline the ethical foundation of the Vegan Organic Network (VON), (the certifying body for SOA in the United Kingdom), and the specific practices emanating therefrom. Their ethics is grounded by a rejection of animal-based agriculture, and particularly 'chemical' farming's historical and present relation to industrialized mass killing of both human and nonhuman beings. That history, and the history of synthetic fertilizers and pesticides in particular, cannot be told without Jewish chemist Fritz Haber (1868–1934) who won the Nobel prize in 1918 for inventing the Haber-Bosch process, which to this day is used to fix nitrogen from the air (Smil, 2011).

In the First World War, Haber led the German development of gas-based weapons for use in trench warfare. He also developed pesticides for Degesch, the German society for pest control, which after Haber's death were not only used to kill off nonhuman 'pests' in agriculture, but also in the form of Zyklon B to murder Jews, Slavs, Leftists, Disabled, Sinti and Romanies, Homosexuals, and other minorities in Nazi Germany's extermination camps (Kalthoff and Werner, 1998). Without intending to lose sight of human culprits and victims, it is worthwhile accounting for the nonhuman agency of pesticides and their effect on the life of the soil. Even if their most inhumane use during the Holocaust is a thing of the past (or is it?), the chemical agency of pesticides and the lethal work they are capable of, largely remains the same. Killing unwanted insects, rodents, weeds, and fungi has the collateral effect of also killing worms and the microbial life of the soil important to its fertility. If the main target is simply to produce maximal amounts of food, however, a loss of soil vitality does not matter as long as synthetic fertilizers are available to become the artificial nutrient medium for plant growth on relatively inanimate soil.

Taking a food security angle, this offers little consolation for future generations considering that the fossil fuels driving that nutrient flow are finite, and given that topsoil, taking a (too) long time to replenish, is practically finite. Another important angle is a posthumanist perspective which refrains from making humans the single source of agency or addressee of ethical concern (Barad, 2003; Cooren, 2020). In this case, the biochemical agency of pesticides and synthetic fertilizers which industrialized, intensive agriculture is based on, and the slaughter which animal-based agriculture intrinsically relies on (although cellular agriculture is trying to change that see Stephens et al., 2018), play major parts in the ecological and social crises we—all life on Earth—face. Considering the various forms of violence, both in society and in agriculture, chemical farming is historically linked to, it may be surprising to learn that Zyklon B, (then under the name of Cyanosil), was a licensed plant 'protectant' in Germany until 2001 (BVL, 2018). In the face of 'an ever-growing population', the company that continued to produce the pesticide after the war today assures us that '[l]ooking to the future, the family company will be living up to its responsibility to help safeguard global food supplies' (Detia-Degesch, 2021). The particularly detestable part of their history, the biochemical agency of their pesticides used in extermination camps, is not mentioned on the company's website. All the while remaining largely unchanged, that biochemical agency is what conventional farming practically draws on.

The founders of VON, however, emphasize that 'good' food must be 'satisfying both physically and psychologically' and thus 'omits the killing element'. Due to traumatic experiences in their own family history during the Holocaust, their advocacy of SOA is an explicit resistance to 'chemical farming' and its perverse synergetic entanglement with the Holocaust (Hirth, 2019b: 165–7). While SOA rejects the use of chemicals or animal derivatives, it also relies on important 'more-than-human' (Whatmore, 2006), 'biomaterial' (Moser et al., 2021) forms of agency to function. For example, it is a fascinating capacity of chicory, which has roots that go 3 metres down, to bring phosphates and potassium up from the subsoil, where these nutrients then become available for less deep-rooted crops. Chicory is just one of many examples for green manures which SOA draws on to replenish soil fertility; the legume family, to give another, maintains the nitrogen cycle (Hall and Tolhurst, 2015; Hirth, 2019b). The agency of green manures thus affect how SOA is organized as a biomaterial practice. Rather than producing crops in monoculture nourished by synthetic fertilizers, SOA cultivation relies on a socio-spatial and temporal arrangement of crops that respects their diversity, their different needs for nutrients in the soil, and their different biomaterial capacities to interact with soil and other plants.

Another key factor is to build up humus soil by maturing compost to a degree that it becomes a long-lasting 'nutrient battery' which then requires plants to actively access nutrients by producing root acids, rather than being 'force-fed' water-soluble synthetic fertilizers. This is said to strengthen crops' immune system and make over-fertilization impossible (Anders and Eisenbach, 2017). As a practice, SOA actively works with the multiplicity of remarkable qualities and agencies certain plant species and varieties are endowed with. According to its proponents and initial evidence from field experiments (Eisenbach et al., 2018; 2019), soils can thus be maintained and productive without intrinsic violence against human or nonhuman animals. To date, visions linked to permaculture or small-scale farming (e.g. Smaje, 2020) tend to presuppose that some degree of animal agriculture is desirable, if not a natural, biomaterial necessity (for an exception from the SOA movement see *The Vegan Book of Permaculture*; Burnett, 2014). The presumption is that manure of large mammals or birds cannot be dispensed with in soil maintenance, although even the term 'green *manure*' suggests that decomposing plants can also drive the nutrient replenishment otherwise attributed to the manure of animals.

So far, there is no long-term evidence for or against that stance, but it is one which debates on 'good' agro-ecological practice will have to grapple with in the future. A practical reason for why this matters is that the growth of plant milks and plant meats already affects animal-based meat and dairy production. As Seymour and Utter (2021: 19) note, 'this raises questions for the future availability of the dominant animal-based fertilizers'. Thus, a degrowth of animal agriculture is needed to prevent climate breakdown and further extinction but a controlled organization of that degrowth also requires openness for and further research on consistently stockfree alternatives such as SOA.

Discussion: Towards Stockfree Food Practices

Despite their incremental normalization, vegan and vegetarian diets can still lead to fierce debates between people with different dietary identities. I argue that overemphasizing dietary identity and the implicit moralization of 'good' food choices hinder effective academic, public, and policy debates on the material and organizational characteristics of sustainable food practices. Conserving the material conditions for thriving on this planet should naturally be a primary concern. Provided animal agriculture's 'long shadow' (FAO, 2006) is accepted as a biomaterial reality, even people with dissimilar dietary identities, values, and political attitudes (e.g. no versus better meat) have nonetheless a *converging* practical interest in, first, reducing animal agriculture's absolute output to an ecologically safe level and, secondly, undoing the favourable conditions globalized, intensified methods have created for disease outbreaks (Wienhues and Hirth, 2021). The latter is worth some additional reflections on the 'long shadow' animal agriculture casts on biosafety and biodiversity conservation.

It is part of animal-sourced foods biomateriality that, on average, 10 grams of plant protein in form of feed crops are needed to produce 1 gram of animal protein (Reijnders and Soret, 2003: 665). Thus, 9 grams serve the farm animal's energy needs, dissipate into the environment, and are lost for human nutrition. These conversion losses of nutritional energy not only create feed-food competition compromising human food security, but are also an indicator of resource use (e.g. fertilizers and pesticides), land use, and thus pressure on ecosystems. Producing 1 gram of meat protein, for example, uses 6–17 times more land than 1 gram of soya protein (Reijnders and Soret, 2003: 665; see also Poore and Nemecek, 2018). That disproportionate land use matters in the context of biosafety.

Concerned virologists and biologists have highlighted that risks from coronaviruses and other zoonotic diseases are increased by human appropriation of land and the globalized economy. By citing sources from before 2019, I want to emphasize that scientists have been addressing how human domination over and destruction of ecosystems created perfect conditions for the outbreak of pandemics long before COVID-19. Next to isolating and habitat-compressing land use influences through deforestation, agriculture, water projects, and urbanization (Aguirre and Tabor, 2008; Bosco-Lauth and Bowen, 2013; Calisher et al., 2006), there are proximity-creating influences such as global air travel, (which enables viruses to spread far and quickly), but also domestic animal farming, exotic animal farming, animal transportation, keeping endangered species in captivity, and even keeping dogs and cats as pets creating favourable conditions for transmission or mutation of coronaviruses (Fornace et al., 2013; Vinnerås et al., 2012; Vlasova and Saif, 2013).

The increased public awareness of the biosafety problems of COVID-19, and the socio-ecology behind them, also gives additional momentum to debates of nature conservation (IPES-Food, 2020; Settele et al., 2020). Due to its disproportionate land use, reducing animal agriculture holds possibilities for stopping the destruction of ecosystems and lessening the pressure on them (e.g. Sun et al., 2022). The EAT-Lancet commission (Willett et al., 2019) has raised awareness for the necessity of dietary change towards plants and particularly away from red meat. They demand a ban on 'future land conversion of natural ecosystems into farmland' (p. 23) and suggest a conservation strategy by which half of the Earth's surface is put under protection. While this reveals good intentions, it is insufficient in two ways. First, the focus is on reductions in the *consumption* of animal-sourced foods, while it is production that needs to decrease for actual change. Secondly, preventing future land-use change is not the same as reverting the past conversions, that is, turning farmland *back* into nature reserves.

Both points would require absolute reductions of animal agriculture and would significantly challenge the power relations (Fuchs et al., 2016), first, behind animal agriculture's normality and, secondly, capitalism's imperative towards growth. A transition towards a sustainable food system will require the abolition of certain organizing practices and the birth of new ones. However, the focus on changing dietary identities hinders the relational and political economic depth that would be necessary for organizing and materializing this transition. Recently, the economic disruption through COVID-19 led to optimism over falling emissions and anecdotal 'evidence' on nature's resurgence, such as wild goats roaming town centres, but this apparent recovery should rather be seen as a 'circumstantial occurrence' of the lockdown situation than a significant step towards sustainability (Searle and Turnbull, 2020). Without action at a systemic level, changed practices are likely to 'bounce back' (Ehgartner and Boons, 2020). The food-biodiversity-biosafety complex requires a clear acknowledgement that it is not simply eating practices that need to change but that the material practices at production level need to change, including the degrowth of animal agriculture, which requires systemic changes to the dominant growth-based political economy. What matters from a perspective of organizational ecology is how agricultural production can shift away from corporate organizations based on extractivism, growth, and private profits, to organizations that cultivate the commons through agrinatural food provisioning practices. Such posthumanist food provision would require a new kind 'of economically productive practice' and 'curiosity-driven [and value-driven] knowledge practice' that does not 'coincide with the profit motive of cognitive capitalism' (Braidotti, 2019: 53).

Unless hampered by moralized identity debates, stockfree organic agriculture may bear the material-discursive potential to develop into an agrinatural revolution that provides food for everyone and restores that relatively 'safe operating space' Earth provides us. Reasons for conceptualizing veganism as practice, not identity, are: its clear, consistent definition as a pattern of action (Dutkiewicz and Dickstein, 2021); ease of adoption without moralized identification forced upon new practitioners (Kurz et al., 2020); as well as the inclusion of producers and a focus on processes, relations, and materiality of vegan food practices (Hirth, 2021). What matters ecologically is that somebody has a vegan meal or a grower performs vegan cultivation practices, not whether either of them self-identifies as 'vegan'. Restoring planetary safety does not necessarily require everybody to become 'a vegan', but it may require most people to have vegan meals most of the time. In recognition of livestock's long and stockfree's short shadow, I think that an undogmatic, and yet value-driven, practice approach to vegan or stockfree food practices, performed by vegans and nonvegans, producers and consumers alike, may help with the necessary systemic shifts towards just and sustainable land use, safe and diverse naturalcultural habitats, and a convivial planet.

References

Aguirre, A.A. & Tabor, G.M. (2008). Global factors driving emerging infectious diseases. *Annals of the New York Academy of Sciences, 1149*, 1–3. https://doi.org/10.1196/annals.1428.052

Anders, A. & Eisenbach, J. (2017). Biocyclic-vegan agriculture. *Growing Green International, 39*, 32–4.

Barad, K. (2003). Posthumanist performativity: Toward an understanding of how matter comes to matter. *Signs: Journal of women in culture and society* 28, 801–831.

Barad, K. (2007). *Meeting the universe halfway: Quantum physics and the entanglement of matter and meaning*. Durham, London: Duke University Press.

Barnett, C. et al. (2011). *Globalizing responsibility: The political rationalities of ethical consumption*. Chichester: Wiley-Blackwell.

Bosco-Lauth, A.M. & Bowen, R.A. (2013). Biological significance of bats as a natural reservoir of emerging viruses. In S.K. Singh (Ed.), *Viral infections and global change* (pp. 195–211). Hoboken: John Wiley and Sons, Ltd. https://doi.org/10.1002/9781118297469.ch11

Braidotti, R. (2019). A theoretical framework for the critical posthumanities. *Theory, Culture and Society, 36*, 31–61. https://doi.org/10.1177/0263276418771486

Bristow, E. & Fitzgerald, A.J. (2011). Global Climate Change and the Industrial Animal Agriculture Link: The Construction of Risk. *Society & Animals* 19, 205–224. https://doi.org/10.1163/156853011X578893

Burnett, G. (2014). *The Vegan Book of Permaculture*. East Meon: Permanent Publications.

Butler, J. (1993). *Bodies that matter: On the discursive limits of 'sex'*. New York: Routledge.

BVL – Bundesamt für Verbraucherschutz und Lebensmittelsicherheit. (2018). Abgelaufene Pflanzenschutzmittel. https://www.bvl.bund.de/SharedDocs/Downloads/04_Pflanzenschutzmittel/Abgelaufene_PSM.html.

Calisher, C.H. et al. (2006). Bats: Important reservoir hosts of emerging viruses. *Clinical Microbiology Reviews, 19*, 531–45. https://doi.org/10.1128/CMR.00017-06

Ceballos, G. et al. (2015). Accelerated modern human–induced species losses: Entering the sixth mass extinction. *Science Advances, 1*, e1400253. https://doi.org/10.1126/sciadv.1400253

Cole, M. & Morgan, K. (2011). Vegaphobia: Derogatory discourses of veganism and the reproduction of speciesism in UK national newspapers. *The British Journal of Sociology, 62*, 134–53. https://doi.org/10.1111/j.1468-4446.2010.01348.x

Cooren, F. (2020). Beyond entanglement: (Socio-) materiality and organization studies. *Organization Theory,* —https://doi.org/10.1177/2631787720954444

Detia-Degesch. (2021). History: A success story featuring 200 years of family tradition. https://detia-degesch.de/the-company/historie/?lang=en.

Dutkiewicz, J. & Dickstein, J. (2021). The ism in veganism: The case for a minimal practice-based definition. *Food Ethics, 6*, 2. https://doi.org/10.1007/s41055-020-00081-6

Ehgartner, U. & Boons, F. (2020). *COVID-19 and practice change in the everyday life domains of hygiene, eating, mobility, shopping, leisure and work. Implications for environmental and social sustainability*. Manchester: Sustainable Consumption Institute. December 2020. https://www.sci.manchester.ac.uk/research/covid-19/

Eisenbach, L.D. et al. (2019). Effect of biocyclic humus soil on yield and quality parameters of processing tomato (lycopersicon esculentum mill). *Bulletin of UASVM Horticulture, 76*, 47–52.

Eisenbach, L.D. et al. (2018). Effect of biocyclic humus soil on yield and quality parameters of sweet potato (ipomoea batatas L.). *Scientific Papers. Series A. Agronomy, LXI*, 210–17.

FAO. (2006). *Livestock's long shadow: Environmental issues and options*. Rome: Food and Agriculture Organization of the United Nations.

Forchtner, B. & Tominc, A. (2017). Kalashnikov and cooking-spoon: Neo-Nazism, veganism and a lifestyle cooking show on YouTube. *Food, Culture and Society, 20*, 415–41. https://doi.org/10.1080/15528014.2017.1337388

Fornace, K. et al. (2013). Effects of land-use changes and agricultural practices on the emergence and reemergence of human viral diseases. In S.K. Singh (Ed.), *Viral infections and global change* (pp. 133–49). Hoboken: John Wiley and Sons, Ltd. https://doi.org/10.1002/9781118297469.ch8

Foucault, M. (1980). *Power/knowledge: Selected interviews and other writings, 1972–1977*. New York: Pantheon Books.

Fuchs, D. et al. (2016). Power: The missing element in sustainable consumption and absolute reductions research and action. *Journal of Cleaner Production, 132*, 298–307. https://doi.org/10.1016/j.jclepro.2015.02.006

Gibson-Graham, J.K. (2006). *A postcapitalist politics*. Minneapolis: University of Minnesota Press.

Hagemann, N. & Potthast, T. (2015). Necessary new approaches towards sustainable agriculture—innovations for organic agriculture. In D.E. Dumitras, I.M. Jitea, & S. Aerts (Eds.), *Know your food—food ethics and innovation* (pp. 107–13). The Netherlands: Wageningen Academic Publishers. https://doi.org/10.3920/978-90-8686-813-1_15

Hall, J. & Tolhurst, I. (2015). *Growing green: Organic techniques for a sustainable future*, 3rd Edition (first published March 2006). Manchester: The Vegan Organic Network.

Hirth, S. (2021). Food that matters: Boundary work and the case for vegan food practices. *Sociologia Ruralis, 61*, 234–54.

Hirth, S. (2019a). All food is 'plant-based'—particularly meat and dairy. *Discover Society, 71*. https://archive.discoversociety.org/2019/08/07/all-food-is-plant-based-particularly-meat-and-dairy/

Hirth, S. (2019b). *Food that matters: Sustainability and the material-discursive boundaries of carnist and vegan food practices*. Manchester: University of Manchester. https://www.research.manchester.ac.uk/portal/files/122884960/FULL_TEXT.PDF

IAASTD – International Assessment of Agricultural Knowledge, Science and Technology for Development. (2009). *Agriculture at a crossroads - Global report*. Washington, DC: Island Press.

IPCC. (2019). *Climate Change and Land: an IPCC special report on climate change, desertification, land degradation, sustainable land management, food security, and greenhouse gas fluxes in terrestrial ecosystems*. https://www.ipcc.ch/srccl/cite-report/

IPES-Food. (2020). *SPECIAL REPORT: COVID-19 and the Crisis in Food Systems—Symptoms, causes, and potential solutions* (Communiqué by IPES-Food, April 2020).

Kalthoff, J. & Werner, M. (1998). *Die Händler des Zyklon B: Tesch and Stabenow: eine Firmengeschichte zwischen Hamburg und Auschwitz*. Hamburg: VSA.

Kurz, T. et al. (2020). Could vegans and lycra cyclists be bad for the planet? Theorizing the role of moralized minority practice identities in processes of societal-level change. *Journal of Social Issues, 76*, 86–100. https://doi.org/10.1111/josi.12366

Moser, C. et al. (2021). Biomateriality and Organizing: Towards an Organizational Perspective on Food. *Organization Studies 42*, 175–193. https://doi.org/10.1177/0170840621991343

Poore, J. & Nemecek, T. (2018). Reducing food's environmental impacts through producers and consumers. *Science, 360*, 987–92. https://doi.org/10.1126/science.aaq0216

Reijnders, L. & Soret, S. (2003). Quantification of the environmental impact of different dietary protein choices. *The American Journal of Clinical Nutrition, 78*, 664S–668S.

Rockström, J. et al. (2009). A safe operating space for humanity. *Nature, 461*, 472–5. https://doi.org/10.1038/461472a

Schatzki, T.R., Knorr Cetina, K., & von Savigny, E. (Eds.) (2001). *The practice turn in contemporary theory*. London: Routledge.

Schmutz, U. & Foresi, L. (2017). Vegan organic horticulture—standards, challenges, socioeconomics and impact on global food security. *Acta horticulturae, 1164*, 475–84. https://doi.org/10.17660/ActaHortic.2017.1164.62

Searle, A. & Turnbull, J. (2020). Resurgent natures? More-than-human perspectives on COVID-19. *Dialogues in Human Geography, 10*, 291–5. https://doi.org/10.1177/2043820620933859

Seymour, M. & Utter, A. (2021). Veganic farming in the United States: Farmer perceptions, motivations, and experiences. *Agric Hum Values 38*, 1139-1159. https://doi.org/10.1007/s10460-021-10225-x

Settele, J. et al. (2020). COVID-19 stimulus measures must save lives, protect livelihoods, and safeguard nature to reduce the risk of future pandemics. https://ipbes.net/covid19stimulus.

Smaje, C. (2020). *A Small Farm Future: Making the Case for a Society Built Around Local Economies, Self-Provisioning, Agricultural Diversity, and a Shared Earth.* London: Chelsea Green Publishing.

Smil, V. (2011). Nitrogen cycle and world food production. *World Agriculture, 2,* 9–13.

Stephens, N. et al. (2018). Bringing cultured meat to market: Technical, socio-political, and regulatory challenges in cellular agriculture. *Trends in Food Science and Technology, 78,* 155–66.

Sun, Z. et al. (2022). Dietary change in high-income nations alone can lead to substantial double climate dividend. *Nature Food* 3, 29–37. https://doi.org/10.1038/s43016-021-00431-5

Twine, R. (2018). Materially constituting a sustainable food transition: The case of vegan eating practice. *Sociology, 52,* 166–81. https://doi.org/10.1177/0038038517726647

Vinnerås, B. et al. (2012). Biosecurity aspects and pathogen inactivation in acidified high risk animal by-products. *Journal of Environmental Science and Health, Part A 47,* 8, 1166–1172. https://doi.org/10.1080/10934529.2012.668383

Vlasova, A.N. & Saif, L.J. (2013). Biological aspects of the interspecies transmission of selected coronaviruses. In S.K. Singh (Ed.), *Viral infections and global change* (pp. 393–418). Hoboken: John Wiley and Sons, Ltd. https://doi.org/10.1002/9781118297469.ch21

Warde, A. (2005). Consumption and theories of practice. *Journal of Consumer Culture, 5,* 131–53.

Warde, A. (2016). *The practice of eating.* Cambridge: Polity Press.

Whatmore, S. (2006). Materialist returns: Practising cultural geography in and for a more-than-human world. *Cultural Geographies, 13,* 600–9. https://doi.org/10.1191/1474474006cgj3770a

Wienhues, A. & Hirth, S. (2021). Intensive animal agriculture, land-use and biological conservation: Converging demands of justice, In: H. Schübel & I. Wallimann-Helmer (Eds.), *Justice and Food Security in a Changing Climate* (pp. 277–282). Conference Proceedings, EurSafe 2021, Fribourg. Wageningen: Wageningen Academic Publishers. https://doi.org/10.3920/978-90-8686-915-2_42

Willett, W. et al. (2019). Food in the Anthropocene: The EAT–Lancet Commission on healthy diets from sustainable food systems. *The Lancet Commissions 393,* 10170, 447–492. https://doi.org/10.1016/S0140-6736(18)31788-4

Worm, B. et al. (2006). Impacts of biodiversity loss on ocean ecosystem services. *Science, 314,* 787–90. https://doi.org/10.1126/science.1132294

Wrenn, C.L. (2017). Trump veganism: A political survey of American vegans in the era of identity politics. *Societies, 7,* 32. https://doi.org/10.3390/soc7040032

CHAPTER 21

HONEYBEE BIAS AND BEE-WASHING

Effects of Vertebrate-centric Care?

OLIVIA DAVIES AND THOMAS D.J. SAYERS

Introduction

INSECTS are the most abundant form of animal life on the planet, present in countless modes of organizing and organizational settings. The ways in which organizations attend (or not) to our invertebrate companions, therefore, hold significant ecological and social implications. Yet, to date, insects remain largely absent from (Animal) Organization Studies. On the rare occurrence they are mentioned, it is usually in passing, and typically to emphasize their economic contribution as pollinators (Reade et al., 2015), problematize them as pests or a bothersome presence (Beacham, 2018; Kwon and Constantinides, 2018; Brummans, Hwang, and Cheong, 2020), or to mobilize them symbolically (e.g. Deleuze and Guattari, 1988) or metaphorically (Cassill, 2002; Rodgers, 2008) regarding modes of human organization. Notable exceptions in which insects are afforded deeper, sustained consideration include Moore and Kosut's rich ethnographic exploration of urban beekeeping (2013), and their subsequent proposal of an ethics of intra-species mindfulness (2014). Valtonen, Salmela, and Rantala (2020) also pay close attention to organizational insects, applying a feminist lens to human-mosquito encounters in tourism settings, while Davies and Riach (2018) offer an ecofeminist reading of biosecurity practices associated with commercial honeybee pollination. On the whole, however, there has been little engagement with insects in (Animal) Organization Studies, let alone consideration of how organizations may care for them.

In response, this chapter works on two levels. Given the current sparsity of literature on the topic, we first provide an extended overview of insects' importance and influence, highlighting the need for greater care towards them than most organizations currently afford. We then explore a rare example of organizational attempts to care for insects, bees specifically. While debates concerned with the morality and ethics of insect care are ongoing in Philosophy, we argue the necessity of caring for insects through an ecologically-informed paradigm. We draw on the empirical examples of 'bee hotels' and rooftop hives, discussing how these contemporary organizational attempts to care for bees emerge from and, in part, perpetuate the interrelated organizational phenomena of honeybee bias (social and scientific attention directed towards this single species disproportionate to their ecological importance) and bee-washing (organizational greenwashing tactics specific to bees). In turn, we point to how these may give rise to ecologically unsound outcomes for bees as well as other insects and the environment more widely.

We suggest this discord between caring intentions and harmful outcomes can, in part, be understood as an effect of the vertebrate-centric nature of organizational expressions of care towards animals. Underpinned by the tenets of singularity and universality, these efforts are formulated through an approach focused on individual species, isolated from their ecologies, replicating the historically dominant mode of caring for vertebrate species. Conversely, we advocate an approach which, at its foundation, understands all beings—vertebrates and invertebrates—as entangled in their situated, co-constitutive ecosystems. To this end, we conclude with a call for others to join the long-term project of thinking further about how organizations can better care for insects, other invertebrates, and vertebrates alike, through a more-than-vertebrate perspective.

INSECTS AND ORGANIZATIONS: WHY SHOULD WE CARE?

When we think of organizational human-animal relationships, the species that typically spring to mind are fellow vertebrates (subphylum Vertebrata), usually mammals, birds, reptiles, and fish. Yet vertebrates (including humans) comprise a minority of the world's animal biomass and species richness, accounting for only ~65,000 species out of more than 1.5 million described animal species (May, 1988; Bar-On, Phillips, and Milo, 2018). By contrast, insects (phylum Arthropoda: Hexapoda: Insecta), the largest group of invertebrates (animals which do not possess a spinal column), are the most dominant animal group on earth, comprising approximately 66 per cent of all the world's known animal species (Zhang, 2011). Even more astonishingly, an average of species richness estimates suggests there are around 5.5 million insect species, indicating that 80 per cent of insect species remain undescribed (Stork, 2018).

Despite their pervasiveness, insects remain an obscure and alien lifeform to most people. In part, this is due to the contrast in human-insect scale, meaning access to their diversity and fascinating intricacy is often only available through specialized magnification, as illustrated in Figure 21.1. In the absence of a macro camera lens or

FIGURE 21.1 Top row: examples of four bee species of the insect order Hymenoptera—European honeybee, neon cuckoo bee, hylaeine bee, and blue banded bee. Rows two-four offer a glimpse into the diversity of other insect groups, all of which contribute to their local ecology whether it be through predation, herbivory, pollination, or as food for other organisms. (Copyright: Thomas Sayers). Displayed left to right from second row (insect order in parentheses): paper wasp (Hymenoptera), flower-feeding march fly (Diptera), drone or flower fly (Diptera), bee fly (Diptera), skipper butterfly (Lepidoptera), thorn bug (Hemiptera), weevil (Coleoptera), fan beetle (Coleoptera), spotted ladybird (Coleoptera), green lacewing (Neuroptera), praying mantis (Mantodea), and dragonfly (Odonata).

microscope, however, most people continue relating to insects predominantly via common narratives. These entrenched narratives reflect society's conflicting attitudes towards insects (Lemelin et al., 2017) and the significant disparity between how various taxa are perceived. Interestingly, these perceptions are not typically aligned with ecological value but rather influenced by multifaceted commercial needs, culture, and sporadic and often unwanted lived encounters (Lemelin et al., 2017). For example, wasps and flies have been identified as significantly more disliked by the public, compared to bees and butterflies, despite the formers' critical roles in pest regulation and pollination (Sumner, Law, and Cini, 2018). Bees, specifically, have been associated with positive public attitudes, linked to an appreciation of their usefulness and conservation value (Schonfelder and Bogner, 2017).

In general, however, negative perceptions towards insects predominate (Kellert, 1993). Raffles (2010: 44) summarizes this widespread disdain, noting that unlike our perception of, and relationships with, other vertebrate species, as humans 'we simply cannot find ourselves in these creatures—it is worse than indifference—it is a deep, dead space without reciprocity, recognition, or redemption'. Hence, while other vertebrate species, which are more evolutionarily like humans, are recognized as deserving a place nearer the pinnacle of the hierarchy of moral and welfare-based consideration (Peggs, 2010; Rozzi, 2019), invertebrates' lack of spine has been associated with deficiencies in forms of cognition that we as humans value, such as sentience, intentionality, and the ability to feel emotion and pain (Adamo, 2016). Critiques of this practice of dichotomizing life and devaluing those belonging to the 'inferior' category—such as man/woman, human/animal, self/other—are commonplace in ecofeminist literature, arguing that this oppressive patriarchal practice and emergent social attitudes and structures are detrimental to both people and planet (Cudworth, 2016: Gaard, 1993). One example of how the pervasiveness and potency of this binarized messaging emerges in relation to vertebratism (the privileging of vertebrates over invertebrates) is via children's television. Vertebrate animal characters 'like us' have often been portrayed as beings capable of feeling in ways we feel, while the suffering of invertebrate characters is construed as something of little or no concern (Paul, 1996). In the context of these cultural norms, ingrained from a young age, it is unsurprising that real insects have also been largely excluded from moral consideration, echoing Canetti's (1981: 205; original emphasis) observation that 'the destruction of these tiny creatures is the only act of violence which remains unpunished even *within* us'.

It was a similar observation that inspired May's (1988: 1446) coinage of the term 'vertebrate chauvinism', referring to the disproportionate philosophic and scientific focus on, and privileging of, species that have a backbone (Rozzi, 2019). This vertebrate chauvinism remains evident in the significant social and scientific attention received by vertebrates (Leather, 2009a), while invertebrates, including insects, continue to be 'deemed less worthy of moral and scholarly consideration' (Wilkie, Moore, and Molloy, 2019: 3). Consequently, studies of these beings are comparatively lacking throughout various fields including biology, animal behaviour, conservation, and human-animal studies (see e.g. May, 1988; Clark and May, 2002; Fazey, Fischer, and Lindenmayer, 2005; Rosenthal et al., 2017; Gangwani and Landin, 2018; Wilkie et al. 2019). In fact, Wilkie et al.'s (2019) keyword search identified invertebrates in only 11 per cent and 15 per cent of articles in the multidisciplinary journals *Anthrozoös* and *Society & Animals*, respectively, both of which focus on human-animal interactions. This was reduced to 2 per cent of search hits for each journal when restricted to title, abstract, and keywords. This dearth of insect knowledge and institutional bias or 'institutional vertebratism' (Leather, 2009b: 414) belies the extent to which insects are critical for ecosystem functioning and their overwhelming impact on human wellbeing and society. What's more, this systemic undervaluing of insects is occurring against a backdrop of continued anthropogenic threats to, and destabilization of, insect richness and abundance, globally (Basset and Lamarre, 2019; Wagner, 2020).

These trends should be of great concern. Insects are deeply entangled with Earth's ecology, their myriad forms having existed for ~479 million years (Misof et al., 2014). They are 'the little things that run the world' (Wilson, 1987: 344), and as such are often utilized as indicators of environmental quality and change (Cardoso et al., 2011). Through deep evolutionary time they have developed innumerable functions and relationships with other co-evolved organisms and the abiotic world. These 'free' ecosystem functions or services include the pollination and seed dispersal of a diversity of wild and crop plants, predation, and parasitism (i.e. agricultural pest control), waste decomposition, energy and nutrient cycling, and sustenance for wild and domesticated animals and organisms across trophic levels (Huis and Ooninex, 2017; Saunders, 2018; Cardoso et al., 2020).

Increasingly, insects are also fulfilling other profit-oriented organizational functions as protein-rich food (Bear, 2019; Van Huis et al., 2013), design, technology (biomimicry) and pharmaceutical resources (Holbrook et al., 2010), model research organisms (i.e. *Drosophila*), and recreational resources (e.g. entomotourism, Chinese fighting crickets) (Raffles, 2010; Lemelin, Boileau, and Russell, 2019). Simultaneously, invertebrates are also considered the costliest animal group to human society. Insects, specifically, have the potential to damage infrastructure (e.g. wood-eating termites), spread disease (e.g. Malaria-carrying mosquitoes), and engage in devastating crop and plantation herbivory (e.g. locust plagues), with invasive insects alone estimated to cost a minimum of US$76.9 billion globally per annum in relation to goods, services, and human health (Bradshaw et al., 2016). Hence, there are plentiful reasons for organizations to care about (if not for) insects.

SAVE THE *BEES*? OR, SAVE THE *BEE*?

Against the above-described paradoxical context of, on the one hand, insects' abundance, diversity, and myriad ecological and economic roles, and on the other, their comparatively underappreciated status, there is one species that has bucked the trend of institutional vertebratism. Valued globally for its importance in crop pollination and honey production, the European honeybee (*Apis mellifera* L.) has become an economic keystone. Pollination is one of the most significant and tangible ecosystem services provided by invertebrates, with 87 per cent of the world's flowering plants pollinated by animals, the majority of which are insects (Ollerton, Winfree, and Tarrant, 2011). Thirty-nine of the 57 main food crops worldwide assessed by Klein et al. (2007) depend upon animal pollination to varied extents, accounting for an estimated 35 per cent of agricultural production. As such, Gallai et al. (2009) estimated the total economic value of insect pollination to be €153 billion based on global agricultural food production in 2005. While non-bee insects (including flies, wasps, beetles, butterflies) play a significant role in plant pollination (Buchmann and Nabhan, 1996; Rader et al., 2016; Sayers et al., 2019), wild and managed bees are widely regarded as the most dominant pollinators of global food crops and wild plants (Klein et al., 2007; Aizen et al., 2009; Ollerton, 2017). Of these, the European honeybee (constituting a number of subspecies) has historically been considered the most effective and economically valuable (Southwick and Southwick, 1992; Klein et al., 2007; Rader et al., 2009).

A process of continual domestication and transportation of honeybees, aided by the development of human beekeeping practices over millennia (vanEngelsdorp and Meixner, 2010), has resulted in today's cosmopolitan 'super-generalist'. From its native range in Europe, Central Asia, and Africa (Ruttner, 1988), the species has been introduced to virtually all habitable regions on earth, correlating with an increase in global demand for pollinator-dependent crops and honey (Aizen and Harder, 2009). In fact, far from being a 'natural' presence, the European honeybee is often formally classified as 'livestock', likened to 'the cow of the insect world' (Bobiwash in Giaccone, 2020: n.p.). The associated over-reliance on this single pollinator species in modern agricultural monocultures has made recent honeybee declines in feral and managed colonies all the more concerning for agricultural production and food security (Watanabe, 1994; Aizen et al., 2009; Lautenbach et al., 2012). Honeybees have seen periodic declines in different parts of the globe for centuries (Oldroyd, 2007), but there have been more sustained and concurrent declines in recent decades in North America and Europe (Ellis, Evans, and Pettis, 2010; Potts et al., 2010) and elsewhere throughout the world (Paudel et al., 2015).

Unprecedented declines in North American honeybee colonies in 2006, attributed to Colony Collapse Disorder (CCD), sparked heightened concerns of an impending 'pollination crisis' (Holden, 2006; vanEngelsdorp et al., 2009; Smith and Saunders, 2016). Emerging as a totem for global sustainability concerns more generally (Geldmann and González-Varo, 2018), honeybees have become a cultural phenomenon that have 'merged within media and consumer culture to become a part of nature that is significant and potentially saveable' (Moore and Kosut, 2014: 521). A series of recent studies highlighted the prevalence of this 'honeybee bias'. A Canadian survey revealed that 51.4 per cent of survey respondents mistakenly identified the European honeybee as native to North America (Trip et al., 2020). Furthermore, Smith and Saunders (2016) found only 15 per cent and 17 per cent of pollination-related articles in Australian media between 2006 and 2015 mentioned native bees and non-bee pollinators, respectively, compared to 80 per cent for the honeybee.

Yet, despite the hype surrounding honeybees, there is currently little evidence of a global pollinator crisis due to honeybee shortages (Aizen et al., 2008; Martin, 2015). Although honeybee stocks are decreasing in certain regions, they are actually increasing overall on a global scale (Aizen and Harder, 2009; Martin, 2015). Conversely, there is growing evidence of declines in the abundance and diversity of insects more broadly, including native bees and non-bee pollinators (Burkle, Marlin, and Knight, 2013;

Goulson et al., 2015; Ollerton, 2017), with terrestrial insect abundance estimated to decline on average by 9 per cent per decade (Klink et al., 2020). From both an ecological and utilitarian perspective, this decline in wild pollinators and their ability to provide a baseline pollination service, insuring against honeybee losses (Winfree, 2008), is alarming. They have been shown to provide effective crop pollination services equivalent or superior to that of honeybees (Kremen, Williams, and Thorp, 2002; Winfree et al., 2007; Rader et al., 2016; Angelella, McCullough, and O'Rouke, 2021), and increasingly, studies cast doubt over the importance of honeybees in providing pollination services globally (Breeze et al., 2011).

Notably, Garibaldi et al. (2013) found that fruit set increased significantly with wild insect visitation in all 41 crops assessed, whereas honeybee visitation resulted in a significant increase in only 14 per cent of crops. Hence, without wishing to downplay their current importance in global crop production (Klein et al., 2007), given the European honeybee is only one of countless insect pollinator species (Ollerton, 2017), including a further ~20,000 bee species, the comparative levels of attention they receive has been characterized as disproportionate (Smith and Saunders, 2016), misleading, and ecologically harmful (Colla and MacIvor, 2017; Geldmann and González-Varo, 2018).

The pervasiveness of this honeybee bias has meant that various organizations' efforts to be seen as caring about bees and insect pollinators in general are often conflated with a commitment to save the European honeybee specifically. Furthermore, rather than committing to substantive, wide-scale changes scientists have identified as necessary for insect conservation (Cardoso et al., 2020), most organizations have opted for less disruptive responses that offer greater short-term profitability; namely the production of a wave of 'bee friendly' products and services. This species-specific claim of 'bee-friendly', and the more general term 'pollinator-friendly', are both positively correlated with consumer willingness to pay (Khachatryan et al., 2017). And while there is a handful of independent farming-focused certifications (including Bee Friendly Farming; Bee Better Certified), the ability to make this claim of bee-friendliness remains under-regulated, and at the discretion of organizations.

One approach that organizations have taken to assuming this label has been via asserting their supply chain processes and components of products intended for human use are of benefit, or at least not to the detriment, of (honey)bee sustainability. Examples of this include textiles, cosmetics, and consumables produced with organic ingredients, thereby avoiding insecticide exposure. Others make more tangential claims, donating a portion of their profits to 'bee saving' initiatives with no mention of the bee-friendliness of their material production systems (such as non-organic certified clothing printed with bee-related slogans/images). Alternatively, some organizations have located themselves as 'bee-friendly' through creating lines of products and services directly aimed for usage by, and the conservation of, bees themselves. Ordinarily, these take the form of packets of flowering plant seeds, beehives, and bee-hotels; products which represent organizational attempts to capitalize on the favourable public perception of bees (Wilson, Forister, and Carril, 2017), and society's desire to play a role in their conservation. This has led to a practice known as 'bee-washing'; a term coined by MacIvor and

Packer (2015: 10) who defined it as 'greenwashing as applied to potentially misleading claims for augmentation of native and wild bee populations' regarding the increasing popularity of artificial nesting aids. Whereas greenwashing speaks to unfounded organizational claims of eco-friendliness, bee-washing, in its broad sense, occurs when a product, service, or organization is marketed as being 'bee-friendly' when, in fact, it does little to promote bee health and wild insect pollinator recovery in any substantive way (Königslöw et al., 2019). In fact, as we discuss below, some bee-washing can be downright deadly for bees. Like greenwashing, bee-washing is not unique to a specific mode of organization. And for as long as widespread honeybee bias prevails, it will remain easy for organizations to 'mislead people into believing that honeybees need to be saved in order to sell their products' (Giaccone, 2020: n.p.). Of course, not all bee-washing is deliberate, and not all bee-friendly products and services are bee-washed. Yet, irrespective of intentions, it remains the case that many organizational efforts to care (or be seen as caring) for bees, even those that appear ecologically sound, may have detrimental wellbeing outcomes.

This tension between organizational imperatives of bee-care and their sometimes-harmful consequences is evidenced in Davies and Riach's (2018) ecofeminist critique of commercial pollination biosecurity practices. Identifying how the discourses and practices of a governmental biosecurity framework were informed by a masculine logic, they point to three motifs via which unintended harm to bees emerged. Indicative of the sense of human mastery evoked through the masculine 'colonial image of the conquest of nature' (Ingold, 2000: 82), particular methods of bee-care deployed as part of the biosecurity mission to 'Save the Bees' were shown to instead result in human inspectors potentially becoming vectors of the very diseases they were supposedly protecting the bees from.

While bee-washing practices may also be understood as emerging through a masculinist organizational culture of competition (as opposed to collaboration), mastery (as opposed to cohabiting), and linearity (as opposed to cyclicity), the point we seek to impress from this example is the way in which foundational principles and assumptions underpinning how care is demonstrated hold significant material ramifications for the recipients of that care. It is this point we develop within the remainder of the chapter. We ask how the values and assumptions associated with vertebrate-centrism, emergent from the pervasive vertebrate/invertebrate dichotomy, contributes to honeybee bias and subsequent bee-washing, locating it as a legitimate mode of care despite its potential for harm.

Vertebrate-centric Care

Organizational bee-washed efforts surely fail to satisfy an ethic of care, which Held (2006: 71) considers 'the most basic moral value'. As elaborated by Tronto (1993: 103), this ethic of care incorporates 'everything that we do to maintain, continue and repair our "world" so that we can live in it as well as possible. That world includes our bodies, ourselves, and our environment, all of which we seek to interweave in a complex, life-sustaining web.' While initially developed with a focus on anthropocentric settings, we understand this approach as appropriate for more-than-human modes of care as it foregrounds the fundamental ecological understanding of life as a process sustained through the interaction of biotic and abiotic phenomena. Instead of situating humans as outside, above, or somehow exempt from our embodied, earthly reality, Tronto's (1993:103) definition speaks to a mode of caring that 'is not restricted to human interaction with others'. Rather, it may entail a broad spectrum of companion species: forms of life that 'make each other up, in the flesh' (Haraway, 2003: 2). In turn, companion species are always entangled in broader 'bio-social-technical apparatuses ... in which particular ways of being emerge and are sustained' (Haraway, 2008: 134), including organizational and institutional practices and processes. This means that recognition of the situated specificities and relational dimensions of organizational human-insect relations is key to ethical considerations (Valtonen et al., 2020). The existence of bee-washing, however, is suggestive of organizations' current widespread inability to adequately recognize and respond to animals' situated ecological complexities, particularly those of insects. This is not surprising given that, historically, insects have largely been excluded from any considerations of organizational care at all.

Even within organizations that have animal ethics policies, insects have been omitted. This omission has been rationalized through citing insects' small nervous systems and the inconclusiveness surrounding their ability to suffer and experience an emotional response to pain (Adamo, 2016). While such approaches to organizational nonhuman care have been criticized for denying invertebrates 'welfare protections despite their considerable cognitive, behavioural, and evolutionary diversity' (Mikhalevich and Powell, 2020: 1), this exclusionary approach remains the norm. For example, the National Health and Research Council of Australia's Code for the Care and Use of Animals (2021) defines an animal as 'any live non-human vertebrate ... and cephalopods'. While cephalopods (such as octopus) are admittedly invertebrates, their inclusion is based on their extreme intelligence and complex nervous system (Mather, 2020): traits typically associated with vertebrate species. Displaying their vertebrate chauvinism, many research institutions consider cephalopods 'honorary vertebrates' (Mather, 2020: 5). It is little wonder then, given this blatantly vertebrate-centric approach, that even the rare expressions of organizational care that do afford extension to insects have been largely insufficient, as evidenced by the above-cited insect declines.

We suggest that vertebrate-centrism should be understood as more than this literal focus on vertebrates to the exclusion of invertebrates. Rather, it is a paradigm premised on the tenets of singularity and universality: terms that simultaneously convey the symbolic and conceptual content of vertebrate-centric care. By symbolic content we are referring to historical assumptions that remain ingrained in the social psyche, pervading contemporary modes of care applied to both human and nonhuman life. For instance, the term singularity speaks to the cultural eminence of the spine, a singular structure that provides beings with structural (and moral) integrity. This idea echoes through the concepts of individualism and self-sustenance that singularity encompasses. In addition, universality speaks to the long-held notion that the possession of a spine is a shared feature of all 'higher' beings, with membership of the vertebrate classification often considered the most fundamental defining factor of a species. In emphasizing this binary above all else, between-species differences are overlooked and the ethical requirement to pay attention to specific needs and desires is erased, creating the conditions for a universal approach to care to be deemed sufficient.

From a conceptual standpoint singularity refers to the way in which the subject(s) of care are situated as ontologically distinct individuals. Such an approach overlooks that being part of the world's 'complex, life-sustaining web' entails that all beings are companion species (Haraway, 2003). In many respects it is easier to comprehend this idea, which muddies the notion of what it means to be an 'individual', when thinking of insects as opposed to vertebrate species. Insects form part of the foundations of animal food webs and their unmatched diversity in species, behaviour, interactions, and ecosystem roles makes it clear that they must be considered and cared for at the ecosystem level. In fact, it is often impossible to care for a single insect, especially those with 'collective cognition' who exist as a superorganism, relying on a synergistic relationship with their conspecifics (and other companion species) to survive (Feinerman and Korman, 2017). Yet, even 'solitary' species are in a perpetual process of relating to others and their abiotic environment (Cardoso et al., 2020).

Despite this, there remains an overwhelming tendency to approach care as something that can be directed to singular individuals and/or species, as though they can be cordoned off from the rest of the world. Increasing recognition of the flaw in this approach, and the associated inefficiency of caring for specific individuals/species, has seen a paradigm shift in the conservation biology literature and on-the-ground environmental management. Moving beyond the singularity-based care exemplified in the familiar discourse of high-profile conservation campaigns to protect specific species (typically charismatic vertebrate fauna), there is a growing focus on conservation at the landscape level. This is not to suggest it is 'wrong' to practice care with a predominant being or species in mind, but rather to point out that caring is an inherently relational, ongoing process (Puig de la Bellacasa, 2017) through which world-making occurs. As such, approaches to care are always affected by, and always have effects on, a broader ecological community. Therefore, as well as necessitating thinking about organisms as inextricably situated in their broader environmental context, a non-singularity-based approach also requires understanding the approach to conservation (or care) itself as a generative component of the ecology being cared for (Carolan, 2006). In doing so, ecosystem processes and functioning, and interaction networks (including human intervention) across temporal and spatial scales are considered in the architecture of care (Harvey et al., 2017; Pickett, Parker, and Fiedler, 1992).

In addition, the tenet of universality refers to how the same type of care is often assumed to be applicable to all members of the same species and broader groups (phylum). A pertinent example of this is how species have traditionally been segregated according to the broad categorizations of vertebrate or invertebrate, with only the former considered as requiring care on a moral level. Not only is this obviously damaging for those deemed unworthy of care, it also 'obscure[s] relevant cognitive diversity among animals' (Mikhalevich and Powell, 2020: 3), reducing the massive diversity within these groups, and in turn allowing an impoverished, universal approach to care to become seen as an adequate, default method. This is not to say that a broad view of the typical needs of different species is not a useful starting point when attempting to practise appropriate care, but that it is not sufficient. The unique, situated specificities of the intended recipients of care must be taken into consideration, for it is through situated, relational dynamics that life is sustained.

Vertebrate-centric care is not only about insects being overlooked when it comes to care. It speaks to a mode of care that has vertebrate-centric assumptions such as singularity and universality at its foundation, often leading to unintended harm. To provide empirical examples of this, we now return to the insect group which arguably receives the most care from organizations and society: bees (Geldmann and González-Varo, 2018; Smith and Saunders, 2016), to show how honeybee bias and bee-washing emerge through and reinforce this paradigm of care.

Bee-washing as a Vertebrate-centric Mode of Organizational Care

Despite being the catalyst for the term bee-washing, artificial nesting aids or 'bee hotels' remain popular with organizations and consumers, particularly in urban settings. These structures come in myriad forms, made from a variety of hollow bundled materials (often bamboo, plastic pipes, wood), marketed as providing artificial nesting cavities to protect native bees. At first glance, these hotels are a welcome change from the usual insect-specific products on the market aimed at extermination and control. Yet this organizational expression of care for bees is revealed as a material manifestation of care premised on the singularity and universality common to a vertebrate-centric approach. Though presumably sold and purchased with the intention of providing genuine care, these structures have been found to be ineffective (Königslöw et al. 2019), with the potential to adversely impact both the health of native bees and the wider ecology of the settings in which they are installed (MacIvor and Packer, 2015).

Though aimed at 'native bees'—a group incorporating a wide spectrum of species—these structures are rarely made in accordance with the preferences and requirements of local target species. For instance, most bee species require deep nesting sites below ground. Yet even for shallow cavity and above-ground nesting bees, the generic (universal), commercially available bee hotels sold by numerous national and international retailers have been shown (both anecdotally and scientifically) to underperform compared to custom-designed bee hotels informed by species-specific nesting requirements and preferences (i.e. resulting in higher occupancy rates, species diversity, and more brood cells) (Königslöw et al., 2019). Furthermore, the design and installation of these structures is insensitive to emergent impacts within the local ecological context and reflect an assumption that native bees are ontologically distinct from their local ecosystem. This is evident in their failure to adequately anticipate and account for the inevitable presence of other non-target species (bees' symbiotic, neutral, and parasitic companion species) and their emergent effects. These structures have been found to accommodate a high abundance of introduced species (Geslin et al., 2020), and may artificially facilitate the increase of harmful parasites, predators, and disease in an area, in addition to distorting the sex-ratios of nesting bees (MacIvor and Packer, 2015). As such, rather than providing additional accommodation to help 'save the bees', these hotels may often generate broader, harmful, ramifications for native bees and their ecosystems. Hence, they may, in fact, only succeed in making our own species feel good (Alton and Ratnieks, 2020).

Another common instance of bee-washed organizational expressions of care is the proliferation and promotion of rooftop hives. Touted as a powerful solution to 'save the bees' in the context of CCD, these elevated urban honeybee hives foster positive public perception of the organizations maintaining them and provide social benefits to the human residents of these areas (Egerer and Kowarik, 2020). However, the effects they have on the honeybees residing within, and native pollinator communities around them, is less clear-cut (Mallinger et al., 2017). Like the singularity of bee hotels, the installation of these hives and consequent bolstering of honeybee populations in urban areas is often considered in isolation, with little forethought as to the impact this may have on native species due to increased resource competition. For example, Cane and Tepedino (2017) calculated that during the northern hemisphere's summer months, the average European honeybee colony collects the equivalent pollen required to rear 100,000 solitary native bees. As such, the introduction of these hives can be a potential risk to local insect conservation. Similarly, the visitation rate of certain wild pollinators, including native bees, has been shown as negatively related to the density of honeybee colonies in the city of Paris (Ropars et al., 2019). In fact, when a journalist queried which data Alvéole, a leading Canadian rooftop hive company, use to determine what constitutes a sustainable population of city-dwelling honeybees and their plans for preventing and managing the spread of disease, they conceded: 'We aren't scientifically qualified to answer those questions' (cited in Giaccone, 2020: n.p.). This speaks to Carolan's (2006) imperative of considering the impacts of potential and realized conservation policy as an active part of the specific ecology in focus. With sparse knowledge surrounding the impacts of urban beekeeping on local ecologies, it is premature, and at times irresponsible, to promote this form of honeybee proliferation.

A further related detrimental effect of rooftop hives, and an example of universality-informed care, is their role in perpetuating honeybee-centric narratives that detract from more meaningful efforts by organizations to curb declines in broader insect populations. The narratives around these hives often encourage the mistaken perception that honeybees are in decline on a global level, and the false belief that the presence of these hives will improve general pollinator wellbeing. This is an extremely narrow, overly simplistic approach to the complex issue of pollinator conservation and decline which fails to adequately take situated context into account. It also obscures the necessity, and subdues public demand, for a shift towards organizations and built environments that actively facilitate broader wild pollinator and insect wellbeing (Cardoso et al., 2020). Ultimately, then, 'keeping hives on roofs appears to be more about the needs of people and organisations' than those of bees (Alton and Ratnieks, 2016; 67).

Conclusion: Towards More-than-Vertebrate Care

As Clark (2016: para. 6) asserts, 'At its best, our scholarship moves animals out of people's ethical blindspot and into their line of vision'. With this motivation, this chapter has integrated literature from Ecology, Entomology, and Organization Studies to contribute to remedying the scarcity of consideration of invertebrates, insects particularly, in (Animal) Organization Studies. Identifying the concept of care as integral to the organizational/insect nexus, we outlined the historical and continuing influence of the vertebrate/invertebrate dichotomy as it pertains to organizational attempts to care for insects. Introducing the interrelated phenomena of honeybee bias and bee-washing, we questioned organizational animal care as vertebrate-centric, characterized by the tenets of singularity and universality. We highlighted examples of contemporary organizational expressions of care for insects to reinforce our argument that the sheer diversity and variation in behaviour, preferences, and needs across the breadth of insect richness demands a more nuanced approach than vertebrate-centric care allows.

Yet, given the lack of attention insects and other invertebrates have received in contrast to their vertebrate counterparts, organizational animal care, by default, remains innately vertebrate-centric. As we have suggested, this is of concern both from an ethical and ecological standpoint. In overlooking the diversity and complexity of insects' everyday interactions, varying through space and time, this homogenizing approach (and the products and services to result from it) are incompatible with achieving true insect care and conservation. In response, we proposed that effective care for insects requires an ecologically informed approach that focuses on relationships (not singular individuals or species) and is informed by the specificities of situated ecologies (not universal principles). On this note, we call for further enquiry into modes of caring that are more-than-vertebrate. This is not a call for an approach exclusive to invertebrates. Rather, we envision this research trajectory as one that requires the development of modes of organizational care that transcend the vertebrate/invertebrate dichotomy entirely, entailing 'rethinking our analytical categories as they pertain to all beings' (Schneider, 2013: 27). In contrast to the singularity and universality of traditional vertebrate-centric modes of care, this approach requires comprehension of the quotidian relational, situated context insects are embedded within in ongoing processes of co-constitution. Effective care, and therefore conservation, necessitates an understanding of specific 'sociobiophysical relationships in all their complexity, even in those cases that require a well-grounded understanding of ecosystem processes' (Carolan, 2006: 153). This is but one of many 'biodiversity issues' which, traditionally, 'are not well understood by corporate actors' (Reade et al., 2015: 451). For this reason, we see the future development of more-than-vertebrate care as a necessarily interdisciplinary project, both for scholars and practitioners. Of course, it must also be a more-than-human pursuit, giving due attention to the ecologies, and their co-constitutive creatures, we seek to care for. As Mather (2020: 3) points out, 'It is obviously difficult to work for the welfare of animals that have not been well described or, worse still, you don't even know exist'. As such, before further significant theoretical development of more-than-vertebrate care is pursued, something far more fundamental is required. That is, for us, as Animal Organization Studies scholars, to reflect on our own vertebrate-chauvinism, both in our scholarship and everyday lives, and take proactive steps to redress it.

References

Adamo, S. (2016). Do insects feel pain? A question at the intersection of animal behaviour, philosophy and robotics. *Animal Behaviour, 118*, 75–9.

Aizen, M. et al. (2008). Long-term global trends in crop yield and production reveal no current pollination shortage but increasing pollinator dependency. *Current Biology, 18*, 1572–5.

Aizen, M. et al. (2009). How much does agriculture depend on pollinators? Lessons from long-term trends in crop production. *Annals of Botany, 103*, 1579–88.

Aizen, M. & Harder, L. (2009). The global stock of domesticated honey bees is growing slower than agricultural demand for pollination. *Current Biology, 19*, 915–18.

Alton K. & Ratnieks, F. (2016). Roof top hives: Practical beekeeping or publicity stunt? *Bee World, 93(3)*, 64–7.

Alton, K. & Ratnieks, F. (2020). Caveat emptor: Do products sold to help bees and pollinating insects actually work? *Bee World, 97*, 57–60.

Angelella, G., McCullough, C., & O'Rourke, M. (2021). Honey bee hives decrease wild bee abundance, species richness, and fruit count on farms regardless of wildflower strips. *Scientific Reports, 11*, 3202.

Bar-On, Y., Phillips, R., & Milo, R., (2018). The biomass distribution on Earth. *Proceedings of the National Academy of Sciences, 115*, 6506–11.

Basset, Y. & Lamarre, G. (2019). Toward a world that values insects. *Science, 364*, 1230–1.

Beacham, J. (2018). Organising food differently: Towards a more-than-human ethics of care for the Anthropocene. *Organization, 25(4)*, 533–49.

Bear, C. (2019). Approaching insect death: Understandings and practices of the UK's edible insect farmers. *Society and Animals, 27*, 751–68.

Bradshaw, C. et al. (2016). Massive yet grossly underestimated global costs of invasive insects. *Nature Communications, 7*, 12986.

Breeze, T. et al. (2011). Pollination services in the UK: How important are honeybees? *Agriculture, Ecosystems and Environment, 142*, 137–143.

Brummans, B., Hwang, J., & Cheong, P. (2020). Recycling stories: Mantras, communication, and organizational materialization. *Organization Studies, 41(1)*, 103–26.

Buchmann, S. & Nabhan G. (1996). *The forgotten pollinators*. Washington: Island Press.
Burkle, L., Marlin, J., & Knight, T. (2013). Plant-pollinator interactions over 120 years: Loss of species, co-occurrence, and function. *Science, 339,* 1611–15.
Cane, J. & Tepedino, V. (2017). Gauging the effect of honey bee pollen collection on native bee communities. *Conservation Letters, 10(2),* 205–10.
Canetti, E. (1981). *Crowds and power* (trans. C. Stewart). New York: Noonday Press.
Cassill, D. (2002). Yoyo-bang: a risk-aversion investment strategy by a perennial insect society. *Oecologia, 132,* 150–8.
Cardoso, P. et al. (2011). The seven impediments in invertebrate conservation and how to overcome them. *Biological Conservation, 144,* 2647–55.
Cardoso, P. et al. (2020). Scientists warning to humanity of insect extinctions. *Biological Conservation, 242,* 108426.
Carolan, M. (2006). Conserving nature, but to what end? Conservation policies and the unanticipated ecologies they support. *Organization and Environment, 19(2),* 153–70.
Clark, J. (2016). *Which animals do we study?* Animals in Society. Cited 23 February 2021: www.animalsinsocietygroup.wordpress.com
Clark, J. & May, R. (2002). Taxonomic bias in conservation research. *Science, 297,* 191–2.
Colla, S. & MacIvor J. (2017). Questioning public perception, conservation policy, and recovery actions for honeybees in North America. *Conservation Biology, 31,* 1202–4.
Cudworth, E. (2016). Ecofeminism and the animal. In M. Phillips and N. Rumens (Eds.), *Contemporary perspectives on ecofeminism*. London: Routledge.
Davies, O. & Riach, K. (2018). From manstream measuring to multispecies sustainability: A gendered reading of bee-ing sustainable. *Gender, Work and Organization, 26(3),* 246–66.
Deleuze, G. & Guattari, F. (1988). *A thousand plateaus: Capitalism and schizophrenia*. London: Bloomsbury Publishing.
Egerer, M. & Kowarik, I. (2020). Confronting the modern gordian knot of urban beekeeping. *Trends in Ecology and Evolution, 35,* 956–9.
Ellis, J., Evans J., & Pettis, J. (2010). Colony losses, managed colony population decline, and Colony Collapse Disorder in the United States. *Journal of Apicultural Research, 49,* 134–6.
Fazey, I., Fischer, J., & Lindenmayer, D. (2005). What do conservation biologists publish? *Biological Conservation, 124,* 63–73.
Feinerman, O. & Korman, A. (2017). Individual versus collective cognition in social insects. *Journal of Experimental Biology, 220,* 73–82.
Gaard, G. (1993). *Ecofeminism: Women, animals, nature*. Philadelphia: Temple University Press.
Gallai, N. et al. (2009). Economic valuation of the vulnerability of world agriculture confronted with pollinator decline. *Ecological Economics, 68,* 810–21.
Gangwani, K. & Landin, J. (2018). The decline of insect representation in biology textbooks over time. *American Entomologist, 64,* 252–7.
Garibaldi, L. et al. (2013). Wild pollinators enhance fruit set of crops regardless of honey bee abundance. *Science, 339,* 1608–11.
Geldmann, J. & González-Varo, J. (2018). Conserving honey bees does not help wildlife. *Science, 359,* 392–3.
Geslin, B. et al. (2020). Bee hotels host a high abundance of exotic bees in an urban context. *Acta Oecologica, 105,* 103556.
Giaccone, C. (2020). 'Beewashing' and the business of honey bees. *Ricochet—Public Interest Journalism,* 10 December. https://ricochet.media/en/3404/beewashing-and-the-business-of-honey-bees

Goulson, D. et al. (2015). Bee declines driven by combined stress from parasites, pesticides, and lack of flowers. *Science, 347,* 1255957.

Haraway, D. (2003). *The companion species manifesto: Dogs, people and significant otherness.* Chicago: Prickly Paradigm Press.

Haraway, D. (2008). *When species meet.* Minneapolis: University of Minnesota Press.

Harvey, E. et al. (2017). Bridging ecology and conservation: from ecological networks to ecosystem function. *Journal of Applied Ecology, 54,* 371–9.

Held, V. (2006). *The ethics of care: Personal, political, and global.* Oxford: Oxford University Press.

Holbrook, C. et al. (2010). Social insects inspire human design. *Biology Letters, 6,* 431–3.

Holden, C. (2006). Report warns of looming pollination crisis in North America. *Science, 314,* 397.

Huis, A. & Ooninex, D. (2017). The environmental sustainability of insects as food and feed. A review. *Agronomy for Sustainable Development, 37,* 43.

Ingold, T. (2000). *The perception of the environment: Essays on livelihood, dwelling and skill.* London: Routledge.

Kellert, S. (1993). Values and perceptions of invertebrates. *Conservation Biology, 7,* 845–55.

Khachatryan, H. et al. (2017). Visual attention to eco-labels predicts consumer preferences for pollinator friendly plants. *Sustainability, 9(1743),* 1–14.

Klein, A-M. et al. (2007). Importance of pollinators in changing landscapes for world crops. *Proceedings of the Royal Society B, 274,* 303–313.

Klink, R. et al. (2020). Meta-analysis reveals declines in terrestrial but increases in freshwater insect abundances. *Science, 368,* 417–20.

Königslöw, V. et al. (2019). Benchmarking nesting aids for cavity-nesting bees and wasps. *Biodiversity and Conservation, 28,* 3831–49.

Kremen, C., Williams, N., & Thorp, R. (2002). Crop pollination from native bees at risk from agricultural intensification. *Proceedings of the National Academy of Sciences of the United States of America, 99,* 16812–16.

Kwon, W. & Constantinides, P. (2018). Ideology and moral reasoning: How wine was saved from the 19th century phylloxera epidemic. *Organization Studies, 39(8),* 1031–53.

Lautenbach, S. et al. (2012). Spatial and temporal trends of global pollination benefit. *PLoS One, 7,* 1–16.

Leather, S. (2009a). Institutional vertebratism threatens UK food security. *Trends in Ecology and Evolution, 24,* 413–14.

Leather, S. (2009b). Taxonomic chauvinism threatens the future of entomology. *Biologist, 56,* 10–13.

Lemelin, R. et al. (2017). Perception of insects: A visual analysis. *Society and Animals, 25,* 553–72.

Lemelin, R., Boileau, E., & Russell, C. (2019). Entomotourism: The allure of the arthropod. *Society and Animals, 27,* 733–50.

MacIvor, J. & Packer, L. (2015). 'Bee hotels' as tools for native pollinator conservation: A premature verdict? *PLoS One, 10,* e0122126.

Mallinger, R., Gaines-Day, H., & Gratton, C. (2017). Do managed bees have negative effects on wild bees?: A systematic review of the literature. *PLoS One, 12,* e0189268.

Martin, C. (2015). A re-examination of the pollinator crisis. *Current Biology, 25,* 811–15.

Mather, J. (2020). Why are octopuses going to be the 'poster child' for invertebrate welfare? *Journal of Applied Animal Welfare Science, 22,* 1–10.

May, R. (1988). How many species are there on Earth? *Science, 241*, 1441–9.

Mikalevich, I. & Powell, R. (2020). Minds without spines: Evolutionary inclusive animal ethics. *Animal Sentience, 5(29)*, 1–25.

Misof, B. et al. (2014). Phylogenomics resolves the timing and pattern of insect evolution. *Science, 346*, 763–7.

Moore, L. & Kosut, M. (2013). *Buzz: Urban beekeeping and the power of the bee*. New York: New York University Press.

Moore, L. & Kosut, M. (2014). Among the colony: Ethnographic fieldwork, urban bees and intra-species mindfulness. *Ethnography, 15(4)*, 516–39.

Oldroyd, B. (2007). What's killing American honey bees? *PLoS Biology, 5*, e168.

Ollerton, J., Winfree, R., & Tarrant, S. (2011). How many flowering plants are pollinated by animals? *Oikos, 120*, 321–6.

Ollerton, J. (2017). Pollinator diversity: Distribution, ecological function, and conservation. *Annual Review of Ecology, Evolution, and Systematics, 48*, 353–76.

Paudel, Y. et al. (2015). Honey bees (*Apis mellifera* L.) and pollination issues: Current status, impacts, and potential drivers of decline. *Journal of Agricultural Science, 7*, 93–109.

Paul, E. (1996). The representation of animals on children's television. *Anthrozoos, 9*, 169–81.

Peggs, K. (2010). Nonhuman animal experiments in the European community: Human values and rational choice. *Society and Animals, 18(1)*, 1–20.

Pickett, S., Parker, V., & Fiedler P. (1992). The new paradigm in ecology: Implications for conservation biology above the species level. In P. Fiedler and S. Jain (Eds.), *Conservation Biology*. Boston: Springer.

Potts, S. et al. (2010). Declines of managed honey bees and beekeepers in Europe. *Journal of Apicultural Research, 49*, 15–22.

Puig de la Bellacasa, M. (2017). *Matters of care: Speculative ethics in more than human worlds*. Minnesota: University of Minnesota Press.

Raffles, H. (2010). *Insectopedia*. New York: Random House Inc.

Rosenthal, M. et al. (2017). Taxonomic bias in animal behaviour publications. *Animal Behaviour, 127*, 83–9.

Rozzi, R. (2019). Taxonomic chauvinism, no more! Antidotes from Hume, Darwin and biocultural ethics. *Environmental Ethics, 41(3)*, 249–82.

Rader, R. et al. (2009). Alternative pollinator taxa are equally efficient but not as effective as the honeybee in mass flowering crop. *Journal of Applied Ecology, 46*, 1080–7.

Rader, R. et al. (2016). Non-bee insects are important contributors to global crop pollination. *Proceedings of the National Academy of Sciences, 113*, 146–51.

Reade, C. et al. (2015). Invisible compromises: Global business, local ecosystems, and the commercial bumble bee trade. *Organization and Environment, 28(4)*, 436–57.

Rodgers, D. (2008). *Debugging the link between social theory and social insects*. Louisiana: LSU Press.

Ropars, L. et al. (2019). Wild pollinator activity negatively related to honey bee colony densities in urban context. *PLoS One, 14*, e0222316.

Ruttner, F. (1988). *Taxonomy and biogeography of honey bees*. Munich: Springer.

Saunders, M. (2018). Ecosystem services in agriculture: Understanding the multifunctional role of invertebrates. *Agricultural and Forest Entomology, 20*, 298–300.

Sayers, T., Steinbauer, M., & Miller R. (2019). Visitor or vector? The extent of rove beetle (Coleoptera: Staphylinidae) pollination and floral interactions. *Arthropod-Plant Interactions, 13*, 685–701.

Schneider, K. (2013). Pigs, fish, and birds: Toward multispecies ethnography in Melanesia. *Environment and Society, 4*, 25–40.

Schonfelder, M. & Bogner, F. (2017). Individual perception of bees: Between perceived danger and willingness to protect. *PLoS One, 12*, e0180168.

Smith, T. & Saunders, M. (2016). Honey bees: The queens of mass media, despite minority rule among insect pollinators. *Insect Conservation and Diversity, 9*, 384–90.

Southwick, E. & Southwick Jr, L. (1992). Estimating the economic value of honey bees (Hymenoptera: Apidae) as agricultural pollinators in the United States. *Journal of Economic Entomology, 98*, 790–5.

Stork, N. (2018). How many species of insects and other terrestrial arthropods are there on Earth? *Annual Review of Entomology, 63*, 31–45.

Sumner, S., Law, G., & Cini, A. (2018). Why we love bees and hate wasps. *Ecological Entomology, 43*, 836–45.

Trip, N. et al. (2020). Examining the public's awareness of bee (Hymenoptera: Apoidea: Anthophila) conservation in Canada. *Conservation Science and Practice*, e293.

Tronto, J. (1993). *Moral boundaries: A political argument for an ethic of care*. New York: Routledge.

Valtonen, A., Salmela, T., & Rantala, O. (2020). Living with mosquitoes. *Annals of Tourism Research, 83*, 1–10.

vanEngelsdorp, D. et al. (2009). Colony collapse disorder: A descriptive study. *PLoS One, 4*, e6481.

vanEngelsdorp, D. & Meixner, M. (2010). A historical review of managed honey bee populations in Europe and the United States and the factors that may affect them. *Journal of Invertebrate Pathology, 103*, S80–S95.

Van Huis, A. et al. (2013). *Edible insects: Future prospects for food and feed security*. Rome: UN Food and Agriculture Organisation.

Wagner, D.L., (2020). Insect declines in the Anthropocene. *Annual Review of Entomology, 65*, 457–480.

Watanabe, M. (1994). Pollination worries rise as honey bee declines. *Science, 265*, 1170.

Wilkie, R., Moore, L., & Molloy, C. (2019). How prevalent are invertebrates in human-animal scholarship? Scoping study of *Anthrozoös* and *Society and Animals Society and Animals, 27*, 656–77.

Wilson, E. (1987). The little things that run the world (the importance of conservation of invertebrates). *Conservation Biology, 1*, 344–6.

Wilson, J., Forister M., and Carril O. (2017). Interest exceeds understanding in public support of bee conservation. *Frontiers in Ecology and the Environment, 15*, 460–6.

Winfree, R. et al. (2007). Native bees provide insurance against ongoing honey bee losses. *Ecology Letters, 10*, 1105–13.

Winfree, R. (2008). Pollinator-dependent crops: An increasingly risky business. *Current Biology, 18*, R968.

Zhang, Z. (Ed.) (2011). *Animal Biodiversity: An introduction to higher-level classification and taxonomic richness*. Auckland: Magnolia Press.

CHAPTER 22

EMPATHY AND INCLUSION

A Philosophical Reading of the Ethics of Nonhuman Animals in Organizations

ELISA AALTOLA

INTRODUCTION

This chapter explores the potential uses of empathy within organizations. It focuses on the moral dimensions of these uses, particularly in the context of animal ethics. The fundamental questions raised in this chapter are threefold, first; what are the social and moral benefits of empathy? Secondly, how do these benefits manifest in de facto animal ethics? Thirdly, should organizations seek to enhance empathy, so as to better pay heed to the wellbeing of nonhuman animals? To help provide a means of thinking about such questions, I introduce six different varieties of empathy and analyse their potential role in making sense of the perspectives and moral consideration of nonhuman animals. I examine recent critiques of empathy, which posit that empathy hinders rather than aids moral inclusion, together with some possible counter arguments. By providing a framework for thinking with, this chapter contributes a new type of organizational philosophy that demonstrates how to pay attention to the experiences and moral worth of nonhuman animals.

EMPATHY, PRO-SOCIAL BEHAVIOUR, AND ORGANIZATIONS

Why is empathy relevant to organizational theory and management? One answer is that it is vital for the sort of pro-social behaviour that ideally lays the foundation for organizational structures. Here, empathy is both theoretically and practically significant: it helps to explain the history and constitution of phenomena such as cooperation, and on a very tangible level, it illuminates the nature of everyday social engagement. Empathy has been linked to the development of pro-social behaviour (Minio-Paluello et al., 2009; Slote, 2007; Soenens et al., 2007). It facilitates the ability to understand and communicate with others, and thus constitutes one cornerstone of social cognition and engagement. Moreover, it encourages us to take restorative action in instances of harm caused to others, thus intertwining with pro-social guilt (Davis, 1996; Decety et al., 2016; Roberts, Strayer, and Denham, 2014). Empathy also invites us to help others in distress (Batson et al., 2002), whilst inhibiting aggressive behaviour (Ali, Amorim, and Chamorro-Premuzic, 2009; Kaukiainen et al., 1999). On these grounds, it has been argued that empathy forms a universal basis for pro-social beliefs and actions (Hoffman, 2001).

Due to its pro-social nature, empathy is important in individual development (Cummins, Piek, and Dyck, 2005; Decety et al., 2016; Hoffman, 2001; Roberts, Strayer, and Denham, 2014): it allows human beings to grow into socially capable agents. Further, empathy plays a part in species development, as it augments our ability to form groups based on mutual trust and cooperation, which again boosts the survival of—not only individuals—but also populations and entire species. Thus, the prominent primatologist Frans de Waal, who has explored empathy's evolutionary roots and manifestations among our closest kin, has claimed that empathy holds an essential role in social interaction and cooperation, and ultimately in the development of *Homo sapiens* (de Waal, 2008: 282). In short, it allows us to stay tuned to the mental states of others, which again is pivotal for survival—'Being in sync is often a matter of life or death' (de Waal, 2008: 288). Since empathy has been observed in certain animals, it has been argued to form the basis of pro-social and helping behaviours also among some nonhuman beings which means this need not be viewed as an exclusively human quality (see Bartal, Decety, and Mason, 2011.)

Empathy has been argued to play a fundamental role in morality too (Blair and Blair, 2009; Deigh, 2011; Haidt, 2003; Hoffman, 2001). As the philosopher David Hume argued in the eighteenth century, our ability to 'reverberate' with and form ideas of the emotions of others is a capacity worth celebrating, since it facilitates moral agency (Hume, 1969). One of the moral benefits of empathy is motivational: empathy makes rational beliefs, which otherwise might remain abstract, matter to us on an affective level and thus motivates moral action (Decety and Cowell, 2014; Dadds et al., 2009). Another moral benefit is derived from the ties between empathy and the content of moral judgements, as the former can influence the latter (Decety and Cowell, 2014; Eisenberg, 2010).

With the above in mind, it is little wonder some have argued that empathy forms a cornerstone of a thriving society (Rifkin, 2009), thus acting as a capacity we collectively ought to enhance in ourselves and others. Indeed, the influential historical figure of liberalism, Adam Smith, dedicated a whole book to what he termed 'sympathy', but which correlates better with the contemporary term 'empathy'. According to Smith, empathy forms a central facet of human interaction, as it allows us to identify with others and thereby invites us to consider the wellbeing of those around us. In his corpus, successful societies rest on empathy, and Smith even presumed that empathy would guide individuals to make morally sound choices in the absence of rules (Smith, 2009.) It is arguable that Smith was excessively optimistic as we also need norms and rules for a morally functioning society. However, there is merit to his claim that empathy deserves more focus on a societal level: it may very well be vital for a morally operational society.

Empathy is central to society and, by extension, can also be positioned as a central element of a functional organization. It has been argued that without empathy, there is a risk of a Machiavellian ethos which focuses on egoistic gains, ruthless competition, hierarchies and the manipulation of others (Smith, 2006). This is a risk organizations face. When empathy is sidelined, organizations may become coloured by overt egoistic competition which erodes trust and increases the sort of hierarchies, conflicts, and inequalities that lessen members' wellbeing. In short, empathy is required for pro-social, morally functioning organizations inclusive of cooperation, pro-social action, and shared wellbeing. Many working within organizational theory have highlighted empathy as a unifying factor behind thriving organizations, capable of enhancing pro-social and altruistic action (Pavlovich and Krahnke, 2012).

Empathy's relevance is evident on an empirical level (Costa et al., 2018). For instance, some state organizations, such as those concerning health care and social work, afford space for empathy (Stanley, Mettilda Buvaneswari, and Meenakshi, 2018) because the consequences tend to be positive. In health care organizations, empathy correlates with better performance and leadership (Mortier, Vlerick, and Clays, 2016) and in the marketing sector, it has been manifested to increase customer satisfaction (Weaven et al., 2019). Further, empathy can facilitate positive public relations (Yeomans, 2016), which is often vital for commercial success. Empathy has also been incorporated into the design used in different organizations (for instance, the design of digital platforms and architecture) (Sustar and Mattelmäki, 2017). Indeed, the actual and potential uses of empathy within different organizational structures are vast.

Unfortunately, however, large organizations have often manifested reluctance to incorporate empathy and pro-social behaviours such as assistance and cooperation (Brandon-Jones, Wagner, and Ramsay, 2010). From the viewpoint of morality, this can be depicted as a major problem in need of urgent attention. Since large corporations hold enormous power on a global scale, their potential failures in empathy will have widespread societal implications, including disregard for the suffering of both human and nonhuman animals.

Empathy in Animal Ethics

Animal ethics—a field of philosophy that studies the norms and values concerning nonhuman animals—has tended to follow a rationalist meta-ethic, according to which our values and norms are primarily founded on rational analysis (see e.g. Singer 1975). However, some authors have argued that the role of emotions needs to be acknowledged as the companion of reason. Feminist animal ethics, for example, has underscored the role of emotions and empathy (Donovan, 2007; Gruen, 2015) while other philosophers have stressed the need for an empathetic animal ethic such as Mary Midgley (Midgley, 1983), Ralph Acampora (Acampora, 2006), and myself (Aaltola, 2018).

The relevance of empathy in animal ethics is based on a simple claim: if empathy plays a vital part in the constitution of pro-social behaviour and morality, it is needed in pro-social and moral engagement with nonhuman animals as well. First, it can motivate one to alleviate the suffering of other animals and to assist their wellbeing. Second, it can also invite us to conceptualize other animals and their treatment in moral terms. In relation to the first of these claims, the very first step of pro-social behaviour—the recognition of another being as a subject—is partly founded on empathy. Simon Baron-Cohen (2011) is among those who have posited that without empathy, others appear to us as objects rather than subjects. Arguably, this applies in relation to other animals, whose subjectivity empathy allows us to notice. Indeed, lack of empathy may have paved the way for conceptualizing nonhuman creatures as objects rather than subjects.

The philosopher René Descartes was an influential figure behind the traditional denial of animal subjectivity, which undermines the existence of nonhuman awareness and/or cognition (Harrison, 1992). As a result, *mechanomorphism*, which likens other animals to biological machines, has been common in the modern era (Crist, 1999). The moral consequences have been dire, as such mechanomorphism has facilitated the questionable treatment of nonhuman beings, particularly within animal industries (Aaltola, 2012). Contemporary psychology has used the term 'de-mentalization' in this context, and manifested that especially the minds of those animals, who are farmed and consumed, tend to be underrated (Bastian et al., 2011; Loughnan, Haslam, and Bastian, 2010). It has also shown that what tends to be missing from such instrumentalizing and de-mentalizing attitudes towards animals, is empathy (Camilleri, Gill, and Jago, 2020). Therefore, if we are to take pro-social action towards animals and support their wellbeing, we first need to acknowledge that other animals are also minded subjects—and this, again, requires the use of empathy.

In relation to the second claim, empathy is helpful for forming moral judgements concerning other animals. Midgley argued that reason alone cannot do justice to the fact that nonhuman animals are individuals with their own felt perspectives onto the world. In order to fully appreciate this fact, we also need emotion, and particularly emotive identification with other animals (Midgley, 1983). Rational analysis is necessary, but so is empathy. Midgley is referring to what in philosophy of mind is called 'phenomenal consciousness'—the ability to feel one's existence as *something*. Beings with phenomenal consciousness can experience their lives as having different qualities: it feels like something to be them (Nagel, 1974). If we are to gain a deeper understanding of the phenomenal consciousness of others, we must put our own phenomenal consciousness—our affective, emotive, experiential core—into use, and empathize with them. Midgley follows many other animal ethicists (Regan, 1983; Singer, 1975) in arguing that their ability to have a felt perspective on the world constitutes the fundamental reason for including also nonhuman animals in the sphere of moral consideration (Midgley, 1983).

This being so, empathy emerges as a channel via which we can better note the moral consideration (or perhaps consider-ability) of our nonhuman kin.

Applying empathy to other animals is epistemologically warranted. There are sound, scientific grounds to argue that phenomenal consciousness is a widespread capacity in the animal world (Allen and Bekoff, 2007; Edelman and Seth, 2009; Griffin and Speck, 2004;). Many animal species consist of what Tom Regan termed 'subjects of a life', that is, individuals with their own felt perspectives on the world, interlinked with cognitive capacities such as perception, memory, learning, and intentionality (Regan, 1983). If empathy—broadly construed—consists of identifying with the felt perspective of another (we shall come to its definitions shortly), then logically all beings with such a perspective can be empathy's legitimate recipients—including other animals.

Organizational Empathy for Animals

On an organizational level, the above means that, if organizations are to pay heed to pro-social behaviour and moral considerations, they need to afford room for empathy in their dealings with nonhuman animals. One way to approach such empathy is to designate animals as legitimate members of organizations, thus recognizing them as morally valuable subjects worthy of pro-social action. Indeed, the interesting task is to consider what type of membership nonhuman animals could have in different forms of organization, and what form of duties would be owed to them due to this membership. As a starting point, it needs to be acknowledged that such membership often requires human representation, whereby nonhuman beings have spokespeople representing their cause—one example being wild animal populations which, some environmental philosophers have argued, have legal rights to their habitats and need human representatives in the legal system (Hadley, 2016).

Indeed, when considering judicial organizations, many working in the field of animal law have argued that animals should be defined as legal subjects and thus as legitimate members, who bear basic species-specific rights in human societies, corresponding with human duties to respect their wellbeing (Kurki, 2019; Wise, 2000). When considering the state as an organization, Will Kymlicka and Sue Donaldson have posited that nonhuman animals can be considered as citizens and thereby as members (Donaldson and Kymlicka, 2013). In both instances, human representatives can defend the membership claims of the nonhuman beings; their legal, political, or moral rights. Therefore, both the legislative and state membership of nonhuman animals has been a topic of discussion. The future task is to map out what type of membership nonhuman beings can have in different organizations, such as those related to health care, education, and the media.

Should the health of nonhuman animals—particularly those in our guardianship—be protected through institutional health care? Should other animals have representatives in the education system and the media, whereby children are taught about their capacities and needs (as is the case in 'humane education', see Saari, 2020), and whereby the media would hold an obligation to discuss also the interests of nonhuman animals? Further, should financial organizations include animal interests through, for instance, innovations and investments aimed at bettering nonhuman wellbeing via protecting the natural habitats of wild animals, or replacing industrial animal agriculture with cultured meat, for example? Considering the power of financial organizations, it is timely to ask: should they include nonhuman animals as stakeholders, and what form would this inclusion take? Some valuable analyses of this issue exist (e.g. García-Rosell and Tallberg, 2021), but more are needed.

Human organizations have tended to remain hopelessly anthropocentric. Recognition of nonhuman interests has remained regrettably rare and limited, as for instance societal and legal protection afforded to other animals has frequently been both minimal and poorly administered (Rudlof, 2017). Therefore, one significant future challenge for organizations and theory thereof is to broaden their scope to nonhuman perspectives and wellbeing. Indeed, we can speak of the need for 'multispecies inclusion', whereby different forms of organization take into account nonhuman interests, based on animals' biological and psychological needs. Beyond reason, this multispecies inclusion requires empathy, which motivates pro-social actions towards, and the construction of moral categories concerning, other animals. Such an inclusion poses a radical challenge but also holds promise of guiding us out of the crises of the Anthropocene (climate change, the sixth mass extinction of species, the unsustainable growth of animal industries, etc.). In fact, it can be argued that it forms one important answer to these crises—an innovative step towards sustainable solutions.

Varieties of Empathy

One danger is that empathy is used instrumentally, as a way to increase one's own gains at the expense of others (the typical example being empathy as superficial pretence, which is solely aimed at bringing in more customers). This problem is particularly pertinent for business relations, and has led to a call to distinguish genuine empathy from its instrumental sibling (Yeomans, 2016). What, therefore, is empathy? Empathy is a heterogenic mental state and takes different forms, which can be contradictory in relation to each other (Decety and Ickes, 2009). My own taxonomy distinguishes empathy into six categories (Aaltola, 2018) and can be seen in Figure 22.1.

Briefly summarized, 'projective empathy' refers to imagining what oneself would feel in the situation of another, whilst 'simulative empathy' refers to imagining what another feels in their own situation. In the context of other animals, the first of these invites us to think, how we would feel when confined into a farrowing crate commonly used in animal agriculture (a cage, which restricts the movement of the sow to an extent that she cannot turn around), for example. Thus, we would project our own human existence into the situation of a sow: what would it be like for a human being to live

```
Projective empathy
Simulative empathy
Cognitive empathy
Embodied empathy
Affective empathy
Reflective empathy
```

FIGURE 22.1 Types of empathy.

in a cage? Simulative empathy, on the other hand, seeks to envision what the sow is undergoing: what is it like for a sow to live in a cage? Without using these precise terms, Adam Smith accentuated both, as he posited that empathy is both about projection of similarity and imagination of difference (Rick, 2007; Smith, 2009).[1] Arguably, both projective and simulative empathy are needed for skilled moral agency, as they allow us to better our understanding of the experiences of other individuals (Aaltola, 2018).

Cognitive empathy, on the other hand, refers to a relatively non-affective perception or inference of the mental states of another. Here, the empathizer perceives or rationally surmises the other's emotions. Thus, she may conclude, on the basis of perceiving hesitant gestures, that the other individual is afraid, for example. This form of empathy was sketched by Smith's friend David Hume (Hume, 1969), and has later become a standard in empathy research (e.g. Schnell et al., 2011). Cognitive empathy is easily applied to other animals, as certain branches of science can infer their possible affective states from their behaviour. This is needed in moral agency, particularly since it allows us to form more rationally considered interpretations of the mental states of others (Aaltola, 2014b).

The fourth category is embodied empathy. Its philosophical roots are in phenomenology, which underscored the embodied nature of all cognition. Edith Stein (1989) stressed that empathy is embedded in our somatic abilities and responses: when I feel empathy towards another, I do so as a bodily being, whose somatic nature responds to that of another (Stein, 1989; Zahavi, 2007). Embodied empathy can be applied to other animals. Indeed, Stein uses dogs as an example: a human individual can empathize with dogs by simply focusing on aspects of somatic similarity (Stein, 1989). Even when very distinct in comparison, the body forms a point of mutuality and relative likeness,

---

[1] Smith and other contemporaries, such as Hume, used the term 'sympathy' rather than 'empathy'.

which acts as a basis for empathy, allowing human beings to empathize with seagulls, octopuses, or cows—on these grounds, Ralph Acampora has spoken of 'corporeal compassion' towards nonhuman beings (Acampora, 2006). Moreover, embodied empathy can facilitate a deeper and more nuanced understanding of other individuals, and thus aid in moral agency.

The fifth category is affective empathy. It refers to an affective resonation with the emotions of another, whereby the empathizer shares the sorrow or joy of another. Hume is one historical source for this variety, as he depicts how individuals can 'reverberate' with the emotions of others (Hume, 1969: 367). It was also celebrated by Arthur Schopenhauer (2005), who used the term 'compassion' in its place. On a more contemporary level, affective empathy is frequently referred to in empirical empathy studies, and the neurological underpinnings of resonation have been of continuing interest (e.g. Eres et al., 2015). I argue that it is affective empathy which acts as a necessary foundation of moral agency: in short, without the ability to resonate with the emotions of others and to viscerally comprehend their affective states, we cannot be moral creatures. One indication of this is that amoral individuals, such as those with strong psychopathic tendencies, tend to lack affective empathy towards other human beings (Aaltola, 2014a). Now, as Schopenhauer argued, this type of resonation can be extended to include nonhuman animals; we can feel compassion for them (Schopenhauer, 2005). Indeed, I argue it to be the most important variety of empathy in the context of animal ethics. If we are to be motivated to act in support of animal wellbeing, we need affective care towards nonhuman creatures, which again requires that we foster affective empathy towards them (Aaltola, 2018).

The sixth variety of empathy is reflective empathy. Whilst the five other varieties tend to take place on the first-order level of mentation, focusing on the immediate stream of emotions, perceptions, and thoughts; reflective empathy takes a step back and rests on the second-order level, from which it evaluates the first-order mental events and contents. Importantly, reflective empathy is not a combination of empathy and rational analysis (which would constitute two separate mental phenomena). Instead, it makes use of *attention* as a pre-lingual and pre-rational metacognitive state developed, for instance, via mindfulness training (Kang, Gruber, and Gray, 2012; Norman, 2017), and attaches this attention integrally to empathic contents. Therefore, the meta-level 'reflection' here refers to the sort of clarity and recognition facilitated by (mindful) attention—quite literally, it is a moment of illumination, which allows us to note our first-order mental states reflected in a new light. More specifically, reflective empathy permits us to recognize and re-evaluate the first-order instances of empathy, and to reflect on their background, causes, content, form, and scope. In a state of reflective empathy I can, for instance, notice and consider why I empathize strongly with dogs, what moral implications empathy for dogs comes with, whether I should utilize other varieties of empathy in order to understand dogs more comprehensively, and whether I should expand my empathy to, for example, pigs and pikes (Aaltola, 2018).

Reflective empathy is fruitful in animal ethics. Societal and cultural influences guide empathy, and if these influences invite one to empathize strongly with companion animals whilst leaving farmed animals aside, the moral consequences are evident. Indeed, psychological studies manifest that it is precisely lack of empathy towards particularly farmed animals, which keeps many stuck in the dilemma of loving some animals whilst eating others (Camilleri, Gill, and Jago, 2020). Reflective empathy holds promise of inviting us to note the potential limits of our empathy, and to extend that empathy to include all those beings, who are its legitimate recipients (i.e. all creatures, who have phenomenal consciousness).

All of the above varieties of empathy are needed to gain a fuller grasp of other individuals—including members of other species. I suggest that affective empathy is the necessary foundation of moral concern, but that also the other varieties are beneficial, as they offer more nuance and depth to our appreciation of others. Moreover, due to its ability to invite us to consider the origins and scope of our empathy, I argue that cultivating reflective empathy holds promise of advancing our moral ability further—in short, developing reflective empathy allows us to improve moral agency.

I suggest that organizations and organizational theory would benefit from making use of these six varieties of empathy. Doing so will arguably strengthen the type of co-operation and pro-social behaviour which ideally stand at the root of organizations. These varieties of empathy allow organizations to better acknowledge the moral relevance and interests of nonhuman animals, and to practise moral agency in relation to them. Moreover, highlighting the need for reflective empathy will allow organizations to keep on cultivating empathy skills, thus becoming more aware of how to better include all those beings who stand as empathy's valid receivers.

Amelié Rorty has spoken of the responsibility of institutions to better individuals' moral ability—an argument, which echoes Aristotle's claims, according to which *the polis* is to make its citizens more virtuous (Rorty, 1997). In line with this, I posit that institutions and organizations also have some responsibility to enhance the empathy skills of their members—to each other and towards nonhuman animals. Thus, for instance organizations related to education, law, media, marketing, and finance (to offer a few examples), would all share the responsibility of refining their members' abilities to empathize with nonhuman beings.[2] Therefore, they would not only face the obligation to take empathy towards animals into account, but also to foster it among their human members. In this, reflective empathy is pivotal.

Prejudiced Empathy?

Not all agree that empathy is needed or even beneficial for morality. Paul Bloom is among those who have argued that empathy rests on the sort of biases that stand in the

---

[2] The results would also benefit human beings, as it has been shown that enhancing empathy towards other animals within early education will increase empathy towards human individuals (Thompson and Gullone, 2003).

way of morality (Bloom, 2016). In short, he argues that we feel most empathy towards those who are closest to or most like us, which means that morality based on empathy would be hopelessly partial. Such criticism is not new. Hume (1969: 631) acknowledged that empathy (or 'sympathy', as he termed it) is prone to prejudice, as we undergo it most towards those most familiar, proximate, or similar to ourselves. There is no denying that empathy can rest on and reaffirm biases.

We have a tendency to immediately empathize most with those who are similar to us, and on the other hand, people tend to empathize less with those whom they consider to be members of out-groups (Cikara, Bruneau, and Saxe, 2011). These considerations are highly pertinent to animal ethics. It appears evident that most human beings tend to feel more empathy towards their conspecifics than other animals (Miralles, Raymond, and Lecointre, 2019). If we were to rely solely on empathy in our moral beliefs concerning animals, those beliefs would likely be highly species-partial. Thus, organizations that accentuate the role of empathy may risk simply reaffirming the anthropocentric order.

However, empathy can also be extended to outgroups. For instance, among primates, positive experiences of strangers will increase empathy (de Waal, 2008: 291), and among humans, positive social beliefs and norms concerning members of out-groups can expand empathy (Tarrant, Dazeley, and Cottom, 2009). These examples suggest that empathy is not restricted to in-groups. Indeed, the very notion of universal human rights arguably rests partly on extending empathetic concern beyond the immediate social setting—without empathy's ability to cross divides, it would appear likely that we would be even more biased than we currently are. A better way of conceptualizing it, perhaps, is that empathy has a dual nature and consequences: it can rest on and reaffirm biases, but it can also challenge those biases by making us pay heed to out-groups.

Hume noted that there are ways to diminish empathy's biases. He spoke of the need to seek a general point of view, which allows us to evaluate our different affective responses before following them (Rick, 2007). I argue that reflective empathy includes such a general point of view, from which to evaluate the limits and potentialities of our empathic responses, and with which to combat biases. Whilst the other varieties of empathy are prone to biases simply because they tend to take place on the immediacy of the first-order level, which often echoes learned prejudices, reflective empathy avoids this trap. By inviting us to move to a meta-level, from which to evaluate first-order empathic responses (or lack thereof), it also invites us to acknowledge and correct biases. This applies in the context of animal ethics.

Because of the prevalence of in-group motivations (Greene, 2013), it is beneficial to evaluate the potential biases impacting one's moral judgements. Reflective empathy provides only one anchor for such evaluation. Other anchors include rational analysis, engagement with distant groups, and scientific knowledge of the relevant empirical facts. In sum, avoiding biases requires constant and broad focus, in which reflective empathy acts as only one (albeit important) evaluative foundation. Within organizations, reflective empathy offers a method of avoiding biases. It provokes us to question, why is empathy seemingly limited to the human species and its companion animals, whilst other animals are disregarded? This question urges organizations and their human members to question the anthropocentric social norms that limit empathy, and to render their empathy and ethics less partial. As a potential end-result stands a society in which all minded individuals, regardless of species, have more chances of flourishing—a society of shared, interspecies wellbeing.

Concluding Words

Extending empathy towards other animals on an organizational level is arguably one of the necessary factors behind a successful response to contemporary crises such as climate change, species extinction, and factory farming. This is because empathy helps us to recognize the relevance of nonhuman perspectives and the moral worth of other-than-human beings, which will allow us to make choices that are both morally and environmentally more sustainable. Without such an extension of empathy, there is little hope of the sort of widespread change in our value priorities that is needed to tackle these crises.

In practice, this would require different organizational sectors, ranging from businesses to, for instance, governmental entities, to take into consideration how their actions impact the wellbeing of other species and individual animals. Nonhuman beings should be approached as stakeholders, whose flourishing is constantly taken into account on the level of organizational decision-making. Today, often such decision-making apparently concerns only (given groups of) human beings, whilst the nonhuman realm is left without due attention. This failure to acknowledge the importance of animal wellbeing needs to be urgently rectified.

This is the era of catastrophes, but also the era of possibilities, wherein the type of creative thinking that is willing to burst through old anthropocentric restrictions can improve the living conditions of all species. In such creative thinking, organizations can either be obstacles or—as is suggested in this chapter—catalysts for beneficial social change. Indeed, if they take empathy seriously, organizations and organizational theory have a chance of standing as vanguards of empathy education and its wider positive consequences for the nonhuman world.

References

Aaltola, E. (2012). *Animal suffering: Philosophy and culture*. Palgrave MacMillan.
Aaltola, E. (2014a). Affective empathy as core moral agency: Psychopathy, autism and reason revisited. *Philosophical Explorations, 17*(1), 76–92. doi: 10.1080/13869795.2013.825004.
Aaltola, E. (2014b). Varieties of empathy and moral agency. *Topoi, 33*(1), 243–53. doi: 10.1007/s11245-013-9205-8.
Aaltola, E. (2018). *Varieties of empathy: Moral psychology and animal ethics*. London: Rowman & Littlefield Int.

Acampora, R. (2006). *Corporal compassion: Animal ethics and philosophy of body*. Pittsburgh: University of Pittsburgh Press.

Ali, F., Amorim, I., & Chamorro-Premuzic, T. (2009). Empathy deficits and trait emotional intelligence in psychopathy and Machiavellianism. *Personality and Individual Differences, 47*, 758–62. doi: 10.1016/j.paid.2009.06.016.

Allen, C., & Bekoff, M. (2007). Animal consciousness. In *The Blackwell companion to consciousness* (pp. 58–71). John Wiley & Sons, Ltd. doi: https://doi.org/10.1002/9780470751466.ch5.

Baron-Cohen, S. (2011). *Zero degrees of empathy: A new theory of human cruelty*. London: Penguin Books.

Bartal, I. B.-A., Decety, J., & Mason, P. (2011). Empathy and pro-social behavior in rats. *Science, 334(6061)*, 1427–30. doi: 10.1126/science.1210789.

Bastian, B. et al. (2011). Don't mind meat? The denial of mind to animals used for human consumption. *Personality and Social Psychology Bulletin, 38(2)*, 247–56. doi: 10.1177/0146167211424291.

Batson, C. et al. (2002). Empathy, attitudes, and action: Can feeling for a member of a stigmatized group motivate one to help the group? *Personality and Social Psychology Bulletin, 28*, 1656–66.

Blair, R., & Blair, K. (2009). Empathy, morality, and social convention: Evidence from the study of psychopathy and other psychiatric disorders. In J. Decety, & W. Ickes (Eds.), *The social neuroscience of empathy* (pp. 139–52). Massachussets: MIT Press. doi: 10.7551/mitpress/9780262012973.003.0012.

Bloom, P. (2016). *Against empathy*. New York: Ecco.

Brandon-Jones, A., Wagner, B., & Ramsay, J. (2010). 'Trading interactions: Supplier empathy, consensus and bias. *International Journal of Operations & Production Management, 30(5)*, 453–87. doi: 10.1108/01443571011039588.

Camilleri, L., Gill, P.R., & Jago, A. (2020). The role of moral disengagement and animal empathy in the meat paradox. *Personality and Individual Differences, 164*, 110103. doi: https://doi.org/10.1016/j.paid.2020.110103.

Cikara, M., Bruneau, E.G., & Saxe, R.R. (2011). Us and them: Intergroup failures of empathy. *Current Directions in Psychological Science, 20(3)*, 149–53. doi: 10.1177/0963721411408713.

Costa, E. et al. (2018). Empathy, closeness, and distance in non-profit accountability. *Accounting, Auditing & Accountability Journal, 32(1)*, 224–54. doi: 10.1108/AAAJ-03-2014-1635.

Crist, E. (1999). *Images of animals: Anthropocentrism and animal mind*. Philadelphia: Temple University Press.

Cummins, A., Piek, J.P., & Dyck, M.J. (2005). Motor coordination, empathy, and social behaviour in school-aged children. *Developmental Medicine & Child Neurology, 47(7)*, 437–42. doi: https://doi.org/10.1111/j.1469-8749.2005.tb01168.x.

Dadds, M.R. et al. (2009). Learning to "talk the talk": The relationship of psychopathic traits to deficits in empathy across childhood. *Journal of Child Psychology and Psychiatry, 50(5)*, 599–606. doi: https://doi.org/10.1111/j.1469-7610.2008.02058.x.

Davis, M. (1996). *Empathy: A social psychological approach*. Boulder: Westview Press.

Decety, J. et al. (2016). Empathy as a driver of prosocial behaviour: Highly conserved neurobehavioural mechanisms across species. *Philosophical Transactions of the Royal Society B: Biological Sciences, 371(1686)*, 20150077. doi: 10.1098/rstb.2015.0077.

Decety, J., & Cowell, J.M. (2014). The complex relation between morality and empathy. *Trends in Cognitive Sciences, 18(7)*, 337–9. doi: https://doi.org/10.1016/j.tics.2014.04.008.

Decety, J., & Ickes, W. (Eds.) (2009). *The social neuroscience of empathy*. Massachusetts: MIT Press.

Deigh, J. (2011). Empathy, justice, and jurisprudence. *The Southern Journal of Philosophy*, 49(s1), 73–90. doi: https://doi.org/10.1111/j.2041-6962.2011.00058.x.

Donaldson, S., & Kymlicka, W. (2013). *Zoopolis: A political theory of animal rights*. Oxford: Oxford University Press.

Donovan, J. (2007). Attention to suffering: Sympathy as a basis for ethical treatment of animals. In J. Donovan, & C. Adams (Eds.), *The feminist care tradition in animal ethics*. New York: Columbia University Press.

Edelman, D.B., & Seth, A.K. (2009). Animal consciousness: A synthetic approach. *Trends in Neurosciences*, 32(9), 476–84. doi: https://doi.org/10.1016/j.tins.2009.05.008.

Eisenberg, N. (2010). Empathy-related responding: Links with self-regulation, moral judgment, and moral behavior. *Prosocial Motives, Emotions, and Behavior: The Better Angels of Our Nature*, 129–48. doi: 10.1037/12061-007.

Eres, R. et al. (2015). Individual differences in local gray matter density are associated with differences in affective and cognitive empathy. *NeuroImage*, 117, 305–10. doi: https://doi.org/10.1016/j.neuroimage.2015.05.038.

García-Rosell, J.-C., & Tallberg, L. (2021). Animals as tourism stakeholders: Huskies, reindeer, and horses working in Lapland. In C. Kline & J.M. (Eds.), *From beasts of burden to K9 security: The working animals of the tourism industry*, (pp. 103–22). Leiden: De Gruyter Oldenbourg. doi: doi:10.1515/9783110664058-008.

Greene, J. (2013). *Moral tribes: Emotion, reason, and the gap between us and them*. London: Penguin Press.

Griffin, D.R., Speck, G.B. (2004). New evidence of animal consciousness. *Animal Cognition*, 7(1), 5–18.

Gruen, L. (2015). *Entangled empathy: An alternative ethic for our relationships with animals*. Herndon: Lantern Books.

Hadley, J. (2016). *Animal property rights: A theory of habitat rights for wild animals*. Lexington Books.

Haidt, J. (2003). The moral emotions. In R. Davidson, K. Goldsmith, & H. Scherer (Eds.), *Handbook of affective sciences*. Oxford: Oxford University Press.

Harrison, P. (1992). Descartes on animals. *The Philosophical Quarterly (1950-)*, 42(167), 219–27. doi: 10.2307/2220217.

Hoffman, M. (2001). *Empathy and moral development*. Cambridge: Cambridge University Press.

Hume, D. (1969). *A treatise of human nature*. London: Penguin Books.

Kang, Y., Gruber, J., & Gray, J.R. (2012). Mindfulness and de-automatization *Emotion Review*, 5(2), 192–201. doi: 10.1177/1754073912451629.

Kaukiainen, A. et al. (1999). The relationships between social intelligence, empathy, and three types of aggression. *Aggressive Behavior*, 25(2), 81–9. doi: https://doi.org/10.1002/(SICI)1098-2337(1999)25:2<81::AID-AB1>3.0.CO;2-M.

Kurki, V. (2019). *A theory of legal personhood*. Oxford: Oxford University Press.

Loughnan, S., Haslam, N., & Bastian, B. (2010). The role of meat consumption in the denial of moral status and mind to meat animals. *Appetite*, 55(1), 156–9. doi: 10.1016/j.appet.2010.05.043.

Midgley, M. (1983). *Animals and why they matter*. Athens, Georgia: University of Georgia Press.

Minio-Paluello, I. et al. (2009). Absence of embodied empathy during pain observation in Asperger syndrome *Biological Psychiatry, 65*(1), 55–62. doi: 10.1016/j.biopsych.2008.08.006.

Miralles, A., Raymond, M., & Lecointre, G. (2019). Empathy and compassion toward other species decrease with evolutionary divergence time. *Scientific Reports, 9(1),* 19555. doi: 10.1038/s41598-019-56006-9.

Mortier, A.V., Vlerick, P., & Clays, E. (2016). Authentic leadership and thriving among nurses: The mediating role of empathy. *Journal of Nursing Management, 24*(3), 357–65. doi: https://doi.org/10.1111/jonm.12329.

Nagel, T. (1974). What is it like to be a bat? *The Philosophical Review, 83(4),* 435–50. doi: 10.2307/2183914.

Norman, E. (2017). Metacognition and mindfulness: The role of fringe consciousness. *Mindfulness, 8(1),* 95–100. doi: 10.1007/s12671-016-0494-z.

Pavlovich, K., & Krahnke, K. (2012). Empathy, connectedness and organisation. *Journal of Business Ethics, 105*(1), 131–7. doi: 10.1007/s10551-011-0961-3.

Regan, T. (1983). *The case for animal rights*. Berkeley: University of California Press.

Rick, J. (2007). Hume's and Smith's partial sympathies and impartial stances. *Journal of Scottish Philosophy, 5*(2), 135–58. doi: 10.3366/jsp.2007.5.2.135.

Rifkin, J. (2009). *The empathic civilization: The race to global consciousness in a world in crisis.* New York: TarcherPerigee.

Roberts, W., Strayer, J., & Denham, S. (2014). Empathy, anger, guilt: Emotions and prosocial behaviour. *Canadian Journal of Behavioural Science, 46,* 465–74.

Rorty, A.O. (1997). The social and political sources of akrasia. *Ethics, 107(4),* 644–57. doi: 10.1086/233763.

Rudlof, L. (2017). The lack of implementation and enforcement of the Animal Welfare Act. *Syracuse Law Review, 67(173),* 173–190.

Saari, M.H. (2020). Re-examining the human-nonhuman animal relationship through humane education. In A. Cutter-Mackenzie-Knowles, K. Malone, & E. Barratt Hacking (Eds.), Research Handbook on Childhoodnature: Assemblages of childhood and nature research. (pp. 1263–73). Springer International Publishing. doi: 10.1007/978-3-319-67286-1_69.

Schnell, K. et al. (2011). Functional relations of empathy and mentalizing: An fMRI study on the neural basis of cognitive empathy. *NeuroImage, 54*(2), 1743–54. doi: https://doi.org/10.1016/j.neuroimage.2010.08.024.

Schopenhauer, A. (2005). *The basis of morality*. Dover publications.

Singer, P. (1975). *Animal liberation*. London: Harper Collins.

Slote, M. (2007). *The ethics of care and empathy*. London: Routledge.

Smith, A. (2006). Cognitive empathy and emotional empathy in human behaviour and evolution. *The Psychological Record, 56,* 3–21.

Smith, A. (2009). *The theory of moral sentiments*. London: Penguin Books.

Soenens, B. et al. (2007). The intergenerational transmission of empathy-related responding in adolescence: The role of maternal support. *Personality and Social Psychology Bulletin, 33(3),* 299–311. doi: 10.1177/0146167206296300.

Stanley, S., Mettilda Buvaneswari, G., & Meenakshi, A. (2018). Predictors of empathy in women social workers. *Journal of Social Work, 20*(1), 43–63. doi: 10.1177/1468017318794280.

Stein, E. (1989). *On the problem of empathy*. Washington: ISC Publishing.

Sustar, H., & Mattelmäki, T. (2017). Whole in one: Designing for empathy in complex systems. DESIGN+POWER. *7(7),* 8, available at: http://www.nordes.org.

Tarrant, M., Dazeley, S., & Cottom, T. (2009). Social categorization and empathy for outgroup members. *British Journal of Social Psychology, 48(3)*, 427–46. doi: https://doi.org/10.1348/014466608X373589.

Thompson, K.L., & Gullone, E. (2003). Promotion of empathy and prosocial behaviour in children through humane education. *Australian Psychologist, 38(3)*, 175–82. doi: https://doi.org/10.1080/00050060310001707187.

de Waal, F.B.M. (2008). Putting the altruism back into altruism: The evolution of empathy. *Annual Review of Psychology, 59(1)*, 279–300. doi: 10.1146/annurev.psych.59.103006.093625.

Weaven, S. et al. (2019). Empathy and apology: The effectiveness of recovery strategies. *Marketing Intelligence & Planning, 37(4)*, 358–71. doi: 10.1108/MIP-03-2018-0080.

Wise, S. (2000). *Rattling the cage: Towards legal rights for animals.* Hachette Books.

Yeomans, L. (2016). Imagining the lives of others: Empathy in public relations. *Public Relations Inquiry, 5(1)*, 71–92. doi: 10.1177/2046147X16632033.

Zahavi, D. (2007). Expression and Empathy. In D. Hutto, & M. Ratcliffe (Eds.), *Folk psychology re-assessed* (pp.25–40). Dordrecht: Springer.

PART IV

CARE, CULTURES, AND AFFECT IN ANIMAL WORK RELATIONS

CHAPTER 23

OLLY THE CAT

Excerpts from a Feline Ethnography in Business and Management Studies

DAMIAN O'DOHERTY

Introduction

On the grand marble steps that lead to the corporate headquarters of Manchester Airport group sits a mangy marmalade-streaked cat. This is Olly, or 'Olly the cat', sitting outside Olympic House. She gives an 'introduction' to the organization, but in a tricksy and felinely reflexive kind of way. You have to pay particular attention to the position of the ears and the tail because, as a description of her posture, 'sits' is not quite right. Get this description wrong and you are possibly in big trouble. Things can rapidly get out of hand with cats. If you want to avoid the worst of the industrial relations consequences that will potentially follow any misreading of her attitudes or behaviour you need to pay particular attention. Corporate resignations, walk-outs, strikes, distress, demotivation, guilt and shame, all manner of human resource-related calamities might radiate and ricochet out through networks of communication and sociality. We don't teach these skills of attention to students of business and management studies, but get it right and you might just land a new million-pound contract for an airport terminal refurbishment. Perhaps Olly is best described, then, as poised, guarding, coiled, or even prowling. Is she looking at you? Are you being stripped naked under the gaze of this semi-feral creature (Derrida, 2008)? We might want to say she is imperious in her grandeur, but of course she is clearly gesturing in a whole set of ways unique to her species (Alger and Alger, 2003) that new medical and feline science is becoming increasingly adept in its reading (Little, 2011). Is this an introduction or a warning?

Many businesses have animals like Olly, which makes the neglect of the animal in business and management studies surprising. It is perhaps not so much neglect as disavowal given the fact that this ignorance can never be fully complete or successful.

From the early days of sedentary civilization and agriculture permitting grain stores to be established (Rogers, 2006), to the officially designated 'chief mouser' at the UK cabinet office (Kraemer and Sleeter, 2019), life as we know it is not possible without the cat. Unfortunately, the current business school lacks the imagination and nerve to offer specialist courses to undergraduates and MBAs in how to acknowledge and manage their animals. This is potentially catastrophic for the economic wellbeing of the UK, or 'UK plc' (public limited company) as it is sometimes ironically referred to in the press. One searches the corpus of textbooks or syllabi in vain for concern with the nonhuman animal, and even the most venturous and controversial avant-garde texts pushing at the frontiers of curriculum reform (e.g. Jones and O'Doherty, 2005) only devote a few pages to the ill-defined category of 'animality' (Borgerson, 2005). There is money to be made from animals though. The influence on Henry Ford's thinking after his visit to the *dis-assembly* lines of animal destruction in Chicago's Swift and Company meatpacking house are well documented (Barratt, 2002). There may be a strong case that the modern global capitalist political economy and associated liberal democracy is founded on oil, but there are equally strong claims that the most essential element that drives neoliberal production systems, whilst inflicting the most self-destructive damage to land, ecology, and health, is meat-eating and the industries that promote and serve these tastes (Shukin, 2009; Pollan, 2006).

In this chapter, I draw on two and a half years of ethnographic fieldwork at Manchester Airport Group in the UK, part of which included extended study of Olly the cat (Olly existed in a liminal state using both she/he pronouns), where I grappled with the significance of his presence in matters of management and organization and sought to answer the question about the role of the animal in contemporary organization. This question is one that has preoccupied a number of specialists in management and organization studies and forms part of a turn to 'animal studies' that has now begun to establish a fairly coherent genealogy of foundations and seminal texts (Ackroyd and Crowdy, 1990; Boyd, 2001; ten Bos, 2004; Desmond, 2010; Hamilton and Taylor, 2012; 2013, 2017; Lennefors and Sköld, 2015). Specialists in organization studies draw inspiration from an eclectic range of work including the ever popular Agamben (2004), Deleuze and Guattari (1987), Derrida's late studies on the animal (Derrida, 2008; 2009), and Donna Haraway's (2003; 2007) remarkable series of texts on human/nonhuman relations and what she calls 'companion species'. As always, organization studies benefits from a certain feral ill-discipline that means it can lay claim to have largely pioneered this animal turn in business and management studies drawing on theory and writings far from the mainstream (see Sayers, 2016; Doré and Michalon, 2017; Skoglund and Redmalm, 2017; Clarke and Knights, 2022; Huopalainen, 2020).

The feline and multispecies ethnography in this chapter develops this work to show how we can learn from the nonhuman animal in ways that ask us to reach beyond the modern principles of management knowledge and rationality (O'Doherty and De Cock, 2017). It opens a space where management can be seen to inhabit a *constitutive impossibility* where ontology is highly uncertain and paradoxical. Management finds its limits in a dimension of organization that simultaneously gives rise to incredible creativity and innovation that leaves organization poised in multiple and undecidable co-existing realities. It forms part of an attempt to develop a 'feline ethnography' on which I have been working for the past 10 years (O'Doherty, 2016; 2017; 2018) to help redress the lack of resources in business and management studies for registering or attending to the role of animals that often lurk as a shadow or disavowed presence in work organizations. In this chapter, I try to find the descriptive and narrative resources equal to the challenge that Olly the cat posed to management at Manchester Airport. I am also looking to practise a form of ethnographic analysis and description that eschews the divide between theory and method so that it can respond to the kind of sensorial or affective and embodied experiences to which one is exposed when entering human/nonhuman relations, in this case relations and practices that formed around Olly the Cat at Manchester Airport between 2009 and 2013. In these ways, I am seeking a deliberate *superficiality* that attempts to shed as much theoretical knowing and meta-explanation whilst making tentative cat-like steps towards theorizing its prey.

Entrance to Olympic House and the Manchester Airport Group

Those marble steps are quite a thing. They tower up with grandeur and monumentalism designed perhaps, as scholars of corporate architecture suggest, to acclimate or glorify, intimidate or stupefy (Dale and Burrell, 2008; Decker, 2014; Jackson and Carter, 2010). And yet if you pay attention to the cat something else appears. Olly appeared on the first day of my ethnography, but she/he was visually registered at first only out of the corner of my eye. Not trained by the disciplines of management and organization to pay much attention to these seeming irrelevancies and marginalia of corporate life I was too preoccupied with the chief executive officer (CEO) (I came to know as Rupert) striding ahead less than 10 yards ahead of me. I was trying to keep my distance in order to avoid a premature meeting that would demand informalities and pleasantries for which I was not yet prepared. I had a meeting with him in less than an hour during which he would decide whether to grant access to the airport for my ethnographic research. I kept my distance, but attentive and mindful of his movements I followed him.

Suddenly, Rupert made a move that took him to the left of his intended path. This shift of body weight soon became a swerve that traced an arc in the form of a semi-circle, away and then back towards the glass entrance doors. As he shifted to the left, Olly appeared directly in front of me. A cat. Sat on a mat. I smiled. Was that a Cheshire grin, I remember thinking? Behind the cat was an impressive and imposing wooden kennel, complete with a high Swiss chalet style roofline. Others might describe the shelter as Shaker in inspiration or a New England style wooden cathouse or 'catio' (Galaxy and Benjamin, 2014), and it cannot help but attract attention, placed immediately to the left of the revolving door entrance. The catio is also festooned in gifts, flowers, colour postcards, pinwheel wind spinners, blankets, makeshift trinkets that shine and twinkle in the sun. I later come to understand that this is 'Olly's house' paid for by donations and voluntary contributions. Olly's house presents something like a 'mise-en-abime' of Olympic House, productive of what is known as the 'Droste effect' (named after the Dutch cocoa advertising), a recursive or abyssal visual effect in which one expects to find a series of nested miniatures set one inside the other (see also Woycicki, 2016). It is Olly's house all the way down, but who had designed this, and with what intentions?

Rupert had now gained access to his glass portal. It was quite a digression and as my gaze returned to his stride I became aware of comportment and what might be described as his generous and corpulent figure. A typical, rotund chief executive, well-fed and exuding an air of satisfaction. Eyes were upon him. He was supposed to be the star of this show. By contrast to this plump and portly demeanour I noticed how thin his legs looked, fragile even, 'pins holding up a cannonball' I recorded in my diary, with not too much concern for its lack of diplomacy. Olly was now on her side. Her head tilts ever so slightly and then appears to track the path of what might be a human sentinel who has emerged from the revolving glass entrance doors. It's difficult to tell from this angle, lying on the ground, twisting your head whilst recumbent on a marble plinth, up and around from left shoulder to right, an arc of some 180 degrees. The human is carrying a bucket with a mop. In the bucket there is a sanitizer spray and a large roll of blue kitchen paper. Yes, unfortunately Olly has become rather incontinent of late, and little discharges and other offerings have begun to appear, staining the marble plinth courtyard with mottled corn yellow 'clouds'.

Carnival and Parody

Sat on its mat outside Olympic House, the headquarters of Manchester Airport Group, the last UK-owned conglomerate in airport operations and management, we would be forgiven for assuming the cat seems to exude a certain air of indifference or insouciance. With this attention to the cat one might be struck by a certain Bakhtinian quality to the scene, one recorded in other studies where its subversive and carnivalesque features are found to complexly resist managerial pretension and its official narratives of organization (Boje, 2001; Rhodes, 2002; Slustskaya and De Cock, 2008). An analysis of this kind could produce a fascinating narrative, with opportunities to cite and build on Foucault or Haraway. There is no shortage of 'data'. And yet, what does the cat think of all this? She might be faking with this 'sitting' or lounging (O'Doherty, 2017). Her posture might be better described as 'poised'. Is Olly simply the object of a human social construction of culture at Manchester Airport? Licking her paws, stretching, arching her back, rolling over in the sun: what agency might we have to ascribe to Olly? How are we to read these signs? What are their effects? What language must we learn to listen and speak in order to take the measure of the organizational significance of Olly the cat?

Olly has become quite a celebrity, and regularly featured on the local BBC news during my research. Of course, she also became the subject of academic research that led to a series of academic articles and debates (de Rond, 2019; O'Doherty, 2016; 2017). In addition to my ostensible object of research—project managers making airports (O'Doherty, 2017)—I too found myself increasingly drawn to Olly as I sought to collect, study, and triangulate the data that might help explain what contribution to organization Olly was making. However, her appearance was also reminiscent of the 'ethnographic moment' that Marilyn Strathern (1999) talks about, an event-like happening (see also Knox et al., 2015) in which complexity and unpredictability begin to play between the field site and the site of writing. Marked by both what Strathern calls an excess and a shortage of information (Strathern, 1999: 4), the ethnographic moment opens a relationship of infinite regress that 'joins the understood (what is analysed at the moment of observation) to the need to understand (what is observed at the moment of analysis)' (Strathern, 1999: 6). This is the moment in which the people and the ethnographic field start to make their demands about what is relevant, in contrast to those the ethnographer thought relevant when designing the study, and when things first start to appear for which there is no wider encompassing whole through which to define or make meaning—whether 'culture', 'society', 'theory', or academic 'discipline'. In that sense the 'data collection' was not conscious and well-planned because this event marked an impossible demand, namely my becoming open to that which might later prove relevant. On the steps of Olympic House, there is then this opening to the recursive abyss of Olly's house and from here I mark this step into a 'cat's cradle' (Haraway, 1994) that will eventually defy management and organization. It requires a different style of narration.

There is an origin myth that tells how Olly was first found at the airport. In fact 'Olly' arrived as 'Olivia', a female cat. At least that is what was thought. Olly might have come from Miami FLA ... ♫ hitch hiked all the way from the USA ♫♫—and if it was not Lou Reed providing the soundtrack then other versions of an omniscient 'pop-culture' certainly helped inform the tales told of Olly. If Olly helped members of the airport find a portal into other worlds, the fantasy of a global village is also made present in the names of streets around the airport. There is Atlanta and Chicago Avenue, World Way and Ringway Road; Chicago Avenue gives way to Melbourne Avenue, Melbourne to Sydney Avenue, which in turn gives way to a local rite of passage, the ancient and labyrinthine Thorley Lane that promises spectres and other historical revenants for psychogeographic researchers influenced by writers such as Iain Sinclair (2005). As a liminal space of international hiatus, of exchange, and transformation, the airport binds and separates the local and the global; it is the quintessential site of Czarniawska's (2002) 'glocal'. Olivia was limping and her left ear was torn. Mangy and scrawny, she looked, according to some, neglected and 'badly treated'. Someone put out a saucer of milk and over time Olivia's confidence grew and she soon let the airport staff handle her. Workers at the airport then clubbed together to pay for expensive dental repair, and funds are currently being brokered for explorative hip replacement surgery. That was when they discovered Olivia was actually a boy and the *Manchester Evening News* covered the story of an airport cat with a sex-change.

The airport is often deemed to be a site of suspended animation, a non-place that generates opportunities for duty-free (purchases or otherwise), transgression, and change. Their spectacular promise of internationalism and open-borders helped to realize a modernity of mass 'democratic' travel and transport, but at the same time the tedium of queues and the disorientation of its architecture also ushered in disappointment and fear. For Pascoe (2001: 10), airports are situated at the 'threshold' of airspace and as such 'should be treated as the sterile transitory zones with which we are familiar, but as 'vessels of conception' for the societies passing through them'. Cats occupy a similar status and since the deification of the cat in ancient Egypt, they are considered animal of liminal spaces, of doorways and thresholds (Rogers, 2006). Powerful teachers of the dark arts of transformation or spiritual elevation and the ancient mysteries of passage between this world and the next, cats have also suffered from association with witches familiar propagated through Christian interpretation of pre-Christian and pagan beliefs and rites. It is tempting to see the fantasy of freedom and escape offered by airports offering a contemporary version of this witches familiar, expressed most clearly in the launching of the 'Escape Lounge' at Manchester Airport whose *en-trance* takes passengers into a fantasy world of escape composed of fine dining and high fashion, corporate pampering, ointments, and rubs (O'Doherty, 2017). These fantasies have been cultivated and shaped by a tremendous managerial effort that stimulates passion and energy which then circulates in various forms through the terminals and spaces of the airport. Like the status of temple guardian in ancient Egypt, Olly the cat appears to sit on the threshold opened up by the modern airport, but whether the cat serves as a warning or part of the seduction apparatus is not clear. Indeed, in the light of recent pandemics, airports are perhaps the first ruins of a society that once passed through them (cf. Pascoe,2001), and yet it is still productive to see the drama unfolding around Olly as a version of Geertz's (1973) 'cock-fight', a vessel of conception through which the airport tries to work through its barely conscious frustrations and disappointments.

Teaching People to Care

'Olly teaches people to care' and 'people learn to be more giving and generous', I am told on a number of occasions by Bob Molloy, head of Olympic House reception. A cat committee is formed, at first to administer Olly's fan mail and to help organize care. A Facebook account is set up and Olly soon has over 2000 friends. Food and bedding is donated. Postcards begin arriving from well-wishers around the world, and then one day a cushion appears hung above Olly's house, sealed in a clear plastic bag. The cushion is embroidered with thick red cotton and reads in capital letters: 'OLLY's PLACE'. It takes pride of place on the marble steps of Olympic House. On Christmas day in 2008, American Airlines staff present Olly with a whole salmon freshly caught from the upper Hudson valley. A local Manchester pop-band goes viral on YouTube with a song they have written about Olly. A competition is then announced by British Midland Airlines for Manchester Airport staff to name one of their new BMi baby Boeing 737s, and it comes as little surprise that the winning answer is 'Olly cat baby'. Indeed, so extravagant becomes this gift-giving that a letter is published in the company newsletter asking for moderation, explaining that Olly has become slightly overwhelmed by the gift-giving: 'Olly asked me if he could share some of his food and bedding with his many feline and canine friends at the *Society for Abandoned Animals* who have not been as fortunate as him'. A new doormat appears and for a few days it sits outside Olly's house. Inscribed in bold letters are the words: 'The Boss'.

One explanation that could be offered for this 'logic of excess' (see Rehn and O'Doherty, 2007), is that Olly helped to rally or recover otherwise neglected emotions of care and empathy. The airport had once been 'all family', I am told. You would see someone and say, 'there's [Rupert's] lad'. Marriages and divorces, sons and daughters, sometimes three generations of family have worked at the same trade in the airport. The cat is of course the archetypal family pet. In recent years, however, the airport had been formally sold or incorporated into a new corporate entity, the 'Manchester Airport Group' and there were many voices expressing discontent and frustration. 'Some say this airport has got a little bit above its station', one of the older terminal operations staff tells me. A more commercially-minded approach to airport operations had begun to develop and increasing numbers of professional managerial appointments made to new corporate positions in finance and human relations set against a backdrop of the privatization and commercialization of the wider UK air transport industry (Graham, 2008; Humphreys, 1999). Stories would circulate of a disgruntled engineering team, cut to the bone in staffing levels, of chaotic operational structures, a lack of role clarity and leadership in terminal operations, of tensions in runway safety and maintenance teams, and customer service teams subject to restructure after restructure. A more distant and impersonal corporate executive had emerged, with little regard for the sentiments of 'family' when set against the realities of cost and competition.

It is possible the cat offered a surrogate means for restoring some of the older but now repressed emotions of family and care. It also might help to displace and transmute anger or frustration into empathy. Olly 'brings out the better side in a lot of us', Bob explained. I recalled my first encounter with Olly and the figure of the chief executive. I had taken pleasure in recording in my diary my impression of his rather unwieldy corporeality and his 'pins holding up a cannonball'. The cat seemed to help displace the seriousness or pretension of this commanding presence of the chief executive, the boss of Manchester Airport Group. On the one hand the observation seems rather trivial or juvenile, but it could be used to generate important data through the methods of free association applied in 'social photo-matrix' and other techniques developed in contemporary Tavistock group-psychodynamic research (Mersky and Sievers, 2018; Sievers, 2008). Later, I came to experience a greater sense of empathy for the chief executive, and this might have been partly the work of Olly. After 17 years as chief executive it was announced in a bulletin that the chief executive was retiring and a new chief executive would be appointed in due course. I thought now of possible arthritis and of the fragility of the aging human body, corporate executive or otherwise. I had previously oscillated between a sense of intimidation at the power I presumed this CEO to wield and a desire to ridicule, a tension perhaps reflecting the schooling of critical management studies

(Alvesson and Willmott, 1992, 1996; Parker, 2002) and the subversive traditions of organizational symbolism as advanced in the work of scholars such as Carl Rhodes and colleagues (Rhodes, 2001a, Rhodes and Westwood, 2007; Rhodes and Parker, 2008).

BECOMING FELINE: THE BREAKDOWN OF ORGANIZATION

Teaching people to care was a story that could be told. Was there something more to this than simply displaced expressions of anger and empathy? Was this, moreover, serious or parodic? I started spending more time watching Olly and the effects he had on people around him during the working day. Throughout the day Olly would receive a stream of visitors, sometimes people on their own, or in groups, and occasionally couples: airline staff, contract cleaners, corporate management, secretaries, construction workers, and passengers. It was not uncommon for people to have their photograph taken with this celebrity, but intimacy went far beyond the visual souvenir. Airport staff would periodically arrive and crouch down to the level of the cat, who would often reciprocate by lifting himself up and arching his back to reach out for the hand. People would stroke and pet the cat, rubbing their hand slowly down the back of the cat and up and over the tail if Olly was responding positively. People would tickle and nuzzle, getting right down on the floor to bury their nose in the cat's fur, smelling, hugging, and kissing (see Beetz and Podberscek, 2005). Both partners seemed to take pleasure in activities that exchanged bodily properties including scent, moisture and perspiration, skin and hair. On occasion Olly would lick a hand or even nuzzle into those with long hair, reaching deep into the neck and ear of the human, who would invariably smile or giggle. Most people would greet the cat with formalities and spoken word, 'Hello Olly' in a soft purring voice, or occasionally a slightly more flirtatious 'have you been a good girl, Olly?', or 'who's been a naughty boy?', with some expressing a promiscuous tone in greetings of the kind 'Who's been a naughty pussy then?'

The attachment to Olly was so significant that when the CEO sought to get rid of the cat soon after he arrived: the level of anger and discontent this provoked was sufficient for the proposal to be withdrawn. People spoke of an impassioned and spontaneous defence of Olly delivered by one of the female secretaries that left the CEO so shaken with the possible consequences of getting rid of the cat that he decided the airport could keep Olly. Over time this story was repeated so frequently that I began to think of it as having a kind of legendary status, but Olly was not universally popular. 'Olly basically divides the organization in two', the terminal manager tells me: 'there are those who love her, and those who hate her'. The deeper I got into my studies the more significant but complex his contribution to organization became. I wondered, for example, about the commercial and economic cost-benefit of the cat. No one had done a formal study of this to work out the 'commercial value' of Olly, but it was a question I was often asked, sometimes aggressively and often, I thought, in a defensive and counter-projective way (O'Doherty, 2017). Everyone was under pressure to prove their commercial worth, although I sensed that I was being asked because the questioners themselves were unclear what was of commercial value, or what could be made commercially valuable. Olly was widely considered to be good publicity for the airport, but this had emerged spontaneously and in many ways *despite* the efforts of the newly employed ranks of corporate strategy and business development managers equipped with MBAs and professional accreditation. Some executives did appear embarrassed about Olly when I had occasion to steer conversation in this direction, but, as already noted, the press interest, the Facebook fan club, and the postcards from around the world helped to promote the airport and its increasing preoccupation with 'brand'. Despite the best efforts of marketing and commercial management to build affection for the airport, to develop loyalty and the 'wow' factor in airport design (Graham, 2019), it was the cat that seemed to elicit the most genuine expressions of delight and surprise otherwise sought in the 'retail offer' of the new terminal design. On one occasion, a young girl of eight or nine years of age breaks away from a queue that has formed for an airport transfer bus and her face breaks open with the most spontaneous delight and enchantment: 'Look, a cat', she shouts as she runs over to Olly, sitting down to stroke and play with the cat.

One might wonder if Olly had been 'put to work' by senior management so ubiquitous had they(?) become. She was by now writing regular monthly columns in several in-house magazines and farmed out to media with regular press releases but reflections and empirical trials to further test this hypothesis led me to reflections about my own status in the airport. Indeed, forces seemed to conspire in such a way that Olly's experience offered a salutary lesson of my own fate. I was increasingly asked, for example, to cover media duties and to talk about my research and answer questions from reporters for which scripts were prepared, and negotiations were conducted concerning what was appropriate and how I could preserve my academic impartiality and independence. As every ethnographer will know, keeping access going in any meaningful way requires constant vigilance and negotiation, which at times resembles a game of cat and mouse. Ethnographers must keep their counsel. They are often deemed a little untrustworthy as they silently watch the happenings of events around them as they are said to prowl, snoop, or crawl through the 'underbelly of organizational life' (Taylor and Hansen, 2005).

Was there a possibility that, like others in the airport, I was taking on certain properties of cat-like behaviour, drawn in like prey to the seductive ploys of Olly the cat? Who was in control here? For a while I could see nothing but cats. I became attentive to cat-talk, the way that the supervision of floor layers working on the Escape Lounge project was being talked about, for example, as 'herding cats'. Meanwhile, offices and desk-space were filling up with cat paraphernalia. Were these spaces always covered in this regalia? Or was I just becoming increasingly sensitive? Or is it possible that I was a part of a movement enrolled into producing more feline ontology with all its obscure and indeterminate qualities? I spent more time at the Rampant Lion pub, where it was said all the most important business of the airport once was conducted, where construction projects were signed, and differences sorted out over drink (cf. Van Maanen, 1992). Meanwhile, there was a Jaguar, in the form of a car, for sale inside terminal 1. I was seeing cats everywhere—the stripes on the shoulder boards of the pilots and co-pilots indicating rank and status, the tiger bread pizza available in the terminal concessions, and Kenzo World Wild Collector Tiger perfume from the zone of desire in terminal 1, and then the fleet of cougar Boeing 727s with cats spread all over the fuselage. With all these trans-species conversations and couplings, I was struck with a sense of fear that I had been living in a cat's 'iron cage' of organization that at moments evoked the kind of existential paranoia popularized in Peter Weir's *The Truman Show*.

These cats, together with the ubiquitous circulation of greeting cards, screen savers, cute kitten photographs, calendars, and keyrings in the modern workplace (see Berland, 2008), now join the internet cat meme that has become so prolific and prolix that, for some researchers, the cat has become a 'hyper meme' or 'memeplex'. Productive of its own increasingly powerful semiotic and meaning structure, the feline memeplex creates a new modus operandi for internet and social media users based on the circulation of 'lolcats' that has now spawned its own language 'appropriately called lolspeak' (Thibault and Marino, 2018: 475). From a cultish, marginal phenomenon, the lolcats infect more mainstream social media, multiply and proliferate through variations and various levels of meta-commentary and inter-textuality, often to the point where it is difficult to distinguish what is originary or derivative, supportive of a status quo or subversive—whether wilful or accidental.

Many people, it seemed, were living a kind of 'cat life' at the airport. Others might even be becoming 'cat people', a veritable modernist cultural icon according to Willmott (2010: 854), for whom the proliferation of cat-becomings in high and low art, from catwoman in DC comics to the George Herriman's hugely popular comic strip *Krazy Kat* to the literature of Pound, Lawrence, and Lovecraft, express both fear and fascination with the feline as modern subjectivities seek out 'new structures of feeling for social kinship'. With all this obsession it is perhaps not surprising that another corporate executive coup was being planned to try and oust Olly from her position as 'the Boss'. However, rumours soon circulated and people started to post threats of strikes and walkouts on various social media channels. This time the campaign took on a much more sophisticated strategy, enrolling members of the cat committee into the plans. The concern now was with the health and wellbeing of Olly. Was an airport the most appropriate place for a cat to be living? Was it safe? The communications informed staff that the local Royal Society for the Prevention of Cruelty to Animals had either made overtures (or had been contacted by the airport—it not clear), and their advice was that Olympic House was not ideal for a cat. We want the best for Olly; he is getting old and perhaps it is time to think about 'retirement'. Located at the juncture of a roundabout and a busy airport road system, Olly was deemed vulnerable; indeed, there was a case that the airport was negligent in its care for animals.

Management Incredulity and Undecidability

No MBA student has been trained to register the intricacies and complexities of trans human-feline organizational relations, but the official communiqués were written with subtlety and guile that suggests growing expertise and attunement to relations other-than-human. Indeed, it seems that things are starting to become a little other-worldly, if they are not already quite beyond the pale for the syllabus of business and management studies. Perhaps management was extending what we might call a 'catiavellian taste' for the diplomatic arts of circuitous and indirect conduct. A project team was established to explore the possibilities for the design and commission of an alternative cathouse that would be cleaner and safer for Olly. Vector Design Concepts were duly commissioned by the airport as client architect and published their eight-page 'project brief' on 20 August 2010. The project archive contains detailed and elaborate paperwork that adheres to the language and methodology of PRINCE 2 project management, widely being adopted at that time around the airport. The brief includes summaries of what it calls the 'main parameters of acceptability', presumably those expressed by the client to the architect: 'It has to look like a piece of street art', the brief explains, so that 'those who hate her can appreciate the art, [while] those who love her can appreciate the new Olly house'. A clause of some significance for deciphering the motivations for the project can be found in this document where we read 'It has to be fitting to be outside the Head Office of a multi-million pound business'. The existing cat shelter is perhaps a little too rustic which 'gets buried in blankets that then get sprayed by foxes, other cats etc. and it then smells like we have a permanent tramp outside our building'.

The completed design is a feat of remarkable imagination and creativity that was rare at the airport where functionality and utility had become more typical of architectural ambition in line with the wider eclipse of high modern romance with air travel (Pearman, 2004; Schaberg, 2015). By contrast, Olly was obviously quite an inspiration. The brief explains the proposed design is informed by a 'set of principles' and 'a philosophy of aesthetics' associated with flight and aviation. The philosopher John Gray (2020) would rather call this an expression of 'feline philosophy', a philosophy he deems to be completely unmarked by self-consciousness, and certainly the detailing of design and rendering is remarkable and appears to be almost unencumbered by customary human restraint or modesty (cf. Derrida, 2008). Using the latest acrylic materials, the design references the more corporate architectural minimalism of glass and steel whilst ingeniously making use of the plasticity of the materials to sculpt an aircraft caught in the moment of take-off. It is a design that recalls the work of Zaha Hadid, whose controversial designs for the swimming pool for the 2012 London Olympics were widely in circulation at the time of the commission for Olly's new house.

The briefing notes explain that cats will not sleep and eat in the same space, and so the design incorporates a complex tripartite structure made up of a 'sleeping zone', a 'feeding zone', and a 'watering hole'. At the time, Manchester Airport had recently opened its new £80 million terminal redevelopment scheme that featured an innovative 'zoning' of different spaces through which passengers move, including the 'zone of transference' that took people out of the security checking hall into the 'zone of reassurance' and then on into the 'zone of desire' where duty-free alcohol, perfume, and tobacco were on display, bathed in lights and music. However, the 'watering hole' zone for Olly seemed to equal, if not trump, the intricacy of design sought for human travellers. As the proposed design explains, this is a system based on running water—because 'cats prefer it'—collected from rainwater, which is then channelled from the roof through a carbon filter and then pumped into a drinking receptacle at ground level. The architect notes that this circulation of cold water could also be adapted so that it could be used as a 'method of cooling the sleeping zone in the summer months'.

The design appears to play with credulity but, since this work of Vector Designs in Manchester, there has appeared a whole series of innovations in cathouse architecture that seem to confirm a wider preoccupation with sophisticated architecturally-designed cat shelters. These include the fantastical designs for a 'spiral kitty shelter' by DSH// architecture, a 'Lunar Cat Lander' by Knowhow Shop that Medlock (2016) describes as 'a cheeky construction which brings kitties on a space exploration adventure', the 'Catleidoscope' by Purrrkins + Will architects, and finally CallisonRTKL's 'Silhouette' that features dramatic curves that serve as a *trompe l'oeil* to distract and disguise the entrance that leads to a private inner sanctum for the cat (Medlock, 2016). The energy invested in this project and resulting design for Olly's new house, perhaps offers a more insightful expression of the state of mind in which organization existed at Manchester Airport, than the more customary artefacts poured over in management research, such as formal charts of structure and reporting lines. Whether serious, playful, parodic, sincere, or subversive, it is difficult to tell, but these artefacts are good to think with and can help tune ethnographic attention to the ways in which these qualities of organization are complexly bound together and inseparable in the day-to-day practices of workplace relations.

A Hybrid Human-Cat Assemblage

The design emerges out of a density of practices and relations that form something like a cat's cradle of entanglement and reciprocity across human and nonhuman relations that are also deeply imbued with organizational memory and history, providing insight into the complex and beguiling ontological nature of its organization. Such complexity is not normally registered by management studies, but it can be shown to be an important way in which the airport is together as a community, or which simultaneously holds the airport together and marks out patterns and relations that threaten to tear and pull it apart.

We know that management can be revealed as a practice of gesture and feint, where learning to tell the difference between a nod and a wink is crucial for understanding what is going on, as students of workplace informality have long known, and where the achievement of a 'working order' is accomplished by all manner of subtlety and guile (Batstone, 1984). However, following another creature through the airport shows how these practices are more extensive and intensive, woven into human/nonhuman relations that includes 'companion species' (Haraway, 2003)—other than human animals, but also materials and artefacts, buildings, tools, and technologies. Through the twists and turns of Olly's story we first become attentive to a strange and other set of gestures that 'spoke' in a language for which veterinarian and other specialists in feline studies have long grappled (Alger and Alger, 2003; Bradshaw, 2013). These feline gestures then cast light back on the ways in which day-to-day practices and relations familiar to students of work organization are imbued with their own material-semiotic gestures that form a complexity marked by a poker-game like mentality of calculation, feint, and parry.

We have had occasion here to trace the added complexity that emerges when we register and attend to the entanglement of material-semiotics within human/nonhuman animal relations. Following Olly through Manchester Airport we have been able to collect material that tells stories that record an ever-increasing uncertainty and undecidability: was there a formal project commissioned to design a new shelter for Olly? There is paperwork that confirms this, evidence exists that funds were allocated and outline studies conducted, and many people continued talking about it with passion and (apparent) seriousness. If this was commissioned, was management being sincere? Again, when asking these questions, even after two and half years' presence at the airport could only elicit an 'of course, we are serious' response, followed by, on one occasion, a silent stare which conjured that 'who blinks first' relational tension (O'Doherty, 2017: 238–9). Like those famous rabbit/duck pictures reproduced by Wittgenstein or William Ely Hill's 1915 version of the 'young woman, old woman' cartoon (also known as my wife and mother-in-law) (see Boring, 1930), we are confronted with two very different, alternative realities, both equally plausible. It is always a good rule of thumb for the ethnographer to presume their interlocutors are reflexively one step ahead of them, a lesson that reaches back to Garfinkel (1967) and especially Wieder's (1974) study of the 'convict code', and more recently recalled in Latour (2005). A capacity to hold both in play at the same time whilst simultaneously erasing their difference seemed to mark the practices of the more skilful members of management.

Finally, such experiences do not transpire without a certain degree of anxiety and disorientation that prompts one to ask who or what is in control here? It would be a mistake to overlook Olly's capacity for agency and autonomy. She refused to play ball, for example, when management wanted to use her as a mascot to promote air travel during the 2010 World Cup finals in Germany (O'Doherty, 2017: 235). And what of the incredible feats of imagination and creativity achieved during the designs for the new cat shelter? Olly was surely an inspiration; but was he, perhaps, more active than this? An actor, maybe, or an accomplice even? In John Gray's (2020) recent essay on 'feline philosophy' we are invited to consider recent studies that show how it is more plausible to see cats as the active agents of human socialization. We do not train or domesticate cats, they train and domesticate the human, as explained in Abigail Tucker's (2016) recent popular synthesis of some of the science that she explains as a case of 'how house cats tamed us and took over the world'.

Following Olly seems to have allowed the ethnographer to enter a highly reflexive trans-species set of relations at Manchester airport, a human-cat hybrid assemblage in which properties normally divided and attributed to cats or humans are more mixed and ill-defined, generating practices and behaviours that cannot be categorized as either human or feline. Whilst the corporate 'fat-cats' sit atop the tower of Olympic House there are equally powerful forces and agencies that displace and subvert their pomp and ceremony, or which cast fresh light on their practices, albeit at the risk of a certain anthropomorphism: the weekly terminal 'walk-through' performed by management now seen as a cat-walk, or preening; their politics a cat fight that on one occasion was reported as 'claws out at Manchester Airport' in the *Manchester Evening News* during the second attempted ousting of Olly; and the desire to hunt for 'low hanging fruit' conjuring the pack-life of feline hunters. Being with cats stimulates a thinking-with-cats that gives rise to new and surprising associations and insights, but we must also be wary of our possible seduction and enrolment into the cat's iron cage that leaves us taking on and helping to enact a feline ontology that is unreliable, inconsistent, poised, and ready to pounce. Meanwhile, with a swish of his tail, Olly takes his leave from the marble plinth of Manchester airport and disappears into the night.

Conclusion

Animals continue to be neglected and ignored, most often subject to cruelty and subordination, but at the same time they remain a preoccupation in which a far greater proportion of day-to-day organizational practices are devoted to things like cats, than they are to the writing of reports and the attendance at meetings. This chapter shows the two are in fact intimately folded together with 'animal spirits' as the economist John Maynard Keynes (1936: 161–2) knew only too well. A recent turn to the animal in organization studies has begun to address this neglect in business and management, and this chapter helps extend this work by showing how multispecies ethnography (see Kirksey and Helmreich, 2010, van Dooren et al., 2016) might be practised in ways that learn from human/nonhuman relations and its emergent forms of life in work organizations. These are forms of life highly contingent, uncertain, and unreliable, reflexively complex by virtue of their other-than-human and multispecies origin, and one that leaves management poised at the limits of its comprehension and agency.

In an important paper for animal studies and in particular, studies of cats in management and organization, Hillier and Byrne (2016: 389) draw on Foucault's work on biopolitics to show that 'feral cats are presences enacted into being within representational practices'. They find that a *'dispositif* of ferality structures social fields of action, guides political practices and is realised through state apparatuses' (p.400), but they are not so successful in showing how cats resist these practices, or might even be implicated in practices that simultaneously undoes the *dispositif*. They are not so attentive to the methodological challenges involved in accessing what they declare to be their interest in studying the 'unsaid', silent, absent or othered' (ibid.) which shadows that which is made present by practices of representation and classification. We have seen how the cat meme phenomenon, for example, demands a certain suspension of our customary expectations about sign, referent, and meaning, but this very suspension allows us to track how management is implicated in a phenomenon that it both tries to harness (in the form of corporate branding), but which simultaneously draws management into an excess it cannot contain. By contrast, Hillier and Bryne (2016) are unable to show the creative and often surprising animal agencies and resistances immanent in forces and energies that render organization a lively and volatile state, always ready to uncoil and discharge.

Olly teaches us that animal studies in management and organization research needs to go beyond a human-centred speciesism in which animals serve as symbols, representations, or projections of all-too-human preoccupations and anxieties. The animal always slips out of control and seem to lead its human captives a merry dance, generating transgressive cross-species love, but also industrial relations conflict and dispute. To learn from a cat demands consideration of another way of being with its own semi-autonomous 'cat-culture' (Alger and Alger, 2003) that is also constitutive of what we might otherwise be tempted to consider the exclusively 'human' dimensions of organization culture. It takes us to the edge of reason and asks us to suspend disbelief as we grapple with the credibility and status of things like specialist air-cooled water systems designed for cat housing. But woe betide the manager who doesn't take this seriously. How many managers would have countenanced the credibility of the hula-hoop as a business proposition at the time of its prototyping (see also Rehn, 2013)? Fact and fiction get blurred when we open ourselves to the practices of human-cat communion that we have shown give rise to co-existing and undecidable realities, but this is precisely what is generative of organization at the very same time that it renders management as conventionally understood and practised constitutively impossible.

References

Ackroyd, S., & Crowdy, P.A. (1990). Can culture be managed? Working with 'raw' material: The case of the English slaughtermen. *Personnel Review*. 19(5), 3–13

Agamben, G. (2004). *The open: Man and animal*. Trans. Kevin Attell. Stanford: Stanford University Press.

Alger, J., & Alger, S. (2003). *Cat culture: The social world of a cat shelter*. Vol. 36. Temple University Press.

Alvesson, M., & Willmott, H. (Eds.) (1992). *Critical management studies*. London: Sage.

Alvesson, M., & Willmott, H. (Eds.), (1996). *Making sense of management: A critical introduction*. London: Sage Publications.

Barrett, J. (2002). *Work and community in the jungle: Chicago's packinghouse workers, 1894-1922.* Urbana.

Batstone, E. (1984). *Working order: Workplace industrial relations over two decades.* Oxford: Blackwell.

Beetz, A.M., & A.L. Podberscek (Eds.) (2005). *Bestiality and zoophilia: Sexual relations with animals.* West Lafayette: Purdue University Press.

Berland, J. (2008). Cat and mouse: Iconographics of nature and desire. *Cultural studies, 22(3-4),* 431-54.

Borgerson, J. (2005). *Animality.* In C. Jones, & D. O'Doherty. (Eds.), *Manifestos for the business school of tomorrow.* (pp. 10-13). Turku, Finland: Dvalin Books.

Boring, E.G. (1930). A new ambiguous figure. *American Journal of Psychology,* 42, 444-45.

Boje, D.M. (2001). Carnivalesque resistance to global spectacle: A critical postmodern theory of public administration. *Administrative Theory and Praxis, 23(3),* 431-58.

ten-Bos, R. (2004). The fear of wolves: Anti-hodological ruminations about organizations and labyrinths. *Culture and Organization, 10(1),* 7-24.

Boyd, W. (2001). Making meat. Science, technology and American poultry production. *Technology and Culture,* 42, 631-64.

Bradshaw, J. (2013). *Cat sense: The feline enigma revealed.* Harmondsworth: Penguin.

Clarke, C., & Knights, D. (2022). Milking it for all it's worth: Unpalatable practices, dairy cows and veterinary work?. *Journal of Business Ethics, 176(4),* 673-688.

Czarniawska, B. (2002). *A tale of three cities: Or the glocalization of city management.* Oxford University Press on demand.

Dale, K., & Burrell, G. (2008) *The spaces of organisation and the organisation of space: Power and materiality at work.* Basingstoke: Palgrave.

Decker, S. (2014). Solid intentions: An archival ethnography of corporate architecture and organizational remembering. *Organization, 21(4),* 514-42.

De Rond, M. (2019). Why is a Raven like a writing desk? *Ephemera, 18(4),* 837-40.

Deleuze, G., & Guattari, F. (1987). *A thousand plateaus,* trans. Brian Massumi. Minneapolis: University of Minnesota Press.

Derrida, J. (2008). *The animal that therefore I am* (Perspectives in Continental Philosophy, trans. D. Wills, series ed. J.D. Caputo). New York: Fordham University Press.

Derrida, J. (2009). *The beast and the sovereign,* vol. 1 (Eds. M. Lisse, M.-L. Mallet, with G. Michaud, trans. G. Bennington). Chicago and London: University of Chicago Press

Desmond, J. (2010). A summons to the consuming animal. *Business Ethics: a European Review 19(3),* 238-252

Doré, A., & Michalon, J. (2017). What makes human–animal relations 'organizational'? The description of anthrozootechnical agencements. *Organization, 24(6),* 761-80.

Galaxy, J., & Benjamin, K. (2014). *Catification: Designing a happy and stylish home for your cat (and you!).* New York: Penguin.

Garfinkel, H. (1967). *Studies in ethnomethodology.* Englewood Cliffs: Prentice-Hall.

Geertz, C. (1973). *The interpretation of cultures.* New York: Basic books.

Graham A. (2008) *Managing airports: An international perspective.* Oxford: Butterworth-Heinemann.

Graham, A. (2019). Aerotropolis: London's Airports as Experiences and Destinations. In: Smith, A. and Graham, A. (eds.) *Destination London: The Expansion of the Visitor Economy,* (pp. 61-89). London: University of Westminster Press

Gray, J. (2020). *Feline philosophy: Cats and the meaning of life*. New York: Farrar, Straus and Giroux.
Hamilton, L., & Taylor, N. (2012). Ethnography in evolution: Adapting to the animal 'other' in organizations. *Journal of Organizational Ethnography*, 1(1), 43–51.
Hamilton, L., & Taylor, N. (2013). *Animals at work: Identity, politics and culture in work with animals*. Leiden: Brill.
Hamilton, L., and Taylor, N. (2017). *Ethnography after humanism: Power, politics and method in multispecies research*. Springer.
Haraway, D.J. (1994). A game of cat's cradle: Science studies, feminist theory, cultural studies, *Configurations*, 2, 59–71.
Haraway, D.J. (2003). *The companion species manifesto: Dogs, people, and significant otherness*. Chicago: Prickly Paradigm Press.
Haraway, D. (2007). *When species meet*. Minnesota: University of Minnesota Press.
Hillier, J., & Byrne, J. (2016). Is extermination to be the legacy of Mary Gilbert's cat? *Organization*, 23(3), 387–406.
Huopalainen, A. (2020). Writing with the bitches. *Organization*, online first. doi:10.1177/1350508420961533.
Humphreys, I. (1999). Privatisation and commercialisation: Changes in UK airport ownership patterns. *Journal of Transport Geography*, 7(2), 121–34.
Jackson, N., & Carter, P. (2010). A IX EF: Symbols in the everyday life of the city. *Culture and Organization*, 16(3), 247–58.
Jones, C., & O'Doherty, D. (Eds.) (2005). *Manifestos for the business school of tomorrow*. Turku, Finland: Dvalin Books.
Keynes, J.M. (1936). *The general theory of employment, interest and money*. London: Macmillan.
Kirksey, S.E., & Helmreich, S. (2010). The emergence of multispecies ethnography. *Cultural anthropology*, 25(4), 545–76.
Knox, H. et al. (2015). Something happened: Spectres of organization/disorganization at the airport. *Human Relations*, 68(6), 1001–20.
Kraemer, D., & Sleator, L. (2019). The new PM's first job: Impress the cat. *BBC*. Archived from the original on 24 July 2019 https://www.bbc.co.uk/news/uk-politics-49049852 . Retrieved July 24, 2019.
Latour, B. (2005). *Reassembling the social: An introduction to social life*. Oxford: Oxford University Press.
Little, S. (2011). *The cat-e-book: Clinical medicine and management*. Elsevier Health Sciences.
Medlock, K. (2016). Architects create extraordinary homes for Los Angeles' feral cats. *Inhabitat* 28 March 2016, available at https://inhabitat.com/architects-design-incredible-cat-shelters-to-raise-money-for-las-strays/catshelters14/ (last accessed 31 March 2022).
Mersky, R. R., & Sievers, B. (2018). Social photo-matrix and social dream-drawing. In K. Stamenova, & R.D. Hinshelwood (Eds.), *Methods of research into the unconscious: Applying psychoanalytic ideas to social science* (pp. 145–68). Abingdon: Routledge.
O'Doherty, D.P. (2016). Feline politics in organization: The nine lives of Olly the cat. *Organization*, 23(3), 407–33.
O'Doherty, D.P. (2017). *Reconstructing organization: The loungification of society*. London: Palgrave Macmillan.
O'Doherty, D. (2018). On the beginning of formal organization. *Journal of Cultural Economy*, 11(6), 598–601.

O'Doherty, D., & De Cock, C. (2017). Management as an Academic Discipline?. In A. Wilkinson, S.J. Armstrong, & M. Lounsbury. (Eds.), *The Oxford handbook of management*. Oxford University Press (pp. 461–80). Oxford: Oxford University Press.

Parker, M. (2002). *Against management: Organization in the age of managerialism*. Cambridge: Polity.

Pascoe, D. (2001). *Airspaces*. London: Reaktion Books.

Pearman, H. (2004). *Airports: A century of architecture*. London: Laurence King Publishing.

Pollan, M. (2006). *The omnivore's dilemma: A natural history of four meals*. New York: Penguin Press.

Rehn, A. (2013). *Frivolous business*. Bloomington: Booktango.

Rehn, A., & O'Doherty, D. (2007). Organization: On the theory and practice of excess. *Culture and Organization, 13(2),* 99–113.

Rhodes, C. (2001). *Writing organization: (Re) presentation and control in narratives at work*. Amsterdam: John Benjamins.

Rhodes, C. (2002). Coffee and the business of pleasure: The case of Harbucks vs. Mr. Tweek. *Culture and Organization, 8(4),* 293–306.

Rhodes, C., & Parker, M. (2008). Images of organizing in popular culture. *Organization, 15,* 627–37.

Rhodes, C., & Westwood, R. (2007). *Critical representations of work and organization in popular culture*. Routledge.

Rogers, K. (2006) *Cat*. London: Reaktion Books.

Sayers, J.G. (2016). A report to an academy: On carnophallogocentrism, pigs and meat-writing. *Organization, 23(3),* 370–86.

Shukin, N. (2009). *Animal capital: Rendering life in biopolitical times*. University of Minnesota Press.

Sievers, B. (2008). Perhaps it is the role of pictures to get in contact with the uncanny: The social photo-matrix as a method to promote the understanding of the unconscious in organizations. *Organisational and Social Dynamics, 8(2),* 234–54.

Sinclair (2005). As a liminal space of inter-national hiatus, of exchange, and transformation, the airport binds and separates the local and the global; it is the quintessential site of

Skoglund, A., & Redmalm, D. (2017). 'Doggy-biopolitics': governing via the First Dog. *Organization, 24(2),* 240–66.

Slutskaya, N., & De Cock, C. (2008). The body dances: Carnival dance and organization. *Organization, 15(6),* 851–68.

Strathern, M. (1999). *Property, substance, and effect: Anthropological essays on persons and things*. London: Athlone Press.

Taylor, S.S., & Hansen, H. (2005). Finding form: Looking at the field of organizational aesthetics. *Journal of Management studies, 42(6),* 1211–31.

Thibault, M., & Marino, G. (2018). Who run the world? Cats: Cat lovers, cat memes, and cat languages across the web. *Int J Semiot Law, 31,* 473–90.

Tucker, A. (2016). *The lion in the living room: How house cats tamed us and took over the world*. Simon and Schuster.

Van Dooren, T, Kirksey, E., & Münster, U. (2016). Multispecies studies: Cultivating arts of attentiveness. *Environmental Humanities, 8(1),* 1–23.

Van Maanen, J. (1992). Drinking our troubles away: Managing conflict in a British police agency. In D. Kolb, & J. Bartunek (Eds.), *Hidden conflict in organizations; uncovering behind-the-scene disputes* (pp. 32–62). London: Sage.

Wieder, D.L (1974). *Language and social reality: The case of telling the convict.* The Hague: Code Mouton.

Willmott, G. (2010). Cat people. *Modernism/modernity, 17(4),* 839–56.

Woycicki, P. (2016). Recursive game structures as emergent post-capitalist creative strategies. *Performance Research, 21(4),* 20–5.

CHAPTER 24

CATCHING CRAB TRUTH IN SEAWATER

On Rockpooling, Affect, and Charisma

LINDSAY HAMILTON

INTRODUCTION

Up until the mid-twentieth century, family holidays in the United Kingdom were synonymous with going to the seaside. After international travel became more affordable, however, many coastal resorts fell into decline as the typical tourist fare of circus sideshows, slot machine arcades, fish and chip shops, and donkey rides faded into obscurity. Many seaside towns have sought to recover their historic popularity with young families and the trend for domestic 'bucket and spade' holidaymaking has been strengthened by the recent pandemic. This was the context for my own experiences in a town I have anonymized as Cobbly Cove in Cornwall—a region on the Southwestern peninsula of England. Known for its rocky shoreline and thriving tourist market, Cobbly Cove has retained its prestige for domestic tourism (in contrast to many resorts that have been tarnished by a reputation for low-end holiday accommodation, criminal activity, and the drinking culture of rowdy stag and hen parties). Its rocky outcrop is situated on the east side of a river estuary where the remains of shipwrecks can occasionally be sighted on the foreshore. The area around the headland is dotted with caves, boulders, and sheltered inlets and is replete with opportunities for rockpooling, the investigation of the contents of rocky pools filled with seawater left exposed by the outgoing tide (Martens, 2016).

From these semi-safe margins, families can investigate natural forms while also remaining shielded from the ocean and its powerful currents. They may develop skills of hunting and gathering, but rockpooling is not a 'serious' means of 'procuring food from the sea, causing the death of living creatures and risking one's own life' (Martens, 2016: 447). In contrast to commercial fishing, this is a playful and child-centred pursuit involving informal and embodied practices of 'curatorship' with rudimentary tools such as brightly coloured buckets, spades, and nets. Human observation, foraging, and collecting activity is, however, limited by weather, terrain, and tides. The surface of a rockpool can be completely flat and clear or it may be corrugated by rain, gusts of wind or tiny breezes, the contents rendered obscure. As the encroaching waves slop up, rockpools are engulfed and become inaccessible. Unlike an inland pond where exhibits might well remain undisturbed for years, the intertidal rockpool is in more or less constant flux. Hence, tides 'materialize and dematerialize these watery habitats at varied temporal intervals' (Martens, 2016: 448), thereby limiting (or encouraging) human activity.

Rather than pursuing 'bookended' categories and paired contrasts (O'Doherty, 2017) that demarcate human observer from animal subject, land from sea, this chapter presents rockpools as material-semiotic assemblages (Law, 2004); material, human, and animal 'multiplicities' (Mol, 2002) or 'compounds' (Helmreich, 2010) which provide 'glimmering enclosures' of multispecies activity (Nicolson, 2021). Specifically, these companies of 'critters infolded into a one' (Haraway, 2008: xvii) highlight the value of *affect* for theorizing the relationality rather than the distinction between 'cleanly oppositional elements or primary units' (Gregg and Seigworth, 2010: 4) of humans and sea animals, vegetables and other natural forms. This lens helps to reveal how the range of subjective impressions and feelings arising from interspecies interactions can impact upon individual animals as well as entire habitats, ecosystems, and species. In other words, affect contours the micro-moment of interaction but also contributes to broader values and cultural norms which play out in the biopolitics of human-animal relations. Unravelling this political process is significant if, as multispecies organization scholars, we are to fully understand (and thereby challenge) the way that certain animals are prioritized in global conservation efforts for example, while others are overlooked or denigrated as food, objects, swarms, or pests.

The 'Affect' of the Seashore

Rockpools are metaphorically similar to organizations where 'objects are better conceived as projects bound into complex relations of maintenance and repair' that 'drift laterally so that the object is never quite the same from one day to the next' (O'Doherty, 2017: 20). This is quite literally the case at the coast where winds, weather patterns, and tides rearrange and reform the contents of each rockpool every day. The seashore is, therefore, ripe for organizational symbolism and, indeed, maritime language already abounds in commercial discourses of 'drowning in paperwork', or projects becoming fatally 'holed under the water'. Managers commonly refer to 'headwinds' that restrict the 'glide path' of their strategic endeavours. While there is some reflective potential in considering these devices, this chapter is concerned with the physical as well as semiotic features of rockpools as spaces of wonder, curiosity, surprise, or fear when 'the ongoing ebb and flow of agency' (Barad, 2003: 817) enables or constrains human foraging and sets the physical conditions through which the species can meet (Haraway, 2008). It may appear that rockpoolers and their basic apparatus constitute the dominant actors of the intertidal zone, but as a land-dwelling species, the edge of the sea is not a truly human world and there are both obstacles to access as well as potential dangers. There is enchanting wonder as well as unsettling, tentacular potential (Haraway, 2008). In its embrace of 'thresholds and tensions, blends and blurs' (Gregg and Seigworth, 2010: 7), affect theory is useful for describing these hard-to-measure experiences and non-lingual interactions.

Affect is the 'force of encounter' emerging from a 'point of connection' (Gregg and Seigworth, 2010: 4) which is apposite to the act of rockpooling because the coast forms a literal point of connection between land and sea at which human and nonhuman agencies come into contact. Different strands of affect theory emerge in phenomenology (e.g. Shilling, 2017), neuroscience and philosophy (see e.g. Braidotti, 2002), psychology and psychoanalysis (e.g. Tomkins, 1962), cultural studies, anthropology, and the broader humanities (e.g. Hollin and Giraud, 2017). The growing literature on commercially orientated affective phenomena including workplace 'atmospheres' (Borch, 2010), emotions (Fineman, 2010), identity and gender politics (Pullen and Rhodes, 2013), and taste, materials, and consumption (Vachhani, 2017) also provides useful points of reference for thinking about a variety of organizational 'planes of experience that intersect' (Tucker, 2006 p.15). This chapter, however, draws on 'charisma' (Lorimer, 2008) which emerges from geographic conceptualizations of affect.

Charisma is a concept already familiar to business and management (particularly leadership/followership) studies where scholarship has investigated the powerful nature of magnetism and charm; how particular personality effects are experienced and become motivational spurs to action. Weber, of course, saw charisma as the necessary counterpart to bureaucracy, but only imagined it as something embodied by influential human leaders and politicians (O'Doherty, 2021; Weber, 1968). In considering the 'relatedness' of social actors through unseen influences there are parallels between these readings and the form of affect I draw on here although charisma (as presented here) is not concerned with human actions alone. As a descriptor of the affect emerging between humans and animals, it focuses upon the features of nonhuman entities as they come to be perceived, a process which influences how other-than-human organisms become known.

This frame helps locate the *felt feeling* that can emerge from an encounter with a nonhuman form and explains the impulse or physical drive that results from it—the instinctive desire to reach out or to recoil; to coax or to kill. In the rockpool, the motion of a sea anemone's fronds, the sway of seaweed, the quicksilver flash of a tiny shrimp might provoke subjective, interiorized responses which are as much about the human participant's perception of place as they are about these tiny physical details. Charisma, then, is a property contingent upon the perceiver and the context in question, often a natural habitat, and it describes the attraction and ease with which a particular entity is experienced (Hollin and Giraud, 2017). The reference points of species, habitats, and ecosystems make this different from organizational theories of charisma that stress the unseen (but felt) aspects of contact between human actors, or between humans and objects within human repertoires of economic activity, dwelling spaces, and materials (Vachhani, 2013).

Charisma recognizes the human in that it 'emerges in relation to the parameters of different technologically enabled, but still corporeally constrained, human bodies, inhabiting different cultural contexts' (Lorimer, 2007: 916) and has an anchoring point in the physicality and embodied nature of sensory experience. It also accounts for the political nature of human-nonhuman relations in 'nature' by showing how and why the appeal of some species leads them to be favoured in their designation as 'companions' or why negatively experienced others may enjoy limited care or interest. Interspecies meetings are sometimes mysterious and hard to articulate, but charisma puts a name to the relationships between affect and ecology (Hollin and Giraud, 2017) and how it is that the objects or animals in human purview come to be seen and acted upon in the manner that they are. In making these connections, the powerful entanglements between micro-sensory human experiences and the broader politics of interspecies interaction are exposed for scrutiny.

To some readers the emphasis upon affective entanglements may sound vague, carrying a danger of getting lost in the subjectivities of others with 'an over-abundance of swarming, sliding differences: chasing tiny firefly intensities that flicker faintly in the night' (Gregg and Seigworth, 2010: 4), but affect theory—and charisma in particular—is highlighted here for its broader applicability to other multispecies 'compounds' (Helmreich, 2010) and its value for description of the 'affective interface' (Gregg and Seigworth, 2010: 5) of rockpooling. To highlight this, the next section presents the first of two 'moves' which describe first-hand experiences of rockpooling with family members to evoke the attraction and lure of interspecies encounters. The following section then turns more closely to the possibility of threat and repulsion at the seashore. Moving from light to shade through these two different sections, the chapter holds a variety of material, semiotic, and metaphoric readings of the seashore in tension and underlines the biopolitical as well as epistemological difficulty of *knowing animals*.

THE CONVIVIALITY OF ROCKPOOLING WITH CHARISMATIC CRITTERS

As liquid spaces of playful learning and wonder, rockpools are the setting of myriad sensory experiences and imaginaries. The words of Charles Darwin (1839: iv) capture it well: 'We feel surprise when travellers tell us of the vast dimensions of the Pyramids and other great ruins, but how utterly insignificant are the greatest of these when compared to these mountains of stone accumulated by the agency of various minute and tender animals!'. The attributes that rockpoolers assign to their 'finds' are structured through

FIGURE 24.1 At the edge of the sea, seaweed covers the craggy rocks and pools. Photo by Michael Richardson-Moore on http://www.unsplash.com.

affective senses of what matters; or what matters matter (Barad, 2003) during their limited temporal opportunities, something that informal conversations with fellow rockpoolers supported.

> Family member: I saw tiny shrimps, very see-through, and they were darting quickly about, hiding in the seaweed. Crabs were so quick after being found under the rocks. They just buried themselves in the sand and I wasn't fast enough to photograph them. I think I got a shot of the back of one as it was swallowed up by sand.

Here, one may perceive that rockpooling is preoccupied with zooming in on the close detail of fish, crustaceans, and plant matter, but is contextualized by an infrastructure of rocks, pebbles, shells and sand that can 'swallow up' animals that choose not to be discovered. Reference is made to the *size* of the creatures in the rockpool, 'tiny', their *colour* 'see-through', *bodily motion*—'darting' or 'burying themselves'. There is also self-reflection, 'I wasn't fast enough'. Together these comprise expressions of perceived charisma, finding descriptive power through a (human) experience of intentionality but dependent upon the immediate sensory contact with lively bodies, expressing unique behaviours in a microcosmic setting populated by colours, shapes, and the wave-worn textures of nature.

Lorimer (2007) breaks down such experiences into three interrelated forms of charisma: ecological, aesthetic, and corporeal. *Ecological charisma* uses an ethological or phenomenological reading of human-nonhuman interaction, the way the human's body and senses filter and interpret the particular animals in ways that 'disproportionately endow' them with qualities of attraction (p. 916). The capacities and activities of shrimps (their 'affordances' as Lorimer terms them), for example, working in tandem with human capacities and activities of kneeling, bending, searching, seeing and photographing create the context that best sums up ecological charisma: the meeting of human senses and technologies with animal agencies in a particular setting. These points of contact lead to surprise, joy, excitement (or potentially disgust or fear) which explains human endeavours to experience these nonhuman others:

> Family member: I think the 'rock fish' were quite a surprise to me. They were bigger than I thought they'd be. They were in one of the larger pools where the rocks were covered in slippery greenery. Barnacles clung on to the sides of the pool and they took a lot of getting off.

Here, the rockpooler is surprised at the scale of the fish, the tenacity of the barnacles, and the texture of the slippery rocks which not only signifies the feeling of seeing particular species in ecological context but also illustrates *aesthetic* and *corporeal charisma*. Aesthetic charisma is evident when the observer denotes a physical quality (here, the size of the 'rock fish') and in other interspecies meetings might also refer to some perceived quality such as 'cuteness', 'dangerousness', 'slipperiness', and so on. Corporeal charisma refers to the emotions engendered by such meetings, here denoted by 'surprise' but in other scenarios might refer to longer-term engagements with a particular animal or group of animals, a rapport or connection of some sort.

In the rockpool, where animals are depicted as 'quick', 'darting', and 'hiding', these are traits that lead some humans to use particular techniques and rudimentary technologies to maximize their chances of contact, as one interviewee highlights:

> Family member: One dad that I spotted had a crab line and was pulling barnacles off the rocks and attaching them to the line, and the fish would come for that.

This adult had a specialized crab line, temporarily repurposed for the capture of fish by means of prizing barnacles off the rock to form bait. Implicit in the fact that the 'dad' had chosen this particular tool is that fish and crabs are treasured while barnacles are deemed worthy only by their utility as food for creatures higher up the pecking order; what Lorimer terms a 'flagship' or 'target' species. Flagship species hold a lasting place in a person's memory, attachment, concern or interest, and leaving home with a 'crab line' implies the experience of corporeal charisma, evident in the hope of encountering a previously known or experienced animal and 'becoming' with them *in situ*, albeit in the roles of hunter and prey.

As multispecies ethnographer Eben Kirksey (2015) notes, there is something distinctively human and deeply political in watching, interpreting, and seeking to interact with other-than-human lives. Whether we are talking about fish, barnacles, or crabs, these represent 'flexible persons' who may well be 'incorporated into human lives, and addressed with kinship terms. But they can be demoted at any moment … as household income or personal circumstances shift' (p. 135). Flexibility of categorization means fish, barnacles, or seaweed may be perceived positively as 'finds' or 'target species' but they may also be regarded as potential food, as objects of wonder, or the toys of play. Their traits can materialize and dematerialize depending on the charisma with which they are experienced; emerging not only from their physical qualities perceived in the sparkling water of the rockpool but also the tropes of natural history and personal recollection that make their behaviours relatable for human onlookers. Feelings of attraction and wonder structure the meeting point between hand, bucket, and organism and characterize rockpooling as a value-laden process that prizes certain organisms as *worth capturing*. This is not to suggest that the value of the animals described is purely to the inquisitive hands and eyes of rockpoolers, rather what intrigues here is the potential for describing and making sense of the affective experience of contact.

Whether humans read the actions of animals as strategy and design or mechanistic and impulsive evolutionary behaviour, manifold readings emerge from observations of the lifeways of the 'liminal critters' (Kirksey, 2015) that dart about or submerge themselves in the sandy bottom of the rockpool. The sensory pleasure of rockpooling is about finding joy in the 'unforeseen capacities and potentialities' (O'Doherty, 2017: 139) of those 'rose-columned forests' (Gosse, quoted in Stott, 2002) and species that we can only speculate on from above the waterline. Rockpooling is concerned with informal acts of searching, finding, naming, and curating, rather than looking to get to the bottom of things. One might perceive the crab resting on grains of sand and gravel on the bottom of the pool, through the glittering reflection of sea water. There is no need to scoop out the water to get a better view but rather accept the blurred refractive qualities of the sand and the crab. Charisma places emphasis upon these informal, sensory, and refracted moments of interspecies contact and embraces a blurring of haptic, optic, and cognitive 'data'. This is well captured by Berlant (2010: 5) who speculates that 'living demands both a wandering absorptive awareness and hypervigilance that collects the material that might help to … maintain one's sea legs … ' (quoted in Stewart, 2011: 447). This applies both literally and metaphorically during rockpooling; it is absorbing, engrossing, and playful but nonetheless fosters the development of a distinct logic, the development of 'sea legs' by collecting and making sense of physical and semiotic material within a specific ecological setting.

Seaweed Tentacles, Solitude, and Fear of Drowning

Thus far, I have focused upon the sensory attractions of rockpooling. I now turn to a darker story which begins with the observation of a minor incident at the shoreline which is recalled by another family member:

Family member: It was very slippery, all the pools were slippery. The day was overcast and drizzly, with huge grey clouds building overhead. We spotted a lady rockpooling quite far away. She fell. She seemed to have broken her arm, she was quite far out so the lifeboat came to pick her up.

It was an event that I reflected on later that afternoon. We had been rockpooling for the day and decided to eat dinner at 'The Smuggler's Inn'—a pub (public house/bar) on a rocky outcrop above the cobbled cove where we had been foraging. Inside the heavily-grockled sixteenth-century hostelry was a profusion of low-hanging ornaments and clutter of the seashore. Lobster pots and coloured glass lanterns adorned the interior. The low-beamed ceilings seemed atmospherically appropriate for the ghost story that was printed for the tourists in the back of the menu. The dingy setting for this surprise discovery was relevant to the chill that I experienced when reading this short text:

> The sun blared down onto the sandy beaches, once untouched in the dead of night, now adorned with many footprints of children and adults. It was here, on this sunny beach in Cornwall, that Mary Lapreina disappeared. 'Come on, Alice! I want to look in the rockpools!' the voice of Mary Lapreina rung out, and her friend, Alice Dewdon, followed on. They ran to one rockpool after another, looking in joy at the contents of each pool. Then Mary slipped on the cursed moss and fell into a large rockpool. 'Are you alright, Mary?' cried Alice. 'I'm fine!' Mary replied, 'Could you get help?' 'Of course!' replied Alice, 'Don't go any further, it goes deep!' She ran away. Mary was a curious and adventurous person; she liked to explore. So, of course, she trudged a little deeper, just to see how deep. Without warning, something slimy groped at her ankle, and wrapped itself tightly. Mary shrieked, and kicked her leg. Then, beneath the water, she saw it was seaweed. She relaxed slightly. Just seaweed. But then, another slimy rope of seaweed shot from the water, wrapping itself around her upper arm. She shrieked again; more seaweed came, wrapping around her legs, her arms. Mary shrieked and shrieked—until a particularly slimy seaweed wrapped itself around her mouth. The shrieks and screams became muffled; the seaweed wrapped over her whole body, like an Egyptian mummy. Eventually, it reached her nose and eyes, and she fell into the water. When Alice returned, all they could see was a green shape—a hand covered in seaweed, being pulled under the surface to her death. There were still disappearances after that, until 1964, when a gnarled figure was seen beside the pool in the dead of night; many shouted to her: she must get away. She did not turn. She was putting something in the water. She then turned, and due to a sudden whisk of sand, they were unable to see her. By the time it had cleared, she had gone. To this day, people still celebrate the Coming Of The Lady, and grieve over those who had lost their lives. Lost their lives to The Seaweed.

The feelings that arose on reading this are best described as a manifestation of corporeal charisma directed at seaweed. The text evokes a sense of being strongly moved, entangled, or affected by its imagined presence. Lorimer describes such moments as an 'epiphany' of awareness of a nonhuman organism although most experiences of this sort are characterized as formative, powerful, and above all *positive* experiences which can lead to a lifelong interest or preoccupation with a certain species. One would not describe the chilling experience of reading this story in precisely these terms however, particularly since the power of the sea is encoded by devices of 'cursed moss' and a 'hand covered in seaweed'. The Seaweed Lady has tentacles that can drag, submerge, kill, and hide unwary human prey.

The exact nature of the dates and names in this story appear to add historic specificity to the tale and are no doubt designed to lend a degree of credence. Yet the encoded warnings about desire, temptation, over-confidence, and curiosity materialize commonly in many other seaside legends that call on a basic human fear of interaction with unknown plants, animals, and other components of the marine environment. Together they instill fear of immersion and drowning. In Shetland, the myth of the Tangi, for example, carries many of these common tropes: a shapeshifting spectre dwelling at the seashore that demonstrated 'amorous propensities towards young women' (Kavanagh and Bates, 2019; Teit, 1918: 187–8) and could transform between human and equine form. In maritime legends such as these, handsome but solitary young men and old crones are common. Ghosts, spectral ships, smugglers, sailors, lockers, storms and shipwrecks, mists, bells, chests, lights, castles, jewels, coves, and caverns also proliferate. Common shapeshifting organisms include horses but also monsters, giant lobsters, and seaweed. So repetitive are these semantic devices, that they also surface in popular culture (e.g. blockbuster films such as *Jaws* and *The Meg*) and have also provided rich metaphoric resources for academics (Helmreich, 2010). They also become valuable symbols for interpreting the superstitions of those who work at sea (McCormack and Forde, 2020) where myths retain literal power and broker a sort of 'saltwater sociality' (Schneider, 2012) contoured by everyday work practices and superstitions (Moore, 2012). The following transcript of an archived interview with a fisherman demonstrates the charismatic absent-presence of pigs, rats, and salmon as signs of foreboding (https://www.bl.uk/collection-items/fishermen-superstitions):

> FISHERMAN: You know, you only need to mention rats on boats. That was a dreadful thing, don't mention a rat.
> INTERVIEWER: Oh [laughs].
> FISHERMAN: Don't mention a pig.
> INTERVIEWER: Yeah, yeah.
> FISHERMAN: Don't mention a salmon.
> INTERVIEWER: Any reason for that? I mean, is that—or is it—how did that come about, you know?
> FISHERMAN: There were certain people in the village and, you know, I've no memory of this, but my father would have told me that some of the skippers that he fished along as a young man, if any of them met a certain lady walking to the harbour in the morning or in the evening to fish for herring, they would have turned and called it off.
> INTERVIEWER: Right.
> FISHERMAN: Because they—and we would all say, 'Oh, a load of silly nonsense,' but the fella would have said the day that you went on to the fishing was the day

you tore your nets or you lost something, or— ... And then, for fun, you know—
and I would have been involved in this when I was younger, we would have left
tins of salmon on the wheelhouse window and things for men that were very
superstitious—
INTERVIEWER: [Laughs].
FISHERMAN: Just for the fun of it, and [laughs] we would have been watching and
you would have seen the tin of salmon hurtling across the harbour [both laugh].
And somebody would always say, now—somebody would say, ['Wish me any luck
today' 0:01:58], you know [laughs].
INTERVIEWER: A tin of salmon bounce off your head [both laugh].
FISHERMAN: We used to do it, and folk would have tied pigs feet up on the
foremast to the boat and things for [inaudible 0:02:08] and—you know?
INTERVIEWER: Such goings on, but it's such goings on in the fishing industry.

As this interview suggests, legends are not simply coded messages about a land-dwelling animal's common fear of drowning but help to strengthen 'what there is about a wet and fishy productive regime that defines the social, cultural, and economic life of fishing communities' (McCay, 1978: 397). Lorimer states that affects are 'contagious' and spread culturally, and it appears precisely thus when considering how stories about lucky (and cursed) plants and animals help annotate the patterns of living with the mutually constitutive nature of work on sea and land (McCormack and Forde, 2020). Clearly, the materialization and dematerialization of dry land and deep water at the intertidal edge provokes deep concern. It is a place where it is all too easy to be tempted, driven mad, enchanted, or killed by nature's tentacular practices (Haraway, 2008). The atmosphere conjured up by sea legends plays to a fear of liminality, that 'betwixt and between' state that sits between worlds.

The monsters of rockpool legends and fishermen's tales are liminal actors in the sense that they hold a societal position in which they are not strictly definable but occupy a symbolic or mythic status which humans cannot fully relate to. Organization studies parallels this by retaining focus upon those labouring at, or between, boundaries with studies of 'contingent workers', 'temps' (Winkler and Mahmood, 2015), or 'loungers' (O'Doherty, 2017: 143). The 'shell-lessness' of the in-between is a fear of destruction, volatility, resistance, and unpredictability and is anchored in all human thinking. After all, acts of management and organization themselves rely upon the haunting background of the ghastly terrors of disorganization where the unwary can slip, become entangled, and drown. The preoccupation with algorithms, data, strategy, and leadership seek to render the threats harmless, but reified thus they so often unfurl their own threatening tentacles and trap us.

There are existential threats for the 'liminal critters' that seek to survive at the intertidal zone. As long as the tide maintains the water-level in a rockpool, for example, the water will continue to heat up and evaporate which means that salinity increases and oxygen falls, making it increasingly difficult to 'breathe'. Why would a creature like a prawn choose to live in such a hostile place? 'Because lower down the tide, where conditions are not so difficult, is filled with enemies and rivals. That is the choice intertidal creatures have to make: horrible circumstances or neighbours out to kill you. Daily heat/oxygen/salt stress or minute-by-minute fear for your life' (Nicolson, 2021). Animals and humans alike are exposed to the dangers of *lateral drift* (O'Doherty, 2017), and clearly this is no place for overconfidence as multiple actors are vulnerable to destabilization and exposure.

It is an error to dismiss seashore stories charged with warnings about sex, sacrifice, disempowerment, and death as mere folklore, enrolled cynically by seaside traders to boost custom. They are not simply old fishermen's tales. The solitary figures of the Tangi, like the enchanted Seaweed She-Monster are commonplace reminders of the concern sparked by the materialization and dematerialization of 'others' across spatial and temporal boundaries. Here charisma involves both fear and threat, rather than attraction, associated with their otherworldly appearance, mysterious powers, and intoxicating capacities. That these exceed the rational and human makes them as concerning to us now as at any time in history.

Discussion and Conclusion: Rockpools as 'Wunderkammer'

Orwell's (1939) novel *Coming up for Air* provides a literary reminder of the value of exploratory playfulness in rockpools. The central character, suburban insurance salesman George Bowling, recalls childhood memories of rockpooling and asks, 'Why don't people, instead of the idiocies they do spend their time on, just walk around LOOKING at things?' p.68 Juxtaposing the dull formality of formalized work against the sparkling agility of pools, teeming with entities that may be impressively crusted, silkily insubstantial, elusive, or tentacular, he ponders 'the mystery of their lives, down there under water'. Orwell's warning to the reader remains relevant, particularly as the pandemic has prompted many workers to adopt increasingly indoor and screen-based patterns of interaction. Consider, for example, the 'dad' who was observed at the rockpool with a crab line. Did he spend his days in a high-rise office block, or perhaps sitting at his kitchen table plugged into a series of online meetings, hardly ever contemplating the attractions of his 'target species'? When away from the carefully curated workplace with its soft lights and comfortable swivel chairs, did he—like George Bowling—rediscover child-like vitality (Deleuze and Guattari, 1987) to look at, capture, and interact with fish and crabs?

During the activity of rockpooling, haptic and ocular encounters with pool-dwelling lifeforms generate affective responses along a spectrum of attraction. Whether such responses are positive or negative; real or imagined is not entirely determined by the inherent properties of the organisms in question. Crabs, for instance, could be viewed as cooperative organizers, elusive prey, or aggressive pugilists and it is important to note that these classificatory traits may well be arbitrary components of a human imaginary,

FIGURE 24.2 The craggy coastline, a liminal zone imbuing fear of nature's tentacular power. Photo by Jamie Street on http://www.unsplash.com.

imperceptibly crafted from exposure to repeating cultural devices and narratives that lend characteristics that may well attract, repulse, or spark superstition but are not intrinsic to the bodies or cognitive capacities of such creatures. Indeed, it is likely that crabs (like many other rockpool critters) are almost entirely oblivious of human attention and the interpretations that are afforded them. Searching for crab truth in seawater is, perhaps, an elusive if not impossible task.

In seeking to make sense of the mix of knowledge, emotion, feeling, and connection, charisma is helpful. It complements a broader range of affect theory, for example, Lugli's (2006) concept of *Wunderkammer* and MacLure's (2013: 228) emphasis on wonder 'as an untapped potential in qualitative research'. The relevance of this to rockpooling is simple to draw out for, as Gherardi (2021 p.44) explains, the 'pastime of gathering very different objects and materials together started in the sixteenth century marked the beginning of the phenomenon of Wunderkammer or cabinets of curiosities which brought together various pieces from the world around us, a world deemed wonderful and full of amazing surprises. They were places where things were accumulated and piled up without any clear order and where connections came into being without there having to be a logical reason for them'. This echoes the casual, disorderly curatorship involved in rockpooling as well as its dry-land offshoot, the domestic aquarium.

What charisma offers, then, is a theoretical lens that helps us better interrogate the source, meaning, and political impacts of such collections; what lies behind practices of gathering and the values placed upon individual plants and animals within material-semiotic assemblages (Law, 2004). Charisma helps explain why a large rock-coloured fish can be designated as a surprising find, while the tenacious barnacle could be regarded a useful form of bait and a tangle of seaweed could be denigrated as a slippery source of danger. These are acts of deterritorialization and reterritorialization (Deleuze and Guattari, 1987) within a process of meaningful gathering and informal ordering that relies upon the fact that the heterogenous collection of actors and objects in a rockpool are never entirely settled. It is this changeable flux which holds potential for surprise, wonder, and joy for humans, as well as intense existential relief for animal life such as prawns as the tide brings freshly aerated, cooler, and less salty water from the open sea.

Deleuze and Guattari's (1987) theorization of the affective as a state of potential, intensity, and vitality (see also Guattari, 1995) seems particularly apposite to the acts of entangled 'becoming' when humans enter bodily contact with animals and plants along certain 'lines of flight' mediated through eyes, hands, or rudimentary technologies like spades and fishing lines. Yet there is a clear danger of anthropocentrism in defining and highlighting rockpool-dwelling species by their capacity to affect humans, and we must bear in mind that the physical look and feel of certain organisms is only part of the story we labour to create for them. Deleuze and Guattari (1987) explain similar account-making phenomena as a series of 'repeated practices that lead to the reorganisation, or the deterritorialisation and reterritorialisation, of the human organism within the cultural frames in which they are enmeshed'. These political acts of meaning-making, resonant with the ways individuals feel affected by others have the potential to produce patterns of logic, becoming routinized and embedded in informing how experiences with these others are forged, organized into activities, and embodied in 'cultural frames' including local superstitions and myths as well as global conservation agendas (Lorimer, 2007; 2008).

Unravelling this process is about apprehending the 'cosmic' expression of myriad agencies as they come together although, as O'Doherty (2021) ponders, whether such agencies are 'staring back' or are 'indifferent, impervious, defeating all attempts to know them' is difficult to grasp. Whether acts of human vigilance or semiotic meaning-making provide a sufficient analytic pathway to do justice to any nonhuman actor or assemblage is, of course, a persistent puzzle for the multispecies researcher. What charisma offers is pragmatic in nature; a degree of analytical purchase on the subjective, interiorized logics that arise from human perceptions of animals and habitats and a means of making sense of the ways that affective relations (whether on land or sea) emerge as both spontaneous and as a consistent pattern of response (Hollin and Giraud, 2017), within a particular ecological setting and over time and space. Charisma thereby complements but also exceeds theories of affect as it directs attention away from the human and towards the holistic assemblage or multiplicity (Law, 2004; Mol, 2002) of life in context, making space to examine the powerful biopolitics of entanglement between the imagined and the fleshy, the human and the animal, in conditions forever exposed—and reinvigorated by—the lateral drift of the tide.

References

Barad, K. (2003). Posthumanist performativity: Toward an understanding of how matter comes to matter. Signs, *40(1)*, 801–31.

Berlant, L. (2010). *Cruel optimism*. Durham: Duke University Press.

Borch, C. (2010). Organizational atmospheres: Foam, affect and architecture. *Organization, 17(2)*, 223–41.

Braidotti, R. (2002). *Metamorphoses: Towards a materialist theory of becoming*. Cambridge: Polity Press.

Darwin, C. (1839). *The structure and distribution of coral reefs*, reprint edition, 1984. Tucson: University of Arizona Press.

Deleuze, G., & Guattari, F. (1987). *A thousand plateaus*. Minneapolis: University of Minnesota Press.

Fotaki, M., Kenny, K., Vachhani, S.J. (2017). Thinking critically about affect in organization studies: Why it matters. *Organization 24(1)*, 3–17

Fineman, S. (2010). Emotion in organizations—A critical turn. In B. Sieben, & Å. Wettergren (Eds.), *Emotionalizing organizations and organizing emotions* (pp. 23–41). Basingstoke: Palgrave Macmillan.

Gherardi, S. (2021). In the worlding of Kathleen Stewart: Daydreaming a conversation with she. Unpublished working paper. University of Trento, Italy.

Gregg, M., & Seigworth, G.J. (2010). *The affect theory reader*. Durham: Duke University Press.

Guattari, F. (1995). *Chaosmosis: An ethico-aesthetic paradigm*. Trans. P. Bains, & J. Pefanis. Sydney: Power.

Haraway, D.J. (2008). *When species meet*. London: University of Minnesota Press.

Helmreich, S. (2010). How like a reef: Figuring coral, 1839–2010. Retrieved from https://drum.lib.umd.edu/bitstream/handle/1903/11834/How%20Like%20a%20Reef%20Figuring%20Coral,%201839-2010.htm?sequence=1.

Hollin, G., & Giraud, E. (2017). Charisma and the clinic. *Social Theory & Health, 15*, 223–40.

Kavanagh, K.E., & Bates, M.R. (2019). Semantics of the sea–stories and science along the Celtic seaboard. *Internet Archaeology, 53*, xx.

Kirksey, E. (2015). *Emergent ecologies*. Durham: Duke University Press.

Law, J. (2004). *After method: Mess in social scientific research*. London: Routledge.

Mol, A. (2002). *The body multiple: Ontology in medical practice*. Durham: Duke University Press.

McCormack, F., & Forde, J. (2020). Fishing. Anthropology, Oxford research encyclopaedias. https://doi.org/10.1093/acrefore/9780190854584.013.183.

Moore, A. (2012). the aquatic invaders: Marine management figuring fishermen, fisheries, and lionfish in the Bahamas. *Cultural Anthropology, 27(4)*, 667–88.
Lorimer, J. (2007). Nonhuman charisma. *Environment and Planning D: Society and Space, 25(5)*, 911–32.
Lorimer, J. (2008). Counting corncrakes: The affective science of the UK corncrake census. *Social Studies of Science, 38(3)*, 377–405.
Lugli, A. (1997[2006]). *Wunderkammer. Le stanze delle meraviglie*. Torino: Allemandi.
MacLure, M. (2013). The wonder of data. Cultural studies. *Critical Methodologies, 13(4)*, 228–32.
Martens, L.D. (2016). From intergenerational transmission to intra-active ethical-generational becoming: Children, parents, crabs and the activity of rockpooling. *Families, Relationships and Societies, 5(3)*, 447–62.
McCay, B.J. (1978). Systems ecology, people ecology, and the anthropology of fishing communities. *Human Ecology, 6*, 397–422.
Nicolson, A. (2021). Come hell or high water. Country Life Issue 31, 4 August 2021.
O'Doherty, D.P. (2017). *Reconstructing organization: The loungification of society*. London: Palgrave Macmillan.
O'Doherty, D.P. (2021). These boots were made for talking: Speaking landscape socialities against the 'businification' of the Dee estuary. In H. Knox, G. John (Eds.), *Speaking for the social: A catalogue of methods* (forthcoming). Goleta, California: Punctum Books.
Orwell, G. (1939). *Coming up for air*. London: Penguin.
Pullen, A., & Rhodes, C. (2013). Corporeal ethics and the politics of resistance in organizations. *Organization, 21(6)* 782–796.
Schneider, K. (2012). *Saltwater sociality: A Melanesian island ethnography*. New York: Berghahn Books.
Shilling, C. (2017). Body pedagogics: Embodiment, cognition and cultural transmission. *Sociology, 51(6)*, 1205–21.
Stewart, K (2011). Atmospheric attunements. *Environment and Planning D: Society and Space, 29(3)*, 445–53.
Stott, R. (2002). Through the eyes of God's naturalist. *Nature, 420*, 608.
Teit, J.A. (1918). Water-beings in Shetlandic folk-lore, as remembered by Shetlanders in British Columbia. *The Journal of American Folklore, 31(120)*, 180–201. http://www.jstor.org/stable/534874.
Tomkins, S. (1962). *Affect, imagery and consciousness: The positive affects*. New York: Springer.
Tucker, I.M. (2006). *Deterritorialising mental health: Unfolding service user experience*. (PhD thesis, Loughborough University, UK).
Vachhani, S. (2013). (Re)creating objects from the past—Affect, tactility and everyday creativity. *Management & Organizational History, 8(1)*, 91–104.
Weber, M. (1968). On *Charisma and Institution Building*. S.N. Eisenstadt (Ed.). Chicago: University of Chicago Press.
Winkler, I., & Mahmood, M.K. (2015). The liminality of temporary agency work: Exploring the dimensions of Danish temporary agency workers' liminal experience. *Nordic Journal of Working Life Studies, 5(1)*, 51–68.

CHAPTER 25

WHEN DISASTER HITS, DISSONANCE FADES

Callings and Crisis at an Animal Shelter

LINDA TALLBERG AND PETER J. JORDAN

The floods reached the animal shelter at 8 am and all we could think of was to save the animals. I wasn't prepared for the scene as an eerie apocalyptic mood hung heavy in the hot sticky Australian summer air, mixed with fried electrics and chemical leaks in the ever-increasing water-levels engulfing the office-buildings and animal kennels. A quiet anxious fear shone in determined eyes as the pressure of getting the animals to safety increased. But this was why we [shelter-workers] did what we did, to try to save as many as possible. The floods ended up saving so many from being killed [by us], water inundating the killing-room and halting our rationalised processes. In the wake of the devastation, many animals got a second chance at family-life framing the floods positively in spite of the toxic clean-up we endured and organizational chaos. (First author autoethnographic narrative)

NATURAL disasters do not discriminate: their effects are harmful for human and nonhuman animals being displaced, injured, or killed in the devastation. While organizations develop procedures to manage day-to-day processes and rules, these systems are rarely developed to deal with the extraordinary in crisis. These unusual moments of organizational life can reveal insights into the nature of relationships between humans, but also into the interspecies relationships at work, and such trigger events can serve as context for deeper understanding of organizational values and power. The opening excerpt illustrates the first author's insider experience of such a crisis—when a flood forced the sudden evacuation of the large Australian animal shelter she was working in, thus displacing the vulnerable animals in care as well as halting the everyday bureaucratic organizational processes. This crisis serves as the illustrative context for this chapter.

One way of thinking about shelter work is that it is human-animal work (HAW). This is defined as 'human work that is substantially focused on live non-human animals' (Hannah and Robertson, 2017: 116). Yet, it would be an error to focus exclusively on the *human* experience as separate in the work, with the nonhuman treated as a symbol or object of interest at the expense of developing an integrated understanding of relationality (see Cunha et al., 2019; Skoglund and Redmalm, 2017; Tallberg et al., 2021). In this chapter, we use a posthuman approach to illustrate the entangled and affective elements (Braidotti, 2019) that illustrate the tensions in *becoming-with* (Haraway, 2008) the nonhuman animals in an animal shelter during a crisis, and how wellbeing in such a work-setting is deeply intertwined among the human and nonhuman animal actors. This *becoming-with* includes a 'metaphysics that is grounded in connection, challenging delusions of separation' (Gherardi, 2019: 7) between the animal and researcher/worker creating an entangled *Umwelt* (lifeworld) which reduces human-animal boundaries and offers embodied knowledge in multispecies encounters. We suggest that understanding the underlying affective and ethical aspects of the animal shelter-worker and nonhuman shelter animal produces insights into the human-nonhuman emotional and ethical challenges involved. We also consider how these entangled affective elements are linked to a work-calling, and dirty work stigma: a further complication to understanding the lived experience of work with animals.

The trigger event of a flood provides the context for this exploration. We use affective, embodied, insider ethnographic data produced by the first author within an autoethnographic animal shelter study where long-term, deep relationships were formed with multiple species in the organization. Gherardi (2019: 1) refers to this as 'affective attunements'. The rest of the chapter is organized as follows: first, we theoretically contextualize the care-based animal work explaining dirty work 'taints'; second, we briefly explain our ethnographic data material, analysis, and context of the shelter; third, we illustrate the crisis event as elevating the importance of saving nonhuman animals, reframing the disaster positively as it disrupted killing processes; and finally, we conclude by framing our discussion through the interwoven human-animal lived experience suggesting a need for organizations to better consider the importance of human-nonhuman interconnectedness of wellbeing and justice in multispecies work-settings.

Animal Shelters as Entangled Sites of Dirty Work and Human-Animal Interactions

Animal shelters exist to societally manage unwanted, abused, and neglected nonhuman animals. They are run by public and private organizations of various sizes, ideologies, and financial means whose missions often explicitly revolve around animal protection and helping animals in distress. Most animal welfare organizations depend on donations in addition to adoption fees (and other fundraising activities), while some receive government subsidies. Lately, animal shelter studies have become popular sites for advancing organizational knowledge on worker wellbeing, callings, emotions, and stress (see Baran et al., 2012; Schabram and Maitlis, 2017; Rogelberg et al., 2007).

Shelter work with animals is often seen as 'dirty'. 'Dirty work' is a social construct defined to include work that has a physical, social, moral (Ashforth and Kreiner, 2002), and/or emotional taint (McMurray and Ward, 2014). These four 'taints' contribute to workers feeling stigmatized by wider society, and by often seeing themselves as 'dirty' (Ashforth and Kreiner, 2002; Baran et al., 2012) through an identity-framing of their work. Animal shelter work carries a *physical taint* in work tasks, such as cleaning animal waste in kennels (or being a 'shit-picker' as one of our interviewees explained) and dealing with dead bodies. Also, shelter-workers experience physical danger (part of physical taint), as the often-traumatized nonhuman animals are unpredictable, and physical injuries such as bites, scratches, and bruises are a normal part of the job. However, animal shelter work can also be socially, morally, and emotionally tainted—and these factors seemingly impact human wellbeing to a higher degree than physical taint. *Social taint* comes from work with stigmatized populations or the proximity to these, such as criminals and drug-addicts (Dick, 2005), which in animal shelters comes from dealing with the unwanted and abused animals that, within the domesticated animal population, may be seen to have a lower value as 'discarded' animals.

Moral taint comes from work of a 'dubious nature' (Ashforth and Kreiner, 2002; see also Grandy, 2008) that is highly task-based, reflecting an iniquitous characteristic of the work. In animal shelter work this can involve killing, often under less-than-ideal circumstances. The preferred shelter linguistic term of killing is 'euthanasia' which problematically implies consent and attempts to destigmatize the act and process, hence silencing both animal interests as well as workers' (often) conflictual feelings about this central work-task to manage limited shelter resources (such as kennel-spaces or care). Finally, *emotional taint* includes the internalized emotions linked to emotional labour (McMurray and Ward, 2014). Animal shelters can be considered highly emotive contexts as workers deal with complex, often difficult feelings, paradox, and dissonance.

These taints are all exacerbated by the emotional contagion of other workers, volunteers, managers, and the public, as well as the distress of the nonhuman animals. By having all four taints affecting animal shelter work, we have suggested this occupation group has a 'dirty' shadow (see Tallberg and Jordan, 2021). As with much dirty work, those not in the occupation may wonder 'why would anybody want to do this job?' Those undertaking the stigmatized, physically and psychologically challenging work are often those who self-identify as 'animal lovers' and being 'called' to help animals, as the work firmly resides within the animal welfare industry. Wrzesniewski et al. (2009: 115) define a calling as a decision to move towards activities that are 'morally, socially, and personally significant' and evidence suggests that individuals who answer their callings have higher job commitment and higher job performance (Kim et al., 2018). These aspects surely provide motivation for the low-paid work in the not-for-profit sector. Hence, callings can generally be seen as favourable from an organizational perspective leading to an intrinsically motivated workforce who often go beyond their work-duties, engaging in pro-social behaviour at work. Yet, for the workers, the hidden realities involved in societal animal management processes may be a stark contrast to the mission and animal-centred image of the organizations involved in maintaining 'order' of animals in our communities.

Work-Callings in Animal Dirty Work

Despite the potentially meaningful work based on a calling, there can be negative personal outcomes such as workaholism, burnout, and exploitation (Bunderson and Thompson, 2009). Although ideology is a highly salient work-motivator in occupations based on a calling, care-based animal work requires a great deal more from workers who highly value the nonhumans in care, yet often feel morally challenged due to the realities of the tasks involved. Much of the moral taint in animal shelters is hidden from public scrutiny through marketing positive stories of adoptions or advocating rescue efforts on behalf of the organization, ignoring facts such as kill-counts or processes that human and nonhuman actors face in their daily dealings based on economic rationalization. Although many larger animal welfare organizations today offer some euthanasia statistics, this is a new development, often downplayed and often shrouded in secrecy by administrative efforts of how such figures are devised (see Tallberg and Jordan, 2021). Bunderson and Thompson (2009) argue that employee expectations, based on a calling, create a specific type of psychological contract between the individual and the organization effecting the lived experience. Hence, those with a calling often have altruistic and moral motivations that drive their occupational choice but their expectations of the job often do not match realities.

To cope with the emotional strain, animal shelter-workers utilize different (but at times layered), coping identities to make sense of their work. We describe these coping mechanisms elsewhere (see Tallberg et al., 2014) as four storylines informing animal shelter-worker identities emerging from the moral paradox in wanting to save those they are tasked to kill. We have suggested that these storylines are: (1) the *'Victim'* (where killing is beyond the individual worker's control and external circumstances force killing those they want to save); (2) the *'Hero'* (when workers take responsibility for 'ignorant' animal 'owners' as well as conflicted co-workers); (3) the *'Professionals'* (long-termers was desensitize and mechanize killing as a 'necessary evil'); and (4) the *'Tourist'* (newcomers who struggle with staying in the organization due to the caring-killing paradox, often exiting the work as a result). These identities are central to how workers cope with the tasks they are assigned in their daily work.

These identities may also be tied to work-callings as most animal shelter-workers describe their work in this way, (i.e., being the 'true animal-lovers'.) According to

Schabram and Maitlis (2017), callings take three distinct paths, two being potentially unhealthy leading to different types of burnout, while one is a 'healthy' calling path. In the first identity-oriented calling path, workers have 'sustained intense negative emotions linked to a threatened identity' and this increases the potential for 'breaking down' as a result of not being able to pursue the 'ideal of the calling' (Schabram and Maitlis, 2017: 596), ending with them leaving the shelter and working in other animal contexts. These authors find that the second contribution-oriented calling path includes increasingly intensifying negative emotions due to a limited impact on the social cause (in this case, to help nonhuman animals). These workers feel defeated and generally leave the shelter to contribute to work on different causes in other contexts. While they find that the third practice-oriented calling path involves individuals who initially are not emotionally animal-motivated, but instead focus on empowerment, innovation, learning, and mastery of work-tasks which allows them to continue the work. Both the four coping identities and three calling paths suggest a complex work situation where workers try to make sense of their motivations of doing the work, mostly seen in the caring task, while tasked with killing those they feel strongest about.

Research Methods and Animal Shelter Context

Post-qualitative and affective methodologies (Gherardi, 2019) were used in the autoethnographic study where the first author worked in a paid frontline animal shelter-position for 10 months documenting affective, embodied, and situational aspects of the work. This included participant observations in the form of field-diaries, reflective notes, pictures, and numerous secondary sources. Nonhuman animal interactions and relationships were included in the multispecies affective ethnography, a common aspect of posthumanist and multispecies epistemologies (see Hamilton and Taylor, 2017). Additionally, 20 semi-structured interviews were conducted with other employees, both before and shortly after the flood. A manual thematic analysis (Glaser and Strauss, 1967) was conducted on all data to find patterns and recurring themes.

The case-shelter managed around 20,000 nonhuman animals during the year of field-research. These were housed in single or group concrete cells for dogs; holding boxes or smaller cells for cats; small animals (such as mice, rats, hamsters) in cages stacked in a trailer; ducks, chicken, and miniature pigs in an outdoor mud enclosure; and horses, sheep, and goats in a field with a three-walled concrete stable. In addition, there were injured Australian wildlife treated in the shelter veterinary centre, and a bird enclosure. There was high turnover among the animal shelter-workers consistent with other studies that have drawn on this occupational group (Rogelberg et al., 2007), but on average, there were around 10 paid shelter-workers on a work-roster to manage the shelter animals and volunteers.

In this kill-shelter[1] workers undertake daily animal husbandry tasks but also assess, process, and kill the nonhuman animals in care in order to manage organizational resources. As the shelter was generally run on a tight financial budget, decisions of animal life and death were primarily made on a cost-benefit assessment. Volunteers and interns were not allowed inside the kill-building, nor were they privy to the process of what happened behind its closed gates. Hence, this process often came as a surprise to new workers and the first author was among those staff who challenged the 'processing-plant' mentality of managing animals (see Tallberg and Jordan, 2021). However, some workers framed the killing task as a 'last gift' to the nonhuman animals, signifying a variety of ideological perspectives among the frontline workers.

WHEN DISASTER HITS, DISSONANCE FADES

Australia often experiences extreme weather, such as fires, storms, and floods, all with devastating effects on the lives of human and nonhuman animals. With climate change this has intensified and will likely increase in the future. This chapter's flood event was caused by a series of unusual weather patterns during extreme summer months, leading to the area being declared a disaster zone. The major natural disaster lasted two months in total and included state-wide flooding affecting 2.5 million humans with over AUS$5 billion in flood damages. There were 33 human deaths, but the number of nonhuman animal deaths is unknown, as animals were not considered in the government disaster reports. For the animal shelter-workers, the crisis triggered a notable shift in dissonance, highlighting key aspects of the salience of taint in the work impacting wellbeing. Physical dirt increased because of the crisis, but the moral dirt lessened which we believe was due to a reversion to the organizational core values and individuals being able to enact their ideological motivations of saving animals. These actions enacted a narrative of positive outcomes when daily organizational processes were halted, demonstrating the underlying resistance and discontent with the normal day-to-day animal management processes.

The following narrative from the flood draws on researcher diary excerpts and illustrates how workers were able to assume control and help animals who in normal circumstances would have been deemed 'unadoptable' and thus killed.

> We had just transferred the last dogs out of the shelter when I remembered the geriatric ward housing sick and pregnant dogs. A soft whimper came from the dark pens, and a huge grey shadow jumped up, almost toppling me over. The dog tried to climb into my lap, failing miserably as his long hind legs were flopping down in panicked excitement. I looked into his big brown eyes and met the gentle soul who'd become my third foster-dog, an Irish Wolfhound I'd later name Boris.

---

[1] Kill-shelters are also referred to as 'open-door' policy shelters as they often take in all animals. In contrast, 'closed-door' policies of some 'no-kill' shelters restrict access due to limited resources. Both policies raise ethical issues.

In the evacuation, one of my senior colleagues tried to squeeze Boris into a crate. The whole attempt seemed ridiculous and he looked out from behind the wires at me, pleading. My heart ached as we connected in the chaos.

'You're taking him? He scares me' one of my managers quizzed me as I grabbed Boris to take with me home. Despite the surrounding fearful animals propped in cages, awaiting transport to volunteer foster homes, Boris happily bounced next to me, showering me with big kisses each time our eyes met, almost like he knew that I already loved him deeply and would do what I could to ensure he was safe. As an extra-large, unsocialized dog with guarding tendencies who had never been on a leash before, he was a handful to rehabilitate but a great teacher for my multispecies family structure. Eventually, I found his forever home with a doting human caretaker, Rosie, but sadly they only shared six months together, before he died of cancer. (First author autoethnographic narrative)

The narrative illustrates the breakdown of power and control in the organization on multiple levels, not only by disregarding managerial subjective assessments of what types of dogs could be rehomed and thus saved—Boris would have been killed in normal circumstances due to the level of care he required to be 'adoptable'—but also by assuming personal responsibility for individuals like him. There was empowerment in finding alternative solutions to confinement and death for those deemed as societally and organizationally 'challenging'. The experience with Boris demonstrates the limitations of many of the organizational policies (such as those regarding the processing, adoptions, and assessments of dogs) and how time, patience, and a safe space could provide balance for some of the troubled nonhumans animals and provide meaning for doing the work, enhancing wellbeing for both the human and nonhuman actors.

During this crisis, instead of challenging workers' intrinsic values most exemplified by the moral and emotional strain of the caring-killing paradox, workers were able to enact their ideological reasons for doing the job—which many reported to be all about saving and helping animals. Thus, killing stopped for some time as part of the shelter's 'tool' to manage their human, spatial, and financial resources, and the animals were seen as getting a chance away from the bureaucratic processes and tight timeframe of being assessed as desirable or not. Rather than the rationalized 'processing-plant' mentality, the core organizational mission of helping animals in need became the focus. As the premises had to be evacuated of both human and nonhuman animals, the shelter-workers were forced to pull together, finding alternative solutions quickly to ensure safety. The evacuation was chaotic and dangerous, with dirty floodwater inundating the buildings creating an extremely toxic environment with dead bodies, toxic chemicals, as well as surgical waste and equipment as there was an in-house shelter veterinary clinic on-site which was fully flooded.

Following the floods, many workers were ill, some having swum in the contaminated water to get the terrified animals to safety. Without official evacuation plans being in place, some of the workers took charge of the evacuation resulting in enacting the 'hero' storyline mentioned earlier. The workers ended up saving all the nonhuman animals from the flood in their efforts, thus highlighting to others, and themselves, their motivations of placing the vulnerable animals first and the valuable nature of their jobs. The crisis resulted in the breakdown of official processes which meant workers were able to align their actions to the core organizational values of saving lives, a value which otherwise became shrouded in normal daily routines. Under official policy, positive tasks such as adoption processes were handled by customer services, not by the frontline shelter-workers who cared for and directly managed the nonhuman animals. Thus, the crisis offered an experiential re-alignment for frontline workers enacting their work-calling.

> The first thing I said when I got into the shelter that morning was 'have we lost anything?' You know, because the kennels had gone under and we'd left dogs in them the night before. It was chaos ... I guess it's a sight to see somebody dragging a sheep down the road and another with a peacock in their car and in this crisis, we certainly all pulled together, but it was manic. (Lauren, Animal shelter-worker)

For workers, reverting to the core values of the organization, typified by working together to get the nonhuman animals to safety, created a sense of camaraderie in place of the pre-crisis conflictual organizational environment when workers often disagreed on how best to help those in care. Breaking processes and hierarchical rules created a situation for swift action and trust in others also being able to help, rather than the 'lone crusader' attitude of many prior to the crisis. However, the societal risks to breaking protocol was felt post-flood, as one interviewee reflected:

> Ultimately when it comes down to it, we [the frontline shelter-workers] make it work ... it was a big risk asking the public just to come and grab a dog. HUGE risk [for the organization] (Sue, Animal shelter-worker).

This refers to how the organization and some workers framed their duty, not only to care for the nonhuman animals, but also to protect the public (predominantly referring to the human public but also 'pets' already in society) from those deemed 'dangerous' (i.e. the unwanted and, at times, behaviourally 'challenged', traumatized nonhuman animals). Although there were limited human incidents with misplacements of animals in improper foster care, little is known about how the nonhuman animals fared as the humans taking them in had not been investigated (the usual protocol for foster care arrangements can be stringent and bureaucratic including house-checks and interviews with both human and nonhuman foster family members). Yet, as Sue's comment shows, the organization (and some long-term workers like Sue) concerned itself with the human safety factor echoing Irvine's (2003: 562) institutional framing of animal shelters as protecting 'people more than they do animals' when offering the public service to manage unwanted or abused animals. Nevertheless, the reversion to the core values of saving animals (despite the uneasiness in public safety aspects), created an alignment to the core purpose of doing the work leading to a reduced level of dissonance for workers.

Sensemaking of the Disaster for Entangled Human-Animal Wellbeing

> The communication from management was awful, but the vibe, the positivity [on the ground], it was just astounding. Seeing people queue and help shovel mud and clean, shelter-workers showing up on their days off saying 'right, what do we need to do?' Evacuating the animals was like Noah's ark … to me, that hideous, awful event just brought out the best in people … it was nice for staff to see all these people falling over themselves to come and help us and seeing that positive side of the human race. (Betty, senior manager)

In addition to not being killed, many nonhumans were adopted by their foster families and, in this way, the flood was constructed as 'a small win' (Weick, 1984) for those saved. As the manager above reflects, the crisis inspired frontline staff and the public to work together to fulfil what, throughout our data and lived experience of the shelter, was seen as the underlying organizational responsibility—to help animals in need. Workers felt more contented in their ideological reasons for doing the animal shelter-work: to save rather than 'process' nonhuman animals and 'shield' the public from the realities behind managing society's 'feline and canine inconveniences' (Irvine, 2003: 562).

Ashforth et al. (2017) suggest managers can limit taint in dirty work through the alignment of a worker's affinity to the organizational cause. This was not an issue in our case study as the animal shelter-workers were aligned to the core organizational mission, in fact, this was seen as a factor contributing to negative worker wellbeing as the reality of the work was dominated by a 'processing-plant' mentality (Tallberg and Jordan, 2021). Working in a job that aligns with strong personal convictions or passions can be seen as work based on a 'moral duty' (Thompson and Bunderson, 2003), a source of pride for many animal shelter-workers. But this can be a 'double-edged sword' as workers may be exploited to benefit organizational functioning (Bunderson and Thompson, 2009). In our case study, this included financial aspects (such as unpaid overtime), physical health aspects (such workers risking their own welfare in the floods), but most notably, the emotionally and psychologically challenging moral aspects of killing those they wanted to save.

There is a 'flourishing of the human condition' that can excel in value-driven circumstances creating meaningful work (Cameron and Spreitzer, 2012). The evacuation of the shelter presented the workers with a chance to regain their ideological reasons for working in a dirty work context as no lives were lost. The core organizational and individual values aligned in this event, minimizing the felt dissonance and the moral dirt. Value-based organizations largely rely on the intrinsic motivation and ideological alignment of their organizational members (Rothschild and Milofsky, 2006). As such, value-based organizations may need to recognize that in specific types of organizations (such as an animal shelter or animal protection organization), the moral paradoxes that give rise to employee dissonance are especially detrimental. Unchecked, this can become more than an individual employee problem, as costly high turnover and negative emotional contagion may disrupt the care of the nonhuman animals. We believe the pro-social motivation resulting from a workforce high in intrinsic motivations based on calling is an opportunity missed, particularly if the occupation is devalued by managers and the public to line-workers who 'just' clean cages. The business case rationalities and thinking dominating the animal welfare organization was considered by many workers as an affront to its charity status and ideological values, yet one could argue their organizational success may be based on aspects of efficiency, control, and protocol in running the shelter.

Other research on animal shelter work (done from an 'outsider' researcher perspective), concludes that the caring-killing paradox creates dissonance which is presented as an intense problem only for shelter newcomers, and that, over time, negative emotions are replaced with more manageable ones objectifying the animals into 'virtual pets' (Arluke, 1994). This perspective could be argued to support the economic rationalities used in the shelter as it reduces and objectifies both the workers and nonhuman animals to support organizational functioning. However, we argue that such a managerial framing of the work is one of the core limitations of outsider methods missing nuances among the workforce, as understanding the affective aspects of this work may be limited due to the reluctance of workers to discuss morally dirty work with others who do not share this experience, and talking about the paradoxical issues with outsiders may stigmatize the individual worker further.

Some workers used emotional management techniques to distance themselves from the shelter animals to cope with the moral conflict. In fact, there was a resilience-training workshop held during the first author's fieldwork where workers were given instructions to this effect. This distancing has been a central way shelter organizations suppress the moral concern of workers for coping with the difficult task of killing. Similar distancing methods are used in overtly profit-driven contexts (reliant on animal death and instrumentality) such as animals-as-food processing facilities. Despite this technique, workers experience massive negative wellbeing beyond factors related to taint and status (see the quantitative research conducted by Baran et al., 2016 on Danish slaughterhouse workers). From a work wellbeing perspective, providing coping mechanisms may seem beneficial, but applying a critical posthuman and post-anthropocentric lens to such activities may suggest that toning down conflictual worker emotions served organizational functioning more than serving the nonhuman animals' interests. As such, human resilience training in multispecies organizations such as animal shelters, could be framed as silencing opposition to organizational processes and protocol, whereby those not being able to reframe the moral taint mostly left the organization.

Despite many dirty workers seeing their roles as contributing to the fabric of society at a macro-level, often the specific work-tasks involved can result in them questioning their reasons for continuing this work and experiencing cognitive and emotional dissonance (Rogelberg et al., 2007). Cognitive dissonance arises when individuals face situations where their actions are at odds with their beliefs or values (Festinger, 1957), a familiar experience for many shelter-workers. Their ideological values can be at odds with organizational processes, creating tensions through 'ideologies of care' contra 'ideologies of control' in managing nonhumans specifically related to killing (Tallberg and Jordan, 2021). This also results in emotional dissonance as their feelings may not match the professional demeanour expected at work. Workers, who often self-identify as 'animal lovers', experience a work-based caring-killing paradox when caring for the nonhuman animals while also being required to kill them due to limited resources, resulting in emotional strain (Reeve et al., 2005; Rogelberg et al., 2007). Arluke (1994: 86) notes it is 'a painful process' that results in a 'complex emotional state' where 'you have to believe it is right' to undertake the work. This implies a moral paradox and hence, there is a moral toll (also referred to as moral dirt) to animal shelter work that goes beyond emotional strain and makes it different to other types of dirty work.

In the flood, workers were able to enact their intrinsic motivations of saving nonhuman animals—both from the flood and from the organizational processes. As argued earlier, moral taint is the most salient aspect beyond other forms of taint in this context (such as physical 'dirt'). Moral behaviour and actions are of specific importance in this low-status work, which organizations founded on ideological principles should consider in greater depth. Our contribution is to highlight how a crisis, which was highly disruptive, gained a positive flavour by giving new opportunities for nonhuman animals who would otherwise have been killed in everyday organizational processes. In this way, both the frontline human worker and the nonhuman animal clients' wellbeing are intricately linked in the multispecies organization.

Concluding Thoughts on Wellbeing and 'Being in this Together'

Being in this 'together' refers to the entangled, multilayered, complex challenge human and nonhuman animals today face in the Anthropocene (Braidotti, 2019). As Johnsen et al. (2021) explain, the mapping and understanding of co-dependence in a posthumanist framing needs to take management and organizing to another level of understanding; the more-than-human level. These authors explain how the 'complex assemblages, interspecies entanglements, and excessive relational potentials ... encompasses a revised managerial sensitivity based on the realization that whether we want it or not, we are all in this "together", inseparable and without control, defeated yet eco-ethically enlightened' (Johnsen et al., 2021: 6). In a natural disaster, such as our flood example, human and nonhuman animals both face suffering because of forces beyond their control. Yet, as humans, we have more resources than nonhuman animals in society to effect change, and it is also us who are responsible for much of the suffering. There are many advantages to refocusing human and nonhuman animal wellbeing as intricately entangled, rather than discrete.

Foremost, if we start to consider nonhuman wellbeing and justice as pillars of human wellbeing and thriving, surely more can be achieved both inside organizations but also in how we organize society from a multispecies lens. As Betty's comment exemplifies in the crisis bringing out the 'positive sides of the human race'; humans can find ways to work together to benefit nonhumans and other humans during extraordinary times. In COVID-19 times we have seen the trend in adoptions with animal shelters around the world being initially emptied during lockdown measures when humans realized their need for companionship in coping with the crisis and solitary life at home. However, as societies opened up in late 2021 there was an increasingly worrisome trend of more animals being surrendered to shelters; increased companion animal-breeding, capitalizing on the high demand, leading to untold long-term issues for the animals who face uncertain futures when life returns to some normalcy; and very limited public debate on the dark side of the animal companion industry (such as the 'pet' carbon paw print, as well as ethical issues involved in companion animal breeding which, at its root, is often based on exploitation and commodification of female bodies). These points do not see the interconnectedness of wellbeing, but rather focus on instrumentalizing nonhuman animals for the benefit of human wellbeing without much long-term concern for the nonhuman animal.

Hence, in this chapter we call for multispecies wellbeing based on our fieldwork: a wellbeing which is relationally affected by, for, and with the nonhumans in human-animal work. In this sense, interspecies wellbeing is a practice of *becoming-with* nonhumans, of being *more* through the entangled relationship between species. When the nonhuman animal suffers, so do often those closest to them—the human workers (or in private spheres, the human families if affectively close to the animal). Hence, to create positive organizational and societal functioning, entangled interspecies wellbeing must be better recognized. Furthermore, in work based on a calling, ideology is highly relevant and for such organizations it becomes even more crucial to consider how values are enacted in organizational practices. For nonhuman animals, it may serve them if organizations better consider workers' conflictual emotions when providing care so that new policies and processes of managing unwanted nonhuman animals can be developed as management better listen to those closest to the animals—both in proximity and affectivity (which is often the frontline workers in shelter contexts). Hence, for multispecies organizations, where nonhuman animals are part of everyday human-animal work, the wellbeing of the humans cannot be separated from the wellbeing of the nonhuman animals. In such work, wellbeing at work is truly connected across species, just as interspecies wellbeing is more generally connected in the wellbeing of the planet.

References

Arluke, A. (1994) Managing emotions in an animal shelter. In A. Manning, & J. Serpell (Eds.), *Animals and human society: Changing perspectives* (pp. 145–65). New York: Routledge.

Ashforth, B., & Kreiner, G. (2002). Normalizing emotion in organizations: Making the extraordinary seem ordinary. *Human Resource Management Review, 12*, 215–35.

Ashforth, B. et al. (2017). Congruence work in stigmatized occupations: A managerial lens on employee fit with dirty work. *Journal of Organizational Behavior, 38*, 1260–79.

Baran, B. et al. (2012). Shouldering a silent burden: The toll of dirty tasks. *Human Relations, 65(5)*, 597–626.

Baran, B., Rogelberg, S., & Clausen, T. (2016). Routinized killing of animals: Going beyond dirty work and prestige to understand the well-being of slaughterhouse workers. *Organization, 23(3)*, 351–369.

Bunderson, J., & Thompson, J. (2009). The call of the wild: Zookeepers, callings, and the double-edged sword of deeply meaningful work. *Administrative Science Quarterly, 54*, 32–57.

Braidotti, R. (2019) *Posthuman knowledge*. Cambridge: Polity Press.

Cameron, K., & Spreitzer, G. (Eds.) (2012) *Oxford handbook of positive organizational scholarship*. New York: Oxford University Press.

Cunha, M., Rego, A., & Munro, I. (2019). Dogs in organizations. *Human Relations, 72(4)*, 778–800.

Dick, P. (2005). Dirty work designations: How police officers account for their use of coercive force. *Human Relations, 58(11)*, 1363–90.

Festinger, L. (1957). *A Theory of Cognitive Dissonance*. Stanford, CA: Stanford University Press.

Glaser, B.G., & Strauss, A.L. (1967). *The discovery of grounded theory: Strategies for qualitative research*. New York: Aldine de Gruyter.

Gherardi, S. (2019). Theorizing affective ethnography for organization studies. *Organization, 26(6)*, 741–60.

Grandy, G. (2008). Managing spoiled identities: Dirty workers' struggles for a favourable sense of self. *Qualitative Research in Organizations and Management: An International Journal, 3(3)*, 176–98.

Hannah, D., & Robertson, K. (2017). Human-animal work: A massive, understudied domain of human activity. *Journal of Management Inquiry, 26(1)*, 116–18.

Hamilton, L., & Taylor, N. (2017). *Ethnography after humanism*. London: Palgrave Macmillan.

Haraway, D. (2008) *When species meet*. Minneapolis, London: University of Minnesota Press.

Irvine, L. (2003). The problem of unwanted pets: A case study in how institutions 'think' about clients' needs. *Social Problem, 50(4)*, 550–66.

Johnsen, R. et al. (2021). Management learning and the unsettled humanities: Introduction to the special issue. *Management Learning, 52(2)*, 135–143.

Kim, S.S. et al. (2018). How do callings relate to job performance? The role of organizational commitment and ideological contract fulfillment. *Human Relations, 71(10)*, 1319–47.

McMurray, R., & Ward, J. (2014). 'Why would you want to do that?': Defining emotional dirty work. *Human Relations, 67(9)*, 1123–43.

Reeve, C.L. et al. (2005). The caring-killing paradox: Euthanasia-related strain among animal-shelter workers. *Journal of Social Applied Psychology, 35(1)*, 119–43.

Rogelberg, S.G. et al. (2007). Impact of euthanasia rates, euthanasia practices, and human resource practices on employee turnover in animal shelters. *Journal of American Veterinary Medical Association, 23(5)*, 713–19.

Rothschild, J., & Milofsky, C. (2006). The centrality of values, passions, and ethics in the nonprofit sector. *Nonprofit Management and Leadership, 17(2)*, 137–43.

Schabram, K., & Maitlis, S. (2017). Negotiating the challenges of a calling: Emotion and enacted sensemaking in animal shelter work. *Academy of Management Journal, 60(2)*, 584–609.

Skoglund, A., & Redmalm, D. (2017). 'Doggy-biopolitics': Governing via the First Dog. *Organization, 24(2)*, 240–66.

Tallberg, L., Jordan, P.J., & Boyle, M. (2014). The 'green mile': Crystallization ethnography in an emotive context. *Journal of Organizational Ethnography, 3(1)*, 80–95.

Tallberg, L., & Jordan, P.J. (2021). Killing them 'softly' (!): Exploring work experiences in care-based animal dirty work. *Work, Employment and Society*. https://doi.org/10.1177/0950017021 1008715

Tallberg, L., García-Rosell, J-C., & Haanpää, M. (2021). Human–animal relations in business and society: Advancing the feminist interpretation of stakeholder theory. *Journal of Business Ethics*. https://doi.org/10.1007/s10551-021-04840-1

Thompson, J.A., & Bunderson, J.S. (2003). Violations of principle: Ideological currency in the psychological contract. *Academy of Management Review, 28(4)*, 571–86.

Weick, K. (1984). Small wins: Redefining the scale of social problems. *American Psychologist, 39(1)*, 40–9.

Wrzesniewski, A., Dekas, K., & Rosso, B. (2009) Calling. In S.J. Lopez, & A. Beauchamp (Eds.), *The encyclopedia of positive psychology* (pp. 115–18). West Sussex: Wiley-Blackwell Publishing.

CHAPTER 26

HUSKY KENNELS AS ANIMAL WELFARE ACTIVISTS

Multispecies Relationships as Drivers of Institutional Change

JOSÉ-CARLOS GARCÍA-ROSELL

INTRODUCTION

THE role played by animals and the treatment of animals in organizations have raised ethical questions that have been the focus of activism and public debate. In this chapter, I examine the efforts of a group of husky kennels to promote higher animal welfare standards in Lapland, Finland. There are more than 4000 huskies working in the business of dog sledding tours, which are currently the most important tourism activity in this Nordic destination (García-Rosell and Äijälä, 2018). Dog sledding is not only the most popular tourism activity in Finnish Lapland, but is also affected by a wide range of ethical issues pertaining to the welfare of the working dogs. For example, while kennel practices such as euthanasia and keeping dogs without regular exercise during the summer months are not illegal, they are morally questionable. These current practices have led some kennels to take a political stance on promoting change towards more ethical sled dog practices.

There is a flourishing field of literature on corporate activism that explores the role of companies and chief executive officers (CEOs) in influencing institutional and social change through political action (see e.g. Corvellec and Stål, 2019; de Bakker, 2012; Eilert and Nappier Cherup, 2020). Most of these studies have focused on large companies and on public debates relating to social and environmental issues. As a result, a number of significant questions remain unaddressed. First, we know relatively little about how small companies involve themselves in corporate activism, despite the fact that many small companies assume a political role in order to address regulatory gaps in their business environments (Wickert, 2016). Second, although animal rights and welfare have been discussed in relation to activism (Beers, 2006) and several studies have drawn attention to the way in which some corporations have addressed these issues as part of their corporate social responsibility (CSR) strategies (van de Ven, Nijhof, and Jeurissen, 2009), little attention has been given to how corporate activism can impose pressure in the institutional environment to improve the conditions of animal workers.

By studying husky kennels' activism through the lenses of institutional theory (Eilert and Nappier Cherup, 2020) and care ethics (Connolly and Cullen, 2018; Engster and Hamington, 2015), I offer insights into the role played by care relationships in multispecies businesses for driving political action and change towards more ethical dog sledding business practices. The empirical data is based on a six-year ethnographic study conducted with husky kennels and other animal-based tourism companies in northern Finland. The chapter is structured as follows. First, I introduce the empirical context of the study. Then, I discuss corporate activism in general and in relation to animal welfare and the notion of care in particular. Finally, the methodology and the results of the research are presented before speculating further on the ethics of inclusion relating to huskies, and other species, within economic and social life.

Dog Sledding as a Multispecies Business

There are more than 50 all-year-round husky kennels operating in the tourism industry in Finnish Lapland. These kennels generate millions of euros in annual revenues and employ hundreds of workers and thousands of sled dogs (García-Rosell and Äijälä, 2018). A husky kennel employs between 4–20 people—the owner, as well as permanent and seasonal workers. The dogs live in outdoor kennels and on running circle chains in populations that vary from a dozen to 500 dogs per company. Due to the growing popularity of dog sledding, all-year-round husky kennels are not able to cope with the high demand for husky tours, especially during the busiest months of the season (December to February). In such situations, the additional demand is covered by temporary kennels who bring their dogs in from southern regions of the Nordic countries as well as other parts of Europe. The keeping, handling, and killing of huskies working in kennels is regulated by the Finnish Animal Welfare Act.

In this chapter, I use the term husky kennels to refer to micro and small tourism companies offering sled dog rides in which it is possible for a tourist to drive a sled and lead their own team of huskies. Sled dog rides can range from short (0.5–2km) to medium length (10–40km), and can be multi-day rides (2–8 days). In these rides, sleds are pulled by a group of four to six dogs depending on the size and weight of the driver and passenger(s). Most of the sled dogs in Finnish Lapland are Alaskan huskies, which are a blend of different northern breeds, chosen because of their extraordinary pulling skills. It is also common to find Siberian huskies in the kennels; this particular breed is used for commercial marketing and advertising, contributing to the creation of exotic Nordic tourism images. Sled dog rides are organized according to strict safety rules and procedures in which good communication, trust, and close collaboration between humans and dogs are key to ensuring a successful tourism experience (Äijälä, 2019; Hoarau-Heemstra and Nazarova, 2021). Safety and driving instructions are generally provided by a guide who demonstrates the appropriate way to handle the sled and team of dogs.

In addition to providing customer services before, during, and after the sled dog ride, human workers are responsible for a variety of animal husbandry tasks (such as feeding, medical care, cleaning, and socializing), as well as training practices. Although huskies may start training alongside older sled dogs when they are six months old, they begin to pull sleds with tourists when they are between one and a half and two years old. Husky kennels put a lot of emphasis on planning the working shifts and resting periods of their working animals. The practices illustrated here show how dog sledding involves a series of multispecies performances, in which humans and nonhuman animals jointly engage in the co-creation of service experiences (Bertella, 2014; Dashper, 2020; Haanpää and García-Rosell, 2020). Considering this, I suggest, in line with Haraway (2008), that dog sledding represents a form of multispecies business in which sled dogs and humans (be they workers or tourists) work together to create a meaningful experience and achieve organizational goals.

The average working life of a husky is 10 years. Some dogs may retire earlier and some later, depending on their strength and motivation. When the sled dogs reach their retirement age, they work on less demanding tasks, such as being cuddled or photographed by tourists, and some will be given for adoption while others are euthanized. Indeed, according to the Finnish Animal Welfare Act, a dog may be killed, even though there is no serious reason for it, by a veterinarian administering a lethal substance, using gas, or shooting it in the brain (this last option can also be chosen by the owner or an authorized person holding a firearm permit) if this causes an immediate loss of consciousness and death. What happens to huskies after they retire depends to a great extent on the practice of each kennel, and this is one of the issues driving the political activity of some kennels—they would like, among other things, to make no-killing policies common practice in this particular business context.

Animal Welfare Corporate Activism as Care

According to Branicki et al. (2020), activism is a form of direct political action informed by a moral position that leads the activist to criticize the political status quo on ethical grounds, using that critique to justify direct political intervention. Although the notion of an activist was usually reserved for people who actively work for social and political causes (Curtin and McGarty, 2016), there is a stream of management research addressing the role of business organizations in promoting social change through institutional pressure (Den Hond and de Bakker, 2007; Eilert and Nappier Cherup, 2020). Indeed, activism is not just about sporadic political protests by concerned citizens, but is also reflected in a dense network of civic organization (Youngs, 2019), which nowadays has been expanded to include companies, covering a wide range of social issues. For example, activism has focused on climate change, immigration, land rights, gender equality, LGBTQI rights, and animal rights, among other issues that require urgent changes in social, political, and legislative arenas. Therefore, activism emerges out of situations where values are in conflict, demanding change in industries and social institutions in general.

When it comes to animal activism, we can refer to more than 150 years of advocacy and lobbying on issues concerning the rights and treatment of nonhuman animals (Beers, 2006). Within this advocacy movement, two perspectives tend to dominate the debate: that of welfarists and that of rightists. While animal welfarists accept the human use of animals as long as it is free of cruelty and mistreatment, animal rightists oppose the use of animals by humans, arguing that using animals is a violation of the animals' rights and thus a serious moral injustice (Beers, 2006). Indeed, the animal rights position is based on the notion of intrinsic value, meaning that animals have value in their own right and exist as ends-in-themselves (Fennell, 2014). Although animal rights activism has been common in the shape of anti-corporate movements challenging business models based on animal exploitation, there are also examples of companies taking a stance on animal rights. For example, Lush has been widely recognized for its campaigns and political stance against animal testing (Aronczyk, 2013). The Body Shop is another cosmetics company that was famous for its strong commitment and activism towards banning the use of animals in cosmetics testing (Hartman and Beck-Dudley, 1999), until it was sold to L'Oréal in 2006.

In a similar way, other companies have engaged in animal activism by relying on a welfarist perspective. The North Face and Patagonia are examples of companies that accept the use of animals but have, to a certain degree, argued for respect for and ethical treatment of the animals used in their supply chains. For instance, both companies have taken a stance on the sourcing of down, and have taken an active role in driving positive change in the industry. Nevertheless, companies engaged in animal welfare activism do not habitually have a direct relationship with the animals involved in or related to their business operations. By focusing on husky kennels in this chapter, I draw attention to these multispecies businesses that take a stance on animal welfare issues in order to drive institutional change by influencing social standards, the existing legislation, and the nature of competition in a Nordic tourism context. Following Eilert and Nappier Cherup (2020: 463), I define animal welfare corporate activism as a company's willingness to take a stand on the treatment of animal workers in order to create societal change by influencing the attitudes and behaviours of actors in its institutional environment.

Within a multispecies business context, human–animal relationships shape not only organizational life, identity, and values, but also the likelihood that organizational human actors will address a social cause that benefits the animals involved in their economic sector (see e.g. Coulter, 2016: 124–31). This likelihood is higher in a multispecies business with direct, concrete human–animal relationships and in which humans place intrinsic value on the life of the animals with which they work (see Connolly and Cullen, 2018: 416–17). In line with the idea of embodied ethics (Hancock, 2008; Pullen and Rhodes, 2015), I argue that the ethics of activism in a multispecies business are based on relational values, that is, on values that prioritize a recognition of, and responsibility and care for, the other (be that a human or an animal). From this perspective, it is not simply justice but also care, relations, and emotions that drive a multispecies business to engage in political action to improve the treatment of animals in society (see Engster and Hamington, 2015).

Methodology

In this chapter, I draw on empirical data collected in an ethnographic study that explored corporate activism in husky kennels located in the Finnish province of Lapland. The study was partly conducted within the realm of two parallel European Union (EU)-funded research and development projects focusing on animal welfare and responsible tourism implemented between 2016 and 2019. The data set used here was organized according to the principles and practices of self-inquiry (Marshall, 2001) and consists mainly of my personal field notes, meeting notes, blog posts, visual material (e.g. pictures and videos), and documentary material gathered during 2016 and 2019. Following the inner and outer arcs of attention suggested by Marshall (2001), I took notes of my experiences and reflections on the development and research process as well as the actions and reactions of the husky kennel owners involved in the two projects. Field notes and documentary material were also collected during the planning of the projects (2015) and after they ended (2020).

By writing analytical field notes and blog posts for the projects, I was able to engage in a reflexive process of questioning my understanding of responsible business in relation to animals, my assumptions about the political status of animals in society, my relationship to animals working in the tourism industry, and my own position as a researcher situated in a multispecies business context (see Hamilton and Taylor, 2017; Hammersley and Atkinson, 1996: 192). Furthermore, it was through this reflexive process and my fieldwork experiences that I noticed how some husky kennels engaged in political action and struggle to promote institutional change. The pictures and video material not only supported my field notes by helping me to recontextualize recorded events and utterances (Hammersley and Atkinson, 1996: 185), but also serve as a trigger for critical reflexivity in exploring multispecies relations (Äijälä, 2021; Haanpää et al., 2021; Hamilton and Taylor, 2017). By being actively involved in the projects, I was able not only to gather rich data, but also to gain access to different perspectives and controversies concerning the keeping and use of sled dogs in tourism.

As my intention is not to explain the point of view of single husky kennels, I approach the empirical data as social texts that are produced, shared, and used in a particular context (see Moisander and Valtonen, 2006: 68). The analysis involved the careful examination of the written and visual empirical material. Reading and re-reading the data made it possible to identify textual elements, recurrences, and arguments that point to the political activity of husky kennels and the resistance this activity encountered among similar companies and institutional actors.

Husky Kennels as Activists

In this section, I first discuss what motivates some husky kennels to act to promote the welfare of sled dogs. For the sake of clarity, I will call these husky kennels 'activist kennels'. I then draw attention to the barriers faced by these companies in their political struggle. Finally, I explain the strategies used by the owner-managers of the activist kennels to overcome these barriers and bring forward their political agenda.

Care Relationships as Motivation

When companies engage in activism, it is because of the organizational culture and value systems on which they are built (Eilert and Nappier Cherup, 2020). Activism is further supported by CEOs who use their leadership position and resources to bring about change (Branicki et al., 2020). This is the case with the activist kennels, where the personal values of the owner-managers play an essential role in informing and shaping their political actions. Nevertheless, their motivation to take a stance on animal welfare issues is based not on a pure notion of justice or rights but on the strong emotional relationships that exists between them and their animal workers (see Tallberg, García-Rosell, and Haanpää, 2021).

> The dogs that are born in our kennel are part of our family and we are responsible for them their whole life ... I make sure that after they have finished their career with us, that they end up with a good life ... It is my responsibility that we find them a good home. (Husky kennel owner-manager media interview)

As the excerpt above shows, the owner-managers of the activist kennel not only share a special connection with their dogs, but also acknowledge the intrinsic value of the animal workers. This is in line with an idea of care that focuses on the welfare, protection, or enhancement of the cared-for (Noddings, 2003: 23). Although the emphasis on finding a new home for huskies who are not good workers or are reaching retirement age may sound ordinary, it is not. In fact, one of the most contentious aspects of dog sledding is that euthanasia is commonly used in kennels to eliminate old dogs and animals which, due to their body structure, injuries, or temperament (aggressive or shy), among other things, are not suitable for work. For the activist kennels, it is not enough to implement adoption programmes and other forward-looking ethical sled dog practices in their own premises; they also want to influence other companies and, thus, have a strong impact on the dog sledding business.

> This was the culmination of a three-year goal, by one of our owners, to bring companies [husky kennels] to the table to challenge current practices in sled dog welfare … [T]he dogs should be treated as living animals with the rights which should come from their intelligence, capacity to love and to feel cared for … [W]e feel a responsibility towards the care of these amazing athletes that we have decided to bring into the world. (Husky kennel website)

My findings show how human–animal relations in a multispecies business may contribute not only to caring for those animals who are part of the organization, but also to having a sense of responsibility and respect for other disadvantaged animal workers (see Tallberg, García-Rosell, and Haanpää, 2021). The close relationship between owner-managers and their huskies, as well as the lack of legal protection for working dogs, lead this group of activist kennels to help and care for all dogs working in this business by raising awareness, using their time, resources, and social capital to induce change.

Barriers to Animal Welfare Activism

Before, during, and after the implementation of the two projects, I noticed two main barriers that were preventing developments on the issue of animal welfare in the husky tourism business. One of these was related to a lack of awareness of the issue among different tourism stakeholders (see Eilert and Nappier Cherup, 2020), including myself and other scholars at the local university. Indeed, despite doing research on responsible business in tourism in Lapland for many years, I had never thought before about responsibility in relation to working animals.

> During our coffee break, we had a conversation on animals and tourism. One of our staff members seemed to have suggested in a meeting the idea of starting a project focusing on ethical animals. I found it funny as I did not understand what they meant by an ethical animal. The idea for the project seems to come from one of the husky kennels. (Field notes 2015, Researcher)

As a researcher, I was not only lacking knowledge about the issue, but also had no relationship or bond with the huskies. As reflected in the extract above, neither my colleagues nor other staff members had a clear idea of the issue or how to frame it. This also points towards the role of the owner of the activist kennel who drew our attention to the issue as part of her political action to promote animal welfare in the dog sledding business. Although the two projects were an excellent tool for raising awareness and making the case for promoting animal welfare in husky kennels, it was also the context in which disagreements, controversies, and resistance became visible.

> Husky kennels disagree on several issues and they seem unable to find a compromise. Some kennels try to push for stricter regulations, which are not accepted by the majority. The no-kill policy is one of the issues that cause most of the controversy… I thought that talking to the vets will help us find a solution to the disagreements in the project. It was a mistake. The vets also have different opinions. Most of them oppose rehoming and adoption programmes. They strongly believe that huskies are born to be working dogs and that they can never become pets. (Field notes 2017, Researcher)

As reflected in the excerpt, most of the resistance to change comes from husky kennels that are not ready to change their practices. This does not mean that they do not care for their working animals. In fact, they do, but they have a different relationship with them. The care relationship is contractual in nature, that is, based on instrumentally-informed human–animal relationships for the sake of financial success (Connolly and Cullen, 2018; García-Rosell and Tallberg, 2021). Indeed, introducing new practices such as adoption programmes and increasing the summer exercising are seen as an additional cost. For example, they may require additions to the workforce and further investments. Although close human-animal relationships are present in these kennels, the owners tend to see their dogs as workers whose employment contracts can be terminated at any time on economic grounds. In such situations, euthanasia is justified by the owners on the basis of a widely shared belief that sled dogs are working animals that are not suitable for life in a home environment. This belief is supported by the majority of federal veterinarians, who see rehoming as a threat to the welfare of huskies, who, as working animals living in packs and outdoors, may experience anxiety and stress when living indoors in their new role as companion animals. It may also be the case, as shown in the study by Clarke and Knights (2022), that the veterinarians' point of view is reinforced by a suppression of affect and a rationalization of their work in terms of the demands of the owners of the kennels. The attitude of most kennels and veterinarians contributes to the maintenance of the status quo and the effective rejection of information and new practices that question it, slowing down change (see Eilert and Nappier Cherup, 2020)

Animal Welfare Activist Strategies

As discussed in the corporate activist literature (e.g. Den Hond and de Bakker, 2007; Eilert and Nappier Cherup, 2020), activist kennels rely on different strategies to influence institutional actors and, thus, change well-established market practices. In the data, there is evidence of two main strategies: the institutionalization of ethical sled dog practices and persuasion in the institutional environment. Indeed, activist kennels engaged in animal welfare activism have been influencing their markets by institutionalizing ethical practices within their own premises. For example, as shown in the previous excerpts, these kennels already have no-kill policies, adoption programmes, and exercise plans to keep dogs active during the summer, among other practices. Furthermore, they are continually putting pressure on their competitors by taking an active role in educating consumers concerning ethical sled dog practices, as is presented in the excerpt below.

> Ask about the end of life plan for the working dogs ... Most owners know that clients won't like to hear that the dogs are put down when ill or old and will fudge the truth on this subject, or, indeed, just try to change the subject. However, if kennels claim that they follow this principle but you do not see many older dogs hanging out there, apart from, maybe, for a token one or two, it is probably not true. (Husky kennel website)

The animal welfare projects implemented between 2016 and 2019 were also a way of putting pressure on other kennels to adopt more responsible practices. Nevertheless, the projects could not have been carried through without the support of an academic institution such as the local university. As an institutional actor involved in the creation and dissemination of knowledge, the local university was seen as a way of legitimizing the ethical sled dog practices already in use by some of the activist kennels.

> After working for several months on the project, I still do not see the discussions moving forward. Still the same companies [kennels] trying to impose their will on the rest of the group. It seems that they don't have any interest in having a dialogue. Their only aim is to put through their ideas. I feel that we [the university] are being used for that purpose. (Field notes 2017, Researcher)

The excerpt shows my frustration and the feeling that the university was being used for the personal agenda of the activist kennels. Nonetheless, when approached from an activist perspective (Eilert and Nappier Cherup, 2020), it makes sense that the owners of the activist kennels would strategically target the university to influence the legitimacy of the issue at stake. This strategy has an additional benefit of establishing a care relationship between the huskies and the researchers.

> It was because of [kennel X] that we started applying for project funding. Without their idea and insistence with the topic, we would never have come up with the idea of studying sled dogs ... The project and the close work with the entrepreneurs and the animals have definitely created a strong connection with the topic. The project ended years ago and I'm still giving time to the cause, helping to develop ethical guidelines and animal welfare criteria. I don't see myself as activist, but I am highly

motivated to improve the working condition of the huskies and support a no-kill policy. (Field notes 2020, Researcher)

Participating in the project activities, visiting the kennels, and writing reports and academic papers contributed to building a care relationship with the huskies working in Lapland. Although I do not have a concrete close relationship with any particular sled dog, I developed a sense of responsibility for these working animals, who possess intrinsic value and deserve better treatment for the work they perform (see Connolly and Cullen, 2018; Hoarau-Heemstra and Nazarova, 2021).

Discussion and Conclusions

By illustrating the animal welfare activism of a group of husky kennels in Finnish Lapland, I offer a concrete example of how small tourism businesses engage in political action to improve the conditions of working dogs. In doing so, I draw particular attention to the way in which care relationships in a multispecies business prompt the taking of a political position to address and fill gaps in animal welfare legislation. As I demonstrate in this chapter, animal welfare activism is based on an ethics that privileges care, compassion, and other feelings that are experienced through entangled human–animal stakeholder relationships (see Tallberg, García-Rosell, and Haanpää, 2021).

In terms of theoretical contributions, I shed light on corporate activism in small companies and within a multispecies business context. Furthermore, I provide insights into corporate activism that aims to improve the working conditions of nonhuman workers. My aim has been to enrich the corporate activism literature by connecting it to a small business context, to human-animal relations and to ethics of care. In doing this, I highlight the embodied and situated nature of multispecies relations in organizations (see Hancock, 2008; Pullen and Rhodes, 2015).

An important question for future research is related to the current pandemic and its impact on husky kennels. Indeed, as Tallberg, Huopalainen, and Hamilton (2020) argue, COVID-19 offers an opportunity to explore human-animal relationships as well as the ethical inclusion of animals as social agents. Global travel restrictions have brought tourism to a standstill, disrupting the working routines of thousands of sled dogs as well as bringing husky kennels to the brink of bankruptcy. This situation has reinforced and raised to new levels the political activity of husky kennels, which have absolutely refused to accept the killing of their animals as an option to mitigate their economic losses. These circumstances are evidence of the ability of dogs to shape and affect relationships and new arrangements (see Äijälä, 2019; Cunha, Rego and Munro, 2019). As animals capable of agency, sled dogs have even entered into new relationships outside the tourism industry. For example, members of local communities located close to the kennels have volunteered to keep the huskies fit by driving sleds and taking them for walks. Similarly, ordinary citizens and private organizations have donated money and food to help the huskies during these difficult times. Overall, the pandemic reveals interesting aspects of collective action and shared solidarity between animals and humans.

REFERENCES

Äijälä, M. (2019). Knowing through interspecies relationality in tourism? Animal agency in human-sled dog encounters. *Matkailututkimus*, 15(2), 45–50.

Äijälä, M (2021). Mobile video ethnography for evoking animals in tourism. *Annals of Tourism Research*, 89. https://doi.org/10.1016/j.annals.2021.103203

Aronczyk, M. (2013). Market(ing) activism: Lush cosmetics, ethical oil, and the self-mediation of protest. *JOMEC Journal Journalism, Media and Cultural Studies*, 4, 1–21.

Beers, D.L. (2006). *For the prevention of cruelty: The history and legacy of animal rights activism in the United States*. Athens: Swallow Press/Ohio University Press.

Bertella, G. (2014). The co-creation of animal-based tourism experience. *Tourism Recreation Research*, 39(1), 115–25.

Branicki, L. et al. (2020). The morality of 'new' CEO activism. *Journal of Business Ethics*, 170, 269–85.

Clarke, C., & Knights, D. (2022). Milking it for all it's worth: Unpalatable practices, dairy cows and veterinary work? *Journal of Business Ethics*, 176, 673-688. https://doi.org/10.1007/s10551-020-04666-3

Connolly, L., & Cullen, J.G. (2018). Animals and organisations: An ethic of care framework. *Organization & Environment*, 31(4), 406–24.

Corvellec, H., & Stål, I.S. (2019). Qualification as corporate activism: How Swedish apparel retailers attach circular fashion qualities to take-back systems. *Scandinavian Journal of Management*, 35(3),101046.

Coulter, K. (2016). *Animals, work, and the promise of interspecies solidarity*. New York: Palgrave Macmillan.

Cunha, M.P., Rego, A., & Munro, I. (2019). Dogs in organizations. *Human Relations*, 72(4), 778–800.

Curtin, N., & McGarty, C. (2016). Expanding on psychological theories of engagement to understand activism in context(s). *Journal of Social Issues*, 72(2), 227–41.

Dashper, K. (2020). More-than-human emotions: Multispecies emotional labour in the tourism industry. *Gender, Work & Organization*, 27, 24–40.

de Bakker, F. (2012). Exploring network of activism on corporate social responsibility: Suggestions for a research agenda. *Creativity and Innovation Management*, 21(2), 212–23.

Den Hond, F., & de Bakker, F. (2007). Ideologically motivated activism: How activist groups influence corporate social change activities. *Academy of Management Review*, 32(3), 901–24.

Eilert, M., & Nappier Cherup, A. (2020). The activist company: Examining a company's pursuit of societal change through corporate activism using an institutional theoretical lens. *Journal of Public Policy & Marketing*, 39(4), 461–76.

Engster, D., & Hamington, M. (2015). *Care ethics and political theory*. Oxford: Oxford University Press.

Fennell, D.A. (2014). Exploring the boundaries of a new moral order for tourism's global code of ethics: An opinion piece on the position of animals in the tourism industry. *Journal of Sustainable Tourism*, 22(7), 983–96.

García-Rosell, J.-C., & Äijälä, M. (2018). Animal-based tourism in Lapland. In J. Ojuva (Ed.), *Animal welfare in tourism services: Examples and practical tips for the well-being of animals used for tourism in Lapland* (pp. 10–24). Rovaniemi: Lapland University of Applied Sciences.

García-Rosell, J.-C., & Tallberg, L. (2021). Animals as tourism stakeholders: Huskies, reindeer, and horses working in Lapland. In J.M. Rickly, & C. Kline (Eds.), *Exploring non-human work in tourism: From beasts of burden to animal ambassadors* (pp. 103–21). Berlin: De Gruyter Oldenbourg.

Haanpää, M., & García-Rosell, J.C. (2020). Understanding performativity and embodied tourism experiences in animal-based tourism in the Arctic. In S.K. Dixit (Ed.), *The Routledge handbook of tourism experience management and marketing* (pp. 229–37). New York: Routledge.

Haanpää, M. et al. (2021). The disruptive "other"? Exploring human-animal relations in tourism through videography. *Tourism Geographies, 23(1–2)*, 97–117.

Hamilton, L., & Taylor, N. (2017). *Ethnography after humanism: Power, politics and method in multi-species research*. London: Palgrave Macmillan.

Hammersley, M., & Atkinson P. (1996). *Ethnography: Principles in practice*. London: Routledge.

Hancock, P. (2008). Embodied generosity and an ethics of organization. *Organization Studies, 29(10)*, 1357–73.

Haraway, D.J. (2008). *When species meet*. Minneapolis: University of Minnesota Press.

Hartman, C.L., & Beck-Dudley, C.L. (1999). Marketing strategies and the search for virtue: A case analysis of the Body Shop, International. *Journal of Business Ethics, 20*, 249–63.

Hoarau-Heemstra, H., & Nazarova, N. (2021). Distributed leadership in tourism experiences: Russian sled dogs and Icelandic horses leading the way. In J.M. Rickly, & C. Kline (Eds.), *Exploring non-human work in tourism: From beasts of burden to animal ambassadors* (pp. 123–41). Berlin: De Gruyter Oldenbourg.

Marshall, J. (2001). Self-reflective inquiry practices. In P. Reason and H. Bradbury (Eds.), *Handbook of action research: Participative inquiry and practice* (pp. 433–9). Los Angeles: Sage Publications.

Moisander, J., & Valtonen, A. (2006). *Qualitative marketing research: A cultural approach*. London: Sage Publications.

Noddings, N. (2003). *Caring: A feminine approach to ethics and moral education*, 2nd Edition. Los Angeles: University of California Press.

Pullen, A., & Rhodes, C. (2015). Corporeal ethics and the politics of resistance in organizations. *Organization, 21(6)*, 782–96.

Tallberg, L., García-Rosell, J.C., & Haanpää, M. (2021). Human-animal relations in business and society: Advancing the feminist interpretation of stakeholder theory. *Journal of Business Ethics*. https://doi.org/10.1007/s10551-021-04840-1

Tallberg, L., Huopalainen, A., & Hamilton, L. (2020). Can methods do good? Ethnology and multi species research as a response to Covid-19. *Ethnologia Fennica, 47(2)*, 103–12.

van de Ven, B.W., Nijhof, A., & Jeurissen, R.J.M. (2009). Sticking to core values: The case of the Body Shop. In C.A. Malin (Ed.), *Corporate social responsibility: A case study approach* (pp. 59–78). Cheltenham: Edward Elgar Publishing.

Wickert, C. (2016). 'Political' corporate social responsibility in small- and medium-sized enterprises: A conceptual framework. *Business & Society, 55(6)*, 792–824.

Youngs, R. (2019). *Civic activism unleashed: New hope or false dawn for democracy?* New York: Oxford University Press.

CHAPTER 27

ROBOTIC ANIMALS IN DEMENTIA CARE

Conceptions of Animality and Humanity in Care Organizations

DAVID REDMALM, MARCUS PERSSON, AND CLARA IVERSEN

INTRODUCTION

THE number of older people is increasing worldwide, both proportionally and in absolute numbers (World Health Organization (WHO), 2015), creating a labour shortage in elderly care work. One response to the increasing pressure on nursing homes and other care services for elderly people is social robots. These are often designed to look like animals—cats, dogs, and seals—with life-like fur, sound, and movements. They are usually equipped with sonic or tactile sensors built to be able to respond to users' talk or touch, and are used both to calm and activate patients. The history of robotic animals in care starts with the robot seal Paro developed in 1993 at Japan's National Institute of Advanced Industrial Science and Technology, as a response to Japan's relatively high percentage of older adults. Nevertheless, the robots tend to raise heated debates—according to a *Wall Street Journal* article (Tergesen and Inada, 2010: n.p.), published after Paro's introduction on the US market, it was still an open question whether Paro 'represents a disturbing turn in our treatment of the elderly or the best caregiving gadget since the Clapper [a sound sensitive electrical switch]'. This tension between a technocritical position arguing that robotization may entail a dehumanized society and an optimistic stance towards the new use of technology is a recurring theme in the debate around the use of robotic animals in care organizations (Sharkey and Wood, 2019). Critics have argued that providing nursing home residents with robotic plush toys reveals a demeaning view of elderly people. At the same time, the robots have proved to have a positive effect on people with dementia, reducing stress and negative behaviour (Kachouie et al., 2014).

In this chapter we take a closer look at these robots and argue for the utility of an animal studies approach to the use of robotic animals in care organizations. We focus on how robotic animals are perceived and deployed within care organizations, and how they become part of interactions between caregivers and patients. The discussion is based on previous research, news articles, marketing materials, and examples from our fieldwork in two research projects on the use of social robots in dementia care and their impact on care workers' work environment.[1] We argue that the care organization is hard-wired into the robotic animals: the robots are designed according to certain expectations on encounters between patients and caregivers, as well as conceptions of other animals and of basic human needs. As we will suggest, robotic animals can be used not only as a calming device or as entertainment, but also as tools that can evoke memories of companion animals, thus contributing to meaningful reflections and interactions. At the same time, animal robots also raise questions of humans' more general relationship to other animals. The fact that humans build low-maintenance animal robots providing their users with unconditional love may risk reinforcing an idea of nonhuman animals as valuable only insofar as they benefit humans.

The study of non-sentient robotic animals is relevant to animal studies as the robots raise questions concerning their animal design and how these design choices affect human beings. Because robotic animals are designed based on certain conceptions of animals and animality, they also reproduce these conceptions as they are deployed in care organizations, thus also affecting wider human-animal relations. Therefore, we can still ask the questions that Birke (2009: 1) puts forward as central to the field of animal studies: 'What's in it for the animals? How could/might they benefit? Do they?' Studies that take the role of animals in organizations seriously should not focus exclusively on evaluating the robots' efficiency but also pay attention to the messy realities when species meet—and when humans and technology meet.

We begin the chapter by drawing on Donna Haraway's concept of companion species to discuss the different choices of model animals—dogs, cats, seals—and what they mean for the robots' deployment in care work. We go on to discuss these notions of animality in relation to culture. In the following section, the materiality of the robots is in focus, and we apply posthumanist thinking to consider robotic animals as actors in care settings. Our discussion on human-technology interaction leads us into the debate about whether robotic animals risk dehumanizing humans by turning care work into an engineering issue. While there is legitimate concern over the effects of the automation of care work tasks, we also give examples of how the robots can speak to humans' empathic

---

[1] 'Material relationships in action: the social psychology of social robots in dementia care', founded by the Swedish Research Council (project no. 2019-02575), and 'Work environment in robotized dementia care: Social robots' impact on caregivers' ways of working and work environment', founded by AFA Insurance (project no. 190170).

and caring sides. We end the chapter stressing the need to stay attentive to this ambiguity in future research of robotic animals' role in care organizations.

THE ANIMALITY OF ROBOTIC ANIMALS

Lévi-Strauss (1991: 89) famously suggested that 'animals are good to think [with]', underlining humans' persistent habit of using animals as metaphors to describe and understand each other. The way animals are deployed in organizations as metaphors, models, and marketing tools indicates both how humans think about these animals and how humans mirror themselves in other animals to understand themselves and their collective ventures (Labatut et al., 2016; Taro Lennerfors and Sköld, 2018). Although not a cohesive field, we suggest that a number of studies could be gathered under the label 'organizational animality studies'—studies that focus on how animals are given meaning and how they are used as symbols in organizations. As such, these studies belong to a wider field of 'animality studies'—the study of how constructions of animality vary in different cultural contexts over time and intersect with constructions of humanity (Lundbladh, 2009).

Studies from a great variety of contexts can be placed within an organizational animality studies framework. Scholars have for example shown how the presence of nonhuman animals in organizations change the social cohesion of workplaces and the identity of the organization (O'Doherty, 2016; Wagner et al., 2021). Studies of slaughterhouses and the meat industry have exposed how the construction and commodification of the animals involved have influence on people's understanding of their work and their occupational identity (Hamilton and McCabe, 2016; Pachirat, 2011). There is also an intersection of animality studies and leadership studies exploring animal symbolism in the creation of leadership myths (Śliwa, 2012), as in Vladimir Putin's wildlife encounters (Mikhailova, 2012) and the Obama family's press conferences together with their dogs (Skoglund and Redmalm, 2017). Animals are furthermore important status symbols in organized crime—even illegal dogfighting can be studied as an entrepreneurial activity (Maher and Pierpoint, 2011; Smith, 2011). These studies give an insight into humans' understanding of other animals, and how that understanding influences leadership, organizations, and work life. Many of these studies also take living nonhuman animals themselves into consideration. Humans' categorization and understanding of other animals are connected to power, and the power imbalance between humans and other animals shapes human-animal relations in organizations (Hamilton and Taylor, 2012).

An organizational animality studies approach can be fruitfully applied to the study of how robotic animals are marketed and put to use in care organizations. Robot cats, dogs, and seals are not only expressions of humans' understanding of these species. Their construction also highlights humans' conceptions of interspecies relationships. Haraway (2003; 2008) has argued that cats, dogs, and other animals should be understood as members of different 'companion species'. Humans' self-understanding as humans, and the thriving of the human species, are dependent on humans' relationships with other animals. Humans and dogs, for example, provide each other with 'significant otherness' (Haraway, 2004): they are each other's significant other in that both species share entangled cultural and natural histories. Haraway uses the word 'species' in a wide sense and also regards categories of non-animal life as companion species, such as mushrooms (Haraway, 2008: 19; see also Tsing, 2012), and human artifacts, such as crutches (Haraway, 2008: 165f.). Using 'companion species' as a tool in research means being attentive to how different 'species' are constructed in relation to each other, and how these constructions shape interspecies relations.

Robotic animals used in care practices are companion species in a twofold sense. They are materializations of humans' ideas of some of their most central companion species; at the same time, these robots may very well become a crucial companion species as they proliferate in care organizations in countries with ageing populations. Looking at the marketing of one of the more popular models it is clear that it emphasizes familiarity. The robots, called The Joy for All Pups, have a 'lifelike coat'[2] and have an electronic heart that can be felt through the synthetic fur. They come as two popular 'pups' or 'family dogs'—a cavalier king Charles spaniel or a golden retriever (see figure 27.1). An interesting difference between the dogs and cats is that the dogs respond to motion, touch, and talk—through 'BARKBACK technology'—while cats only respond to motion and touch. This feature draws on practices of cat-dog-human interactions: while people regularly talk to their companion animals (see Charles, 2016; Roberts, 2004), cats are rarely expected to listen to commands. The robotic cats (see figure 27.2) are described as 'inspired by real felines', with cat-like movement and sounds ('MEOW!'). They are also equipped with 'VibraPurr' technology that creates vibrations and purring sounds. The purring can be understood as an especially salient feature in cats: it is an expression of otherness that humans have difficulty imitating, yet it is deeply familiar to anyone who has had a cat in their lap.

Robotic animals are, however, not just marketed based on similarities with animals: one of the repeated sales pitches for the electronic pets is that they provide effortless love: 'No vet bills, just love' the slogan reads. Such slogans miss an essential part of the meaning of 'pet love'. Although pets are often associated with 'unconditional love', mutual affection between human and companion is achieved through continuous attention to the animals' needs (Redmalm, 2021; Rehn et al., 2014). The work put into a human-animal relationship is an integral part of what makes the relationship meaningful to both human and animal—a companion species relationship presupposes mutual exchanges and interdependency. Therefore, Haraway (2008: 206) has argued that the term 'unconditional love' is in fact misleading, as it suggests a clear power imbalance: a one-way relationship that reduces the animal to a means for human purposes. An emphasis on unilateral 'unconditional love' can risk reproducing a view of companion

---

[2] Quotes retrieved from http://www.joyforall.com, accessed on 16 March 2021.

FIGURE 27.1 The Joy for All Pup. Press photo, used with permission from the manufacturer.

FIGURE 27.2 The Joy for All Cat. Press photo, used with permission from the manufacturer.

animals as emotional servants for humans, or 'affectional slaves' to use Haraway's (2008: 206) wording. Companion animal ownership is predicated upon a biopolitical logic: paraphrasing Foucault (2003: 241) pets are made to live and let die to fulfil human needs. Pets are given life through breeding practices that often take industrial proportions, and humans let unwanted pets die regularly, because of their behaviour, for economic reasons, or because of an abundance of pets on the market (Redmalm, 2019). However, individual human-animal relationships need to partly transcend this logic for them to be perceived as meaningful and reciprocal.

Perhaps as a way of avoiding a one-way relationship of commodification, and to create a sense of reciprocity, it is common that people interacting with the robots perform a real human-animal relationship and do more for the robots than needed. In a study of care workers using therapeutic animal cats in nursing homes (Persson, 2020: 13), a care worker described a resident who actively cared for the cat, 'taking care of it, feeding it, and taking it out on walks so it may pee and poop'. The care worker had encouraged the resident, buying a water bowl and a leash for the cat, as the activities seemed meaningful to the resident and provided exercise. This highlights how the resident and care worker together made the 'unconditional love' of the robot conditional in order to enact a meaningful animal guardianship.

Culture in Robotic Animals

Because of Japan's ageing population there is a shortage of care workers; at the same time, the number of migrant workers has been limited by nursing union organizations (Wright, 2019). A common position taken in the debate is that elderly people will not be able to interact well with care workers if they are unfamiliar with Japanese customs and do not speak Japanese fluently. In contrast, the humanoid robot Pepper that Wright observed is 'culturally odorless' (Iwabuchi, 2002 quoted in Wright, 2019): it can communicate in flawless Japanese. Wright (2019) observes that this argument is also used when Paro is introduced into a nursing home. Animals are not associated with cultural otherness and are thus a response to the xenophobic notion that foreign workers will import their native culture and challenge a cultural equilibrium.

The idea that animals would be culturally odorless builds on a strict separation between nature and culture that obscures the way animals are affected by, and affect, culture (Latour, 2004). There are examples of behaviours being passed down from generation to generation among nonhuman primates, so the idea that animals are culturally blank is flawed (de Waal, 1999). Yet more importantly in this case, social robots have an impact on humans because they are designed based on a cultural conception of animals, and built to meet culturally rooted expectations. In fact, many nonhuman animals are culturally over-determined: to many people, cats and dogs are so familiar and loaded with so many ideas and preconceptions that it will be difficult to make them respond to an animal-like robot. Consequently, robotic animals are generally designed to be more similar to a plush animal than a real cat or dog. The 'uncanny valley' effect (Mori, 1970) may be a partial explanation: humans' acceptance of humanoid robots increases the more lifelike a robot is, but only up to a certain point, after which the robot evokes uneasiness and disapproval. Research suggests that it is easier to accept and like a robotic animal than a humanoid robot, but robotic animals can also be perceived as eerie if they look too much like a real animal (Löffler et al., 2020). The most negative responses to robotic animals were given to robots with clear inconsistencies in realism, for example a robot covered in realistic fur but with a simple and 'dead' looking face (MacDorman and Chattopadhyay, 2016). If the lifelike appearance of the robot inflates expectations it can lead people to terminate the interaction—in a study comparing humans' interaction with the robot dog Aibo and a real dog, the people in the study terminated the interactions with the robot more often compared to the human-dog interactions (Kerepesi et al., 2006).

Another way of sidestepping culturally rooted expectations and avoiding the uncanny valley effect is to choose a less common model animal. Shibata et al. (1996) chose to make Paro a seal because few people have first-hand experiences of seals and will have greater difficulty seeing through the design than they would with cat or dog robots. Furthermore, users might also have negative experiences with animals they met in real life. In an interview, a nurse working with dementia patients told us about a man who exclaimed 'Ugh! Not that black cat!' when the staff tried to give a robotic cat to him—a tool that was otherwise appreciated in the nursing home. In contrast, a baby seal brings with it the same positive connotations as a kitten or a puppy, without the more specific knowledge and associations often connected to more common species (see further Shibata et al., 2000; Pfadenhauer and Dukat, 2015). Paro displays a generic cub-like behaviour, with small, tentative movements and bright squealing sounds, accentuated by its neotenized appearance: a relatively large head and big shiny, winking eyes (Pfadenhauer and Dukat, 2015).

Robotic animal designers have picked up on some of the central features of humans' most positive experiences with other animals—the soft fur, the shiny eyes, the purring, the tender movements, the high-pitched affirmative sounds—which are built into the robots. But experiences with animals vary from person to person, and may also vary across cultural contexts. For some, the robotic seal's appearance may evoke caring impulses, bringing to mind the photos of baby animals looking straight into the camera that are a common feature in the imagery of the animal rights movement (Redmalm, 2011). A robotic seal might be less effective in a society with a tradition of hunting seals for their meat and fur—although Hung et al. (2019) spoke to a research participant who said that she loved Paro *because* her grandfather was a seal hunter, and she liked the taste of seal meat. This is yet another instance of the cultural over-determination of many animal species, as well as a striking example of humans' ambivalent relation to other animals.

Cultural conceptions may also explain the scepticism towards robotic animals. McHugh (2004: 87) identifies a history of misogynist connections between pet ownership, sentimentality, vanity, single-mindedness, and femininity, and concludes that 'prejudices against people with pet dogs remain socially acceptable'. Some of the resistance against robots in the form of companion animals may thus be due to the fact that they represent characteristics and values, and speak to needs, that are widely downgraded. Furthermore, social robots also enter a cultural context characterized by a biomedical understanding of human health. A biomedical model of dementia focused on finding a cure for dementia is generally prioritized over a psychosocial that underlines the importance of social interventions and improved care practices (Vernooj-Dassen et al., 2021), which is another reason social robotics may be downplayed in dementia care, in favour of medication.

Robotic Animals as Actors

A posthumanist perspective opens up possibilities of understanding beings and relations that traverse the boundaries between subject and object, human and animal, and technology and organic life, thus challenging both anthropocentrism and the notion of the rational autonomous human subject rooted in the humanist tradition (Wolfe, 2010). A posthumanist perspective does not dismiss human-robot interaction as a nonsocial phenomenon. Pfadenhauer and Dukat (2015) observe that Paro is either used by care workers in interactions with patients, or it is given to patients, while care workers passively observe the patients. In either case, the robots are treated as capable of engaging users into interaction—with other humans or the robots themselves. A posthumanist analysis of robotic animals pays attention to how matter and meaning are entangled in this encounter, and how the design and materiality of the robots affect human bodies and meaning-making practices.

Robotic animals engineered for care purposes are not passive entities with a clean surface ready for human meaning inscription. The material specificity of the robots shapes interactions between human and robot and between caregiver and recipients of care. They are 'evocative objects' (Turkle, 2007) engaging people into interaction through the way they are designed, engineered, and perceived. Barad's (2003) posthumanist performativity is a useful approach to understand encounters with these objects. Barad (2003: 803) regards matter not as a passive 'end product' of social processes but 'as an active participant in the world's becoming, in its ongoing "intra-activity"'. Informed by insights within quantum physics she argues that the world is not divided into separate entities interacting with each other; instead, bounded subjects and objects emerge through intra-action—processes involving both materiality and meaning at the same time. Phenomena are 'relations without preexisting relata' according to Barad (2003: 815), and therefore objects can never be studied or understood in isolation.

Relying on Barad's theoretical work, as well as concepts from actor-network theory (Latour, 2005), Ericka Johnson (2008) observed that a pelvic exam simulator would work successfully in the United States but was deemed less useful by Swedish teachers and students. Through participant observations Johnson discovered that the mechanical robotic body was designed based on how pelvic exams are conducted in the United States. The simulator was built to measure and respond to certain kinds of pressures created during the exam, in the manner that North American students were taught. The practices of the examinations were thus materialized through the design and construction of the gynaecological simulators. In Sweden, where students are taught a slightly different form of examination, the simulator did not work as well, as the students' examination did not synchronize with the simulator's design. This is a reminder that the simulator cannot be a 'pure' reproduction of the female body; instead, it is built according to the anatomy of a body as it is experienced during an exam. The simulator is not built to mimic a body, but to represent the practice of an examination. Johnson argues that '[t]he body built into the simulator has a history, as models and understandings of a body do' (Johnson, 2008: 124). Similarly, animals with a history are built into robotic animals, as robotic animals are materializations of humans' experiences with and cultural conceptions of other animals. In the meeting between human and robotic animal, two sets of experiences collide: the experiences of those who make the robots and of those who use the robots. Whether or not those experiences correspond is consequential for how the robots are employed, and for their success in care work. Interactions with robotic animals can therefore be seen as complex 'intra-actions' of meaning and matter from which a plethora of bounded objects emerge: clients, caregivers, designers, engineers, focus group members interviewed during the construction process, as well as the real animals who originally gave these humans their experiences. With Latour (2005: 46), the robot becomes a node in a network of actors engaging each other into action.

A caregiver interviewed in our current project on social robots in dementia care explained that when she puts the robotic cat in the lap of one of her patients, the patient becomes overjoyed and shouts happily: 'The cat jumps up to me, he jumps up to me! He wants to be with me!' The patient also has a brush that she uses to brush the cat when laying in her lap. In contrast, if the caregiver does not actively present the robotic cat to a patient, the patient does not react to it or ask for it. At first glance, the robotic cat appears to be a piece of dead matter that the staff makes use of to create an illusion of something living. However, it is also possible to conceive of this event as an intra-action from which 'cat' and 'animal caregiver' emerge. To some extent, matter 'makes itself felt' (Barad, 2003: 810) through material presence of the robot that creates an impression—a felt physical impression on the legs of the patient, as well as a psychological impression (cf. Hayward, 2010). Using Haraway's conception of 'species', Hayward (2010) has suggested that 'species are impressions, thresholds of emergence' through touch (p. 580). Species are not just abstract categories—they emerge from 'corporeal enunciation' (p. 592).

In one of his lectures on animals and animality, Derrida (2008) describes an encounter with his 'little cat' who challenges Derrida's own impulse to treat the cat as 'an allegory for all the cats on the earth' (Derrida, 2008: 6). By asking 'And say the animal responded?' Derrida (2008: ch. 3) challenges his readers to take seriously animals' resistance against humans' categorizations and metaphorical use of them. But robots are rarely designed to 'respond' in Derrida's sense. Although the Joy for All Pups are equipped with 'BARKBACK technology', they are not designed to imitate disobedient or aggressive behaviour. During our fieldwork we were told about one resident who initially had shown interest in a robotic cat, and had interacted with it repeatedly over the course of a few days. At one point he asked the caregivers if the cat would bite him if he patted it too much. The caregivers told him it would not happen. Clearly disappointed that the cat lacked wilfulness, the resident lost all interest in the cat and stopped using it. Wishes for independence in (robotic) animals connect back to our discussion of the one-way character of 'unconditional love'. The interaction with a companion animal who acts with perfect obedience risks being experienced as 'a little machine' (Redmalm, 2021: 446; see also Fox, 2006) without the capacity to respond, or to make a real impression on others. Similarly, the expressions of undivided and affirmative attention that robots are programmed to give is a reason of concern among some users—as was the case with this man and his lost interest in the cat robot.

Animals' capability of *failing* to live up to humans' ideas of a 'good dog' or a 'nice cat' is integral to many humans' experiences of living with animals. Dogs in organizations do not only symbolize loyalty and obedience, but playfulness and sometimes unleashed liveliness (Cuncha et al., 2019 Skoglund and Redmalm, 2017;). Therefore, erratic or random responses from a robot can be more engaging than a perfectly timed automatic bark. As Pfadenhauer and Dukat (2015) point out, Paro to some extent displays a capability of 'disobedience' as it is programmed to give irregular and diverse output, which in turn 'brings the care workers to regard the conversational situation with the residents as special or out of the ordinary' (Pfadenhauer and Dukat, 2015: 402). But it should be underlined here that robots are designed only to be 'disobedient enough'—they are still marketed as low-maintenance alternatives to real, living animals. In this way, users' memories of caring human-animal relationships are commodified and used in the design of the robots built to suggest reciprocity. The robots' capacity of unpredicted behaviour thus suggests a sense that anything might happen, although the robots will at most bark back, and never bite back.

Robotization and Dehumanization

So far, we have focused on notions of animality and how they are related to the design, use, reception, and agency of robotic animals. We will now turn our focus to the notion of humanity and how it is played out in discussions of the use of robotic animals in care work. Marx (1975) connected human, animal, and machine in his *Economic and Philosophical Manuscripts* written in 1844 and first published in 1932. Here, Marx discusses the process of alienation, which is the loss of self that workers experience when they perform repetitive tasks in the capitalist mode of production. Human beings are creative by nature, Marx argues, so when the capitalist system inhibits workers from enjoying the fruits of their labour and from channelling their creativity through their work, they are estranged from their own human nature. This also means that the worker is reduced to a state below that of a nonhuman animal—the worker is turned into a machine:

> The savage and the animal at least have the need to hunt, to move about, etc., the need of companionship. The simplification of machinery and of labour is used to make workers out of human beings.... The machine accommodates itself to man's *weakness*, in order to turn *weak* man into a machine. (Marx, 1975: 360, emphasis in original)

Marx's theory of alienation has had a persistent impact on work life studies, and the colonialist connection between animal and 'savage' aside, it is still highly relevant in studies of the digitized workplaces of today. Marx's insights are integral to Braverman's (1974) influential critique of the deskilling or 'degradation' of work, and critical studies of work in the capitalist mode of production since then (see e.g. Thompson and Smith, 2009). Marx's notion of alienation also influenced criticisms of how some employers make use not only of workers' labour, but also of their emotions (Hochschild, 1983), and their personality, values, and sense of self (Fleming, 2014).

Marx's theoretical constellation of human-animal-machine is echoed in studies of robotics in the workplace. Several authors have suggested that social robots risk deskilling care labour. For instance, Wright (2019: 350) writes that social robots 'could reduce the need for human-human verbal interaction in the future, turning care work into straightforward manual labor', such as lifting and caring for patients' personal hygiene (tasks which are also increasingly robotized, see e.g. Beedholm et al., 2010). While Hochschild warned that emotional labour can lead to stress and burnout, managing one's emotions to be able to offer emotional support can also be integral to making care work meaningful (Lewis, 2005). If robots take over the concrete interpersonal and embodied aspects of care work the fundamentally human aspect of care work is diminished. Care workers become machine operators, bound to following and assisting the machine—and are thus in a sense turned into machines, to use Marx's phrasing.

To continue paraphrasing Marx, there is also a concern that robotic animals accommodate themselves to patients' weaknesses. Leeson (2017: 30) uses the term 'entrapment', that is, 'the capacity of technology to entice and seduce people through appealing to their specific qualities and preferences', to describe how robotic animals are designed to keep the users' attention and engagement. The term is also used more widely to describe how different kinds of technologies attract the attention of the user, such as video games (Essig, 2012) and websites (Miller, 2000). Here we can connect back to the resident of a nursing home who more or less organized her life around her cat robot, caring for it and taking it on walks. We learned of one clearly problematic example of entrapment in our current project about social robots in dementia care: in one nursing home it had been necessary to take away a robotic cat at meal situations, since it distracted the residents to the extent that they forgot to eat, and instead patted, talked to, and tried to feed the cat.

A central aspect of becoming entrapped in a technologically simulated situation is to at least momentarily forget that the simulation is not real (Essig, 2012). In a *New York Times* article about the Joy for All Companion Pets, a 97-year-old woman is interviewed while stroking the robotic cat. She comments upon the cat's movement and says that '[s]he must have some kind of mechanism inside', but nevertheless goes on to talk to the cat: 'You're my pussycat—do you love me?' (Newman, 2016: n.p.). Another anecdotal example is a woman interviewed about Paro in the *Wall Street Journal*, who during the interview whispers to the robot: 'I know you're not real, but somehow, I don't know, I love you' (Tergesen and Inada, 2010: n.p.). Calo et al. (2011) mention several similar examples of partial 'self-deception'.

Just as the 'entrapment' does not have to be complete, it is not negative by necessity. The lure of the robot can be used to increase human contact. Persson (2020) observed in a study of the therapeutic JustoCat that it could break dementia patients' stressful repetitive behavioural loops in favour of new conversations. Persson also learned that patients would recurrently call the cats by names of cats they had owned previously in their lives. These naming practices would sometimes lead patients to talk about past companion animals, and by extension, places where they had lived and people connected to those places. Caregiving staff described exchanges like these as meaningful conversations strengthening the bond between care worker and resident. This example interconnects the four aspects of robotic animals discussed in this chapter: (1) the feline *animality* of the robot which evokes memories; (2) the import of the cultural or social role of cats; (3) the robot's role as actor as it mediates between caregiver and resident; and (4) the humanizing effect of the robot, as it brings the two humans engaged in the interaction closer to each other on a personal level.

In this section we have highlighted concerns raised in the literature regarding the replacement of human caregivers with robots. However, the fact that they can also replace therapeutic animals is rarely discussed. Therapeutic animals risk being subjected to draining emotional labour (Coulter, 2016: 73), stress (MacNamara et al., 2015), or unintentional maltreatment and injuries from patients (Tedeschi et al., 2015). Therefore, to return to Birke's (2009) question, 'What's in it for the animal?', nonhuman animals may in some instances benefit from being replaced by robotic animals.

Conclusion

The replacement of humans and other animals with robotic simulacra is commonly associated with dystopian visions. In Ridley Scott's film *Blade Runner*, most nonhuman animals have died from radioactive dust that spread during a world war. The few real animals left are sought-for status symbols. Those who cannot afford a real animal can buy a lifelike robotic animal to acquire some of the status of real animal owners. These robotic animals become a sad reminder of the ongoing extinction of animals in current times—often referred to as the sixth extinction. 'In the last two centuries,' Berger (2009: 11) writes, 'animals have gradually disappeared.' He describes a 'new solitude' in which humans have reduced animals to mere biological 'machines' and have forgotten about their unique characteristics. Simultaneously, both modern science and consumption society tends to reduce humans to the same mechanical empty shells. When animality is lost in oblivion, so is humans' sense of humanity, according to Berger.

We have shown that rather than a representation of humans' animal oblivion, robotic animals can help people remember important human-animal relationships in their lives. Actual human-animal encounters are materialized in the robotic bodies of the animal simulators, and robots that appear too much as smoothly operating, pre-programmed technological tools risk being rejected as uninteresting by the users. The manufacturing and consumption of therapeutic robotic animals can thus be seen as testament to the importance of nonhuman animals in the lives of humans. The fact that robots resembling plush toys with some animal-like characteristics can spur people to reminisce and interact with others suggest that these robots might resonate with a deeper empathy and connection with nonhuman animals.

In this chapter we have suggested that robotic animals are materializations of cultural conceptions of nonhuman animals, and of therapeutic intra- and interspecies interaction. In this way, robotic animals can be seen as technological incorporations of the care organization. Even if the implementation of robotic animals seems promising when the robots are used in certain ways in care work, they should not be considered a miracle cure. We have pointed to some of the concerns raised in relation to the robots—their potential dehumanizing effects, and the risk that passive and cuddly robots reproduce a view of companion animals as emotional servants for humans. Robotic animals are ambiguous, in the same way as humans' more general relationship to other animals, mirroring both humans' devotion and instrumental approach to other animals. We therefore suggest that animal-centred research of robotic animals needs to stay attentive to this ambiguity, and to the meaning as well as the material otherness of this emerging technological companion species.

Acknowledgements

We would like to take the opportunity to extend our gratitude to the research participants of the projects referred to in this chapter. Thank you for your time and for allowing us to take part of your work routines and your everyday lives.

References

Barad, K. (2003). Posthumanist performativity: Toward an understanding of how matter comes to matter. *Signs, 28(3),* 801–31.

Beedholm, K., Frederiksen, K., & Lomborg, K. (2016). What was (also) at stake when a robot bathtub was implemented in a Danish elder center: A constructivist secondary qualitative analysis. *Qualitative Health Research, 26(10),* 1424–33.

Berger, J. (2009). *Why look at animals?* London: Penguin.
Birke, L. (2009). Naming names—Or, what's in it for the animals? *Humanimalia, 1(1)*, 1–9. http://www.depauw.edu/humanimalia/issue01/pdfs/Lynda%20Birke.pdf.
Braverman, H. (1974). *Labor and monopoly capital.* New York: Monthly Review Press.
Calo, C.J., Hunt-Bull, N., Lewis, L., & Metzler, T. (2011). Ethical implications of using the paro robot, with a focus on dementia patient care. *Workshops at the twenty-fifth AAAI conference on artificial intelligence.*
Charles, N. (2016). Post-human families? Dog-human relations in the domestic sphere. *Sociological Research Online, 21(3)*, 83–94.
Coulter, K. (2016). *Animals, work, and the promise of interspecies solidarity.* Basingstoke: Palgrave Macmillan.
Cunha, M.P.E., Rego, A., & Munro, I. (2019) Dogs in organizations. *Human Relations, 72(4)*, 778–800.
Derrida, J. (2008). *The animal that therefore I am.* New York: Fordham University Press.
Essig, T. (2012). The addiction concept and technology: Diagnosis, metaphor, or something else? A psychodynamic point of view. *Journal of Clinical Psychology, 68(11)*, 1175–84.
Fleming, P. (2014). When 'life itself' goes to work: Reviewing shifts in organizational life through the lens of biopower. *Human Relations, 67(7)*, 875–901.
Foucault, M. (2003). *Society Must Be Defended: Lectures at the Collège de France, 1975–1976.* New York: Picador.
Fox, R. (2006). Animal behaviours, post-human lives: Everyday negotiations of the animal-human divide in pet-keeping. *Social and Cultural Geography, 7(4)*, 525–37.
Hamilton, L., & Taylor, N. (2012). Ethnography in evolution: Adapting to the animal 'other' in organizations. *Journal of Organizational Ethnography, 1(1)*, 43–51.
Hamilton, L., & McCabe, D. (2016). 'It's just a job': Understanding emotion work, de-animalization and the compartmentalization of organized animal slaughter. *Organization, 23(3)*, 330–50.
Haraway, D.J. (2003) *The companion species manifesto: Dogs, people, and significant otherness.* Chicago: Prickly Paradigm Press.
Haraway, D.J. (2008). *When species meet.* Minneapolis: University of Minnesota Press.
Hayward, E. (2010). Fingeryeyes: Impressions of cup corals. *Cultural Anthropology, 25(4)*, 577–99.
Hochschild, A. (1983). *The managed heart: Commercialization of human feeling.* Berkeley: University of California Press.
Hung, L. et al. (2019). Exploring the perceptions of people with dementia about the social robot PARO in a hospital setting. *Dementia, 20(2)*, 485–504.
Iwabuchi, K. (2002). *Recentering globalization: Popular culture and Japanese transnationalism.* Durham: Duke University Press.
Johnson, E. (2008). Simulating medical patients and practices: Bodies and the construction of valid medical simulators. *Body and Society, 14(3)*, 105–28.
Kachouie, R. et al. (2014). Socially assistive robots in elderly care: A mixed-method systematic literature review. *International Journal of Human-Computer Interaction, 30(5)*, 369–93.
Kerepesi, A. et al. (2006). Behavioural comparison of human-animal (dog) and human-robot (AIBO) interactions. *Behavioural Processes, 73(1)*, 92–9.
Labatut, J., Munro, I., & Desmond, J. (2016). Animals and organizations. *Organization, 23(3)*, 315–29.
Latour, B. (2004). *Politics of nature: How to bring the sciences into democracy.* Cambridge, MA: Harvard University Press.

Latour, B. (2005). *Reassembling the social: An introduction to actor-network-theory*. Oxford: Oxford University Press.

Leeson, C. (2017). *Anthropomorphic robots on the move: A transformative trajectory from Japan to Danish healthcare*. (PhD thesis, Faculty of Social Sciences, University of Copenhagen).

Lévi-Strauss, C. (1991). *Totemism*. London: Merlin Press.

Lewis, P. (2005). Suppression or expression: An exploration of emotion management in a special care baby unit. *Work, employment and society, 19(3)*, 565–81.

Lundblad, M. (2009). From animal to animality studies. *PMLA, 124(2)*, 496–502.

Löffler, D., Dörrenbächer, J., & Hassenzahl, M. (2020). The uncanny valley effect in zoomorphic robots: The U-shaped relation between animal likeness and likeability. *Proceedings of the 2020 ACM/IEEE International Conference on Human-Robot Interaction*, 261–70.

MacDorman, K., & Chattopadhyay, D. (2016). Reducing consistency in human realism increases the uncanny valley effect; increasing category uncertainty does not. *Cognition, 146*, 190–205.

MacNamara, M., Moga, J., & Pachel, C. (2015). What's love got to do with it? Selecting animals for animal-assisted mental health interventions. In A.H. Fine (Ed.), *Handbook on animal-assisted therapy* (pp. 91–101). Amsterdam: Academic Press.

Maher, J., & Pierpoint, H. (2011). Friends, status symbols and weapons: The use of dogs by youth groups and youth gangs. *Crime, law and social change, 55(5)*, 405–420.

Marx, K. (1975). *Early writings*. London, New York, Ringwood, Toronto, New Delhi, Albany, Rosebank: Penguin Books.

McHugh, S. (2004). *Dog*. London: Reaktion Books.

McHugh, S. (2012). Bitch, bitch, bitch: Personal criticism, feminist theory, and dog-writing. *Hypatia, 27(3)*, 616–35.

Mikhailova, T. (2012). Putin as the Father of the Nation: his family and other animals. In H. Goscilo (Ed.), *Putin as Celebrity and Cultural Icon* (pp. 85–101). London: Routledge.

Miller, D. (2000). The fame of Trinis: websites as traps. *Journal of material culture, 5(1)*, 5–24.

Mori, M. (1970). The uncanny valley. *Energy, 7*, 33–5.

Newman, A. (2016). Therapy cats for dementia patients, batteries included. *The New York Times*, 15 December. https://www.nytimes.com/2016/12/15/nyregion/robotic-therapy-cats-dementia.html.

O'Doherty, D.P. (2016). Feline politics in organization: The nine lives of Olly the cat. *Organization, 23(3)*, 407–33.

Pachirat, T. (2011). *Every twelve seconds: Industrialized slaughter and the politics of sight*. New Haven: Yale University Press.

Persson, M. (2020). Introducing social robots in Swedish dementia care: Exploring the interaction between care workers, residents, and robotic cats. *Journal of Sociology and Social Work, 8(1)*, 8–19.

Pfadenhauer, M., & Dukat, C. (2015). Robot caregiver or robot-supported caregiving?. *International Journal of Social Robotics, 7(3)*, 393–406.

Redmalm, D. (2011). In-your-face-ethics: Phenomenology of the face and social psychological animal studies. In P. Segerdahl (Ed.), *Undisciplined animals: Invitations to animal studies* (pp. 73–104). Newcastle upon Tyne: Cambridge Scholars Publishing.

Redmalm, D. (2019). To make pets live, and to let them die: The biopolitics of pet keeping. In T. Holmberg, A. Jonsson, & F. Palm (Eds.), *Death Matters: Cultural Sociology of Mortal Life* (pp. 241–63). London: Palgrave Macmillan.

Redmalm, D. (2021). Discipline and puppies: The powers of pet keeping. *International Journal of Sociology and Social Policy, 41(3–4)*, 440–54.

Rehn, T. et al. (2014). I like my dog, does my dog like me? *Applied Animal Behaviour Science*, 150, 65–73.

Roberts, F. (2004). Speaking to and for animals in a veterinary clinic: A practice for managing interpersonal interaction. *Research on Language and Social Interaction*, 37(4), 421–46.

Sharkey, A., Wood, N., & Aminuddin, R. (2019). Robot companions for children and older people: Ethical issues and evidence. In C. Hasse & D. M. Søndergaard (Eds.), *Designing Robots, Designing Humans* (pp. 132–46). London: Routledge.

Shibata, T., Inoue, K., & Irie, R. (1996). Emotional robot for intelligent system-artificial emotional creature project. *Proceedings 5th IEEE International Workshop on Robot and Human Communication*, 466–71.

Shibata, T., & Tanie, K. (2000). Influence of a priori knowledge in subjective interpretation and evaluation by short-term interaction with mental commit robot. In *Proceedings 2000 IEEE/RSJ International Conference on Intelligent Robots and Systems*, vol. 1, 169–74.

Śliwa, M. et al. (2012). Profaning the sacred in leadership studies: A reading of Murakami's A Wild Sheep Chase. *Organization*, 20(6), 860–80.

Skoglund, A., & Redmalm, D. (2017). 'Doggy-biopolitics': Governing via the First Dog. *Organization*, 24(2), 240–66.

Smith, R. (2011). Investigating financial aspects of dog-fighting in the UK. *Journal of Financial Crime*, 18(4), 336–46.

Taro Lennerfors, T., & Sköld, D. (2018). The animal. *Culture and Organization*, 24(4), 263–67.

Tergesen, A., & Inada, M. (2010). It's not a stuffed animal, it's a $6,000 medical device: Paro the robo-seal aims to comfort elderly, but is it ethical? https://www.wsj.com/articles/SB10001424052748704463504575301051844937276.

Tedeschi, P. et al. (2015). On call 24/7: The emerging roles of service and support animals. In A. H. Fine (Ed,), *Handbook on animal-assisted therapy* (pp. 321–32). Amsterdam: Academic Press.

Thompson, P., & Smith, C. (2009). Labour power and labour process: Contesting the marginality of the sociology of work. *Sociology*, 43(5), 913–30.

Tsing, A. (2012). Unruly edges: Mushrooms as companion species, for Donna Haraway. *Environmental Humanities*, 1(1), 141–54.

Turkle, S. (2007). *Evocative objects: Things we think with*. Cambridge, MA: MIT Press.

Vernooij-Dassen, M. et al. (2021). Bridging the divide between biomedical and psychosocial approaches in dementia research: The 2019 INTERDEM manifesto. *Aging and Mental Health*, 25(2), 206–12.

de Waal, F.B. (1999). Cultural primatology comes of age. *Nature*, 399(6737), 635–6.

Wagner, E., & Pina e Cunha, M. (2021). Dogs at the workplace: A multiple case study. *Animals* 11(1), 89. https://doi.org/10.3390/ani11010089

Wolfe, C. (2010). *What is posthumanism?* Minneapolis: University of Minnesota Press.

World Health Organization. (2015). World report on ageing and health. World Health Organization. https://apps.who.int/iris/handle/10665/186463

Wright, J. (2019). Robots vs migrants? Reconfiguring the future of Japanese institutional eldercare. *Critical Asian Studies*, 51(3), 331–54.

CHAPTER 28

TE AO MĀORI AND ONE WELFARE IN AOTEAROA NEW ZEALAND

The Case of Kurī, Dog Registration, the Law, and Local Councils

JANET SAYERS AND RACHEL FORREST

IN 1898 there was a confrontation between the Crown and a group of Northern Māori opposed to the enforcement of a 'dog tax' by local county councils, which is now known colloquially as the 'The Dog Tax War' (see Figure 28.1). Forty summonses were served on Māori to force them to register their dogs. There had been (and continued to be) widespread Māori opposition to dog registration. Most Māori at the time had little involvement with the cash economy and owned many dogs, especially for hunting. They saw the annual 'dog tax' of 2 shillings 6 pence per dog as discrimination. Hone Toia, a local leader and priest, led 150 men to the area's administrative centre and stated they would not pay any taxes and that 'they would die on account of these taxes', and they would rather resist than be driven further into poverty and hardship. The situation escalated, the men threatened armed resistance against the Crown although no shots were ever fired, local settlers fled, an armed militia moved in, and eventually a respected Māori Member of Parliament negotiated the men's surrender. Two leaders were sent to hard labour for two years and others were fined, although the Crown eventually voided expectation of any payment since the people could not afford it.[1]

Dog taxes did not stop being a sore point in 1898. During the writing of this chapter, one author (Rachel) revisited a piece of family history that brought the Dog Tax War into clear focus. Rachel's great granny's—Hinetehuanga Te Whare—husband (Tiriana Te

---

[1] Sources are: https://nzhistory.govt.nz/page/dog-tax-war; and https://natlib.govt.nz/schools/topics/5e28c68c0158b1000961ba7b/the-dog-tax-war-1898

426 JANET SAYERS AND RACHEL FORREST

STRAINED RELATIONS: OR "DOGGED" RESISTANCE.

FIGURE 28.1 A Māori man lets Premier Richard Seddon know what he thinks about the dog tax. Used with permission from the Alexander Turnbull library. By Ashley Hunter, 1898, Reference Number: 23009191.

Omeka Kingi) and grandfather (Tieme Te Whare) were arrested in 1908 for unpaid dog tax and costs which had accumulated over several years. They owned five unregistered dogs between them and were imprisoned. The Prime Minister, Sir Joseph Ward, directly interceded in their case (at one in the morning!) and liberated the two after saying he had promised the Native Department would pay the dog tax in this instance, which was £48/19s/3p. This was meant to be a one-off case 'to prevent the disturbance in connection with the 1904 Dog Tax from spreading among the Maoris' (Robinson and Christoffel, 2011: 195–6). The written record conjectures that Ward was trying to avoid confrontation with the recognized jurisdiction of Kingitanga[2] (a Māori political movement within Aotearoa), who had been collecting their own dog tax since 1894, but there was clearly simmering conflict between Māori and local councils over this revenue-generating tax. Most historical records describe the Dog Tax War as if it was the last 'armed insurrection' event at the tail end of the Land Wars (1845–72), as if conflict over the dispossession of land was resolved at that time (it wasn't and still isn't) and the tension over the dog tax was similarly resolved (it wasn't and still isn't).

An Unfolding Story

He ihu kurī, he tangata haere.
(As a dog follows a scent, a wayfarer looks for an open door.)

Our contention in this chapter is that it is necessary to take an historical and cultural approach to animal organizational studies. This is particularly important in countries such as Aotearoa New Zealand,[3] where the study we discuss in this chapter was set. This chapter arose out of a project on companion animal (CA) welfare and specifically looks at the dog (kurī) in the contexts of their lives and welfare in Aotearoa. Consequently, we begin this chapter with some background on kurī because they have their own history in Aotearoa New Zealand in relation to Māori; and this story, as we foreshadow in our introduction above, is still unfolding.

Polynesian dogs have a rich role in Pacific cosmology and culture which goes back for thousands of years (Luomala, 1958). The original kurī were Polynesian dogs brought to Aotearoa New Zealand by ancestors of Māori, who travelled from Polynesia by waka (canoe) in the thirteenth century. In tikanga Māori the origins of the kurī are explained through the trickster demigod Māui, who transformed his brother-in-law Irawaru into the first kurī. Māori have many legends and tales about kurī, and place names often function to remember certain valued animals or events involving them (Potts et al., 2013). The original kurī were long-haired, with short legs and a bushy tail, with no specific colour, and they did not bark, but they had a long melancholy howl—which Māori called anau. Kurī are genetically confirmed to belong with all Pacific domesticated dogs within the category of *Canis familiaris* (King, 2005). As well as being beloved

---

[2] See more on this period of New Zealand history here https://teara.govt.nz/en/kingitanga-the-maori-king-movement/

[3] We use New Zealand and Aotearoa together and interchangeably, reflecting current practice in Aotearoa.

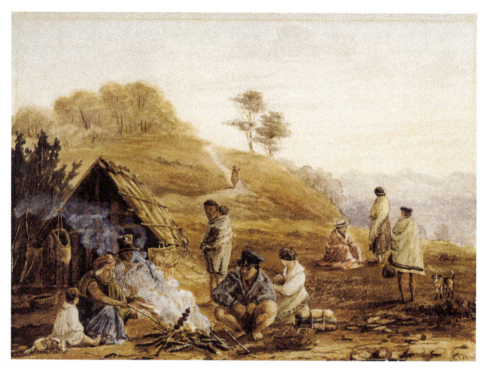

FIGURE 28.2 Kai Time with Kurī. Used with permission from the National Library of New Zealand. By Charles Hemus, 1849–1925. Kai time. [ca 1900] Reference Number: A-367-030.

companions, kurī were an important food source for Māori in a land with no land mammals as a source of protein (early European visitors also ate dog meat). Dog skins were used for cloaks, and bones were made into fishhooks and necklaces. Kurī were also good hunters and were used for this skill. See Figure 28.2 above for an historical depiction of the everyday life of Māori and kurī.

Scientific sources report the original kurī breed died out after intermingling with dogs who arrived with European settlers though King (2005) reported there may be some genetic remnants in certain places in New Zealand. Popular accounts often stress that the kurī population declined because of competition from 'superior' imported dogs: 'The small pups—prized for their hunting skills and fur, but not looks—were common in Aotearoa New Zealand when Europeans first arrived but quickly interbred with or were ousted by newly brought canines' (Wannan, 2015). Also, the decline of 'pure-breed kurī' was associated with the 'decline of Māori culture throughout the second half of the nineteenth century' (King, 2005: 260), with feral 'hybrid' kurī often shot on sight by shepherds.

Two main historical tensions have been highlighted in this chapter so far. The first relates to humans: the simmering conflict between settler government and Māori over self-determination, land, and dog tax. The second tension relates to the ways that kurī are represented in accounts of their demise, with the history of Māori-dog relations thus becoming obscured. We frame this chapter with these two tensions because it is essential to take an historical approach to the issue of human-dog relations in Aotearoa New Zealand. In present-day Aotearoa New Zealand, the effects of colonization[4] are ongoing and underpin socio-economic and health inequities impacting not only on hauora Māori (Māori health and wellbeing) but also the capacity of Māori to act as kaitiaki (guardians and protectors) of the natural environment (Moewaka Barnes and McCreanor, 2019; Te Ahukaramū, 2021).

We elaborate upon three themes in this chapter—registration (tax), cost of animal care, and hunting—and note at the outset that the fines for not registering and microchipping dogs are significant.[5] No information is kept on the demographic characteristics of owners, and so no one knows now if registration and microchipping (or lack of) creates a barrier to Māori seeking health care and welfare advice for their dogs. We discuss the implications of this gap in knowledge more in our discussion of our empirical observations later in this chapter.

Te Ao Māori and One Welfare Aotearoa

From a Te Ao Māori perspective, there is a deep connection and relationship between people, the land, and nature which is vital to hauora and which is not typically acknowledged in traditional Western approaches to human health. Sir Mason Durie, a key advocate for Māori wellbeing, stated: 'Māori health development is essentially about Māori defining their own priorities for health and then weaving a course to realise their collective aspirations' (1998: 1). Māori health initiatives are thus focused on realizing principles of self-determination regarding their health needs. Durie (1998: 2) went on to say, 'Enough is known about health to justify an integrated approach to cultural, social and economic development and to recognise the futility of designing highly sophisticated treatment procedures while blatantly ignoring educational failure or inadequate housing'. In Durie's Te Whare Tapa Whā model, hauora has five sustaining

---

[4] Colonization is a term defining a Westernized cultural construct in relation to land and communities, that entails the displacement and destruction of Indigenous peoples' traditional knowledge and ways of living, along with usurpation of the environment. The impacts of colonization extend into the ways that knowledge is produced in research and consequently has an ongoing impact upon science, research institutions, and other organizations associated with implementing the outcomes of scientific endeavour (Hammerton, 2018).

[5] Penalties relating to animal mistreatment can involve imprisonment and significant fines. Not registering or microchipping a dog can result in a NZ$300 fine. See https://www.govt.nz/browse/law-crime-and-justice/paying-fines/dog-owners-fines-and-offences/. We could not locate any demographic statistics relating to registration rates or penalties. Dog Control Statistics from the Department of Internal Affairs—National Dog Database and Accident Compensation Corporation do not include any demographic information about the owners.

dimensions, four of which form the pou (supporting structures—walls) of a whare (house) and the fifth being the whenua (land) which provides the foundations of all things. The four walls are: Taha whānau (extended family health), Taha hinengaro (mental health, including emotions), Taha wairua (spiritual health), and Taha tinana (physical health).

Māori researchers have a pivotal role in science, health, and government policy to advance knowledge about Rangahau Māori (Māori research epistemologies) which challenges the accepted anthropocentrism of Western knowledge systems, contemporary Aotearoa New Zealand society, and much research and policy along with the organizations that support them (Durie, 1998; Smith, 1999; Denzin, Lincoln, and Smith, 2008). Te Ao Māori is increasingly being woven into research and policy approaches because it provides a holistic perspective that sees humans, animals, and the environment as integrated and interdependent. Globally the latter has been reflected in the concepts of One Health and One Welfare.

One Health originated in the United States (US) with a concord between the American Medical Association and the American Veterinary Medical Association, which recognized the need for interdisciplinary approaches to animal health and welfare and human health and wellbeing. Animal welfare, which is intrinsically associated with health, can be defined as the state of how an animal is coping with the conditions in which it lives:

> An animal is in a good state of welfare if (as indicated by scientific evidence) it is healthy, comfortable, well nourished, safe, able to express innate behaviour, and if it is not suffering from unpleasant states such as pain, fear and distress. Good animal welfare requires disease prevention and veterinary treatment, appropriate shelter, management, nutrition, humane handling and humane slaughter/killing. (Pinillos et al., 2016: 2)

Issues around animal-human-environment health are being addressed in Aotearoa New Zealand through platforms such as One Health Aotearoa which works within Te Ao Māori. One Health Aotearoa's focus is currently on three main pou (pillars) which are antimicrobial resistance, freshwater quality, and emerging infectious diseases (Harrison et al., 2020), reflecting the significance of the agricultural and food sector to Aotearoa New Zealand's economy. One Health Aotearoa sees building meaningful partnerships with Māori as critical to the development of science and innovative solutions to food security, and agricultural and horticultural development. One Health Aotearoa recognizes the relationship between socio-economic factors such as poverty and the threat of infectious diseases, an issue brought very much into the spotlight through the COVID-19 pandemic.

One Welfare is based on One Health and their purposes overlap with One Welfare, broadening the scope of One Health concerns which focus on the clinical aspects of disease states and health, to include aspects of living well; human and animals living a sustainable good life (Pinillos et al., 2016; Pinillos, 2017). Proponents of One Welfare argue 'Global ethical and policy decisions about human and animal welfare should be based on considerations of the wellbeing of animals and humans within their ecosystem' (Colonius and Earley, 2013: 310). As with human health and wellbeing, there has been a move in animal 'welfare science towards the promotion of positive states whilst continuing to minimise negative states' (Mellor and Beausoleil, 2015: 241), thereby promoting a good life.

Researchers in Aotearoa New Zealand have noted that One Welfare aligns well with tikanga Māori (Forrest et al., 2019). Tikanga Māori entails the customary system of values and practices that have developed over time and are deeply embedded in the social context and underpinned by Mātauranga Māori; knowledge created by Māori according to their experiences, history, worldview, values, culture, and aspirations (Harrison et al., 2020).[6] In this chapter we use the term Te Ao Māori, which means Māori worldview, to describe the perspective used in the One Welfare project.

In what follows, we illustrate a Te Ao Māori approach by describing research conducted through the One Welfare prism, on New Zealanders and their attitudes to animal welfare of CA,[7] with the overall purpose and philosophy being one of holism and inclusivity and working towards a good life for all inhabitants of Aotearoa New Zealand, animal, and human alike. The research project consisted of two independent studies undertaken to understand welfare issues for CA from the perspective of their guardians. One was a nationwide internet survey to gather information on guardian attitudes to animal welfare, and the other a regional study in which a tailored 'intervention' was conducted with a Māori organization dedicated to Māori wellbeing—Patu™ Aotearoa. The latter was called Patu Pets and its explicit intention was to establish mutually beneficial community relationships. Reciprocity was a key component; whānau got their pets health-checked for free regardless of registration status, and educators and students had an experiential learning opportunity. The researchers provided the vehicle to bring everyone together and in return, the researchers got data from a hard-to-access population so they could in turn provide insight into pro-equity approaches to promote human and animal wellbeing. By discussing this project, we aim to illustrate not only how One Welfare concepts have both cultural and species strands, but also how alternative Indigenous approaches to animal questions can promote a holistic One Welfare community perspective on both human and animal welfare. In the following discussion, we focus upon differences and similarities in the findings of the two approaches to understanding guardian attitudes to CA, and what they may reveal about the construction of knowledge about human-dog relations in Aotearoa.

---

[6] More detail about Māori research methodology is available at http://www.rangahau.co.nz/research-idea/27/.

[7] In this chapter we use the term companion animals (CA) interchangeably with 'pet'. The naming of the relationships between people and domesticated animals signifies the history of values associated with the human-animal bond. Thus, terms such as 'owner', still the preferred term in legislation and animal control, signifies the animal is the property of the owner. Guardianship or kaitiakitanga signifies a relationship of care and responsibility which is more reciprocal and mutual.

The New Zealand Companion Animal Trust (NZCAT) Furry Whānau Wellbeing Research Study

With increasing pet ownership comes an increasing array of animal welfare concerns globally (Forrest et al., 2019). In Aotearoa few studies explore the attitudes of people towards their pets and their welfare needs. Therefore, there is limited information concerning sociological factors that may influence pet welfare.[8] Factors such as gender and ethnicity are known to impact on animal welfare issues. For example, research has found that female owners in Aotearoa New Zealand are more likely to sterilize their dog or cat and there are age differences concerning attitudes towards sterilization (McKay, Farnworth, and Waran, 2009), which might influence communication campaigns to increase rates of sterilization. Regarding ethnicity, although, as mentioned earlier, no official statistics are available regarding rates of registration of dogs by ethnicity of the owner, it seems reasonable to assume rates will be lower for Māori due to cost (often in exceeding $100 per annum)[9] and their lower average income.

The rationale for the NZCAT Furry Whānau Wellbeing project was that if pet welfare is to be improved then human behaviour concerning pets needs to be understood to inform human behaviour change programmes. Given that Aotearoa New Zealand hosts a diversity of cultures, has a strong conservation and biodiversity focus, and farming is a primary industry, there are differing cultural values placed on pet animals such as dogs (who may work on farms, be used for hunting, and can be pets) which may impact on their welfare.[10] Consequently, the project employed both a targeted study aimed at Māori and their pets (the Patu Pets study) and a broad nationwide internet survey approach to capture as wide a range of opinions as possible from the general population.

One Welfare Project, Two Methodologies

The NZCAT Furry Whānau Wellbeing Research Project followed on from the Eastern Institute of Technology (EIT) and Patu research with the Patu Pets study part of a

---

[8] Māori have higher rates of cat and dog ownership than any other ethnicity (NZCAC, 2016). Pet ownership has increased in Māori households since 2011, whereas nationally pet ownership rates decreased (NZCAC, 2016).

[9] Registration fees for a dog in Auckland area, the most populous region of New Zealand, is currently $33 for a working dog (e.g. farm herding is specified as an example) to $149 for regular dogs. https://www.aucklandcouncil.govt.nz/dogs-animals/register-your-dog/Pages/renew-registration-for-dog.aspx

[10] For instance, many working dogs on farms are killed if they: are injured; unable or unsuitable for work; excess to work requirements; or in excess of legal limits (Fladeboe, 2015). Different ethical frameworks are used to deal with farm animals according to Spencer et al. (2006).

larger collaborative healthy lifestyles intervention project between EIT and Patu Aotearoa (see Forrest et al., 2014; 2016). Patu Aotearoa (often referred to as Patu) is an initiative dedicated to the holistic health and wellbeing of local communities and runs gyms nationwide that combine group exercise and healthy lifestyle education with Māori language and culture, with the majority of Patu gym members identifying as Māori. Patu members and staff (the Patu whānau) create a supportive community that empowers individuals to change their lifestyles for the better (Forrest et al., 2014; 2016). Patu staff use a variety of behaviour change techniques such as commitment, visual images, prompts, and reminders; and the creation of their own social norms and branding along with incentives, strong social support, and feedback. (Forrest et al, 2019).

As referred to earlier, the Patu Pets study was a reciprocal intervention study to co-create value for the local Māori community and their pets. The Patu study consisted of a team from EIT Napier (staff and students) and was designed to engage with the local Māori community and their pets with the specific purpose of promoting human and animal welfare together. The EIT Patu Pets project implemented pet health checks for dogs and cats alongside existing regular Patu whānau health checks to explore the link between human and animal health and to develop an owner-friendly pet wellbeing assessment tool (the pet Meke Meter based on the human Meke Meter). Both the human and pet health checks were co-facilitated by Patu staff, and EIT staff and students. The pet check clinics were run by EIT researchers along with EIT Centre of Veterinary Nursing (CVN) staff and students. The approach allowed the CVN staff and students to engage with and educate a local community that is often referred to as 'hard-to-reach', thus providing a unique platform to facilitate positive human behaviour change towards animals. A sharing of knowledge occurred, however, as this approach also provided EIT CVN staff and students the opportunity to practise their skills and connect with the local community broadening their experiential knowledge (both as educators and students), and for the researchers to collect further information about attitudes towards animal welfare, which interviewers did after the pet check. Similar questions were asked in both this study and the more conventional internet survey.

The nationwide internet survey was distributed through social networks such as Facebook, and snowball methods were used to encourage participation.[11] The survey consisted of 42 questions with several text fields to enable respondents to provide further information. The number of respondents was 2744. The project overall found guardians in both studies felt deep love and affection for their CA. Similarly, guardians

---

[11] Nationally, an online survey was developed and offered to New Zealanders via SurveyMonkey. The survey was developed by EIT researchers Dr Rachel Forrest (Associate Professor, Research) and Maria Pearson in consultation with Natalie Waran (Professor, One Welfare, EIT), EIT CVN staff, Patu staff, Jeal Reiri (Kaitiaki Māori, Lecturer, School of Nursing, EIT) and Mark Farnworth (Associate Professor, Animal Welfare, Nottingham Trent University). The SurveyMonkey link was distributed through email networks and distributed online via social media (e.g. Facebook) and Patu websites with a snowball sampling approach being used to promote the survey and recruit participants.

had similar attitudes supporting animal welfare and their pets having a 'good life' (Mellor and Beausoleil, 2015). Full findings are available in the published final report (Forrest et al. 2019).

One Welfare Project, Multiple Participant Types

Some notable participant differences are explained in this section as opportunities for further conversation to promote One Welfare. Differences introduced in this section include the predominantly European and female participants in the online survey; the Māori participants of the Patu Pets study; and the potential of including the species-specific history of CA into account when interpreting the results of the One Welfare project overall. In this regard we focus on the kurī.

First, the participants of the online survey were overwhelmingly female (92.3 per cent) and European (New Zealand and Other) (93.5 per cent). This demographic characteristic is informally recognized as a common occurrence in non-random research sampling often used in CA qualitative studies. European women often want to participate in research about animals. Also, the method of distribution through snowball sampling through online social media meant that any tendencies for sampling homogeneity were accentuated through the ways online sharing behaviour and social media algorithms work to reinforce social and attitudinal predisposition. Consequently, results seem likely to be skewed towards the concerns of European women.

Second, the participants in the Patu project were predominantly Māori, which was an intentional design element of the study which built on previous success reaching Māori in the district through human health checks. Consequently, some characteristics of the group are relevant and here we elaborate upon the significance of the words family and whānau, which were used to entitle the project because of the regularity with which the participants used the terms to describe their relationship with, and obligations to, CA. An additional reason for the significance of whānau is that students doing the pet checks were mainly local and several of them are Māori. Consequently, students' whānau were notable in their support of the project and brought their animals in to be checked because whānau were doing the research and the checks.

Family used in the European sense usually means close relative and usually in the context of CA research, the nuclear family that lives in the household. 'Furry family' when discussing CA signifies that the pet is thought of as a child, a close sibling, or a comfort figure such as a parent (Charles and Davies, 2008). People are of course aware that their pets are not human but nevertheless they are still often thought of as kin.[12] The concept of furry family emphasizes families are socially and culturally constructed, and they can be interspecies. However, when a CA is called whānau, the concept of family

---

[12] Sometimes in research the relationship between guardians and CA is described as more-than-human, or posthuman (Charles, 2016).

achieves a much broader and more flexible meaning. Whānau includes a much broader concept of family to include extended family (including ancestors and descendants not yet born), and has an emotional, ethical, and spiritual dimension. Whānau is used in contemporary contexts to adapt values, histories, and traditions through whakapapa (genealogy) to life now; it is a flexible term whose meaning changes according to the circumstances of its use. Whānau can include those that are whāngai (or fostered) and includes a strong element of responsibility to mana whenua (Māori who belong to this place). The relationships of mana whenua with their place, which includes ancestral water and land, are based in a Māori cosmology that describes a shared whakapapa as the basis for what is a familial relationship between te ira tangata (mankind) and te taiao (the environment).

> Whakapapa describes a Māori lineage that extends beyond human relationships, a lineage that reflects the Māori creation narratives of Rangi-nui and Papatūānuku. These are the narratives that relate the individual to mountains, rivers, trees and even birds as a part of larger extended family. This strengthens the bond between the individual and the natural world, and just like human relationships, guides behaviours and interactions that ensure mutually beneficial outcomes. (Rangi, 2017)

Third and finally, there are species as participants that can be delineated. Guardians identified dogs and cats as their main CA. In the Patu Pets study CA were given a more equivalent status with their human guardians because of the Te Ao Māori approach as they both engaged in health checks together. At the Patu checks there were rich interactions between student vet nurses, Patu participants, and their dogs, taking place in a high-trust environment, which enabled researchers to then engage in more meaningful dialogues with participants about their knowledge of, and attitudes towards, their animal's welfare.

In the Patu Pets study, kurī and their guardians were given respect and attention in an environment which recognized and facilitated whānau ora (family wellbeing) and mauri (life-force). Mauri is in everything and everywhere; a person or animal's mauri is their essential life-force, and it must be guarded and protected by ensuring their wellbeing. For Māori, there are also obligations to help whānau with their mauri (Thorpe, 2015). In the next section, we discuss in more detail the differences between findings from the two studies and discuss them in relation to the historical relations raised earlier.

Implications: Kurī and Dog Registration

Interviewer: What motivated you to bring your pet along to the health check?
Respondent: Um, that it was free.

Interviewer: Yeah. Anything else?
Respondent: Um, and to see if my dog was alright.
(Excerpt from Patu interview)

In this implications section, we discuss three issues that arise from the Furry Whānau project: registration, costs of welfare, and animal welfare in relation to hunting.

It is important to preface this discussion by noting again that human and animal health are interrelated in One Welfare Aotearoa, and the Patu Pets study provides a model for the pro-equity significance of human and animal health and welfare found in Te Ao Māori. The approach is not top down, bottom up, nor even 'participatory' in the usual sense of organizational ethnographic research, even human-animal research (Hamilton and Taylor, 2017). Instead, the Patu Pets approach finds its centre in communities of reciprocal care, within which organizations are merely facilitators, and researchers are partners who serve their communities, and any knowledge derived must benefit those communities. Constellations of reciprocal care enacted through research methodology are embedded in ongoing processes of political and cultural relations that have a species dimension.

The issue of non-registration of dogs is thus discussed in this section in the context of improving the quality of life for both Māori and their dogs. In this context, we note that most of the dogs brought to the pet checks were not registered although deeply loved. This issue of non-registration needs to be understood historically to adequately address the issues of welfare that may or may not be associated with non-registration.

Here we conjecture that the expense of registration, microchipping, and fines may have an unintentionally negative impact on animal welfare. Dog registration is a form of tax that pays for dog control; a proviso of the Dog Control Act 1996, section 9. The barrier to animal welfare in the context we investigated emerges if non-registered dogs do not receive adequate care because guardians avoid taking an animal to a veterinary clinic in case they get into trouble because the animal is not registered (or microchipped).[13] There are additional implications for human welfare: not microchipping and registering a dog may have negative psychological implications as most people have absorbed the societal message that to register and microchip means one is a good/responsible owner and so not registering and microchipping may bring feelings of judgement or shame, being harmful to one's mauri. In highlighting this issue of unintended effects, we note that, in general, veterinarians do not ask owners if their dogs are registered because that question has no direct relevance to the wellbeing of the dog. Nevertheless, the perception of judgement from veterinary professionals may be a barrier to people seeking veterinary treatment. One implication arising from our chapter is the necessity for further studies on this issue relating to pet health outcomes so that appropriate policy and practices can be either introduced or extended (here we note the good work many animal control officers already do to work with 'hard-to-reach' populations, including the homeless who are also disproportionately Māori). At any rate, a social cost-benefit analysis of this issue seems timely in Aotearoa to support One Welfare Aotearoa goals.

---

[13] Other animal welfare issues such as dog fighting are also relevant, but are beyond the scope of this chapter.

As well as fear of falling afoul of the law, the cost of pet ownership and care is a valid and central concern for health and welfare. Māori, like anyone else, will spend money on their pet's health and their own health if they need to, but are reluctant to go to the veterinarian or doctors and pay money only to be told it's nothing to worry about. The NZCAT Furry Whānau project overall identified that pet care practices are mainly affected by household income.[14] The issues of financial difficulty or cost in relation to pet welfare was often mentioned by participants in both studies but is particularly pertinent for Māori. Regarding standard veterinarian treatments, participants at Patu were pro-vaccination but thought it was acceptable not to vaccinate regularly as it is expensive, with similar attitudes expressed towards flea and worm control. For example, one participant said, 'there's a lot of animal lovers out there that can't afford to take their animals to the vet … Even just for basic stuff'. The free nature of the Patu Pet health check clinics made them accessible, and access to knowledge and expertise gave reassurance that their pets were healthy or at least gave them the knowledge they needed to help them achieve a wellness state and that a veterinary clinic visit would not be wasted money. This issue of access to free pet health checks underlines the significance of socio-economic factors across the board for guardians. Considering the socio-economic position of Māori, which is still below that of non-Māori in New Zealand, achieving One Welfare, like One Health, is dependent on understanding and ameliorating the impact of socio-economic inequality (Harrison et al., 2020), especially considering Māori have the fastest growth of pet ownership in New Zealand. Two quotes below from participants in the Patu Pets study underscore the necessity of making information about pet welfare more freely available and accessible. Both quotes communicate deep affection alongside a poor understanding of the downsides of overconsumption of food and alcohol for both human and animal welfare. 'Um, yes we have slowed down on her drinking … Um, she really prefers bourbon, anything sweet.' And 'I was killing her by feeding her pies and chocolate … she's, yeah she's starting to come right'.

Regarding dog welfare, one interesting topic was tail docking and ear cropping, often now interpreted in animal welfare as being unnecessary and cruel. Although both study groups (survey and Patu whānau) were generally against tail docking and ear cropping, a few Patu (male) respondents said they thought it was alright if it was functional—for example, to prevent ripping and tearing of the ears and tail of the dog when confronting wild boar during a pig hunt. This issue of animal welfare in relation to hunting dogs requires more research. Dogs are often kept for hunting purposes in whānau, and Māori have higher demographic populations in less urban areas, near hunting areas and game which puts food on the table for whānau and marae. Hunting in Aotearoa has specific cultural[15] practices around Māori customary rights to hunt and gather kai (food) which align with self-determination goals. New Zealand animal welfare systems and institutions were originally imported from the United Kingdom and Europe, and

---

[14] Also, number of children in the household, rural upbringing, and whether the respondent lived in a town/city.

[15] See 'Hunting Aotearoa', a New Zealand television series, for a sense of the significance of hunting and the cultures associated with hunting animals. Note that almost all hunting in Aotearoa involves wild animals that have been introduced and compete with native wildlife. https://www.Māoritelevision.com/shows/hunting-aotearoa/S14E001/hunting-aotearoa-series-14-episode-1

similar value systems underpin key New Zealand animal welfare institutions (e.g. the Society for the Prevention of Cruelty to Animals (SPCA)) (Swarbrick, 2013). Potentially animal welfare and conservation institutions, if they are not in partnership with Māori, can apply animal welfare ethical judgements in a way that misses Aotearoa cultural differences. We suggest further research examining welfare discourses in the Aotearoa context.

We have identified three issues—registration, cost of welfare, and hunting—which arise out of further focused consideration of the Patu Pets initiative. Returning to our opening remarks on framing Māori-dog relations historically, we suggest here that understanding historical human-animal relations is critical to understanding contemporary CA welfare challenges. Broad and sweeping assumptions about what constitutes animal welfare, and even One Welfare, need culturally sensitive, politically nuanced, 'local histories of the roles that animals and their representations have played—or been made to play—in colonial and postcolonial transactions' (Armstrong, 2002: 416).

The Story Continues...

Our story about kurī in Aotearoa New Zealand has three main contributions for the development of a multispecies organizational and management studies. The first contribution is empirical. This chapter provides an Indigenous perspective on a One Welfare issue and such studies are so far non-existent. Since much scientific health and welfare work around the world is concerned with animal-human interfaces, we hope this study will assist other One Welfare researchers to also question their research design and see Indigenous knowledge as indispensable to the development of One Welfare.

Our second contribution is theoretical and relates to the development of organizational studies theory. We have shown not only the usefulness of Indigenous perspectives to give voice to perspectives usually silenced in organizational theory, but also the significance of historical and cultural analyses of human-animal relations to the development of organizational theory. By placing dog registration in historical perspective and drawing attention to how an Indigenous perspective can change the questions being asked about practice, we can start to appreciate how historical settler relations have impacted beyond the human. We suggest further work in animal organization studies which use decolonized, Indigenous methodologies and perspectives to enrich theory but ultimately practice for the betterment of both humans and animals since neither humans and animals nor the fields of theory and practice are separate.

The third contribution relates to animal management practice. By taking an historical perspective on a real-world problem, we have hinted at how management practice might shift to focus on welfare outcomes for both humans and animal through taking a One Welfare Aotearoa approach. We have only tentatively suggested where practice might go: by making access to veterinary services more available through targeted interventions such as the Patu project; by developing management partnership models with Māori; and by thinking outside legal and enforcement systems for solutions.

In this chapter we have explored some insights available from the Furry Whānau project which can help develop the capacity of One Welfare to contribute to animal-human knowledge and quality of life for all species. One Welfare Aotearoa is potentially an avenue through which government, corporate, and not-for-profit institutions can work in a transdisciplinary manner to achieve human and animal wellness in the most challenging of times. The crises of our era are our own (human) fault, and many of them involve dysfunctional relations with animals and the larger ecology, not to mention disparities of wealth that continue to fuel conflicts around the globe which ultimately destroys habitat and quality of life for all things human and nonhuman. A Te Ao Māori approach provides a model for the development of One Welfare internationally.

Glossary of Māori words*

Aotearoa New Zealand, literally the 'land of the long white cloud'.
Kurī Dog.
Mauri Life force, a prerequisite for life to exist and is pervasive in that it is present everywhere.
Māori The Indigenous people of Aotearoa.
Mātauranga Māori Knowledge created by Māori according to their experiences, history, worldview, values, culture, and aspirations.
Meke Meter™ A self-reported wellbeing or quality of life measurement tool. There is both a human and dog version.
Pou Pillars or support structures both actual and metaphorical, or central themes.
Te Ao Māori The Māori worldview which acknowledges the interconnectedness and inter-relationship of all living and non-living things.
Tangata whenua The Indigenous people born of the land.
Tikanga Māori The customary system of values and practices belonging to Māori that have developed over time and are deeply embedded in the social context.
Whakapapa Genealogy or lines of descent.
Whānau Often translated as 'family', but its meaning is more complex and flexible, even extending, if appropriate, to describe all ethnicities in Aotearoa and overseas. Whānau includes ancestors and descendants not yet born, and has a spiritual meaning and incorporates a sense of responsibility for others, including the nonhuman world.
Whānauora Family health and wellbeing.

*Source: Mainly https://Māoridictionary.co.nz/ and references used in this chapter.

References

Armstrong, P. (2002). The postcolonial animal. *Society and Animals, 10(4)*, 413–19.

Charles, N. (2016). Post-human families? Dog-human relations in the domestic sphere. *Sociological Research Online, 21(3)*, 83–94. doi:10.5153/sro.3975.

Charles, N., & Davies, C. (2008). My family and other animals: Pets as kin. *Sociological Research Online, 13(5)*, 13–26. doi:10.5153/sro.1798.

Colonius T., & Earley R. (2013). One welfare: A call to develop a broader framework of thought and action. *Journal of the American Veterinary Medical Association, 242(3)*, 309–10.

Denzin, N.K., Lincoln, Y.S., & Smith, L.T. (2008). *Handbook of critical and indigenous methodologies*. Los Angeles: Sage.

Durie, M. (1998). *Whairoa: Māori health development*. Auckland: Oxford University Press.

Fladeboe, A. (2015). *New Zealand's working dogs*. Nelson, New Zealand: Potton and Burton.

Forrest R. et al. (2014). The PATU® initiative as cultural praxis: Constructing tools to appropriately evaluate health and fitness programmes developed by and for Māori. In Congress Proceedings: New Zealand Population Health Congress, 6–8 October, 2014 (pp. 129–34). Auckland, New Zealand.

Forrest, R. et al. (2016). PATU™ Fighting fit, fighting fat! The Hinu Wero approach. *AlterNative: An International Journal of Indigenous Peoples, 12(3)*, 282–97.

Forrest, R. et al. (2019). Furry whānau wellbeing: Working with local communities for positive pet welfare outcomes. Final Report 2019. Prepared for the New Zealand Companion Animal Trust (NZCAT). ISBN: 978-0-9951429-2-3.

Hamilton, L., & Taylor, N. (2017). *Ethnography after humanism: Power, politics and method in multi-species research*. London: Palgrave Macmillan UK.

Hammerton, Z. (2018). Decolonising the waters: Interspecies encounters between sharks and humans. *Animal Studies Journal, 7(1)*, 270–303.

Harrison, S. et al. (2020). One Health Aotearoa: A transdisciplinary initiative to improve human, animal and environmental health in New Zealand. *One Health Outlook, 2(1)*, 4.

King, C. (Ed.) (2005). *The handbook of New Zealand mammals*. Dunedin, New Zealand: Oxford University Press.

Luomala, K. (1958). Polynesian myths about Maui and the dog. *Fabula*. Berlin: Walter de Gruyter. 2(1), 139–62. doi:10.1515/fabl.1959.2.1.139

McKay, S.A., Farnworth, M.J., & Waran, N.K. (2009). Current attitudes toward, and incidence of, sterilization of cats and dogs by caregivers (owners) in Auckland, New Zealand. *Journal of Applied Animal Welfare Science, 12(4)*, 331–44.

Mellor, D.J., & Beausoleil, N.J. (2015). Extending the 'Five Domains' model for animal welfare assessment to incorporate positive welfare states. *Animal Welfare, 24(3)*, 241.

Moewaka Barnes, H., & McCreanor, T. (2019). Colonisation, hauora and whenua in Aotearoa. *Journal of the Royal Society of New Zealand, 49(sup1)*, 19–33.

New Zealand Companion Animal Council Inc. (NZCAC) (2016). Companion animals in New Zealand 2016. Auckland, New Zealand: The New Zealand Companion Animal Council Inc.

Pinillos, R.G. (2017). 'One Welfare': A framework to support the implementation of OIE animal welfare standards. *OIE Animal Welfare Bulletin*, 3–7.

Pinillos, R.G. et al. (2016). One Welfare—A platform for improving human and animal welfare. *Veterinary Record, 179(16)*, 412–13.

Potts, A., Armstrong, P., & Brown, D. (2013). *A New Zealand book of beasts: Animals in our culture, history and everyday life*. Auckland, New Zealand: Auckland University Press.

Rangi, T. (2017). Gods, whānau, body parts—making sense of health with whakapapa. *The Spinoff*. https://thespinoff.co.nz/atea/06-11-2017/gods-whanau-body-parts-making-sense-of-health-with-whakapapa/)

Robinson, H., & Christoffel, P. (2011). Aspects of Rohe Potae political engagement, 1886 to 1913: A report commissioned by the Waitangi Tribunal for the Te Rohe Potae (Wai 898) district inquiry. Available from Rachel Forrest.

Smith, L.T. (1999). *Decolonizing methodologies: Research and indigenous peoples*. London: Zed Books.

Spencer, S. et al. (2006). History and ethics of keeping pets: Comparison with farm animals. *Journal of Agricultural and Environmental Ethics*, 19(1), 17–25.

Swarbrick, N. (2013). *Creature comforts: New Zealanders and their pets. An illustrated history*. Dunedin, New Zealand: Otago University Press.

Te Ahukaramū, C.R. (2021). 'Kaitiakitanga—guardianship and conservation', Te Ara—the Encyclopaedia of New Zealand http://www.TeAra.govt.nz/en/kaitiakitanga-guardianship-and-conservation)

Thorpe, J.A.R. (2015). *Tihei Mauri Ora!* Knowledge in Indigenous networks. Digital Iwi. https://indigenousknowledgenetwork.net/2015/11/14/tihei-mauri-ora/)

Wannan, O. (2015, October 7). Extinct dogs' voyage from Indonesia to NZ. Stuff. https://www.stuff.co.nz/science/72787645/extinct-dogs-voyage-from-indonesia-to-nz

CHAPTER 29

DOGS AT WORK

Gendered Organizational Cultures and Dog-Human Partnerships

NICKIE CHARLES, REBEKAH FOX, MARA MIELE, AND HARRIET SMITH

INTRODUCTION

DOGS work with and for humans in organizational contexts ranging from the armed forces and search and rescue to hospital wards, nursing homes, and schools. In this chapter our focus is on interspecies working relationships in two contrasting organizational settings, the police and a charitable organization established to provide assistance dogs to those with physical impairments. In these two organizations we focus particularly on how human-animal relationships are constructed through training. Dog-human partnerships have been analysed in various ways with Donna Haraway referring to them as 'more than one but less than two' (Haraway, 2008: 244) and Vinciane Despret using 'attunement' (Despret, 2013) to capture the idea of 'a shared trans-species being in the world' (Wolfe, 2010: 141). Those taking a symbolic interactionist approach have developed insights into the dynamics of the partnership and how it is understood and experienced by the human partner (Michalko, 1999; Sanders, 1999; 2006). Sanders, for instance, investigates the tension between object and subject in the status of guide dogs, the most frequently researched type of assistance dog, and police dogs and the ambivalence in the dog-handler relationship (Sanders, 1999; 2006). Others see dogs primarily as workers: they explore their professionalization, arguing, for police dogs, that their career trajectory mirrors that of police officers and, for assistance dogs, that they are care workers both caring and being cared for by the person they assist (Coulter, 2016; Mouret, 2019; Mouret et al., 2019).

Most of these researchers, whatever their approach, consider that the affective bond between dog and human is central to the ability of the partnership to do its work effectively (d'Souza et al., 2019; Handy et al., 1961; Michalko, 1999; Mouret, 2019; Mouret et al., 2019; Pemberton, 2019; Sanders, 1999; Sanders, 2006; Shukin, 2013; Smith et al., 2021) but few address the organizational context of dog-human partnerships. There are some exceptions. Michalko analyses the way an assistance dog organization in the United States constructs the partnership through the arrangement of institutional space and sometimes contradictory beliefs about dog-human relationships. Thus, dogs are seen as pack animals in need of a leader, but those being assisted are exhorted to 'follow your dog', thereby abandoning ideas of human leadership (Michalko, 1999). Similarly, the work of therapy dogs in university settings and the limited possibility of students establishing a relationship with them is shaped by organizational goals (Charles and Wolkowitz, 2019). We take these insights further, exploring how the dog-human partnership is conditioned by the organizational context within which it exists.

For police dogs the organizational context of their work is the masculinized, coercive state apparatus where they help police officers to track down and detain suspects and, for assistance dogs, it is the feminized, voluntary sector where they help people who have a physical impairment. In what follows, we explore these differences and ask how they shape dog-human partnerships and the work they do. We first describe the research and the progress of police and assistance dogs through the training process; we then explore the culture of risk shaping police dog training and the culture of care shaping assistance dog training before discussing the nature of the partnerships and the affective connection at their heart. We argue that, while both organizations create the conditions for the development of strong interspecies affective ties, they also require the instrumentalization of affect and a consequential expenditure of emotional labour on the part of dogs and humans.

Researching Dog Training Cultures

The research on which this chapter is based is part of a larger multispecies ethnography exploring how different dog training cultures shape the dog-human relationship.[1] Our methodology combines observation of training over a period of several months, interviews with key human participants, and visual recording of training events. Here we draw on our fieldwork with the dog sections of three police forces and the charitable organization anonymized here as Canine Helpers UK. In both cases we followed dogs through from their selection for the training programme to completion of training. In Canine Helpers we followed dogs from puppyhood to their qualifying as assistance dogs

---

[1] 'Shaping inter-species connectedness: training cultures and the emergence of new forms of human-animal relations' was funded by the Leverhulme Trust and based at the universities of Warwick and Cardiff. https://warwick.ac.uk/fac/soc/sociology/research/currentresearch/interspeciesconnectedness/

and with the police we followed dogs undergoing their training as general purpose police dogs.[2]

General purpose police dogs have an initial training course of 12 weeks with their handler, at the end of which the dog-human partnership is licensed. They start this course when they are 12 months or older, prior to which some have been living with experienced dog handlers, some have been with puppy walkers, some have been bred by professional breeders, and some have been pets. They and their handler continue to have formal top-up training throughout their working lives; indeed, training is an ongoing process and most handlers spend a great deal of time training their dogs inside and outside working hours. Assistance dogs spend their first year or so with a volunteer puppy walker before they go into formal training at around 14 months of age; this involves them leaving their puppy walker and establishing a relationship with their trainer who is employed by Canine Helpers. Their training takes five months at the end of which they are matched with the person who they will work with, the assistance dog owner.[3] They spend a period of time getting to know each other and becoming familiar with the work they will be doing before qualifying as a partnership. For the purposes of this chapter we draw on our observations of training, fieldnotes, and interviews with those who were involved with the dogs either as trainers/instructors or as owners/handlers. In Canine Helpers, we interviewed five puppy walkers (four women and one man), six trainers (five women and one man), and eight assistance dog owners (five women and three men) while in the police we interviewed one puppy walker (a woman), four instructors (all men), and eight trainee dog handlers (two women and six men).

Gendered Organizations

Police and assistance dog training share their origins in Europe in the first half of the twentieth century (Handy et al., 1961; Michalko, 1999; Pemberton, 2019; Pearson, 2016;). Most of the literature relating to the history of assistance dogs focuses on guide dogs and, in the early years, both the police and organizations training guide dogs shared a preference for working with German Shepherds. Furthermore, their development influenced dog training more generally, and has been characterized in terms of the emergence of 'disciplinary institutions' where dogs are understood to be driven by natural instincts

---

[2] General purpose police dogs are trained to track and immobilize suspects, by barking or biting, and locating objects a suspect might have dropped or hidden; they are also used for crowd control. The breeds used for this work are usually herding dogs such as German Shepherds, Belgian Shepherds, or Dutch Herders.

[3] The term 'owner' is somewhat contentious but is used here to reflect the language in use at the case study organization. Similarly we use the term 'handler' for those who work in partnership with a police dog as this is the language used by the police.

and in need of physical subjugation to human will (Wlodarczyk, 2018: 14). The cultures characterizing these institutions in the early years were associated with forms of masculinity exhibiting 'firmness, strength and courage' (Wlodarczyk, 2018: 16). It was men who trained dogs and the clients in need of guiding were assumed to be men of working age (Pemberton, 2019). Assistance dogs were always female but police dogs—at least in Paris—could be male or female (Pearson, 2016). Since then, the gendering of these organizations has changed with police forces retaining their masculinist culture and the organizational culture of Canine Helpers becoming more feminized.

Reflecting this, in the police dog sections most of the dog handlers are men while the kennel staff tend to be women and, in Canine Helpers, the majority of the workforce, particularly those involved in training and caring for the dogs, are women. In both organizations those working with dogs are overwhelmingly white. Canine Helpers' client base includes women and men of different ages and with a wide range of needs and abilities. Assistance and police work can be carried out by dogs of both sexes and, while the police still use German Shepherds and other herding breeds, Canine Helpers rely mainly on retrieving breeds and their crosses. What has not changed significantly are the tasks that the dogs are being trained to do—helping a person with a physical impairment or tracking and detaining a suspect—although training methods, the technologies of training, and the way dogs are understood have changed considerably (Charles et al., 2021; Pemberton, 2019; Wlodarczyk, 2018).

Despite these changes, echoes of the view that dogs are driven by instinct remain. In the police dog sections training is understood as a means of harnessing dogs' natural instincts for human ends. We were told that it is important to transform the prey drive into 'ball drive' so that the dogs are highly motivated by a ball being thrown as a reward. In contrast assistance dog trainers speak about how the training process teaches the dogs to go against their natural instincts (Michalko, 1999; Sanders, 1999). So, while assistance dogs may not be allowed to sniff or chase while working, this is precisely what trainee police dogs are encouraged to do, under human control and for specific ends. In line with this, assistance dogs are neutered, apart from those who are selected to join the breeding programme and, while neutering policies vary in police dog sections, male dogs are not usually castrated.

Within masculinist police cultures there are views about the ability of human gendered bodies to cope with the physicality of police work; men are assumed to be more able than women to use physical force to control an 'arrestee' (Westmarland, 2017: 308). These views are reflected in assumptions about the different aptitudes of male and female dogs for general purpose work. Thus, in one dog section, males were preferred because they were seen as more able than females to work under pressure. Such a preference was not evident in the other two dog sections but even there one of the instructors said that, while male and female dogs 'work the same':

> [I]t's a macho thing and if you put ten dogs in kennels dog handlers will go for the biggest and toughest looking and bitches will get left because they tend to be smaller and have smaller heads. (Fieldnotes)

This gendering of dogs' bodies is not apparent in Canine Helpers where there was no preference on the basis of sex and, in any case, differences that might be attributed to sex were minimized through the organization's neutering policy. This practice not only helps to reduce the risk of dogs being distracted from their work by their sex hormones but also reflects an assumption that the ability to undertake the work they are trained for is not related to sex.

Cultures of Risk and Care

This notwithstanding, care work is culturally feminized while policing is masculinized and this is reflected in the work undertaken by police and assistance dog partnerships. The work of an assistance dog is about providing care and ensuring the safety of trainers, clients, and dogs; it is characterized by a culture of care. Policing, in contrast, is characterized by a culture of risk: it is dangerous and police officers and dogs can and do lose their lives in the course of doing their work. Danger and risk taking add an excitement and 'buzz' to the work and are associated with masculinities (Butler and Charles, 2012). As one of the police dog handlers said:

> I wake up every day excited to go to work now.... It's like I want to get there and I want to get there now because I'm doing it with my mate who is equally as excited.

However, while police dog handlers have chosen this risky work, police dogs have not and, as one of the trainee handlers commented:

> [W]e sign up to come on a dog unit. They don't... they've got no choice in the matter.

This highlights the anthropocentric hierarchy within which the dogs are working (Clarke and Knights, 2019) where, while they are highly valued members of a dog-human team and visibly enjoy the training they do with their human partner, their collaboration does not involve an understanding of the risks entailed. It also shows the discomfort some handlers felt with the organization's assumption that training dogs to do dangerous work is ethically unproblematic (cf. Wlodarczyk, 2021). In practice, handlers do as much as they can to protect their dogs while ensuring that they do their jobs effectively. At the same time they recognize that it may sometimes be necessary to send a dog into a potentially life threatening situation and they are very aware that they 'are relying on them to potentially save your life one day' (for a personal account, see Wardell, 2019).

As with other jobs involving danger, such as firefighting (Thurnell-Read and Parker, 2009), group loyalty is part of police culture (Westmarland, 2017) and there is a camaraderie in the dog sections which were often small in terms of the number of dog-handler teams. The culture is marked by banter and storytelling, particularly about the bites dogs have had which make an arrest possible. Storytelling is a feature of police culture 'and the retelling of the catch or fight confers added kudos upon the participants', in this case, the dog-human partnership (Westmarland, 2017: 302). The difference between the risks involved in police work and the risk aversion of Canine Helpers is reflected in the temperaments of the dogs required for these different types of work. We noticed a difference in terms of energy levels with police dogs being high energy and raring to go while assistance dogs, whatever their breed, have lower levels of energy and are much calmer. An assistance dog trainer said that they need dogs who have 'a calm, relaxed demeanour' and 'want to please' while a police instructor said that police dogs need to have 'energy, enthusiasm, confidence, boldness, courageousness'. These characteristics can be understood as gendered, reflecting the types of work that police and assistance dogs undertake.

Becoming Partners

The dog-human partnership is dependent on the formation of an emotional connection and the dog's willingness to engage with the training process. This affective connection is understood as a bond and is seen as critical to the ability of both dog and human to engage in the training and working relationship (cf. Shukin, 2013; Pearson, 2016). Establishing this connection requires emotional labour on the part of dog and human through engaging in play and caring activities (Smith et al., 2021). Trainee police handlers cared for their dogs from the beginning of the course; they fed, groomed, and walked them, checked them for injury and made sure their kennel (at the handler's home) was comfortable and secure. Assistance dog trainers bond with the dogs by playing and spending time with them and the owners and their dog bond when they are in partnership training.[4] This is encouraged through lavish use of food and praise, the dogs being with their new owners 24 hours a day, and owners playing with and caring for their dog (cf. Michalko, 1999). The dog is encouraged to see the owner as the source of all things good[5] and, according to the trainers, most bond quickly. This process of bonding is not automatic as was evident in the police when dogs and their handlers met each other for the first time. At this stage neither understood what the other was trying to communicate which contrasted significantly with their ability to communicate some

---

[4] This is the period of time a dog spends with the person they will be partnered with, getting to know each other, bonding, training together, and learning the work that they will be doing together. They may spend this time at a hotel or at the assistance dog owner's house. At the end of this period the partnership is assessed and, if they qualify, they are able to work on their own.

[5] In both organizations measures are in place to support the dog-human partnership. These involve no other family member feeding or grooming the dog and all their needs being met by their handler/owner. An exception is made with assistance dogs who may need another person to take them for exercise off lead. These practices ensure that the dog's affective orientation is to the person they are working with.

weeks into training. And an assistance dog owner told us how her new dog had taken quite a long time to establish the emotional connection with her which she felt was vital for them to be able to work together.

Dogs as Active Partners

Establishing the emotional connection on which partnerships depend is a two-way process in which dogs actively engage, an engagement which is also evident in their ability to take the initiative and make decisions independently of their handler. This includes acting against what their handler is indicating, 'taking responsibility' when working, and resisting the process of becoming a working dog. There are examples from both organizations. Police dogs, for instance, when following a track, may go against the wishes of their handler. A dog handler recounted, 'I thought I knew where the track went, so I tried to influence where Tai was going.' He continued, 'She knew where the track went … and I actually physically stopped her because I thought we'd gone way past it—we hadn't—and she was actually doing the right thing, … she's doing the work, I'm just helping her do that work.'

Assistance dog trainers talk about the responsibility that the dogs assume when helping someone. Some dogs, in the trainers' words, are not able to cope with that responsibility and find the pressure to make decisions for themselves, rather than relying on support from the trainer or owner, too much. Decisions involve complex behaviours and require the dogs to think for themselves and choose to disobey. As Sanders points out, however, this sort of behaviour, such as a guide dog deciding not to cross a road when a vehicle is coming, is learned and this leads some to question whether it is accurate to describe it as 'intelligent disobedience' (Sanders, 1999; Pemberton, 2019). What this also shows is that those working with an assistance or police dog need to learn to trust their dog and recognize the dog's authority. In the words of a police instructor:

> [T]he dog is doing what you're asking it to do and you trust and follow your dog. If the dog's telling you to go that way, you go that way.

This is part of learning to work in an interspecies partnership where the animal's decisions are respected. It also points to the reliance of the dog-human partnership on their combined sensory abilities (Hart et al., 2000; Warren, 2013). The dog's senses are different from those of their human handlers—police dogs can follow scent and assistance dogs use senses such as hearing and sight which may be impaired in those they are helping—and it is the combination of the dog's and human's sensory apparatuses that makes the dog-human partnership effective.

A dog's willingness and ability to do the work are taken into account in both organizations and there is a view that a dog cannot be made to do the work if they do not want to (see also Mouret, 2019). To us as researchers, it seemed that assistance dog trainers were very aware of how a dog is feeling about their work; they can tell if a dog is happy, bored, stressed, confident and so on and they use that language to describe the dog's feelings. They also know when a dog does not want to do something and are respectful of the dog's wishes. One of the police dog handlers told us that the dog he had first licensed with wasn't a 'natural police dog'; he had been unable to rely on him in potentially dangerous situations and the dog had been re-homed as a pet where he was much happier. And in Canine Helpers we were told about a dog who had simply lain down and refused to move during training; after everything had been tried to persuade her to move and nothing had worked she was withdrawn from the programme and re-homed. In this sense, dogs are able to influence the way they do their work or whether they do it at all; they are active agents in a two-way relationship albeit operating within organizational constraints (Carter and Charles, 2013).

Describing Partnerships

These working partnerships were described in different ways with assistance dog owners seeing their dogs as extensions of themselves and police dog handlers talking about them as best friends and workmates; for both they were also family members (see also Hart et al., 2000). A police dog handler said, '[O]nce you've bonded with him, you don't want to lose the dog ... You want to keep him. He's, like, your best friend, part of the family,' and others told us that that they spend more time with their dog than with their (human) family. Trust is central to the relationship, a trust that is seen as two-way. Police dog handlers need to be able to trust their dogs to work when they are away from them, often out of sight, and assistance dog owners trust their dogs to listen for important events such as doorbells and alarms or to guide them safely in public places. A police dog handler said that the relationship is, 'about trust and protection but you build up the relationship through training but also through working together and realizing that you can trust each other. The dog trusts you and you trust the dog. It's a bond, a partnership.'

There was, however, a tension, particularly in the police, between the affective bond at the heart of the partnership and the dog's status as an asset of the organization akin to any other piece of equipment (Mouret et al., 2019; Sanders, 2006, Shukin, 2013). This emerges in references to the dog as a piece of kit and is particularly noticeable at the beginning of the training course when the possibility of dogs being reallocated is stressed. This upset trainee handlers who became attached to their dogs very quickly and worried that the dog might be taken away. While trainee police dogs are matched more or less randomly with handlers, this was not the case with assistance dogs and their owners who are matched very carefully. This is the relationship that the training and previous relationships are geared towards and involves a profound bodily attunement when it is working well. One assistance dog owner said:

I feel closer to her in a way when we're working because she's almost me and I'm almost her ... It's this closeness that I don't think you would even get with a pet, because you *become* this working partnership when you're almost just one entity really.

Michalko, in his writing on the guiding relationship, understands this in terms of the 'two-in-one'. He says of his own guide dog, 'we cannot be separated. *My* self is now *our* self. Smokie's self too is *our* self' (Michalko, 1999: 91) and Mouret writes about a 'common bodiliness', referring to the dog's understanding that their embodied travel through the world includes the person who they are guiding (Mouret, 2019: 108).

Provisional Partnerships

Even though in both organizations the work dogs do is highly valued and the importance of a strong emotional bond for the ability of the partnership to work effectively is recognized, partnerships are provisional in two senses: dogs undergo a series of transitions before being paired with the person with whom they will work and partnerships only persist as long as they are working well. Thus, if an assistance dog is unable to handle the responsibilities of their work or a police dog hides behind their handler rather than accompanying them into a potentially dangerous situation, then the partnership is not working and the dog is likely to be withdrawn. A partnership is always provisional and dependent on both the ability to do the job and the needs of the organization. In what follows, we look first at the transitions that are intrinsic to the training programme before discussing the dissolution of partnerships for other reasons.

In both organizations the creation of a successful working dog-human partnership is the end point of their training programmes and transitions are part of the training process. In Canine Helpers, efforts are made to ensure the dogs can cope with transitions and that any stress is reduced to a minimum; indeed a trainer told us that one of the characteristics the dogs are bred for is 'adaptability'. During their time with a puppy walker, puppies become accustomed to being handled by different people and, when they move from their puppy walker's home to the training environment of kennels, vans, a boarder's home, and other dogs, trainers do all they can to ensure that the dogs are not stressed. Part of this involves encouraging an attachment to their trainer and a dog's ability to bond is seen as assisting them in coping with transitions.

In both organizations it is assumed that dogs can easily move on and that the provisional nature of the partnership is not problematic for them (although in Canine Helpers there was also a view that so many transitions may not be ideal for the dog). One of the police dog handlers said, 'It's quite basic with dogs: whoever feeds me, whoever walks me, whoever plays with me, that's who I become attached to. And that's how dogs really think.' Potential police dogs are expected to be able to cope with stressful situations and their ability to do so is an indication of their suitability for police work. A young dog was deemed unsuitable because, in the words of the instructor, he did not have the 'heart' to become a police dog and was too 'sensitive'. His training was abandoned and he was returned to the breeder who had supplied him 'on approval'. If a dog does not live up to expectations they will be moved on and, in this sense, they are treated as if they were faulty equipment (cf. Mouret et al., 2019); this means that it is risky for handlers to form an emotional attachment.

For both organizations dogs are an investment; they contribute to meeting organizational goals and the cost of production of a fully-trained partnership is substantial so organizations have an interest in their longevity. And while police forces have an interest in dog-human partnerships succeeding and recognize the importance of the emotional dimension of the relationship for it to work effectively, dogs belong to the force not to the individual handler. This means that organizational change and operational priorities can disrupt dog-human relationships with little regard for the emotional fall-out for the dog, their handler, and other family members.

In Canine Helpers the relationship between assistance dog and owner is regarded as permanent until the dog retires and, once qualified, this is part of the arrangement between the organization and the assistance dog owner.[6] The organization is keen that dogs are not seen as tools or equipment and they discourage people from talking about them as such; despite this some of the owners we spoke to used these terms (see also Sanders, 1999). Assistance dog trainers told us that it is important that owners do not regard the dog as a tool, 'because at the end of the day they're still a dog that needs to do dog things', such as playing and exercising off lead, and owners are expected to interact with their dog when the dog is not working. There is an organizational awareness of language which reflects the care taken over the dog's physical and emotional wellbeing and the recognition of dogs as subjects.

Emotional Labour

The provisional nature of the partnerships and the transitions that are part of the dogs' training means that people adopt a range of strategies to minimize emotional distress; this can be understood as emotional labour (Mouret et al., 2019). It is work that is relied on by both organizations to achieve their goals which take precedence over the interspecies affective ties on which partnerships depend. Even in retirement assistance dogs do not necessarily stay with their owners, although it is for the owners to decide whether they wish and are able to keep them. If they are re-homed it involves a transition for both dog and owner which requires emotional work on the part of the owner as they experience the loss of an animal who is an 'extension' of themselves. One owner told us:

---

[6] Canine Helpers are able to remove assistance dogs from their owners if it is in the interests of the dog's welfare or if the partnership breaks down.

> Emotionally it's like a complete disaster in your head, because you're going, 'I need to just go, I need to not think about you because I need to focus on the new dog.'

Not thinking about the dog you are parting from and focusing instead on the new one was a coping strategy also used by assistance dog puppy walkers, some of whom made a distinction between their assistance dog puppy and their own pet dog/s. They see the puppy as a working dog and have a responsibility to Canine Helpers to treat them differently from a pet dog; they do not regard the puppy as 'theirs' (it is owned by the organization) and this helps them to cope emotionally when the puppy moves into training. For trainers a commitment to 'changing the life' of someone who requires an assistance dog and enabling a dog to have a happy and fulfilling life helps them accept the inevitability of dogs moving on.

Referring to a dog as a 'piece of kit' can also be understood as a form of emotional labour. A police instructor spoke about it as, '[A] coping mechanism for handlers … to be able to kind of try to detach emotionally from grief around something happening to the dog.' It is also a form of language that de-emphasizes the emotional nature of the relationship. More experienced handlers tried to avoid emotional investment in the partnership until it was clear the dog would make the grade and, as a police instructor told trainee handlers on day one of the course, 'Love your dog, don't fall in love with it'. Less experienced handlers found this advice almost impossible to follow. Seeing the dogs as having a job of work to do, belonging to the organization, being a 'piece of kit', or not becoming emotionally attached too early in the partnership are all ways of creating an emotional distance and can be understood as the emotional labour needed in order to be able to cope with the impermanence of partnerships. This emotional labour is part of the work done by those involved in dog-human partnerships which depend precisely on an emotional investment for their effectiveness.

Instrumentalizing Affect

In this chapter we have explored the shaping of interspecies partnerships, arguing that the organizational contexts within which they operate are key to understanding the work they do, the affective ties on which they depend, and the emotion and care work that are required to establish an emotional connection and to cope with their provisional nature. Furthermore, these partnerships are subject to contradictory pressures. On the one hand, affect is instrumentalized to meet organizational goals with dog-human partnerships only persisting insofar as they contribute to those goals and, on the other hand, emotional involvement is recognized as essential for a partnership to work and is supported and encouraged. It is in the interests of the organization, as well as the dog-human dyad, that a partnership succeeds and there are costs (financial and operational) to the organization when a partnership fails. The emotional costs, however, are borne exclusively by the partnership.

We have also argued that the work done by these interspecies partnerships is gendered: in the police it is dangerous, physical work, putting bodies on the line—both dog and human—while, in Canine Helpers it is care work that ensures dog and owner are safe and risk is minimized; and it takes place within differently gendered organizational cultures. For Canine Helpers, creating a successful assistance dog-owner partnership is the goal of the organization while, for the police, the partnership is a means to an end rather than an end in itself. In Canine Helpers every attempt is made, through training and matching, to ensure that the partnership will last and, during their training, dogs are given support to enable them to adapt to new people and are acclimatized early in their organizational lives to spending time with others. These practices reflect the organization's gendered culture of care. In the police there is an organizational assumption that police dogs and their handlers can cope with the sudden ending of partnerships and the stress of transitions although, in the dog sections, the strength of the affective ties between dog and handler—especially on the part of the handler—are acknowledged and efforts made to ensure that partnerships are not disrupted. This is not always possible and the culture of risk characterizing the dog sections involves a form of masculinity which, while celebrating a strong emotional connection, also recognizes that both dogs and handler have to submit to organizational demands and be able to cope with the consequences. Hence an apparent objectification of dogs as a 'piece of kit', sits alongside an understanding of them as subjective beings entangled in strong emotional attachments which are critically important for the partnership to work and which matter.

These findings suggest that interspecies working partnerships cannot be fully understood without taking into account the organizational practices within which they are produced and in which they are embedded. Situating them in their organizational context highlights the way they are shaped for human ends and how the dogs willingly collaborate in this process. It also demonstrates that the affective bond at the heart of the partnership which is essential for that partnership's success is a means to an organizational end rather than an end in itself. As well as instrumentalizing affect, however, the organizational context within which training takes place creates the conditions for the emergences of interspecies trust, respect, care, and communication, and the dog's authority in the work they do is recognized by their human partners. Moreover, if a dog does not want to work their wishes are respected. Thus, while jobs that put animals' lives at risk without their consent raise serious ethical questions, the dogs' consent to and enjoyment of the work itself is an essential pre-requisite of these partnerships. This was evident in both organizational contexts and suggests that interpreting the work dogs do with and for humans as irremediably exploitative fails to capture the complexities of interspecies working partnerships.

Acknowledgments

We thank everyone who has made this research possible: the Leverhulme Trust for funding it, the organisations who so generously gave us access to their training programmes, and the people involved in training and working with dogs in the police dog sections and Canine Helpers UK.

References

Butler, D., & Charles, N. (2012). Exaggerated femininity and tortured masculinity: Embodying gender in the horseracing industry. *The Sociological Review*, 60(4), 676–95.

Carter, B., & Charles, N. (2013). Animals, agency and resistance. *Journal for the Theory of Social Behaviour*, 43(3), 322–40.

Charles, N. et al. (2021). 'Fulfilling your dog's potential': changing dimensions of power in dog training cultures in the UK. *Animal Studies Journal*, 10(2), 169–200.

Charles, N., & Wolkowitz, C. (2019). Bringing dogs onto campus: Inclusions and exclusions of animal bodies in organisations. *Gender, Work and Organization*, 26(3), 303–21.

Clarke, C., & Knights, D. (2019). Who's a good boy then? Anthropocentric masculinities in a veterinary practice. *Gender, Work and Organization*, 26, 267–87.

Coulter, K. (2016). Beyond human to humane: A multispecies analysis of care work, its repression, and its potential. *Studies in Social Justice*, 5(2), 199–219.

Despret, V. (2013). Responding Bodies and Partial Affinities in Human-Animal Worlds. *Theory, Culture & Society*, 30(7–8), 51–76.

D'Souza, R., Hovorka, A., & Niel, L. (2019). Conservation canines: Exploring dog roles, circumstances, and welfare status. In C. Blattner, K. Coulter, & W. Kymlicka (Eds.), *Animal labour: A new frontier of interspecies justice?* (pp. 65–87). Oxford: Oxford University Press.

Handy, W.P., Harrington, M., & Pittman, D.J. (1961). The K-9 corps: The use of dogs in police work. *Journal of Criminal Law and Criminology*, 52(3), 328–37.

Haraway, D. (2008). *When species meet*. Minneapolis: University of Minnesota Press.

Hart, A.L. et al. (2000). The role of police dogs as companion and working partners. *Psychological Reports*, 86, 190–202.

Michalko, R. (1999). *The two in one: Walking with Smokie, walking with blindness*. Philadelphia: Temple University Press.

Mouret, S. (2019). Guide dogs: Care workers. In J. Porcher, & J. Estebanez (Eds.), *Animal Labor: A new perspective on human-animal relations* (pp. 101–12). Berlin: De Gruyter.

Mouret, S., Porcher, J., & Mainix, G. (2019). Military and police dogs: Weapons or colleagues? In J. Porcher, & J. Estebanez (Eds.), *Animal Labor: A new perspective on human-animal relations* (pp. 129–46). Berlin: De Gruyter.

Pearson, C. (2016). Between instinct and agency: Harnessing police dog agency in early 20th century Paris. *Comparative Studies in Society and History*, 58(2), 463–90.

Pemberton, N. (2019). Cocreating guide dog partnerships: Dog training and interdependence in 1930s America. *Medical Humanities*, 45, 92–101.

Sanders, C.R. (1999). *Understanding dogs: Living and working with canine companions*. Philadelphia: Temple University Press.

Sanders, C.R. (2006). 'The dog you deserve': Ambivalence in the K9 officer/patrol dog relationship. *Journal of Contemporary Ethnography*, 35(2), 148–72.

Shukin, N. (2013). Security bonds: On feeling power and the fiction of an animal governmentality. *English Studies in Canada*, 39(1), 177–98.

Smith, H. et al. (2021). Becoming with a police dog: Training technologies for bonding. *Transactions of the Institute of British Geographers*, 46(2), 478–494.

Thurnell-Read, T., & Parker, A. (2009). Men, masculinities and firefighting: Occupational identity, shopfloor culture and organisational change. *Emotion, Space and Society, 1*(2), 127–34.

Wardell, D. with Barrett-Lee, L. (2019). *Fabulous Finn: The brave police dog who came back from the brink*. London: Quercus.

Warren, C. (2013). *What the dog knows: Scent, science, and the amazing ways dogs perceive the world*. New York: Simon and Schuster.

Westmarland, L. (2017). Putting their bodies on the line: Police culture and gendered physicality. *Policing, 11*(3), 301–17.

Wlodarczyk, J. (2018). *Genealogy of obedience: Reading North American dog training literature, 1850s–2000s*. Leiden, Boston: Brill.

Wlodarczyk, J. (2021). Beyond bizarre: The spectacular failure of B.F. Skinner's pigeon-guided missiles, paper presented to the BASN conference, May (online).

Wolfe, C. (2010). *What is posthumanism?* Minneapolis: University of Minnesota Press.

Index

For the benefit of digital users, indexed terms that span two pages (e.g., 52–53) may, on occasion, appear on only one of those pages.

Tables and figures are indicated by *t* and *f* following the page number

A

Aaltola, E. 168–69
aboutness knowledge 183n.2
absence-of-knowledge 62, 63
Acampora, R. 333–34, 337–38
acculturation 107–8
activists/activism 3, 11, 53, 69, 302
    animal activists unwilling to see life from farmers' perspective 279–80
    corporate 12–13
    dairy farmer and vegan discourses on animal consumption 277–78
    education through animal-industrial complex (AIC) 75, 76–77, 81
    food 284
    hurt and disruption caused by animal protests/activism 280–81
    speciesism 241–42, 245, 255
    vegan activists at out-of-touch with realities of rural life 278–79
    veterinary work in Dutch farm animal care 288–89, 297
    see also husky kennels in Finland as animal welfare activists
Actor Network Theory (ANT) 195–97, 200, 201–2, 203, 205–4, 206, 416–17
Adams-Hutcheson, G. 105, 110
aesthetic inquiry 247
affect 369–71, 378–80, 384
    see also rockpooling, affect and charisma
affected ignorance 274
Agamben, G. 262, 350
agency 37–38, 362–63
    animal metaphors 195–96, 197

animals as labour and capital 36–37
biosphere management 47, 48–49
education in animal studies: critical inquiry 77–78
horse-human relationships and leadership 88, 89, 96, 97
husky kennels in Finland as animal welfare activists 406–7
rockpooling, affect and charisma 371–72
urban coyotes in USA 137–38
see also agency and responsibility paradoxes in the Anthropocene: posthumanist praxis; moral agency
agency and responsibility paradoxes in the Anthropocene: posthumanist praxis 42–53
    animals in Anthropocene 50–52
    Anthropocene and the anthropos 44–46
    biosphere management 46–50
agnoses (ignorance) 58–59, 64, 67, 69
agribusiness 20–21, 64–65, 77, 79
    dairy farmer and vegan discourses on animal consumption 274, 276, 281–82, 284
alibi research 65
alienation 77, 216–17, 418–19
alien thought experiment 246–47, 249, 254
Alvesson, M. 169–70
analytical lens 201–2
anchor institutions 230
Andrighetto, L. 198
animal-based foods 264–65, 266, 282
animal caretaking 80
animal companion industry 394

458   INDEX

animal consumption 64
    see also dairy farmer and vegan discourses on animal consumption
animal dirty work 12, 276, 386–87
animal fertilizers 301
animal-industrial complex (AIC) 20–21, 74–80
    see also Covid-19, zoonotic disease and animal-industrial complex (AIC)
animality 410–14, 418–19, 420
animal liberation perspective 146, 265, 273, 275, 278
animal metaphors and strategic human resource management (SHRM) 210–20
    'big hat, no cattle' 210, 214–17
        context 215, 219220–16
        interpretation 216–17
    conceptual metaphor theory (CMT) 213, 214
    'dog does not bark' metaphor 214
    high-performance work systems (HPWS) and managerial perceptions of HR departments 211, 217–19
        context 217–18
        interpretation 218–19
    Human Resource Management (HRM) 211, 212
    multispecies metaphor conceptual frame 212–15
    SHRM as field of scientific inquiry 211–12
    storytelling 212, 213, 216, 220
animal metaphors and workplace interactions 194–207, 411
    Actor Network Theory (ANT) 195–97, 200, 201–2, 203, 205–4, 206
    animal costumes ('too animally') 204–5
    animals as resolution to problems 202–4
    cultural 'buy-in' 200–2
    Fireco 195–96, 199, 200–1
    Gung Ho culture 195–96, 199–202, 203, 204
        Gift of the Goose 199, 200, 201–2, 204, 205–6
        Spirit of the Squirrel 199, 200, 202, 205–6
        Way of the Beaver 199, 200–1, 202, 203, 205–6
    organizational culture 198–99

    Organizational Zoo 198, 200
    trust relationships 203–4
Animals Australia 277
animal shelter in Australia: natural disaster and work calling 383–94
    altruistic motivations 386
    animal protection and animals in distress 384–85
    becoming-with 394
    burnout 386–87
    caring-killing paradox 389, 392–93
    coping identities 386–87, 392
    dissonance 385, 388–90, 391–93
    emotional challenges 384–85, 386
    emotional contagion 385–86, 391–92
    emotional taint 385–86
    empowerment 389
    euthanasia/killing 385, 386, 388, 392–93
    frontline staff and public working together 391
    Hero identity 386, 389–90
    identity framing 385, 386–87
    institutional framing 390
    moral motivations 386
    moral paradoxes 391–92
    moral taint 385–86, 393
    negative emotions 386–87, 392
    negative personal outcomes 386
    paradox 385
    physical challenges 385–86
    physical danger 385
    physical taint 385–86
    power and control, breakdown of 389
    processing plant mentality 391
    Professionals identity 386
    psychological challenges 385–86
    research methods 387–88
    resilience-training workshop 392
    resistance and discontent 388
    sensemaking of disaster for entangled human-animal wellbeing 391–93
    shelters as entangled sites of dirty work and human-animal interactions 384–86
    social taint 385–86
    stigma 384, 385–86, 392
    taints 385–86, 391
    Tourist identity 386

turnover, high 387, 391–92
unwanted and abused animals 385
Victim identity 386
wellbeing 384, 385, 389, 391, 392, 393–94
work-calling in animal dirty work 386–87
animals as labour and capital 28–38
  agency, objects and posthumanism 36–37
  commercial competitors 31–34
  domestic economy (cattle and sheep) 29–31
  wild displays 34–36
'animal spirits' 362
animal symbolism 411
'animal turn' 231
animal welfare 11, 12–13
  dairy farmer and vegan discourses on animal consumption 272–73, 277–78, 280, 281
  foundational economy 233, 234, 235–36
  veterinary work in Dutch farm animal care 288, 289, 294–96, 297, 298
  see also companion animal (CA) welfare; dog registration and One Welfare in New Zealand; husky kennels in Finland as animal welfare activists; wellbeing
Anthony, R. 156
anthroparchy 116, 125, 126
Anthropocene 2–3, 6, 8, 36, 67–68, 141, 159–60, 336, 393–94
  see also agency and responsibility paradoxes in the Anthropocene: posthumanist praxis
anthropocentrism
  biosphere management 47–49
  Covid-19, zoonotic disease and animal-industrial complex (AIC) 57–59, 64, 65, 66–67, 68, 69
  dairy farmer and vegan discourses on animal consumption 275
  dog registration and One Welfare in New Zealand 430
  dogs and space-time and labour organization in multispecies homes 115–16
  education in animal studies: critical inquiry 73–74, 76–77
  empathy, inclusion and ethics 336, 340–41
  foundational economy: infrastructures of everyday multispecies life 231
  horse-human relationships and leadership 88–89, 90–91, 96, 97
  rockpooling, affect and charisma 380
  tracking craft of the Southern African San 160
  vertebrate-centric care, honeybee bias and bee-washing 320–21
  see also anthropocentrism and industrial capitalism: industrial food systems
anthropocentrism and industrial capitalism: industrial food systems 258–69
  capitalist food system 264–68
  control 260–61, 265–66
  death 258–59, 260
  domination 258–59, 260–62, 268–69
  feed production 259–60
  force 260
  hierarchical anthropocentrism 259–60, 262, 263–65, 267–68
  intensification 259–60, 262–63, 264–67
  reproductive controls 264, 265–66
  slaughter 259–60
  torture 260
  violence, systematic 258–59, 260–63, 268–69
  war against animals 259–63
anthropogenic biomass 50
anthropogeny 60–62
anthropomorphism 155–56
anthropozootechnical agencement 74–75
antibiotics and antimicrobial resistance 290, 291, 293, 295
anti-capitalist social movements 268–69
Arcari, P. 58–59
Arendt, H. 106
Aristotle 262, 339
Arluke, A. 392–93
artificial intelligence (AI) and autonomous systems 102
Ashforth, B. 391
assemblages 160–61
assistance animals 24, 156
  see also gendered organizational cultures and dog-human partnerships
assistance dog animal charity see gendered organizational cultures and dog-human partnerships

asymmetrical animal-human
    relationships 58–60
Attenborough, D. 35
Aull Davies, C. 117
Australia 137, 235, 318
    Bureau of Statistics 285
    dairy farmer and vegan discourses on
        animal consumption 272–73, 274
    see also animal shelter in Australia: natural
        disaster and work calling; totem
        animals in Australia

B

'bad foods' 300–1, 302–3
badgers 33–35
Bak, S. 165f
Bame, R. 198
Barad, K. 132, 304, 416–17
Barney, J. 219
Baron-Cohen, S. 334
Barua, M. 131, 132
Bates, V. 104
Bear, C. 37
bears 34–35
Beck, U. 43
Belgium 95
Bell, G. 284
Benatar, D. 62, 63, 64–65
Bennett, J. 79–80, 132
Berger, J. 420–21
Berlant, L. 374
Bhattacharya, T. 266
Big Agriculture 59–60
'big hat, no cattle' *see under* animal metaphors
    and strategic human resource
    management (SHRM)
Bignall, S. 67–68
biodiversity loss 21–22, 42–43, 50–51
biomaterial practices 301–2, 303, 304–5, 306,
    307–8
biosafety crises 300
biosphere management 46–50
bird flu 64, 65–66
birds 50
Birke, L. 90, 146–47, 410, 420
Blanchard, K. 199
Bloom, P. 339–40

Blue, G. 131
bonding 442–43, 447–48, 449, 450, 453
boundary-crossing 87
Bowden, V. 63
Bowles, S. 199
Braidotti, R. 230–31
Brain, R.M. 110
Branicki, L. 399–400
Braverman, H. 419
Broussine, M. 213
BSE crisis 36
Buddle, E. 278–79
Bunderson, J. 386
Bureau of Animal Population (Canada) 31–32
burnout 386–87
'business as usual' practices 59
Butler, J. 66–67
Byrne, J. 362–63

C

Calarco, M. 160–61
Calo, C.J. 419–20
Cameron, L. 214
Canada 318, 324
Cane, J. 324
Canetti, E. 316
capitalism, accelerated 2–3
capitalist food system 264–68
capitalist modernity 31
care farms 24
care organizations *see* robotic animals in
    dementia care
care theory 147–48
caring-killing paradox 389, 392–93
Caring Vets (Netherlands) 288–89, 290, 298
Carolan, M. 324
Carson, R. 60
Cassidy, A. 33–34
cats 32
    robotic 410–12, 414–15, 417–18, 419, 420
cattle farming 7, 29–31, 37, 235, 281, 285, 296
    see also sensor technologies in cattle
        farming
Causey, A. 168
Caviola, L. 246
Center for Disease Control (CDC) (United
    States) 65–66

Cerolo, K. 197
Chakrabarty, D. 131–32
change theory (Lewin) 242, 244, 245, 249, 251, 253, 255
charisma *see* rockpooling, affect and charisma
Charles, N. 117, 118
Cheeke, P.R. 63
chickens *see* poultry farming
chicory (green manure) 306
China 22, 29–30, 62
Clark, B. 264–65
Clarke, C. 404
Clark, J. 325
Clay, N. 234
climate change 1, 2–3
   agency and responsibility paradoxes in the Anthropocene 42–44, 45, 50–51
   animal shelter in Australia: natural disaster and work calling 388
   animals as labour and capital 38
   anthropocentrism and industrial capitalism: industrial food systems 264–65
   biosphere management 47–48, 49
   Covid-19, zoonotic disease and animal-industrial complex (AIC) 60–61, 66–67
   empathy, inclusion and ethics 336, 341
   factory farming 21–22
   foundational economy: infrastructures of everyday multispecies life 227
   sensor technologies in cattle farming 109
   speciesism 245
   stockfree organic agriculture (SOA) and sustainability 300, 302, 307
   Vegan Wellbeing Project 283
close reading techniques 210–11
co-becoming 87
co-habitation with animals 87
Cole, M. 77–78
collective sense-making 197
colonialism 45–46, 53, 87–88, 170–71, 181–82, 191, 232–33, 259, 261, 272–73, 320, 419, 438
   see also neo-colonialism; postcolonialism
commercial competitors 31–34
companion animal (CA) welfare 118, 427, 431, 433–35, 438

competitive advantage 210, 211
complacency 59
Conan Doyle, A. 214
Concentrated Animal Feed Operations (CAFOs) 20–21
conceptual metaphor theory (CMT) 213, 214
consent and horse-human interactions 93, 146
conservation movement 33
conservation projects 35
contract farming 75–76
control 260–61, 265–66
Convention of Migratory Species 64–65
Cooke, F. 212
cooperation 332, 333
Cooper, R. 103, 106, 108
coping identities and mechanisms 386–87, 392, 452
corporate social responsibility (CSR) 397–98
COVID-19
   animal shelter in Australia: natural disaster and work calling 394
   anthropocentrism and industrial capitalism: industrial food systems 263
   dog registration and One Welfare in New Zealand 430
   dogs and space-time and labour organization in multispecies homes 126
   foundational economy: infrastructures of everyday multispecies life 227, 229
   husky kennels in Finland as animal welfare activists 406–7
   stockfree organic agriculture (SOA) and sustainability 308–9
COVID-19, zoonotic disease and animal-industrial complex (AIC) 57–69
   anthropogeny 60–62
   asymmetrical animal-human relationships 58–60
   knowledge/power relations 62–66
   multispecies organization 66–68
Cow Compass (CC) (Netherlands) 295–97
cows *see* dairy farming
coyotes *see* urban coyotes in United States
Creighton, E. 146–47

critical organizational phenomena 242
cruelty 116, 362
    see also suffering and violence
cultural aspects and robotic animals in dementia care 414–16, 420
cultural 'buy-in' 200–2
cultural issues and dog registration in New Zealand 427, 432, 437–38
Czarniawska, B. 353

D

Dairy Australia 284–85
dairy farmer and vegan discourses on animal consumption 272–86
    Dairy Farmers' Wellbeing Project 273, 277–81, 285
        animal activists unwilling to see life from farmers' perspective 279–80
        animal protests, hurt and disruptions caused by 280–81
        vegan activists as out-of-touch with realities of rural life 278–79
    future possibilities 284–85
    identity 276–77
    Vegan Wellbeing Project 273, 281–84, 285
        against animal cruelty 282–83
        carnism, challenging 283–84
dairy farming 22, 23, 30, 34, 37, 77–78, 265–66
    robotic milking technologies 37, 77–78, 232–34
    veterinary work in Dutch farm animal care 289, 292, 294–95
Danby, P. 145–46
Darwin, C. 371–72
Dashper, K. 93, 94
Davies, O. 313, 320
de-animalization process 77
decarbonization 49
deer 33
defending others and ourselves 243–44
Degesch (German society for pest control) 305–6
dehumanization and robotic animals 409–11, 418–20, 421
Deleuze, G. 74, 79–80, 350, 380
dementia care see robotic animals in dementia care
Denis, J.L. 92–93

Denzin, N. 212
Derrida, J. 417
Descartes, R. 334
Desmond, J. 74–75
Despret, V. 442
de Waal, F. 332
Dhont, K. 243, 246
Dickstein, J. 303
dietary problems and dairy industry 274
dining tourism 23–24
dissonance 243–44, 385, 388–90, 391–93
dirty work, 384–86, 391–92
    see also animal dirty work
distancing 76–77, 107
'dog does not bark' metaphor 214
dogfighting, illegal 411
dog registration and One Welfare in New Zealand 425–39
    animal management practice 438–39
    animal mistreatment penalties 429n.5
    behaviour change techniques 432–33
    companion animal (CA) welfare 427, 431, 433–35, 438
    costs of welfare 436–37, 438
    cultural issues 427, 432, 437–38
    Dog Control Act (1996) 436
    dog tax and Dog Tax War 425–27, 428–29
    euthanasia 432n.10
    guardian attitudes 431
    health development 429–30, 432–33
    historical approach 427
    hunting 427–28, 436, 437–38
    Kingitanga (political movement) 427
    kurī 427–29, 428f, 435–38
    Mātauranga Māori 431
    Native Department 427
    New Zealand Companion Animal Trust (NZCAT) Furry Whānau Wellbeing Research Study 432–35, 436, 437, 439
        One Welfare Project and methodologies 432–34
        One Welfare project, multiple participant types 434–35
    non-registration 436
    One Health 425–31, 437
    One Welfare Aotearoa 429–31, 436–37, 438–39

Patu Pets study (Eastern Institute of
       Technology) 431, 432–33, 434, 435, 436,
       437–39
   pet Meke Meter (wellbeing assessment
       tool) 433
   pro-equity approaches 431
   quality of life 436
   reciprocal care 431, 436
   Society for the Prevention of Cruelty to
       Animals (SPCA) 437–38
   tail docking and ear cropping 437–38
   Te Whare Tapa Whā model 429–30
   Tikanga Māori 431
   wellbeing 429–30, 432–33
dogs 30–31
   puppy breeding industry 116
   rescue dogs 116
   robotic animals 410–12, 414–15, 418
   see also animal shelter in Australia:
       natural disaster and work calling;
       dog registration and One Welfare
       in New Zealand; dogs and space-
       time and labour organization in
       multispecies homes; gendered
       organizational cultures and dog-
       human partnerships
dogs and space-time and labour organization
       in multispecies homes 115–26
   anthroparchy 116, 125, 126
   community, sense of 121
   doggy day care 123–24
   dog walking 116–17
   homeworking 126
   home and work, organization of 122–25
   household connectivity 121
   household damage 119
   invitation, exclusion and disturbance
       triad 125–26
   outside activities: time, space and
       walking 118–22
   private space, organization of 117–18
   reciprocal care 121
   reproductive labour 124, 125
   separation anxiety 124, 125, 126
   smells 119–20
   socializing and friendships 120–22
   spatial organization 120
   walking, temporalized and
       spatialized 121–22
   working time, space and species 125–26
domination
   anthropocentrism and industrial
       capitalism: industrial food
       systems 258–59, 260–62, 268–69
   dairy farmer and vegan discourses on
       animal consumption 275, 285–86
   dogs and space-time and labour organization
       in multispecies homes 116
   horse-human interactions 88, 89–90, 146
   see also anthroparchy
dominionistic attitudes 132–33
Donaldson, S. 335
Doré, A. 74–75, 115–16
Dowling, R. 197
Dukat, C. 416, 418
Durie, Sir M. 429–30
Dutkiewicz, J. 303

E
East Africa 34–35
EAT-Lancet commission 301–2, 308
eco feminist research
   agency and responsibility paradoxes in the
       Anthropocene 46
   anthropocentrism and industrial
       capitalism: industrial food
       systems 264, 266–67
   dogs and space-time and labour organization
       in multispecies homes 115–16
   empathy, inclusion and ethics 333–34
   horse-human relationships and
       leadership 90–91
   human-mosquito encounters in tourism
       settings 313
   vertebrate-centric care, honeybee bias and
       bee-washing 316, 320
ecological degradation and crises
   agency and responsibility paradoxes in the
       Anthropocene 45
   biosphere management 49–50
   foundational economy: infrastructures of
       everyday multispecies life 227
   tracking craft of the Southern African
       San 159–60

eco-social reproduction 24–25
ecosophical approach 67–68
education in animal studies: critical
    inquiry 73–81
    animal-industrial complex (AIC) 74–80
ego 244
Eilert, M. 400
Ellis, W. 169
Elton, C. 31–32
emergent ecologies 160–61
emotional labour/emotional
    connection 447–48, 450–53
empathy 170, 246–47, 251, 254
    embodied 168–69, 337–38
    factory farming 19–20
    horse-human interactions 148
    Olly the Cat and Manchester Airport
        Group 355–56
    see also empathy, inclusion and ethics
empathy, inclusion and ethics 331–41
    affective empathy 338
    cognitive empathy 337
    embodied empathy 337–38
    empathy 331–35
    empathy as superficial pretence 336
    moral agency 336–37, 338, 339
    moral considerations 334–35
    morality 332, 333, 334, 339–40
    moral judgements 332, 334–35
    moral rights 335
    organizational empathy 335–36
    prejudiced empathy 339–41
    projective empathy 340
    pro-social behaviour 331–33, 334, 335, 336, 339
    reflective empathy 338–39, 340–41
    simulative empathy 340
    social and moral benefits of empathy 331
    varieties of empathy 336–39, 337f
    wellbeing 331, 333, 334, 335–36, 340–41
Emschwiller, C. 206–7
Enclosure movement 29
environmental impacts/degradation
    agency and responsibility paradoxes in the
        Anthropocene 45
    anthropocentrism and industrial capitalism:
        industrial food systems 264–65

dairy industry 274
speciesism 245
Vegan Wellbeing Project 283
veterinary work in Dutch farm animal
    care 288
see also ecological degradation and crises
environmental sustainability 1, 22, 42–44
ethical issues
    agency and responsibility paradoxes in the
        Anthropocene 43–44, 50–51, 52–53
    animal companion industry 394
    animal shelter in Australia: natural disaster
        and work calling 384
    animals as labour and capital 28–29, 32, 33–34
    dairy farmer and vegan discourses on
        animal consumption 272–73
    dog registration and One Welfare in New
        Zealand 432n.10, 437–38
    education in animal studies: critical
        inquiry 74–75, 79–80
    factory farming 17, 18, 19–20, 22, 23, 25
    gendered organizational cultures and dog-
        human partnerships 446, 453
    horse-human interactions 156
    horse-human relationships and
        leadership 88, 93, 94, 96, 97–98
    husky kennels in Finland as animal welfare
        activists 397, 398, 399–401, 403, 405–7
    situational 38
    speciesism 242, 245, 246–47, 251, 254, 255
    stockfree organic agriculture (SOA) and
        sustainability 303
    tracking craft of the Southern African
        San 171
    Vegan Wellbeing Project 282
    vegetarianism 243
    vertebrate-centric care, honeybee bias and
        bee-washing 313–14, 320–22, 325–26
    veterinary work in Dutch farm animal
        care 288–89, 290, 291, 297
    see also empathy, inclusion and ethics
Europe 22, 29–30, 49, 117, 235–36
euthanasia
    animal shelter in Australia: natural disaster
        and work calling 385, 386, 388, 392–93
    husky kennels in Finland as animal welfare
        activists 397, 399, 402–3, 404, 405

exceptionalism 59, 88, 89–90
exploitation 90–91, 146
eyewitnessing 76–77

F

factory farming 17–25
  anthropocentrism and industrial capitalism: industrial food systems 265
  contextual aspects 18–20
  critical data 20–22
  education in animal studies: critical inquiry 75
  empathy, inclusion and ethics 341
  generative thinking 23–25
  speciesism 243, 247
family farming 23–24
farmed fish 259–60
farming *see* agribusiness; cattle farming; dairy farming; factory farming; fur farming/fur trade; livestock industry; pig farming; poultry farming; sheep farming; veterinary work in Dutch farm animal care
Farmonline 284
farms without fences 181–82, 189–90
feed conversion rates 266–67
feed production 259–60
feline ethnography in business and management studies *see* Olly the Cat and Manchester Airport Group
Fernández, L. 245
fertilizers 234, 301, 304, 305–8
Finkel, R. 145–46
Finland 89, 93, 94
  see also husky kennels in Finland as animal welfare activists
Food and Agriculture Organization (FAO) 259–60
  Livestock's Long Shadow report 302
food animals: structural position 267–68
food-biodiversity-biosafety complex 308–9
food consumption 10
food production 10, 20–21, 75, 77, 79, 288, 300, 317–18
food safety 290, 294, 295, 296, 298
Foot and Mouth Disease outbreak (UK) 36, 298

foraging/hunting-gathering 20–21
force 260
Ford, H. 349–50
Fordist division of labour 76–77
Foster, C. 169
Foster, J.B. 264–65
Foucault, M. 261–62, 352, 362–63, 412–14
foundational economy: infrastructures of everyday multispecies life 227–38
  dairy farming and milking machines 232–34
  future research directions 236–38
  rare breeds and provenance 234–36
Foundational Economy Challenge Fund (Wales) 230
Foundational Economy Collective 231–32
four N's 247, 278–79
foxes 33–35
France 101–2, 103, 106, 107–10
Freud, A. 245
Fudge, E. 168–69
fur farming/fur trade 31–32, 58–59, 79

G

Gabb, J. 118
Gallai, N. 317–18
game birds 31–32
Garfinkel, H. 361
Garibaldi, L. 319
gender and dog registration and One Welfare in New Zealand 432, 434
gendered organizational cultures and dog-human partnerships 116–17, 442–53
  ambivalence 442
  animal assistance dogs charity (feminized organization) 442–43, 444–45, 446
  bonding 442–43, 447–48, 449, 450, 453
  coping mechanisms 452
  describing partnerships 449–50
  dogs as active partners 448–49
  dogs as family members 449
  emotional labour/emotional connection 447–48, 450–53
  gendered organizations 444–46
  German Shepherds 444–45
  group loyalty 446–47
  instrumentalizing affect 452–53

gendered organizational cultures and dog-human partnerships (*cont.*)
   neutering policy 445, 446
   police dogs (masculinized organization) 442, 444–45, 446, 453
   provisional partnerships 450–51
   reallocation of unsuitable dogs 449, 450
   researching dog training cultures 443–44
   responsibility 448
   risk and care cultures 446–47, 453
   storytelling 446–47
   training 444–45, 446, 447–48, 449
   transitions pre-pairing 450
   trust 449
   wellbeing, physical and emotional 451
gendered, racialized and power dynamics of human-animal relationships 89–90
gender inequality 45, 46, 53
gender relations and totem animals in Australia 189
generative thinking 23–25
geo-engineering 47–48, 53
geographical indications (GI) schemes 235–36
Gherardi, S. 379–80, 384
Giacon, J. 183
Gibb, R.W.J. Jr. 213
Giedion, S. 76
Gillespie, K. 264
glass horse metaphor 95
global biomass 50
'good foods' 300–1, 302–3, 306, 307
Graham, J.E. 197
Gray, J. 359, 361–62
graylag geese near Schiphol Airport 130–31
green care 24
'green growth' thinking 49–50
green jobs 23
Green New Deal agendas 49, 51, 53
Greger, M. 62, 64
Gressier, C. 235
gross domestic product (GDP) 229–30
Guattari, F. 74, 79–80, 350, 380
Guenther, M. 164, 167, 169, 171
guide dogs 442, 444–45
Gung Ho culture *see under* animal metaphor use and workplace interactions 194–207

H

Haber-Bosch process 305
Haber, F. 305–6
Hadid, Z. 359
hailed-as-symbols-of-the-wilderness charismatic megafauna 33
Halfacre, A.C.H. 104
Half-Earth proposals 48, 53
Hamilton, L. 105, 276, 406–7
Hamington, M. 155–56
Hannah, D.R. 145
Haraway, D.J. 132, 161, 168, 170–71, 212, 219, 350, 352, 399, 410–14, 417, 442
Harguess, J. 245
harm, normalized 21
Harvey, D. 264–65
Hawthorne studies 211–12, 220
Hayward, E. 417
health and safety in factory farming 21–22
Held, V. 320–21
Herman, A. 104
Herriman, G. 358
Heslop, J. 230
hierarchical anthropocentrism 259–60, 262, 263–65, 267–68, 446
high-performance work systems (HPWS) and managerial perceptions of HR departments 211, 217–19
Hillier, J. 362–63
Hochschild, A. 419
Hockenhull, J. 90, 146–47
Hodson, G. 246
Holloway, L. 37, 77–78, 104
Homer 262
honeybees *see* vertebrate-centric care and honeybee bias and bee-washing
horse-human interactions 145–56
   caring imagination 155
   embodied caring knowledge 155
   ethic of care approach 156
   Listening Guide method 146–48, 156
     'I' in text 148, 152–53
     memory writing 148
     plot of the narrative 147–48
     voices of relationship 148
   Listening Guide in practice 148–52
     first listening 149

    fourth listening 152
    second listening 149–51
    third listening 151
  responsiveness and bodily actions 155
  voice poems 148, 150–51, 152–54, 155–56
  'voicing' animals 146–47
horse-human relationships and leadership 87–98
  body language, gestures and affective moods 97–98
  body language, movements and gestures 87–88, 93
  care, gentleness and respect 97–98
  celebrity horses 91–92
  conceptualization 89–91
  dressage 90–91
  feelings, emotions and intentions 90
  horse-assisted leadership learning 92
  horse handling sessions 92
  join-up and follow-up exercises 87–88
  masculine leadership 88–89
  mental health improvement 90n.2
  methodological considerations 93
  more-than-human leadership 93–96
    mismatchings 96
    relational co-being and listening to horse in multispecies leadership 94–95
    taking the side of the horse 95–96
  nonverbal, affective aspects 97
  prior experiences, personalities and characters 90
  relationality 89–91, 93
  relational leadership 88, 89, 93–94, 96, 97
  relational leadership and posthuman or more-than-human leadership 91–93
  riding 90–91
  sensory attention and relational listening 94
  therapeutic riding and physical disabilities 90n.2
  trust and mutual understanding 94
  verbal language, dialogue and conversation 92–93, 97
horsemeat scandal 36
horseracing industry 79
horticulture 20–21, 24
Hosking, D.M. 183n.2, 184, 191

Hudson Bay Company 31–32
humane jobs 23
Hume, D. 332, 337, 338, 339–40
Hung, L. 415
Huopalainen, A. 406–7
husky kennels in Finland as animal welfare activists 397–407
  adoption programmes 404–5
  all-year-round kennels 398
  animal husbandry tasks 399
  Animal Welfare Act 398, 399
  animal welfare corporate activism as care 399–401
  barriers to welfare activism 403–4
  communication, trust and collaboration 398–99
  customer services 399
  dog sledding as multispecies business 398–99
  educating consumers 404–5
  emotional relationships 402
  ethical issues 397, 398, 399–401, 403, 405–7
  euthanasia 397, 399, 402–3, 404, 405
  exercise plans 404–5
  institutionalization of ethical sled dog practices 404–5
  legal protection, lack of for working dogs 403
  methodology 401–2
  no-kill policies 399, 404–5, 406–7
  outdoor kennels 398
  owner-managers and close relationships with dogs 402–3
  permanent and seasonal workers 398
  political struggle 402
  rehoming and adoption programmes, opposition to 404
  retirement 399
  rightist perspective 400
  running circle chains 398
  safety rules and procedures 398–99
  summer exercising 397, 404
  temporary kennels 398
  welfare activists 400, 402–3, 404–6
  working life of husky dependent on strength and motivation 399
  working shifts and resting periods 399

I

id 244
identity and dairy farmer and vegan discourses on animal consumption 276–77
Ijäs, M. 164
inclusion *see* empathy, inclusion and ethics
incorporation of animal life 77
Indigenous philosophies 67–68
industrial capitalism 49
industrialization 29, 31, 34
industrial revolution 28–29
industry standards 22
insects *see* vertebrate-centric care and honeybee bias and bee-washing
institutional theory 398
institutional vertebratism 316–18
intellectualization 244, 255
intensification 34, 58–59, 61, 258, 302
  industrial food systems 259–60, 262–63, 264–67
interrelationships 198
interspecies solidarity 19–20, 197
'invented needs' 59–60
Irvine, L. 388

J

Japan 409–10, 414
Johnsen, R. 393–94
Johnson, E. 416–17
Johnstone, M.A. 68
Jones, O. 109
justice 12–13, 18, 384, 394
  economic and social 49
  environmental 45, 46, 53
  racial and global 22

K

Karlsson, F. 155–56
Kaufman, B. 211n.1
Kavanagh, D. 107
Keynes, J.M. 362
killing
  anthropocentrism and industrial capitalism: industrial food systems 259–60
  dog registration and One Welfare in New Zealand 432n.10

economic rationalization 386
industrial food systems 258–59, 260
see also caring-killing paradox; euthanasia; slaughterhouses
Kim, C.J. 259
King, C. 428
King-Eveillard, F. 109
Kirksey, E. 160, 373–74
Knight, C. 197
Knights, D. 404
knowledge
  aboutness 183n.2
  absence of 62, 63
  discovering 182–84
  -making sensory practices 106
  politics 4
  and power relations 62–66
  practices 105
  production 75
  situated 212
  suppression 63
Kosut, M. 313
Kuch, D. 107–8
Kurz, T. 303–4
Kymlicka, W. 335

L

Labatut, J. 74–75, 195, 275
labour process theory 17–18
Langley, A. 92–93
Lathrop, A. 32
Latour, B. 42–43, 168, 170–71, 195, 196, 201–2, 361, 416–17
Law, J. 298
leadership *see* horse-human relationships and leadership
Leeson, C. 419
Lefebvre, H. 105
legume family and nitrogen cycle 306
Leite, A.C. 246
Lennerfors, T.T. 74–75
Leopold, A. 33
Levi Martin, J. 115
Lévi-Strauss, C. 411
Lewin, K. 242, 244, 245, 249, 251, 253, 255
Liebenberg, L. 161–62, 164, 167, 169–70, 172
lion metaphor 201–2

livestock industry 23, 36–38–, 50, 51, 64, 411
   precision livestock farming (PLF) 102, 108–9
'Livestock's Long Shadow' 301–2
Lloro, T. 140–41
Lorimer, J. 372–73, 375–76, 377
Lovelock, J. 60–61
'Lucy the Human Chimp' 206
Lugli, A. 379–80

M

McCombie, W. 30
Macfarlane, R. 160, 161
McHugh, S. 415–16
MacIvor, J. 319–20
Mack, K.S. 104
MacLure, M. 379–80
Macpherson-Grant, Sir G. 30
Maitlis, S. 386–87
Manchester Airport Group *see* Olly the Cat and Manchester Airport Group
manure, green 306–7
Marshall, J. 401
Marxist view of labour exploitation 266–67
Marx, K. 258–59, 266–68, 418–19
masculinist organizational culture 320, 442, 444–45, 446, 453
mass species extinctions 2, 21–22, 43, 264–65, 301–2, 336, 341
Mather, J. 325–26
matsutake mushrooms tracking 160–61, 164, 168, 169, 170–71
Mayo, E. 211
May, R. 316–17
Mazzucato, M. 229, 234–35, 236
meat consumption, global per capita 266
Meat and Livestock Australia 285
meat production *see* livestock industry
mechanomorphism 334
Medlock, K. 360
Meijer, E. 130–31
Metaphor Conceptual Frame (MCF) 212
mice 34
Michalko, R. 442–43, 450
Michalon, J. 74–75, 115–16
Midgley, M. 333–35
'missing masses' 201–2

Mitchell, Sir T. 181–82, 189–90
Mol, A. 196
Molloy, B. 354–55
Monbiot, G. 24–25
Moore, J. 264–65, 266
Moore, L. 313
Moore, M. 60–61
moral agency 336–37, 338, 339
moral issues
   animal metaphors 203
   animal shelter in Australia: natural disaster and work calling 386, 391–92
   dairy farmer and vegan discourses on animal consumption 272–73, 274
   empathy and inclusion 332, 333, 334–35, 339–40
   industrial food systems 260
   Vegan Wellbeing Project 282
   vertebrate-centric care, honeybee bias and bee-washing 313–14
   see also ethical issues
moral judgements 332, 334–35
moral lens 196–97, 198, 201–2
moral reasoning 210
moral rights 335
moral shock 245, 281
moral taint 385–86, 393
moral theory 197
moral worth 202
Morris, C. 104
Morrison, R.L. 198–99
Mouret, S. 450
multispecies turn 161
Munro, I. 74–75
Myburgh, P.J. 164
'Myth of Wild Africa' narrative 36

N

Napoli, J. 282
Nappier Cherup, A. 400
National Health and Research Council of Australia - Code for the Care and Use of Animals 321
natural history programming 35–36
Natural Resource Use Programming (Sweden) 80
negativistic attitudes 132–33

neglect 116
neo-colonialism 45, 46, 48–49, 53
neo-Keynesian sustainability measures 49–50
Netherlands 233–34
　Food and Consumer Safety Authority (NVWA) 288, 295, 296
　see also veterinary work in Dutch farm animal care
neutering policy 445, 446
New Zealand 272–73
　see also dog registration and One Welfare in New Zealand
New Zealand Companion Animal Trust (NZCAT) Furry Whānau Wellbeing Research Study see under dog registration and One Welfare in New Zealand
Nimmo, R. 107
Nippert-Eng, C. 168
Noddings, N. 155
no-kill policies 399, 404–5, 406–7
non-governmental organizations (NGOs) 69, 76–77
North America 22, 29–30
Norway 24, 104
Noske, B. 19, 20–21, 75–76, 77, 79
Nussbaum, M. 229–31

O

objectification and horse-human interactions 146
objects of care 290–91
occupational identity 411
O'Doherty, D.P. 133–34, 275, 285–86, 380–81
Offringa, C. 290
Olly the Cat and Manchester Airport Group 197, 285–86, 349–63
　agency and autonomy (Olly) 361–62
　attachment to Olly 356–57
　breakdown of organization 356–58
　care and empathy 355–56
　carnival and parody 352–54
　cat committee and fan mail 354–55
　cat meme phenomenon 362–63
　celebrity status 352–53
　commercial and economic cost-benefit 356–57
　Facebook account 354–55, 356–57
　feline memeplex 358
　food and bedding donations and gift-giving 354–55
　health and wellbeing concerns 357–58
　hybrid human-cat assemblage 360–62
　lolcats and lolspeak 358
　love and hate relationships with Olly 356–57
　management incredulity and undecidability 359–60
　Olly's house 351–52
　Olympic House entrance 351–52
　origin myth 353
　postcards 354–55, 356–57
　promotion of airport and brand 356–57
　publicity and press interest 356–57
　teaching people to care 354–56
　Vector Design Concepts and new Olly house 359–60, 361–62
One Health (New Zealand) 24, 425–31, 437
One Welfare Aotearoa see under dog registration and One Welfare in New Zealand
ontology 182
　blending 164
　mutability 163–64, 163f
oppression and horse-human interactions 146
organizational culture 198–99
Organizational Zoo 198, 200
Organization for Economic Cooperation and Development (OECD) - Environmental Outlook (2012) 227
Orwell, G. 378
Ouschan, R. 282
Owler, K. 198–99
ownership and horse-human interactions 146
oxen 29

P

Pachirat, T. 76–77
Packer, L. 319–20
Pasco, E. 353–54
Patel, R. 264–65, 266
Patu Pets study see under dog registration and One Welfare in New Zealand
Pauchard, A. 167

Persson, M. 420
pesticides 42–43, 305–6, 307–8
Peters, T. 198–99
pet food industry and meat-based
    products 59–60, 64
pets 30–31, 36, 37–38, 118
  puppy breeding industry 116
  see also cats; dogs
Pfadenhauer, M. 416, 418
pharmaceutical industry 79
phenomenal consciousness 334–35
Philo, C. 119
Piazza, J. 246, 278–79
Pierce, C. 78
pig farming 22, 29–30, 75, 265–66, 276–77, 285
  veterinary work in Dutch farm animal
    care 289, 290, 293, 294–95
Pinker, S. 198
planetary boundaries 44–45
plant-based foods 23–24, 234
  see also veganism
Plumwood, V. 262
police dogs 197
  see also gendered organizational cultures
    and dog-human partnerships
pollution 60, 109
postcolonialism 4, 36, 261, 438
post-growth or de-growth models 51
posthumanist perspective
  animal shelter in Australia: natural disaster
    and work calling 387, 392, 393–94
  animals as labour and capital 28, 36–37
  anthropocentrism and industrial
    capitalism: industrial food
    systems 259, 266–67
  Covid-19, zoonotic disease and animal-
    industrial complex (AIC) 67
  foundational economy: infrastructures of
    everyday multispecies life 227–28,
    230–31, 234
  horse-human relationships and
    leadership 88, 89–90, 96
  robotic animals in dementia care 410–11, 416
  stockfree organic agriculture (SOA) and
    sustainability 304, 306, 308–9
  see also agency and responsibility paradoxes in
    the Anthropocene: posthumanist praxis

poultry farming 22, 29, 30, 34, 50, 77
power relations 77–78, 116
  dairy farmer and vegan discourses on
    animal consumption 275, 285–86
  horse-human relationships and
    leadership 90–91, 92–93, 97–98
Precht, R.D. 246–47
precision livestock farming (PLF) 102, 108–9
Preston model for community
    wealth-building 230
'Preventing the Next Pandemic Zoonotic
    Diseases and How to Break the Chain
    of Transmission' report 61
Prins, F.E. 162
Proctor, R.N. 62 , –63, 64–65, 66
pro-social behaviour 331–33, 334, 335, 336, 339
pro-social guilt 331–32
providential domain 228–29
psychoanalytical theory of defence
    mechanisms (Freud) 242, 244–45, 251,
    253, 255
public interest in nature and wild animals 35
puppy breeding industry 116

Q

quality assurance schemes 290, 295
Quammen, D. 61
Quinn, C.E. 104

R

Rader, K. 32
Raffles, H. 316
Raffnsøe, S. 92, 94
Rantala, O. 313
rare breeds and provenance 234–36
rationalization 244, 251, 255–56
Raworth, K. 230
reciprocity 137, 190, 192, 360–61, 414, 418, 431
Redmalm, D. 91–92
reflexive ignorance 65–66
refreezing 245, 249, 255
Regan, T. 335
registration practices 294–95
  see also dog registration and One Welfare in
    New Zealand
relational constructivism 180–81, 183, 186,
    191, 192

relational meaning 198
relational ontology 180–81
relational system 196–97
relearning 161
Repka, M. 79
repressive authenticity 162
reproductive controls 264, 265–66
rescue dogs 116
resilience-training workshop 392
resistance 362–63
Resource-Based View 211
respect and totem animals in Australia 180, 183–84, 192
responsibility *see* agency and responsibility paradoxes in the Anthropocene: posthumanist praxis
rewilding 24–25, 51
Riach, K. 313, 320
risks, calculated 64
Ritvo, H. 30–31
Robertson, K. 145
robotic animals in dementia care 409–21
  actors, robotic animals as 416–18
  Aibo (robotic dog) 414–15
  alienation 418–19
  animality 410–14, 418–19, 420
  calming device or entertainment 410
  cats 410–12, 414–15, 417–18, 419, 420
  companion species 410–14
  cultural aspects 414–16, 420
  dehumanization 409–11, 418–20, 421
  design and materiality 416, 418–19
  dogs 410–12, 414–15, 418
  entrapment 419, 420
  evocative objects 416
  humanizing effect 420
  intra-actions 416–17
  Joy for All Cat 413*f*
  Joy for All Companion Pets 419–20
  Joy for All Pup 412, 413*f*, 417–18
  JustoCat 420
  materiality 410–11
  misogynist connections 415–16
  Paro (robot seal) 409–10, 414, 415, 416, 418, 419–20
  partial self-deception 419–20
  Pepper (humanoid robot) 414
  role as actor 420
  seals 410–12
  social robots 109, 409–10
  tools evoking memories of companion animals 410
  uncanny valley effect 414–15
  unconditional love 412–14, 417–18
  unpredicted, erratic or random responses, desire for 417–18
robotic technologies in farming 37, 77–78, 101–10
rockpooling, affect and charisma 368–81
  aesthetic charisma 372–73
  affect 369–71, 378–80
  charisma 370–71, 374, 378, 379–81
  conviviality with charismatic creatures 371–74
  corporeal charisma 372–73, 375–76
  deterritorialization and reterritorialization 380
  ecological charisma 372–73
  exploratory playfulness 378
  felt feeling 370–71
  flagship or target species 373–74
  lateral drift 377–78
  maritime legends 375–76, 377, 378
  organizational symbolism 369–70
  physical features 369–70
  pigs, rats and salmon as signs of foreboding 376–77
  rockpools as material-semiotic assemblages 369–70, 380
  rockpools as 'wunderkammer' 378–81
  seaweed tentacles, solitude and fear of drowning 374–78
  sensory attractions 374
rodent control 32
rodents for experiments and testing 32
Rollin, B. 291
Rorty, A. 339
Royal Dutch Veterinary Association (KNMvD) 288–90
Royal Society for the Prevention of Cruelty to Animals (UK) 357–58
Rural Skills Australia 285
Rutherford, S. 141

S

Sagarin, R. 167
Sage, D. 125-26
Salmela, T. 313
Sandbrook, C. 36
Sanders, C.R. 442, 448
Sang, K. 197
Saunders, M. 318
Sauvagnargues, A. 78-79, 81
Sayer, K. 32
Sayers, J. 75, 81, 276-77, 285-86
Scarry, R. 115
Schabram, K. 386-87
Scheibinger, L. 62
Schjelderup-Ebbe, T. 34
Schlosberg, D. 131-32
Schön 214
Schopenhauer, A. 338
Schuurman, N. 94-95
Schwartz, B. 274
Scientific Management 211
Scott, R. 420-21
Seddon, R. 426f
self-responsibility 202, 203
Sen, A. 230-31
'Sensemaking in Organizations' course 171
sensor technologies in cattle farming 101-10
    different senses at work 105-6
    imaginaries of the absurd 108-10
    modern sensorium 106-8
    senses and sensory practices 103-4
Sergi, V. 92-93
Serres, M. 170, 174
Seymour, M. 307
sharing economies and mutual aid 230
sheep farming 29-31, 285
Shelley (founder of Organizational Zoo) 198, 201-2
Shibata, T. 415
Sinclair, I. 353
Sinclair, U. 76-77
Singer, P. 265
singularity 314, 321-22, 323, 325-26
Skinner, W. 215-17
Skoglund, A. 91-92
Sköldberg, K. 169-70
Sköld, D. 74-75

slaughterhouses 21-22, 64, 103, 115-16, 235-36, 243, 247, 251, 392
    education in animal studies: critical inquiry 76-77
    mechanized facilities 20-21
    occupational identity 411
    and routinization of animal death 276
    veterinary work in Dutch farm animal care 294-95
Smart, A. 61
smart algorithms 107
Smart, J. 61
Smith, A. 332-33, 336-37
Smith, T. 318
Snell 218
social consequences and animals as labour and capital 28-29
social desirability bias 253
social interaction 198, 332
social movements 69
social pressures 253-54
social relations 267-68
social reproduction 266-67
Society for the Prevention of Cruelty to Animals (SPCA) (New Zealand) 437-38
socio-ecological transformation/crisis 46, 47, 49, 52-53
speciesism 241-56
    anthropocentrism and industrial capitalism: industrial food systems 265
    baseline measures 248f
    change theory (Lewin) 242, 244, 245, 249, 251, 253, 255
    changing 245
    Covid-19, zoonotic disease and animal-industrial complex (AIC) 58, 68, 69
    defending others and ourselves 243-44
    findings and discussion 249-55
    how change happens 245
    methods - speciesism scale 246
    overview results 250f
    psychoanalytical theory of defence mechanisms 242, 244-45, 251, 253, 254-55
    psychological approach to social and organizational problem 242

speciesism (cont.)
 refreezing 245, 249, 255
 research process 246–47
 unfreezing 245, 249, 251, 253, 255
'species turn' 159–60, 161
Spencer, S. 432n.10
Srinivasa, K. 130
Stander, P.E. 167
status symbols, animals as 411, 420–21
Staunæs, D. 92, 94
Stein, E. 337–38
sterilization 432
Stibbe, A. 276–77
stigma in animal shelter in Australia 384, 385–86, 392
stockfree organic agriculture (SOA) and sustainability 300–9
 approaching veganism as practice not identity 303–4
 'bad foods' 300–1, 302–3
 biomaterial practices 301–2, 303, 304–5, 306, 307–8
 'good foods' 300–1, 302–3, 306, 307
 'Livestock's Long Shadow' 301–2
 omitting violent food practices 305–7
 towards stockfree food practices 307–9
storytelling 212, 213, 216, 220, 446–47
strategic human resource management (SHRM) *see* animal metaphors and strategic human resource management (SHRM)
Strathern, M. 352–53
subject-to-eradication-programmes (vermin) 33
subordination 362
subsistence farming 20–21
Suen, A. 146
suffering and violence 22, 90–91, 242–43, 245, 255
 routinized 276–77
 systematic violence 258–59, 260–63, 268–69
super-ego 244, 255
sustainability 1, 5, 6, 11, 230, 288
 environmental 1
 factory farming 23
 future 102

global 318
neo-Keynesian 49–50
socio-ecological 49
vertebrate-centric care, honeybee bias and bee-washing 318, 319–20
see also stockfree organic agriculture (SOA) and sustainability
sympoiesis 161

T
Tallberg, L. 406–7
Taylorism 211–12
Taylor, N. 105, 276
teamwork 201–2
Tepedino, V. 324
Thaxton, Y.V. 64
Thomas, K. 30–31
Thompkins, B. 30
Thompson, J. 386
Tomaselli, K. 162
Topsell, E. 29
torture 260
totem animals in Australia 179–92
 action, knowing how and script knowledge distinctions 179
 biiwii-lizards and biiwii-humans 185, 188, 190
 Burruguu (the Creation) and Rainbow Serpent story 184–86
 Community of Communities (CoC) 181, 182, 188, 191–92
 Crane and the Crow, The 186–88, 187*f*
 farms without fences 181–82, 189–90
 fish and crustaceans 189–90
 inter-acting respectfully: Law story 186, 190*t*
 kangaroo totem collective 190
 kinship 188
 knowledge, discovering 182–84
 Kurrajong tree planting 189
 'Law Book' (scripts) 183
 Law collectives 189
 Law totems 185
 Longnecked turtle 185
 Marriage Law collective 188, 189, 191–92
 Nhunggabarra Law stories 180, 181, 182
 Nhunggabarra people 181–82, 188, 191–92

organizing respectfully with collectives 188
respect 180, 183–84, 192
sand goanna 179, 180f, 185–86
symmetrical reciprocity 190, 192
winanga (covering both knowledge and respect) 183
tracking craft of the Southern African San 159–74
   bodily and sensory nature of 164
   interpreting spoor 169–70
   lion spoor 166f
   Observation, Becoming with and Reflexivity (OBR) learning cycle 167–73
   reflexivity 167
   relational connectedness 167
   sensemaking 172
   sympathy bond between hunter and hunted 167
   wildness 159–67
   wild pedagogy 170–73
   wild way forward 173–74
transformative goals 18
Tronto, J. 320–21
trust 94–95, 203–4, 332
Tsing, A. 160–61, 164, 168, 169, 170–71
Tuan, Y.F. 106
Tucker, A. 361–62
Twine, R. 59, 74n.1, 75–76
Tyler, T. 259
Tyson Foods (United States) 21

U

Uhl-Bien, M. 91, 92
unconditional love 412–14, 417–18
unfreezing 245, 249, 251, 253, 255
United Kingdom 160
   animals as labour and capital 31–32, 33–35, 36
   biosphere management 49
   dogs and space-time and labour organization in multispecies homes 117–18, 124, 125, 126
   domestic economy (cattle and sheep) 29–30
   foundational economy: infrastructures of everyday multispecies life 232–33
   sensor technologies in cattle farming 101–2, 103, 106, 107–10

   see also gendered organizational cultures and dog-human partnerships; Olly the Cat and Manchester Airport Group; rockpooling, affect and charisma
United Nations Environment Programme (UNEP) 61, 64–66
United States
   animals as labour and capital 34–35
   anthropocentrism and industrial capitalism: industrial food systems 265–66
   biosphere management 49
   Bureau of Biological Survey 33
   Covid-19, zoonotic disease and animal-industrial complex (AIC) 64
   education in animal studies: critical inquiry 76–77
   foundational economy: infrastructures of everyday multispecies life 235
   One Health 430
   see also gendered organizational cultures and dog-human partnerships; urban coyotes in United States
universality 314, 321–23, 324–26
unlearning 161
urban coyotes in United States 129–41
   apex predators 132–33
   attacks on young children 133
   Buena Vista Park Coyotes (BVPC) Facebook group 134
   conflict-prevention perspective 134–35
   cooperation and reciprocity 137
   dog-coyote interactions 136
   Eastern coyotes (coywolves) 138, 141
   eco-political challenges 133–34
   feeding coyotes 136
   Friends of the Wissahickon (FOTW) Facebook page 138–39
   hospitality and mutual respect 141
   injuries 135
   interspecies etiquette 134–35, 137
   leash-walking etiquette 136–37
   multispecies hospitality and neighbourliness 133–34
   physical risks to adult humans 133
   predation on free-roaming cats 134–35
   predator paradox 137

urban coyotes in United States (*cont.*)
   responsible pet-keeping practices 140
   social media images and living well with urban coyotes 132–40
      Buena Vista Park, San Francisco 134–38, 141
      Wissahickon Valley, Philadelphia 138–40, 141
   territorial disputes with dogs 134–35
   territoriality 134, 135–36
   virtual contact zones and more-than representational visual methodologies 131–32
urbanization 30, 31
Utter, A. 307

V

Valtonen, A. 313
value orientation 290
Varner, G. 117, 118
veganism 10, 11, 58–59, 64–65, 69
   global rise in 272–73
   speciesism 244, 245, 247, 251, 253, 254
   see also dairy farmer and vegan discourses on animal consumption; stockfree organic agriculture (SOA) and sustainability
Vegan Organic Network (VON) 305, 306
vegan organizations 69
Vegan Wellbeing Project *see under* dairy farmer and vegan discourses on animal consumption
vegaphobia 303–4
vermin 31, 33, 38
vertebrate-centric care and honeybee bias and bee-washing 313–26
   bee-friendliness 319–20
   'bee-friendly' products and services 319
   beehives 319–20
   bee hotels 313–14, 319–20, 323–24
   bee saving initiatives 319–20
   bee-washing 313–14, 319–21, 323, 325
   Colony Collapse Disorder (CCD) 318
   commercial honeybee pollination 313
   crop pollination 317–18
   European honeybee 317–18
   flowering plant seeds 319–20
   honeybee bias 313–14, 319–20, 323, 325
   honeybees 317–20
   honey production 317–18
   insects and organizations 314–17
   institutional vertebratism 316–18
   invasive insects 317
   negative perceptions 314–16
   North American honeybee 318
   rooftop hives 313–14, 324–25
   singularity 314, 321–22, 323, 325–26
   universality 314, 321–23, 324–26
   urban beekeeping 313
   vertebrate chauvinism 316–17, 321
   vertebratism 316
   wild and managed bees 317–18
vertebrate chauvinism 316–17, 321
vertebratism 316–18
veterinary education 79–80
veterinary work in Dutch farm animal care 288–98
   Caring Vets 288–89, 290, 298
   Cow Compass (CC) 295–97
   improvement through advice 292–94
   improvement through inspection 294–97
   livestock production 290–92
   Netherlands Food and Consumer Safety Authority (NVWA) 288, 295, 296
   Royal Dutch Veterinary Association (KNMvD) 288–90
Vince, R. 213
violence *see* suffering and violence
viruses and totem animals in Australia 181–82
vocational animal care-taker education 79–80
voles 31–32
von Clausewitz, C. 260–61
Von Humboldt, A. 170–71
von Thünen, J.H. 233–34

W

Wadham, H. 197
Wales 235–36
Walker, A. 59
war against animals 259–63
Ward, Sir J. 425–27
Watson, H. 30
Watson, J. 213–14
wellbeing 331, 333, 334, 335–36, 340–41

animal shelter in Australia: natural disaster and work calling 384, 385, 389, 391, 392
factory farming 17–18, 22, 23–24
gendered organizational cultures and dog-human partnerships 442–51
horse-human relationships and leadership 90–91, 93
Wellbeing of Future Generations Act (UK) 230
White, S. 29–30
Wieder, D.L. 361
Wilbert, C. 119
wild animals 38, 50
   ecology 31–32
   identification in fieldwork 34–35
wild displays 34–36
wilderness 33, 48–49
wild fish capture and aquaculture 259–60
Wilkie, R. 33, 316–17
Williams-Jones, B. 197
Willmott, G. 358
wolves 33, 34–35
working conditions in factory farming 23–24

workplace interactions *see* animal metaphor use and workplace interactions
workplace turnover, high 387, 391–92
World Health Organization (WHO) 61
Wright, J. 414, 419
Wright, M. 219
Wrzesniewski, A. 385–86

X

Xenophon 90

Y

Yellowstone National Park and wolves reintroduction 33
Youngt 218

Z

'zookeeper for a day' programmes 35
zoonotic disease 21–22
   prevention and control 290
   see also Covid-19, zoonotic disease and animal-industrial complex (AIC)
Zyklon B 305–6